Pro Java 8 Programming

Brett Spell

Apress®

Pro Java 8 Programming

ISBN-13 (pbk): 978-1-4842-0642-3

ISBN-13 (electronic): 978-1-4842-0641-6

Managing Director: Welmoed Spahr
Lead Editor: Steve Anglin
Technical Reviewer: Chad Darby
Editorial Board: Steve Anglin, Louise Corrigan, Jonathan Gennick, Robert Hutchinson,
    Michelle Lowman, James Markham, Susan McDermott, Matthew Moodie, Jeffrey Pepper,
    Douglas Pundick, Ben Renow-Clarke, Gwenan Spearing, Steve Weiss
Coordinating Editor: Mark Powers
Copy Editor: Lori Jacobs
Compositor: SPi Global
Indexer: SPi Global
Artist: SPi Global
Cover Designer: Anna Ishchenko

Distributed to the book trade worldwide by Springer Science+Business Media New York, 233 Spring Street, 6th Floor, New York, NY 10013. Phone 1-800-SPRINGER, fax (201) 348-4505, e-mail orders-ny@springer-sbm.com, or visit www.springeronline.com. Apress Media, LLC is a California LLC and the sole member (owner) is Springer Science + Business Media Finance Inc (SSBM Finance Inc). SSBM Finance Inc is a Delaware corporation.

For information on translations, please e-mail rights@apress.com, or visit www.apress.com.

Apress and friends of ED books may be purchased in bulk for academic, corporate, or promotional use. eBook versions and licenses are also available for most titles. For more information, reference our Special Bulk Sales–eBook Licensing web page at www.apress.com/bulk-sales.

Any source code or other supplementary material referenced by the author in this text is available to readers at www.apress.com/9781484206423. For detailed information about how to locate your book's source code, go to www.apress.com/source-code/.

Dedicated to Shari, Ashleigh, and Kaitlin with love.

Contents at a Glance

Contents

About the Author

Brett Spell has been programming professionally in Java since 1996 and is a Sun-certified Java programmer, developer, and architect. Brett is the author of numerous articles on Java development and design patterns and he holds a bachelor's degree in Computer Science and a master's degree in Security Engineering. Brett has experience in wide a variety of industries and currently lives in Plano, Texas, with his wife, Shari, and daughters, Ashleigh and Kaitlin.

About the Technical Reviewer

Chád (shod) Darby is an author, instructor, and speaker in the Java development world. As a recognized authority on Java applications and architectures, he has presented technical sessions at software development conferences worldwide (United States, UK, India, Russia, and Australia). In his 15 years as a professional software architect, he's had the opportunity to work for Blue Cross/Blue Shield, Merck, Boeing, Red Hat, and a handful of startup companies.

Chád is a contributing author to several Java books, including *Professional Java E-Commerce* (Wrox Press), *Beginning Java Networking* (Wrox Press), and *XML and Web Services Unleashed* (Sams Publishing). Chád has Java certifications from Sun Microsystems and IBM. He holds a B.S. in Computer Science from Carnegie Mellon University.

Visit Chád's blog at www.luv2code.com to view his free video tutorials on Java. You can also follow him on Twitter @darbyluvs2code.

Acknowledgments

Writing or even updating a book is a grueling task, but the other folks involved in this effort did a great job of minimizing the pain involved in updating this title. I'd like to thank everyone involved, especially Mark Powers, Steve Anglin, and Matthew Moodie at Apress along with ChádDarby who did an excellent job of reviewing the material and providing helpful feedback.

Introduction

It's been a while since I last revised this material and even longer than that since the first edition was published. In that time the technologies that Java programmers use have changed quite a bit and there's no doubt that if I were writing this book for the first time I would do some things differently. For example, I'd place more of an emphasis on technologies related to web development to reflect the dominance that it has in the industry today. Even so, it's a little surprising to find out how relevant most of the original material still is, and I hope that you'll find both the principles and specific technology topics covered here useful in learning how to program in Java.

CHAPTER 1

■ ■ ■

Going Inside Java

Java has been described as "a simple, robust, object-oriented, platform-independent, multithreaded, dynamic, general-purpose programming environment." Living up to this definition allowed Java to grow and expand into so many niches that it's almost unrecognizable from its earliest days. Today you can find Java just about anywhere you can find a microprocessor. It's used in the largest of enterprises to the smallest of devices, and it's used in devices from cell phones to supercooled mainframes. For Java to support such a wide range of environments, an almost bewildering array of application programming interfaces (APIs) and versions have been developed, though they're built around a common set of core classes.

In order to become a good Java programmer, it's important to be able to do the basics well. Being able to produce a highly complex user interface is all very well, but if your code is bloated, memory hungry, and inefficient, your users won't be happy. This book isn't about the huge array of development options available to you as a Java developer but about how to do the common tasks that as a Java developer you'll encounter again and again. Over the course of the book, we'll examine some of the core language features, such as threading and memory management, that can really make the difference in a professional-quality Java application.

At the core of Java's adaptability, and hence popularity, is that it's platform-independent. Its "write once, run anywhere" (WORA) capability stems from the way Java itself operates and in particular from the use of an abstract execution environment that allows Java code to be separated from the underlying operating system. Whereas the rest of this book will be about exploring the programming language and APIs of Java, in this chapter we'll look at the foundations of how Java really operates under the hood, with the Java Virtual Machine (JVM). Understanding the inner workings of Java will give you as a programmer a better understanding of the language, which should make you a better programmer.

In this chapter, we'll cover the following:

- The various components of the Java platform

- How the JVM allows Java to be platform-independent

- What happens when you run a Java program

- What a Java class file really contains

- The key tools needed to work with a JVM

First, then, let's look at what Java actually is.

Java's Architecture

It's easy to think of Java as merely the programming language with which you develop your applications—writing source files and compiling them into bytecode. However, Java as a programming language is just one component of Java, and it's the underlying architecture that gives Java many of its advantages, including platform independence.

The complete Java architecture is actually the combination of four components:

- The Java programming language
- The Java class file format
- The Java APIs
- The JVM

So, when you develop in Java, you're writing with the Java programming language, which is then compiled into Java class files, and those in turn are executed in the JVM. In fact, these days the Java language is just one of the options available if you want to use the rest of the Java platform. Scala, for example, has generated a great deal of interest as an alternative to the Java language and is only one of many different languages that use Java technology without also using the Java language.

The combination of the JVM and the core classes form the Java platform, also known as the Java Runtime Environment (JRE), sits on whatever operating system is being used. Figure 1-1 shows how different aspects of Java function relative to one another, to your application, and to the operating system.

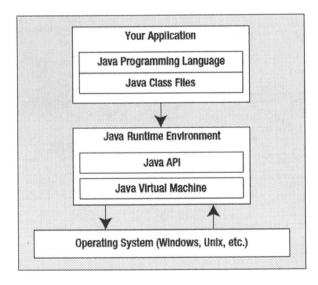

Figure 1-1. *An overview of Java's role*

The Java API is prewritten code organized into packages of similar topics. The Java API is divided into three main platforms:

- **Java Platform, Standard Edition (Java SE):** This platform contains the core Java classes and the graphical user interface (GUI) classes.

- **Java Platform, Enterprise Edition (Java EE):** This platform contains the classes and interfaces for developing more complex "enterprise" applications; it contains servlets, JavaServer Pages, and Enterprise JavaBeans, among others.

- **Java Platform, Micro Edition (Java ME):** In this platform, Java goes back to its roots. It provides an optimized runtime environment for consumer products such as Blu-ray disc players, cell phones, and various other types of hardware such as smart appliances.

The Java Virtual Machine

Before we cover the various aspects of writing powerful Java applications, in this section we'll spend some time examining the engine that makes this possible. That engine is the JVM, which is an abstract computing machine that interprets compiled Java programs.

With other programming languages such as C or C++, a compiler, which is specific to the processor and often also the operating system, compiles the source code into an executable. This executable is then self-sufficient and can be run on the machine.

One drawback of this is the lack of portability: code compiled under one operating system can't be run on another operating system but must be recompiled on every different system on which it is to run. In addition, because of vendor-specific compiler features, code compiled under a certain operating system for a certain processor family (for example, Intel x86, SPARC) may not run on a different type of processor, even if that processor supports the same operating system.

This problem occurred particularly when people began writing applications for the Internet. Their applications were intended for users running many different operating systems on various different platforms through different browsers. The only way to resolve this problem was to develop a platform-independent language.

In the early 1990s, developers at Sun Microsystems were working on a platform-independent language for use in consumer electronic devices, which unfortunately was somewhat ahead of its time and was therefore shelved. With the advent of the Internet, these developers saw a much greater potential for the language they had created and therefore Java was born.

The key to the portability of the Java language is that the output of the Java compiler isn't standard executable code. Instead, the Java compiler generates an optimized set of instructions called a *bytecode* program. Bytecodes are sequences of bytes that follow a documented pattern, and we'll cover them in more detail later. The bytecode program is interpreted by the runtime system, otherwise known as the JVM, and a bytecode program generated on one platform can be run on any other platform that has a JVM installed.

This is generally true even though some specifics of the JVM may differ from platform to platform. In other words, a Java program that's compiled on a Linux workstation can be run on a PC or a Mac. The source code is written in a standard way in the Java language and compiled into a bytecode program, and each JVM interprets the bytecode into native calls specific to its platform (that is, into a language the specific processor can understand). This abstraction is the way various operating systems achieve such operations as printing, accessing files, and handling hardware in a consistent manner across platforms.

One feature (and some would say disadvantage) of bytecode is that it's not executed directly by the processor of the machine on which it's run. The bytecode program is run through the JVM, which interprets the bytecode, and that's why Java is referred to as an *interpreted language*. In reality, Java's days of being a purely interpreted language are long gone, and the current architecture of most JVM implementations is a mixture of interpretation and compilation. Interpretation is a relatively slow process compared to compilation, and it was during the days of purely interpreted Java that it gained a reputation for being slower than other languages. However, the newer interpreted/compiled hybrid model has largely eliminated the speed difference in Java programs and those of other programming languages, making it appropriate for all but the most resource-intensive applications.

Table 1-1 lists compiled versus interpreted languages.

Table 1-1. *Compiled vs. Interpreted Languages*

Language	Compiled or Interpreted?	Portable Code?	Minimal Execution Overhead?
C++	Compiled	No	Yes
Java	Interpreted	Yes	No

It's also worth noting that Java includes an API for interfacing with native applications (those written in non-Java languages such as C and C++). This API is the Java Native Interface (JNI) API and allows developers to call code written in a non-Java language from Java code, and vice versa. JNI accomplishes two things, one of which is to allow your application to take advantage of operating system–specific features that wouldn't be available directly through Java. More to the point, JNI allows you to use a compiled language such as C or C++ for functions used by your Java application where performance is critical. Using JNI does, however, negate some of the platform independence of Java, as the native code is generally platform-specific, and therefore the Java code will be tied to the target platform as well if it relies on the native code for some functionality.

For machine portability to work, the JVM must be fairly tightly defined, and that's achieved by the JVM *specification*. That specification dictates the format of the bytecode recognized by the JVM as well as features and functionality that must be implemented by the JVM. The JVM specification is what ensures the platform independence of the Java language; you can find it on the Oracle web site.

In this context, referring to a "JVM" can mean any one of three different things:

- An abstract specification, such as the specification for Java 8.

- A concrete implementation of the specification.

- A runtime execution environment.

Different JVM Implementations

Sun Microsystems, the original company that developed Java, initially provided its own implementations of various Java technologies, including the JVM, and these were referred to as the *reference implementations*. However, Sun (and now Oracle, which acquired Sun in 2010) has also granted licenses that allow other organizations to create their own implementations. Although the reference implementations of the JVM and other Java technologies have always been widely used, they're far from the only implementations available and licensees include IBM, Apple, Hewlett-Packard, and many other organizations. Following the standards defined in the JVM specification means that Java code will behave the same in one-on-one implementation as it does in any other.

In 2006, Sun began transitioning Java from its original proprietary model—where Sun tightly controlled the standards and reference implementation—to an open model. That transition resulted in changes in how Java was managed, including the following:

- The full source code was made publicly available, or at least as much of it as Sun could legally publish given associated licensing restrictions.

- Future changes and additions to Java have been handled through the Java Community Process (JCP) instead of internally within Sun. The JCP is an open and collaborative process for making decisions about the future of Java, though Sun (and now Oracle) continued to play a prominent role in the decision-making process.

- The reference implementation of Java is now produced using an open source model and is referred to as the Open Java Development Kit (OpenJDK).

Many JVM implementations still exist, but the OpenJDK remains the most commonly used implementation. Why do different versions of the JVM exist? Remember, the JVM specification sets down the required functionality for a JVM but doesn't mandate how that functionality should be implemented. In an attempt to maximize the use of Java, some flexibility to be creative with the platform was given. The important thing is that whatever the implementation, a JVM must adhere to the guidelines defined by the Java specification. In terms of platform independence, this means a JVM must be able to interpret bytecode that's correctly generated on any other platform.

The JVM As a Runtime Execution Environment

Every time you run a Java application, you're in fact running your application within an instance of the JVM, and each separate application you run will have its own JVM instance. So far you've seen that Java uses an interpreted form of source code called *bytecode*, but how do the instructions you code in the Java programming language get translated into instructions that the underlying operating system (OS) can understand?

The JVM specification defines an abstract internal architecture for this process. You'll learn about the components of this internal architecture in a moment, but at a high level, class files (compiled Java files have a .class extension and are referred to as *class files*) are loaded into the JVM where they're then executed by an execution engine. When executing the bytecodes, the JVM interacts with the underlying OS through means of native methods, and it's the implementation of those native methods that tie a particular JVM implementation to a particular platform (see Figure 1-2).

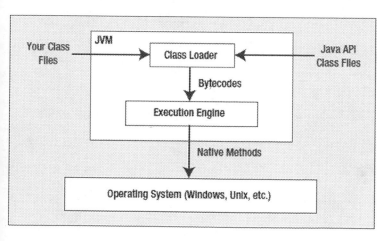

Figure 1-2. Role of the JVM

In addition to the previous components, a JVM also needs memory in order to store temporary data related to code execution, such as local variables, which method is executing, and so on. That data is stored within the runtime data areas of the JVM, as explained next.

The Runtime Data Areas of the JVM

Although the individual implementations may differ slightly from platform to platform, every JVM must supply the runtime components shown in Figure 1-3.

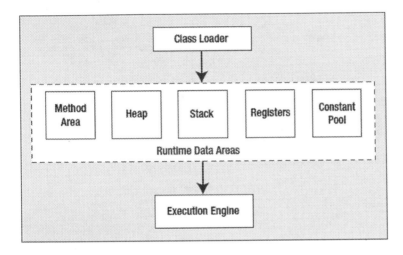

Figure 1-3. *Runtime data area*

The Heap

The *heap* is a region of free memory that's often used for dynamic or temporary memory allocation. The heap is the runtime data area that provides memory for class and array objects. When class or array objects are created in Java, the memory they require is allocated from the heap, which is created when the JVM starts. Heap memory is reclaimed when references to an object or array no longer exist by an automatic storage management system known as the *garbage collection*, which you'll learn more about later.

The JVM specification doesn't dictate how the heap is implemented; that's left up to the creativity of the individual implementations of the JVM. The size of the heap may be constant, or it may be allowed to grow as needed or shrink if the current size is unnecessarily large. The programmer may be allowed to specify the initial size of the heap; for example, on the Win32 and Solaris reference implementations, you can do this with the -mx command-line option. Heap memory doesn't need to be contiguous. If the heap runs out of memory and additional memory can't be allocated to it, the system will generate an OutOfMemoryError exception.

The Stack

A Java *stack frame* stores the state of method invocations. The stack frame stores data and partial results and includes the method's execution environment, any local variables used for the method invocation, and the method's operand stack. The operand stack stores the parameters and return values for most bytecode instructions. The execution environment contains pointers to various aspects of the method invocation.

Frames are the components that make up the JVM stack. They store partial results, data, and return values for methods. They also perform dynamic linking and issue runtime exceptions. A frame is created when a method is invoked and destroyed when the method exits for any reason. A frame consists of an array of local variables, an operand stack, and a reference to the runtime constant pool of the class of the current method.

When the JVM runs Java code, only one frame, corresponding to the currently executing method, is active at any one time. This is referred to as the *current frame*. The method it represents is the current method, and the class that includes that method is the current class. When a thread invokes a method (each thread has its own stack), the JVM creates a new frame, which becomes the current frame, and pushes it onto the stack for that thread.

As with the heap, the JVM specification leaves it up to the specific implementation of the JVM how the stack frames are implemented. The stacks either can be of fixed size or can expand or contract in size as needed. The programmer may be given control over the initial size of the stack and its maximum and minimum sizes. Again, on Win32 and Solaris, this is possible through the command-line options -ss and -oss. If a computation requires a larger stack than is possible, a StackOverflowError exception is generated.

Method Area

The *method area* is a common storage area shared among all JVM threads. It's used to store such things as the runtime constant pool, method data, field data, and bytecode for methods and constructors. The JVM specification details only the general features of the method area but doesn't mandate the location of the area or dictate how the area is implemented. The method area may be a fixed size, or it may be allowed to grow or shrink. The programmer may be allowed to specify the initial size of the method area, and the area doesn't need to be contiguous.

Registers

The *registers* maintained by the JVM are similar to registers on other computer systems. They reflect the current state of the machine and are updated as bytecode is executed. The primary register is the program counter (the pc register) that indicates the address of the JVM instruction that's currently being executed. If the method currently being executed is native (written in a language other than Java), the value of the pc register is undefined. Other registers in the JVM include a pointer to the execution environment of the current method, a pointer to the first local variable of the currently executing method, and a pointer to the top of the operand stack.

Runtime Constant Pool

The *runtime constant pool* is similar to a symbol table used in other programming languages. As the name suggests, it contains constants including numeric literals and field constants. The memory for each runtime constant pool is allocated from the method area, and the runtime constant pool is constructed when the JVM loads the class file for a class or interface.

The Garbage Collector

Older languages such as C require the programmer to explicitly allocate and release memory. Memory is allocated when needed and released when no longer needed by the application.

Unfortunately, this approach often causes "memory leaks," where memory is allocated and for one reason or another never released. When that takes place repeatedly, the application will eventually run out of memory and terminate abnormally or at least no longer be able to function. In contrast, Java never requires the programmer to explicitly allocate or release memory, preventing many of the problems that can occur. Instead, Java automatically allocates memory when you create an object, and Java will release the memory when references to the object no longer exist.

Java uses what's known as a *garbage collector* to monitor a Java program while it runs and automatically releases memory used by objects that are no longer in use. Java uses a series of *soft pointers* to keep track of object references and an object table to map those soft pointers to the object references. The soft pointers are so named because they don't point directly to the object but instead point to the object references themselves. Using soft pointers allows Java's garbage collector to run in the background using a separate thread, and it can examine one object at a time. The garbage collector can mark, remove, move, or examine objects by changing the object table entries.

The garbage collector runs on its own, and explicit garbage collector requests are generally not necessary. The garbage collector performs its checking of object references sporadically during the execution of a program, and when no references to an object exist, the memory allocated to that object can be reclaimed. You can request that the garbage collector run by invoking the static gc() method in the System class, though this represents a request that may or may not be honored and there's no guarantee that an object will be garbage collected at any given time.

The JVM: Loading, Linking, and Initializing

For the JVM to interpret a Java bytecode, it must perform three steps for the required classes and interfaces:

1. **Loading:** When the JVM loads a class, it finds a binary representation of a class or interface and creates a Class object from that binary representation (usually a class file created by a Java compiler). A Class object encapsulates the runtime state of a class or interface.

2. **Linking:** Linking is the process of taking the loaded class or interface and combining it with the runtime of the JVM, preparing it for execution.

3. **Initializing:** Initialization occurs when the JVM invokes the class or interface initialization method.

The First Step

The first thing the JVM does when a stand-alone Java application starts is create a Class object representing the Java class that contains the public static void main(String[] args) method. The JVM links and initializes this class and invokes the main() method, and that method drives the loading, linking, and initializing of any additional classes and interfaces that are referenced.

Loading

The loading process itself is carried out by a class loader, which is an object that's a subclass of ClassLoader; the class loader will do some of its own verification checks on the class or interface it's loading. An exception is thrown if the binary data representing the compiled class or interface is malformed, if the class or interface uses an unsupported version of the class file format, if the class loader couldn't find the definition of the class or interface, or if circularity exists. Class circularity occurs if a class or interface would be its own superclass.

Two general types of class loader exist: the one supplied by the JVM, which is called the *bootstrap class loader*, and user-defined class loaders. User-defined class loaders are always subclasses of Java's ClassLoader class and can be used to create Class objects from nonstandard, user-defined sources. For instance, the Class object could be extracted from an encrypted file. A loader may delegate part or all of the loading process to another loader, but the loader that ultimately creates the Class object is referred to as the *defining loader*. The loader that begins the loading process is known as the *initiating loader*.

The loading process using the default bootstrap loader is as follows: The loader first determines if it has already been recorded as the initiating loader of a class corresponding to the desired class file. If it has, the Class object already exists, and the loader stops. (You should note here that loading a class isn't the same as creating an instance of it; this step merely makes the class available to the JVM.) If it's not already loaded, the loader searches for the class file and, if found, will create the Class object from that file. If the class file isn't found, a NoClassDefFoundError exception is generated.

When a user-defined class loader is used, the process is somewhat different. As with the bootstrap loader, the user-defined loader first determines if it has already been recorded as the initiating loader of a class file corresponding to the desired class file. If it has, the Class object already exists and the loader stops, but if it doesn't already exist, the user-defined loader invokes the loadClass() method. The return value of that method is the desired class file, and the loadClass() method assembles the array of bytes representing the class into a ClassFile structure. It then calls the defineClass() method, which creates a Class object from the ClassFile structure; alternatively, the loadClass() method can simply delegate the loading to another class loader.

Linking

The first step in the linking process is verifying the class files to be linked.

Java Class File Verification

Because the JVM is completely separate from the Java compiler, the JVM, which interprets the class file, has no guarantee that the class file is properly formed or that it was even generated by a Java compiler. Another problem arises with inheritance and class compatibility. If a given class file represents a class that inherits from a superclass represented by another class file, the JVM must make sure the subclass class file is compatible with the superclass class file.

The JVM verifies that each class file satisfies the constraints placed on it by the Java language specification, although the Java class verifier is independent of the Java language. Programs written in certain other languages can also be compiled into the class file format and (if everything has been done correctly) pass the verification process.

The verification process itself happens in four steps:

1. In the first step, the class file is loaded by the JVM and checked to make sure it adheres to the basic format of a class file. The class file must be the correct length. The magic number (which identifies a class file as really being a class) is checked. The constant pool must not contain any unrecognizable information, and the length of each attribute is checked to be sure it's the correct length.

2. The second step in the verification process occurs when the file is linked. The actions performed in this step include ensuring that the final keyword constraint is respected. This means final classes can't be subclassed and final methods can't be overridden. The constant pool is checked to make sure the elements don't violate any language constraints. All field and method references in the constant pool are validated, and every class except the Object class is checked to see if it has a direct superclass.

3. The third verification step also occurs during the linking phase. Every method referenced in the class file is checked to ensure it adheres to the constraints placed on methods by the Java language. The methods must be invoked with the correct number and type of arguments. The operand stack must always be the same size and contain the same types of values. Local variables must contain an appropriate value before they're accessed. Fields must be assigned values of the proper type only.

4. The final step in the verification looks at events that occur the first time a method is invoked and ensures that everything happens according to the specification. The checks include ensuring that a referenced field or method exists in a given class, verifying that the referenced field or method has the proper descriptor, and ensuring that a method has access to the referenced method or field when it executes.

Preparation

Once the class file has been verified, the JVM prepares the class for initialization by allocating memory space for the class variables and also sets them to the default initial values. These are the standard default values, such as 0 for int, false for Boolean, and so on. These values will be set to their program-dependent defaults during the initialization phase.

Resolution

At this (optional) step, the JVM resolves the symbolic references in the runtime constant pool into concrete values.

Initialization

Once the linking process is complete, any static fields and static initializers are invoked. Static fields have values that are accessible even when there are no instances of the class; static initializers provide for static initialization that can't be expressed in a single expression. All these initializers for a type are collected by the JVM into a special method. For example, the collected initializers for a class become the initialization method <clinit>.

However, when initializing a class, not only must the class initialization method be invoked by the JVM (only the JVM can call it) but in addition any superclasses must also be initialized (which also involves the invocation of <clinit> for those classes). As a result, the first class that will always be initialized is Object. The class containing the main() method for an application will always be initialized.

Bytecode Execution

The bytecode from a class file consists of a series of 1-byte opcode instructions specifying an operation to be performed. Each opcode is followed by zero or more operands, which supply arguments or data used by that operation. The JVM interpreter essentially uses a do...while loop that loads each opcode and any associated operands and executes the action represented by the opcode. The bytecode is translated into an action according to the JVM instruction set, which maps bytecode to operations represented by the bytecode as specified by the JVM specifications. This process continues until all the opcode has been interpreted.

The first set of instructions in the JVM instruction set involves basic operations performed on the primitive data types and on objects. The nomenclature used is generally the data type followed by the operation. For instance, the `iload` instruction (`iload` is merely a mnemonic representation of the actual instruction) represents a local variable that's an `int` being loaded onto the operand stack. The `fload` instruction is for loading a local variable that's a `float` onto the operand stack, and so on. There are a series of instructions to store a value of a certain data type from the operand stack into a local variable, to load a constant onto the operand stack, and to gain access to more than one local variable.

The second set in the instruction set concerns arithmetic operations, and the arithmetic operation generally involves two values currently on the operand stack, with the result of the operation being pushed onto the operand stack. The nomenclature is the same as before; for instance, the `iadd` operation is for adding two integer values, and the `dadd` operation is for adding two double values.

Similarly, some operations represent basic mathematical functions (add, subtract, multiply, and divide), some represent logical operations (bitwise OR, bitwise AND, and bitwise NOT), and some specialized functions including remainder, negate, shift, increment, and comparison.

The JVM adheres to the IEEE 754 standards when it comes to things such as floating-point number operations and rounding toward zero. Some integer operations—divide by zero, for instance—can throw an `ArithmeticException`, while the floating-point operators don't throw runtime exceptions but instead will return a `NaN` ("Not a Number"—the result is an invalid mathematical operation) if an overflow condition occurs.

The JVM instruction set includes operations for converting between different types. The JVM directly supports widening conversions (for instance, `float` to `double`). The naming convention is the first type, then 2, and then the second type. For example, the instruction `i2l` is for conversion of an `int` to a `long`. The instruction set also includes some narrowing operations, the conversion of an `int` to a `char`, for instance. The nomenclature for these operations is the same as for the widening operation.

Instructions exist for creating and manipulating class and array objects. The `new` command creates a new class object, and the `newarray`, `anewarray`, and `multilinearray` instructions create array objects. Instructions also exist to access the static and instance variables of classes, to load an array component onto the operand stack, to store a value from the operand stack into an array component, to return the length of an array, and to check certain properties of class objects or arrays.

The JVM instruction set provides the `invokevirtual`, `invokeinterface`, `invokespecial`, and `invokestatic` instructions that are used to invoke methods, where `invokevirtual` is the normal method dispatch mode. The other instructions are for methods implemented by an interface, methods requiring special handling such as private or superclass methods, and static methods. Method return instructions are also defined for each data type.

Another JVM instruction worth mentioning is `invokedynamic`, which was added to the JVM specification for Java 7. Ironically, the instruction actually had little impact on the Java language in that release, but it did provide the framework for a major change introduced in Java 8, namely, lambda expressions which are covered in detail in Chapter 3. The older invocation instructions (`invokevirtual`, `invokeinterface`, etc.) only supported what's referred to as "static linking"; that is, the type of an object that's referenced is established at compile time. For example, when `invokevirtual` is used, the specific method that's called is known to exist because the type (class) of the object in which that method is defined is known. That approach is referred to as static linking because it's defined at compile time and can't change or be substituted later for a different type. In contrast to static linking, `invokedynamic` supports dynamic linking, where the type of the object for which a method is invoked is determined at runtime, and any type is valid as long as it meets certain criteria. Specifically, the method must accept parameters that are consistent with what's specified by the invocation, and any data type with a method satisfying that condition is acceptable. Although `invokedynamic` didn't really impact the Java language until Java 8, it did allow for better implementations of other languages besides Java that use the JVM.

Finally, there's a collection of miscellaneous instructions for doing various other operations, including managing the operand stack, transferring control, throwing exceptions, implementing the `finally` keyword, and synchronizing.

For example, consider the following simple Java class:

```
class Hello {
  public static void main(String[] args) {
    System.out.println("Hello World!");
  }
}
```

If you compile this class and then use the javap utility with the -c switch (covered later) to disassemble the class file, you can get a mnemonic version of the bytecode.

```
Compiled from "Hello.java"
class Hello {
  Hello();
    Code:
       0: aload_0
       1: invokespecial #1              // Method java/lang/Object."<init>":()V
       4: return

  public static void main(java.lang.String[]);
    Code:
       0: getstatic     #2              // Field java/lang/System.out:Ljava/io/
                                           PrintStream;
       3: ldc           #3              // String Hello World!
       5: invokevirtual #4              // Method java/io/PrintStream.println:
                                           (Ljava/lang/String;)V
       8: return
}
```

The main set of mnemonics we're interested in consists of the three lines under the main() method, which translate the single System.out.println("Hello World"); line of code.

The first instruction, getstatic, retrieves a PrintStream object from the out field of the java.lang.System object and places it onto the operand stack. The next line, ldc, pushes the String "Hello World!" onto the operand stack. Finally, invokevirtual executes a method, in this case println (on the java.io.PrintStream class). For that method to successfully execute, it expects there to be a String and an instance of java.io.PrintStream in the stack, in that order. Upon execution these items are removed from the stack.

The Java Class File Format

As already explained, the JVM can't interpret the Java programming language directly, so when Java code is compiled, the result is one or more class files containing bytecode, a symbol table, and other information. The class file structure is a precisely defined binary format that ensures any JVM can load and interpret any class file, no matter where the class file was produced.

The class file itself consists of a stream of 8-bit bytes. All higher-bit quantities (16, 32, or 64 bits) are created by reading in a combination of 8-bit bytes, and multibyte quantities are stored in big-endian order (the high bytes come first). The Java language provides I/O (input/output) streams (supported by the DataInput, DataInputStream, DataOutput, and DataOutputStream interfaces from the java.io package) that can read and write class files.

The data types in the class file are unsigned 1-, 2-, or 4-byte quantities. These are denoted by the syntax u1, u2, and u4. The class file can also contain a series of contiguous fixed-size items that can be indexed like an array. These are designated using square brackets ([ ]).

The class format contains a single ClassFile structure, and that structure contains all the information about the class or interface that the JVM needs to know. The general structure of the ClassFile is as follows:

```
ClassFile {
  u4 magic;
  u2 minor_version;
  u2 major_version;
  u2 constant_pool_count;
  cp_info constant_pool[constant_pool_count - 1];
  u2 access_flags;
  u2 this_class
  u2 super_class;
  u2 interfaces_count;
  u2 interfaces[interfaces_count];
  u2 fields_count;
  field_info fields[fields_count];
  u2 methods_count;
  method_info methods[methods_count];
  u2 attributes_count;
  attribute_into attributes[attributes_count];
}
```

The magic parameter is the magic number assigned to the class file format. This will have the value 0xCAFEBABE and identifies the code as being a class file.

The major_version and minor_version items are the major and minor versions of the class file format. To the JVM, the version numbers indicate the format to which the class file adheres. JVMs can generally load class files only within a certain version range (for example, within a single major version but a range of minor versions) and will generally reject files from a newer specification than that of the JVM itself.

The constant_pool_count item is equal to the number of elements contained in the constant pool plus one. This variable determines if a constant_pool index is valid. The constant_pool[ ] item is a table of cp_info structures containing information on the elements in the constant_pool.

The access_flags item is a mask of flags reflecting whether the file is a class or interface and the access permissions of the class or interface. The mask will be off or will be a combination of public, final, super, interface, or abstract flags.

The this_class parameter points to a CONSTANT_Class_infor structure in the constant_pool table representing the class or interface defined by this class file. The super_class item points to a similar element in the constant_pool representing the direct superclass or interface or zero if no superclass exists.

The interfaces_count parameter represents the number of direct superinterfaces for the class or interface. The interfaces[ ] item contains the location of those superinterfaces in the constant_pool table.

The fields_count variable gives the number of field_info structures contained in the ClassFile. The field_info structures represent all fields, both static and instance, declared by the class or interface. The methods[ ] item is a table containing the method_info structures.

Finally, the attributes_count variable gives the number of attributes in the attributes table of the class or interface. The attributes[ ] item is a table containing the attributes' structure.

The Java Programming Language and APIs

All that we've covered so far happens transparently from the perspective of an application developer. In fact, you don't really have to know any details of Java's internal architecture to program in Java. However, what you do need to know is how to use Java as a programming language and also how to use the various APIs that come with the different platforms to communicate with the underlying software and operating system. In fact, this is essentially what the remainder of the book will be about—how to develop effectively with Java.

The Java Programming Language

Although knowledge of the various APIs is essential to achieving anything with Java, a solid foundation in the core Java language is also highly desirable to make the most effective use of the APIs. In this book, you'll explore the following features of core Java programming:

Method, interface, and class design: Writing the main building blocks of your applications with Java objects can be simultaneously quite straightforward and very complex. However, if you take the time to follow some basic guidelines for creating methods, classes, and libraries, it's not too difficult to develop classes that not only provide the required functionality but are also reliable, maintainable, and reusable.

Threading: Java includes built-in support for multithreaded applications, and you'll often find it necessary or desirable to take advantage of this. To do so, you should be familiar with Java's multithreading capabilities and know how to implement threads correctly within an application.

The Java APIs

As discussed earlier in the chapter, three major versions of the Java platform exist, and each consists of some significantly different APIs. In this book, we'll concentrate on some (although by no means all) of the APIs that form the Standard Edition. More specifically, we'll cover the following:

User interface components: We'll take an in-depth approach to show some of the more complex user interface components; you'll also learn how to use a layout manager to arrange components within an interface.

The data transfer API: Closely related to providing the user interface for your application is the need to provide cut-and-paste and drag-and-drop capabilities.

The printing API: Another common feature often required is the ability to print, which you'll examine through the use of Java's printing capabilities.

JDBC: All but the most trivial of applications require data to be loaded, manipulated, and stored in some form or another, and a relational database is the most common means for storing such data. The Java Database Connectivity (JDBC) API is provided for that purpose; we'll discuss it in detail.

Internationalization: Most commercial applications and those developed for internal use by large organizations are used in more than one country and need to support more than one language. This requirement is sometimes overlooked and treated as an implementation detail, but to be done successfully, internationalization should be considered as part of an application's design. To create a successful design that includes internationalization support, you should be familiar with Java's capabilities in that area, and we'll discuss them in detail in this book.

Metadata: Java provides the ability to easily associate data with classes, interfaces, methods, and fields. Java also includes an API that allows the metadata to be read programmatically and used by tools to provide various useful functions such as code generation.

Java Utility Tools: Making the Most of the JVM

Java SE comes with a number of development tools that you can use to compile, execute, and debug Java programs; we'll discuss some of the tools that relate to the JVM in the next sections. You can find a description of all the utility tools on the Oracle web site at http://docs.oracle.com/javase/8/docs/technotes/tools/.

The Java Compiler

The compiler that comes with the J2SE is named javac; it reads class and interface definition files and converts these into bytecode files. The command to run the Java compiler is as follows:

```
javac [options] [source files] [@file list]
```

The options are command-line options. If the number of source files to be compiled is sufficiently short, the files can just be listed one after another. However, if the number of files is large, a file containing the names of the files to be compiled can be used preceded by the @ character. Source code file names must end with the .java suffix.

You can use the command-line options described in Table 1-2 to include additional functionality in the standard compile command. This is only a partial list of options; for a complete list, including some that may be specific to the Java compiler implementation, enter javac -help at the command line.

Table 1-2. *Standard Options Supported by Java Compilers*

Option	Description
-classpath	This command, followed by a user-specific class path, overrides the system CLASSPATH environment variable.
-d	This command, followed by a directory path, sets the destination directory for the class files generated by the compiler.
-deprecation	This command displays a description of any deprecated methods or classes used in the source code.
-encoding	This command sets the source file encoding name. Otherwise, the default encoding is used.
-g	This command provides more complete debugging information, including local variable information.
-g:none	This command turns off all debugging information.
-g:keyword	This command allows the user to specify the type of debugging information provided. Valid keyword options are source, lines, and vars.
-help	This command displays information about the compiler utility options.

(continued)

Table 1-2. (*continued*)

Option	Description
−nowarn	This command prevents warning messages from being displayed. Warnings occur when the compiler suspects something is wrong with the source code but the problem isn't severe enough to stop compilation.
−source	This command indicates that features added after the specified release aren't supported. For example, specifying −source 1.3 will cause the compiler to fail if it encounters the assert keyword, since assertions weren't available until Java 1.4.
−sourcepath	This command, followed by a source path, specifies the path that the compiler will use to search for source code files.
−verbose	This command produces additional information about the classes that are loaded and the source files that were compiled.
−X	This command displays information about nonstandard options. These are options that need not be implemented by a compiler to be considered a valid implementation, and as such may or may not be supported by a given compiler implementation.

The Java Interpreter

The java utility launches a Java application by loading and running the class file containing the main method of the application. The java utility will interpret the bytecode contained in that file and any other class files that are part of the application. The general command syntax for the java utility is as follows:

```
java [options] class [arguments]
```

Alternatively, you can run it as follows:

```
java [options] -jar file.jar [arguments]
```

You can provide the initial class file as a separate file or as part of a Java Archive (JAR) file. The options are command-line options for the JVM, and the class is the name of the class file containing the static main() method to execute. The arguments are any arguments that need to be passed to main().

Table 1-3 describes some of the standard options for the java utility and, as with the compiler, you can enter java -help at the command line to see a complete set of options supported by the implementation you're using.

Table 1-3. *Standard Options Supported by JVM Implementations*

Option	Description
-client	This command specifies that the Java HotSpot Client Virtual Machine should be used. This is the default and is optimized for executing client/desktop application code.
-server	This command specifies that the Java HotSpot Server Virtual Machine should be used. This Virtual Machine is optimized for executing server code, such as that used to support web applications.
-classpath or -cp	This command, followed by a user-specified class path, overrides the system CLASSPATH environment variable.
-Dproperty=value	This command provides a system property with a value.
-enableassertions or -ea	This command enables assertions, which are disabled by default.
-disableassertions or -da	This command disables assertions.
-enablesystemassertions or -esa	This command enables assertions in all system classes.
-disablesystemassertions or -dsa	This command disables assertions in all system classes.
-help or -?	This command displays information about the java utility.
-jar	This command executes a program contained in a JAR file, as shown previously.
-showversion	This command shows version information and continues running.
-verbose	This command provides information about each class that's loaded.
-verbose:gc	This command reports garbage collection events.
-verbose:jni	This command displays information about native methods and other JNI activity.
-version	This command shows version information and then exits.
-showversion	This command shows the version number and then continues.
-X	This command displays information about nonstandard options and then exits.

The Java Class Disassembler

You can use the javap utility to look inside a class file, which can be helpful if you want to have only the compiled code and want to want to understand what the source code looked like or if you want to understand how Java source code is mapped to bytecode. The standard command lists declarations of nonprivate and nonstatic fields, methods, constructors, and static initializers for a specific class file. You can also use the javap utility to provide a printout of the JVM bytecode instructions that are executed for each method as we did earlier in the chapter to examine the bytecodes generated by compiling the source. The basic syntax for the javap command is as follows:

```
javap [options] class
```

The options are command-line options for the javap utility (see Table 1-4).

Table 1-4. *Some of the Options Supported by the javap Utility*

Option	Description
-b	This command ensures backward compatibility with earlier versions of javap.
-bootclasspath	This command, followed by a path, specifies the path from which to load the bootstrap classes. Normally these would be classes contained in the /lib/rt.jar archive.
-c	This command prints the JVM instructions for the execution of each method. This tells you what the bytecode for each method actually does.
-classpath	This command, followed by a user-specified class path, overrides the system CLASSPATH environment variable.
-extdirs	This command, followed by a directory, overrides the location the system searches for installed extensions. The default location is /lib/ext.
-help	This command prints information about the javap utility.
-Jflag	This command passes the specified flag directly to the runtime system.
-l	This command displays line and local variables.
-package	This command shows only package, protected, and public classes and members. This is the default.
-private	This command shows information about all classes and members.
-protected	This command displays information about protected and public classes and members only.
-public	This command shows information only about public classes and members.
-s	This command prints internal type signatures.
-verbose	This command prints additional information for each method including stack size, local variable information, and arguments.

Summary

This chapter has been a bit of a whirlwind tour inside Java, poking in the corners of Java's internal architecture that don't get explored very often. You should now have a better appreciation of what's actually going on when you type java MyClass at the command prompt.

We've covered the following:

- The components of Java's architecture

- What the JVM is and how it functions

- The internals of the JVM architecture

- The Java class file format

Now that you've taken a bit of time to explore the foundations of Java, you're ready to start the main work of learning how to use all the different components of the Java platform in detail, starting with library, class, and method design.

■ ■ ■

CHAPTER 2

Designing Libraries, Classes, and Methods

Understanding the mechanics of creating Java code is relatively easy, but creating a good object-oriented design is much more complex. In this context, *good* means that the code works correctly and is reasonably easy to understand, maintain, extend, and reuse. This chapter describes some guidelines that can help you create code with those characteristics.

Reusability is an important goal and is one of the primary advantages of using object-oriented programming languages. Creating reusable code saves time and effort by avoiding the duplication that occurs when software must be created that's similar or identical to something that was written previously.

Although creating reusable code should always be your goal, the reality is that it's not always possible or practical to do so. Some classes are good candidates for reuse while others aren't, and creating reusable software usually requires more work in the short term than creating "throwaway" code. However, as you become more experienced in creating good object-oriented designs, you'll learn to recognize good candidates for reuse and become better at creating classes, interfaces, and packages that aren't tied too closely to a single application. This chapter provides some of the basic concepts that will help you learn those skills.

Library Design

Since it's almost certain that some of the code you write won't be reusable, it's a good idea to segregate your classes into those that are reusable and those that aren't. For example, if you're creating a class containing functionality that's useful throughout the application—and perhaps even in other applications—it's usually a good idea to put that class and other reusable ones that are related to it in their own package. On the other hand, when you're creating classes that aren't likely to be reusable because they serve a very specific purpose it's best to put those groups of related single-use classes in a separate package or packages. In other words, the goal should be for each individual package to represent either code that's reusable or code that isn't. By doing this, you can begin to assemble a library of reusable classes and can easily import them into another application. You should try to treat these reusable classes the same way most programmers do the Java core classes: as code that can't (or at least shouldn't) be changed. To avoid making changes, you should put a great deal of thought into the initial design of a class. In particular, you should think about how it might need to be used differently in the future than the initial use you have in mind.

Package Design

Perhaps the first question to be answered concerning packages is when to define them. Ideally, you should define packages early in the design phase, prior to creating class definitions. In practice, however, it's usually easier to create packages once your design is at least partially complete. At that point, it's more evident what sort of logical groupings you can create, and those groupings can be the basis for your package design. Fortunately, modern Integrated Development Environment (IDE) software makes moving classes to different packages trivial to do, which in turn helps facilitate good design.

A package should be kept reasonably focused and have some type of theme or consistency to the classes assigned to it. If the package grows large and contains a subset of classes that can be separated from the main package, you should consider moving them into newly defined subpackages. For example, the java.util.concurrent package contains many classes and interfaces representing utilities associated with concurrent (multithreaded) programming. Instead of putting all of the concurrency classes and interfaces in java.util.concurrent, however, Java's package structure breaks out those related to atomic wrappers into one subpackage (java.util.concurrent.atomic) and those related to locks into another (java.util.concurrent.locks). Multiple levels of subpackage are possible and entirely appropriate when further logical subdivisions can be made, and you should take advantage of this when designing your own libraries.

Keep in mind that package design isn't an exact science; there is no right and wrong, but you should try to make the placement of your classes as predictable and logical as possible and you generally should avoid creating packages with only one or two classes in them. If a given class doesn't seem to be a good fit for a particular subpackage then a good rule of thumb is to keep it in the higher-level package. For example, in the case of the concurrency packages just mentioned a class that's not related to atomic wrappers or to locks would probably be best suited for the java.util.concurrent package, and in fact that's how the concurrency classes are organized.

The recommended approach for package hierarchies is to use something resembling a reverse domain name. For example, if you're writing code for the Acme Corporation whose domain name is www.acme.com, your packages should begin with com.acme and include as many other levels as are necessary to support an effective division of classes. For example, if you're writing code for a project referred to as the *CRM project*, you might use a base package of com.acme.crm with appropriate sublevels below that base.

If you don't have a registered domain name, you can always choose to use geography or other criteria for selecting your base package hierarchy, such as us.tx.plano.bspell which is a combination of country, state, city, and user name. As this example suggests, package names should be kept short and abbreviations and acronyms are commonly used to support that convention. The important point to keep in mind is that packages are primarily intended to prevent naming "collisions" where two classes exist in the same package with the same name. If you're never going to share your code with anyone, you can use any package-naming convention you want or none at all. There's no technical reason you can't define classes in a package such as com.sun or com.microsoft, but doing so may confuse people who want to use your code or even make it difficult for them to use it if they're already using code with the same package/class name combination.

Class Design

An important part of being a professional object-oriented programmer is the ability to create well-designed classes. Practice is an important ingredient in mastering this skill, but some simple principles can help you become more effective. Class design is largely a matter of assigning responsibility, where you identify the functions that must be implemented and assign each one to the class or classes best suited to perform that function. Alternatively, if there's no existing class that's appropriate, you may decide to create a new class. Some classes are identified in the analysis phase and correspond to real-world entities; for example, a Student class might be defined that corresponds to a real-world student. Other classes, though, called *pure abstractions* exist solely to provide needed functionality while allowing you to create a better design. To promote reusability, your classes should have two general characteristics: loose coupling and strong cohesion. A class should also encapsulate its data in an effective manner, and we'll now examine each of these points as they relate to class design.

Loose Coupling

Coupling refers to the degree to which classes depend upon one another, and two classes that are highly dependent upon each other are considered tightly (sometimes called *highly*) coupled. Coupling is inevitable in some cases because classes must maintain references to one another and perform method calls. However, when you implement a class that's a good candidate for reuse, you should limit its dependencies on other classes as much as possible. It's often not obvious how to do this because you usually can't simply eliminate the interaction between classes. In many cases, it's possible to create a pure abstraction that handles the interaction between two classes or to shift the responsibility for the interaction to an existing class that you don't intend to make reusable.

As an example, suppose you need to create a graphical component that allows you to select font properties, enter some sample text, and have that sample text displayed using the selected font properties. When the font or the sample text changes, the display should update to display the sample text value using the current font settings.

To satisfy these requirements, you might first create a class similar to the one in Listing 2-1, which defines a panel that allows you to select the font properties (name, size, bold, italic). (See Figure 2-1).

Listing 2-1. The Initial FontPropertiesPanel Code

```java
import java.awt.*;
import java.awt.event.*;
import javax.swing.*;
import javax.swing.event.*;

public class FontPropertiesPanel extends JPanel {

    protected JList<String> nameList;
    protected JComboBox<Integer> sizeBox;
    protected JCheckBox boldBox;
    protected JCheckBox italicBox;

    protected SampleTextFrame frame;

    public final static int[] fontSizes = {10, 12, 14, 18, 24, 32, 48, 64};

    public FontPropertiesPanel(SampleTextFrame stf) {
        super();
        frame = stf;
        createComponents();
        buildLayout();
    }

    protected void buildLayout() {
        JLabel label;
        GridBagConstraints constraints = new GridBagConstraints();
        GridBagLayout layout = new GridBagLayout();
        setLayout(layout);

        constraints.anchor = GridBagConstraints.WEST;
        constraints.insets = new Insets(5, 10, 5, 10);
```

```
    constraints.gridx = 0;
    label = new JLabel("Name:", JLabel.LEFT);
    layout.setConstraints(label, constraints);
    add(label);
    label = new JLabel("Size:", JLabel.LEFT);
    layout.setConstraints(label, constraints);
    add(label);
    layout.setConstraints(boldBox, constraints);
    add(boldBox);

    constraints.gridx++;
    nameList.setVisibleRowCount(3);
    JScrollPane jsp = new JScrollPane(nameList);
    layout.setConstraints(jsp, constraints);
    add(jsp);
    layout.setConstraints(sizeBox, constraints);
    add(sizeBox);
    layout.setConstraints(italicBox, constraints);
    add(italicBox);
  }

  protected void createComponents() {
    GraphicsEnvironment ge =
        GraphicsEnvironment.getLocalGraphicsEnvironment();
    String[] names = ge.getAvailableFontFamilyNames();
    nameList = new JList<String>(names);
    nameList.setSelectedIndex(0);
    nameList.setSelectionMode(ListSelectionModel.SINGLE_SELECTION);
    nameList.addListSelectionListener(new ListSelectionListener() {
      public void valueChanged(ListSelectionEvent event) {
        handleFontPropertyChange();
      }
    }
    );
    Integer sizes[] = new Integer[fontSizes.length];
    for (int i = 0; i < sizes.length; i++) {
      sizes[i] = new Integer(fontSizes[i]);
    }
    sizeBox = new JComboBox<Integer>(sizes);
    sizeBox.addActionListener(new ActionListener() {
      public void actionPerformed(ActionEvent event) {
        handleFontPropertyChange();
      }
    }
    );
    boldBox = new JCheckBox("Bold");
    boldBox.addActionListener(new ActionListener() {
      public void actionPerformed(ActionEvent event) {
        handleFontPropertyChange();
      }
    }
    );
```

```java
    italicBox = new JCheckBox("Italic");
    italicBox.addActionListener(new ActionListener() {
      public void actionPerformed(ActionEvent event) {
        handleFontPropertyChange();
      }
    }
    );
  }

  protected void handleFontPropertyChange() {
    frame.refreshDisplayFont();
  }

  public String getSelectedFontName() {
    return (String)(nameList.getSelectedValue());
  }

  public int getSelectedFontSize() {
    return ((Integer)(sizeBox.getSelectedItem())).intValue();
  }

  public boolean isBoldSelected() {
    return boldBox.isSelected();
  }

  public boolean isItalicSelected() {
    return italicBox.isSelected();
  }
}
```

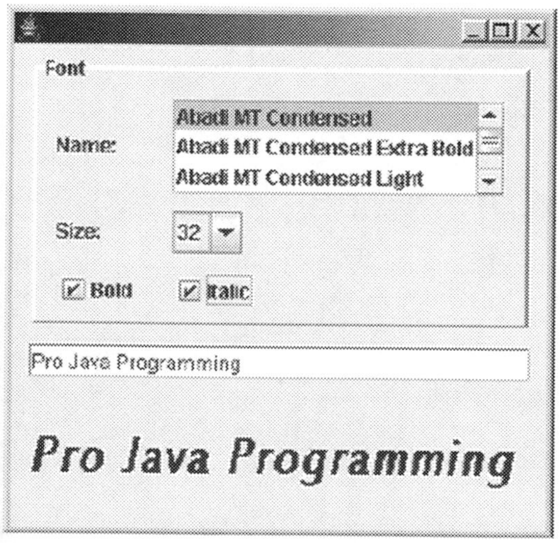

Figure 2-1. *Font testing application interface*

Next, you might create a class similar to the one shown in Listing 2-2 that contains an instance of FontPropertiesPanel, contains a text field that allows you to type the sample text, and contains a label that displays that text using the specified font.

Listing 2-2. The Initial SampleTextFrame Class

```java
import java.awt.*;
import javax.swing.*;
import javax.swing.border.*;
import javax.swing.event.*;
import javax.swing.text.*;

public class SampleTextFrame extends JFrame {

  protected FontPropertiesPanel propertiesPanel;
  protected JTextField sampleText;
  protected JLabel displayArea;

  public static void main(String[] args) {
    SampleTextFrame stf = new SampleTextFrame();
    stf.setDefaultCloseOperation(JFrame.EXIT_ON_CLOSE);
    stf.setVisible(true);
  }

  public SampleTextFrame() {
    super();
    createComponents();
    createDocumentListener();
    buildLayout();
    refreshDisplayFont();
    pack();
  }

  protected void createComponents() {
    propertiesPanel = new FontPropertiesPanel(this);
    sampleText = new JTextField(20);
    displayArea = new JLabel("");
    displayArea.setPreferredSize(new Dimension(200, 75));
    displayArea.setMinimumSize(new Dimension(200, 75));
  }

  protected void createDocumentListener() {
    Document document = sampleText.getDocument();
    document.addDocumentListener(new DocumentListener() {
      public void changedUpdate(DocumentEvent event) {
        handleDocumentUpdate();
      }

      public void insertUpdate(DocumentEvent event) {
        handleDocumentUpdate();
      }
```

```java
      public void removeUpdate(DocumentEvent event) {
        handleDocumentUpdate();
      }
    }
    );
  }

  protected void buildLayout() {
    Container pane = getContentPane();
    GridBagConstraints constraints = new GridBagConstraints();
    GridBagLayout layout = new GridBagLayout();
    pane.setLayout(layout);

    constraints.insets = new Insets(5, 10, 5, 10);
    constraints.fill = GridBagConstraints.HORIZONTAL;
    constraints.weightx = 1;

    constraints.gridx = 0;
    BevelBorder bb = new BevelBorder(BevelBorder.RAISED);
    TitledBorder tb = new TitledBorder(bb, "Font");
    propertiesPanel.setBorder(tb);
    layout.setConstraints(propertiesPanel, constraints);
    pane.add(propertiesPanel);

    layout.setConstraints(sampleText, constraints);
    pane.add(sampleText);

    layout.setConstraints(displayArea, constraints);
    pane.add(displayArea);
  }

  protected void handleDocumentUpdate() {
    displayArea.setText(sampleText.getText());
  }

  public void refreshDisplayFont() {
    displayArea.setFont(getSelectedFont());
  }

  public Font getSelectedFont() {
    String name = propertiesPanel.getSelectedFontName();
    int style = 0;
    style += (propertiesPanel.isBoldSelected() ? Font.BOLD : 0);
    style += (propertiesPanel.isItalicSelected() ? Font.ITALIC : 0);
    int size = propertiesPanel.getSelectedFontSize();
    return new Font(name, style, size);
  }

}
```

25

As you can see from this code, FontPropertiesPanel maintains a reference to its parent SampleTextFrame and, when a font property changes, calls the frame's refreshDisplayFont() method. At first glance this may appear to be an acceptable design, but it has a significant drawback: neither class can be used independently of the other. In other words, SampleTextFrame and FontPropertiesPanel are tightly coupled and as a result are poor candidates for reuse. If you wanted to use FontPropertiesPanel as part of some user interface component other than SampleTextFrame, you'd be unable to do so in its present form, as the current design allows it to operate only in conjunction with an instance of SampleTextFrame. Figure 2-2 shows the relationship between these two classes.

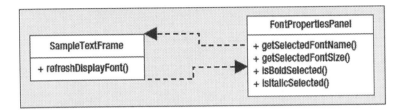

Figure 2-2. *FontPropertiesPanel's dependency upon SampleTextFrame greatly limits the reuse potential of the former class*

Since it provides functionality that might be useful in another context, FontPropertiesPanel appears to be a good candidate for reuse *if* it can be decoupled from SampleTextFrame. The existing dependence is because FontPropertiesPanel calls refreshDisplayFont() directly. Consequently, FontPropertiesPanel depends not only upon the existence of SampleTextFrame but also upon its implementing the refreshDisplayFont() method. Obviously, changes to the font must be communicated to the text display somehow, but ideally it should be done in a way that allows FontPropertiesPanel and SampleTextFrame to be loosely coupled.

One solution to this problem is to use a technique that's simple but powerful: couple a class to an interface instead of to another class. For example, you might create an interface called FontListener that defines a single fontChanged() method, which is called when the font property value changes. In fact, you can use this technique to reduce SampleTextFrame's dependence upon FontPropertiesPanel as well. Notice that currently when a property changes, SampleTextFrame is responsible for extracting the font properties from FontPropertiesPanel and using that information to construct an instance of Font. This is a poor design not only because it makes the two classes more tightly coupled but also because it actually requires more code than building a Font instance inside of FontPropertiesPanel, which has all the information needed to do so.

This illustrates another important point related to class design: functionality should typically be assigned to the class that contains the information needed to perform the function. So, to make these two classes more loosely coupled, we'll specify that the listener's fontChanged() method should be passed a reference to a new font that was built using the newly selected properties. The following is an implementation of such an interface:

```java
public interface FontListener {
  public void fontChanged(java.awt.Font newFont);
}
```

Next, you'll implement the previous interface in SampleTextFrame and have it update the label's font when it receives a message from the FontPropertiesPanel instance (see Listing 2-3).

Listing 2-3. Implementing the FontListener Interface

```java
import java.awt.*;
import javax.swing.*;
import javax.swing.border.*;
import javax.swing.event.*;
import javax.swing.text.*;

public class SampleTextFrame extends JFrame implements FontListener {

  protected FontPropertiesPanel propertiesPanel;
  protected JTextField sampleText;
  protected JLabel displayArea;

  public static void main(String[] args) {
    SampleTextFrame stf = new SampleTextFrame();
    stf.setDefaultCloseOperation(JFrame.EXIT_ON_CLOSE);
    stf.setVisible(true);
  }

  public SampleTextFrame() {
    super();
    createComponents();
    createDocumentListener();
    buildLayout();
    displayArea.setFont(propertiesPanel.getSelectedFont());
    propertiesPanel.setFontListener(this);
    pack();
  }

  protected void createComponents() {
    propertiesPanel = new FontPropertiesPanel();
    sampleText = new JTextField(20);
    displayArea = new JLabel("");
    displayArea.setPreferredSize(new Dimension(200, 75));
    displayArea.setMinimumSize(new Dimension(200, 75));
  }

  protected void createDocumentListener() {
    Document document = sampleText.getDocument();
    document.addDocumentListener(new DocumentListener() {
      public void changedUpdate(DocumentEvent event) {
        handleDocumentUpdate();
      }

      public void insertUpdate(DocumentEvent event) {
        handleDocumentUpdate();
      }
```

27

```
        public void removeUpdate(DocumentEvent event) {
          handleDocumentUpdate();
        }
      }
    );
  }
  protected void buildLayout() {
    Container pane = getContentPane();
    GridBagConstraints constraints = new GridBagConstraints();
    GridBagLayout layout = new GridBagLayout();
    pane.setLayout(layout);

    constraints.insets = new Insets(5, 10, 5, 10);
    constraints.fill = GridBagConstraints.HORIZONTAL;
    constraints.weightx = 1;

    constraints.gridx = 0;
    BevelBorder bb = new BevelBorder(BevelBorder.RAISED);
    TitledBorder tb = new TitledBorder(bb, "Font");
    propertiesPanel.setBorder(tb);
    layout.setConstraints(propertiesPanel, constraints);
    pane.add(propertiesPanel);

    layout.setConstraints(sampleText, constraints);
    pane.add(sampleText);

    layout.setConstraints(displayArea, constraints);
    pane.add(displayArea);
  }

  protected void handleDocumentUpdate() {
    displayArea.setText(sampleText.getText());
  }

//  public void refreshDisplayFont() {
//     displayArea.setFont(getSelectedFont());
//  }

//  public Font getSelectedFont() {
//     String name = propertiesPanel.getSelectedFontName();
//     int style = 0;
//     style += (propertiesPanel.isBoldSelected() ? Font.BOLD : 0);
//     style += (propertiesPanel.isItalicSelected() ? Font.ITALIC : 0);
//     int size = propertiesPanel.getSelectedFontSize();
//     return new Font(name, style, size);
//  }

  public void fontChanged(Font newFont) {
    displayArea.setFont(newFont);
  }
}
```

Finally, you can modify FontPropertiesPanel so it no longer maintains a reference to SampleTextFrame but instead keeps a reference to a FontListener. You can also implement a getSelectedFont() method that can be used to create a new Font instance using the currently selected properties (see Listing 2-4).

Listing 2-4. Decoupling FontPropertiesPanel and SampleTextFrame

```java
import java.awt.*;
import java.awt.event.*;
import javax.swing.*;
import javax.swing.event.*;

public class FontPropertiesPanel extends JPanel {

  protected JList<String> nameList;
  protected JComboBox<Integer> sizeBox;
  protected JCheckBox boldBox;
  protected JCheckBox italicBox;

// protected SampleTextFrame frame;
  protected FontListener listener;

  public final static int[] fontSizes = {10, 12, 14, 18, 24, 32, 48, 64};

  public FontPropertiesPanel() {
    super();
    createComponents();
    buildLayout();
  }

  protected void buildLayout() {
    JLabel label;
    GridBagConstraints constraints = new GridBagConstraints();
    GridBagLayout layout = new GridBagLayout();
    setLayout(layout);

    constraints.anchor = GridBagConstraints.WEST;
    constraints.insets = new Insets(5, 10, 5, 10);

    constraints.gridx = 0;
    label = new JLabel("Name:", JLabel.LEFT);
    layout.setConstraints(label, constraints);
    add(label);
    label = new JLabel("Size:", JLabel.LEFT);
    layout.setConstraints(label, constraints);
    add(label);
    layout.setConstraints(boldBox, constraints);
    add(boldBox);

    constraints.gridx++;
    nameList.setVisibleRowCount(3);
    JScrollPane jsp = new JScrollPane(nameList);
    layout.setConstraints(jsp, constraints);
```

```
    add(jsp);
    layout.setConstraints(sizeBox, constraints);
    add(sizeBox);
    layout.setConstraints(italicBox, constraints);
    add(italicBox);
  }

  protected void createComponents() {
    GraphicsEnvironment ge =
      GraphicsEnvironment.getLocalGraphicsEnvironment();
    String[] names = ge.getAvailableFontFamilyNames();
    nameList = new JList<String>(names);
    nameList.setSelectedIndex(0);
    nameList.setSelectionMode(ListSelectionModel.SINGLE_SELECTION);
    nameList.addListSelectionListener(new ListSelectionListener() {
      public void valueChanged(ListSelectionEvent event) {
        handleFontPropertyChange();
      }
    }
    );
    Integer sizes[] = new Integer[fontSizes.length];
    for (int i = 0; i < sizes.length; i++) {
      sizes[i] = new Integer(fontSizes[i]);
    }
    sizeBox = new JComboBox<Integer>(sizes);
    sizeBox.addActionListener(new ActionListener() {
      public void actionPerformed(ActionEvent event) {
        handleFontPropertyChange();
      }
    }
    );
    boldBox = new JCheckBox("Bold");
    boldBox.addActionListener(new ActionListener() {
      public void actionPerformed(ActionEvent event) {
        handleFontPropertyChange();
      }
    }
    );
    italicBox = new JCheckBox("Italic");
    italicBox.addActionListener(new ActionListener() {
      public void actionPerformed(ActionEvent event) {
        handleFontPropertyChange();
      }
    }
    );
  }

  public void setFontListener(FontListener fl) {
    listener = fl;
  }
```

```
protected void handleFontPropertyChange() {
  listener.fontChanged(getSelectedFont());
}

public Font getSelectedFont() {
  String name = (String)(nameList.getSelectedValue());
  int style = 0;
  style += (boldBox.isSelected() ? Font.BOLD : 0);
  style += (italicBox.isSelected() ? Font.ITALIC : 0);
  int size = ((Integer)(sizeBox.getSelectedItem())).intValue();
  return new Font(name, style, size);
}

//  public String getSelectedFontName() {
//    return (String)(nameList.getSelectedValue());
//  }

//  public int getSelectedFontSize() {
//    return ((Integer)(sizeBox.getSelectedItem())).intValue();
//  }

//  public boolean isBoldSelected() {
//    return boldBox.isSelected();
//  }

//  public boolean isItalicSelected() {
//    return italicBox.isSelected();
//  }

}
```

Figure 2-3 illustrates the relationships between the two classes and the new interface after these changes have been made.

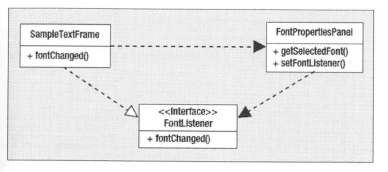

Figure 2-3. *Reducing dependencies can also result in improved reuse*

Although the design is slightly more complex than the original one, it's much more desirable from a reuse standpoint. FontPropertiesPanel is now dependent only upon FontListener and isn't coupled to SampleTextFrame. Any user interface component that needs to incorporate FontPropertiesPanel can do so and must simply implement the FontListener interface (and its fontChanged() method) in a class that's responsible for monitoring the font properties. In this case, the method was implemented with just a single line of code that refreshes the display so that it uses the updated font properties.

Although SampleTextFrame isn't as good a candidate for reuse as FontPropertiesPanel, you can make it more reusable by eliminating its dependence upon FontPropertiesPanel. You've already removed one dependency by preventing SampleTextFrame from building a new Font instance based on the properties in the panel, but dependencies still exist. For example, in the createComponents() method, an instance of FontPropertiesPanel is created. In addition, the SampleTextFrame constructor makes calls to the panel's getSelectedFont() and getFontListener() methods.

Let's assume that SampleTextFrame will always contain a JPanel subclass called propertiesPanel but that you don't want to couple it specifically to FontPropertiesPanel. This would allow you to use other panel types and greatly reduce the coupling between these two classes, but how can you achieve this?

Another helpful guideline for creating reusable classes is to divide the functionality into two segments: functionality that's common and reusable and functionality that's specific to one application and isn't reusable. Given this division, you can improve reusability by putting the common functionality in a superclass and the application-specific logic in a subclass. For example, in this case, you can eliminate SampleTextFrame's references to the FontPropertiesPanel class and move them into a subclass of SampleTextFrame. Listing 2-5 shows the modified SampleTextFrame.

Listing 2-5. SampleTextFrame, Modified

```
import java.awt.*;
import javax.swing.*;
import javax.swing.border.*;
import javax.swing.event.*;
import javax.swing.text.*;

public class SampleTextFrame extends JFrame implements FontListener {

//  protected FontPropertiesPanel propertiesPanel;
    protected JPanel propertiesPanel;
    protected JTextField sampleText;
    protected JLabel displayArea;

    public static void main(String[] args) {
      SampleTextFrame stf = new SampleTextFrame();
      stf.setDefaultCloseOperation(JFrame.EXIT_ON_CLOSE);
      stf.setVisible(true);
    }

    public SampleTextFrame() {
      super();
      createComponents();
      createDocumentListener();
      buildLayout();
//      displayArea.setFont(propertiesPanel.getSelectedFont());
//      propertiesPanel.setFontListener(this);
      pack();
    }
```

```
   protected void createComponents() {
//    propertiesPanel = new FontPropertiesPanel();
     sampleText = new JTextField(20);
     displayArea = new JLabel("");
     displayArea.setPreferredSize(new Dimension(200, 75));
     displayArea.setMinimumSize(new Dimension(200, 75));
   }

   protected void createDocumentListener() {
     Document document = sampleText.getDocument();
     document.addDocumentListener(new DocumentListener() {
       public void changedUpdate(DocumentEvent event) {
         handleDocumentUpdate();
       }

       public void insertUpdate(DocumentEvent event) {
         handleDocumentUpdate();
       }

       public void removeUpdate(DocumentEvent event) {
         handlcDocumentUpdate();
       }
     }
     );
   }

protected void buildLayout() {
     Container pane = getContentPane();
     GridBagConstraints constraints = new GridBagConstraints();
     GridBagLayout layout = new GridBagLayout();
     pane.setLayout(layout);

     constraints.insets = new Insets(5, 10, 5, 10);
     constraints.fill = GridBagConstraints.HORIZONTAL;
     constraints.weightx = 1;

     constraints.gridx = 0;
     BevelBorder bb = new BevelBorder(BevelBorder.RAISED);

     TitledBorder tb = new TitledBorder(bb, "Font");
     propertiesPanel.setBorder(tb);
     layout.setConstraints(propertiesPanel, constraints);
     pane.add(propertiesPanel);

     layout.setConstraints(sampleText, constraints);
     pane.add(sampleText);

     layout.setConstraints(displayArea, constraints);
     pane.add(displayArea);
   }
```

```
protected void handleDocumentUpdate() {
  displayArea.setText(sampleText.getText());
}

public void fontChanged(Font newFont) {
  displayArea.setFont(newFont);
}

}
```

Listing 2-5 removes all explicit references to FontPropertiesPanel, which can be added to a new subclass of SampleTextFrame (see Listing 2-6).

Listing 2-6. The FontPropertiesFrame Subclass

```
public class FontPropertiesFrame extends SampleTextFrame {

  public static void main(String[] args) {
    FontPropertiesFrame fpf = new FontPropertiesFrame();
    fpf.setVisible(true);
  }

  public FontPropertiesFrame() {
    super();
    FontPropertiesPanel fontPanel = (FontPropertiesPanel)propertiesPanel;
    displayArea.setFont(fontPanel.getSelectedFont());
    fontPanel.setFontListener(this);
  }

  protected void createComponents() {
    propertiesPanel = new FontPropertiesPanel();
    super.createComponents ();
  }

}
```

Figure 2-4 illustrates the relationship between these components.

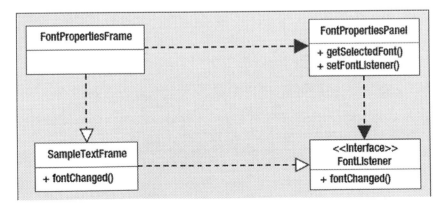

Figure 2-4. *Class diagrams such as this one illustrate the dependencies between classes and can be helpful in identifying design weaknesses*

Although it was necessary to create a small class (FontPropertiesFrame) and an interface (FontListener), you've now converted two tightly coupled and practically impossible to reuse classes into good candidates for a reusable code library.

Strong Cohesion

In addition to loosely coupling classes, another characteristic of good class design is a high level of cohesion. If a class is highly cohesive, it means that all its responsibilities are closely related and that it's complete. In other words, the class isn't cohesive if it contains methods that perform unrelated functions or if some set of closely related functions is split across that class and one or more others. You saw an example of this in the application just described, where the original implementation of FontPropertiesPanel didn't contain a method to create an instance of Font based on the selected property settings.

Cohesion most commonly becomes a problem when too much functionality is added to a single class. To avoid that problem, a good rule of thumb is to keep the responsibilities of a class limited enough that they can be outlined with a brief description. For another example of classes that aren't cohesive, suppose you're given the code in Listing 2-7, which is part of a larger application. StudentReport is responsible for printing out students' reports.

Listing 2-7. StudentReport

```java
import java.util.List;

public class StudentReport {

  public void printStudentGrades(Student[] students) {
    List<TestScore> testScores;
    int total;

    for (Student student : students) {
      testScores = student.getTestScores();
      total = 0;
      for (TestScore testScore : testScores) {
        total += testScore.getPercentCorrect();
      }
      System.out.println("Final grade for " + student.getName() + " is " +
                          total / testScores.size());
    }
  }

}
```

Student holds students' names and an array containing their test results:

```java
import java.util.List;

public class Student {

  private List<TestScore> testScores;
  private String name;
```

```
  public Student(List<TestScore> scores, String name) {
    this.testScores = scores;
    this.name = name;
  }

  public String getName() {
    return name;
  }

  public List<TestScore> getTestScores() {
    return testScores;
  }

}
```

Finally, TestScore is as follows:

```
public class TestScore {

  private int percentCorrect;

  public TestScore(int percent) {
  this.percentCorrect = percent;
}

  public int getPercentCorrect() {
    return percentCorrect;
  }

}
```

This code will function correctly but is an example of poor design. StudentReport is responsible for printing a list of students and the average of their grades, but it has also been assigned responsibility for calculating the average. It's coupled both to Student and to TestScore, because TestScore contains the information needed to calculate the averages. Figure 2-5 illustrates the relationships among these three classes.

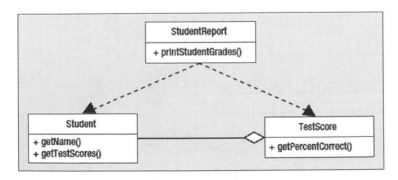

Figure 2-5. *This diagram illustrates the relationship between the StudentReport, TestScore, and Student classes*

Notice that both StudentReport and Student depend upon TestScore. This code is poorly designed because it violates both of the guidelines outlined previously.

- The classes are tightly coupled because of an unnecessary dependency (specifically StudentReport's dependency upon TestScore).

- StudentReport suffers from weak cohesion, because it performs two functions: printing a report and calculating each student's average.

This poor design is a result of the decision to assign StudentReport the responsibility for calculating averages. A better design would involve assigning responsibility for the calculation to Student and creating a method that allows StudentReport to obtain the information from that class. StudentReport's printStudentGrades() method is therefore much simpler.

```java
public class StudentReport {

  public void printStudentGrades(Student[] students) {
    for (Student student : students) {
      System.out.println("Final grade for " + student.getName() +
          " is " + student.getAverage());
    }
  }

}
```

And Student gains a getAverage() method:

```java
import java.util.List;

public class Student {

  private List<TestScore> testScores;
  private String name;

  public Student(List<TestScore> scores, String name) {
    this.testScores = scores;
    this.name = name;
  }

  public String getName() {
    return name;
  }

  public List<TestScore> getTestScores() {
    return testScores;
  }
```

```java
public int getAverage() {
  int total = 0;
  for (TestScore testScore : testScores) {
    total += testScore.getPercentCorrect();
  }
  return total / testScores.size();
}

}
```

TestScore is unchanged. This code is not only more readable but also more reusable, since there are fewer dependencies, as illustrated in Figure 2-6.

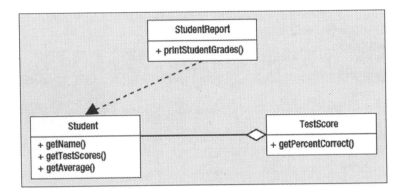

Figure 2-6. *Modifying the classes results in fewer dependencies, which in turn results in application code that's easier to understand and support*

In general, you should assign responsibilities carefully and minimize the number of dependencies among different classes. As mentioned earlier, you should usually assign responsibility for manipulating data to the class that has access to it. In this case, Student had access to all the necessary information while StudentReport didn't, which made Student a better choice for performing the task of calculating an average.

Encapsulation

One of the most basic ways of ensuring good class design is to provide effective encapsulation of your data. For example, suppose you create a class called Employee that contains all the information an application needs to describe an individual.

```java
public class Employee {

  public int employeeID;
  public String firstName;
  public String lastName;

}
```

Since the three fields are public, it's possible to access them from any other class, as in the following code segment:

```
Employee emp = new Employee();
emp.employeeID = 123456;
emp.firstName = "John";
emp.lastName = "Smith";
```

Although Java allows you to read and modify fields this way, you shouldn't normally do it. Instead, change the visibility of the fields to restrict their accessibility and create a pair of accessor (get) and mutator (set) methods (sometimes called *getters* and *setters*) for each field that will allow you access to it, as in Listing 2-8.

Listing 2-8. Adding Accessor and Mutator Methods

```
public class Employee {

  private int employeeID;
  private String firstName;
  private String lastName;

  public int getEmployeeID() {
    return employeeID;
  }

  public void setEmployeeID(int id) {
    employeeID = id;
  }

  public String getFirstName() {
    return firstName;
  }

  public void setFirstName(String name) {
    firstName = name;
  }

  public String getLastName() {
    return lastName;
  }

  public void setLastName(String name) {
    lastName = name;
  }
}
```

Encapsulation and object-oriented "purity" are nice concepts, but this approach also has some practical advantages. First, if it becomes necessary for Employee to be made thread-safe, which we'll discuss in detail in Chapter 3, then it's relatively easy to do so if access to its fields is controlled this way. In contrast, when implementation details—such as the fields that contain the data—are visible externally, there's really no way to control how those fields are used.

Another advantage of using accessor and mutator methods is that they insulate you from changes to a property's implementation. For example, you could change employeeID from an int to a String without affecting other classes, as long as you perform the appropriate conversions in the accessor and mutator methods, as shown in Listing 2-9.

Listing 2-9. Encapsulation Hides Implementation Details

```java
public class Employee {

  private String employeeID;
  private String firstName;
  private String lastName;

  public int getEmployeeID() {
    return Integer.parseInt(employeeID);
  }

  public void setEmployeeID(int id) {
    employeeID = Integer.toString(id);
  }

  public String getFirstName() {
    return firstName;
  }

  public void setFirstName(String name) {
    firstName = name;
  }

  public String getLastName() {
    return lastName;
  }

  public void setLastName(String name) {
    lastName = name;
  }

}
```

Although the implementation of employeeID changed, other classes that read or modify it won't see any change in its behavior, because the change in implementation is concealed by the accessor and mutator methods.

Finally, encapsulating the class properties this way allows you to define derived values that can be made accessible. For example, you might define a getFullName() method in Employee that returns the first and last name together as a single string.

```java
public String getFullName()  {
  return firstName + " " + lastName;
}
```

Of course, it's possible to obtain derived values without creating an accessor method, but often that means duplicating the code that derives the value. For example, to derive the "full name" property in several places within your application, you'd have to copy the implementation (`firstName + " " + lastName`) to each of those places. This has the same disadvantage that always accompanies duplicated code: if the implementation ever changes, you'll need to change every place in the code that relied upon the old implementation. If you decided to include a middle name, for instance, using a `getFullName()` method would allow you to make the change in a single place within your code.

Visibility

In this example, the fields were `private` and the methods `public`. As a rule, you should assign fields and methods the most restrictive visibility possible while still providing the functionality you need (see Table 2-1). The methods in `Employee` are `public` because it's assumed it should be possible for any other class in any package to be able to access and manipulate the state of an `Employee` instance. As mentioned earlier, though, overly permissive scope leaves a class open to usage in ways that weren't anticipated or desirable. More importantly, the more a class exposes its methods and fields to other classes the more likely it becomes that other classes will be tightly coupled to that class and the harder it becomes to maintain and modify that class without breaking other code.

Table 2-1. *Variable and Method Scope*

Visibility	Description
public	Accessible by all classes
protected	Accessible by subclasses and by other classes within the same package
(Default)	Accessible by classes within the same package
private	Not accessible from any class other than the one in which it's defined

Following are some rules of thumb for selecting visibility area:

- If access is needed across a variety of classes in different packages use `public`.
- If access is only needed by subclasses use `protected`.
- If access is only needed for other classes in the same package use default visibility.
- If none of the above applies use `private`.

Except for constants, which are marked `static` and/or `final`, fields should almost always be made `private`, with access provided through an appropriate method as described earlier. Usually the hardest decision related to scope is whether to use private, default, or protected visibility for a method. It is, of course, a technically trivial change to increase a method's scope later, but sometimes circumstances—such as your organization's processes or expectations—make code changes difficult or impossible. In that latter case, where changes are discouraged or impossible, you may prefer to provide more visibility than is known to be needed. In general, though, you should aim to provide the most restrictive scope possible at every level of design: fields, methods, and classes.

Constant fields, as just mentioned, are somewhat of an exception to the rule of thumb regarding scope. Constants are sometimes represented by primitive (`int`, `char`, etc.) values but can also be represented by objects and to understand how this is accomplished it's helpful to examine how to create and use what are referred to as *immutable objects*.

Immutable Objects

To say that an object is *immutable* means that its state can't be changed, which is most commonly implemented by allowing its state to only set during construction. Some examples of this in Java's core class library are the wrapper classes defined in the java.lang package (Integer, Float, Boolean, etc.), which are called *wrapper classes* because they "wrap" a primitive value with an object. String instances are probably the most commonly used type of immutable object, even though it might appear on the surface that you're able to modify them. For example, the following three lines will compile and run successfully:

```
String myString = "Hi";
System.out.println(myString);

//...

myString = "Hello";
System.out.println(myString);
myString += " there";
System.out.println(myString);
```

Running this code segment will produce the following output:

```
Hi
Hello
Hello there
```

From this example, it may seem that the object instance referenced by myString was modified twice after it was initially created: once when it was assigned a new value of "Hello" and a second time when "there" is appended. In reality, an entirely new String instance was created for each distinct value shown, and the reference was changed to point to the new instance. In other words, none of the objects was modified; instead, a new object was created and a reference to it replaced the reference to the previous value. Any references to the original string that existed before the two "changes" would still refer to the original "Hi" text.

Although String and the wrapper classes for primitive values are part of Java's core library, it's easy to create your own immutable class. In the case of the Employee class, for example, it can easily be made immutable by declaring its fields to all be final, which in turn has two implications for the rest of the class:

- At least one constructor must be defined that allows a value to be assigned to each field.

- The mutator (setter) methods must be removed because modifying the fields after construction is no longer possible and code that attempts to do so will result in a compiler error.

For example, we can easily convert the Employee class defined earlier into an immutable class by adding a constructor and removing the mutator methods as shown in Listing 2-10.

Listing 2-10. An Immutable Version of the Employee Class

```java
public class Employee {

  private String employeeID;
  private String firstName;
  private String lastName;

public Employee(String id, String first, String last) {
    employeeID = id;
    firstName = first;
    lastName = last;
}

public int getEmployeeID() {
    return Integer.parseInt(employeeID);
}

  public String getFirstName() {
    return firstName;
  }

  public String getLastName() {
    return lastName;
  }

}
```

Instances of Employee are now immutable because the properties are set during construction and can never be modified after that. Note that we can—and arguably should—mark the three fields as final, though this will have no functional impact on the code. What it would accomplish, though, is to make it obvious to anyone looking at the class that its properties are immutable; otherwise it's necessary to browse the entire class to determine that no mutator methods exist. Browsing the entire class isn't a problem in a small, simple case like this one, but in a larger and more complex class it's helpful to make clear by the use of final which fields can't be modified after construction.

On the other hand, it's also important to understand that making all the fields in a class final doesn't automatically mean that the class is immutable. Remember that being immutable means that an object's state can't be modified, but if the object contains references to other objects and the state of those objects can change then the containing class isn't immutable. If this explanation sounds a little confusing it may help to consider another example using a different class that we used before, specifically, the Student class, which defines a name and collection of test scores. Both the name and the test score collection are initialized at construction and no mutator is defined for either, so on the surface it may appear that Student is immutable, but in reality that's not the case. Recall that one of its accessor methods returned a reference to the test scores as shown next.

```java
public List<TestScore> getTestScores() {
  return testScores;
}
```

The problem is that the Student class returns a reference to part of its internal state, specifically, the collection of test scores, and that collection can be changed by adding or removing entries, which in turn means that Student is mutable. Making the testScores field final wouldn't have any effect at all because that wouldn't prevent the collection from being modified; it would only prevent the reference stored in Student from being overwritten after construction. There are different ways this can be addressed but one easy solution is to wrap the list passed to the Student constructor in an unmodifiable list.

```java
public Student(List<TestScore> scores, String name) {
  this.testScores = Collections.unmodifiableList(scores);
  this.name = name;
}
```

Now when the getTestScores() method is called it will return a reference to a list that can't be modified. Depending on the design of your application this may be sufficient, but there's still one potential cause for concern: the class that created the Student instance could still modify the original List that was passed to the constructor or could pass a reference to that List to some other object that might modify it. To be certain that the test score data can't be modified it's necessary to create an object that's never exposed outside of Student, and an example of how this is done is shown in Listing 2-11, which shows a fully immutable version of Student:

Listing 2-11. An Immutable Version of the Student Class

```java
import java.util.ArrayList;
import java.util.Collections;
import java.util.List;

public class Student {

  private List<TestScore> testScores;
  private String name;

  public Student(List<TestScore> scores, String name) {
    this.testScores = Collections.unmodifiableList(
        new ArrayList<TestScore>(scores));
    this.name = name;
  }

  public String getName() {
    return name;
  }

  public List<TestScore> getTestScores() {
    return testScores;
  }

  public int getAverage() {
    int total = 0;
    for (TestScore testScore : testScores) {
      total += testScore.getPercentCorrect();
    }
    return total / testScores.size();
  }

}
```

This gives us the immutability we wanted; the List inside Student can't be modified because that class doesn't contain any code to change it after it's constructed and because there's no way for any other class to obtain a reference to the collection or otherwise modify it once it's created.

We just spent a bit of time discussing how to make classes immutable, but why bother? What's the benefit of spending the additional effort it takes to make a class immutable? Aside from their simplicity, the biggest advantage of an immutable class over a mutable one is that an immutable class is inherently thread-safe. In other words, any number of threads can safely reference and use an immutable object, such as an instance of Student, without any explicit synchronization between the other threads. Thread safety is an important topic, and one that we'll discuss in more detail in Chapter 3.

Overriding Object Methods

The java.lang.Object class is the direct or indirect superclass of all Java classes, and it's often necessary or desirable to override some of the methods in Object. The following sections cover the methods that are commonly overridden, along with a description of how each one is used and what information you need to know before overriding it.

clone( )

The implementation of this method defined in Object returns a copy of the object instance, assuming that the class implements the Cloneable interface. Cloneable is a tag interface—that is, it's an interface that doesn't define any methods but is used to mark instances of a class as having some property. In this case, the interface indicates it's acceptable to create a *clone*, or copy, of an instance of the class. The following code checks to see whether the object unknown implements Cloneable, and it displays a message indicating whether that's the case:

```
Object unknown = getAnObject();
if (unknown instanceof Cloneable) {
  System.out.println("I can create a clone of this object");
} else {
  System.out.println("I might not be able to create a clone of this object");
}
```

The indefinite wording of the second message reflects the fact that the Cloneable interface only applies to the clone() implementation in Object. In other words, a class that inherits the clone() method from Object can only be cloned if it implements Cloneable, but a class is free to override clone() with its own implementation that ignores the presence or absence of that interface. The default implementation of clone() defined in Object creates a shallow copy of the object, where *shallow copy* is defined as a copy of the object that contains references to the same objects to which the original contained references. For example, suppose that we have an implementation of Employee like the one defined earlier, but this time implementing Cloneable (see Listing 2-12).

Listing 2-12. An Employee Class That Implements Cloneable

```
public class Employee implements Cloneable {

  private int employeeID;
  private String firstName;
  private String lastName;

  public Employee(int id, String first, String last) {
    employeeID = id;
    firstName = first;
    lastName = last;
  }

  public int getEmployeeID() {
    return employeeID;
  }

  public String getFirstName() {
    return firstName;
  }

  public String getLastName() {
    return lastName;
  }

}
```

Let's also suppose that an instance of this class is created and initialized, and the clone() method is called to create a copy of it. Note that Object's implementation of clone() is protected, so you must either call it from a subclass or class in the same package or override it and make it public, and for this example we'll assume that one or both of those to approaches was used.

```
Employee original = new Employee(123456, "John", "Smith");
Employee myClone = (Employee)(original.clone());
```

In this code segment, a shallow copy of the Employee instance is created, and a reference to it is stored in myClone. Since it's only a shallow copy, the object references in the clone will point to the same objects—not copies of those objects—that are referenced in the original. Figure 2-7 illustrates this. Both the original and the clone have their own copy of employeeID, because it's a primitive (integer) value and primitives are always copied by value instead of by reference. Note, however, that the other (object) fields contain references to the same object instances.

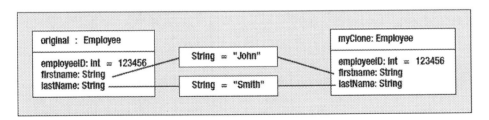

Figure 2-7. *A shallow copy of an object is one that shares with the original object references to the same instances of other referenced objects*

Shallow copies are sometimes acceptable, but not in all cases. For example, when you create a clone of an object, you'll often do so intending to modify the contents of the clone without changing the original. In that case, a shallow copy may not be sufficient. For example, suppose you're using the following class:

```
public class MailMessage implements Cloneable {

  protected String sender;
  protected String recipient;
  protected StringBuffer messageText;

  public MailMessage(String from, String to, String message) {
    sender = from;
    recipient = to;
    messageText = new StringBuffer(message);
  }

  public StringBuffer getMessageText() {
    return messageText;
  }

}
```

If you use clone() to create a duplicate instance of this class, you'll have a shallow copy that points to the same object instances as the original. If you then make changes to the StringBuffer instance referenced by messageText, your changes will affect both the original MailMessage instance and its cloned copy. For example,

```
// Create a new instance of MailMessage
MailMessage original = new MailMessage("bspell", "jsmith",
                                "This is the original text");

// Create a shallow copy
MailMessage shallowCopy = (MailMessage)(original.clone());

// Get a reference to the copy's message text
StringBuffer text = shallowCopy.getMessageText();

// Modify the message text using the clone/shallow copy
text.append(" with some additional text appended");

// Now print out the message text using the original MailMessage
System.out.println(original.getMessageText().toString());
```

Running this code segment results in the following message being displayed:

```
This is the original text with some additional text appended
```

To prevent this from happening, you must override the `clone()` method in `MailMessage` so it creates a "deep" copy. For example,

```
public class MailMessage implements Cloneable {

  protected String sender;
  protected String recipient;
  protected StringBuffer messageText;

  public MailMessage(String from, String to, String message) {
    sender = from;
    recepient = to;
    messageText = new StringBuffer(message);
  }

  public StringBuffer getMessageText() {
    return messageText;
  }

  protected Object clone() CloneNotSupportedException {
    MailMessage mm = (MailMessage)(super.clone());
    mm.messageText = new StringBuffer(messageText.toString());
    return mm;
  }

}
```

Note that although it was necessary to create a new `StringBuffer` for `messageText`, it wasn't necessary to create new objects for either `sender` or `recipient`. This is because those two fields point to instances of `String`, which are immutable objects. Since their state can't be changed, it's usually acceptable for the original and the clone to reference the same object instance.

As these examples illustrate, it's generally true that shallow copies are acceptable for objects that contain references to immutable objects and/or to primitives, while more complicated object structures usually require deep copies. When a deep copy is needed, it's your responsibility to implement the functionality yourself.

equals()

This method returns a `boolean` value (true or false) and determines whether two object instances should be considered equal to one another. What determines equality between two instances is left up to the programmer to decide, and this method can be overridden to perform any type of comparison that's useful to you. The default implementation provided in `Object` tests to see whether the two objects being compared are actually the same object instance and, if so, returns `true`. However, if you define a class for which instances will be compared to one another, you'll often want to use some other criteria.

For example, you might decide that two instances of Employee should be considered equal if the value of employeeID is the same in both instances. In that case, you'd add a method similar to the following to the class:

```
public boolean equals(Object obj) {
  if ((obj != null) && (obj instanceof Employee)) {
    Employee emp = (Employee)obj;
    if (this.employeeID == emp.employeeID) {
      return true;
    }
  }
  return false;
}
```

This method first checks to ensure that the parameter passed to the equals() method isn't null and is an instance of Employee and, if so, casts it to a reference of that type. It then checks to see whether the employeeID field in both instances contains the same value and, if so, returns a value of true, indicating that the two instances are equal. Although this simple example uses only a single field to determine equality, you can use any criteria that are meaningful to your application when overriding equals() in your own classes.

finalize()

The garbage collector calls this method when it determines there are no more references to the instance but before the object is destroyed. The most common use of this method is to ensure that any resources held by the instance are released.

Java makes no guarantees about when or even if this method will ever be called for an instance, so you shouldn't use it for normal cleanup. Instead, provide a separate method that releases active resources, and encourage programmers who use the class to call that method to perform the cleanup. Listing 2-13 shows an example.

Listing 2-13. Using the finalize() Method

```
public class MyFinalizeTest {

  private boolean resourcesInUse;
  public synchronized void allocateResources() {
    performAllocate();
    resourcesInUse = true;
  }

  public synchronized void releaseResources() {
    performRelease();
    resourcesInUse = false;
  }

  /**
   * If we're still holding resources, release them now
   */
```

```
  protected synchronized void finalize() throws Throwable {
    if (resourcesInUse) {
      releaseResources();
    }
  }

  // Allocate resources here
  protected void performAllocate() {
  }

  // Release resources here
  protected void performRelease() {
  }

}
```

hashCode()

An object's hash code value is used primarily to improve the performance of some collection classes, such as java.util.HashMap. It's not necessary for each instance of a class to return a different hash code from every other instance, but you should attempt to make them as unique as possible. Greater uniqueness will generally translate into improved performance for collections that use hashing, such as HashMap. The following are the two requirements for values returned from this method:

- Two objects that are considered equal when compared using the equals() method must return the same hash code value.

- When this method is invoked on an object two or more times during a single execution of an application, the method should return the same value. However, this requirement doesn't need to be met if the object's state changes in such a way that the object would no longer be considered equal to an instance to which it was previously equal.

For example, given the previously defined Employee class, you might choose to simply use the employeeID field as the hash code for each instance. This is an appropriate choice since it could be expected to provide a reasonable degree of uniqueness from one instance to the next.

```
public int hashCode() {
  return employeeID;
}
```

This would satisfy the first requirement mentioned previously because the value of employeeID would be used to determine equality and would be used as the hash code value. In other words, two instances that have the same employeeID value are considered equal to one another, and they will return the same hash code value. The second requirement is also satisfied, because as long as the employeeID value remains unchanged, the hashCode() method will return the same result each time it's called.

When you have multiple properties that you want to use in performing the hash code calculation, and particularly if those properties are object references, you should consider using the hash() method defined in the java.util.Objects class. That method allows you to specify a variable number of arguments and will produce a hash code generated using the arguments supplied.

In general, the default implementation of hashCode() will return values that are reasonably unique, and you won't find it necessary to override this method. However, when you override the equals() method, you must also override hashCode() to ensure it meets the two requirements listed previously. If you don't, the collections that use hash codes may not function correctly.

toString()

This method returns a string representation of the object instance. You can call this method explicitly whenever it's useful to do so (such as while debugging), but it's also called implicitly whenever you specify an object reference as part of a string expression. For example, if you create an instance of MailMessage and include it in a string expression, the toString() method is called to obtain its string representation.

```
MailMessage message = new MailMessage("bspell", "jsmith", "This is a test");
System.out.println("Calling toString(): " + message);

// The following line is equivalent to the previous one and would produce
// exactly the same output if it were compiled and executed:
// System.out.println("Calling toString(): " + message.toString());
```

The default implementation of this method in Object simply displays the name of the object's class and the object's hash code value, separated by the at (@) symbol:

```
MailMessage@71eaddc4
```

Since this information usually isn't very helpful, you'll normally want to override toString() so it returns more useful information. Typically, that information should include a partial or complete description of the object's state. For example, you might choose to add the following method to MailMessage:

```
public String toString() {
   return "MailMessage[sender=" + sender + ", recipient=" + recipient +
         ", messageText=" + messageText + "]";
}
```

With this implementation of toString(), running the code segment shown previously will result in the following output:

```
MailMessage[sender=bspell, recipient=jsmith, messageText=This is a test]
```

You can use this information when debugging or at any other time when you need to obtain a string representation of an object's state.

Method Design

Many of the guidelines previously mentioned for classes also apply to methods. For example, methods should be loosely coupled and strongly cohesive, with each method having a single responsibility that can be easily described, and should be independent of other methods as much as possible.

One indication that a method may not be cohesive is the existence of many levels of code blocks, which are easy to identify if the blocks are properly indented. For example,

```
public void doSomethingComplex(int a, int b, Object c, int d) {
  if (a < b) {
    if (c instanceof Number) {
      for (int i = 0; i < count; i++) {
        if (getSomeData(i) == null) {
          while (d < 5) {
            if (d == 0) {
              handleSpecialCase();
            }
          }
        }
      }
    }
  }
}
```

It's sometimes necessary to create such complex logical constructs. However, it's never necessary to include the entire construct in a single method, and splitting it into two or more methods can make the code much easier to understand. Most people find it difficult to follow more than a few levels of logic and would probably find the following implementation more readable:

```
public void doSomethingComplex(int a, int b, Object c, int d) {
  if (a < b) {
    if (c instanceof Number) {
      for (int i = 0; i < count; i++) {
        doPartOfSomethingComplex(i, d);
      }
    }
  }
}

public void doPartOfSomethingComplex(int i, int d) {
  if (getSomeData(i) == null) {
    while (d < 5) {
      if (d == 0) {
        handleSpecialCase();
      }
    }
  }
}
```

Although this may not be the best implementation for these methods, it illustrates that by separating pieces of functionality from a method, you can make its responsibilities simpler and clearer. In addition to greater clarity, structuring your code this way can also make it easier to enhance and debug.

One basic but extremely important point worth mentioning concerning method design is the use of an obscure, complex algorithm when a simpler alternative exists. Although the more complicated approach may provide minor benefits such as slightly faster execution, that advantage is usually outweighed by the added complexity involved in the maintenance and debugging of the code. Stated more simply, readability, extensibility, and reliability are important, and you should be hesitant to sacrifice those qualities for an algorithm that seems elegant and clever unless doing so provides some important advantage to your application.

Passing Parameters

When deciding what parameters to pass to a method, you should avoid using "flags" or "control" parameters that tell the method how to perform its function. For example, assume you're responsible for a Roster class that maintains a list of students. In addition, let's assume a limit exists to the number of students that can normally be included on the roster. However, in some cases, you want to be able to override that maximum, so you might create a class like the one shown in Listing 2-14.

Listing 2-14. Initial Roster Implementation

```
import java.util.*;

public class Roster {

  protected int capacity;
  protected List<String> students;

  public Roster(int max) {
    capacity = max;
    students = new ArrayList<>();
  }

  /**
   * Attempts to add the student name to the List that is used to
   * maintain the list. There is a capacity value that normally will
   * limit the number of students that can be on the list, but the
   * caller can override that constraint if the student has been
   * given permission from their advisor to add the class even though
   * it's already full.
   *
   * @param  name      Student to add to the list.
   * @param  allowExcess  Override capacity check when adding student
   * @return        <code>true</code> if the student was added
   *          to the list, <code>false</code> otherwise.
   */
  public boolean addStringToList(String name, boolean allowExcess) {
    if (!allowExcess) {
      if (students.size() >= capacity) {
        return false;
      }
    }
    students.addElement(name);
    return true;
  }

}
```

At first glance, this method may appear to be reasonably well-designed, but in fact, it possesses a number of undesirable characteristics. For one thing, it requires callers to pass a parameter that indicates whether the student should be added when the capacity value has already been reached. This makes the method less cohesive, because it not only has responsibility for adding the student's name to the List but it also must determine whether it's acceptable to add the student.

Given that the method isn't cohesive, how can it be improved? For starters, you should eliminate the allowExcess flag, since it's used as a way for the caller to communicate with the method concerning how the method should operate. You should avoid using parameters for that purpose, since they tend to make the function of your method less clear and cohesive. In this example, a better solution is to create a separate method that always ignores the capacity value and remove the allowExcess flag, as shown in Listing 2-15.

Listing 2-15. Eliminating Flag Usage

```java
import java.util.*;

public class Roster {

  protected int capacity;
  protected List<String> students;
  public Roster(int max) {
    capacity = max;
    students = new List<>();
  }

  /**
   * Adds the student name to the List that is used to maintain the
   * list.
   *
   * @param name     Student to add to the list.
   */
  public void addStringToList(String name) {
    students.addElement(name);
  }

  /**
   * Attempts to add the student name to the List that is used to
   * maintain the list. There is a capacity value that normally will
   * limit the number of students that can be on the list, but the
   * caller can override this check if desired.
   *
   * @param name     Student to add to the list.
   * @return     <code>true</code> if the student was added
   *         to the list, <code>false</code> otherwise.
   */
  public boolean conditionalAddStringToList(String name) {
    if (students.size() >= capacity) {
      return false;
    }
    addStringToList(name);
    return true;
  }

}
```

This is an improvement over the original design, as there's more cohesion in these two methods than in the original one. Instead of passing a flag to the method as in the previous implementation, the caller can now call the method that provides the desired behavior. Notice that conditionalAddStringToList() doesn't actually add the student but instead calls addStringToList(). Since the "add" operation requires just a single line of code, it might be tempting to copy the contents of addStringToList() to conditionalAddStringToList(). However, not doing so makes the code more cohesive, and the lack of code duplication makes the class easier to maintain.

Method Naming

One final point to make about the addStringToList() and conditionalAddStringToList() methods in the previous example is that they're poorly named. You should avoid names that describe the method implementation and instead use names that describe what the method does conceptually. For example, these method names imply that the purpose of the method is to add a String to a List, which is true in this implementation. However, this approach has two problems. First, the names don't provide any useful information that couldn't be obtained from a quick glance at the code, and naming these methods enrollStudentConditionally() and enrollStudent() provides the reader with helpful information about the responsibilities of these methods.

Second, choosing a name that describes a method's implementation is a bad idea because the implementation may change over time. If the Roster class were modified to use a different type of collection, the method name would need to be changed to avoid being a misleading representation of what occurs in the code. For example, if the student names were to be stored in a TreeSet instead of a List, you either must change every occurrence of the method names or resign yourself to having method names that no longer describe the implementation, which is at best confusing to programmers who read your code. Listing 2-16 shows an improved version of the Roster class.

Listing 2-16. Roster Class, Improved

```java
import java.util.List;

public class Roster {

    protected int capacity;
    protected List<String> students;

    public Roster(int max) {
        capacity = max;
        students = new List<String>();
    }

    /**
     * Enrolls the student in this course.
     *
     * @param name Name of the student to enroll.
     */
    public void enrollStudent(String name) {
        students.addElement(name);
    }
```

```
/**
 *  Attempts to enroll a student in this course. The student is added
 *  only if the capacity limit for the course has not been reached.
 *
 *  @param name Name of the student to enroll.
 *  @return <code>true</code> if the student was added
 *      to the list, <code>false</code> otherwise.
 */
public boolean enrollStudentConditionally(String name) {
  boolean isEnrolled = false;
  if (students.size() < capacity) {
  enrollStudent(name);
  isEnrolled = true;
  }
  return isEnrolled;
}

}
```

Avoiding Code Duplication

In the previous example, we placed the logic for adding a student in one method and called that method from a different one that needed the same functionality. Minimizing duplication is an important step in creating maintainable code, as it prevents you from having to make identical changes to many methods when some implementation detail must be modified. This is particularly important when multiple programmers are involved in creating an application and it applies not only to methods but also to constructors, since you can call one constructor from another. For example, the following class shows an example of how duplication can occur in constructors:

```
public class DuplicationSample {

  protected int firstValue;
  protected String secondValue;
  protected Integer thirdValue;

  public DuplicationSample(int first, String second, Integer third) {
    firstValue = first;
    secondValue = second;
    thirdValue = third;
  }

  public DuplicationSample(int first, String second) {
    firstValue = first;
    secondValue = second;
    thirdValue = new Integer(0);
  }

}
```

Only the last statement differs in these two constructors, and you can eliminate the duplicate code without changing the behavior of the constructors by modifying the class, as follows:

```java
public class DuplicationSample {

  protected int firstValue;
  protected String secondValue;
  protected Integer thirdValue;

  public DuplicationSample(int first, String second, Integer third) {
    firstValue = first;
    secondValue = second;
    thirdValue = third;
  }

  public DuplicationSample(int first, String second) {
    this(first, second, new Integer(0));
  }

}
```

Similarly with methods, it's often helpful to use overloading and identify a method implementation that contains a superset of the functionality defined in the other implementations. The following example illustrates this point:

```java
public class AddingMachine {

  /**
   * Adds two integers together and returns the result.
   */
  public static int addIntegers(int first, int second) {
    return first + second;
  }

  /**
   * Adds some number of integers together and returns the result.
   */
  public static int addIntegers(int[] values) {
    int result = 0;
    for (int value : values) {
      result += value;
    }
    return result;
  }

}
```

Although there's no code duplication here, there's duplicate functionality, and eliminating that duplication will make the class simpler and more maintainable. Both methods add numbers together, and it's necessary to decide which one should retain that functionality. One of the methods adds two numbers together, and the other adds zero or more numbers together. In other words, the first method provides a subset of the functionality of the second one. Since that's the case, you can eliminate the duplication by delegating responsibility for adding the two numbers to the more flexible method. The following is an alternative implementation:

```
public class AddingMachine {

  /**
   * Adds two integers together and returns the result.
   */
  public static int addIntegers(int first, int second) {
    return addIntegers(new int[] {first, second});
  }

  /**
   *  Adds some number of integers together and returns the result.
   */
  public static int addIntegers(int[] values) {
    int result = 0;
    for (int value : values) {
      result += value;
    }
    return result;
  }

}
```

This simplistic example illustrates an important point concerning something that's common in method design. Specifically, you can often reduce code or functional duplication by identifying a method that represents a "special case" of some other method and delegating the request to the more generic implementation. Although it does represent an improvement over the original implementation there are still a couple of features of the implementation that are not ideal.

- The caller of the second addIntegers() method is required to construct an array.

- Unless additional error checking is added it's possible to specify zero or one integers to the method, neither of which is very meaningful. In other words, it doesn't make much sense to define a method that adds zero or one numbers together and returns the result.

Variable Arguments

This code can be improved further in a way that will both make it "cleaner" and also reduce the amount of code involved, specifically by creating a method that uses *variable arguments*, or *varargs*, adds the values specified, and returns the result. As the name implies, varargs are a way of defining a method that can accept a variable number of arguments, which in this case means that a variable number of integer values can be added. In other words, instead of explicitly identifying each individual argument, varargs allow you to indicate that zero or more arguments of a particular type can be specified. The following is an example of how you can declare such a method:

```
/**
 * Add at least two integers together and returns the result.
 */
public static int addIntegers(int value1, int value2, int... values) {
  int result = value1 + value2;
  for (int value : values) {
    result += value;
  }
  return result;
}
```

The values parameter is identified by the ellipses (…) after its type as representing a variable number of int values and it follows a pair of parameters that require the user to specify integer values. In other words, the caller must specify at least two int values that correspond to the value1 and value2 parameters and can also specify zero or more additional int values that will be assigned to the values vararg parameter. For example, the caller could specify a pair of numbers, as shown.

```
int result = addInteger(37, 23);
```

Or, as in the following example, the caller can specify additional integers:

```
int result = addInteger(37, 23, 59, -2, 0);
```

Notice that when iterating through the varargs parameter values, we're able to use Java's enhanced for looping just as we would with a collection or array. That's possible because varargs are implemented internally as arrays, so any code that will work with an array will work with a vararg parameter.

Varargs do have an important limitation: you can have only one vararg entry in a method signature. So, for example, the following isn't a valid method signature:

```
public void doSomething(String... firstList, int... secondList);
```

Using Exceptions

Exceptions provide a useful capability, and properly using exceptions is an important part of good method design in Java. However, a number of questions arise when designing a class.

- When should an exception be thrown?
- What type of exception should be thrown?
- When should a new exception subclass be created, and what should its superclass be?
- What information should be included in the exceptions that are thrown?
- Where should exceptions be caught and handled?

When to Throw an Exception

In general, your method should throw an exception when some sort of condition is detected that the method can't or shouldn't handle. It's usually obvious when a method can't handle an exception, but it may be less clear how to determine when it should handle some condition. Sometimes the method may be able to handle the condition but it isn't the best choice for doing so. For example, suppose you define a simple user interface that allows the user to enter a name and an age. Let's also assume that your interface provides a button that ends the application when pressed, as illustrated in Figure 2-8.

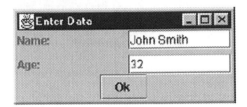

Figure 2-8. *A simple application with an interface that prompts the user to enter some basic information*

The following two classes provide this functionality; the DataFrame class displays a frame with a button and an instance of DataPanel (see Listing 2-17).

Listing 2-17. Initial DataFrame Implementation

```java
import java.awt.*;
import java.awt.event.*;
import javax.swing.*;

public class DataFrame extends JFrame {

  public static void main(String[] args) {
    DataFrame df = new DataFrame();
    df.setVisible(true);
  }

  public DataFrame() {
    super("Enter Data");
    buildLayout();
    pack();
  }

  protected void buildLayout() {
    Container pane = getContentPane();
    pane.setLayout(new BorderLayout());
    pane.add(new DataPanel(), BorderLayout.CENTER);
    JButton button = new JButton("Ok");
    button.addActionListener(new ActionListener() {
      public void actionPerformed(ActionEvent event) {
        System.exit(0);
      }
    }
    );
```

```
      JPanel panel = new JPanel();
      panel.setLayout(new FlowLayout(FlowLayout.CENTER, 0, 0));
      panel.add(button);
      pane.add(panel, BorderLayout.SOUTH);
   }

}
```

The DataPanel class defines the text fields that allow the user to enter a name and an age (see Listing 2-18).

Listing 2-18. Initial DataPanel Implementation

```
import java.awt.GridLayout;
import javax.swing.*;

public class DataPanel extends JPanel {

  protected JTextField nameField;
  protected JTextField ageField;

  public DataPanel() {
    buildDisplay();
  }

  protected void buildDisplay() {
    setLayout(new GridLayout(2, 2, 10, 5));
    JLabel label = new JLabel("Name:");
    add(label);
    nameField = new JTextField(10);
    add(nameField);
    label = new JLabel("Age:");
    add(label);
    ageField = new JTextField(10);
    add(ageField);
  }

}
```

Now let's assume the requirements change after these two classes have been created, and it's now required that the user must enter valid data before exiting the application. Specifically, the "Name" field shouldn't be blank, and the "Age" field should contain a positive integer. In addition, let's specify that if either of these two conditions isn't met, then an error dialog should be displayed and the input focus set to the field that contains invalid data.

Given these requirements, you must decide where to assign responsibility for the new functionality. The design guidelines covered previously indicate that the responsibility for validation belongs in DataPanel, since it already has access to the data being validated. The other new responsibility that must be assigned is the error message display, and DataFrame stands out as the more desirable choice, because putting the error display logic into DataPanel would make it less cohesive and less flexible. For example, another application might need to reuse DataPanel but might not want to use dialogs to display validation errors.

This scenario provides an example of what was referred to previously as an error that a method shouldn't handle. The validation method in DataPanel shouldn't be responsible for displaying the error dialog because doing so would make it less cohesive, flexible, and extensible. Instead, it should throw an exception and let its caller in DataFrame display the error.

Choosing the Exception Type

Now that you've determined an exception will be thrown, what type of exception should be used? Many subclasses of Exception are defined with the Java core classes, and it's appropriate for applications to create and throw instances of those. In fact, nothing prevents you from throwing an exception that's totally unrelated to the problem that has occurred. For example, when the validation routine determines that the user has entered a non-numeric age value, it could throw any type of exception, such as a NullPointerException, a SocketException, or an InterruptedException. However, those are inappropriate choices because those exceptions are normally used to indicate specific problems that have no relationship to our user interface validation. While it's possible to use the exception classes defined as part of Java, you should do so only if the exception is an appropriate choice for signaling the type of error your application experienced. Otherwise, you should instead create your own Exception subclass and throw an instance of that class. Besides a situation where no existing exception class accurately describes the condition that has occurred, there's at least one other case where you'll want to create a custom exception class. Specifically, you'll do so when you need to return more information than a simple text message to the caller who's responsible for handling the exception; you'll see an example of this later in the chapter.

Choosing a Superclass for a Custom Exception Class

When creating your own exception classes, you'll normally want to extend one of two classes: either Exception or RuntimeException. You should subclass Exception when you want your exception classified as a checked exception. A checked exception is one that must be declared when you create a method that can throw the exception, while unchecked exceptions (subclasses of RuntimeException) need not be declared or caught.

For example, the doSomething() method in the class shown in Listing 2-19 can throw either MyFirstException or MySecondException, but only MyFirstException must be identified, because it's a checked exception (in other words, it subclasses Exception).

Listing 2-19. ExceptionSampler Implementation

```java
public class ExceptionSampler {

  /**
   * Not declaring that this method can throw MyFirstException will
   * cause the Java compiler to generate an error message when this
   * class is compiled. However, declaring MySecondException is
   * optional.
   */
  public void doSomething(boolean throwFirst) throws MyFirstException {
    if (throwFirst) {
      throw new MyFirstException();
    } else {
      throw new MySecondException();
    }
  }

  class MyFirstException extends Exception {
  }

  class MySecondException extends RuntimeException {
  }

}
```

Determining which type of exception to create is usually based on the nature of the error or errors that can cause the exception to be thrown. Checked (Exception subclasses) should be used when the condition is one for which the software can provide some type of recovery; on the other hand, if the error is one from which it isn't practical to try to recover then unchecked exceptions are the more appropriate choice. Stated another way, unchecked (RuntimeException subclass) exceptions are best used to represent programming errors. For example, the exception that's probably thrown more frequently than any other is NullPointerException. It's thrown any time you attempt to use a null object reference to access a field or method, which almost by definition indicates a programming error. If NullPointerException were a checked exception, you'd be forced to throw it from virtually all methods or to catch it at hundreds or even thousands of places within a single application, but because it's an unchecked exception you can selectively choose when (or if) to catch it, which makes code less tedious to write and easier to understand.

In the case of our input validation routine for DataFrame and DataPanel, though, we actually intend to recover from the error by indicating to the user that invalid data was entered and giving the user a chance to enter something different. To accommodate that behavior we'll create a checked exception and call it InputValidationException:

```
public class InputValidationException extends Exception {
}
```

Using a Common Superclass for Different Exception Types

Another issue you'll commonly need to address regarding exceptions occurs when you throw exceptions for different but related types of error conditions. For example, suppose you create a method called attemptLogon() that can throw a LogonFailedException if either the username or password specified is invalid. It's possible to use only a single LogonFailedException class in both cases and simply create an appropriate message that describes which type of condition caused the exception to be thrown. Alternatively, you may consider creating subclasses of that exception (perhaps calling them InvalidUseridException and InvalidPasswordException) and throwing instances of those subclasses instead of an instance of LogonFailedException.

To determine which approach is better you need to consider how the exceptions will be handled. If you plan to create error handling for the entry of an invalid password that's different from the handling for an invalid username, you should create the two subclasses and throw instances of those. However, if your application will simply display the message encapsulated within the exception object and it doesn't care which type of error occurred, you should create and use only a single exception class. In other words, splitting an exception class into a hierarchy with additional subclasses gives you extra flexibility in terms of how you handle specific exception causes and their corresponding types. For example, the following code illustrates how you might just display the error message contained within the exception class:

```
String userid, password;
// ...
try {
  attemptLogon(userid, password);
} catch (LogonFailedException lfe) {
  System.out.println("Logon failed: " + lfe.getMessage());
}
```

In contrast, the following code assumes that the `InvalidPasswordException` is handled differently from other errors (for example, `InvalidUseridException`):

```
String userid, password;
// ...
try {
  attemptLogon(userid, password);
}
// Handle the case where the password was invalid
catch (InvalidPasswordException ipe) {
  // Log the logon attempt and possibly lock the userid
  // to prevent more logon attempts
  recordFailedLogon(userid);
  System.out.println("Logon failed: " + ipe.getMessage());
}
// Handle all other types of errors
catch (LogonFailedException lfe) {
  System.out.println("Logon failed: " + lfe.getMessage());
}
```

Although it's not necessary to make `InvalidUseridException` and `InvalidPasswordException` share a single superclass, doing so has a significant advantage. Instead of specifying that it throws both types of exception, the `attemptLogon()` method can be defined to throw instances of `LogonFailedException` as follows:

```
public void attemptLogon(String userid, String password)
    throws LogonFailedException {
```

instead of the following:

```
public void attemptLogon(String userid, String password)
    throws InvalidUseridException, InvalidPasswordException {
```

Besides making your code slightly simpler, the first approach shown also makes it possible for you to modify `attemptLogon()` so it throws additional exception types without also changing the code that calls the method. In fact, you can add any number of new exception types without affecting the method signature as long as the new exception types are subclasses of an exception type already declared. For example, you might change `attemptLogon()` so it also throws an exception called `AlreadyLoggedOnException`. As long as that new exception type is a subclass of `LogonFailedException`, you're not required to make any changes to the code that calls `attemptLogon()`.

Adding Information to an Exception

When creating your exception, you should include a message that describes the nature of the error that occurred, along with any information that exception handlers will need. Keep in mind that exceptions are a mechanism for communicating with your method's callers, and any information that's needed to process the error should be included. In the case of our input validation, the validation routine will pass back to the handler two pieces of information: an error message and a reference to the field that contains invalid information. The `Exception` class inherits the ability to store a message from its parent, so the only additional field you need to define is a reference to the component associated with the error. By returning a reference to the component, you make it possible for the frame to move the input focus to that component as a convenience for the user.

```java
import java.awt.Component;

public class InputValidationException extends Exception {

  protected Component errorSource;

  public InputValidationException(String message, Component source) {
    super(message);
    errorSource = source;
  }

  public Component getErrorSource() {
    return errorSource;
  }

}
```

Now that the exception class is created, you can implement the validation routine in DataPanel and make it throw an exception when it encounters an error, as shown in Listing 2-20.

Listing 2-20. Throwing InputValidationException

```java
import java.awt.GridLayout;
import javax.swing.*;

public class DataPanel extends JPanel {

  protected JTextField nameField;
  protected JTextField ageField;

  public DataPanel() {
    buildDisplay();
  }

  public void validateInput() throws InputValidationException {
    String name = nameField.getText();
    if (name.length() == 0) {
      throw new InputValidationException("No name was specified",
                                         nameField);
    }
    String age = ageField.getText();
    try {
      int value = Integer.parseInt(age);
      if (value <= 0) {
        throw new InputValidationException("Age value must be " +
                                           "a positive integer",
                                           ageField);
      }
    }
  }
```

```
   catch (NumberFormatException e) {
      throw new InputValidationException("Age value is missing " +
                                         "or invalid", ageField);
   }
 }
}

protected void buildDisplay() {
   setLayout(new GridLayout(2, 2, 10, 5));
   JLabel label = new JLabel("Name:");
   add(label);
   nameField = new JTextField(10);
   add(nameField);
   label = new JLabel("Age:");
   add(label);
   ageField = new JTextField(10);
   add(ageField);
 }

}
```

Notice that there are three cases where you throw InputValidationException: when the "Name" field is empty, when the "Age" field is less than or equal to zero, and when the "Age" field isn't a valid integer. It's easy to create more than one exception class, such as one for a missing name and one for an invalid age, as shown in Figure 2-9.

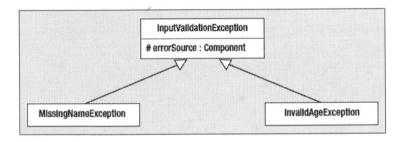

Figure 2-9. *Creating more granular exception classes gives you more control over exception processing*

However, the only time you should do this is when there are multiple possible error conditions and some of them are handled differently from others. This example has three different error conditions, but they're all handled the same way and by the same caller. Therefore, you have no need to define more than one new Exception subclass.

Finally, you must modify DataFrame so that it catches any validation errors and displays them in a dialog (see Listing 2-21). In addition, we'll use the reference to the component with the invalid data to set the input focus to that component after the error message is displayed that indicates why the data is invalid.

Listing 2-21. Handling the Exception

```java
import java.awt.*;
import java.awt.event.*;
import javax.swing.*;

public class DataFrame extends JFrame {

  protected DataPanel panel = new DataPanel();

  public static void main(String[] args) {
    DataFrame df = new DataFrame();
    df.setVisible(true);
  }

  public DataFrame() {
    super("Enter Data");
    buildLayout();
    pack();
  }

  protected void buildLayout() {
    Container pane = getContentPane();
    pane.setLayout(new BorderLayout());
    pane.add(panel, BorderLayout.CENTER);
    JButton button = new JButton("Ok");
    button.addActionListener(new ActionListener() {
      public void actionPerformed(ActionEvent event) {
        onOk();
      }
    }
    );
    JPanel panel = new JPanel();
    panel.setLayout(new FlowLayout(FlowLayout.CENTER, 0, 0));
    panel.add(button);
    pane.add(panel, BorderLayout.SOUTH);
  }

  protected void onOk() {
    try {
    panel.validateInput();
    System.exit(0);
  }
  catch (InputValidationException ive) {
    ive.getErrorSource().requestFocus();
    JOptionPane.showMessageDialog(this, ive.getMessage(),
                                  "Validation Error",
                                  JOptionPane.ERROR_MESSAGE);
    }
  }

}
```

When to Catch Exceptions

Two final points should be made concerning where exceptions should be caught and handled. As mentioned earlier, the main factor that will determine where to catch an exception is often simply a matter of good class design. In other words, your choice of where to handle an exception should be one that maintains the cohesiveness and flexibility of the classes involved. However, when no particular class stands out as an appropriate place to handle an exception, a rule of thumb is that you should catch the exception as early as possible. For example, suppose you have the following nested calls:

```
Method A() calls method B()
  Method B() calls method C()
    Method C() calls method D()
      Method D() calls method E(), which can throw SomeException
```

In this scenario, if method E() can throw SomeException, it's better to catch that exception as far down the call stack as possible. For example, if SomeException can be handled appropriately in method D() while still maintaining cohesion and loose coupling, then you should do so. If SomeException is a checked exception, handling it in D() will prevent you from having to declare that SomeException can be thrown from A(), B(), or C(), which simplifies your code. Depending upon the nature of the exception condition and the design of your application, it may be necessary to allow the exception to propagate all the way back to method A(). However, you should do so only if handling the exception earlier would cause you to violate object-oriented design principles such as cohesion and loose coupling. In other words, throw exceptions as often as necessary but handle them as early as possible.

Lastly, you'll often find yourself creating a block of code that contains multiple statements that can throw exceptions, either a particular type of exception or several different types. In this situation, you should enclose all the statements within a single try/catch instead of creating a separate one for each statement. For example, suppose you've created the following segment of code that creates a database connection and uses it to execute and process the results of a query:

```
Connection connection = DriverManager.getConnection(url, userid, password);
Statement statement = connection.createStatement();
ResultSet results = null;
results = statement.executeQuery("SELECT * FROM CUSTOMERS WHERE CUSTID = 123");
if (results.next()) {
  String custname = results.getString("CUSTNAME");
  System.out.println(custname.toUpperCase());
}
```

The majority of the statements in this code segment are capable of throwing SQLException, but enclosing each one within its own try/catch block would be tedious and result in code that's difficult to read. Although it may be necessary to do so if your application needs to know specifically which statement caused the exception, it's often appropriate to simply enclose all of the statements in a single try/catch block as follows:

```
try {
  Connection connection = DriverManager.getConnection(url, userid, password);
  Statement statement = connection.createStatement();
  ResultSet results = null;
  results = statement.executeQuery(
      "SELECT * FROM CUSTOMERS WHERE CUSTID = 123");
```

```
  if (results.next()) {
    String custname = results.getString("CUSTNAME");
    System.out.println(custname.toUpperCase());
  }
} catch (SQLException sqle) {
  // Handle exception thrown by one of the statements
}
```

Using a finally Block

One of the more useful features of Java's exception handling facility is the ability to include a finally block, which is simply a section of code that's always executed after the code in the try block regardless of what happens during the execution of the code within that block. For example, suppose you create the following code segment:

```
String value;
// ...
try {
  int intValue = Integer.parseInt(value);
  System.out.println("Is a valid integer value");
}
catch (NumberFormatException nfe) {
  System.out.println("Not a valid integer value");
}
finally {
  System.out.println("This is always executed");
}
```

If the value string in the previous code represents a valid integer value, the try block will complete successfully and the following two messages will be displayed:

```
Is a valid integer value
This is always executed
```

In contrast, if the value string doesn't represent a valid integer, the parseInt() call will cause the try block to be exited, the catch block to be entered, and the following messages to be displayed:

```
Not a valid integer value
This is always executed
```

The most common reason for using a finally block is to ensure that cleanup occurs regardless of what happens within the try block. For example, suppose your application creates multiple threads that are using a Lock instance and you implement code that obtains the lock, performs an operation, and then releases the lock.

```
java.util.concurrent.locks.Lock resourceLock;
.
.
.
resourceLock.lock();
doSomething();
```

What's missing is a call to the Lock object's unlock() method that will cause the lock to be released. Placing the unlock() call inside a try/catch block as follows is a solution:

```
resourceLock.lock();
try {
  doSomething();
  resourceLock.unlock();
}
catch (Exception e) {
  resourceLock.unlock();
}
```

Note that a call to unlock() was defined both inside the try block and inside the catch block. This was done to ensure that the lock is released regardless of whether the call doSomething() throws an exception. If it doesn't throw an exception the unlock() call within the try block will release the lock; otherwise the one inside the catch block will release it. One possible way of eliminating the duplicate code is to put the unlock() call after the try/catch.

```
resourceLock.lock();
try {
  doSomething();
}
catch (Exception e) {
}
resourceLock.unlock();
```

Functionally this approach may work, but it's even less ideal than the previous approach. The catch block is empty because we didn't really intend to handle the exception at all, and in fact this design could very well mask a bug if doSomething() does throw an exception. In effect, we declared a catch block for an exception we aren't going to handle and then ignored the exception, which is a very poor coding practice. What we really want is to define code that's executed regardless of the success or failure of the doSomething() invocation, and we want to define that code without having to catch the exception. This is where the finally block is useful, and the following is an example of how it can be used:

```
resourceLock.lock();
try {
  doSomething();
}
finally {
  resourceLock.unlock();
}
```

In effect, the finally block defines code that will be executed regardless of what occurs inside the try block and—if one is defined—within the catch block. Even if, for example, you put a return statement inside the try (or catch) block, the code inside the finally block will be executed. That behavior is somewhat counter-intuitive, though, so for the sake of readability it's preferable to avoid relying on it that way. In practice it's better to define a single exit point inside a method, which would result in more structured and readable code.

You should be aware, too, that although we didn't define a catch block in this example, catch and finally aren't mutually exclusive: it's just as valid to include one, resulting in a try/catch/finally block as shown next, where the previous code has been modified to catch and rethrow the exception generated by doSomething().

```
resourceLock.lock();
try {
  doSomething();
}
catch (Exception e) {
  logError("An error occurred calling doFinally()");
}
finally {
  resourceLock.unlock();
}
```

Although this code is somewhat contrived, it does illustrate some of the important points just covered related to the finally block and its relationship to the try and catch blocks. If doSomething() does throw an exception it will be caught and rethrown by the catch block—but the call to unlock() will also be called. On the other hand, if no exception is generated then execution will continue with the code that follows this segment after unlock() is called.

Nested Exceptions

An interesting point to consider related to the last example is what will happen if the logError() invocation causes an exception to be thrown, since that invocation occurs inside the catch block that handles a different exception. In practice, of course, logging doesn't generally cause exceptions, but it's worthwhile to consider what would happen if one did occur. With the code in its current state the original exception generated by doSomething() would effectively be discarded and the one generated by logError() would be thrown.

Discarding the original exception obviously isn't ideal, and in fact it's not substantially different from the code shown earlier with the empty catch block that caught the exception from doSomething() and ignored it. Again, this is very undesirable behavior, but having two exceptions does present something of a problem, because Java doesn't support the ability to throw two different exceptions from a single method invocation—at least not directly.

The best solution to this is to use exception *nesting*, where one exception is essentially wrapped by another, and the original or "inner" exception is said to be the "cause" of the second "outer" exception. In this scenario the inner exception is the one generated by doSomething() while the outer exception is the one generated by logError(). Support for exception nesting is built in to the exception facility, with the Exception class (and most of its subclasses) defining constructors that accept both a message like the ones we've been creating and also a reference to an inner exception to be wrapped. We can take advantage of this design by putting the call to logError() inside its own try/catch block, and creating and throwing a new exception that encapsulates both the original exception and the one generated by the logError() call.

```
resourceLock.lock();
try {
  doSomething();
}
catch (Exception e) {
  try {
    logError("An error occurred calling doFinally()");
  }
  catch (Exception le) {
    throw new LoggingException(
        "An error occurred during logging: " + le.getMessage(), le);
  }
  throw e;
}
finally {
  resourceLock.unlock();
}
```

As mentioned before, we don't want to just ignore the original exception from doSomething() but want to wrap it in our custom exception class, so we'll implement a constructor that accepts a reference to the original exception and maintains a reference to it as shown here.

```
public class LoggingException extends Exception {

  public LoggingException(String message, Exception cause) {
    super(message, cause);
  }

}
```

When the LoggingException is thrown, the caller can retrieve information on both exceptions: the Exception that occurred when attempting to create the log message and the original exception generated by doSomething(). Accessing the original exception is done by calling the getCause() method defined in the Throwable class and inherited by Exception and its subclasses.

Stack Traces and Message Text

When an exception class is instantiated, a stack trace is created and associated with the exception object. A stack trace is nothing more than information that describes the path of execution of a thread at some point in time, including the name of each method that was called, the class in which each method is defined, and in most cases the line number within the class. It's the stack trace information that's displayed when you execute an application that terminates with an exception. For example, suppose you create a class like the following one that attempts to read the contents of a file:

```
import java.io.*;

public class ShowStack {

    public static void main(String[] args) throws IOException {
        ShowStack ss = new ShowStack();
    }
```

```
public ShowStack() throws IOException {
    initialize();
}

protected void initialize() throws IOException {
    readFileData();
}

protected void readFileData() throws IOException {
    File f = new File("test.txt");
    FileReader fr = new FileReader(f);
    BufferedReader br = new BufferedReader(fr);
    String line = br.readLine();
}

}
```

If the file doesn't exist, this application will terminate by displaying a stack trace like the following:

```
C:\brett\temp>java ShowStack
Exception in thread "main" java.io.FileNotFoundException: test.txt
(The system cannot find the file specified)
        at java.io.FileInputStream.open(Native Method)
        at java.io.FileInputStream.<init>(FileInputStream.java:138)
        at java.io.FileReader.<init>(FileReader.java:72)
        at ShowStack.readFileData(ShowStack.java:19)
        at ShowStack.initialize(ShowStack.java:14)
        at ShowStack.<init>(ShowStack.java:10)
        at ShowStack.main(ShowStack.java:6)
```

This information indicates that the exception was generated from within the native open() method defined in the FileInputStream class. Prior to that method being called, two levels of constructors were invoked, which are indicated by the <init> entries, with the class name and line numbers indicating which Java class's constructors were involved. The original FileReader constructor was called as part of the instantiation that's found on line 19 of our ShowStack class, which is a statement within the readFileData() method.

By examining the stack trace entries, you can determine the complete execution path of the thread that generated an exception, which in this case began with the execution of the static main() method in StackTrace. That information is very useful for debugging purposes, but it raises the question of how to handle the stack trace information in the case of a nested exception.

Returning to our implementation of LoggingException, the obvious question is which stack trace should be displayed in the case of a nested exception: the one from the original exception or the one associated with the outer exception? The answer is that both are potentially useful, so both should be displayed, and in fact the support in Exception for nested exceptions ensure that both will be shown when there is a cause (nested/inner exception) associated with the exception for which a stack trace is generated.

This behavior can be illustrated by making a small change to the ShowStack class that wraps the generated exception in an outer exception and throws the outer exception as follows:

```
protected void initialize() {
  try {
    readFileData();
  }
  catch (IOException e) {
    throw new RuntimeException("An error occurred during initialization", e);
  }
}
```

Running the ShowStack example now produces a very different stack trace from the original as shown next.

```
Exception in thread "main" java.lang.RuntimeException:
    An error occurred during initialization
        at ShowStack.initialize(ShowStack.java:18)
        at ShowStack.<init>(ShowStack.java:10)
        at ShowStack.main(ShowStack.java:6)
Caused by: java.io.FileNotFoundException: test.txt
    (The system cannot find the file specified)
        at java.io.FileInputStream.open(Native Method)
        at java.io.FileInputStream.<init>(FileInputStream.java:138)
        at java.io.FileReader.<init>(FileReader.java:72)
        at ShowStack.readFileData(ShowStack.java:24)
        at ShowStack.initialize(ShowStack.java:15)
        ... 2 more
```

Now the user is shown information about both the original/inner and wrapper/outer exceptions and the original problem of the first exception being ignored has been addressed.

Avoiding Exceptions

There are some situations where an exception might initially seem appropriate when in fact it's not the best choice. For example, suppose you define a method that performs a search and returns a value, as in the following case:

```
public Student findStudent(int studentID) {
  // ...
}
```

One question that would need to be answered in designing and implementing this method is what should happen when no student is found for the associated identifier. Depending upon the nature of your application it might be entirely appropriate to throw an exception. However, if the method could reasonably be expected to not find a Student instance that matches the specified criteria, it's probably more appropriate to return a null value instead of throwing an exception. An even better approach would be to return an instance of the new Optional class introduced in Java 8, and we'll discuss the application of that approach in depth in Chapter 3.

Similarly, if you define a method that returns some integer value that should always be positive or zero, returning a negative value could be used in place of an exception to indicate an error. For example, the indexOf() method in the String class does just that if it can't find an occurrence of the character you specify.

```
String test = "Hello";
// Prints the index of the first occurrence of 'e', in this case 1
System.out.println(test.indexOf('e'));
// Prints -1, since the character 'z' isn't found in the string
System.out.println(test.indexOf('z'));
```

In some cases, such as the two just described, what constitutes an error can be subjective and dependent upon the context. Is it really an error at all when a given character isn't found in a string? Maybe, and maybe not—it depends upon the context. If the application were designed in such a way that the character should be found, most people would classify the results as an error. Otherwise, it's just one possible outcome of the method call, in which case you should avoid throwing exceptions.

Assertions

Since version 1.4, Java has included support for a feature called *assertions*. Assertions are related to exception processing but with some important differences. Before we examine how assertions are to be used, let's examine how to add an assertion to your code. The format is quite simple, with the assert followed by either a single boolean argument or a boolean and an expression separated by a colon, as follows:

```
boolean systemValid;
.
.
.
assert systemValid;
```

Alternatively, it's as follows:

```
assert systemValid : "Invalid System State";
```

In both cases, if systemValid is false, an AssertionError is thrown, and if the expression is specified as with the "Invalid System State" message shown previously, the string representation of that expression is used as the message for the AssertionError.

So, what's the advantage of using an assertion instead of throwing an exception directly? One advantage is that assertions can be enabled and disabled without making any code changes. Assertions are disabled by default and must be explicitly enabled using the -enableassertions command-line option or its abbreviated -ea equivalent as follows:

```
java -enableassertions MyClass
```

If you don't enable assertions, any assert statements in your code will be ignored at execution time. For this reason, you shouldn't include in an assertion's boolean expression any functionality that must be executed for your code to work correctly. For example, let's suppose you have a method that updates a database and returns a boolean value indicating whether it was successful. If you use the following code, that code will be executed only when assertions are enabled:

```
assert updateDatabase(parms);
```

In most cases, what you'll want is to perform the operation unconditionally (that is, whether assertions are enabled) and then check the results of the update operation, generating an assertion if the operation failed to complete successfully. You can easily accomplish this with the following code:

```
boolean success = updateDatabase(parms);
assert success;
```

For essentially the same reason, you also shouldn't use assertions for checking the validity of parameters passed to public methods. In other words, checking the validity of those parameters is something you should do whether or not assertions are enabled, and for that purpose, you should use the existing exception classes such as IllegalArgumentException and NullPointerException.

Note that assertions are specifically intended to be used in debugging and not in production code. So, what are some situations where it's appropriate to use assertions? A good place is any section of code that theoretically should never be executed, such as an if/else that shouldn't be reached, as in the following example:

```
int age;
.
.
.
if ((age > 12) && (age < 20)) {
  // Handle teenagers here
}
else if (age >= 65) {
  // Handle seniors here
}
else if (age >= 0) {
  // Handle all other valid ages here
}
else {
  assert false;
}
```

Similarly, another good candidate is the default block of a select statement as in the following example:

```
public class processPassenger(Passenger passenger) {
    int cabinClass = passenger.getCabinClass();
    switch (cabinClass) {
        case TYPE_COACH:
            processCoachPassenger(passenger);
            break;
        case TYPE_BUSINESS:
            processBusinessPassenger(passenger);
            break;
```

```
        case TYPE_FIRST_CLASS:
            processFirstClassPassenger(passenger);
            break;
        default:
            assert false;
    }
}
```

Another possible use of assertions is to verify that an object is in a state that's valid and/or adequate for the application to continue execution. For example, as you'll see in another chapter, the interfaces that Java uses for database access such as Connection, Statement, and ResultSet contain methods called getWarnings() and clearWarnings(). Those methods are provided because some of their "sibling" methods can result in warnings being quietly attached to the object when called. For example, calling the getInt() method for a ResultSet can cause a warning to be added to the ResultSet if there was a loss of precision when the value retrieved is returned as an integer.

In this scenario, you might use assertions at some point in your code to ensure that no warnings exist for the object, as in the following example:

```
ResultSet results;
.
.
.
// Create a passenger object from the current row of the ResultSet
Passenger passenger = createPassenger(results);
// See if any warnings were generated for the ResultSet
assert (passenger.getWarnings() == null);
```

Enumerations

In the switch statement you just saw, which was an example of how assertions can be used, an integer was expected to have a value that corresponds to one of several valid categories, and being assigned any other value was considered to be an incorrect state. This is a situation that's encountered often; you can use several different approaches to handle it. The problem with the technique used previously is that it's easy for errors to occur because there's no way to ensure that a particular parameter represents a valid value. For example, let's suppose that you define a Passenger class with a constructor that takes a string and an integer and that the integer should correspond to one of the constants in the following class:

```
public class TicketType {
    public int TYPE_COACH = 1;
    public int TYPE_BUSINESS = 2;
    public int TYPE_FIRST_CLASS = 3;
}
```

Given these values, there's nothing to prevent a Passenger object from being created with a constructor like the following:

```
Passenger passenger = new Passenger("Del Griffith", -1);
```

Although it's technically possible for the Passenger object to perform error checking on its parameters, it's not really desirable to do so. For example, suppose you implemented the constructor as follows:

```java
public class Passenger {

    private String name;
    private int cabinClass;

    public Passenger(String nm, int type) {
        name = nm;
        switch (type) {
           case TicketType.TYPE_COACH:
           case TicketType.TYPE_BUSINESS:
           case TicketType.TYPE_FIRST_CLASS:
               break;
           default:
               assert false;
        }
        cabinClass = type;
    }
}
```

The problem with this approach is that the Passenger constructor is now tightly coupled to the list of valid values, and the Passenger class would have to change if a new value is added to the application or an existing one is removed. An alternative is to add a method to the TicketType class that checks the validity of a value and call that method from the previous constructor, but an even better approach is to simply ensure that an invalid value can't be passed to the constructor at all. One way of implementing this in Java is to define a single private constructor for the relevant class (TicketType in this case) and then create a public instance for each valid state as follows:

```java
public class TicketType {

    public static final TicketType TYPE_COACH = new TicketType();
    public static final TicketType TYPE_BUSINESS = new TicketType();
    public static final TicketType TYPE_FIRST_CLASS = new TicketType();

    private TicketType() {
    }

}
```

Since the available selections are now represented as instances of the TicketType class instead of integer values, you'd also need to make the corresponding changes to Passenger.

```java
public class Passenger {

    private String name;
    private TicketType cabinClass;

    public Passenger(String nm, TicketType type) {
        name = nm;
        cabinClass = type;
    }
```

```
    public TicketType getCabinClass() {
        return cabinClass;
    }
}
```

Although this prevents a Passenger from being constructed with an invalid type, there's one potential problem: it's possible for multiple instances of the TicketType class to be created that correspond to the same type. Without going into the details of how that can occur, suffice it to say that with the current code, there's no guarantee the following code will be evaluated as true even if both variables represent the same type:

```
if (oldPassenger.getCabinClass() == newPassenger.getCabinClass())
```

A better option is to use an enumeration, which allows you to define a class-like structure that identifies a finite list of valid instances/values. To define an enumeration for your TicketType class, create code like the following:

```
public enum TicketType {
    TYPE_COACH,
    TYPE_BUSINESS,
    TYPE_FIRST_CLASS
}
```

Once you've defined an enumeration this way, you can access the values the same way they were accessed with the class implementation shown earlier:

```
TicketType type = TicketType.TYPE_COACH;
```

Despite this simplistic example, enumerations aren't limited to simply being instantiated; you can define attributes, methods, and constructors just as you would in a standard class. For example, suppose you wanted to associate each type in the previous example with a numeric value so you could store a representation of the type in a database (for example, coach = 1, business = 2, and so on). In that case, you could simply add a property and corresponding accessor method to the enumeration, specifying a different value for each enumeration instance as follows:

```
public enum TicketType {

    TYPE_COACH(1),
    TYPE_BUSINESS(2),
    TYPE_FIRST_CLASS(3);

    private int value;

    private TicketType(int intValue) {
        value = intValue;
    }
    public int getValue() {
        return value;
    }

}
```

As you can see, enumerations are similar to classes in terms of the functionality that's available. However, they offer a more reliable way of defining a finite set of values from which you can choose, and doing so makes your code simpler and more maintainable.

Summary

In this chapter, we covered a number of issues related to the design of packages, classes, and methods, including the following:

- You can make a library of classes more manageable by organizing the classes into packages.

- Creating classes, interfaces, and packages with loose coupling and strong cohesion tends to make those items more reusable.

- Encapsulation provides many advantages, including the ability to hide implementation details and insulation from changes in implementation.

- Immutable objects and fields can simplify an object-oriented design.

- The Object class contains a number of important methods that it may be necessary or helpful to override.

- Method design and naming are an important part of a good design. Method design greatly influences the reusability of your code, while naming is an important part of making your code intuitive and easy to understand.

- Minimizing code duplication not only saves time but also makes your code more reliable and maintainable.

- Java's exception handling mechanism is a powerful, flexible facility that can handle conditions that require attention during the execution of your application.

- Assertions can improve your code's correctness by checking for a condition that you expect to be true under normal circumstances.

- Enumerations are useful when defining a finite set of values that are employed to identify a selection or some kind of state.

CHAPTER 3

Lambdas and Other Java 8 Features

Rarely, if ever, has there been a new release of Java that created as much interest as Java 8, which was officially released in early 2014. By far the most talked-about change was the introduction of lambda expressions, although the new release also included a number of other changes, such as the following:

- Implementation of default methods.

- The Streams API.

- A new API for the representation and manipulation of date and time values.

Other less notable changes and additions were included in Java 8, but these items represent the ones that have generated the most interest and as a result will be covered in this chapter along with lambda expressions.

Lambda expressions generated by far the most "buzz" and rightly so, because they represent the most radical change to the syntax of the language since at least the introduction of generics and arguably the biggest change since the language was first created. In fact, several of the other new features in Java 8 support lambdas either directly or indirectly and some of those other new features, along with lambda expressions themselves, will be examined here.

Lambda Expression Concepts

From a functional perspective lambda expressions represent something Java programmers—and programmers in other languages—have been doing for a long time, at least conceptually. Specifically, lambdas support the ability to define and pass method (or "function") references within application code. Initially it might seem that Java programmers haven't been doing this and can't in earlier versions of Java, because Java has only supported passing references at an object level, not at a method/function level. To understand how this has been supported, consider the common scenario where a class is instantiated that's an implementation of `Runnable` and a reference to that instance is passed to a method such as `execute()` defined in `ThreadPoolExecutor`. A simple example of such a class is shown in Listing 3-1.

Listing 3-1. A Skeleton Runnable Implementation

```java
class MyRunnable implements Runnable {

    public void run() {
        performLongRunningTask();
    }

    private void performLongRunningTask() {
        // Do some work here
    }

}
```

Creating and passing a reference to MyRunnable is easily done as shown in Listing 3-2.

Listing 3-2. Supplying a Runnable Reference to ThreadPoolExecutor

```java
public void startExecution()
{
    ThreadPoolExecutor executor = getExecutor();
    Runnable newInstance = new MyRunnable();
    executor.execute(newInstance);
}
```

Very often the Runnable implementation is trivial and only used in a single class, in which case it's common practice to define it as an anonymous inner class. This is particularly appropriate and easy if the functionality executed by the run() method is already defined or can be defined in the same class that creates the Runnable, as in Listing 3-3.

Listing 3-3. It's Common for a run() Method to Delegate Processing to Some Other Method

```java
public void startExecution() {
    ThreadPoolExecutor executor = getExecutor();
    Runnable newInstance = new Runnable() {
        public void run() {
            performLongRunningTask();
        }
    };
    executor.execute(newInstance);
}

void performLongRunningTask() {
    // Do some work here
}
```

This implementation results in slightly less code and, more importantly, one less source file that must be created and maintained, so it's generally considered a faster and more convenient approach.

To understand how this relates to lambda expressions and to passing a function reference it's helpful to consider what the Runnable interface and its run() method represent. Most classes and methods represent a specific type of behavior; for example, it's obvious from their names and documentation that the add() method in the Collection interface adds an object to a collection. In contrast, the run() method—and for that matter the Runnable class that defines it—is named very generically, and for good reason: because there is no prescribed behavior and the documentation of the interface itself can't specify what will happen when the run() method is called. What, then, does Runnable represent? It's an object that's known to have exactly one method defined, namely, run(). In other words, when a Java programmer creates an implementation of Runnable and passes a reference to it, what's effectively being passed is a reference to a specific method. The receiver of that reference knows which method to invoke because there's only one method that can be guaranteed to exist and the purpose of that method is to serve as an entry point into the object's functionality. So in a sense, when a reference to Runnable is passed it's really just a reference to a method, and the Runnable interface is a wrapper around that method.

In contrast, other languages allow function references to be passed directly, such as in JavaScript where the following code will display a "Hello world" dialog five seconds after it's executed:

```
setTimeout(function() {alert('Hello world');}, 5000);
```

This JavaScript code calls a function named "setTimeout" and passes two parameters to it: a function that displays a message ("Hello world"), and a numeric value representing the number of milliseconds to wait before calling the function. The function can be said to be "anonymous" because it's not assigned a specific name, and that type of anonymous function is what lambda expressions represent in Java. In fact, the term "lambda expression" has been used for decades in the context of computer programming to refer to a function that's not assigned a name. The term was borrowed from an area of calculus represented by the eleventh letter (lambda) of the Greek alphabet and was first used in the 1950s to describe the feature of the Lisp programming language that allowed anonymous functions to be defined and used.

Programming that involves the use of function references is referred to as "functional programming," and the purpose of lambda expressions is to provide Java with better, more direct support for functional programming than what was possible before. With that understanding in mind we can now look at an example of how lambdas can be used, specifically in this case to pass a value to the ThreadPoolExecutor's execute() method as was done before using an inner class (see Listing 3-4).

Listing 3-4. Using the execute() Method in ThreadPoolExecutor with a Lambda Expression

```
ThreadPoolExecutor executor = getExecutor();
executor.execute(() -> performLongRunningTask());
```

Notice that the lambda expression fits easily on the same line as the call to execute() because the "boilerplate" code—that is, the code that's essentially identical each time something like this is implemented—is eliminated.

It's also worth pointing out that nowhere in the lambda expression is the run() method ever referenced. The compiler knows that execute() requires a Runnable parameter and it also knows that Runnable defines a single run() method, so when this code is compiled and executed the result is the same as the earlier implementations, but again it's done without having to write all the boilerplate code.

At this point we've implemented the call to execute() three different ways: using a top-level Runnable implementation, an implementation using an anonymous inner class, and one that uses a lambda expression. Comparing the three implementations illustrates clearly how much the use of lambda expressions can reduce the volume of code produced for something like this (see Table 3-1).

Table 3-1. *Statistics Representing the Creation and Use of the Parameter Passed to* `execute()` *Using Normal Code Formatting Standards*

Implementation	Class Files	Lines of Code
Top-Level Class	2	11
Anonymous Inner Class	1	5
Lambda Expression	1	< 1

Using lambda expressions won't reduce the amount of code in an application by 80%, but it can greatly decrease the amount of code needed for functional programming.

Analyzing the Example

Before going further in discussing lambda expressions it's helpful to break the example down into its component parts and understand what each one represents (see Table 3-2). The code in Listing 3-4 can be broken down into three components, all three of which must be present in some form, although there is some flexibility in how they're specified.

Table 3-2. *The Elements of a Lambda Expression in* `executor.execute(() -> performLongRunningTask());`

	Name	Description
`()`	Parameters	Defines parameters used by the expression
`->`	Arrow Token	Separates the parameters from the body
`performLongRunningTask()`	Expression Body	The code to be executed

The first component identifies the function's parameters. The format is essentially the same one used for method or constructor parameters, with the individual parameters separated by commas and the set of parameters enclosed in a pair of open and closing parentheses. In this no parameters are specified, which is because the `run()` method's signature doesn't define any parameters.

To illustrate an example of how parameters are used, let's suppose that there is an array of `String` values that needs to be sorted and that the values all contain only numeric digits and should be sorted based on the corresponding numeric value. A naïve implementation would use the `sort()` method as shown in Listing 3-5.

Listing 3-5. Sorting Strings Using `Arrays.sort()`

```
String[] stringsToSort;
.
.
.
Arrays.sort(stringsToSort);
```

This wouldn't produce the desired results because, for example, "12" would be considered less than "2" due to the fact that the first character in "12" (the "1") is less than the first—and only—character in "2". What's needed is something like the following (see Listing 3-6) where customized sort logic is defined for the text:

Listing 3-6. A Comparator Implementation for Sorting Strings Containing Numeric Values

```
Comparator<String> numericStringSorter = new Comparator<String>() {
    public int compare(String s1, String s2) {
        int i1 = Integer.valueOf(s1);
        int i2 = Integer.valueOf(s2);
        int relativeValue = Integer.compare(i1, i2);
        return relativeValue;
    }
};
Arrays.sort(stringsToSort, numericStringSorter);
```

The anonymous inner class implementation of Comparator can be shortened somewhat by combining the logic into a single line as shown in Listing 3-7.

Listing 3-7. Sorting Numeric Strings with an Anonymous Inner Class Implementation of Comparator

```
Comparator<String> numericStringSorter = new Comparator<String>() {
    public int compare(String s1, String s2) {
        return Integer.compare(Integer.valueOf(s1), Integer.valueOf(s2));
    }
};
```

In effect, what this code does is to convert each pair of strings into their equivalent integer values and to perform the comparison on those values instead. Implementing this as a lambda expression not only greatly reduces the amount of code involved but also illustrates how parameters are specified (see Listing 3-8).

Listing 3-8. Implementing a Numeric String Sort Using Lambda Expressions

```
Arrays.sort(stringsToSort, (String s1, String s2) ->
        Integer.compare(Integer.valueOf(s1), Integer.valueOf(s2)));
```

Unlike the empty parentheses from the first example, this one in Listing 3-8 defines a pair of parameters, s1 and s2, both of type String. That's because the function being called, specifically the Comparator interface's compare() method, requires that a pair of values be passed to it and that they must be of the same type, which in this case is String. As mentioned before, lambdas are very good at removing boilerplate code, which is partly accomplished by having the compiler determine automatically things like which interface (Comparable) and method (compare()) are to be used. In fact, the preceding lambda expression can be made even shorter by omitting the parameter types and allowing them to be inferred (see Listing 3-9).

Listing 3-9. The Parameter Types Can Often Be Omitted in Lambda Expressions

```
Arrays.sort(stringsToSort, (s1, s2) ->
        Integer.compare(Integer.valueOf(s1), Integer.valueOf(s2)));
```

Additionally, the parentheses themselves are only necessary when there's more than one parameter to be specified. If, for example, a lambda expression is used with a functional interface where the method accepts a single parameter then it's possible to specify just a parameter name as in Listing 3-10.

Listing 3-10. The Parentheses Can Be Omitted When There's Exactly One Parameter Value Specified

```
javax.swing.JButton button;
.
.
.
button.addActionListener(actionEvent ->
        System.out.println(actionEvent.getActionCommand()));
```

In all of the examples presented so far the body of the lambda expression consisted of a single statement, such as the call to `System.out.println()` in Listing 3-10. Multiple statements are supported, though, and are implemented the same way that a block of code is normally defined: by placing the statements inside a pair of braces ({}) and ending each statement with a semicolon. For example, to separate the retrieval of the `ActionEvent` command property from the call to display it could be implemented as shown in Listing 3-11.

Listing 3-11. Braces Are Needed When More Than One Line of Code Is to Be Executed

```
button.addActionListener(actionEvent -> {
        String command = actionEvent.getActionCommand();
        System.out.println(command);
        });
```

Functional Interface Methods

When discussing the `Runnable` interface it was mentioned that the method to be invoked is implicitly identified by its having only one method defined, and the same could be said for the `ActionListener` method in the preceding example. However, it would be an oversimplification to say that a functional interface can only define one method, because in fact the `Comparable` interface referenced earlier actually defines two methods: `compare()` and `equals()`. In the example provided in Listing 3-8, the lambda expression was obviously (and correctly) associated with the `compare()` method instead of `equals()`, but the selection of `compare()` is simpler than finding a method with parameters that match the lambda parameters. In fact, the requirement is that for an interface to be considered a functional interface it must define only a single abstract (non-implemented) method. So why does `Comparable` qualify as having only a single abstract method? Because the `equals()` method it defines matches exactly the signature of the `equals()` method defined in the `Object` class, and by definition any class that implements the `Comparable` interface is a subclass of `Object` and therefore does provide an implementation of `equals()`.

Default Methods

The definition of a functional interface as one for which there's only a single unimplemented method is somewhat complicated by the addition in Java 8 of another new feature, specifically that of "default methods." Default methods are concrete method implementations implemented for interfaces, in which case the interface much more closely resembles that of an abstract class. For example, suppose an `ApplicationManager` interface is designed that contains a pair of methods for processing used to initialize and shut down an application environment as in Listing 3-12.

Listing 3-12. A Simple Interface That Defines a Pair of Methods for Activating and Deactivating a System

```
public interface ApplicationManager {
    public void activate();
    public void deactivate();
}
```

At this point the ApplicationManager doesn't qualify as a functional interface because it defines two methods for which there's no implementation. However, that's no longer true if one of them is modified to have a default implementation, which is done using the new default keyword and providing an implementation as would be done with any abstract or concrete class (see Listing 3-13).

Listing 3-13. The ApplicationManager Interface with a Default deactivate() Method

```
public interface ApplicationManager {
    public void activate();
    public default void deactivate() {
        System.exit(0);
    }
}
```

The ApplicationManager interface now qualifies as a functional interface and can be used with lambda expressions. Default methods do complement lambda expressions but that isn't their only purpose or even their primary one. Default methods allow additions to be made to an interface without "breaking" older implementations of the interface that don't implement the newly defined method. Specifically, for example, a new forEach() method has been added to Java's collection interfaces, and by including a default implementation for that method with Java 8 the change can be made without invalidating any existing collection implementations or instances that were created prior to the existence of the forEach() method. As this example illustrates, default methods are primarily useful in the context of supporting an interface that's used by application code and that has a new method added to it that shouldn't force existing implementations to be updated.

Default methods are just that: a default, and like non-default methods defined in an interface a class (either abstract or concrete) that implements the interface is free to provide its own implementation that overrides the default version. In the case of the ApplicationManager interface just described, for example, an implementation can provide its own version of deactivate() that contains completely different logic that will be used instead of the version contained in the default method.

Multiple Inheritance Ambiguity

Interfaces have always been considered Java's mechanism for implementing multiple inheritance: that is, the ability for a class to inherit methods from more than one type, though in the past it could only inherit the method signatures and not their implementations. The fact that no implementation could be inherited from an interface also meant that there could be no conflict between two interfaces that define methods with identical signatures. For example, let's suppose that we have another interface called ResourceController that defines a deactivate() method with no parameters and that we want to define a class that implements both ResourceController and the previously defined ApplicationManager as shown here.

```
class ApplicationFacade implements ResourceController, ApplicationManager
{
}
```

This presents something of a dilemma because it's not immediately obvious whether ApplicationFacade should inherit the default implementation of deactivate() from the ApplicationManager class, and becomes even more complex if ResourceController also defines its deactivate() method to have a default method. In that scenario we will have defined a class that inherits from two different interfaces, each with its own implementation of deactivate(). Java 8 addresses this by requiring you to provide an implementation for the ambiguous method in the relevant class, in this case ApplicationFacade. In fact, if you try to compile the foregoing code you'll receive a message like the one shown next.

```
ApplicationFacade.java:1: error: ApplicationFacade is not abstract and does not override
abstract method deactivate() in ResourceController
```

As the message implies, you can resolve this issue by providing an implementation of the deactivate() method in ApplicationFacade. If you do want it to use the default implementation provided by ApplicationManager, you can invoke it using syntax similar to that normally used in a subclass to explicitly indicate that a superclass method should be called, specifically by using the super keyword as shown in Listing 3-14.

Listing 3-14. Invoking a Default Method from a Class That Implements Its Interface

```java
class ApplicationFacade implements ResourceController, ApplicationManager
{
    public void deactivate() {
        ApplicationManager.super.deactivate();
    }
}
```

Streams

Another major change introduced in Java 8 is the Streams API, which provides a mechanism for processing a set of data in various ways that can include filtering, transformation, or any other way that may be useful to an application.

To understand what streams are meant to improve or replace it's helpful to look at an example of how you'd perform a filtering operation without them. Suppose that you have a List that represents a collection of String values and you want to remove the entries that begin with some prefix text. In that case, you could iterate through the List elements, test each one to see if it begins with the target text, and remove the ones that do begin with that text as shown in Listing 3-15.

Listing 3-15. Filtering the Items in a Collection Without Using the Streams API

```java
List<String> items;
String prefix;
.
.
.
for (ListIterator<String> iterator = items.listIterator(); iterator.hasNext(); ) {
    String item = iterator.next();
    if (item.startsWith(prefix)) {
        iterator.remove();
    }
}
```

This type of code where the iteration is explicitly coded is sometimes referred to, appropriately enough, as "explicit" iteration and is also sometimes referred to as "active" or "external" iteration. However, the Streams API in Java 8 supports a different type of iteration where you simply define the set of items to be processed, the operation(s) to be performed on each item, and where the output of those operations is to be stored. That type of iteration is referred to as "implicit," "passive," or "internal" iteration in contrast to the processing shown previously.

As just described, a "stream" consists of three parts.

- Data source: As its name implies, this part of the stream defines where the data comes from, such as a List or other object representing a collection.

- Intermediate operations: These are the operations to be performed on the data, such as filtering or transformation operations.

- Terminal operation: This describes what to do with the processed data, as well as determines when (or if) to stop processing the data. Only one terminal operation can be specified per stream.

Probably the best way to understand these parts and how they relate to the Streams API is to see an example, and the most obvious candidate for this is an example that performs the same function as the code in Listing 3-15. So, take a look at Listing 3-16 to see the implementation.

Listing 3-16. Filtering the Items in a Collection Using the Streams API

```
List<String> filteredList = items.stream().
        filter(e -> (!e.startsWith(prefix))).
        collect(Collectors.toList());
```

To understand what has been done here, let's break down the code in Listing 3-16 into its component parts and determine what each one is doing.

```
List<String> filteredList =
```

This is just a standard declarative assignment statement. In this case we're defining a local variable named filteredList that represents a reference to a List containing String values.

```
items.stream()
```

This indicates that we wish to have the data in the items collection (List) processed using the Streams API and is an example of a data source. In this case the List is our data source because it contains the collection of values that are to be processed.

```
filter(e -> (!e.startsWith(prefix)))
```

This is an example of an intermediate operation. As its name implies, the filter() function filters the stream data; that is, it excludes items that do not match the criteria defined by the filter. The filter in this specific case is simply a lambda expression that determines whether a String value starts with the text associated with the prefix variable.

```
collect(Collectors.toList())
```

Finally, this portion of the statement represents a terminal operation and identifies what should be done with the items that are processed. Specifically, it indicates that they should be stored in a new collection (List), and it's that collection that will be returned and assigned to the filteredList variable defined at the beginning of the statement.

This is a simple example, but as you may have guessed, the Streams API allows you to specify more than one intermediate operation. For example, suppose that we have both a prefix and a suffix and want to determine which values both begin with the specified suffix and end with the prefix. In that case we could use a multi-stage "pipe" like the one shown in Listing 3-17, where the suffix is defined in a variable by that same name.

Listing 3-17. Filtering the Items in a Collection Using a Multi-stage Pipe

```
List<String> items;
String prefix;
String suffix;
.
.
.
List<String> filteredList = items.stream().
        filter(e -> (e.startsWith(prefix))).
        filter(e -> (e.endsWith(suffix))).
        collect(Collectors.toList());
```

As the name implies, the "pipe" in this case represents a series of operations through which the data flows and is very similar conceptually to a "pipeline" used on UNIX/Linux systems to perform some sort of processing on the data.

This example only illustrates the Stream API's support for filtering, but if you browse the API documentation for the Stream class you'll find that it supports a large number of very useful methods, including the following:

Method	Description
distinct()	Returns a stream consisting of only the distinct items as determined by toString()
limit(int n)	Returns a stream consisting of only the first "n" elements corresponding to the int parameter value.
skip(int n)	Returns a stream consisting of all elements except the first "n" ones.
sort()	Returns a stream that generates the elements in their natural sort order.

In addition to the foregoing, there are a number of terminal operations that can be used to transform the results of the intermediate operations. For example, using our previous example with the prefix and suffix operations we could use the count() terminal operation to obtain the number of items that contain the specified prefix and suffix instead of a collection that encapsulates those values.

```
long matchCount = items.stream().
        filter(e -> (e.startsWith(prefix))).
        filter(e -> (e.endsWith(suffix))).
        count();
```

Another example of a terminal operator is `findFirst()`, which in this example shown in Listing 3-18 will return just the first item that matches the prefix and suffix value.

Listing 3-18. An Example of the `findFirst()` Terminal Operator

```
Optional<String> firstItem = items.stream().
        filter(e -> (e.startsWith(prefix))).
        filter(e -> (e.endsWith(suffix))).
        findFirst();
```

This example illustrates another important concept that makes the Streams API potentially very efficient, namely, the idea of "short-circuiting." In the original example provided here where explicit iteration was used, the code will iterate once for every item in the collection, which is necessary because we need to examine each item to determine whether or not it matches the criteria (that is, contains a particular prefix) that's being used. In Listing 3-18, however, we're looking for the first match and once that item is found no additional iteration is necessary. Of course, if the first match happens to be the last item in the list then we'll still wind up iterating through every item, but if we were doing this using explicit iteration then we'd probably include a break statement that would be executed once the first (and only) match is identified.

Fortunately, the Streams API was designed with this kind of capability built in, and it will stop processing once a match is found. This is done by having the processing driven by the terminal operator, which will "pull" data from its predecessor(s) until there is no more data or until it finds what it needs. In this case, it will continue to pull values from the intermediate operators—which in turn will pull from the data source—until it finds an item with the appropriate prefix and suffix. Again, that behavior is referred to as "short-circuiting" and it can help ensure that your applications written using the Streams API execute as efficiently as possible.

Optional

Another point worth mentioning regarding the previous code segment is the usage of the `Optional` class, which is yet another new feature introduced in Java 8. In short, the `Optional` class acts as a wrapper around a value that may or may not be `null`, and is used to reduce the frequency of `NullPointerException` in applications that take advantage of it. It does this by ensuring that a method always returns a non-null value because instead of directly returning the expected result the method returns an `Optional`, which in turn contains and can return a reference the value the user intends to access. In other words, `Optional` is meant to "force" a programmer to recognize and handle the possibility that a return value may be `null` and to handle it gracefully instead of naïvely writing code that will eventually generate a `NullPointerException`. In the previous example, the stream will produce a null value if there are no matches found that have the expected suffix and prefix, but even if that occurs the `firstItem` variable will never be null. That's because the `findFirst()` method always returns an `Optional` that encapsulates the first value if there is one or `null` if there isn't one. The application code can access the wrapped value by calling the `Optional` object's `get()` method, and `Optional` also includes other useful methods like `isPresent()` for determining whether it encapsulates a non-null value.

Parallel Streams

Another major advantage of the Streams API is that it may greatly improve performance where large volumes of data are being processed. Microprocessors for many years now have been increasing in speed, although in recent years it has become more common for processing power to be increased by the addition of multiple "cores" that allow true multithreading to be performed. In other words, with a multi-core processor you can have two almost completely independent threads executing at the same time. A limitation, though, is that writing code to handle multithreaded applications is potentially very complex and error-prone, so it's often the case that an application that needs a performance boost won't get one unless the programmer(s) working on it are able to effectively write code that makes use of the multiple threads that are available.

Fortunately, the Streams API makes it very simple to take advantage of a multi-core environment, and that feature can be enabled with only a very minor change to your code. Specifically, instead of calling the `stream()` function as was done in the previous example you can call the `parallelStream()` method, which indicates that the stream is allowed to be processed by multiple threads if that capability is supported by the operating system and hardware. An example of this is shown in Listing 3-19.

Listing 3-19. Filtering with Parallel Processing Enabled

```
List<String> filteredList = items.parallelStream().
        filter(e -> (e.startsWith(prefix))).
        filter(e -> (e.endsWith(suffix))).
        collect(Collectors.toList());
```

In practice, you're better off not enabling parallel processing unless you expect the data source to contain a very large set of items that will be processed. That's because there is overhead associated with multithreading and there's a threshold below which that overhead will exceed the performance gain from using multiple threads. In other words, if you use `parallelStream()` with a small set of data, there's a good chance that performance will actually be worse than if you had used the single-threaded `stream()` equivalent. For larger sets of data, though, it may be worthwhile to take advantage of parallel stream support. In fact, this is arguably a bigger advantage of the Streams API than the elimination of boilerplate code: it allows Java applications to easily provide better support for "big data" applications than would be possible otherwise.

Improved Date/Time Handling In Java 8

The Java language is generally very robust, but one area that has been repeatedly criticized is its support for processing date and time values. In fact, as a result of Java's weakness in this area, an open source library called Joda-Time was created by a developer named Stephen Colebourne and over the years had become a popular alternative to Java's built-in date and time handling. To address the problems with the core library support, a decision was made via the Java Community Process (JCP) to improve Java's built-in support and eliminate the need for an add-on library like Joda. With Colebourne as one of the leaders of the JCP group, a new API was included in Java 8 that represents an improved version of Joda-Time.

Date/Time Support Before Java 8

To fully understand and appreciate what the new Date and Time API provides it's necessary to first understand how dates and times were previously handled in Java. In the first (1.0) release of Java the only support for date/time processing was through the `java.util.Date` class, which is essentially just a wrapper around a `long` value. That value represents the number of milliseconds relative to midnight on January 1, 1970, with respect to the Greenwich Mean Time (GMT) time zone, with that instant in time sometimes referred to as the "epoch" or as Coordinated Universal Time (UTC). That point was somewhat arbitrarily chosen and corresponds to a value of 0 for the `long` value of a `Date`, with each millisecond since that time corresponding to an increment in the value. For example, a value of 1,000 corresponds to one second (1,000 milliseconds) after midnight GMT, while a value of -60,000 corresponds to one minute before the epoch.

Date and Time Context

Before going any further in discussing Date, note that the foregoing description qualifies the epoch as occurring relative to a specific time zone (GMT). That's critical because there's a difference between a point in time and a local representation of a point in time. For example, suppose that you send an e-mail to someone and tell that person to call you at 1:00 pm and he agrees to do so, but then 1:00 pm passes and the phone doesn't ring. Later you receive an e-mail saying that the person had called at 1:00 pm but you didn't answer. Even assuming that both of your phones are working correctly it's entirely possible that both of you are correct: this can happen if you and the person who called you are in different time zones. That person called you when his clock said it's 1:00 pm but you were able to answer the call at what *your* clock says is 1:00 pm, but what you refer to as 1:00 pm isn't the same instant in time as what the person refers to as 1:00 pm if you're in different time zones.

This example may seem trivial but it illustrates a very important point related to representing dates and times in Java: what we often refer to as a "time" like 1:00 pm is only meaningful in the context of a specific time zone. This is sometimes overlooked because most communication regarding time takes place between two people in the same time zone, so the time zone is implied to be the one in which both parties reside. For example, if you live in a location that uses Central Time and tell someone to call you at 1:00 pm it's understood to mean 1:00 pm Central Time. A time that's implicitly or explicitly associated with a specific time zone is referred to as a "local time" to indicate that it's associated with a particular geographic area and that area's time zone. In fact, this concept of a time only being meaningful in the context of a specific time zone also applies to dates. For example, when it's October 16th where you are, at some other places in the world it's either October 15th or October 17th.

On the other hand, a Date value is inherently neutral when it comes to time zones: it represents a specific point in time, and it's only by converting that value into a representation that a user understands—typically the user's local time—that the value becomes useful and recognizable. For example, a long value of 1413465227900 isn't meaningful but it becomes meaningful when it's translated into a local time like 8:13:47 am, which is implied to mean 8:13:47 am in the time zone of the person who's viewing the time.

Calendar and GregorianCalendar

When it was introduced in Java 1.0 the Date class included a number of methods for setting and retrieving specific parts of a date value from instances of the class, such as getYear() for returning an integer representing the year and setYear() for updating the Date to correspond to the specified year. This approach was determined to be insufficient for many scenarios and in Java 1.1 the Calendar and GregorianCalendar classes were introduced and the methods in Date that supported updating and retrieving date field values were deprecated. Calendar is meant to represent a generic calendar that can be subclassed, but in practice creating additional calendar implementations is a complex task and as a result GregorianCalendar is the only implementation provided with Java.

Calendar improved Java's support for time and date processing by providing a larger number of methods for setting and accessing date and time components, such as the year, month of the year, etc. In reality, a Calendar is little more than an object that encapsulates an instant in time (Date) value and a time zone, represented by the TimeZone class.

Joda-Time

Even with the introduction of the Calendar class date and time manipulation in Java remained somewhat difficult, partly as a result of the fact that a small number of classes were used to represent many different concepts: a date, a time, a combination date and time (sometimes referred to as a "timestamp"), an interval such as a specific number of hours, days, months, etc. In addition, the poorly named Date and Calendar classes made understanding Java's date support somewhat more difficult due to confusion regarding what they represent. In 2002 Stephen Colebourne began development on the Joda-Time library in order to provide an easier and more flexible way of working with dates and times in Java, and the library eventually became a popular addition to Java for developers needing something more than very simple date and time processing. Later the decision was made to integrate Joda-Time or something similar to it into Java's core libraries, and the Java Community Process was used to create an improved version of Joda-Time that was included in Java 8. That new API is referred to as the Date and Time API.

Date and Time API

As mentioned before, part of the difficulty associated with Java's older classes is that the classes weren't cohesive; that is, multiple concepts (a date, a time, a combination date and time) were represented by a single class. The Date and Time API, like its Joda-Time predecessor, avoids that mistake by defining a larger number of more cohesive classes that represent more specific concepts. Another advantage of the new API is that, unlike GregorianCalendar, the Date and Time API classes are thread-safe, which is largely achieved through the use of immutable classes. Yet another improvement is the names of the classes defined in the new API: while Java previously only supported the badly named Date and Calendar classes, the new API uses names that are more intuitive such as YearMonth, MonthDay, LocalDate, LocalTime, and LocalDateTime. Finally, yet another difference is that while the older classes only support millisecond granularity the Date and Time API classes support nanosecond granularity, allowing them to represent much more fine-grained values.

The root package of the date and time API is java.time, and we'll look at some of the classes supported there and in some of its subclasses to understand how they can be used in place of Java's older date processing classes.

Basic Classes

As you'd expect, the Date and Time API provides a superset of the functionality that was available before and provides superior implementations for some of the classes that were already available. For example, we've already seen that Date represents a point in time, but with the Date and Time API a better alternative to Date is the Instant class. Instant instances are immutable, and the class includes a number of useful static methods that can be called to retrieve an instance that meets some criteria. For example, to obtain an Instant that corresponds to the current point in time you can call the static now() method as follows:

```
Instant currentPointInTime = Instant.now();
```

One of the simpler improvements included in the Date and Time API is the inclusion of DayOfWeek and Month enumerated types. Enumerated types weren't yet supported by Java when Calendar was introduced, so days of the week and months of the year were defined as int constants. Besides the usual problems associated with "simulated" enumerated types, these also had the disadvantage of being zero-based so that, for example, the Calendar.JANUARY int constant corresponds to a value of 0 instead of the more intuitive value of 1 (which is how January is traditionally represented in written/displayed dates). Given the new Month enumerated type, a value corresponding to the month of January can be accessed through the type as shown in the following code:

```
Month firstMonth = Month.JANUARY;
```

Converting Date and Time Values

The new API makes it easy to convert between its classes and the older types supported by Java. For example, if you have code that uses the old Date class, it's also easy to convert between instances of Date and Instant using the methods provided by Instant. For example, given an instance of Date you can obtain a corresponding Instant by using the static ofEpochMilli() method as shown in the following code:

```
Date someDate;
.
.
.
Instant someInstant = Instant.ofEpochMilli(someDate.getTime());
```

If, on the other hand, you want to create a Date from an Instant you can retrieve the number of epoch milliseconds from the Instant as shown in the following code:

```
Instant someInstant;
.
.
.
Date someDate = new Date(someInstant.toEpochMilli());
```

As you'll see if you browse the documentation for the API documentation, these methods defined in Instant are common across many of the different types used to represent different concepts related to date and time. Some of these are listed in Table 3-3, along with a brief description of what each one represents.

Table 3-3. *Some Temporal Types in the Date and Time API*

Class / Type	Description
Year	Represents a year.
YearMonth	A month within a specific year.
LocalDate	A date without an explicitly specified time zone.
LocalTime	A time without an explicitly specified time zone.
LocalDateTime	A combination date and time without an explicitly specified time zone.

Notice that several types are described as not having an explicitly specified time zone. This means that those types represent a local time regardless of what time zone is applicable for the machine on which the code is running. Or, to put it another way, these types represent a "wall clock time" (and date in the case of LocalDateTime) as opposed to a specific point in time.

These types are all implementations of the Temporal interface, which is a type that identifies classes representing various date and time types. Note that none of these, including the LocalDateTime type, includes a time zone, so none of them corresponds to the Calendar class discussed earlier. However, in addition to the previous classes there's also a ZonedDateTime class that does include a time zone. Like the other types related to date and time processing, however, the Java Date and Time API also includes a new class for representing a time zone. In fact, it separates two concepts that were previously combined into Java's TimeZone class into two different classes: ZoneId and ZoneOffset.

Time Zones

Each time zone represents some offset—usually some number of hours—relative to GMT. For GMT itself, the offset is implicitly zero, since it's the basis on which other time zone offsets are defined, while for Eastern Standard Time (EST) in the United States the office is five hours, for Central Standard Time (CST) it's six hours, etc. For those time zones that observe Daylight Savings Time (DST)—and not all do—the offset is reduced by an hour, so Eastern Daylight Time (EDT) corresponds to an offset of four hours, and so on. As implied by these examples, the offset for a given time zone can usually be expressed as some number of hours relative to GMT, though in some cases the offset includes only part of an hour.

Prior to Java 8 the concept of a time zone was represented by instances of the TimeZone class defined in the java.util package, with each instance encapsulating two properties: the actual time zone with which the instance is associated and the associated offset for the time zone. More specifically, TimeZone includes methods for retrieving an identifier such as "CST" or "CDT," as well as methods for retrieving a "display name" like "America/Chicago" that describes a geographic location associated with the time zone. It also includes methods for returning an offset in milliseconds of the time zone relative to GMT.

ZoneId and ZoneOffset

In contrast to the older TimeZone class, the Date and Time API splits the concepts of a time zone identifier and time zone offset into two separate classes, namely, ZoneId and ZoneOffset. As their names imply, the ZoneId and ZoneOffset classes represent specific time zones and the offsets associated with time zones, respectively. The distinction between a time zone (or its associated ZoneId) and a time zone offset (represented by ZoneOffset) is an important one. At any point in time a time zone is associated with exactly one offset value, but that offset can change, such as when DST begins or end and more than one time zone may share the same offset value.

As mentioned earlier most of the Temporal types are defined as not being associated with a particular time zone and as you'd expect none of them supports the ability to retrieve the time zone associated with the type. In contrast, though, there is an additional Temporal type not mentioned earlier, specifically the ZonedDateTime class which, as its name implies, is a combination date and time along with an associated time zone. If this sounds familiar it's because the combination of a specific date, time, and time zone identifies a specific point in time, making ZonedDateTime the conceptual equivalent of a Calendar instance. As you'd expect from this description, the ZonedDateTime class includes getZone() and getOffset() methods that return the ZoneId and ZoneOffset, respectively, of the time zone associated with the ZonedDateTime instance.

In addition to ZonedDateTime, there are also a pair of classes, namely, OffsetTime and OffsetDateTime, that have an associated ZoneOffset.

Temporal Amounts

As mentioned earlier, a large part of the difficulty associated with date and time processing earlier versions of Java was that a small number of classes were required to support various different concepts that are only somewhat related, but Java 8's Date and Time API provides a larger number of more cohesive classes. One of the concepts that was only indirectly supported by Java's earlier date and time classes is that of a time interval, such as some number of minutes, hours, or days. By necessity these types of value were represented using the number of milliseconds corresponding to the interval, which in some cases is appropriate and simple. For example, 1,000 milliseconds always represents one second, so representing some number of seconds is as simple as multiplying that number times 1,000. Representing some number of hours is equally simple, because an hour is always 60 minutes (or 60 * 60 * 1,000 milliseconds) long. Initially it might seem that a day is always 24 hours long, but in fact that's not the case for every day in every time zone. Specifically, a day can at least conceptually be only 23 or 25 hours long, and these odd lengths each occur once every year in time zones where DST is observed. In reality, of course, the earth's rotation hasn't changed but the boundaries that defined where one day ends and another begins are altered in order to adjust the relationship between clock time and when and where the sun is visible in the sky.

As this illustration implies, the concept of a "day" actually is overloaded because it has at least two meanings:

1. A period of exactly 24 hours.

2. The time interval that begins at a given time on one calendar day and ends at exactly the same time on the following calendar day, such as from midnight on one date to midnight of the next date.

Most of the time these meanings can be used interchangeably because usually calendar days also happen to be exactly 24 hours long, but as just mentioned there are exceptions to that rule and to be reliable software must be able to function correctly based on which of the previous two definitions is relevant to it. For example, if you intend to add one week to some instant in time, it's not always appropriate to simply advance the instant by the number of milliseconds (or nanoseconds) that corresponds to seven 24-hour days: if the one-week period includes a DST start or end date then one of the days will be either 23 hours long or 25 hours long.

A "month" is an even less well-defined concept because different months in the Gregorian calendar can be anywhere from 28 to 31 days long, and even in the context of a specific month the number of days can vary, specifically in the case of February which is 29 days long in leap years. When someone refers to a "month" as a time interval, its meaning is normally similar to that of the second definition of "day" described earlier: specifically, they mean the period of time from a given date in one month to the same date in a following month, such as January 1st to February 1st.

Similarly, a Gregorian "year" can be either 365 or 366 days long, depending upon whether it's a leap year, and when someone refers to a "year" they generally mean the interval corresponding to the start of a date in one year to the start of the same date in the following year. A summary of these variations is shown in Table 3-4.

Table 3-4. *Some Temporal Types in the Date and Time API*

Concept	Duration	Comments
Day	23–25 hours	23 hours when DST starts; 25 hours long when it ends
Month	28–31 days	February is normally 28 days long; 29 in a leap year
Year	365–366 days	366 days long in a leap year; otherwise 365 days long

Fortunately, the Date and Time API has taken all of these variations into account and includes built-in support that not only represents the various different concepts but can be used to accurately manipulate date and time values based on the concepts involved. The relevant classes are Duration and Period, both of which implement the TemporalAmount interface.

Duration

A Duration represents some number of elapsed seconds and conceptually can be thought of as representing an amount of time similar to that captured by a stopwatch. A stopwatch strictly records the duration between when it's started and when it's stopped and has no dependency or real relationship to a time zone or any other concept related to calendar dates or wall clock times.

The Duration class includes a handful of methods that allow you to create instances representing various numbers of days, hours, minutes, seconds, milliseconds, or nanoseconds. For example, to create an instance of Duration representing 30 minutes you could use code like that shown here:

```
Duration halfAnHour = Duration.ofMinutes(30);
```

Or, to represent an interval of three days, you could use the following:

```
Duration threeDays = Duration.ofDays(3);
```

As mentioned before, the concept of a "day" is inherently ambiguous, but in the context of the static ofDays() method defined in Duration a day is assumed to be a day that's exactly 24 hours long, so it corresponds to the first definition of "day" identified earlier.

Period

In contrast to the Duration class that represents fixed intervals, the Period class is used to represent the more conceptual intervals like "year," "month," or the second definition of a "day" mentioned earlier. Unlike Duration instances, a Period doesn't represent a specific amount of "wall clock" time but instead represents a conceptual length of time. In other words, a Period can represent a day, month, or year of indeterminate length, and it's only when it's used in the context where it can be resolved to a specific length that its length becomes meaningful. To better understand this, let's construct a Period and see how it behaves.

```
Period oneMonth = Period.ofMonths(1);
```

The call to ofMonths() returned a Period representing a one-month interval, but is it a 28-, 29-, 30-, or 31-day month? It can be any one of these, because what it really represents is the concept of a month as described earlier: from a given day in one month to the same date in the following month, regardless of the start date's month. Let's observe its behavior by creating a LocalDate and seeing how it interacts with the Period we just created.

```
LocalDate newYearsDay = LocalDate.of(2015, Month.JANUARY, 1);
System.out.println(newYearsDay);
```

Running the foregoing code yields the following output:

```
2015-01-01
```

Now let's add the Period to the date just created and display the results.

```
LocalDate newYearsDay = LocalDate.of(2015, Month.JANUARY, 1);
System.out.println(newYearsDay);
Period oneMonth = Period.ofMonths(1);
LocalDate firstOfFebruary = newYearsDay.plus(oneMonth);
System.out.println(firstOfFebruary);
LocalDate firstOfMarch = firstOfFebruary.plus(oneMonth);
System.out.println(firstOfMarch);
```

As expected, this code displays the dates for the first day of January, February, and March.

```
2015-01-01
2015-02-01
2015-03-01
```

To summarize, the Duration class is used to represent a fixed amount of "wall clock" time; the Period class represents a temporal concept like day, month, and year that can vary in duration.

Note that in the previous example each distinct local date is represented by a different instance of LocalDate. As mentioned earlier, the API provides thread safety by making its classes immutable, which means that although we may talk of "manipulating" dates and times, what really occurs is that we create new instances of them based on some criteria. In this case, those criteria represented a period of one month, and we used a starting point (the initial newYearsDay) and Period value to derive two other dates.

Parsing and Formatting

Parsing and formatting dates and times are essentially opposites of each other: parsing involves converting a text representation (usually text entered by a user) into an internal format such as one of the data types mentioned here, while formatting involves converting an internal format into a text representation of that value, usually for the purpose of displaying it.

Parsing and formatting are complicated by the fact that date and time formats vary from one region to another and are further complicated by the fact that even within a single region multiple formats may be used. Within the United States, for example, the format most commonly used mm/dd/yy, consisting of two digits apiece for the month ("mm"), day ("dd"), and year ("yy"). Even within the United States, though, many other date formats are used and the situation is roughly as complicated for times, where there's no single format that's clearly used more frequently than others, though the hh:mm am|pm format (e.g., 2:45 pm) is very common.

Prior to the introduction of the Java Data and Time API formatting and parsing were handled by the abstract DateFormat class, usually with an instance of SimpleDateFormat. DateFormat supports a number of commonly used date and time formats and custom formats can easily be defined by specifying a pattern when creating an instance of SimpleDateFormat. An instance of DateFormat handles both parsing and formatting for the format it's associated with, but like the other classes defined in earlier versions of Java DateFormat has been superseded with the introduction of the new API. Applications written using Java 8 can use the new DateTimeFormatter class, which serves a purpose very similar to that of DateFormat; specifically, an instance of DateTimeFormatter represents a specific format that can be used to format and parse text representing some combination of date and/or time components.

Similar to the way the DateFormat and SimpleDateFormat classes worked, DateTimeFormatter allows you either to use a predefined format that's considered appropriate for your system settings or to define your own custom format. The predefined formats are associated with the FormatStyle enumerated type that defines four styles: SHORT, MEDIUM, LONG, and FULL. The DateTimeFormatter defines three static methods: one for dates, one for times, and one for timestamp (date and time) formatters, and each of the three static methods requires you to specify the format style for which to return a DateTimeFormatter instance.

- ofLocalizedDate() - Returns a DateTimeFormatter for parsing and formatting date text.

- ofLocalizedTime() - Returns a DateTimeFormatter for parsing and formatting time text.

- ofLocalizedDateTime() - Returns a DateTimeFormatter for parsing and formatting date and time text.

Table 3-5 shows the output generated by passing in a ZonedDateTime created using the following code:

```
ZonedDateTime timestamp = ZonedDateTime.of(2015, 7, 4, 12, 30, 0, 0,
ZoneId.systemDefault());
```

Table 3-5. *Results of Various Combinations of FormatStyle and DateTimeFormatter Instances*

	ofLocalizedDate()	ofLocalizedTime()	ofLocalizedDateTime()
SHORT	7/4/15	12:30 PM	7/4/15 12:30 PM
MEDIUM	Jul 4, 2015	12:30:00 PM	Jul 4, 2015 12:30:00 PM
LONG	July 4, 2015	12:30:00 PM	July 4, 2015 12:30:00 PM CDT
FULL	Saturday, July 4, 2015	12:30:00 PM CDT	Saturday, July 4, 2015 12:30:00 PM CDT

Also, as mentioned earlier it's possible to create an instance of DateTimeFormatter using a custom pattern as shown in the following code fragment using the same ZonedDateTime value as before:

```
ZonedDateTime timestamp = ZonedDateTime.of(2015, 7, 4, 12, 30, 0, 0, ZoneId.
systemDefault());
DateTimeFormatter formatter = DateTimeFormatter.ofPattern("HH:mm a zzz MM/dd/yyyy");
System.out.println(formatter.format(timestamp));
```

Running this code results in output like the following with the local time zone:

```
12:30 PM CDT 07/04/2015
```

In the foregoing method we created a ZonedDateTime and passed it as a parameter to the format() method of a DateTimeFormatter instance, but the API also includes convenience methods that support doing the opposite. For example, the following code passes a DateTimeFormatter instance to the format method of a ZonedDateTime and is functionally identical to the previous code fragment:

```
ZonedDateTime timestamp = ZonedDateTime.of(2015, 7, 4, 12, 30, 0, 0, ZoneId.
systemDefault());
DateTimeFormatter formatter = DateTimeFormatter.ofPattern("HH:mm a zzz MM/dd/yyyy");
System.out.println(timestamp.format(formatter));
```

In fact, this second approach is generally preferable, partly because it's also consistent with how parsing can be done. Specifically, you can create a DateTimeFormatter and pass it to the static parse() method of the type that you want to parse. For example, you could use code like that shown next to parse text and return an instance of LocalDateTime that represents the timestamp used in the previous example.

```
DateTimeFormatter formatter = DateTimeFormatter.ofPattern("HH:mm a zzz MM/dd/yyyy");
LocalDateTime dateTime = LocalDateTime.parse("12:30 PM CDT 07/04/2015", formatter);
```

In fact, most of the types defined in the java.time package include a parse() method that allows you to obtain an instance of that type by parsing text using a formatter as shown previously.

Method Naming Conventions

One of the things that makes the Date and Time API easy to use is that it consistently adheres to a set of naming conventions for the methods defined in the various classes we've examined, and gaining an overview of these conventions is a helpful step in being able to effectively use the API. We've already encountered some of these methods in the previous examples, but it's still helpful to review the standards.

now()

The static now() method, when defined for a class, returns an instance of that class representing the current point in time as shown in the following:

```
ZonedDateTime currentTimestamp = ZonedDateTime.now();
LocalDate currentDate = LocalDate.now();
```

of()

The static of() method is used to create an instance of the corresponding class that meets some criteria. For example, the following code will create a LocalDateTime representing noon (12:00 PM) on July 4, 2015:

```
LocalDateTime julyFourthNoon = LocalDateTime.of(2015, Month.JULY, 4, 12, 0, 0);
```

from()

The static from() method is passed one or more input parameters that are used to derive an instance of the class for which this method is called. For example, to retrieve the day of the week from a LocalDate you could use code like the following:

```
LocalDate newYearsDay = LocalDate.of(2015, Month.JANUARY, 1);
DayOfWeek dayOfWeek = DayOfWeek.from(newYearsDay);
```

parse() and format()

As mentioned earlier, the parse() method can be used to convert text into an instance a class that represents the corresponding value, while format() does the opposite: converts text representing a date or time into a representation of that value. For example, to create a LocalDate by parsing some text that contains a date in the mm/dd/yyyy format you could use the following:

```
String dateText;
.
.
.
DateTimeFormatter mmddyyyyFormatter = DateTimeFormatter.ofPattern("MM/dd/yyyy");
LocalDate parsedDateTime = LocalDate.parse(dateText, mmddyyyyFormatter);
System.out.println(parsedDateTime);
```

Similarly, to create text representing a date or time value you can use the format() method as shown in the following code:

```
LocalDate today = LocalDate.now();
DateTimeFormatter mmddyyyyFormatter = DateTimeFormatter.ofPattern("MM/dd/yyyy");
System.out.println(today.format(mmddyyyyFormatter));
```

getXXX()

The Date and Time API classes include various methods prefixed with "get" that provide the ability to retrieve a single component of the corresponding object. This is similar to the get() method defined in the older Calendar class that allows you to specify a component type (e.g., year, month, day, hours, minutes, seconds) and that returns an int value representing that part of the value the Calendar encapsulates. For example, we already saw how a DayOfWeek could be retrieved from a LocalDate using the from() method in DayOfWeek, but the same result could be achieved by calling the getDayOfWeek() method for the LocalDate object as shown in the following:

```
LocalDate newYearsDay = LocalDate.of(2015, Month.JANUARY, 1);
DayOfWeek dayOfWeek = newYearsDay.getDayOfWeek();
```

isXXX()

The various methods prefixed by "is" return information related to the state of the object. For example, to determine if a particular year is a leap year you could use code like the following:

```
Year year = Year.now();
System.out.println(year.isLeap()
        ? "This is a leap year" : "This is not a leap year");
```

In some cases a static method is also provided as a convenience, and in some cases it may be easier to use that. For example, if you want to check an arbitrary year to determine whether it's a leap year you could use the Year.isLeap() method as shown in the following code:

```
System.out.println(Year.isLeap(2015)
        ? "It is a leap year" : "It's not a leap year");
```

Comparing Dates

In addition to implementing the Comparable interface, the Date and Time API classes also include isBefore() and isAfter() methods that in many cases represent a more convenient way of comparing a pair of values. For example, the following will display "true" because the first date is earlier than the second:

```
LocalDate first = LocalDate.of(2015, Month.FEBRUARY, 1);
LocalDate second = LocalDate.of(2015, Month.FEBRUARY, 2);
System.out.println(first.isBefore(second));
```

with()

Variations of the with() method are defined for the API classes, and each one represents a way of returning a copy of the value that has been modified in some way, either by replacing one of the value's components or by adjusting the value in some manner. For example, the following code will create two LocalDate instances: one for the first day of 2015, and the second representing the first day of 2016:

```
LocalDate newYears2015 = LocalDate.of(2015, Month.JANUARY, 1);
LocalDate newYears2016 = newYears2015.withYear(2016);
```

In this example the year was replaced using the withYear() method, but the API classes also contain a more general-purpose with() method that allows you to specify a field and a value for the field. The following code is functionally equivalent to the previous example but uses the LocalDate.with() method that accepts TemporalField and long parameters representing the field to change and the new value to be assigned to it:

```
LocalDate newYears2015 = LocalDate.of(2015, Month.JANUARY, 1);
LocalDate newYears2016 = newYears2015.with(ChronoField.YEAR, 2016);
```

Perhaps even more useful, though, is the with() method that accepts a single TemporalAdjuster value. As the parameter type implies, this value will "adjust" the value by the specified amount. For example, the following will display the date value for February 2, 2015 when executed:

```
LocalDate newYears2015 = LocalDate.of(2015, Month.JANUARY, 1);
MonthDay groundhogDay = MonthDay.of(Month.FEBRUARY, 2);
LocalDate groundhogDate = newYears2015.with(groundhogDay);
System.out.println(groundhogDate);
```

plus() and minus()

Variations of the plus() and minus() methods are included in the API classes and these allow an instance of the corresponding class to be derived and returned by selecting a later (for plus()) or earlier (for minus()) value. For example, to retrieve the last date of a previous year you could use code like the following:

```
LocalDate newYears2015 = LocalDate.of(2015, Month.JANUARY, 1);
LocalDate newYearsEve2014 = newYears2015.minusDays(1);
```

Even more useful are the plus() and minus() methods that accept an instance of TemporalAmount. We already discussed both of the classes that implement this interface, specifically the Duration and Period classes representing a fixed interval (e.g., some specific number of hours) or a more conceptual interval whose exact length can vary, such a day, month, or year. For example, to determine the date that's 90 days into the future from some arbitrary date you could use the following code:

```
Period ninetyDays = Period.ofDays(90);
LocalDate currentDate = LocalDate.now();
LocalDate ninetyDaysFromToday = currentDate.plus(ninetyDays);
```

toXXX()

The to() methods return an instance of some type that's derived from a different type. For example, to retrieve a LocalDate from an instance of LocalDateTime you could use the toLocalDate() method as shown in the following code:

```
LocalDateTime dateTime;
.
.
.
LocalDate dateOnly = dateTime.toLocalDate();
```

atXXX()

The methods prefixed with "at" return a different type from the one for which the method is invoked, specifically an instance of the return type that's derived from the original object and the parameter values specified. For example, given a YearMonth value you can retrieve a LocalDate by calling the atDay() method, passing to it an int value representing the day of the month to be returned.

```
YearMonth december2015 = YearMonth.of(2015, Month.DECEMBER);
LocalDate christmas2015 = december2015.atDay(25);
```

Summary

In this chapter we've examined some—but certainly not all—of the features that have caused Java 8 to receive so much attention, including lambda expressions, default methods, the Streams API, and the new Date and Time API. These are arguably the most important of the new features introduced in Java 8, and when used in a Java application they make that application easier to write, and easier to maintain, and can allow it to process larger volumes of data more efficiently.

CHAPTER 4

■ ■ ■

Using Threads in Your Applications

If you're like most users, you probably have more than one application running on your computer most of the time. In addition, you probably sometimes initiate a long-running task in one application and switch to another application while waiting for that task to complete. For example, you might start downloading a file from the Internet, or begin a search that scans your disk drive for files matching a particular pattern, and then read your e-mail while the download or search is in progress. Running multiple applications simultaneously (or at least appearing to do so) is called *multitasking*, and each application is usually referred to as a *process*.

Multitasking is possible partly because the operating system is designed to make it appear that multiple processes are running at the same time even if your computer only has a single processor. That's done by allocating the available processor time—whether there's a single processor or more than one—across the various tasks that are supposed to be executing. This behavior is useful even on a single-processor system because it makes efficient use of processor time that would otherwise be wasted. In both of the examples mentioned (downloading and searching) a processor would spend much of its time simply waiting for I/O operations to complete unless it has other work to do. From a user's perspective, multitasking is desirable because it allows you to continue to use your computer while some background task is being executed instead of being blocked until that task completes.

Although the previous discussion assumed that there were multiple processes/applications running, the same concept is relevant within the context of a single application. For example, a word processor can automatically check your spelling and grammar while simultaneously (or at least apparently so) allowing you to continue entering new text. Similarly, if your application performs a long-running task such as downloading a large file from the Internet, it's usually desirable to provide a user interface that can respond to a user's request to cancel the download. Java provides built-in support for simultaneous (concurrent) tasks within a single application through its threading capabilities, where a *thread* is simply a unit of execution.

In this chapter, we'll cover the following topics related to using threads in Java:

- We'll examine common reasons for using threads and some of the advantages and disadvantages of using them.

- We'll see examples that illustrate how to create threads and manage their execution.

- We'll cover tips on how to synchronize access to resources that are used by multiple threads, and information on how to prevent problems from occurring.

- We'll study changes that occurred to the `Thread` class in Java 2 and sample code that shows how to create or modify your applications to take into account those changes.

- We'll examine thread pooling, a technique that's used to reduce the overhead associated with creating threads, with an example of how you can take advantage of it.

Threading in Java

It's likely you've built a multithreaded application in Java, even if you didn't do so explicitly. When you execute a Java application, the main() method is executed by a thread, although that fact is largely transparent. In addition, applications that provide a user interface (as most do) will implicitly cause another thread to be created and used: the event dispatch thread.

The EDT is active for both Abstract Window Toolkit (AWT) and Swing-based user interfaces and is responsible for painting lightweight components and for performing event notifications. If you create an interface that includes a JButton instance, the event dispatch thread paints the button when it's made visible and will call the actionPerformed() method for each of the button's listeners when it's clicked.

The fact that the event dispatch thread is responsible for both painting and event notification provides the motivation behind one of the most common uses of threads in Java. As long as the thread is busy with event handling, it can't repaint the user interface, and if you create an event handler that performs some long-running function, the interface may remain unpainted long enough to produce undesirable results.

For example, the code shown in Listing 4-1 calls the performDatabaseQuery() method from actionPerformed(). The called method simulates a long-running query by calling the sleep() method, causing the currently running thread to pause for five seconds before continuing execution. Since actionPerformed() will be called by the AWT event thread, that thread will be busy until the query completes, which prevents it from repainting the user interface during that time. Therefore, the user interface will appear to "hang" during the query, as shown in Figure 4-1.

Listing 4-1. Simulating a Long-Running Query

```java
import java.awt.*;
import java.awt.event.*;
import javax.swing.*;

  public class ButtonPress extends JFrame {

  public static void main(String[] args) {
    ButtonPress bp = new ButtonPress();
    bp.setSize(400, 300);
    bp.setVisible(true);
  }

  public ButtonPress() {
    JMenuBar jmb = new JMenuBar();
    JMenu menu = new JMenu("Execute");
    jmb.add(menu);
    JMenuItem jmi = new JMenuItem("Database Query");
    menu.add(jmi);
    jmi.addActionListener(new ActionListener() {
      public void actionPerformed(ActionEvent event) {
        performDatabaseQuery();
      }
    });
    setJMenuBar(jmb);
  }
```

106

```java
private Object performDatabaseQuery() {

    // Simulate long-running database query
    try {
      Thread.sleep(5000);
    } catch (Exception e) {}
    ;
    return null;
  }
}
```

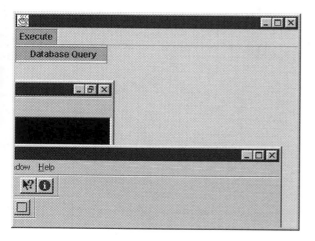

Figure 4-1. *Blocking the event dispatch thread prevents your GUI from being repainted/refreshed, which makes the application look as though it's "hung up" or is otherwise malfunctioning*

This type of confusing display can occur when one window is temporarily overlaid by another and the first window isn't repainted after the second one is hidden or removed.

Creating Threads

As mentioned earlier, Java provides robust built-in support for supporting multithreaded applications, and creating a new thread is simple. Each thread is represented by an instance of the java.lang.Thread class, and to create a new instance, you simply define a class that extends Thread or implements the java.lang.Runnable interface.

You'll often want to create a class with code that runs in its own thread, but if that class extends Thread, it can't inherit functionality from any other class since Java doesn't support multiple inheritance. Extending Thread doesn't provide any functional advantage over implementing Runnable, and neither approach is significantly easier than the other one, so the latter approach (implementing Runnable) is usually better.

The only method defined in Runnable is run() which is called when the thread executes. Once the thread exits run() (either normally or because of an uncaught exception), it's considered dead and can't be restarted or reused. In effect, the run() method serves the same purpose in a thread that the main() method does when executing a Java application: it's the initial entry point into your code. As with the main() method, you shouldn't normally call run() explicitly. Instead, you'll pass an instance of Runnable to a

Thread constructor, and the thread will call run() automatically when it's started. For example, to make the ButtonPress application multithreaded, you could create a DatabaseQuery class like the following one that implements Runnable:

```
class DatabaseQuery implements Runnable {

  public void run() {
    performDatabaseQuery();
  }
}
```

To use this class, all that's necessary is to create a new instance of Thread, passing its constructor a DatabaseQuery instance, and call the Thread's start() method to begin execution. Calling start() indicates that the newly created thread should begin execution, and it does so by calling the object's run() method as mentioned previously.

```
Thread t = new Thread(new DatabaseQuery());
t.start();
```

In fact, the need to perform long-running operations outside the EDT is so common that since Java 1.6 a SwingWorker class has been included in Java that implements Runnable and that makes it easier to support this functionality, and Listing 4-2 shows an example of how it can be used.

Listing 4-2. DatabaseQuery, Modified

```
import java.awt.*;
import java.awt.event.*;
import javax.swing.*;

public class ButtonPress extends JFrame {

public static void main(String[] args) {
  ButtonPress bp = new ButtonPress();
  bp.setSize(400, 300);
  bp.setVisible(true);
}

public ButtonPress() {
  JMenuBar jmb = new JMenuBar();
  JMenu menu = new JMenu("Execute");
  jmb.add(menu);
  JMenuItem jmi = new JMenuItem("Database Query");
  menu.add(jmi);
  jmi.addActionListener(new ActionListener() {
    public void actionPerformed(ActionEvent event) {
      SwingWorker<Object,Object> worker =
              new SwingWorker<Object,Object>() {
        public Object doInBackground() {
          return performDatabaseQuery();
        }
      };
```

```
    Thread t = new Thread(worker);
    t.start();
    }
  });
  setJMenuBar(jmb);
}

private Object performDatabaseQuery() {

  // Simulate long-running database query
  try {
    Thread.sleep(50000);
  } catch (Exception e) {}
  ;
  return null;
}

}
```

When this code is executed and the menu item activated, the AWT event thread will call the actionPerformed() method and create a new thread, passing to it the SwingWorker instance. When that thread executes, it will call run() which in turn invokes the doInBackground() method. Creating a new thread and using it to execute the long-running task prevents the EDT from being blocked, ensuring that the application interface remains responsive to user input and that it can repaint the interface when appropriate.

In addition to the constructor used here that accepts a single Runnable parameter, Thread also provides constructors that allow you to specify a name (in the form of a String) for the thread and to identify the ThreadGroup with which the Thread should be associated. We'll examine thread groups in more detail later in this chapter; they allow you to create logical groupings of threads. A thread's name has no functional significance but may allow you to more easily distinguish one thread from another while debugging a multithreaded application.

Disadvantages of Using Threads

As you can see from the previous example, it's extremely easy to create a thread in Java, but you should avoid doing so when possible. Although not obvious from this simple example, using multiple threads within your applications has several disadvantages, as described in the following sections.

Slow Initial Startup

Although not apparent from the previous ButtonPress class, creating and starting a new thread is a relatively slow operation on some platforms, and in an application where performance is critical, this can be a significant drawback. Thread pooling provides a reasonably simple solution to this problem, and will be discussed in detail later in this chapter.

Resource Utilization

Each thread is allocated its own *stack*, which is an area of storage used to contain local variable values (that is, variables defined within a method) and other information related to execution. Other system resources are used in addition to the stack, although the specific amount and type of those resources used vary from one Java Virtual Machine (JVM) to the next. Although it's typically possible to create a large number of threads, the platform you're using may limit the number that can be created. Even if the platform doesn't explicitly limit the number of threads you can create, there's usually a practical limit determined by the speed of your processor(s) and the amount of available memory on your system.

Although you can't eliminate this problem, you can control it through thread pooling. In addition to eliminating the overhead penalty associated with creating a new thread, you can use thread pools to limit the number of threads that are created. This assumes, of course, that your application voluntarily allows a thread pool manager to control when to create threads and how many to create.

Increased Complexity

By far the biggest disadvantage of using threads within your application is the complexity that it adds. For example, if you're debugging a single-threaded application, it's relatively easy to observe your application's flow of execution, but it can be significantly more difficult to do so when using multiple threads.

Thread safety usually involves designing the object so that its data can't be read or written by one thread while another thread is in the process of modifying that data. In this context, *data* refers to the information encapsulated by the object, and a single data item can consist of a field or collection of fields within the object. An example of a data item is a person's name, which might be contained within a single String field or within several fields (for example, first, middle, and last names).

An even more complex problem is the matter of sharing resources among multiple threads. In this context, a resource is any entity that can be used by more than one thread simultaneously, and in most cases you're responsible for coordinating their use by the threads. For example, Swing components aren't inherently thread-safe, so you're responsible for coordinating how they're used by your application's thread(s) and the AWT event thread. This is usually done using the invokeAndWait() and invokeLater() methods in SwingUtilities to delegate modifications to visible components to the AWT event thread.

In general, if you create an object that contains data that can be modified, and the object is accessible by more than one thread, you're responsible for making that object thread-safe. *Thread safety* refers to ensuring that no partial or otherwise inappropriate modifications can be made to an object's state because of two or more threads attempting to update the state simultaneously; you'll see shortly how this can occur when an object isn't thread-safe.

Sharing Resources

Before discussing how to coordinate using shared resources among threads, we'll first cover which resources are shared. Variables defined locally within a method aren't accessible outside that method and are therefore not shared when multiple threads execute the same method for some object. For example, suppose you run the following application, which creates two threads that use the same Runnable object instance:

```
public class ThreadShare implements Runnable {

  public static void main(String[] args) {
    ThreadShare ts = new ThreadShare();
    Thread t1 = new Thread(ts);
    Thread t2 = new Thread(ts);
```

```
    t1.start();
    t2.start();
  }

  public void run() {
    int nonSharedValue = 100;
    nonSharedValue += 100;
    System.out.println("Value: " + nonSharedValue);
  }

}
```

Because the nonSharedValue variable is defined inside the run() method, it's local to that method and isn't shared by the two threads. Since each thread will get its own copy of nonSharedValue, running this application will always produce the following output:

```
Value: 200
Value: 200
```

However, if the application is modified so that the run() method increments an instance variable, that variable will be a shared resource:

```
public class ThreadShare implements Runnable {

  private int sharedValue = 100;

  public static void main(String[] args) {
    ThreadShare ts = new ThreadShare();
    Thread t1 = new Thread(ts);
    Thread t2 = new Thread(ts);
    t1.start();
    t2.start();
}

  public void run() {
    sharedValue += 100;
    System.out.println("Value: " + sharedValue);
  }

}
```

If you modify and execute this application, it will probably produce the following results:

```
Value: 200
Value: 300
```

However, it's also possible that the output could match the following:

```
Value: 300
Value: 300
```

It's even possible for the program to produce these results.

```
Value: 300
Value: 200
```

To understand why the output can vary, it's necessary to have some knowledge of how threads are managed by operating systems, since Java's threading support uses the native thread capabilities of the platform on which the Java Virtual Machine executes.

Thread Management

For multiple operations to be executed concurrently by a single microprocessor, it's necessary at some point to transfer control of the processor from one thread to another, which is called *context switching*. Context switching can occur when a thread voluntarily gives up control of the processor, and that approach is known as *cooperative multitasking*. In cooperative multitasking, a thread must execute some instruction or call a method to indicate that it's willing to relinquish control over the processor to another thread. Unfortunately, if a programmer deliberately or accidentally creates a thread that doesn't periodically give up control of the processor, that thread can easily cause the application to "hang" and/or prevent other threads from running. Cooperative multitasking is relatively easy to implement and was used by older operating systems, but the voluntary nature of context switching makes it possible for one thread to "lock up" an application or even the entire operating system if that thread doesn't occasionally release control of the processor.

A better approach is *preemptive multitasking*, where control of the processor is arbitrarily transferred from one thread to another, such as after some amount of time has elapsed. Preemptive multitasking has two advantages over cooperative multitasking:

- It can prevent a thread from monopolizing the processor.

- It removes from the programmer the burden of deciding when to perform a context switch, shifting that responsibility to the operating system.

With preemptive multitasking, a programmer doesn't need to be concerned with how or when to perform a context switch, but that convenience comes at a price. Although the programmer doesn't need to be concerned with the details of context switching, it becomes necessary to coordinate the use of resources that are shared by multiple threads.

In the previous example of the ThreadShare class, you saw that the results of running the application could vary. The reason for this is that no effort was made to coordinate the use of the shared resource, specifically the sharedValue variable. In most cases, the sequence of events will proceed as follows, where t1 represents the first thread and t2 the second:

```
t1 enters the run() method
t1 adds 100 to sharedValue, setting it equal to 200
t1 prints the value of sharedValue
t2 enters the run() method
t2 adds 100 to sharedValue, setting it equal to 300
t2 prints the value of sharedValue
```

However, if the native platform uses preemptive multitasking, it's possible that the sequence of steps can be performed slightly differently. In fact, from an application perspective, it's not possible to predict when a context switch will occur, so you must assume a worst-case scenario. In this case, for example, it's possible for the sequence of steps to occur as follows:

```
t1 enters the run() method
t1 adds 100 to sharedValue, setting it equal to 200
(Context switch occurs here and t2 is allowed to run)
t2 enters the run() method
t2 adds 100 to sharedValue, setting it equal to 300
t2 prints the value of sharedValue
(Context switch occurs and t1 is allowed to resume execution)
t1 prints the value of sharedValue
```

This is just one of the possible combinations that can occur, which means the results of the application are unpredictable. This type of situation, where the order in which threads execute can affect the results of running an application, is called a *race condition*. Since unpredictability is obviously not desirable in a software application, it's important to avoid race conditions, and the following code illustrates that point. The application creates two instances of CustomerAccount representing a customer's savings and checking accounts. Once the accounts have been created and initialized so that each one contains $1,000, two threads are created that transfer random amounts of money between the two accounts.

In the case of the ThreadShare application, it wasn't clear what the correct output should be because the purpose behind the code's design wasn't stated, but it should be more obvious here. In this case, the intent is clearly to transfer money between two accounts while still maintaining the same total value. To allow you to determine whether that's actually the case, the sum of the two account balances is printed both before and after the transfers take place. Listing 4-3 shows the initial AccountManager implementation.

Listing 4-3. Initial AccountManager Implementation

```java
public class AccountManager {

  private CustomerAccount savings;
  private CustomerAccount checking;

  public final static int SAVINGS_ACCOUNT = 1;
  public final static int CHECKING_ACCOUNT = 2;

  public static void main(String[] args) {
    int transfers = 1000000;
    try {
      transfers = Integer.parseInt(args[0]);
    } catch (Exception e) {}
    AccountManager am = new AccountManager(transfers);
  }

  public AccountManager(int transfers) {
    savings = new CustomerAccount(SAVINGS_ACCOUNT, 1000);
    checking = new CustomerAccount(CHECKING_ACCOUNT, 1000);
    java.text.NumberFormat formatter =
        java.text.NumberFormat.getCurrencyInstance(
        java.util.Locale.US);
```

```
System.out.println("Total balance before transfers: " +
    formatter.format(savings.getBalance() +
    checking.getBalance()));
TransferManager tm1 = new TransferManager(checking,
    savings, transfers);
TransferManager tm2 = new TransferManager(savings,
    checking, transfers);

// Create two threads
Thread t1 = new Thread(tm1);
Thread t2 = new Thread(tm2);
// Initiate execution of the threads
t1.start();
t2.start();
// Wait for both threads to complete execution
try {
  t1.join();
  t2.join();
} catch (Exception e) {};
System.out.println("Total balance after transfers: " +
    formatter.format(savings.getBalance() +
    checking.getBalance()));
}

class TransferManager implements Runnable {

  private CustomerAccount fromAccount;
  private CustomerAccount toAccount;
  private int transferCount;

  public TransferManager(CustomerAccount fromacct,
      CustomerAccount toacct, int transfers) {
    fromAccount = fromacct;
    toAccount = toacct;
    transferCount = transfers;
  }

  public void run() {
    double balance;
    double transferAmount;
    for (int i = 0 ; i < transferCount; i++) {
      balance = fromAccount.getBalance();
      transferAmount = (int)(balance * Math.random());
      balance -= transferAmount;
      fromAccount.setBalance(balance);
      balance = toAccount.getBalance();
      balance += transferAmount;
      toAccount.setBalance(balance);
    }
  }
}

}
```

```
class CustomerAccount {

  private int accountType;
  private double balance;

  public CustomerAccount(int type, double bal) {
    accountType = type;
    balance = bal;
  }

  public int getAccountType() {
    return accountType;
  }

  public double getBalance() {
    return balance;
  }

  public void setBalance(double newbal) {
    balance = newbal;
  }

  }

}
```

Regardless of how many transfers take place or what the amounts of those transfers are, the total value of the two accounts should be equal to $2,000 once the application completes. However, if you compile and execute this application it can display the following results:

```
Total balance before transfers: $2,000.00
Total balance after transfers: $2.00
```

However, it's also possible that it will display results like the following:

```
Total balance before transfers: $2,000.00
Total balance after transfers: $41.00
```

This variation occurs for the same reason that ThreadShare's output was unpredictable. Specifically, the two threads that are modifying the account balances sometimes produce a conflict as follows, where t1 represents one thread and t2 represents the other:

```
t1 gets the current checking account balance (e.g. $1000).
t1 calculates the transfer amount (e.g. $15)
t1 subtracts the transfer amount from the checking balance (1000 - 15 = $985) (Context
switch occurs)
t2 calculates the transfer amount (e.g. $27)
t2 gets the current savings account balance (e.g. $1000).
t2 subtracts the transfer amount from the savings balance (1000 - 27 = $973)
t2 saves the new savings balance (973) in the CustomerAccount object
t2 gets the current checking account balance ($1000)
t2 adds the transfer amount ($27) to the checking balance (1000 + 27 = $1027)
t2 saves the new checking balance ($1027) in the CustomerAccount object
(Context switch occurs)
t1 saves the new checking balance ($985) in the CustomerAccount object
t1 gets the current savings account balance ($973)
t1 adds the transfer amount ($15) to the savings balance (973 + 15 = $988)
t1 saves the new savings balance ($988) in the CustomerAccount object
```

After this sequence of steps, the checking balance is $985 and the savings balance is $988. Although the total of the two account balances should still be $2,000, their total is only $1,973. In effect, $27 was lost because of context switching and the failure to prevent the two threads from making inappropriate updates to the resources they share.

Understanding the Problem

Before discussing a solution to the problem we just encountered it's helpful to clarify the reasons why a problem like this can occur. One reason the potential exists is that some—in fact most—Java language statements are executed as a series of byte code instructions. For example, suppose that you've defined an instance variable called amount and that you execute the following line of code in the class where it's defined:

```
this.amount += 100;
```

Although this is a single Java statement in practice it's executed as a series of statements:

- Load the value of the amount field.

- Add 100 to the loaded value.

- Store the new value in the amount field.

If two different threads are manipulating the field as just described it's possible that one of them could overwrite the changes made by the other as described earlier. In fact, even if one thread completes all of these steps it's still possible that a second thread could overwrite its changes. That can occur because most modern processors maintain a memory cache, and if one thread has changes that are cached but not stored in the main memory ("flushed") it can wind up overwriting the changes made to that same memory location by a second thread even if the second thread executes later. For example, suppose that thread t1 updates the amount field as described earlier but the change isn't flushed (written to the processor's main memory area); if thread t2 then executes, makes a different change, and flushes its change that change will eventually be overwritten when t1's change is flushed.

The implication of this behavior is that to be effective synchronization has to take into account two factors: the multistage execution of some Java statements and the tendency of modern processors to cache requested changes to memory locations.

Synchronizing the Use of Shared Resources

In the previous example we saw that it's possible for data to effectively become corrupted when it's modified by more than one thread simultaneously. However, Java's synchronized keyword provides an easy way for you to prevent this from happening by allowing you to define methods and blocks of code that can be executed by only one thread at a time. In effect, the synchronized keyword locks the method or block of code while it's being executed by one thread so that no other threads are allowed to enter until the first thread has exited the method or block.

Each instance of java.lang.Object or one of its subclasses (in other words, every Java object) maintains a lock (or monitor), and the synchronized keyword is always implicitly or explicitly associated with an instance of Object (primitives can't be used). Before a thread can enter a synchronized method or section of code, it must obtain the monitor of the object associated with that code. If one thread obtains an object's monitor and a second thread attempts to do so, the second thread becomes blocked and its execution is suspended until the monitor becomes available. In addition to the monitor, each object maintains a list of threads that are blocked because they're waiting on the object's monitor. If a thread can't obtain an object's monitor, it's automatically put on the list, and once the monitor becomes available, one of the threads in the list will be given the monitor and allowed to continue execution. This behavior occurs when you use the synchronized keyword, and you don't need to explicitly obtain or release an object's monitor. Instead, it will be automatically obtained (if possible) when a thread enters a synchronized method or block of code and released when the thread exits that code block or method.

In the following code segment, a synchronized block of code is created that requires a thread to obtain the studentList object's monitor before entering the block:

```java
public class StudentRoster {

  private java.util.Vector studentList;

  public void addStudentToList(Student st) {
    synchronized (studentList) {
      studentList.addElement(st);
    }
    st.setEnrolled(true);
  }

  public void removeStudentFromList(Student st) {
    studentList.removeElement(st);
  }

}
```

In this case, the object that's used for synchronization is an instance of Vector, but it can be an instance of any class. As in this example, it's common (but not necessary) for the synchronization to be performed using the object that's accessed or modified within the synchronized block. There's no technical requirement that you do so, but this approach provides an easy way for you to remember which object's monitor is used to control access to that object's data.

You can also use the synchronized keyword as a method modifier, in which case the entire method is synchronized as follows:

```
public class StudentRoster {

  private java.util.Vector studentList;

  public synchronized void addStudentToList(Student st) {
    studentList.addElement(st);
    st.setEnrolled(true);
  }

  public void removeStudentFromList(Student st) {
    studentList.removeElement(st);
  }

}
```

Since it was mentioned earlier that synchronized is always associated with an instance of Object, you may be wondering which object that is in this case. When synchronized is used with an instance (in other words, nonstatic) method, the object that will be used is the object against which the method was invoked. For example, if you create an instance of the StudentList class and then call its synchronized addStudent() method, the thread that calls the method must obtain the monitor of the StudentList object instance. In other words, the following code is functionally identical to calling removeStudentFromList() after adding synchronized to that method's definition:

```
StudentRoster sr = new StudentRoster();
Student st = new Student();
.
.
.
// Putting the call to removeStudentFromList() in a code block that's
// synchronized on the instance of StudentList is functionally equivalent
// to adding the synchronized keyword to the method definition.
synchronized (studentList) {
  sr.removeStudentFromList(st);
}
```

When you define a class (in other words, static) method that's synchronized, calls to that method will be synchronized on the Class object associated with the class. For example, suppose that a static method is added to StudentRoster.

```
public class StudentRoster {

  private java.util.Vector studentList;

  public synchronized void addStudentToList(Student st) {
    studentList.addElement(st);
    st.setEnrolled(true);
  }
```

```
public void removeStudentFromList(Student st) {
  studentList.removeElement(st);
}

public static synchronized StudentRoster getNewInstance() {
  return new StudentRoster();
}

}
```

Calls to getNewInstance() will be synchronized on the Class object associated with StudentRoster, so specifying synchronized with the getNewInstance() method definition is equivalent to calling that method using the following code:

```
StudentRoster sr;
.
.
.
// The following code is equivalent to adding synchronized to the
// removeStudentFromList() method's definition, because it causes
// the running thread to attempt to obtain the lock of the Class
// object associated with StudentList.
synchronized (StudentRoster.class) {
  sr = StudentRoster.getNewInstance();
}
```

As these examples illustrate, you can use the synchronized keyword to make code thread-safe that wouldn't be otherwise. However, as you'll see later in the chapter, thread safety often isn't as simple as adding this modifier to one or more method signatures. You need to be aware of some potential problems that can occur in multithreaded applications, and synchronizing methods and code blocks is just part of what you need to do to make your application function appropriately.

One final point should be made with respect to the synchronized keyword, specifically with regard to the behavior mentioned earlier where a processor can cache a requested change to a memory location. Synchronizing execution of a block of code is the most obvious outcome of using the synchronized keyword, but in reality it's not the only one. Specifically, when a thread is blocked trying to execute a synchronized block the JVM also flushes that thread's cached memory changes to the processor's main memory before allowing other threads to execute. Likewise, when a thread becomes eligible to resume execution its cache is cleared so that it doesn't contain any outdated ("dirty") cache values. This ensure that not only are two threads prevented from executing the same block of code but that the processor cache doesn't cause any unexpected results to occur.

Nested Calls to Synchronized Methods and Code Blocks

As mentioned earlier, a thread becomes blocked if it tries to enter a synchronized method or section of code while some other thread owns the associated object's monitor. However, you may be wondering what happens if a thread attempts to enter a synchronized method when it already owns the associated object's monitor. For example, you might have two synchronized methods in a class where one of them calls the other as follows:

```
public synchronized void performFirstFunction() {
  // Some functionality performed here
  .
  performSecondFunction()
}

public synchronized void performSecondFunction() {
  // Some other functionality performed here
}
```

When a thread enters the `performFirstFunction()` method, it obtains the monitor for the object for which the method is called. Once `performSecondFunction()` is called, there's no need to obtain the object's monitor because the thread is already the owner of that monitor, so the thread is allowed to continue executing normally.

Each time a thread successfully enters a method or section of code that's synchronized on some object, a count value associated with the object is incremented, and when the thread exits that method or block, the value is decremented.

A thread releases an object's monitor only when the count value associated with the object is zero, which ensures that the thread keeps the monitor until it exits the code that originally caused it to obtain the monitor. In this case, for example, when a thread enters `performFirstFunction()`, it obtains the object's monitor and increments the count value to one. When the call to `performSecondFunction()` occurs, the count value is incremented to two but will be decremented back to one when the thread exits `performSecondFunction()`. Finally, when the thread exits `performFirstFunction()`, the count value returns to zero, and the object's monitor is released by the thread.

Synchronized Blocks vs. Methods

As you've seen, it's possible to synchronize both an entire method and a section of code within a method, and you may wonder which one you should use. To understand which is appropriate in a given situation, it's important to consider what synchronization really provides.

Stated simply, synchronization allows you to prevent multithreaded execution of certain portions of a multithreaded application. In other words, synchronization reduces the concurrency of your application's threads and, if used too extensively, defeats the purpose of using multiple threads. A good rule of thumb is to include as few lines of code as possible within synchronized methods or blocks but only to the extent that you haven't sacrificed thread safety.

Adding the `synchronized` keyword to a method definition is a simple, readable way to provide thread safety, but it's sometimes not necessary and may be undesirable. For example, if only one or two lines of code within the method really need to be synchronized, you should enclose that code within its own synchronized block instead of synchronizing the entire method. This is particularly true if much of the time devoted to executing that method is spent on code that doesn't need to be synchronized. In other words, if you synchronize too much of your code, you'll prevent threads from running when they should be able to run.

Deadlocks

Once you've synchronized access to the shared resources within your application, you may encounter a deadlock. For example, returning to the AccountManager application as an example, let's suppose you decide to synchronize access to the resources (in other words, the CustomerAccount objects) that are used by multiple threads, as shown in Listing 4-4.

Listing 4-4. Synchronizing Code Sections

```
class TransferManager implements Runnable {

  private CustomerAccount fromAccount;
  private CustomerAccount toAccount;
  private int transferCount;

  public TransferManager(CustomerAccount fromacct,
      CustomerAccount toacct, int transfers) {
    fromAccount = fromacct;
    toAccount = toacct;
    transferCount = transfers;
  }

  public void run() {
    double balance;
    double transferAmount;
    for (int i = 0 ; i < transferCount; i++) {
      synchronized (fromAccount) {
        balance = fromAccount.getBalance();
        transferAmount = (int)(balance * Math.random());
        balance -= transferAmount;
        fromAccount.setBalance(balance);
        synchronized (toAccount) {
          balance = toAccount.getBalance();
          balance += transferAmount;
          toAccount.setBalance(balance);
        }
      }
    }
  }

}
```

Although these modifications do fix one potential problem, they introduce the possibility of another: deadlock. The first thread that's started in the CustomerAccount application transfers money from the checking account to the savings account, and the second thread transfers money from savings into checking. Therefore, for each of the first thread's iterations through the run() method, it will obtain the checking account object's monitor and then the savings account monitor. The second thread competes for the same two monitors, but it attempts to obtain them in the reverse order.

Now suppose during an iteration of the run() method that the first thread is interrupted after it obtains the checking account monitor but before it has gotten the savings account monitor. If the second thread then begins executing the loop, it will successfully obtain the savings account monitor, but it will be blocked when it attempts to obtain the checking account monitor. At that point, each thread has successfully obtained one of the two monitors, and each will wait indefinitely for the other monitor to become available, which is an example of deadlock.

Deadlock conditions are common in multithreaded applications and often result in the application becoming "hung." Fortunately, you have at least two ways of preventing this problem, neither of which is terribly complex: high-level synchronization and lock ordering.

High-Level Synchronization

In Listing 4-4, each CustomerAccount's monitor was used to synchronize access to that CustomerAccount instance. Since a transfer operation involved obtaining two locks, it was possible for deadlock to occur if a thread obtained one of the locks but not the other. However, since this form of deadlock can't occur if only one lock is involved, high-level synchronization offers a potential solution to the problem.

As mentioned earlier, it's customary when adding synchronization to your application to cause an operation to synchronize on the object being accessed or modified, but there's no technical reason you must do so. In this case, for example, the application synchronizes access to each CustomerAccount object using that instance's monitor, but it's entirely acceptable to synchronize access to those objects using some other object.

In high-level synchronization, you simply select a single object that synchronizes access to all shared resources that are involved in some operation. In the case of a transfer operation, for example, you can select an existing object or create a new object that will be used to control access to all instances of CustomerAccount. You can do this by creating a new object explicitly for that purpose, as shown in the following variable declaration that might be added to CustomerAccount:

```
private final static Object synchronizerObject = new Object();
```

This new object is defined as a class variable because it will be used to synchronize access to all instances of CustomerAccount as follows:

```
public void run() {
  double balance;
  double transferAmount;
  for (int i = 0 ; i < transferCount; i++) {
    synchronized (synchronizerObject) {
      balance = fromAccount.getBalance();
      transferAmount = (int)(balance * Math.random());
      balance -= transferAmount;
      fromAccount.setBalance(balance);
      balance = toAccount.getBalance();
      balance += transferAmount;
      toAccount.setBalance(balance);
    }
  }
}
```

In effect, you've eliminated the deadlock problem by reducing the number of monitors that a thread must own from two to one. However, the problem with this approach is that it reduces the concurrency of the application, since only one transfer can ever be in progress at any given time. In other words, even a transfer involving two completely separate and unrelated CustomerAccount objects would be blocked while a thread is executing the code inside this synchronized block.

Lock Ordering

As you saw earlier, the deadlock condition occurred because the two threads attempt to obtain the objects' monitors in a different order. The first thread attempts to obtain the checking account monitor and then the savings account monitor, while the second thread attempts to obtain the same two monitors but in the reverse order. This difference in the order in which the monitors are obtained lies at the root of the deadlock problem, and you can address the problem by ensuring that the monitors are obtained in the same order by all threads.

You can accomplish this by creating an if statement that switches the order in which the locks are obtained based on the results of some comparison. In other words, when locking two objects, there must be some way to compare those objects to determine which one's monitor should be obtained first. In this case, the CustomerAccount instances provide a convenient way of doing so, since each one maintains an account type (in other words, checking or savings) that's stored as an integer value. Listing 4-5 shows an example of how you could implement this.

Listing 4-5. Implementing Lock Ordering

```
class TransferManager implements Runnable {

  private CustomerAccount fromAccount;
  private CustomerAccount toAccount;
  private int transferCount;

  public TransferManager(CustomerAccount fromacct,
      CustomerAccount toacct, int transfers) {
    fromAccount = fromacct;
    toAccount = toacct;
    transferCount = transfers;
  }

  public void run() {
    double balance;
    double transferAmount;
    for (int i = 0 ; i < transferCount; i++) {
      balance = fromAccount.getBalance();
      transferAmount = (int)(balance * Math.random());
      transferFunds(fromAccount, toAccount, transferAmount);
    }
  }
}

private void transferFunds(CustomerAccount account1,
    CustomerAccount account2, double transferAmount) {
  double balance;
  CustomerAccount holder = null;
  // We want to always synchronize first on the account with the
  // smaller account type value. If it turns out that the "second"
  // account actually has a larger type value, we'll simply
  // switch the two references and multiply the amount being
  // transferred by -1.
```

```
if (account1.getAccountType() > account2.getAccountType()) {
  holder = account1;
  account1 = account2;
  account2 = holder;
  transferAmount *= -1;
}
synchronized (account1) {
  synchronized (account2) {
    balance = account1.getBalance();
    balance -= transferAmount;
    account1.setBalance(balance);
    balance = account2.getBalance();
    balance += transferAmount;
    account1.setBalance(balance);
  }
}
}

}
```

Since the savings account's type value (1) is less than the checking account type, (2) a savings account's monitor will always be obtained first by this code, regardless of the type of transfer being performed. In this case, you obtain the monitor of the account with a lower type value, but this code would run equally well if it were modified to first obtain the monitor of the account with the higher type value. In other words, it's not the order in which the monitors are obtained that's important: it's simply necessary to ensure that both threads consistently obtain the monitors in the same order.

Thread Priorities

Each Thread is assigned a priority, which is a value between 1 and 10 (inclusive) that's an indication of when a thread should run relative to other threads. In general, a thread's priority determines whether it's given preference by the processor when there are two or more *runnable threads*. A runnable thread is one that's able to execute instructions, which means it has been started, hasn't yet died, and isn't blocked for any reason.

When a context switch occurs, the processor typically selects the runnable thread with the highest priority, which means that higher-priority threads will usually run before and/or more frequently than lower-priority threads. If two or more threads with the same priority are runnable, it's more difficult to predict which one will be allowed to run.

In fact, the factors that determine how long and how often a thread runs are specific to the platform on which it's running and to the Java Virtual Machine implementation in use. One operating system might always select the first available runnable thread with the highest priority, while another system may schedule threads with the same priority in a "round-robin" fashion. In addition, while Java supports ten priorities, the underlying operating system's threading architecture may support a lesser or greater number of priorities. When that's the case, the Java Virtual Machine is responsible for mapping the priority value assigned to the Thread object to an appropriate native priority.

Given these differences between platforms, Java doesn't make any guarantees concerning how priority affects a thread's execution. Therefore, you should avoid making assumptions about the effects of thread priorities on your application or at least test its effects on each platform on which your code will be deployed.

When one Thread creates another, that new Thread (sometimes called the *child thread*) is given the same priority value as the one that created it (the *parent thread*). However, you can explicitly set a Thread's priority by calling its setPriority() method and specifying an int parameter value between 1 and 10. The Thread class provides three constants that correspond to low, medium, and high thread priorities; MIN_PRIORITY, NORM_PRIORITY, and MAX_PRIORITY correspond to values of 1, 5, and 10, respectively. For example, to create a thread and assign it the lowest possible priority, you could use code similar to the following:

```
Runnable myRunnable;
.
.
.
Thread t = new Thread(myRunnable);
t.setPriority(Thread.MIN_PRIORITY);
```

The specific priority you assign to a thread will depend primarily on the nature of the function(s) performed by the thread. For example, if a thread will spend most of its time waiting for input and it performs a task that must be completed quickly, it should normally be assigned a high priority. Conversely, a thread that performs some type of noncritical background task (particularly one that takes a long time to complete) should be given a low priority. The word processor used to create this book, for instance, performs automatic spell checking, but that function is performed in a low-priority thread, at least until the application receives an explicit request to spell check the document.

When selecting thread priorities, be aware that it may be possible for a long-running thread with a high priority to monopolize the processor, even when preemptive multitasking is being used. Therefore, you should use caution in assigning higher priorities and will usually do so only for threads that can be counted on to periodically relinquish control of the processor voluntarily.

Daemon Threads

Each thread is classified as either a daemon thread or a user thread, and Thread's setDaemon() method allows you to specify the thread's type. To use setDaemon(), you must call it before a thread is started, and passing a boolean value of true indicates that the thread should be a daemon thread, while false (the default) indicates it should be a user thread.

The only difference between a daemon thread and a user thread is that one type (user) prevents the Java Virtual Machine from exiting, while the other (daemon) doesn't. For example, if you compile and execute the following application, the JVM will terminate after executing the main() method:

```
public class Test {

  public static void main(String[] args) {
    Test t = new Test();
  }

  public Test() {
    System.out.println("Hello world.");
  }

}
```

However, if you create a similar application that displays a visual component such as a frame or dialog, as shown in Listing 4-6, the JVM doesn't exit.

Listing 4-6. Displaying a Visual Component in Test

```java
import java.awt.*;
import java.awt.event.*;
import javax.swing.*;

public class Test {

  private JFrame frame;
  public static void main(String[] args) {
    Test t = new Test();
  }

  public Test() {
    frame = new JFrame("Hello World");
    frame.addWindowListener(new WindowAdapter() {
      public void windowClosing(WindowEvent event) {
        frame.setVisible(false);
        frame.removeWindowListener(this);
        frame.dispose();
        frame = null;
      }
    });
    Container pane = frame.getContentPane();
    pane.setLayout(new FlowLayout());
    pane.add(new JLabel("Hello world."));
    frame.setSize(400, 300);
    frame.setVisible(true);
  }

}
```

Although the modified Test class shown in Listing 4-6 performs all the appropriate cleanup operations, the JVM doesn't exit when the window is closed and the resources are released. This is because a JVM will not automatically terminate as long as there are any live user threads, even if it may not be obvious which user thread is active. In this case, the user thread preventing the JVM from exiting is the AWT event thread, which is started automatically when the JFrame is created so that rendering and event notification services can be provided. If you want to force the JVM to exit despite the fact that one or more user threads are still executing, you must call the static exit() method in the System class as follows:

```java
System.exit(0);
```

Daemon threads are often used for background tasks that run continuously and that don't need to perform any cleanup tasks before the JVM terminates execution; an example of this is the thread that performs garbage collection. If it's important for a thread to perform some cleanup task(s) before the Java Virtual Machine exits, that thread should be made a user thread. Otherwise, it's appropriate for the thread to run as a daemon thread.

Adding Threads to an Application

We'll now see how to create an application that can benefit from the use of threads and cover some of the issues you'll face when doing so. This application allows you to specify the URL of a file and download it, writing the file to disk. Figure 4-2 illustrates how the application will appear during the download.

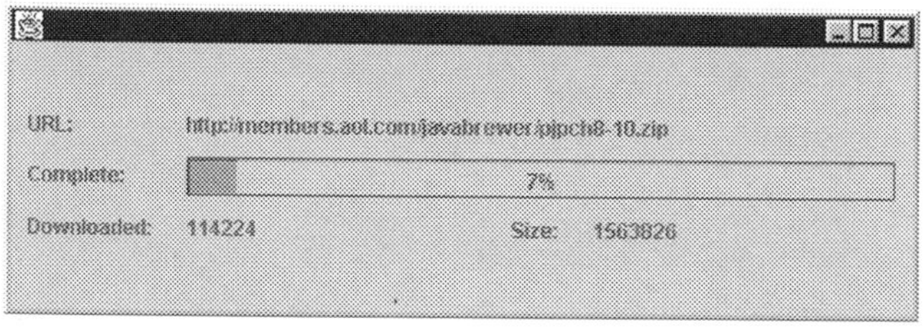

Figure 4-2. *The Downloader class allows you to download a file and displays the progress of the download*

To run this application by itself, you must specify two parameters on the command line: the URL of the file to download and the output file to which the contents of that URL should be written. When you do so, the component will appear in a frame like the one shown in Figure 4-2, and the portion of the file downloaded will be displayed visually through the progress bar. For example, to download the home page from Oracle's Java web site and store its contents in C:/brett/temp/javahome.html, you could enter the following command:

```
java Downloader http://www.oracle.com/java/index.html C:/brett/temp/javahome.html
```

Listing 4-7 shows the initial implementation of this code. The main() method defined here creates an instance of the Downloader visual component, places it in a frame, displays that frame, and initiates the download by calling performDownload().

Listing 4-7. Initial Downloader Implementation

```java
import java.awt.*;
import java.io.*;
import java.net.*;
import javax.swing.*;

public class Downloader extends JPanel {

    private URL downloadURL;
    private InputStream inputStream;
    private OutputStream outputStream;
    private byte[] buffer;

    private int fileSize;
    private int bytesRead;
```

```
  private JLabel urlLabel;
  private JLabel sizeLabel;
  private JLabel completeLabel;
  private JProgressBar progressBar;
  public final static int BUFFER_SIZE = 1000;

  private boolean stopped;

  public static void main(String[] args) throws Exception {
    Downloader dl = null;
    if (args.length < 2) {
      System.out.println("You must specify the URL of the file " +
          "to download and the name of the local file to " +
          "which its contents will be written.");
      System.exit(0);
    }
    URL url = new URL(args[0]);
    FileOutputStream fos = new FileOutputStream(args[1]);
    try {
      dl = new Downloader(url, fos);
    } catch (FileNotFoundException fnfe) {
      System.out.println("File '" + args[0] + "' does not exist");
      System.exit(0);
    }
    JFrame f = new JFrame();
    f.getContentPane().add(dl);
    f.setSize(600, 400);
    f.setVisible(true);
    dl.performDownload();
  }
```

The following portion of the code is passed a URL that identifies the file to be downloaded and an OutputStream that represents the location to which the file's contents will be written. In this case, it will be a FileOutputStream, causing the contents to be written to a local disk file.

```
public Downloader(URL url, OutputStream os) throws IOException {
  downloadURL = url;
  outputStream = os;
  bytesRead = 0;
  URLConnection urlConnection = downloadURL.openConnection();
  fileSize = urlConnection.getContentLength();
  if (fileSize == -1) {
    throw new FileNotFoundException(url.toString());
  }
  inputStream = new BufferedInputStream(
      urlConnection.getInputStream());
  buffer = new byte[BUFFER_SIZE];
  buildLayout();

  stopped = false;
}
```

The following section of the code simply builds the interface that's used to provide feedback to the user on the status of the download and consists of labels and a JProgressBar:

```java
private void buildLayout() {
  JLabel label;
  setLayout(new GridBagLayout());
  GridBagConstraints constraints = new GridBagConstraints();
  constraints.fill = GridBagConstraints.HORIZONTAL;
  constraints.insets = new Insets(5, 10, 5, 10);

  constraints.gridx = 0;
  label = new JLabel("URL:", JLabel.LEFT);
  add(label, constraints);

  label = new JLabel("Complete:", JLabel.LEFT);
  add(label, constraints);

  label = new JLabel("Downloaded:", JLabel.LEFT);
  add(label, constraints);

  constraints.gridx = 1;
  constraints.gridwidth = GridBagConstraints.REMAINDER;
  constraints.weightx = 1;
  urlLabel = new JLabel(downloadURL.toString());
  add(urlLabel, constraints);

  progressBar = new JProgressBar(0, fileSize);
  progressBar.setStringPainted(true);
  add(progressBar, constraints);

  constraints.gridwidth = 1;
  completeLabel = new JLabel(Integer.toString(bytesRead));
  add(completeLabel, constraints);

  constraints.gridx = 2;
  constraints.weightx = 0;
  constraints.anchor = GridBagConstraints.EAST;
  label = new JLabel("Size:", JLabel.LEFT);
  add(label, constraints);

  constraints.gridx = 3;
  constraints.weightx = 1;
  sizeLabel = new JLabel(Integer.toString(fileSize));
  add(sizeLabel, constraints);
}
```

As its name implies, the performDownload() method, shown next, is responsible for performing the download. It does this by repeatedly reading a portion of the file into a buffer, writing the contents of that buffer to the output destination, and updating the user interface so that it illustrates the progress of the download.

```
public void performDownload() {
  int byteCount;
  while ((bytesRead < fileSize) && (!stopped)) {
    try {
      byteCount = inputStream.read(buffer);
      if (byteCount == -1) {
        stopped = true;
        break;
      }
      else {
        outputStream.write(buffer, 0,
            byteCount);
        bytesRead += byteCount;
        progressBar.setValue(bytesRead);
        completeLabel.setText(
            Integer.toString(
            bytesRead));
      }
    } catch (IOException ioe) {
      stopped = true;
      JOptionPane.showMessageDialog(this,
          ioe.getMessage(),
          "I/O Error",
          JOptionPane.ERROR_MESSAGE);
      break;
    }
  }
  try {
    outputStream.close();
    inputStream.close();
  } catch (IOException ioe) {};
}

}
```

One problem with this initial implementation of Downloader is that there's no way to control the download process. Downloading starts immediately when the application is executed and can't be suspended or canceled. This is particularly undesirable since downloading a large file can be time-consuming, especially when the download occurs over a low-bandwidth network connection.

The first step in allowing a user to control the download process is to create a thread that exists specifically to perform the download (see Listing 4-8). By making this change, it will be possible to integrate an instance of Downloader into a user interface that will allow the download process to be controlled (in other words, started, suspended, and stopped) through components such as buttons.

Listing 4-8. Creating a Download Thread

```java
import java.awt.*;
import java.io.*;
import java.net.*;
import javax.swing.*;

public class Downloader extends JPanel implements Runnable {

    private URL downloadURL;
    private InputStream inputStream;
    private OutputStream outputStream;
    private byte[] buffer;

    private int fileSize;
    private int bytesRead;

    private JLabel urlLabel;
    private JLabel sizeLabel;
    private JLabel completeLabel;
    private JProgressBar progressBar;

    public final static int BUFFER_SIZE = 1000;

    private boolean stopped;

    private Thread thisThread;

    public static void main(String[] args) throws Exception {
        Downloader dl = null;
        if (args.length < 2) {
        System.out.println("You must specify the URL of the file " +
            "to download and the name of the local file to which " +
            "its contents will be written.");
        System.exit(0);
    }
    URL url = new URL(args[0]);
    FileOutputStream fos = new FileOutputStream(args[1]);
    try {
        dl = new Downloader(url, fos);

    } catch (FileNotFoundException fnfe) {
        System.out.println("File '" + args[0] + "' does not exist");
        System.exit(0);
    }
    JFrame f = new JFrame();
    f.getContentPane().add(dl);
    f.setSize(600, 400);
    f.setVisible(true);
    dl.thisThread.start();
}
}
```

```java
public Downloader(URL url, OutputStream os) throws IOException {
  downloadURL = url;
  outputStream = os;
  bytesRead = 0;
  URLConnection urlConnection = downloadURL.openConnection();
  fileSize = urlConnection.getContentLength();
  if (fileSize == -1) {
    throw new FileNotFoundException(url.toString());
  }
  inputStream = new BufferedInputStream(
    urlConnection.getInputStream());
  buffer = new byte[BUFFER_SIZE];
  thisThread = new Thread(this);
  buildLayout();

  stopped = false;
}

private void buildLayout() {
  JLabel label;
  setLayout(new GridBagLayout());
  GridBagConstraints constraints = new GridBagConstraints();
  constraints.fill = GridBagConstraints.HORIZONTAL;
  constraints.insets = new Insets(5, 10, 5, 10);

  constraints.gridx = 0;
  label = new JLabel("URL:", JLabel.LEFT);
  add(label, constraints);

  label = new JLabel("Complete:", JLabel.LEFT);
  add(label, constraints);

  label = new JLabel("Downloaded:", JLabel.LEFT);
  add(label, constraints);

  constraints.gridx = 1;
  constraints.gridwidth = GridBagConstraints.REMAINDER;
  constraints.weightx = 1;
  urlLabel = new JLabel(downloadURL.toString());
  add(urlLabel, constraints);

  progressBar = new JProgressBar(0, fileSize);
  progressBar.setStringPainted(true);
  add(progressBar, constraints);

  constraints.gridwidth = 1;
  completeLabel = new JLabel(Integer.toString(bytesRead));
  add(completeLabel, constraints);

  constraints.gridx = 2;
  constraints.weightx = 0;
```

```
    constraints.anchor = GridBagConstraints.EAST;
    label = new JLabel("Size:", JLabel.LEFT);
    add(label, constraints);

    constraints.gridx = 3;
    constraints.weightx = 1;
    sizeLabel = new JLabel(Integer.toString(fileSize));
    add(sizeLabel, constraints);
}

public void run() {
    performDownload();
}

public void performDownload() {
    int byteCount;
    while ((bytesRead < fileSize) && (!stopped)) {
        try {
            byteCount = inputStream.read(buffer);
            if (byteCount == -1) {
                stopped = true;
                break;
            }
             else {
                outputStream.write(buffer, 0,
                    byteCount);
                bytesRead += byteCount;
                progressBar.setValue(bytesRead);
                completeLabel.setText(
                    Integer.toString(
                    bytesRead));
            }
        } catch (IOException ioe) {
            stopped = true;
            JOptionPane.showMessageDialog(this,
                ioe.getMessage(),
                "I/O Error",
                JOptionPane.ERROR_MESSAGE);
            break;
        }
    }
    try {
        outputStream.close();
        inputStream.close();
    } catch (IOException ioe) {};
  }

}
```

Although this application appears correct on the surface, it has one small problem. Specifically, the AWT event thread and the thread that performs the download share two resources that are not synchronized: the JProgressBar and the JTextField that are updated to provide feedback on the download operation's progress. This is actually a common problem with multithreaded applications, but Java's SwingUtilities class provides a simple solution. When you create a multithreaded application that needs to modify components after they've been made visible, you can use the invokeLater() and invokeAndWait() methods in SwingUtilities.

These methods allow you to pass a Runnable object instance as a parameter, and they cause the AWT event thread to execute the run() method of that object. The invokeLater() method represents an asynchronous request, which means it may return before the event thread executes the object's run() method. In contrast, invokeAndWait() represents a synchronous request, meaning that the method waits until the AWT event thread has completed execution of the object's run() method before returning. In the case of Downloader, there's no reason it should wait for the user interface to be updated before it continues downloading, so invokeLater() can be used.

Making this modification solves the problem of having two different threads sharing the same resources, since only a single thread (in other words, the AWT event thread) will access JProgressBar and JTextField once they've been made visible.

```java
public void performDownload() {
  int byteCount;
  Runnable progressUpdate = new Runnable() {
    public void run() {
      progressBar.setValue(bytesRead);
      completeLabel.setText(
          Integer.toString(
          bytesRead));
    }
  };
  while ((bytesRead < fileSize) && (!stopped)) {
    try {
    byteCount = inputStream.read(buffer);
    if (byteCount == -1) {
      stopped = true;
      break;
    }
    else {
      outputStream.write(buffer, 0,
          byteCount);
      bytesRead += byteCount;
      SwingUtilities.invokeLater(
          progressUpdate);
    }
  } catch (IOException ioe) {
    stopped = true;
    JOptionPane.showMessageDialog(this,
        ioe.getMessage(),
        "I/O Error",
        JOptionPane.ERROR_MESSAGE);
    break;
  }
}
```

```
try {
  outputStream.close();
  inputStream.close();
} catch (IOException ioe) {};
}
```

Controlling Threads

It's acceptable in some cases to start a thread and simply allow it to die once it exits the run() method. However, for various reasons, you'll often want to terminate a thread before it exits the run() method, or you may simply want to suspend its execution and allow it to resume later. In the latter case, you may want to suspend its execution for some particular length of time, or you may want it to be suspended until some condition has been met. To provide the functions just described, you can create a new subclass of JPanel that defines five buttons (as shown in Figure 4-3):

- A Start button that causes the download thread to begin execution

- A Sleep button that causes the download thread to suspend its execution for a specific length of time, which is for five seconds in this case

- A Suspend button that causes the thread to suspend its execution indefinitely

- A Resume button that causes the thread to resume execution after the Suspend button was previously clicked

- A Stop button that effectively kills the thread by causing it to exit the run() method

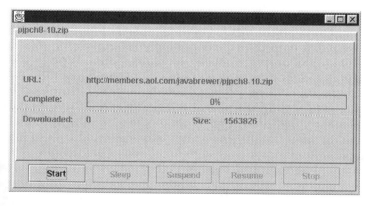

Figure 4-3. *The download code becomes more useful when you add buttons that allow you to control the process*

The DownloadManager class shown in Listing 4-9 displays an instance of Downloader and creates the buttons just described that will be used to control the execution of the Downloader's thread. It takes the same two parameters as the Downloader class, but unlike that class, DownloadManager allows you to interact with the thread performing the download by clicking one of the buttons that are displayed. It does that by adding action listeners to each of the buttons, and you'll see shortly how to create the code needed for each button to perform the function requested.

Listing 4-9. Initial DownloadManager Implementation

```java
import java.awt.*;
import java.awt.event.*;
import java.io.*;
import java.net.URL;
import javax.swing.*;
import javax.swing.border.*;

public class DownloadManager extends JPanel {

  private Downloader downloader;

  private JButton startButton;
  private JButton sleepButton;
  private JButton suspendButton;
  private JButton resumeButton;
  private JButton stopButton;

  public static void main(String[] args) throws Exception {
    URL url = new URL(args[0]);
    FileOutputStream fos = new FileOutputStream(args[1]);
    JFrame f = new JFrame();
    DownloadManager dm = new DownloadManager(url, fos);
    f.getContentPane().add(dm);
    f.setSize(600, 400);
    f.setVisible(true);
  }

  public DownloadManager(URL source, OutputStream os)
      throws IOException {
    downloader = new Downloader(source, os);
    buildLayout();
    Border border = new BevelBorder(BevelBorder.RAISED);
    String name = source.toString();
    int index = name.lastIndexOf('/');
    border = new TitledBorder(border,
        name.substring(index + 1));
    setBorder(border);
  }

  private void buildLayout() {
    setLayout(new BorderLayout());
    downloader.setBorder(new BevelBorder(BevelBorder.RAISED));
    add(downloader, BorderLayout.CENTER);

    add(getButtonPanel(), BorderLayout.SOUTH);
  }

  private JPanel getButtonPanel() {
    JPanel outerPanel;
    JPanel innerPanel;
```

```
    innerPanel = new JPanel();
    innerPanel.setLayout(new GridLayout(1, 5, 10, 0));

    startButton = new JButton("Start");
    startButton.addActionListener(new ActionListener() {
      public void actionPerformed(ActionEvent event) {
      }
    });
    innerPanel.add(startButton);

    sleepButton = new JButton("Sleep");
    sleepButton.setEnabled(false);
    sleepButton.addActionListener(new ActionListener() {
      public void actionPerformed(ActionEvent event) {
      }
    });
    innerPanel.add(sleepButton);
    suspendButton = new JButton("Suspend");
    suspendButton.setEnabled(false);
    suspendButton.addActionListener(new ActionListener() {
        public void actionPerformed(ActionEvent event) {
        }
    });
    innerPanel.add(suspendButton);

    resumeButton = new JButton("Resume");
    resumeButton.setEnabled(false);
    resumeButton.addActionListener(new ActionListener() {
      public void actionPerformed(ActionEvent event) {
      }
    });
    innerPanel.add(resumeButton);

    stopButton = new JButton("Stop");
    stopButton.setEnabled(false);
    stopButton.addActionListener(new ActionListener() {
        public void actionPerformed(ActionEvent event) {
        }
    });
    innerPanel.add(stopButton);

    outerPanel = new JPanel();
    outerPanel.add(innerPanel);
    return outerPanel;
  }

}
```

We'll now see how to create the functionality needed for each of these buttons and will then return to the DownloadManager source code to have each button activate the appropriate functionality.

Starting a Thread

As you've seen, starting the execution of a thread is trivial and simply requires that you call the Thread instance's start() method. Calling start() doesn't necessarily cause the thread to run immediately but simply makes the thread eligible for execution (in other words, makes it runnable). Once that occurs, the thread will be executed by the processor at the first available opportunity, although when that occurs it is platform-dependent and is affected by many factors. However, unless the processor is very busy executing other applications or other threads within the Java Virtual Machine, the thread will usually begin executing almost immediately when its start() method is called.

You can easily modify the Downloader class to provide a startDownload() method that starts the thread's execution, as shown in the following code, and that method will be called when the Start button in a DownloaderManager instance is clicked. For now, however, you'll simply define the startDownload() method and wait until the methods for all five buttons have been defined before going back and calling those methods from the buttons' action event handlers.

```
public void startDownload() {
  thisThread.start();
}
```

Making a Thread "Sleep"

The static sleep() method defined in Thread causes the currently executing thread to temporarily stop executing (in other words, to "sleep") for some specific length of time. You can specify that length of time either as long representing some number of milliseconds or as a combination of milliseconds and an int value representing nanoseconds. However, milliseconds provide enough resolution for most situations, so you'll typically be able to use the simpler implementation of sleep(). For example, to cause the current thread to pause for two seconds, you could use the following code:

```
Thread.sleep(2 * 1000);
```

Similarly, to sleep for 100 nanoseconds, you could use the following code:

```
Thread.sleep(0, 100);
```

Note that both of these methods can throw an InterruptedException if the sleeping thread is interrupted, a scenario that will be discussed shortly. Since sleep() affects only the thread that's currently executing, it must be executed by the thread that should sleep, and that thread can't be "forced" to sleep by any other thread. For example, when the Sleep button is clicked, the actionPerformed() method will be called by the AWT event thread. Since the event thread can't force the download thread to sleep, it must instead send a sleep request to the download thread, and the code executed by the download thread must be designed to recognize and comply with the request. The easiest way to do so is simply to define a boolean flag inside Downloader that's set to true to signal the download thread that it should sleep, and once the download thread wakes up, it can clear the flag. These steps will be taken each time the Downloader is about to read another portion of the file being downloaded, as shown in the bold code of the run() method in Listing 4-10.

Listing 4-10. Implementing the Sleep Function

```java
import java.awt.*;
import java.io.*;
import java.net.*;
import javax.swing.*;

public class Downloader extends JPanel implements Runnable {

    private URL downloadURL;
    private InputStream inputStream;

    private OutputStream outputStream;
    private byte[] buffer;

    private int fileSize;
    private int bytesRead;

    private JLabel urlLabel;
    private JLabel sizeLabel;
    private JLabel completeLabel;
    private JProgressBar progressBar;

    public final static int BUFFER_SIZE = 1000;

    private boolean stopped;
    private boolean sleepScheduled;

    public final static int SLEEP_TIME = 5 * 1000; // 5 seconds

    private Thread thisThread;

    public static void main(String[] args) throws Exception {
        Downloader dl = null;
        if (args.length < 2) {
            System.out.println("You must specify the URL of the file to download and "+
                "the name of the local file to which its contents will be written.");
            System.exit(0);
        }
        URL url = new URL(args[0]);
        FileOutputStream fos = new FileOutputStream(args[1]);
        try {
            dl = new Downloader(url, fos);
        } catch (FileNotFoundException fnfe) {
            System.out.println("File '" + args[0] + "' does not exist");
            System.exit(0);
        }
        JFrame f = new JFrame();
        f.getContentPane().add(dl);
        f.setSize(400, 300);
```

```
      f.setVisible(true);
      dl.thisThread.start();
  }

  public Downloader(URL url, OutputStream os) throws IOException {
    downloadURL = url;
    outputStream = os;
    bytesRead = 0;
    URLConnection urlConnection = downloadURL.openConnection();
    fileSize = urlConnection.getContentLength();
    if (fileSize == -1) {
      throw new FileNotFoundException(url.toString());
    }
    inputStream = new BufferedInputStream(
        urlConnection.getInputStream());
    buffer = new byte[BUFFER_SIZE];
    thisThread = new Thread(this);
    buildLayout();

    stopped = false;
    sleepScheduled = false;
  }

  private void buildLayout() {
    JLabel label;
    setLayout(new GridBagLayout());
    GridBagConstraints constraints = new GridBagConstraints();
    constraints.fill = GridBagConstraints.HORIZONTAL;
    constraints.insets = new Insets(5, 10, 5, 10);

    constraints.gridx = 0;
    label = new JLabel("URL:", JLabel.LEFT);
    add(label, constraints);

    label = new JLabel("Complete:", JLabel.LEFT);
    add(label, constraints);

    label = new JLabel("Downloaded:", JLabel.LEFT);
    add(label, constraints);

    constraints.gridx = 1;
    constraints.gridwidth = GridBagConstraints.REMAINDER;
    constraints.weightx = 1;
    urlLabel = new JLabel(downloadURL.toString());
    add(urlLabel, constraints);

    progressBar = new JProgressBar(0, fileSize);
    progressBar.setStringPainted(true);
    add(progressBar, constraints);
```

```
  constraints.gridwidth = 1;
  completeLabel = new JLabel(Integer.toString(bytesRead));
  add(completeLabel, constraints);

  constraints.gridx = 2;
  constraints.weightx = 0;
  constraints.anchor = GridBagConstraints.EAST;
  label = new JLabel("Size:", JLabel.LEFT);
  add(label, constraints);

  constraints.gridx = 3;
  constraints.weightx = 1;
  sizeLabel = new JLabel(Integer.toString(fileSize));
  add(sizeLabel, constraints);
}

public void startDownload() {
  thisThread.start();
}

public synchronized void setSleepScheduled(boolean doSleep) {
  sleepScheduled = doSleep;
}

public synchronized boolean isSleepScheduled() {
  return sleepScheduled;
}

public void run() {
  performDownload();
}

public void performDownload() {
  int byteCount;
  Runnable progressUpdate = new Runnable() {
    public void run() {
      progressBar.setValue(bytesRead);
      completeLabel.setText(
          Integer.toString(
          bytesRead));
    }
  };
  while ((bytesRead < fileSize) && (!stopped)) {
    try {
      if (isSleepScheduled()) {
       try {
         Thread.sleep(SLEEP_TIME);
         setSleepScheduled(false);
       }
       catch (InterruptedException ie) {
       }
      }
```

```
      byteCount = inputStream.read(buffer);
      if (byteCount == -1) {
        stopped = true;
        break;
      }
      else {
        outputStream.write(buffer, 0,
            byteCount);
        bytesRead += byteCount;
        SwingUtilities.invokeLater(
            progressUpdate);
      }
    } catch (IOException ioe) {
      stopped = true;
      JOptionPane.showMessageDialog(this,
          ioe.getMessage(),
          "I/O Error",
          JOptionPane.ERROR_MESSAGE);
      break;
      }
    }
    try {
      outputStream.close();
      inputStream.close();
    } catch (IOException ioe) {};
  }

}
```

Note that the setSleepScheduled() and isSleepScheduled() methods are synchronized, which is necessary since two threads access a resource. Specifically, that resource is the sleepScheduled flag that will be set by the AWT event thread (when the Sleep button is clicked) and that will be both set and queried by the download thread.

Suspending a Thread

As you just saw, you can suspend a thread's execution for some length of time using the sleep() method. Similarly, you'll often want to suspend a thread for an indefinite length of time, usually until some condition is met and the wait() method defined in Object allows you to do so. However, before a thread can call an object's wait() method, it must own that object's monitor, or an IllegalMonitorStateException will be thrown.

The following modifications to Downloader illustrate how wait() can be used to suspend a thread's execution indefinitely; I'll later show how to modify the DownloadManager class so that it calls the setSuspended() method to suspend the download thread. Here, too, a boolean flag value provides a way for the AWT event thread to communicate with the download thread when one of the DownloadManager buttons (in other words, Suspend) is clicked.

First, add a new member variable.

```
private boolean stopped;
private boolean sleepScheduled;
private boolean suspended;
```

Second, modify the constructor to set this suspended variable to `false`.

```
public Downloader(URL url, OutputStream os) throws IOException {
  downloadURL = url;
  outputStream = os;
  bytesRead = 0;
  URLConnection urlConnection = downloadURL.openConnection();
  fileSize = urlConnection.getContentLength();
  if (fileSize == -1) {
    throw new FileNotFoundException(url.toString());
  }
  inputStream = new BufferedInputStream(
      urlConnection.getInputStream());
  buffer = new byte[BUFFER_SIZE];
  thisThread = new Thread(this);
  buildLayout();

  stopped = false;
  sleepScheduled = false;
  suspended = false;
}
```

Third, add accessor and mutator methods that allow the suspended flag to be set and queried.

```
public synchronized void setSuspended(boolean suspend) {
  suspended = suspend;
}

public synchronized boolean isSuspended() {
  return suspended;
}
```

Finally, modify the `performDownload()` method as appropriate. This code checks the suspended flag and calls `wait()` if the flag is assigned a value of `true`, causing the thread to be suspended. Later, I'll show how to add the ability to resume a suspended thread, and when the thread is resumed, it will clear the suspended flag so that it continues execution unless explicitly suspended again.

```
public void performDownload() {
  int byteCount;
  Runnable progressUpdate = new Runnable() {
    public void run() {
    progressBar.setValue(bytesRead);
    completeLabel.setText(
        Integer.toString(
        bytesRead));
    }
  };
```

```
  while ((bytesRead < fileSize) && (!stopped)) {
     try {
       if (isSleepScheduled()) {
         try {
           Thread.sleep(SLEEP_TIME);
           setSleepScheduled(false);
         }
         catch (InterruptedException ie) {
         }
       }
       byteCount = inputStream.read(buffer);
       if (byteCount == -1) {
         stopped = true;
         break;
       }
     else {
       outputStream.write(buffer, 0,
           byteCount);
       bytesRead += byteCount;
       SwingUtilities.invokeLater(
           progressUpdate);
      }
     } catch (IOException ioe) {
       stopped = true;
       JOptionPane.showMessageDialog(this,
           ioe.getMessage(),
           "I/O Error",
            JOptionPane.ERROR_MESSAGE);
         break;
      }
      synchronized (this) {
        if (isSuspended()) {
          try {
            this.wait();
            setSuspended(false);
          }
          catch (InterruptedException ie) {
          }
        }
      }
    }
    try {
      outputStream.close();
      inputStream.close();
    } catch (IOException ioe) {};
  }

}
```

In this case, the object that's used for synchronization is the instance of Downloader, and that object's wait() method is called to suspend the download thread. The download thread is able to invoke wait() because it will implicitly obtain the object's lock when it enters the synchronized block of code containing the call to wait().

When a thread calls the wait() method and is suspended, it's added to a list of waiting threads that's maintained for each instance of Object. In addition, calling wait() causes the thread to release control of the object's monitor, which means that other threads are able to obtain the monitor for that object. For example, if one thread is blocked because it's waiting to obtain an object's monitor and the thread that owns the monitor calls wait(), the first thread will be given the monitor and allowed to resume execution.

In this case, the wait() method was called with no parameters, which will cause the download thread to wait indefinitely until another thread wakes it up; the following section describes how to do so. However, you may sometimes want to have the thread wait for some finite period of time, in which case you can specify that length of time on the wait() method. Like sleep(), wait() provides one method that accepts a long value representing some number of milliseconds and another implementation that also allows you to specify an int nanosecond value. You can take advantage of these methods to cause a thread to "time out" when it's waiting for some resource to become available and that resource doesn't become available within the desired length of time.

Resuming a Thread

Since calling wait() with no parameters causes a thread to be suspended indefinitely, you may be wondering how you can cause the thread to resume execution. To do so, simply have another thread call either notify() or notifyAll(), both of which are methods defined in Object. As with wait(), a thread must own the object's monitor before it can call notify() or notifyAll(), and if one of those methods is called by a thread that doesn't own the monitor, an IllegalMonitorStateException is thrown.

In this case, you can make the download thread "wake up" after it invokes wait() by having the AWT event thread call notify() or notifyAll() when the Resume button in DownloadManager is clicked. To accommodate this functionality, you can add a resumeDownload() method to Downloader as follows:

```
public synchronized void resumeDownload() {
  this.notify();
}
```

Notice that the resumeDownload() method is synchronized, even though it doesn't modify any resources that are shared between the AWT event thread and the download thread. You want to do this so that the event thread will obtain the Downloader object's monitor, which is necessary for the event thread to be able to call the object's notify() method successfully.

Also note that calling notify() or notifyAll() doesn't cause the waiting thread to immediately resume execution. Before any thread that was waiting can resume execution, it must again obtain the monitor of the object on which it was synchronized. In this case, for example, when the AWT event thread calls notify() by invoking resumeDownload(), the download thread is removed from the Downloader object's wait list. However, you should recall that when the download thread invoked the wait() method, it implicitly gave up ownership of the monitor, and it must regain ownership of the monitor before it can resume execution. Fortunately, that will happen automatically once the monitor becomes available, which in this case will occur when the AWT event thread exits the resumeDownload() method.

Up to this point it has been implied that notify() and notifyAll() are interchangeable, which is true in this case, but there's a difference between those two methods that's important for you to understand. In this application, there will only ever be one thread (the download thread) on the object's wait list, but you'll sometimes create applications that allow multiple threads to call wait() for a single object instance. Calling notifyAll() causes all threads that are waiting to be removed from the wait list, while calling notify() results in only a single thread being removed. Java doesn't specify which thread will be removed when notify() is called, and you shouldn't make any assumptions in that respect, since it can vary from one JVM implementation to the next. It may intuitively seem that the first thread that called wait() should be removed from the list, but that may or may not be the case. Since you can't cause a specific thread to be resumed using notify(), you should use it only when you want to wake up a single waiting thread and don't care which one is awakened.

Stopping a Thread

Most of the code that's needed to stop the download thread is already present, since a stopped flag was previously defined. The download thread tests that flag as it performs the download, and once the flag is set to true, the download thread exits the run() method and dies. However, you'll also want to allow the AWT event thread to set the flag when a DownloadManager's Stop button is clicked. Once you make that change, the flag has effectively become a shared resource that can be used by multiple threads, so access to it must be synchronized through accessor and mutator methods, making it thread-safe, as shown in Listing 4-11.

Listing 4-11. Adding Stop Support

```
public synchronized void setStopped(boolean stop) {
  stopped = stop;
}

public synchronized boolean isStopped() {
  return stopped;
}

public void run() {
  int byteCount;
  Runnable progressUpdate = new Runnable() {
    public void run() {
      progressBar.setValue(bytesRead);
      completeLabel.setText(
          Integer.toString(
          bytesRead));
    }
  };
  while ((bytesRead < fileSize) && (!isStopped())) {
    try {
      if (isSleepScheduled()) {s
        try {
          Thread.sleep(SLEEP_TIME);
          setSleepScheduled(false);
        }
        catch (InterruptedException ie) {
        }
      }
      byteCount = inputStream.read(buffer);
      if (byteCount == -1) {
        setStopped(true);
        break;
      }
```

```
      else {
        outputStream.write(buffer, 0,
            byteCount);
        bytesRead += byteCount;
        SwingUtilities.invokeLater(
            progressUpdate);
      }
    } catch (IOException ioe) {
      setStopped(true);
      JOptionPane.showMessageDialog(this,
          ioe.getMessage(),
          "I/O Error",
          JOptionPane.ERROR_MESSAGE);
      break;
    }
    synchronized (this) {
      if (isSuspended()) {
        try {
          this.wait();
          setSuspended(false);
        }
        catch (InterruptedException ie) {
        }
      }
    }
  }
  try {
    outputStream.close();
    inputStream.close();
  } catch (IOException ioe) {};
}

}
```

    While this implementation will work, it has one weakness: the download thread can't be stopped while it's suspended or sleeping. For example, suppose you start the download operation and decide to suspend the download. If you then decide to terminate the download completely after having suspended it, you're forced to resume the download (in other words, click the Resume button) and then stop the download. Ideally, it should be possible to stop a download that was suspended without first resuming the download; the interrupt() method defined in Thread allows you to do so.

Interrupting a Thread

Each thread maintains a flag that indicates whether the thread has been interrupted, and when you call a thread's interrupt() method, that flag is set to true. In addition, if interrupt() is called while the thread is blocked by a method such as sleep() or wait(), that method will terminate with an InterruptedException. However, in some cases such as when a thread is blocked because it's waiting for an I/O operation to complete, the interrupt flag is set "quietly" (in other words, no exception is thrown) and the thread's execution isn't affected.

To determine whether interrupt() will cause a blocking method to terminate with an exception, you should examine the API documentation for that method. For example, the read() method defined in java.io.InputStream can block a thread, but it doesn't throw InterruptedException. In contrast, the waitForAll() method in java.awt.MediaTracker blocks and will result in an InterruptedException being thrown if the thread that called waitForAll() is interrupted while blocked.

Since some blocking methods throw an InterruptedException and others don't, you'll sometimes need to explicitly test the interrupted flag to determine whether the thread was interrupted. To accomplish this, you can use either the static interrupted() method or the nonstatic isInterrupted(). The interrupted() method returns a boolean value that identifies the state of the currently executing thread's interrupted flag and clears that flag if it was set. The isInterrupted() method similarly returns the value of a thread's interrupted flag but doesn't change the state of the flag. Therefore, interrupted() is appropriate if you want to both test and clear the flag, while isInterrupted() is often a better choice, particularly if you prefer to leave the flag unchanged. Either is acceptable in many cases, and the choice of which one to use will depend upon your application. By making the changes in bold in Listing 4-12, you can interrupt the download thread (and cancel the download) by the AWT event thread, regardless of the state of the download thread.

Listing 4-12. Supporting the Cancel Function

```
public void stopDownload() {
  thisThread.interrupt();
}

public void performDownload() {
  int byteCount;
  Runnable progressUpdate = new Runnable() {
    public void run() {
      progressBar.setValue(bytesRead);
      completeLabel.setText(
          Integer.toString(
          bytesRead));
    }
  };
  while ((bytesRead < fileSize) && (!isStopped())) {
    try {
      if (isSleepScheduled()) {
        try {
          Thread.sleep(SLEEP_TIME);
          setSleepScheduled(false);
        }
        catch (InterruptedException ie) {
          setStopped(true);
          break;
        }
      }
      byteCount = inputStream.read(buffer);
      if (byteCount == -1) {
        setStopped(true);
        break;
      }
```

```
    else {
      outputStream.write(buffer, 0,
          byteCount);
      bytesRead += byteCount;
      SwingUtilities.invokeLater(
          progressUpdate);
    }
  } catch (IOException ioe) {
    setStopped(true);
    JOptionPane.showMessageDialog(this,
        ioe.getMessage(),
        "I/O Error",
        JOptionPane.ERROR_MESSAGE);
    break;
  }
  synchronized (this) {
    if (isSuspended()) {
      try {
        this.wait();
        setSuspended(false);
      }
      catch (InterruptedException ie) {
        setStopped(true);
        break;
      }
    }
  }
  if (Thread.interrupted()) {
    setStopped(true);
    break;
  }
  }
  try {
    outputStream.close();
    inputStream.close();
  } catch (IOException ioe) {};
  }

}
```

Completing DownloadManager

You've now added all the necessary functionality to Downloader and can tie that functionality to the buttons previously defined in DownloadManager by making the changes shown in Listing 4-13. With these changes in place, you can use those buttons to start, suspend/sleep, resume, and stop the download that's in progress (see Figure 4-4).

Listing 4-13. Enabling the Function Buttons

```java
import java.awt.*;
import java.awt.event.*;
import java.io.*;
import java.net.URL;
import javax.swing.*;
import javax.swing.border.*;

public class DownloadManager extends JPanel {

  private Downloader downloader;

  private JButton startButton;
  private JButton sleepButton;
  private JButton suspendButton;
  private JButton resumeButton;
  private JButton stopButton;

public static void main(String[] args) throws Exception {
  URL url = new URL(args[0]);
  FileOutputStream fos = new FileOutputStream(args[1]);
  JFrame f = new JFrame();
  DownloadManager dm = new DownloadManager(url, fos);
  f.getContentPane().add(dm);
  f.setSize(400, 300);
  f.setVisible(true);
}

public DownloadManager(URL source, OutputStream os)
    throws IOException {
  downloader = new Downloader(source, os);
  buildLayout();
  Border border = new BevelBorder(BevelBorder.RAISED);
  String name = source.toString();
  int index = name.lastIndexOf('/');
  border = new TitledBorder(border,
      name.substring(index + 1));
  setBorder(border);
}

private void buildLayout() {
  setLayout(new BorderLayout());
  downloader.setBorder(new BevelBorder(BevelBorder.RAISED));
  add(downloader, BorderLayout.CENTER);

  add(getButtonPanel(), BorderLayout.SOUTH);
}

private JPanel getButtonPanel() {
    JPanel outerPanel;
    JPanel innerPanel;
```

```
  innerPanel = new JPanel();
  innerPanel.setLayout(new GridLayout(1, 5, 10, 0));

  startButton = new JButton("Start");
  startButton.addActionListener(new ActionListener() {
    public void actionPerformed(ActionEvent event) {
      startButton.setEnabled(false);
      sleepButton.setEnabled(true);
      resumeButton.setEnabled(false);
      suspendButton.setEnabled(true);
      stopButton.setEnabled(true);
      downloader.startDownload();
    }
  });
  innerPanel.add(startButton);

  sleepButton = new JButton("Sleep");
  sleepButton.setEnabled(false);
  sleepButton.addActionListener(new ActionListener() {
    public void actionPerformed(ActionEvent event) {
      downloader.setSleepScheduled(true);
    }
  });
  innerPanel.add(sleepButton);

  suspendButton = new JButton("Suspend");
  suspendButton.setEnabled(false);
  suspendButton.addActionListener(new ActionListener() {
    public void actionPerformed(ActionEvent event) {
      suspendButton.setEnabled(false);
      resumeButton.setEnabled(true);
      stopButton.setEnabled(true);
      downloader.setSuspended(true);
    }
  });
  innerPanel.add(suspendButton);

  resumeButton = new JButton("Resume");
  resumeButton.setEnabled(false);
  resumeButton.addActionListener(new ActionListener() {
    public void actionPerformed(ActionEvent event) {
      resumeButton.setEnabled(false);
      suspendButton.setEnabled(true);
      stopButton.setEnabled(true);
      downloader.resumeDownload();
    }
  });
  innerPanel.add(resumeButton);

stopButton = new JButton("Stop");
stopButton.setEnabled(false);
```

```
    stopButton.addActionListener(new ActionListener() {
        public void actionPerformed(ActionEvent event) {
            stopButton.setEnabled(false);
            sleepButton.setEnabled(false);
            suspendButton.setEnabled(false);
            resumeButton.setEnabled(false);
            downloader.stopDownload();
        }
    });
    innerPanel.add(stopButton);

    outerPanel = new JPanel();
    outerPanel.add(innerPanel);
    return outerPanel;
    }
}
```

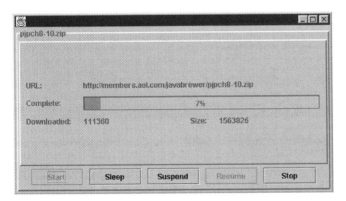

Figure 4-4. *The completed application allows you to start, delay, suspend, resume, and stop the file download*

Deprecated Methods in Thread

You've now seen how to add code to an application that will suspend, resume, and stop a running thread, but if you review the API documentation for the Thread class, you'll see that it includes suspend(), resume(), and stop() methods, even though they're now deprecated. You can probably guess (correctly) from this fact that those functions were handled "manually" within the application to avoid using the deprecated methods, but it may not be as obvious why they're deprecated.

When one thread wants to stop or suspend another thread, the first thread usually can't know whether the second thread is in a state that's appropriate for it to be suspended. For example, suppose you're running the AccountManager example that was defined earlier in this chapter, where money is transferred between two accounts. If a thread is stopped after it has removed money from one account but before it has increased the balance in the other account, that money will again be lost. Similarly, if a thread is suspended while it owns the monitor of some object, it will be impossible for other threads to obtain that object's monitor while the owning thread is suspended.

In effect, suspend() and stop() allow a thread to be suspended or stopped even while it's in a state where such an action is inappropriate. Therefore, instead of using those deprecated methods, you should instead send a request to a thread that will cause it to suspend or stop itself at an appropriate point.

For example, an `AccountManager` thread should allow itself to be stopped or suspended before or after a transfer is performed but not while one is in progress. Similarly, if some resources may be needed by other threads, the thread being suspended can release the monitor(s) of those resources before it's suspended. This reduces the likelihood of deadlock, which is a common problem with multithreaded applications, as I discussed previously.

DownloadFiles

The existing implementations of `Downloader` and `DownloadManager` provide a great deal of flexibility and functionality, but they have one limitation: you can't initiate multiple downloads without running each one in a separate Java Virtual Machine process. To address that limitation, I'll now show how to create a new `DownloadFiles` class that allows you to create instances of `DownloadManager` by entering URLs in a text field, as shown in Figure 4-5.

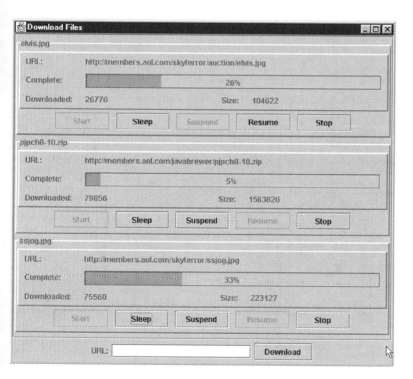

Figure 4-5. The `DownloadFiles` class allows you to use multiple download managers so that multiple files can be downloaded simultaneously

The code shown in Listing 4-14 provides the desired functionality. It creates a user interface like the one shown in Figure 4-5 and creates a new `DownloadManager` instance when the user enters a URL in the text field and presses Enter (or clicks the Download button). To use the application, simply compile and execute it and enter the URL of each file you want to download into the text field. You can then control the downloads using the buttons previously defined in the `DownloadManager` class, and each file will be written to the local drive using the filename portion of its URL.

Listing 4-14. Initial DownloadFiles Implementation

```java
import java.awt.*;
import java.awt.event.*;
import java.io.*;
import java.net.*;
import javax.swing.*;

public class DownloadFiles extends JPanel {

  private JPanel listPanel;
  private GridBagConstraints constraints;

  public static void main(String[] args) {
    JFrame f = new JFrame("Download Files");
    DownloadFiles df = new DownloadFiles();
    for (int i = 0; i < args.length; i++) {
      df.createDownloader(args[i]);
    }
    f.getContentPane().add(df);
    f.setSize(600, 400);
    f.setVisible(true);
  }

  public DownloadFiles() {
    setLayout(new BorderLayout());
    listPanel = new JPanel();
    listPanel.setLayout(new GridBagLayout());
    constraints = new GridBagConstraints();
    constraints.gridx = 0;
    constraints.weightx = 1;
    constraints.fill = GridBagConstraints.HORIZONTAL;
    constraints.anchor = GridBagConstraints.NORTH;
    JScrollPane jsp = new JScrollPane(listPanel);
    add(jsp, BorderLayout.CENTER);

    add(getAddURLPanel(), BorderLayout.SOUTH);
  }

  private JPanel getAddURLPanel() {
    JPanel panel = new JPanel();
    JLabel label = new JLabel("URL:");
    final JTextField textField = new JTextField(20);
    JButton downloadButton = new JButton("Download");
    ActionListener actionListener = new ActionListener() {
      public void actionPerformed(ActionEvent event) {
        if (createDownloader(textField.getText())) {
          textField.setText("");
          revalidate();
        }
      }
    };
```

```
    textField.addActionListener(actionListener);
    downloadButton.addActionListener(actionListener);
    panel.add(label);
    panel.add(textField);
    panel.add(downloadButton);
    return panel;
  }

  private boolean createDownloader(String url) {
    try {
      URL downloadURL = new URL(url);
      URLConnection urlConn = downloadURL.openConnection();
      int length = urlConn.getContentLength();
      if (length < 0) throw new Exception(
          "Unable to determine content " +
          "length for '" + url + "'");
      int index = url.lastIndexOf('/');
      FileOutputStream fos = new FileOutputStream(
          url.substring(index + 1));
      BufferedOutputStream bos =
          new BufferedOutputStream(fos);
      DownloadManager dm = new DownloadManager(
          downloadURL, bos);
      listPanel.add(dm, constraints);
      return true;
    }
    catch (Exception e) {
      JOptionPane.showMessageDialog(this, e.getMessage(),
          "Unable To Download",
          JOptionPane.ERROR_MESSAGE);
    }
    return false;
  }
}
```

Although this application provides an easy and convenient way to create instances of DownloadManager, there's currently no way to remove those instances once they've been added. To address that limitation, you might choose to add a button to DownloadFiles that performs the following operations:

- Interrupts each active thread, terminating its download

- Waits until all threads have died, which may take several seconds depending upon the speed of your network connection

- Removes all the Downloader instances from the user interface display

An easy way to perform the first operation described (interrupt the active threads) is to use a ThreadGroup.

ThreadGroup

Just as packages allow you to organize your Java classes in a hierarchy, the ThreadGroup class allows you to create groups of associated threads and organize them hierarchically. Each ThreadGroup can have one parent and may have child ThreadGroup instances, and you can add a Thread to a particular ThreadGroup when the thread is created by passing a reference to that group to the thread's constructor.

```
Runnable runnable;
ThreadGroup myGroup = new ThreadGroup("My ThreadGroup");
.
.
.
Thread t = new Thread(myGroup, runnable);
```

ThreadGroup wouldn't be very useful if it simply allowed you to create a collection of associated threads, but it also provides a convenient way to control those threads. Specifically, you can use ThreadGroup's interrupt() to interrupt all its threads with a single method call, and you can specify the maximum priority that should be valid for a thread in the group. ThreadGroup also provides suspend(), resume(), and stop() methods that allow you to control the execution of the threads, but those methods have been deprecated for the reasons described earlier, so you shouldn't use them in your application.

As illustrated previously, you can add a Thread to a ThreadGroup by passing a reference to the group as a parameter when creating the Thread instance. As the following bold code illustrates, you can easily modify Downloader to define a ThreadGroup that will contain all download threads, which will allow you to interrupt them all with a single method call:

```
public static ThreadGroup downloaderGroup = new ThreadGroup(
    "Download Threads");

public Downloader(URL url, OutputStream os) throws IOException {
  downloadURL = url;
  outputStream = os;
  bytesRead = 0;
  URLConnection urlConnection = downloadURL.openConnection();
  fileSize = urlConnection.getContentLength();
  if (fileSize == -1) {
    throw new FileNotFoundException(url.toString());
  }
  inputStream = new BufferedInputStream(
      urlConnection.getInputStream());
  buffer = new byte[BUFFER_SIZE];
  thisThread = new Thread(downloaderGroup, this);
  buildLayout();

  stopped = false;
  sleepScheduled = false;
  suspended = false;
}
```

Now that each thread associated with a Downloader instance is part of the same ThreadGroup, the threads can all be stopped with a single call to the ThreadGroup's interrupt() method. In this case, that will be done by a static method called cancelAllAndWait() within the Downloader class.

```
public static void cancelAllAndWait() {
  downloaderGroup.interrupt();
}
```

To obtain a list of the threads that were active before interrupt() was called, it's possible to use the ThreadGroup's activeCount() and enumerate() methods. As the names imply, activeCount() returns the number of active threads in the group, while enumerate() stores a reference to each active thread within a Thread array that's passed to it as a parameter.

```
public static void cancelAllAndWait() {
  int count = downloaderGroup.activeCount();
  Thread[] threads = new Thread[count];
  count = downloaderGroup.enumerate(threads);
  downloaderGroup.interrupt();
}
```

To wait for each thread to die, you can use the join() method defined in Thread. When one thread invokes another's join() method, the first thread will be blocked until the second thread dies or until the first thread's interrupt() method is called. In this case, the AWT event thread will call each download thread's join() method once the download threads have been interrupted.

As with wait() and sleep(), it's also possible to specify a particular length of time (in milliseconds and optionally in nanoseconds) that the caller should wait when calling a thread's join() method. However, if you don't do so, the caller waits indefinitely until the thread dies.

```
public static void cancelAllAndWait() {
  int count = downloaderGroup.activeCount();
  Thread[] threads = new Thread[count];
  count = downloaderGroup.enumerate(threads);
  downloaderGroup.interrupt();

  for (int i = 0; i < count; i++) {
    try {
      threads[i].join();
    } catch (InterruptedException ie) {};
  }
}
```

With the cancelAllAndWait() method available in Downloader, it's easy to add a button to DownloadFiles to use that method. When the new Clear All button is clicked, it will call cancelAllAndWait(), remove the DownloadManager instances, and refresh the user interface display (as shown in Figure 4-6). Listing 4-15 shows the code.

157

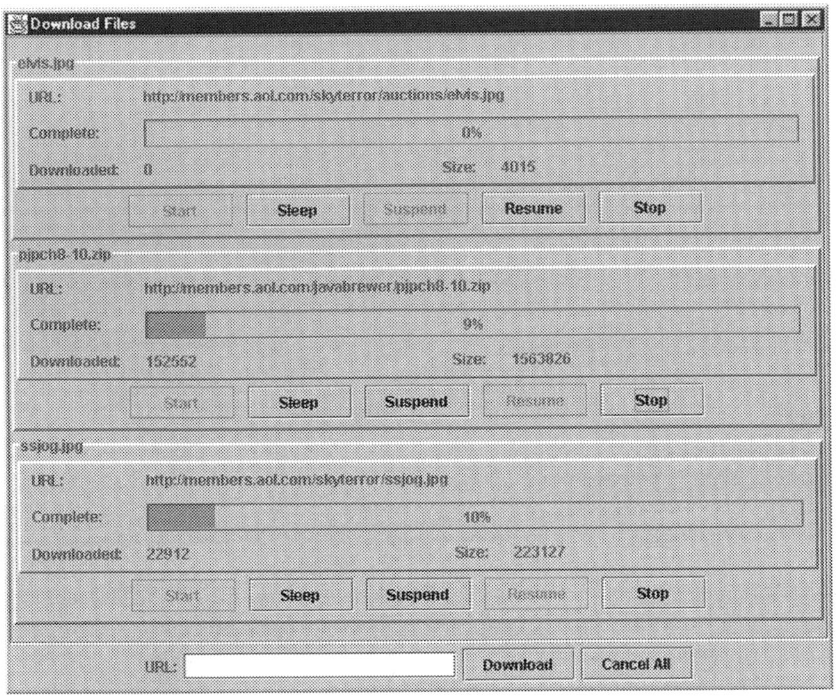

Figure 4-6. *This version of the user interface includes a button that allows you to cancel all the downloads that are in progress*

Listing 4-15. Implementing the Clear All Button Functionality

```
private JPanel getAddURLPanel() {
  JPanel panel = new JPanel();
  JLabel label = new JLabel("URL:");
  final JTextField textField = new JTextField(20);
  JButton downloadButton = new JButton("Download");
  ActionListener actionListener = new ActionListener() {

    public void actionPerformed(ActionEvent event) {
      if (createDownloader(textField.getText())) {
        textField.setText("");
        revalidate();
      }
    }
  };
  textField.addActionListener(actionListener);
  downloadButton.addActionListener(actionListener);
  JButton clearAll = new JButton("Cancel All");
  clearAll.addActionListener(new ActionListener() {
```

```java
    public void actionPerformed(ActionEvent event) {
      Downloader.cancelAllAndWait();
      listPanel.removeAll();
      revalidate();
      repaint();
    }
  });
  panel.add(label);
  panel.add(textField);
  panel.add(downloadButton);
  panel.add(clearAll);
  return panel;
}
```

Uncaught Exceptions

As mentioned earlier, a thread dies when it exits the run() method of the Runnable object with which it's associated. In most cases, this will occur when the thread has executed all the code within that method, but it can also occur if an exception is thrown that's not caught. For example, NullPointerException is perhaps the most common exception that's encountered by Java programmers, and it isn't typically caught and handled because there's usually no way for the application to recover when a NullPointerException is thrown. Assuming that a NullPointerException is thrown during execution of the run() method, either within that method itself or within other code it calls, and assuming that no attempt is made to catch the exception, it will cause the thread to die.

By default, an uncaught exception simply causes the thread's stack trace to be printed before the thread dies, but you can override this behavior using an uncaught exception handler. How you handle uncaught exceptions depends upon whether you want to customize the behavior for all threads in a ThreadGroup or you only want to change the behavior for a single thread. When an uncaught exception occurs for a thread its getUncaughtExceptionHandler() method is called to determine if it has been assigned an instance of the UncaughtExceptionHandler interface. If so, that object's uncaughtException() method is called and is passed a reference to the thread and to the exception that occurred. If, on the other hand, no handler has been assigned to the thread the uncaughtException() method is called for the ThreadGroup associated with the thread and, as mentioned before, the behavior defined there is to simply display the stack trace of the thread for which the exception occurred.

Voluntarily Relinquishing the Processor

As you've seen, the specific details of how threads share the processor's time vary from one platform to the next. The operating system will sometimes ensure that each thread is eventually given a chance to run, but some platforms are more effective at this than others. Therefore, if you create a multithreaded application, it's possible that one or more threads won't be able to run if other threads of a higher priority are constantly executing. To prevent this from happening, you should be aware of situations where a high-priority thread may run for a long time, and you may want to cause it to periodically relinquish control of the processor voluntarily.

One way of making a thread give up control of the processor is to call the static yield() method defined in Thread.

```java
Thread.yield();
```

This method causes the currently executing thread to signal that another thread of the same priority should be allowed to run. Conceptually, you can think of yield() as causing the current thread to be moved to the end of the list of runnable threads with the same priority. In theory, this should allow a different thread to run, but as you saw earlier, the mechanism used to select the next thread to run is undefined and platform-specific. Therefore, it's possible that the same thread that yielded control of the processor will be immediately reselected for execution, even if other runnable threads of the same priority are available. In other words, yield() isn't a completely reliable way to ensure that one thread doesn't monopolize the processor.

A more reliable method of ensuring that a thread is temporarily prevented from running is to use the sleep() method, but this approach has a serious drawback. If you use sleep(), you're effectively overriding the native platform's efforts to allocate the processor's time in an efficient and "fair" manner among the threads. For example, suppose you're given the simple application shown in Listing 4-16.

Listing 4-16. Minimum and Maximum Priority Threads

```
public class Test {

  public static void main(String[] args) {
    Test t = new Test();
  }

  public Test() {
    Runnable runner = new MyRunnable("First");
    Thread t = new Thread(runner);
    t.setPriority(Thread.MIN_PRIORITY);
    t.start();
    runner = new MyRunnable("Second");
    t = new Thread(runner);
    t.setPriority(Thread.MAX_PRIORITY);
    t.start();
  }

  class MyRunnable implements Runnable {

    private String name;

    public MyRunnable(String tn) {
      name = tn;
    }

    public void run() {
      while (true) {
        System.out.println(name);
      }
    }
  }

}
```

On most platforms, the second thread will be given more of the processor's time because it's assigned a higher priority than the first, which is presumably the desired result. If you're concerned that the first thread might be prevented from ever running on some operating systems, you can modify the run() method as follows:

```
public void  run() {
  while (true) {
    try {Thread.sleep(500);} catch (Exception e) {};
    System.out.println(name);
  }
}
```

The problem with this approach is that it has effectively rendered the two threads' priorities meaningless. Since each thread will sleep for half a second as it loops within the run() method, the result on most systems will be that each thread executes for approximately the same length of time.

While it's possible to use sleep() to control how threads are run, you should do so only with caution and understand that you may defeat the platform's attempts to execute the threads in an appropriate manner. In addition, using sleep() for this purpose may succeed on one platform but fail on another because of differences in the behavior of the operating systems. Fortunately, most operating systems do a reasonably good job of ensuring that each thread is given a chance to run, so you can and should normally use yield() instead.

Regardless of whether you use sleep() or yield() you should be aware that there's no way in Java to guarantee that low-priority threads will ever be run, at least not while higher-priority threads are also executing. Given this unpredictability and the increased complexity associated with scheduling threads of different priorities, you should use priorities with caution.

Concurrency Utilities

As mentioned earlier, using threads complicates your application and has the potential to create problems. For example, creating and starting a new thread can be a relatively slow process, and creating a large number of threads can degrade the performance of your application. However, thread pooling is a technique that's commonly used to address this problem, particularly in applications that repeatedly execute tasks that complete in a relatively short amount of time. By using a thread pool, you can avoid the overhead associated with creating a new thread by maintaining a group, or *pool*, of available threads and retrieving one from the pool when necessary. In other words, this technique allows you to reuse a single thread repeatedly instead of creating a new thread for each task and allowing it to be destroyed when the task completes.

Thread pooling is just one function that's often used by multithreaded applications, and in the past it was common for programmers to create and use their own implementations. However, Java 5 included a new set of packages containing interfaces and classes that support services such as a thread pooling that are commonly needed by multithreaded applications.

Pooling is supported by a number of the interfaces and classes in the java.util.concurrent package, one of which is the ScheduledThreadPoolExecutor class; the following shows an example of how it can be used:

```
ScheduledThreadPoolExecutor executor = new ScheduledThreadPoolExecutor(1);
.
.
.
Runnable runner = getNextTask();
executor.execute(runner);
```

The instance of `ScheduledThreadPoolExecutor` created in this sample code maintains a pool that initially contains a single thread, and each time its `execute()` method is called, it will either create a new thread or wait for an existing one to become available to execute the specified `Runnable`.

While the `java.util.concurrent` package contains general utility classes useful in multithreaded applications, the `java.util.concurrent.atomic` package contains classes that provide manipulation and comparison operations for various types of atomic (single-value) variables. For example, it contains classes called `AtomicBoolean`, `AtomicInteger`, and `AtomicLong`, and each of those classes in turn contains methods for examining and updating the encapsulated values in a thread-safe manner.

Another useful package is `java.util.concurrent.locks`, which contains classes that support locking capabilities. At a high level, the *locking* refers to resource locking, which is conceptually similar to Java's synchronization capabilities but provides more robust capabilities. For example, Java's synchronization mechanism provides for serialization of access to resources but doesn't directly provide a way for multiple threads to share a resource in a read-only manner while also facilitating write access to that resource. In contrast, the `ReentrantReadWriteLock` class, for example, provides that ability and much more.

Summary

In this chapter, I covered the following topics:

- Common reasons for using threads and some of the advantages and disadvantages of using them

- How to create threads and manage their execution

- How to synchronize access to resources that are used by multiple threads and how to prevent problems from occurring

- Changes that occurred to the `Thread` class in Java 2 and how to modify your applications to take into account those changes

- Java's concurrency utilities

CHAPTER 5

■ ■ ■

Using Stream APIs and Collections

By definition, an object-oriented application is one that creates and uses objects, and most useful applications create and manage groups of objects. In fact, maintaining a group, or *collection*, of objects is done so often that Java's core library has always included classes designed specifically for that purpose.

   To understand why collection classes are so important, let's briefly examine the alternative and what limitations existed. Before object-oriented programming became popular, procedural languages typically used arrays to maintain groups of related values. Arrays are, of course, supported by Java and heavily used within Java's core classes, but they do have limitations. To illustrate those limitations, let's first suppose your application includes the following class, shown in Listing 5-1, which maintains student information:

Listing 5-1. A Simple Class for Encapsulating Student Information

```java
public class Student {

    private int studentID;
    private String firstName;
    private String lastName;

    public Student(int id, String fname, String lname) {
        studentID = id;
        firstName = fname;
        lastName = lname;
    }

    public int getStudentID() {
        return studentID;
    }

    public String getFirstName() {
        return firstName;
    }

    public String getLastName() {
        return lastName;
    }

    public String getFullName() {
        return getFirstName() + " " + getLastName();
    }

}
```

Now let's also assume your application also uses a database that includes a table containing student information, with one row per student, and you want to retrieve the list of students from that table and load the list into memory using instances of the previous class. You'll obviously need some way to maintain that group of Student objects, and an array can easily be defined with a statement such as the following:

```
Student[] students;
```

The problem is that this statement hasn't really defined an array of Student objects but has merely created a pointer that can be used to reference such an array. To actually create an array, you'll need to include a statement like the following:

```
students = new Student[30];
```

Alternatively, you can replace both of the previous statements with a composite statement, such as the following one, that both defines the pointer and creates the array:

```
Student[] students = new Student[30];
```

In this case we've arbitrarily decided that the array can reference up to 30 instances of Student. That may very well be a valid assumption for this example application, but explicitly specifying the array size this way means the code won't work correctly if you ever need to load more than 30 students at one time. That's because once you create an array, it can never increase or decrease in size; the array just created is always capable of holding 30 students—no more and no less.

Of course, if you know that there will normally be 30 or fewer students but that occasionally the number will be as high as 50, you can simply make the array larger.

```
Student[] students = new Student[50];
```

This works because the array can technically contain fewer objects than its maximum size simply by not changing the default null value for some or all of the array's elements. For example, if you perform a database query that you know will normally return 30 or fewer students, you could store them in the array using code similar to that in Listing 5-2.

Listing 5-2. Defining and Populating an Array

```
Student[] students = new Student[50];
java.sql.ResultSet resultSet;
// Perform query
.
.
.
int index = 0;
while (resultSet.next()) {
    students[index++] = createStudent(resultSet);
}
.
.
.
// Creates and returns a Student from data in current row of the ResultSet
private Student createStudent(ResultSet resultSet) throws SQLException {
```

Assuming you were to execute the previous code and assuming that the query returns fewer than 50 students, the array will effectively contain fewer than 50 students simply because it doesn't reference that number of objects. Although this addresses the potential problem of having more than 30 students by increasing the array size, this solution isn't perfect. For one thing, if your requirements suddenly change again so the maximum number of students is now 100, you'll be forced to modify and recompile your code for it to work correctly. Of course, you could simply choose an extremely large array size that you're certain will never need to be exceeded, as in the following code:

```
Student[] students = new Student[100000];
```

Although this change would allow the code to work with up to 100,000 students, it also wastes memory. When you create the array, an amount of memory is allocated that's sufficient to maintain a number of object references that correspond to the size of the array. In other words, if you allocate an array using the previous code but then store references to only 30 students in it, the other 99,970 entries represent wasted memory. Ideally, you'd like for an array to be able to shrink and grow so that it uses only as much memory as it needs to maintain the number of objects it contains, but arrays just don't work that way. Although arrays are definitely useful, they don't offer as much flexibility as you'd probably like, and this is why Java includes classes and interfaces used for managing collections. Figure 5-1 shows a class diagram with many of the collection classes and interfaces.

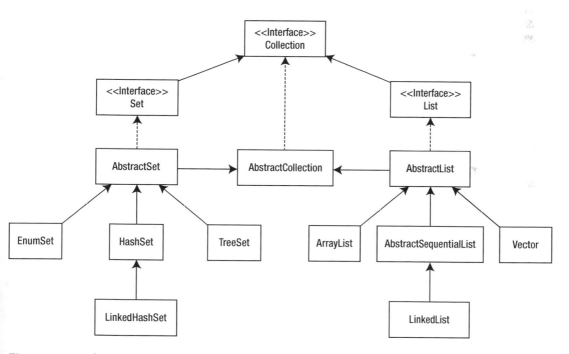

Figure 5-1. Java's collection types include a wide variety of interfaces and classes

The Evolution of Collections

In the earliest versions of Java, the only three collection classes were Vector, Hashtable, and Stack. Although they provided basic collection capabilities, they weren't a completely satisfactory solution. For one thing, they didn't offer enough flexibility to provide programmers with the functionality that's needed in many cases. For another, all the methods were synchronized to make them thread-safe, but that synchronization also caused a performance penalty that's present even in single-threaded situations where thread-safe class design isn't needed.

Java 2/Java 1.2

Most of the collection classes that are now part of Java's core libraries were added in Java 2, and it's those classes that we'll cover in this chapter. Unlike the older classes, however, these new classes weren't designed to be inherently thread-safe, so if you create a collection object that's used by more than one thread, you'll need to take steps to serialize access to the collection.

Java 5/Java 1.5

Another major change occurred in Java 5, when support for new features was added that effectively changed the syntax related to using collection classes. In other words, code that was written for prior versions of Java will by default generate errors when you attempt to compile it with a Java 5 or later compiler. In addition, source code written using the Java 5 syntax can't be compiled using an earlier version of Java. Most of this chapter will use the newer syntax, but you should be aware of the differences in case you need to work with code written using an earlier version.

Prior to Java 5, you couldn't directly add a primitive value to a collection. For example, an int value could be added only if it was first encapsulated in an instance of the corresponding Integer wrapper. However, Java 5 introduced a feature called *autoboxing/unboxing* that allows you to write source code that appears to add primitives to and retrieve them from collection objects. In reality, the objects are still being encapsulated in wrappers while they're inside the collection, but the conversion between primitives and objects is handled automatically and is concealed from the programmer.

Before Java 5, all objects stored in collections were treated as instances of Object, and you had no restrictions on the type of object you could add to a collection. It was the responsibility of the programmer to cast an Object to a more specific type when retrieving it from a collection, and a ClassCastException would occur if you made an incorrect assumption about the class of the object. However, Java 5 introduced a feature called *generics* that allows you to indicate what specific class of objects a collection will hold. If you do, the compiler will use that information to ensure that the code being compiled only adds instances of the specified class.

Java 7/Java 1.7

This release included a relatively minor change to generic support that simplified creating collection objects. Prior to Java 7 it was necessary to define the collection type both on the variable declaration and on the constructor portion of the statement. Java 7, however, introduced a feature called the *diamond operator* that allows you to specify the generic information on just the declaration (left side) of the statement, and it's that notation that will be used in the remainder of this chapter.

GENERICS

Programmers had requested adding generics to Java for years; generics serve two purposes, both of which you'll see in detail later. One advantage of generics is that they eliminate some of the tedious casting that's otherwise necessary, which results in code that's simpler and more readable. The bigger advantage of generics is that they allow some types of errors to be detected at compile time instead of at runtime, which improves reliability when the code runs because of the potential errors that were eliminated.

Collection Classes and Interfaces

Before you examine the classes and interfaces that make up Java's collection library, let's review some of the concepts and terminology you need to understand. An object that has been added to a collection is referred to as an *element*; some collection classes allow duplicate elements, and others don't. In this context, two elements are considered duplicates if a value of true is returned when they're compared using the equals() method. For example, the following two objects are duplicate elements:

```
String first = "Hello";
String second = "Hello";
```

Some differences between collection classes, besides whether they support duplicate elements, are whether the elements are ordered and whether the class allows null elements to be added. The functionality your application requires will determine which class you use; however, some classes are used often, and others are rarely needed.

Collection

At the top of the class hierarchy is the Collection interface, which defines methods that are common to most class implementations. Note, however, that some of the methods aren't applicable to some collection implementations, so just because a method is defined in Collection doesn't necessarily mean it's valid in a given implementation. If you try to call a method that isn't valid, an UnsupportedOperationException will be thrown, indicating that the method isn't meaningful for that object. Table 5-1 describes some of the most commonly used methods that are defined in Collection.

Table 5-1. Commonly Used Methods Defined in Collection

Method	Description
add(Object o)	Adds the specified object to the collection.
remove(Object o)	Removes the specified object from the collection.
clear()	Removes all elements from the collection.
size()	Returns an integer that indicates how many elements are currently in the collection.
iterator()	Returns an object that can be used to retrieve references to the elements in the collection.

Even without the descriptions, you could probably correctly guess what general behavior to expect from most of these methods, but to illustrate the usefulness of generics let's first look at examples of how collections are used without them. Suppose you want to create and use an instance of a class that implements the Collection interface. One of the most frequently used classes is ArrayList, and we'll discuss it in depth in the section "ArrayList," but for now let's say you simply want to create and use an instance using its no-argument constructor.

Using Collection Implementations Without Generics

Prior to Java 5, you'd create an instance of a collection object in the same way you'd create any other object; the following example shows how to do this:

```
Collection collection = new ArrayList();
```

Now let's also assume you have a method that reads from a database and creates instances of Student until there are no more to be read. If you wanted to add those objects to the collection, you could use code like the following:

```
Student student = getNextStudent();
while (student != null) {
    collection.add(student);
}
```

Notice that all you did was call the add() method mentioned previously, and this particular code isn't affected by the use of generics. As you'll see, what changed is primarily how you go about creating collection objects and how you retrieve objects from a collection.

Now that you've created the collection object and added student information to it, how can you go about retrieving references to those student objects? Table 5-1 mentioned an iterator() method that allows you to access the elements in a collection, and the documentation for that method indicates it returns an object that implements the Iterator interface defined in the java.util package. In other words, the iterator() method returns an Iterator object, which is simply an object that provides methods that allow you to access the objects in a collection one at a time. In fact, Iterator is a simple interface and includes only the three methods described in Table 5-2.

Table 5-2. Iterator's Methods

Method	Description
next()	Returns a reference to the next Object in the collection.
hasNext()	Indicates whether the iterator has already returned references to all the objects in the collection.
remove()	Removes from the collection the object most recently returned by the next() method.

Now let's suppose you want to print the first and last name of each Student in the collection, which you can begin to implement by calling the collection's iterator() method and looping through the list of elements.

```
Student student;
Iterator iterator = collection.iterator();
while (iterator.hasNext()) {
}
```

The only thing that's missing is to retrieve a reference to each Student and print the name for each one. To accomplish that, keep in mind you're currently looking at how this would be done without generics and that, as mentioned earlier, using generics involves identifying what type of object a collection holds. Because you intend for your collection to only contain Student instances and because the next() method is defined to return an instance of Object, you'll need to cast the return value as a Student, as shown by Listing 5-3.

Listing 5-3. Iteration Without Generics Often Requires Casting

```
Student student;
Iterator iterator = collection.iterator();
while (iterator.hasNext()) {
    student = (Student)(iterator.next());
    System.out.println(student.getFullName());
}
```

One point worth noting is that if your collection somehow contained an object other than an instance of Student, the previous code would generate a ClassCastException when executed. The problem with treating everything in a collection as an Object is that it becomes more likely that some type of object other than the one you're expecting will be added, and you have no way at compile time to prevent that from occurring. Also, your code is more verbose because to treat an object retrieved from the previous collection as a Student you first have to cast it accordingly.

Another limitation in the collection classes prior to Java 5 was that you could add primitive values to a collection only by first encapsulating them in their corresponding wrapper classes. For example, let's suppose you wanted to create a collection containing a group of random integers. In that case, you'd be required to explicitly create an Integer for each one and add that wrapper to the collection as shown by Listing 5-4.

Listing 5-4. Wrapping Primitives to Store Their Values in Collections

```
Integer integer;
Random random = new Random();
Collection collection = new ArrayList ();
for (int i = 0; i < 10; i++) {
    integer = new Integer (random.nextInt());
    collection.add(integer);
}
```

Similarly, retrieving the objects from the collection would require you to cast the return value to an Integer and then call the intValue() method (see Listing 5-5).

Listing 5-5. Unwrapping to Convert an Object Value into a Primitive

```
Integer integer;
int total = 0;
Iterator iterator = collection.iterator();
while (iterator.hasNext()) {
    integer = (Integer)(iterator.next());
    total += integer.intValue();
}
```

While encapsulating primitive values within wrappers isn't a serious inconvenience, it'd certainly be preferable to be able to add and retrieve primitive values directly.

Collection Support with Generics and Autoboxing

Java 5 introduced two new language features that addressed the limitations just discussed related to collection classes. Generics address the need to explicitly cast objects retrieved from collections and also reduce runtime errors by detecting more potential problems at compile time, and autoboxing/unboxing allows you to treat primitives like objects.

To understand generics, it's first helpful to realize that, within a well-designed application, a collection object should almost always be homogenous in terms of the class of objects it contains. For example, if the Student class were the superclass of the PartTimeStudent and FullTimeStudent classes, it might be appropriate to add instances of those subclasses to a single collection, but it would probably not be appropriate to store both Student and Integer objects in the same collection. In practice, you'll almost never have a reason to store two very different types of object in the same collection; when that does occur, it's more often a mistake rather than done intentionally. However, as long as collections are simply treated as holding Object instances, you have no way to ensure at compile time that a given collection is being used appropriately.

Generics address this by having you specify in your source code the type of object that your collection will hold when you create an instance of a collection class. You do this by specifying the class name between less than (<) and greater than (>) characters when you specify the variable class and the class that's being instantiated. Prior to Java 7 it was necessary to specify a type on both sides of the assignment as follows:

```
Collection<Student> collection = new ArrayList<Student>();
```

As mentioned earlier, though, Java 7 introduced the diamond operator, so-called because of the somewhat diamond-like shape created by a less than/greater than pair as shown in the following, where the type is omitted from the right side of the statement:

```
Collection<Student> collection = new ArrayList<>();
```

Using this notation the compiler simply infers that the generic type on the right side is the same as that specified on the left and we'll use this newer notation for the rest of the chapter.

You've now seen how creating a collection is done using generics, but how is the collection used differently after that? The call to the add() method doesn't change, but the most useful feature of generics is that it provides more error checking at compile time. Let's now suppose you attempt to write code that adds an Integer to the collection of Student objects, something we've already established isn't desirable in a well-designed application.

```
collection.add(new Integer (12345));
```

Attempting to compile this code results in an error because it represents an attempt to add an object of the wrong type to the collection. This ability to recognize problems at compile time prevents you from accidentally adding the wrong type of object to a collection and is the biggest advantage associated with generics.

Another useful feature of generics is that because the type of object a collection holds is now known by the compiler, it's not necessary for you to explicitly cast the collection objects back to the type you expect. Instead, you can simply indicate that the Iterator generates references to the expected type and then omit the explicit cast to the code that retrieves a reference.

```
Student student;
Iterator<Student> iterator = collection.iterator();
while (iterator.hasNext()) {
    student = iterator.next();
}
```

This approach results in code that's more readable and maintainable because it allows you to specify the object type in only one place, specifically when you obtain the Iterator reference. After that, you don't need to specify the type again regardless of how many different places within the code retrieve objects from the Iterator.

AUTOBOXING AND UNBOXING

Another improvement in collection handling was the introduction of autoboxing and unboxing, which eliminates the need to explicitly encapsulate primitive values within wrapper objects and to retrieve them from those objects when the primitives are to be stored within a collection. The result is that you can now simplify your code by eliminating the portions that perform the encapsulation and extraction. In reality, the encapsulation is still being done, but it's handled by the Java compiler rather than being explicitly included in your code. *Autoboxing* is the process of performing the encapsulation before a primitive is stored in a collection, and the following is an example of how this can improve your code:

```
Random random = new Random();
Collection<Integer> collection = new ArrayList<Integer>();
for (int i = 0; i < 10; i++) {
    collection.add(random.nextInt());
}
```

Similarly, *unboxing* is the process of extracting the primitive value from its corresponding wrapper object when retrieving data from a collection:

```
int total = 0;
Iterator<Integer> iterator = collection.iterator();
while (iterator.hasNext()) {
    total += iterator.next();
}
```

Now that you've seen the basics of how to use the Collection methods, let's continue to examine the other interfaces and classes that make up Java's collection API.

List

One of the characteristics of a collection class is whether it maintains a meaningful order for the elements it contains, and the List interface defines such an implementation. In other words, when you use an implementation of List and retrieve references to the elements, those elements will be returned in a predictable sequence. The sequence is defined by the element's position within the collection, and you specify that position either explicitly or implicitly when you add the element. Besides accessing the elements serially as you did earlier, a List also allows you to directly reference a particular element by specifying its zero-based position within the collection. For example, the first element in a collection corresponds to position 0, the second element to 1, and so on.

To better understand how this works, let's assume you're using an implementation of List to maintain a collection of Student objects and you use the add() method defined in Collection.

```
List<Student> students = new ArrayList<>();
students.add(new Student(12345, "John", "Smith");
students.add(new Student(67890, "Jane", "Smith");
```

In this case, the object representing the student John Smith occupies the first position (index 0) within the list, and Jane Smith occupies the second. In other words, when you use the add() method and don't explicitly specify a position for the element being added, the element is added to the end of the list. Alternatively, if you want to add an element to an arbitrary position within the List, you can use the add() method defined in the List interface that includes an index position. For example, continuing the previous code segment, suppose that you executed the following line:

```
students.add(1, new Student(13579, "Adam", "Smith");
```

The first argument specified in this call to the overloaded add() method indicates that the specified Student object should be inserted into the list at the position corresponding to an index of 1, a position that was previously occupied by the Jane Smith object. The result of executing this line of code will be that the newly added object will be inserted between the two originally stored in the collection, and the index of the Jane Smith object effectively becomes 2.

An alternative to add() is the set() method, which performs a similar function; however, while add() inserts the specified object into the collection at the given index, set() replaces the object currently stored at that position with the one specified. For example, the code in Listing 5-6 would result in only two Student objects being stored in the list, the one for John Smith and the one for Adam Smith, because the object associated with Jane Smith would be replaced as part of the call to set().

Listing 5-6. Using set() to Store an Element in a Particular Location

```
List<Student> students = new ArrayList<>();
students.add(new Student(12345, "John", "Smith");
students.add(new Student(67890, "Jane", "Smith");
students.set(1, new Student(13579, "Adam", "Smith");
```

Removing Elements from a List

Just as List defines an add() method that accepts an index position, the interface also includes a remove() method that allows you to specify the index of the object to be removed. Continuing with the previous example, let's suppose you execute the following line of code:

```
students.remove(0);
```

This removes the object at index position 0, which corresponds to the John Smith object added earlier. With that first element in the collection removed, the indices of the remaining objects shift downward to reflect the removal, resulting in Jane Smith becoming the first object and Adam Smith becoming the second object in the collection, with positions of 0 and 1, respectively.

The fact that index positions aren't constant for a given object in a List is an important point to remember; forgetting it can cause you to write code that doesn't work correctly. For example, suppose you have a List of objects and an array of integers identifying index positions of objects that you want to remove from the array and that those index positions are sorted from lowest to highest in the array. Your first thought might be to write code as shown in Listing 5-7.

Listing 5-7. A Naive Approach to Removing Elements Corresponding to a Set of Index Values

```
int[] deleteIndices;
List myList;
//  Populate list, get indices of objects to be deleted
.
.
.
for (int i = 0; i < deleteIndices.length; i++) {
    myList.remove(deleteIndices[i]);
}
```

The problem with this approach is that it will only work correctly when there's no more than one index in the deletion array. That's because as soon as you remove the first entry, the other indices in the array effectively become invalid because they no longer refer to the same elements. To understand this, let's assume you have a list that contains five elements and your deletion array contains two entries, one with a value of 1 and the other with a value of 3, indicating that the second and fourth entries should be deleted.

Once you delete the element corresponding to the position of 1 within the array, the other index no longer refers to the object you intended to delete but instead corresponds to the one that follows it in the list. The result will be that on the second (and later) iterations the code shown previously will remove the wrong objects from the list.

An easy way to address this problem is to simply traverse the index list in reverse order, starting from the last and ending with the first one. Since removing an element affects only the index of the elements that follow it in the list, this approach will ensure that the correct objects are removed from the list.

```
for (int i = deleteIndices.length - 1; i >= 0; i--) {
    myList.remove(deletedIndices[i]);
}
```

Searching for Objects

Although we didn't really discuss it, you may recall that the Collection interface includes a remove() method that takes a single Object argument. Although you can use that method, doing so may limit the scalability of your application; to understand why that's the case, you need to understand how List implementations handle that remove() method.

Internally, a List is nothing more than a sequentially arranged group of objects that isn't really designed for quick searching. It's intended to allow you to easily add and remove elements, to maintain those elements in a particular order, and to access an element at an arbitrary location, as you've just seen. However, what a List isn't designed to do is to allow you to quickly search for a particular object within the collection. As you'll see later, certain other collection objects do a better job of that, but the ability to quickly search for a given element isn't something that List implementations do efficiently. To illustrate this point, let's suppose you have a reference to a List object and you want to remove an object from it that was added earlier. You can use the remove() method that accepts a single Object parameter, as follows:

```
List list;
Object objectToRemove;
// Initialize list, add some objects to it, get reference to object to remove
.
.
.
list.remove(objectToRemove);
```

When the remove() method is called, the entire list will be searched sequentially by comparing each element in the list to the object passed to the remove() method. This will happen quickly if the List contains a reasonably small number of elements and/or the element to be removed is near the front. However, if the List is large and the element to be removed isn't near the beginning of the list, many iterations and comparisons will be needed to locate the object to be removed, and the removal will therefore be relatively slow. In addition, this applies not only to the remove() method but also to any method that needs to locate a particular object within a List that's given a reference to that object. For example, the same limitation affects the contains() method defined in the Collection interface and the indexOf() method defined in List.

Although this may seem like a severe limitation, the truth is that many times searching for an arbitrary object within a large collection isn't needed, in which case a List may be an appropriate choice for your application. As you'll see throughout the course of this chapter, the key is to be aware of the strengths and weaknesses of each collection implementation so you can make an appropriate choice.

Using the equals( ) Method in Collections

Before moving on, it's worthwhile to make one final point about how List implementations locate an object. I already established that they do this by iterating through the objects in the collection and comparing each one to the parameter, such as the one referenced in the call to remove() in the previous example, but how exactly are they compared to one another? As you might expect, the equals() method defined in the Object class is used to compare two objects, which has important implications if you intend to add an instance of a class you've created to a List collection. To understand those implications, let's suppose you execute the following code:

```
List<Student> list = new ArrayList<>();
Student s1 = new Student(12345, "John", "Smith");
Student s2 = new Student(12345, "John", "Smith");
list.add(s1);
list.remove(s2);
System.out.println(list.size());
```

As you can see, this segment creates two objects with identical states, adds the first one to a List, and then attempts to remove the second one, after which it prints the number of elements stored in the array. If you guessed that the value printed is 1 (that is, that the first Student remains an element of the collection even after the remove() method is called), you're correct. However, in practice, you'll typically want two objects with identical states to be treated as if they're both an instance of the same object; in any case, it's helpful to understand what happens here.

The implementation of equals() that's defined in the Object class returns a value of true only if the object passed to the equals() method is the same object as the one for which the method was called. In other words, no attempt is made to compare the state of the two objects, but they're considered "equal" if and only if the two objects are actually the same object instance. Having just said that this often isn't the desired behavior, how can you change it? You can override the equals() method so that it considers two objects equal based on their state. In this case, for example, you might decide that two Student objects should be equal if the identifier value is the same for both, so you might add a method like the following one in Listing 5-8 to the Student class:

Listing 5-8. An Example of How to Implement the equals() Method

```
public boolean equals(Object o) {
    boolean isEqual = false;
    if ((o != null) && (o instanceof Student)) {
        Student target = (Student)o;
        isEqual = (target.getStudentID() == this.getStudentID());
    }
    return isEqual;
}
```

After adding this method to Student, running the code segment listed earlier returns a zero because the reference to the first Student object is removed from the List when the call to remove() is passed a reference to the second Student with an identical state.

Understanding Other List Characteristics

You need to be aware of these other characteristics of List implementations that will help you determine whether one of those implementations is the right choice for your application.

- Unlike some other types of collections, a List normally allows duplicate elements.

- List implementations typically support null elements.

The ability to support duplicate elements means you can have two or more elements equal to one another stored in the List. Those elements could be references to the same object that has been added more than once, or, as in the previous example, they could be two different objects that simply have the same state. For example, if you run the following code segment, it will display a value of 2 to reflect that the same object occurs twice in the List:

```
List<String> list = new ArrayList<>();
String test = "Testing";
list.add(test);
list.add(test);
System.out.println(list.size());
```

In addition, adding the following bold line will cause the code segment to display a value of 3:

```
list.add(test);
list.add(null);
System.out.println(list.size());
```

As you'll see later, some collection types don't allow duplicate elements or null values, but List does support them.

ListIterator

Earlier you saw that the Collection interface defines an iterator() method that returns an implementation of Iterator, and that interface in turn defines methods for accessing the objects in a collection and for removing the most recently retrieved object. As Figure 5-1 showed, ListIterator is a subinterface of List, and, as you might expect, ListIterator defines some additional methods that are appropriate for iterating through List collections. These methods primarily are related to the characteristics of a list, namely, that the objects in the collection are assigned a specific order and by extension that each one is associated with a particular index. So, while the basic Iterator interface allows a forward-only approach to accessing the object, ListIterator provides both forward and backward movement through the collection and allows you to retrieve the appropriate index values, as shown in Table 5-3.

Table 5-3. ListIterator's *Methods for Iterating Through a* List *Implementation*

Method	Description
hasNext()	Returns true if additional forward traversal of the list is possible.
hasPrevious()	Returns true if additional backward traversal of the list is possible.
next()	Returns the next element in the list.
previous()	Returns the previous element in the list.
nextIndex()	Returns the index of the next element in the list.
previousIndex()	Returns the index of the previous element in the list.

To retrieve a ListIterator for a List implementation, simply call the listIterator() method that's defined in the List interface instead of the iterator() method defined in Collection.

ArrayList

Even though we haven't previously discussed its characteristics, we used the ArrayList class in some of the examples, and you'll find that in practice it's a class you'll use often. As its name implies, ArrayList's approach to implementing the List interface is simply to define an Object array and increase the size of that array as necessary to support the number of elements contained within the collection.

If you understand the functionality defined by the methods in the Collection and List interfaces, you don't need to know much else to use ArrayList since it's simply an implementation of those interfaces. However, when considering ArrayList, keep in mind the following characteristics that have been discussed before and that apply to this class:

- An ArrayList can contain duplicate elements.

- You can add null values to an ArrayList.

- ArrayList isn't an inherently thread-safe class, so if you create an instance that's to be used by multiple threads, you're responsible for synchronizing modifications to the list.

Thread Safety

In practice, the need to synchronize access to ArrayList applies only to cases where multiple threads are referencing it while elements are being added or removed. However, if you simply create and populate an ArrayList within a single thread, it's safe to have multiple threads retrieving values from that ArrayList. If you do modify the contents of an ArrayList through its methods while an iterator is being used to retrieve the contents of the list, the iterator will in most cases throw a ConcurrentModificationException the next time you attempt to use it.

In practice, thread safety is usually not necessary, but as you'll see later, Java provides classes that are thread-safe for those situations where that feature is needed.

Constructors

As you've already seen, ArrayList provides a no-argument constructor you can use to create an instance of the class, but it also provides two other constructors you should know. One of the other two allows you to pass a Collection object to the constructor, and using that constructor will cause the ArrayList to be initially populated with the same elements that are stored in that other Collection.

The other constructor that ArrayList provides allows you to specify the collection's "initial capacity." To understand what that means, remember that an ArrayList uses an array to maintain the references to the elements in the collection. The capacity of an ArrayList is simply the size of the array it has allocated to hold those references, although the capacity can change as needed. For example, suppose that an ArrayList has a capacity of ten and it has reached full capacity, meaning the collection already contains ten elements. If you add another element to the ArrayList, it will increase its capacity so it's able to store a reference to the additional element. As you saw at the beginning of the chapter, a capacity that's extremely large (or an array far larger than is needed to maintain the object references) wastes memory, so ideally you'd like the capacity of an ArrayList to be as small as possible.

If you know exactly how many elements an ArrayList will hold, you can specify that number on the constructor, as follows. In this case, you know that the collection will contain exactly ten elements, so you can specify the capacity on construction.

```
List<Student> list = new ArrayList<>(10);
```

On the other hand, if you've already created an ArrayList and then obtain an estimate of the capacity it needs or an exact amount, it can be helpful to call the ensureCapacity() method before adding the elements to the list. In this scenario, imagine that you've previously constructed an ArrayList but know the number of elements it will contain; therefore, you call ensureCapacity() to set its capacity accordingly (see Listing 5-9).

Listing 5-9. Using ensureCapacity() to Make Certain That an Array Is Already Large Enough for Its Intended Use

```
public void populateStudentCollection(ArrayList studentList) {
    studentList.clear();
    int count = getNumberOfStudents();
    studentList.ensureCapacity(count);
    for (int i = 0; i < count; i++) {
        studentList.set(i, getNextStudent());
    }
}
```

Keep in mind that you're never required to set or update the capacity of an ArrayList; if you don't, the capacity will be increased for you automatically. However, if you know or have an estimate of the capacity that will be needed, specifying it as I've shown here will in many cases cause the ArrayList to use less memory than it would if it changes the capacity itself.

LinkedList

The LinkedList implementation of the List interface doesn't provide any behavior that's visibly different from ArrayList, but LinkedList is different in terms of how the list is maintained. Just as the name of the ArrayList class correctly implies that it uses an array, the LinkedList class uses a double linked list to manage the collection of objects. What this means is that each node in the list contains a pointer to the node that precedes it and one to the node that follows it, which in turn means the list can be traversed in either direction (that is, both forward and backward). A *node* is simply an object created by the LinkedList when you add an object to the collection, and the nodes are linked to one another in a way that maintains the proper sequence for the objects in the list.

The advantages and disadvantages of linked lists are well documented, and in theory inserting and removing an element at the beginning or from the end of a linked list should offer a significant performance advantage over the same operation performed using (for example) an ArrayList. In practice, however, the performance advantage is negligible, and the LinkedList is actually slower in cases where an entry is added to the end and the ArrayList hasn't reached full capacity. The reason for this is to a great extent because operations performed on the middle of a linked list are relatively slow because the nodes must be traversed to reach that location within the list. In other words, assuming you have a List that contains one million elements, the following code will execute far more slowly with a LinkedList than with an ArrayList:

```
Object value = list.get(500000);  // Get an element near the middle
```

To execute this line of code, a linked list will need to start with either the first node or the last node and iterate through the list until it reaches the node that corresponds to the specified index. In other words, the amount of time a LinkedList takes to access a given node is proportional to that node's distance from the beginning or end of the list. In contrast, accessing an element in the middle of an ArrayList is no faster or slower than accessing one at any other location.

In addition to generally providing better performance, ArrayList presents another advantage over LinkedList: it uses less memory. That's because it's necessary to create a node object for each element that's added to a LinkedList. On the other hand, an ArrayList needs to maintain only a single object array, and the only time it needs to create a new object is when the capacity needs to increase. The object creation associated with a LinkedList not only results in it using more memory but also is another reason why LinkedList is generally slower than ArrayList, since object creation is a relatively time-consuming process.

The one scenario where you may see a performance improvement when using a LinkedList is when you're adding many entries to the beginning of the list. However, this is relatively rare, and the performance improvement isn't great, so as a general rule, you should use ArrayList when you need a List with the characteristics that it and LinkedList provide.

Vector

As mentioned earlier, Vector is one of the few collection classes that have existed since the first release of Java, and Vector is similar in terms of behavior to ArrayList. Like ArrayList, Vector is an implementation of List, but List didn't exist when Vector was originally defined. However, when Java's collection library expanded in Java 1.2, the Vector class was retrofitted to become an implementation of List to make it consistent with the other collection classes. Like ArrayList, Vector is able to contain duplicate elements and null values. In fact, the biggest difference between ArrayList and Vector is that Vector is inherently thread-safe and ArrayList isn't.

Although thread safety is a desirable feature, it's simply not needed in many cases, and synchronizing is a relatively slow process. In other words, if you use a synchronized collection class when you don't need one, your application may be unnecessarily slow. Even if you do need some level of synchronization, you probably can do a better job of providing it based on how you know the collection will be used by your application. Vector by necessity takes a "worst-case" approach to synchronization, which causes its performance to suffer. For this reason, Vector isn't often used. (However, you'll sometimes still see it used by long-time Java coders and in code written to run on early releases.)

Perhaps the one advantage that Vector does have over ArrayList is that Vector not only allows you to specify the capacity on construction and change it later but also allows you to specify the amount that will be automatically added to its capacity when an increase is needed.

Stack

This is another one of the original collection classes; it extends Vector, and Stack is effectively just a wrapper around Vector that provides operations that make its behavior match that of a stack. Instead of the concept of a beginning or end, the stack's elements are considered to be accessible from the "top" to the "bottom." Elements can be added only to the top of the stack, and the most recently added one is the only one that's accessible at any given time. In other words, this is an implementation of a last-in/first-out (LIFO) algorithm.

For the most part, this is just a matter of defining methods that match the terminology associated with a stack and having those methods function appropriately. For example, while you'd call add() to add an element to a Vector, you'd call push() to "push" an object onto the top of the stack. Similarly, while remove() is used to remove an object from a Vector, you can use pop() to remove the object currently at the top of the stack and retrieve a reference to it.

Although applications do sometimes need the functionality of a stack, it can easily be accomplished with a more commonly used implementation such as ArrayList. The fact that the Stack class provides the more academically correct terminology is of questionable value and may even be confusing to someone who isn't familiar with the concepts or doesn't remember the terminology. In addition, because it's simply a thin wrapper around Vector, the Stack's operations are synchronized and therefore will execute more slowly than one of the newer classes. Given these disadvantages, you'll rarely get any real benefit from using the Stack class, but I mention it here for the sake of completeness.

Set

Now let's examine another major branch of the collection class hierarchy, specifically the Set interface and associated subinterfaces and implementing classes. As its name implies, Set is intended to roughly mimic the idea of a mathematical "set" containing a group of distinct values. In contrast to the List interface, implementations of Set generally have the following characteristics:

- They can't contain duplicate elements.
- The elements may or may not have a predictable order.
- Since the elements can't be assumed to be in a particular order, no mechanism is provided for accessing an element based on its index position.

To better illustrate these points, let's assume you've created a code segment like the following one, in Listing 5-10, which creates an instance of ArrayList and calls its add() method four times, with one instance of Student being added twice:

Listing 5-10. A List with the Same Object Added More Than Once

```
Collection<Student> collection = new ArrayList<>();
Student s1 = new Student(12345, "John", "Smith");
Student s2 = new Student(67890, "Jane", "Smith");
Student s3 = new Student(13579, "Adam", "Smith");
collection.add(s1);
collection.add(s1);
collection.add(s2);
collection.add(s3);
for (Student student : collection) {
    System.out.println(student.getFullName());
}
```

Running this code produces the following results, with "John Smith" being displayed two times because that Student was added to the collection twice:

```
John Smith
John Smith
Jane Smith
Adam Smith
```

However, let's now suppose you make one small change to the code segment, creating an instance of HashSet instead of ArrayList (see Listing 5-11).

Listing 5-11. A Set with the Same Object Added More Than Once

```
Collection<Student> collection = new HashSet<>();
Student s1 = new Student(12345, "John", "Smith");
Student s2 = new Student(67890, "Jane", "Smith");
Student s3 = new Student(13579, "Adam", "Smith");
collection.add(s1);
collection.add(s1);
collection.add(s2);
collection.add(s3);
for (Student student : collection) {
    System.out.println(student.getFullName());
}
```

Now the results are very different. For one thing, the names aren't necessarily displayed in the same order in which they were added to the collection, and for another, "John Smith" is displayed only one time.

```
John Smith
Adam Smith
Jane Smith
```

The fact that the names are displayed in a different order shouldn't be surprising since I already established that the elements in a Set don't necessarily have a predictable sequence. In addition, I said that duplicates aren't allowed, so only one John Smith object in the Set is also the expected behavior.

As you saw earlier, the way the definition of a duplicate element in the context of a List is determined is by whether two objects are considered equal based upon the results of the equals() method. Assuming that the equals() method you added to Student earlier is present, let's extend the code segment with the following changes, noting that you're now adding two Student objects to the collection that will return true when compared using equals(). Specifically, the Jane Smith and Tom Jones objects both have identifier values of 67890, which will cause their equals() methods to return true when compared to one another (see Listing 5-12).

Listing 5-12. A Set with Two "Equal" Objects

```
Collection<Student> collection = new HashSet<>();
Student s1 = new Student(12345, "John", "Smith");
Student s2 = new Student(67890, "Jane", "Smith");
Student s3 = new Student(13579, "Adam", "Smith");
Student s4 = new Student(67890, "Tom", "Jones");
collection.add(s1);
collection.add(s2);
collection.add(s3);
collection.add(s4);
for (Student student : collection) {
    System.out.println(student.getFullName());
}
```

Running this code segment will produce results similar to the following (although the order in which the names will be displayed could vary):

```
John Smith
Adam Smith
Jane Smith
Tom Jones
```

Obviously, simply overriding the equals() method isn't enough to make two elements be considered duplicates in the context of a Set implementation. In fact, one additional step is necessary that's actually documented in the equals() method of the java.lang.Object class: you also need to override hashCode().

Using Collection Objects, Hash Codes, and equals()

If you review the API documentation for the equals() method defined in Object, you'll find the following:

Note that it is generally necessary to override the hashCode method whenever this method is overridden, so as to maintain the general contract for the hashCode method, which states that equal objects must have equal hash codes.

Since you now know you need to override hashCode(), and since that method must return the same integer value for objects that are considered equal, an appropriate implementation of hashCode() can easily be added to the Student class by returning the following identifier value:

```
public int hashCode(){
    return studentID;
}
```

This implementation works well because it satisfies the contract of the hashCode() method and will return a different hash code value for any two instances of Student that are considered to be unequal. If you run the code segment listed earlier, the results now include only the following three entries:

```
Adam Smith
John Smith
Jane Smith
```

You might have expected the Tom Jones object to replace the Jane Smith object when it's added to the collection, but this obviously didn't happen. The reason is that when you attempt to add an object that's considered to be a duplicate, the newer duplicate object is merely discarded instead of replacing the one already in the collection that it appears to duplicate.

Overriding the hashCode() method in Student solved the problem, but it raises the question of why two objects considered duplicates in a List weren't treated as duplicates in a Set. The reason for this is because List simply uses the hashCode() method when locating elements. Remember, when trying to locate an element for a call such as contains(), the List iterates through its elements and uses the equals() method to compare the object it's looking for to each one it contains. In contrast, when you call a method such as contains() for a Set to determine whether it contains an object, the Set uses that object's hash code to determine whether it contains the object or a duplicate of that object. In other words, if you add an object with a hash code of 24680 to a set that doesn't already contain an object with that same hash code, that new object will be added even if its equals() method would return true when compared to one or more other objects within the set.

Understanding Buckets

To better understand why this works the way it does, it helps to understand that hash codes provide functionality in Set implementations similar to that of index values stored in a relational database. When an object is added to the Set, its hash code is used to choose a "bucket" into which to place the object. Objects that aren't equal may have different hash codes and still wind up in the same bucket, but two objects that are considered equal should always wind up in the same bucket. The reason this is important is that when the Set goes to determine whether it contains a particular object, it will use that object's hash code to determine which bucket the object should be stored in and iterate through the objects in that bucket, using the equals() method to determine whether the bucket contains the object. Stated another way, the hashCode() method is used to derive a subset of objects in which a particular instance should occur, and the equals() method is used to examine that subset to determine whether the object is found there.

This concept of how hashCode() and equals() methods are used is an important one, not only for using instances of Set but also for using implementations of the Map interface you'll examine later in the chapter. Overriding hashCode() and equals() isn't an issue when you're using system classes that are part of Java such as String, Date, or the numeric wrappers (Integer, Float, and so on). However, once you begin adding instances of custom classes like Student to a Set or a Map, you need to ensure that the equals() and hashCode() methods will function appropriately, or your code may produce unexpected results.

HashSet

Now that you're already familiar with the basic behavior of Set implementations, you don't need to know much else to understand and use the HashSet class. As previously indicated in the case for Set implementations, HashSet has the following characteristics:

- No guarantee is made concerning the order in which the elements will be returned when you're iterating through them.

- No duplicate elements are allowed, where "duplicate" elements are two objects that have the same hash code and that return true when compared using the equals() method.

- The Set is allowed to contain a null element.

Constructors

Although the basic behavior of a HashSet may now be well understood, the constructors provided may be slightly confusing. Aside from the no-argument constructor used in an earlier example, constructors exist that allow you to specify an "initial capacity" and a "load factor." In reality, those values aren't used directly by the HashSet class itself but by an instance of another collection class that HashSet uses called HashMap. You'll examine the HashMap class in detail later in the section "HashMap," but for now all that's important for you to understand is that HashSet is really just a wrapper around an instance of HashMap. In other words, most of the code that provides the functionality of a HashSet is actually defined in HashMap and its related classes. The reason it's important to know this is because the initial capacity and load factor are used by HashSet only when it's creating the instance of HashMap that it will use; you'll examine their usage in detail later in this chapter.

LinkedHashSet

This class provides functionality similar to that of HashSet but with one important difference: the elements are returned in a predictable order, specifically in the same order in which they were added to the set. This can be useful when fast lookups are needed to determine whether an object is contained within a Set and when it's also important to be able to retrieve the elements and have them returned in the same sequence in which they were added to the set.

TreeSet

TreeSet allows elements to be retrieved in a predictable order, but in this case the elements are maintained and returned based upon a sorting algorithm instead of the order in which they were added to the table. That algorithm can be in one of two places, and the constructor you use when creating a TreeSet will determine which location performs the sorting.

Using Comparable and Natural Order

In many cases, the objects you add to a Set will have what's known as a *natural order*, which means the object implements the Comparable interface defined in the java.lang package. This means for the given class there's a way of sorting instances that's intuitive and appropriate for many or most situations.

For example, the natural order for instances of a numeric wrapper class, a String or a Date, is from lowest to highest. To illustrate this point, let's suppose you execute the following code segment, shown in Listing 5-13:

Listing 5-13. A TreeSet Example to Illustrate How Elements Are Ordered

```
TreeSet<Integer> set = new TreeSet<>();
set.add(new Integer (100));
set.add(new Integer (50));
set.add(new Integer (75));
set.add(new Integer (0));
for (Integer i : set) {
    System.out.println(i);
}
```

The results will appear exactly as follows:

```
0
50
75
100
```

The numbers are sorted and returned in ascending order because the Integer class implements the Comparable interface, and the TreeSet is able to take advantage of that. Comparable defines a single method that returns an integer that identifies the value of an object relative to some other object, as follows:

```
public int compareTo(Object o)
```

If the object for which this method is called is less than the one it's being compared to (represented by the local variable called o), a value less than zero will be returned. Similarly, if it's greater than the one it's being compared to, then it will return a value greater than zero, and if the two are equal, then a value of zero is returned. In other words, when the Integer containing a value of 75 is compared to the one containing 50, a positive (greater than zero) value is returned, and comparing the Integer containing 75 to the one containing 100 causes a negative (less than zero) to be returned.

The Comparable interface is already implemented in Java's system classes where a meaningful and intuitive order exists, but what about user-defined classes such as the Student class you've been using? To be able to sort Students, you can easily implement the Comparable interface in that class to assign a natural order so instances of Student can be sorted by TreeSet. When implementing Comparable, the main question that needs to be answered is, how will users of the class want instances sorted most often? In this case, sorting the students in ascending order by last name and then by first name would seem to be the most useful (or "natural") arrangement.

You can begin your implementation by creating an assertion that the object passed to the compareTo() method is also an instance of Student. Given Java's support for generics, this is likely to be a valid assumption, and if not, there probably isn't going to be a meaningful value that can be returned anyway. In other words, it's reasonable to assume that instances of Student will be compared only to other instances of Student and not to instances of (for example) Date or Integer or some other unrelated class.

```
public int compareTo(Object o) {
    assert (o instanceof Student);
}
```

You can now assume that the object passed to your method isn't an instance of some other class, but what about a null value? Although it's technically possible to add a null value to most collections, and by extension possible to compare one to an instance of Student, it's not common in practice for this to occur, so expand your assertion state as follows:

```
public int compareTo(Object o) {
    assert ((o instanceof Student) && (o != null));
}
```

Now that you've established that the object passed presumably isn't a null and is an instance of Student, you can cast it to the appropriate class.

```
public int compareTo(Object o) {
    assert ((o instanceof Student) && (o != null));
    Student s = (Student)o;
}
```

Now that you have a reference to the Student, you can begin the name comparison with the last name. Since the String class already implements Comparable, you can take advantage of that by simply delegating the comparisons to the object that contains the student's last name.

```
public int compareTo(Object o) {
    assert ((o instanceof Student) && (o != null));
    Student s = (Student)o;
    int relativeValue = lastName.compareTo(s.getLastName());
    return relativeValue;
}
```

This code alone is sufficient for cases where the two students' last names are different, but what about those where they both have the same last name but a different first name? In that case, the call to compareTo() you just added will return a value of 0, meaning that the two last name String values are equal; when that occurs, you need to then perform the same comparison using the students' first names.

```
public int compareTo(Object o) {
    assert ((o instanceof Student) && (o != null));
    Student s = (Student)o;
    int relativeValue = lastName.compareTo(s.getLastName());
    if (relativeValue == 0) {
        relativeValue = firstName.compareTo(s.getFirstName());
    }
    return relativeValue;
}
```

The implementation of the compareTo() method in Student is now complete. The only thing that remains is to indicate that the class now implements Comparable.

```
public class Student implements Comparable {
```

Once you've completed these changes, you could test them using a code segment like the following in Listing 5-14:

Listing 5-14. A Set with Comparable Objects

```
Collection<Student> collection = new TreeSet<>();
Student s1 = new Student(12345, "John", "Smith");
Student s2 = new Student(24680, "Jane", "Smith");
Student s3 = new Student(13579, "Adam", "Smith");
Student s4 = new Student(67890, "Tom", "Jones");
collection.add(s1);
collection.add(s2);
collection.add(s3);
collection.add(s4);
for (Student student : collection) {
    System.out.println(student.getFullName());
}
```

As expected, running this code will print the names of the students in alphabetical order by last name and then by first name, as follows:

```
Tom Jones
Adam Smith
Jane Smith
John Smith
```

Using Comparator

As you've now seen, it's easy to use a TreeSet to sort objects based on their natural order. In fact, no code is required at all as long as the objects to be sorted were created from a class that implements Comparable. However, sometimes this might not be possible or appropriate. For example, you might need to sort instances of a class that you can't modify and that doesn't implement Comparable. Even if the class implements Comparable, what about situations where you want to sort the objects using something other than their natural order? In the example you just used, for instance, what if you wanted to sort the students in descending order instead of ascending order?

Fortunately, Java's collection library provides an easy way for you to sort objects in any way you want regardless of whether they implement Comparable. It does this by defining an interface called Comparator that allows you to write comparison code that's external to a given class. Comparator defines just two methods: an equals() method with a signature matching the one defined in the java.lang.Object class and a compare() method that takes two Object arguments and returns an integer value. That integer value serves exactly the same function as the value returned by Comparable's compareTo() method but in this case indicates the value of the first object relative to the second one.

To see how easily you can use Comparator, let's suppose you want to sort the Student objects based on their student identification number instead of the name values. You could easily create a class like the following one, in Listing 5-15, which performs the comparison:

Listing 5-15. A Simple Comparator for Comparting and Sorting Student Instances

```java
class StudentComparator implements Comparator<Student> {

    public int compare(Student s1, Student s2) {
        int relativeValue = s1.getStudentID() - s2.getStudentID();
        return relativeValue;
    }

}
```

With this class defined, you can now pass an instance of it to the TreeSet constructor to have the TreeSet use the Comparator implementation when sorting the students, instead of using the Student objects' natural order as defined by the Comparable implementation. In addition, note that the line that displays the list of students has been modified to also display the identification number, which makes it easier to verify that the code worked as expected (see Listing 5-16).

Listing 5-16. Using the StudentComparator

```java
Collection<Student> collection = new TreeSet<>(new StudentComparator());
Student s1 = new Student(12345, "John", "Smith");
Student s2 = new Student(24680, "Jane", "Smith");
Student s3 = new Student(13579, "Adam", "Smith");
Student s4 = new Student(67890, "Tom", "Jones");
collection.add(s1);
collection.add(s2);
collection.add(s3);
collection.add(s4);
for (Student student : collection) {
    System.out.println(student.getStudentID() + " " + student.getFullName());
}
```

Running the modified code produces the following results with the students sorted based on their identification numbers:

```
12345 John Smith
13579 Adam Smith
24680 Jane Smith
67890 Tom Jones
```

Comparable vs. Comparator

As this example illustrates, you should use the Comparable interface to implement comparison code that can appropriately be stored inside a given class and when there's a "natural" order for instances of that class that users can intuitively expect to represent the default order. In contrast, Comparator is appropriate when the information needed to perform the sorting isn't available within the object itself and in other situations where it may not be feasible or appropriate to embed the sorting logic within the class.

One final point should be made concerning TreeSet, and it has to do with whether it supports adding a null element. This wasn't mentioned before because its ability to support a null value primarily depends upon whether you use natural ordering or a Comparator implementation. A null value isn't allowed in a TreeSet if you use natural ordering because the null value can't compare itself to other objects within the set. However, if you specify a Comparator object, that object can be designed to compare the null value with a non-null value and return a value that will cause the null to be sorted in whatever way is appropriate. In that case, when you've used a Comparator and the implementation is designed to handle the null value, the TreeSet will be able to contain a null value.

EnumSet

This implementation of Set has a unique function: to serve as a collection for a group of enumeration values from a single enumeration type that has been defined using Java's enumeration syntax. By combining this collection with a variable argument, you can easily define a set that contains an arbitrary group of enumeration values. For example, let's suppose you've defined an enumeration that defines the days of the week as follows:

```
public enum DayOfWeek {
    Sunday, Monday, Tuesday, Wednesday, Thursday, Friday, Saturday;
}
```

Given that enumeration, you could easily create a set containing only the weekdays by using a single line of code as follows. This is possible because one implementation of the overloaded of() method allows you to specify a variable number of arguments.

```
EnumSet<DayOfWeek> schoolDays = EnumSet.of(DayOfWeek.Monday, DayOfWeek.Tuesday,
        DayOfWeek.Wednesday, DayOfWeek.Thursday, DayOfWeek.Friday);
```

You can further verify that this creates a set containing only the weekday values by adding code like the following:

```
for (DayOfWeek day : schoolDays) {
    System.out.println(day);
}
```

This loop results in the following values being displayed:

```
Monday
Tuesday
Wednesday
Thursday
Friday
```

As these results suggest, the order in which the elements of an EnumSet are returned corresponds to the order in which they're defined within the enumeration. In addition, an EnumSet can't contain any null elements, which makes it somewhat different in that respect from other Set implementations.

Although EnumSet instances can be used in a relatively static manner, it's entirely possible to add and remove enumeration elements just as other collections allow you to add and remove objects.

```
schoolDays.add(DayOfWeek.Saturday);
```

In summary, an EnumSet is simply a Set implementation created specifically for use with enumeration values, and its elements are guaranteed to have an order that corresponds to the sequence in which they're defined within the enumeration.

Map

In Figure 5-1 you saw a class diagram with many of the collection interfaces and classes in it. The Map interface is also part of the collection API, but it was omitted from that diagram partly because it doesn't extend Collection or otherwise share a common superinterface, as shown in Figure 5-2.

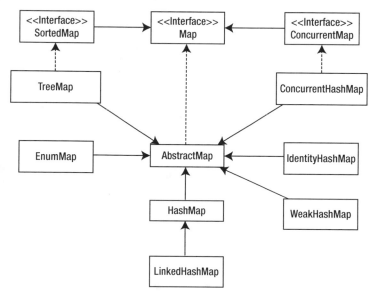

Figure 5-2. *The Map interface and its associated classes aren't part of the same hierarchy as the other components you've seen*

Since the Map interface doesn't extend Collection, you might think that Map is different from any of the classes and interfaces we've discussed up to this point. Although that's partly correct in some ways, Map implementations actually have a great deal in common in terms of their behavior with Set classes. That shouldn't be entirely surprising, since it was already mentioned that most of the behavior of a HashSet is actually provided by that class's use of a HashMap object. In fact, many of the most commonly used set interfaces and classes correspond to equivalent map definitions, as shown in Table 5-4.

Table 5-4. Map and Set Counterparts

Type	Map	Set
Interface	Map	Set
Abstract class	AbstractMap	AbstractSet
Class	HashMap	HashSet
Class	LinkedHashMap	LinkedHashSet
Class	TreeMap	TreeSet
Class	EnumMap	EnumSet

So how is it that a Map and a Set are so different that they don't share a common interface ancestor (Collection) but are so similar that they have implementations that mimic one another? The answer is that while a Set is simply a collection of objects, a Map is a collection of objects with each one having a corresponding value. In other words, a map represents a group of key/value pairs, with the keys being analogous to the elements in a set. Because the functionality of a Map is largely a superset of the functionality defined for a Set, HashSet and TreeSet use HashMap and TreeMap, respectively, to provide most of their functionality.

Since a Map doesn't contain a single data type but instead includes key/value pairs, the syntax that's used to support generics is slightly different. Instead of specifying a single class, you must specify two classes: one for the keys and one for the corresponding values. For example, to create an instance of HashMap, you might use code like the following:

```
HashMap<Integer,Student> map = new HashMap<>();
```

This code creates a HashMap that allows you to use Integer instances for the keys and Student objects for the corresponding values. Adding an entry to a Map is simple, but instead of calling add() and specifying a single object, you call put() and specify two arguments, the first representing the key and the second representing the value. For example, let's suppose you plan to store instances of Student in your newly created HashMap and you want to use each Student object's identifier value as the key. In that case, you could use code as shown in Listing 5-17.

Listing 5-17. Autoboxing with Collection Generics

```
HashMap<Integer,Student> map = new HashMap<>();
Student s1 = new Student(12345, "John", "Smith");
Student s2 = new Student(24680, "Jane", "Smith");
Student s3 = new Student(13579, "Adam", "Smith");
Student s4 = new Student(67890, "Tom", "Jones");
map.put(s1.getStudentID(), s1);
map.put(s2.getStudentID(), s2);
map.put(s3.getStudentID(), s3);
map.put(s4.getStudentID(), s4);
```

Although the student identifier returned by the getStudentID() method is an integer primitive, autoboxing support automatically converts it into an instance of the Integer wrapper before it's stored in the map.

Once you've stored a key/value pair in the map, you can retrieve the value by passing the key value to the get() method. By far the most useful feature of a Map, and arguably the most useful feature of any collection class, is the ability to retrieve a value given the appropriate key. For example, if you have the student identifier and want to retrieve the corresponding Student for it, you could execute code like the following:

```
Student s0 = map.get(13579);
```

This code searches the map for a key equal to 13579 and returns the corresponding Student value if there's one or null if no such key exists. This ability to perform an object lookup is extremely useful, partly because unlike List searches, retrieving an object from a Map using a key value doesn't require iteration through the list of keys in the map. Instead, the key's hash code locates the corresponding value in a "bucket" as described earlier, which means Map lookups can be very fast even with extremely large collections.

To maximize the speed of such lookups, you should try to ensure to as great an extent as possible that two objects that aren't equal to one another return different hash code values.

It's technically possible to have every instance of a given class return the same hash code value, and Map (and Set) implementations will still work correctly in that case. However, their performance will be seriously degraded because all objects will be placed in the same "bucket" because of having identical hash code values. As mentioned earlier, searches are first done by determining which "bucket" an object should be placed in given its hash code, and then a linear search of all objects within that bucket takes place until one that matches the desired value is found.

While the List and Set implementations allow you to retrieve iterators that return the element values, Map instances allow you to retrieve both the list of keys (through the keySet() method that returns a Set containing all keys) and the values (through the appropriately named values() method that returns a Collection containing all values). For example, the following code (in Listing 5-18) shows how you can retrieve the set of key values and then iterate through the set, displaying each key and retrieving its corresponding values:

Listing 5-18. Displaying the Keys in a Map

```
Student student;
Set<Integer> keys = map.keySet();
for (Integer i : keys) {
    student = map.get(i);
    System.out.println("Key: " + i + " Value:" + student.getFullName());
}
```

Aside from the variations discussed here, Map implementations function very much like their corresponding Set classes described earlier.

HashMap

Earlier in the chapter we covered the HashSet class and briefly discussed that it included a constructor that accepts an integer representing an initial capacity and a floating-point number representing a load factor. However, we also deferred a meaningful examination of those values since those arguments are in fact not used directly by the HashSet code but by the HashMap that the HashSet creates to maintain its list of elements.

So, how does HashMap use the initial capacity and load factor? If the words *initial capacity* sound familiar, it's because I previously discussed a parameter by the same name that can be used when constructing an ArrayList, and as you'd expect, it represents essentially the same thing here. In this case, the initial capacity is the number of "buckets" that are created for use by the collection. Once again, it's best to specify on construction the number of elements that will be stored in the collection if you know it, because doing so will minimize the amount of memory used by the collection.

While the capacity is an integer value, the load factor is a floating-point number that essentially represents a percentage value indicating how many elements can be added to the HashSet before the capacity will be automatically increased. For example, if the capacity is set to 100 and the load factor to 0.5, you can add up to 50 elements before the capacity will be increased (10 × .5 = 50). Once you add the 51st element, for example, the capacity will automatically be roughly doubled, and this process will be repeated as many times as needed. In effect, the load factor represents the relative importance to your application of speed vs. memory usage: a low value means that you're more concerned with lookup speed, while a high value is appropriate when saving memory is expected to be more important.

LinkedHashMap

The behavior of LinkedHashMap is essentially the same as that of HashMap with the exception that it maintains its entries in a predictable sequence, specifically, the order in which they were added to the map. In other words, if you add entries to a LinkedHashMap and then retrieve them through an iterator, they will be returned in the same order in which they were added.

TreeMap

This class maintains its keys in a sorted order either by using their natural order or by using an implementation of the Comparator interface. The behavior of TreeMap with respect to its key values is identical to the behavior previously described for the elements in a TreeSet.

EnumMap

Instances of EnumMap allow you to use enumeration values from a single type as keys in the map. The keys (and by extension their associated values) are maintained in the order in which the values are defined in the enumeration.

IdentityHashMap

This implementation of the Map interface is different from all others in terms of how it determines key equality. Like the other Map implementations, it doesn't allow duplicate entries, but it's the way that duplicates are identified within an IdentityHashMap that makes it unique. Instead of using the equals() method to compare entries, IdentityHashMap compares them using the == operator. What this means from a functional standpoint is that no two object references are considered equal unless they're references to the same object instance. With other implementations, the state of the objects is used to determine equality, but in this case an object's identity is the only criterion used to determine uniqueness. To illustrate how this affects the behavior of the map, consider the following code in Listing 5-19:

Listing 5-19. An IdentityHashMap That Contains Equivalent Objects

```
IdentityHashMap<Integer,Student> map = new IdentityHashMap<>();
map.put(new Integer (123), null);
map.put(new Integer (123), null);
for (Integer i : map.keySet()) {
    System.out.println(i);
}
```

If you run this code segment, it will display the value "123" twice. Any other map implementation besides IdentityHashMap would have displayed it only once, because the second Integer would have been considered a duplicate and wouldn't have been added. However, because the IdentityHashMap ignores object state and considers every instance distinct from every other instance, it can contain entries that would be considered duplicates of one another (and therefore discarded) in other Map implementations.

Since IdentityHashMap's behavior is so different from that of other maps, it may be helpful to provide one more example to illustrate an important point. Given the following code segment in Listing 5-20, consider what you'd expect the output to be when it's executed:

Listing 5-20. Unexpected IdentityHashMap Behavior

```
IdentityHashMap<Integer,Student> map = new IdentityHashMap<>();
Student s1 = new Student(12345, "John", "Smith");
map.put(s1.getStudentID(), s1);
map.put(s1.getStudentID(), s1);
for (Student s : map.values()) {
    System.out.println(s.getStudentID() + " " + s.getFullName());
}
```

If you compile and execute this code, the results will be as follows:

```
12345 John Smith
12345 John Smith
```

These results may come as a surprise even to someone with an understanding of how IdentityHashMap works, because at first glance it would appear that the map contains a duplicate key. The map indeed contains two references to the same Student object, but in fact each one has a distinct key value that references it. The student identifier is actually a primitive value, and as you may recall from earlier in the chapter, Java's autoboxing feature simply creates wrappers around primitive values when they're specified. Therefore, the previous two lines of code that add the Student to the map twice are functionally identical to the following:

```
map.put(new Integer(s1.getStudentID()), s1);
map.put(new Integer(s1.getStudentID()), s1);
```

As this illustrates, a separate object is being created for each key value, which explains why the IdentityHashMap was able to hold what initially appeared to be duplicates even by its own very restrictive definition.

WeakHashMap

WeakHashMap is another implementation of the Map interface that's unique, and to fully understand it, one needs to be aware of how Java's garbage collection mechanism works, in particular with respect to references to objects being maintained. Suffice it to say, though, it's usually the case that an object will not be garbage collected (the memory it uses reclaimed) as long as there's at least one reference to the object remaining. However, Java 2 introduced the concept of a weak reference, which simply means a reference that by itself doesn't prevent an object from being garbage collected. An object can have both weak and "strong" (normal) references, and as long as at least one strong reference exists, the referenced object can never be garbage collected. Once an object has no references or has only weak references, it becomes eligible for garbage collection.

Although all other map implementations in the `java.util` package use strong references, instances of `WeakHashMap` use only weak references to their key values. What this means is that at any given time, a particular key that was added to the map might effectively be removed, but only if no strong references exist to that object. To illustrate this point, you can run the following code in Listing 5-21:

Listing 5-21. A `WeakHashMap` Usage Example

```
WeakHashMap<Integer,Student> map = new WeakHashMap<>();
Student s1 = new Student(12345, "John", "Smith");
Student s2 = new Student(24680, "Jane", "Smith");
Student s3 = new Student(13579, "Adam", "Smith");
Student s4 = new Student(67890, "Tom", "Jones");
map.put(s1.getStudentID(), s1);
map.put(s2.getStudentID(), s2);
map.put(s3.getStudentID(), s3);
map.put(s4.getStudentID(), s4);
System.out.println("The map initially contained " + map.size() + " entries");
System.gc();
System.out.println("The map now contains " + map.size() + " entries");
```

Although it's not possible to predict for certain what the garbage collector will do (if anything) when the `System.gc()` method is called, running the previous code may produce the following results:

```
The map initially contained 4 entries
The map now contains 0 entries
```

What happened in this case is that the call to the `System.gc()` method prompted the garbage collector to run. Since it found only weak references to the keys associated with the four `Student` values, it removed them from the system and by extension from the `WeakHashMap`.

Understanding how `WeakHashMap` works also illustrates how it can be valuable. It allows you to provide a caching mechanism for data without forcing you to explicitly remove items from the cache to ensure that your application doesn't run out of memory. Instead, items will be removed automatically when they're garbage collected.

ConcurrentHashMap

In most respects, the `ConcurrentHashMap` is identical to the `Hashtable` class: it doesn't allow duplicates or a null value for the key, its elements aren't returned in a predictable order, and it's thread-safe. However, unlike `Hashtable`, the `ConcurrentHashMap` doesn't implement thread safety by using Java's synchronization/locking abilities and therefore provides better performance than a `Hashtable`. In addition, `ConcurrentHashMap` allows you to optimize its performance if you know in advance how many different threads will be updating its contents. You do this by specifying the *concurrency level* parameter when constructing an instance of the class, but you can't change it after instantiation.

Unlike the other `Map` implementations you've examined, `ConcurrentHashMap` isn't defined in the `java.util` package but instead can be found in the `java.util.concurrent` package that was added in Java 5. That package contains a variety of classes and interfaces that can be used by multithreaded applications, including some other collection implementations discussed later in this chapter.

CopyOnWriteArrayList and CopyOnWriteArraySet

Just as ConcurrentHashMap offers a Map implementation that's thread-safe without using synchronization, CopyOnWriteArrayList and CopyOnWriteArraySet provide List and Set implementations, respectively, that are thread-safe. As their names imply, these work by creating a copy of the collection data whenever a change is made to it, such as an addition, removal, or replacement of an element in the collection. Creating a new copy each time a modification occurs is a somewhat "expensive" operation in terms of computational resources (memory and processor time), but this can be a worthwhile trade-off if your application needs a List or Set that isn't modified frequently during the execution of the application. If your application does need to modify a List or Set frequently then it may be more efficient to use a synchronized collection such as Vector or Hashtable or to use ArrayList or HashMap along with custom synchronization code that you implement yourself to ensure the thread safety of your application.

Queue

This interface was added to the collection API in Java 5, and its implementations are used to define various types of queues. Queues have a great deal in common with lists; in fact, the LinkedList class discussed earlier in the chapter implements both the List and Queue interfaces. In addition, a queue that provides LIFO behavior is usually known as a *stack*, and as described earlier, the java.util package includes a Stack class that also implements the List interface.

As its similarity to a List implies, implementations of the Queue interfaces maintain their elements in a predictable order although the order can vary across implementations. For example, with a LIFO queue, or stack, the first element in the collection (also known as the *head*) is the one that was most recently added. In contrast, the head of a first-in/first-out (FIFO) queue is the element that was added the earliest. Either type (LIFO or FIFO) can easily be simulated with a linear collection such as an ArrayList or other List implementation, but Java provides some helpful Queue implementations, as you'll see later in the chapter.

Even though its behavior is similar to that of a List, the Queue interface defines methods with names that are very different from those of the other collection interfaces and classes. However, the number of methods defined in Queue is small, and Table 5-5 describes them.

Table 5-5. Queue Methods

Method	Description
element()	Returns a reference to the head element without removing it, throwing an exception if the queue is empty.
peek()	Returns a reference to the head element without removing it, returning null if the queue is empty.
offer()	Adds an element to the queue. Some implementations may reject the addition, in which case a value of false is returned.
remove()	Retrieves a reference to the head element and removes it from the queue, throwing an exception if the queue is empty.
poll()	Retrieves a reference to the head element and removes it from the queue, returning null if the queue is empty.

PriorityQueue

Even though it implements the `Queue` interface, a `PriorityQueue` is really more like a `TreeSet` or a `TreeMap` in that its elements are ordered based upon their "priority," which is really just either their natural order or their sequence as determined by an instance of `Comparator`. In other words, unlike most `Queue` implementations, the order of the elements in a `PriorityQueue` isn't affected by the order in which they were added but only by their priorities relative to one another.

PriorityBlockingQueue

This class isn't a subclass of `PriorityQueue`, but the two function in a similar manner, with one important difference: as the name implies, this class represents a blocking queue. A *blocking queue* is one that causes the calling thread to be blocked if the queue is empty, and the thread will remain blocked until at least one element is added to the queue.

As you saw in the earlier method descriptions, the typical behavior for a `Queue` implementation is to return a null value or throw an exception if an attempt is made to retrieve an element when none exists in the queue. However, it's common for applications to create threads that simply wait for some type of event or information to be received and then take some action based on that. This type of behavior is where blocking behavior is useful; a thread can simply request the next element from the queue and will wait until one becomes available. In effect, the thread acts as a consumer of the elements added to the queue, while the thread or threads adding elements to the queue represent producers.

This class is defined in the concurrency (`java.util.concurrent`) package introduced in Java 5 and is inherently thread-safe. That package defines interfaces and implementations of those interfaces that represent functionality often needed by multithreaded applications. Prior to Java 5, it was necessary for an application to include or create its own implementations of many different types of thread-related classes, but this package includes a robust set of classes that an application can use directly.

ArrayBlockingQueue

This class represents a blocking queue that uses an array to maintain its elements, and those elements are returned in FIFO manner. As its name implies, this queue is implemented using an array, and it has an important difference from many of the other collection classes you've examined. Specifically, you're required to specify a capacity when creating an instance of this class, and that capacity can never be exceeded. Attempting to add an element to an `ArrayBlockingQueue` that's already "full" (that is, it's at capacity) will cause the thread attempting to add the element to become blocked until an existing element is removed. This class is defined in the concurrency (`java.util.concurrent`) package introduced in Java 5 and is inherently thread-safe.

You might use this class when threads are creating tasks that need to be processed and all the tasks are considered to be of equal priority. In other words, you want the first task added to the queue to be the first one that's processed regardless of what other tasks may be added afterward. In addition, since instances of this class have a fixed capacity, this is an appropriate choice only when it's acceptable for *producer* threads (those adding elements to the queue) to be blocked without causing your application to function incorrectly.

LinkedBlockingQueue

This is a blocking queue that uses a linked list to maintain its elements, which are returned in FIFO order. Like ArrayBlockingQueue, this class can be used as a *bounded* queue, or one where a fixed capacity is used and attempts to add elements beyond that capacity will cause the producer thread to become blocked. What's different with this class is that you aren't required to specify a capacity, and if you don't do so, the instance is considered to be unbounded. In other words, if you specify a capacity, then an instance of LinkedBlockingQueue behaves similarly to an ArrayBlockingQueue. However, if you create an instance of LinkedBlockingQueue using one of the constructors that doesn't include a capacity argument, there will be no limit to the number of elements that can be added to the queue.

This class is defined in the concurrency (java.util.concurrent) package introduced in Java 5 and is inherently thread-safe. This class is a good choice when your application needs a FIFO queue implementation that should block when retrieving an element but not when adding elements.

ConcurrentLinkedQueue

ConcurrentLinkedQueue represents a queue that returns its elements in FIFO order but doesn't block. It's defined in the concurrency (java.util.concurrent) package introduced in Java 5 and is inherently thread-safe; it's a good choice for applications that need a thread-safe FIFO queue that doesn't block.

SynchronousQueue

This is a blocking queue that can't contain any elements; instead, it blocks each request to add an element to the queue until it receives a request to retrieve an element from the queue, and vice versa. It's defined in the concurrency (java.util.concurrent) package introduced in Java 5 and is inherently thread-safe.

A typical use for this class is in an application that contains the type of producer and consumer threads I've discussed before but wants to block the producer until an element it adds to the queue has been retrieved by the consumer. When you have this type of producer/consumer relationship, it's typically desirable for the producer to generate elements as quickly as it can and allow elements to simply wait until the consumer is able to process them. In other cases, however, it's more appropriate to ensure that there are no "waiting" elements.

Given its behavior, SynchronousQueue doesn't really represent what you'd intuitively expect from a queue implementation but instead provides a way to facilitate the transfer of an element from one thread to another.

DelayQueue

Only objects that implement the Delayed interface can be added to this queue, which orders its elements based upon the amount of time remaining before they can be removed from the queue. That time is identified by calling the getDelay() method of the Delayed interface. An object can be retrieved from the queue only once it has expired (its remaining delay is 0), and if no expired objects exist, attempts to retrieve an object from the queue will fail. For example, a call to the poll() method would return null.

This class is useful when you have a group of elements that are time sensitive. That is, instead of being ordered by their priority/importance or by the order in which they were added to the queue, a specific target time is associated with each element. This might be useful if you had a series of reminders to send to users and each one was associated with a particular point in time. You could add those reminders to a DelayQueue and create a consumer thread that retrieves each one from the queue once its target deadline has been reached. Listing 5-22 provides an example of how you could implement this.

Listing 5-22. Sample Implementation of the Delayed Interface

```
public class DelayedReminder implements Delayed {

    private String reminderText;
    private long delayInSeconds;

    public DelayedReminder(String reminder, long seconds) {
        reminderText = reminder;
        delayInSeconds = seconds;
    }

    public String getReminderText() {
        return reminderText;
    }

    public long getDelay(TimeUnit timeUnit) {
        return TimeUnit.SECONDS.convert(delayInSeconds, timeUnit);
    }

    public int compareTo(Delayed delayed) {
        return (int)(delayInSeconds - delayed.getDelay(TimeUnit.SECONDS));
    }

}
```

Given this implementation of the Delayed interface, you could use it in code like that in Listing 5-23 to add time-sensitive reminders to a DelayQueue.

Listing 5-23. An Example of How to Use DelayQueue

```
DelayQueue queue = new DelayQueue();
DelayedReminder reminder = new DelayedReminder("Wake me up in 60 seconds", 60);
queue.add(reminder);
reminder = new DelayedReminder("Wake me up in 30 seconds", 30);
queue.add(reminder);
```

In this example, the second element added to the queue would actually be returned first because its delay expires prior to that of the first element.

Tips on Using Collections

Now that you've looked at the various collection classes and how they function, we can make some generalizations about how to use them. For example, you should use a List when you want to maintain a collection of objects that need to be referenced in a sequence or that will be referenced based upon their position within the collection. A Map is useful when you want to be able to quickly locate a particular object using a corresponding key, while a Set is helpful when you simply want a collection of unique objects and need to be able to quickly establish whether a given object is a member of that collection. Table 5-6 summarizes some of the collection characteristics and indicates whether the specified characteristic is applicable to each of the classes discussed.

Table 5-6. *Collection Class Characteristics*

Class	Sequential Access?	Random Access?	Thread-Safe?	Allows Duplicates?	Sorted?
ArrayList	Yes	Yes	No	Yes	No
LinkedList	Yes	Yes	No	Yes	No
Vector	Yes	Yes	Yes	Yes	No
Stack	Yes	Yes	Yes	Yes	No
HashSet	No	Yes	No	No	No
LinkedHashSet	No	Yes	No	No	No
TreeSet	No	Yes	No	No	Yes
EnumSet	No	Yes	No	No	No
HashMap	No	Yes	No	No	No
LinkedHashMap	No	Yes	No	No	No
TreeMap	No	Yes	No	No	Yes
EnumMap	No	Yes	No	No	No
IdentityHashMap	No	Yes	No	No	No
WeakHashMap	No	Yes	No	No	No
ConcurrentHashMap	No	Yes	Yes	No	No
PriorityQueue	Yes	No	Yes	Yes	Yes
PriorityBlockingQueue	Yes	No	Yes	Yes	Yes
ArrayBlockingQueue	Yes	No	Yes	Yes	No
LinkedBlockingQueue	Yes	No	Yes	Yes	No
ConcurrentLinkedQueue	Yes	No	Yes	Yes	No
SynchronousQueue	Yes	No	Yes	Yes	No
DelayQueue	Yes	No	Yes	Yes	Yes

Shallow vs. Deep Copies

Some of the collection classes provide a `clone()` method that the documentation says creates a *shallow* copy of the collection. This means the object that's created results in only a copy of the collection itself and not the objects it contains. Instead, a collection is created with references to the same objects that are contained within the collection that was cloned. This is an important concept to understand, particularly if the objects in the collection have state that can be changed. In that situation, a programmer might create a clone of a collection and modify objects in the newly created collection without realizing that they were also modifying the objects in the original collection. If you need to create a *deep* copy of a collection where the collection and its elements are both copied, then you must implement the code yourself that will make copies of the elements and store them in the new collection. To better understand the implications of shallow vs. deep copies and how to implement each, you should refer to Chapter 2.

Referencing an Interface Instead of an Implementation

When you create a new collection object, it's necessary to explicitly identify the class for which you want to create an instance. However, you can improve the maintainability of your code in many cases by maintaining a reference to only the interface the class implements rather than the class itself. For example, let's suppose you've created the following code:

```
HashSet<Student> students = new HashSet<>();
displayAllStudents(students);
.
.
.
private void displayAllStudents(HashSet<Student> students) {
    for (Student s : students) {
        System.out.println(s.getFullName());
    }
}
```

If you reference an object using its class as shown here, your code is less maintainable than it could be; to illustrate this point, let's suppose you decide to change the HashSet to a TreeSet so its elements will be sorted using their natural order. You'd now need to change not only the line of code that creates the collection but also the places where that collection's class is explicitly referenced, which in this case includes the signature of the displayAllStudents() method.

A better approach is to simply define the object as an instance of Set or even Collection if possible, as follows:

```
Collection<Student> students = new HashSet<>();
displayAllStudents(students);
.
.
.
private void displayAllStudents(Collection<Student> students) {
    for (Student s : students) {
        System.out.println(s.getFullName());
    }
}
```

Notice that with this new approach, changing the code to create and use a TreeSet would require that the code be changed in only one place, since it's simply treated as a Collection when passed to the displayAllStudents() method. The effect can be even more significant in a real-world application where you might have many references to a given collection object. In this simplistic example, it was possible to treat the object as a Collection, but in practice, you'll often need one or more of the methods defined in the subinterface. When that's the case, it's usually better to use the more specific interface such as Set instead of the more generic one (Collection); otherwise, you're likely to be forced to simply cast the object to a more specific type in many places.

Keep in mind that this guideline isn't specific to collection objects but is applicable to object-oriented programming in general. It's always better to refer to a less specific type when possible, but collections are one area where you'll often have the opportunity to reference an interface such as List instead of a specific implementation such as ArrayList, and doing so makes your code more maintainable.

Streams API

As mentioned earlier, collections are an important part of Java because it's very common for an application to process a group of items, and as we've seen with the discussion of generics, it's expected that a single collection will normally contain multiple instances of the same type of item. For example, applications often need to filter a collection: that is, to remove objects from the collection that meet (or don't meet) some criteria. Another common operation is transformation, where some or all of the objects in the collection are modified in some way. In other words, you'll often need to execute some set of code using each object instance that's stored in a collection and traditionally that's been done using a for loop as has been done here. In fact, it's because that type of processing is so common that the enhanced for loop was introduced that allows you to just specify the element variable and a collection (or array) as in the following example, where myCollection is defined as an implementation of Collection that was defined as containing instances of Student:

```
for (Student student : collection) {
```

This approach is referred to as "explicit" iteration, because iteration logic is explicitly specified by the programmer: specifically, it indicates that the Student instances should be processed one at a time in the order they're returned by the collection.

As we saw earlier, a major initiative in Java 8 was to reduce the amount of "boilerplate" code needed to create an application in Java, and one part of accomplishing that was through the use of lambda expressions. Another was the introduction of the Streams API, which simplifies many of the tasks that are often performed on collections such as filtering and transformation, and by combining this support with lambda expressions you can greatly reduce the amount of code needed to perform some tasks that involve collections.

Reducing the amount of code needed to perform a task involving collections isn't the only improvement introduced with the Streams API, though. If, for example, you have a collection that is expected to contain a very large number of objects and you want to process that collection quickly, using more than one thread may be the best—or only—way to accomplish that. As we've seen, though, creating thread-safe code can be a complex task, even with the various thread-related capabilities built in to Java's core classes. Fortunately, one aspect of the Streams API is that it allows you to use multithreading to process a collection without doing anything except indicating that you want the processing to take advantage of your system's multiprocessing capabilities. In other words, the Streams API not only provides an easy way to process the objects in a collection but essentially gives you thread-safe processing for "free"—that is, with no work on your part.

Anatomy of a Stream

The Streams API is used by defining a "stream," which is Java code that consists of three parts which are named and described in the following list:

- Data source: As the name implies, this part of the stream defines where the data comes from, such as a List instance.

- Intermediate operations: This part of the stream defines what should be done with the data, such as filtering or transforming it.

- Terminal operation: This procedure describes what should be done with the processed data and when (or if) processing should be stopped. For example, this might specify a collection in which the filtered set of items should be stored.

201

With this brief introduction let's look at an example of how a stream can be defined. Suppose that we have a collection of String instances and we want to filter the collection and create a new collection containing only the objects from the original collection that begin with some prefix. This can easily be accomplished in Java 8 using code like that in Listing 5-24, where the filterPrefix is assumed to be initialized to the prefix text using for the filtering and the original collection (data source) is referenced by the myItems variable.

Listing 5-24. A Simple Stream Implementation

```
List<String> filteredList =
        myItems.stream()
        .filter(item -> item.startsWith(prefix))
        .collect(Collectors.toList());
```

The first line in Listing 5-24 is a simple variable declaration and assignment statement, defining a List of String values called filteredList, while the second, third, and fourth lines represent the stream's data source, intermediate operation, and terminal operation, respectively. Specifically, the myItems collection is used to produce a data source by calling the stream() method defined in the Collection class. That method returns an object of type Stream, an interface that is defined in the new java.util.stream package and that defines a variety of methods. One of those methods is filter(), and as just mentioned that method represents an intermediate operation. Note here that the single parameter passed to filter() is a lambda expression that defines a single parameter assigned to the item variable, and that parameter's startsWith() method is called.

As we saw in Chapter 3, which introduced lambda expressions, the Java compiler is able to infer a great deal of information, especially with regard to data types. In this case it recognizes—thanks to the use of generics—that the items in filteredList are String instances, and one of the methods in String is the startsWith() method that accepts a String parameter and returns true if the object for which it's called starts with the prefix identified by that parameter. And what about the type of object that's passed to the filter() method defined in Stream? Again, based on the previous discussion of lambda expressions you can probably guess that filter() accepts an instance of a functional interface implementation, and if you review the API documentation for filter() you'll find that is in fact the case. Specifically, filter() expects an instance of the Predicate interface that's newly defined in Java 8. Predicate defines a small number of methods but all except one include default implementations. The one that doesn't include an implementation—and therefore the one invoked by the lambda expression—is its test() method that is passed a single parameter and returns a Boolean (true or false) value.

Finally, the last line invokes the collect() method, which is also defined in Stream. That method accepts a single parameter that must be an instance of the Collector class, which again is a new class introduced in Java 8 and defined in java.util.stream. If you review the API documentation for collect() you'll find that the information that describes the method includes the following statement: "This is a terminal operation." As mentioned before, a terminal operation is one that identifies what to do with the processed data, and in this case it's passed to a Collector that stores the data in a List that's returned.

It may be easier to understand what's being done here if the foregoing code is "unraveled" as shown in Listing 5-25.

Listing 5-25. An Expanded Version of the Stream Example

```
// This anonymous inner class is equivalent to the lambda: item -> (item.startsWith(prefix))
Predicate<String> prefixSelector = new Predicate<String>() {
        public boolean test(String candidate)
        {
            return candidate.startsWith(prefix);
        }
};
Stream<String> dataSource = myItems.stream();
Stream<String> filtered = dataSource.filter(prefixSelector);
Collector<String, ?, List<String>> collector = Collectors.toList();
List<String> myList = filtered.collect(collector);
```

Again, note that although each item in the original (myItems) collection will be processed, nowhere is any explicit iteration code implemented. Instead, the iteration is implicit (sometimes called "passive" or "internal" iteration) in the use of the stream. In short, the Streams API has given us a way to eliminate a large amount of "boilerplate" code involved in performing this filter operation.

Intermediate Operation Pipelining

Earlier when discussing the different parts of a stream it was mentioned that the second part is the set of intermediate operations—plural. As this implies, there can be more than one intermediate operation used to process the data. For example, let's suppose that besides filtering items that don't begin with a particular prefix, we also want to transform the data so that a lower-case version of each string is what's stored in the returned collection. In that case, we can just add another intermediate operation to the stream, in this case one that will convert each item into some other value. The best choice for this is the map() method defined in Stream that accepts a parameter and returns a value that's derived from the parameter. In this case, for each String that's processed we want to generate a lower-case equivalent, so we can use a stream like the one shown in Listing 5-26.

Listing 5-26. A Stream Example That Contains Two Intermediate Operations

```
List<String> filteredList =
        myItems.stream()
        .filter(item -> item.startsWith(prefix))
        .map(item -> item.toLowerCase())
        .collect(Collectors.toList());
```

This technique is referred to as "pipelining" and in this case the pipeline is a set of operations that represents a two-stage pipe through which data flows. Conceptually it's very similar to the pipelining support on Linux systems, where data can be passed through a series of commands that perform the same kinds of filtering and transformation that we've seen here. Note that the syntax for pipelining is simplified by the fact that the intermediate operation methods defined in Stream return a reference to a Stream, allowing us to use the builder design pattern syntax, where we "chain" successive calls to the methods in a single class, which in this case is Stream. For example, in the filtering sample just shown the filter() method returns a Stream and the map() method of that returned object is invoked, and so on. This is an important point to keep in mind because at first glance the syntax appears very different from traditional Java code, but in reality it's mostly a combination of the same syntactic elements that Java has always supported—with the obvious exception of the lambda expression embedded in the map() call.

Some Other Intermediate Operation Methods

We've only used two of the intermediate operation methods defined in Stream, but there are many others defined, and some of the most obviously useful ones are listed and described in Table 5-7.

Table 5-7. Some Additional Intermediate Operation Methods Defined in Stream

Method	Description
distinct()	Returns a stream consisting of only the distinct items as determined by toString().
limit(int n)	Returns a stream consisting of only the first "n" elements corresponding to the int parameter value.
skip(int n)	Returns a stream consisting of all elements except the first "n" ones.
sort()	Returns a stream that generates the elements in their natural sort order.

One useful aspect of the API documentation is that it describes the type of operation each method represents with comments such as "This is an intermediate operation." In the case of limit(), for example, the documentation indicates that "This is a short-circuiting stateful intermediate operation." We've already defined what it means to be an intermediate operation, but what about "short-circuiting" and "stateful"? A short-circuiting operation is one that may be able to stop processing before all elements in the data source have been encountered. In this case, for example, the limit() is, by definition, only going to process the first "n" elements that it receives from the preceding stage in the stream. If, for example, your data source is a collection containing 1,000 elements but you include a limit(10) stage, only the first 10 elements will ever be retrieved from the data source and no processing will occur for the others. A stateful operation is just what its name implies: when it processes a given element it may contain and use state information from previously encountered elements. In the case of the distinct() method, for example, the state must necessarily keep track of what values it has already encountered in order to filter out the duplicates that occur, and as expected, reviewing the API documentation for distinct() identifies it as a stateful operation. Another aspect to be aware of is that a stateful operation may need to process the entire collection in order to ensure that it produces the correct results. In the case of sort(), for example, it's impossible to know the sequence in which the elements should be forwarded until all elements have been examined. The significance of this to your application is that a stream containing stateful operations may require more memory—perhaps significantly more memory—than a stream without them.

Terminal Operations

In contrast to intermediate operations, a stream can only contain a single terminal operation that determines what output the stream generates. In the earlier example we used the collection() operation to have the elements placed in a collection, but other methods are also available. In fact, a collection is just one of the types of output that can be generated by a terminal operation, with the specific type determined by what kind of operation is requested. For example, as its name implies, the toArray() operator returns an array containing the elements processed by the stream. Another example is the anyMatch() terminal operation, which checks to see if any of the elements processed meet some criteria, returning a boolean value of true if at least one does or false if none does as shown here.

```
boolean foundMatch = myItems.stream().anyMatch(s -> s.equals("Hello"));
```

This example assumed that myItems is a collection of String values and will assign true to foundMatch if at least one of them equals "Hello." Similarly, the Stream class also defined allMatch() and noneMatch() methods that return true if all or none of the items matches the specified Predicate. Contrast this single line of code with the code you'd create without the use of streams and it becomes apparent how much work can be accomplished with a small amount of code using streams.

Another point is shown by what doesn't appear in this example: specifically, notice that there is no intermediate operation. Instead, there's only a data source and a terminal operation, with no filtering or transformation. There's no restriction that prevents you from including intermediate operations, but there's also no requirement that you do so, and as shown in this example streams can be very useful even when intermediate operations aren't needed or used.

Table 5-8 lists some other terminal operators, their return types, and a description of their function.

Table 5-8. *Some Additional Intermediate Operation Methods Defined in* Stream

Method	Return Type	Description
min()	Optional<T>	Returns the minimum element from the stream as defined by a supplied Comparator.
max()	Optional<T>	Returns the maximum element from the stream as defined by a supplied Comparator.
findFirst()	Optional<T>	Returns the first element produced by the stream.
count()	long	Returns the total number of elements processed by the stream.
forEach()	void	Returns nothing; performs some function on each element in the stream.

Note that the forEach() method described earlier arguably represents one of the more useful methods because it allows you to define code that's executed for each instance processed by the stream. For example, to send the text representation of each object to standard output you could use code like the following:

```
myItems.stream().forEach(t -> System.out.println(t));
```

It's also worth noting the use of the Optional interface as the return type for those terminal operations that may or may not actually return a result. This ensures that those methods will never return a null value, but will instead return an Optional wrapper for whatever is returned. Indeed, a number of different features including lambda expressions, streams, the Optional interface, and generics all work together to make Java code easier to write and more reliable.

Parallel Streams

Earlier in the section titled, "Streams API", it was mentioned that one of the big advantages of the Streams API is that it allows you to take advantage of your system's multitasking capabilities without any effort on your part. In other words, the system can allocate multiple threads that result in multiple elements being processed by the pipeline simultaneously or nearly so, depending upon your system's capabilities and resources. The default behavior is for all processing to be done on a single thread, namely, the thread that executes the stream code, but to request that multiprocessing support be used you simply call the parallelStream() method defined in Collection instead of stream(). Even if your system does support multitasking there are at least a couple of reasons that you may not want a stream to use parallel processing, which is why it's optional for you to request it. First, even if additional threads are available you may not want them assigned to handling the stream processing. Second, due to the overhead associated with multitasking, a stream that processes a small amount of data may actually run *slower* when you specify parallelStream() than it would if you had instead used stream(). That's due to the overhead associated with multitasking and the synchronization associated with more than one thread accessing and updating the same object or set of objects, so you should only use parallelStream() if you have a large volume of data and you need the performance gains that can come from processing that data using more than one thread.

Summary

In this chapter, we've examined several important topics related to collections:

- Why they're needed
- The history of Java's collection API
- How the List, Set, and Map interfaces and their implementations work
- Some general guidelines for using collection objects
- The Streams API introduced in Java 8

■ ■ ■

CHAPTER 6

Using Layout Managers

In Java, you can use the `java.awt.Container` class and its subclasses to display groups of Swing components. For example, you might use a `JPanel` to display a related set of buttons or add components to a `JFrame`. *Layout managers* are classes that control the size and location of each component that's added to a container, and in most cases a layout manager is also responsible for determining the sizes returned from the container's `getMinimumSize()`, `getPreferredSize()`, and `getMaximumSize()` methods. Layout managers are important because they simplify the task of positioning and sizing components and because they allow you to create flexible user interfaces.

Java provides a number of layout managers that you should be familiar with, and each one has advantages and disadvantages. Some are easy to use but provide limited flexibility, and others are flexible but also much more difficult to use. When none of the layout managers provided with Java suits your needs, you can easily create your own, but it's not often necessary to do so if you're familiar with those already available.

In some cases you may be able to create a user interface without being familiar with a layout manager, because every major integrated development environment (IDE)—such as Eclipse, IntelliJ IDEA, and NetBeans—includes a graphical user interface (GUI) builder that allows you to design an interface by dragging and dropping components. Even if you're working with code that was generated using a GUI builder, though, it's sometimes necessary to update the code manually or at least to have some level of understanding of what the code is doing, especially since those GUI builders just generate layout manager code automatically. In other words, UI code that's created using a GUI builder just does what any programmer could accomplish manually. That type of generated code may be appropriate for a simple UI, but it tends to be more difficult to understand and maintain than manually created code, at least code written by someone who's comfortable with Java layout managers. Ultimately, understanding Java's layout managers ends up being helpful regardless of whether you expect to be able to use a GUI builder to construct your UI.

Layout Managers and GUI Construction

To assign a layout manager to a container, you must create an instance of the manager and pass it to the `setLayout()` method defined in `Container`. For example, the following code provides an example of how to create an instance of `BorderLayout` and assign it to a `JPanel`:

```
JPanel panel = new JPanel();
panel.setLayout(new BorderLayout());
```

You can use the overloaded `add()` method defined in `Container` to add a `Component` to a container, which then becomes known as the component's parent container. Similarly, the component added is referred to as a *child component* of the container.

Although `Container` defines a number of different implementations of add(), the following are the two used most often:

- add(Component comp)

- add(Component comp, Object constraints)

In both cases, a reference to the child component is sent to the `Container`. However, the second implementation also includes a constraints parameter that provides information normally used by the layout manager to determine where the component should be placed and/or what its size should be. The specific subclass of `Object` used for this parameter depends upon what type of layout manager is involved. For example, if you're using a `GridBagLayout`, the constraints parameter must be an instance of the `java.awt.GridBagConstraints` class; other layout managers require you to pass a `String` value.

Some layout managers don't support constraints and instead use the order in which components are added to their parent container to determine their positions. When you're using a layout manager that doesn't accept constraints, you should use the simpler add() method shown previously that takes only a single `Component` parameter. Doing so is equivalent to passing a null value for the constraint parameter, which means the following two lines of code are functionally identical to one another:

```
myContainer.add(someComponent);
myContainer.add(someComponent, null);
```

On the other hand, using code like this with a layout manager that does support constraints will cause the layout manager to assign some default constraint information to the component. Therefore, unless you're certain that the default information will produce the results you want, you should always explicitly specify a constraints parameter when using a layout manager that supports constraints.

When add() is called, the container adds the component to a list that it maintains and calls the layout manager's addLayoutComponent() method. That method is passed references to the component being added and to the constraints object specified, and this allows the layout manager to save the constraint information and associate it with the component for later use.

When a layout manager's layoutContainer() method is called, it's passed a reference to the container for which components should be arranged. The layout manager obtains the list of child components by calling the container's getComponents() method and sets the size and location for each visible child using `Component` methods such as setSize(), setLocation(), and setBounds(). If the layout manager supports constraints, it will use them to determine each component's size and location, but if it doesn't, it will arrange the components based on the order in which they occurred in the list returned by getComponents().

To determine what a component's size should be, the layout manager usually also considers the container's size and may call each component's getPreferredSize(), getMinimumSize(), or getMaximumSize() methods. However, the layout manager isn't required to respect the values returned by those methods, and in some cases, Java's layout managers ignore them.

Each container has inset values that indicate the number of pixels around the container's edges that are reserved and can't be used to display child components. Those values are encapsulated by an instance of `java.awt.Insets`, which defines four int values, each corresponding to one side of the container: top, left, bottom, and right. Those values usually describe the width of the border on the sides of the container, but in some cases, additional space may be reserved. For example, `JDialog` and `JFrame` both include a title bar along their top edges; you can reserve that space by setting the top inset value appropriately.

When a layout manager calculates the amount of space available in a container, it subtracts the container's left and right insets from its width and subtracts the top and bottom insets from the height. In addition, when the layout manager arranges the child components, it positions them inside the container's inset area so that none of the components overlays the reserved portion of space around the container's edges.

It's possible to create your own layout manager class, and this chapter describes how to do so, but the Java core classes include a number of layout managers that are flexible enough to meet the needs of most applications. The following list identifies some of the layout manager classes that are provided with Java; the classes are listed in what's arguably their order of complexity starting with the least complex and ending with the most complicated one:

- CardLayout
- FlowLayout
- GridLayout
- BorderLayout
- GridBagLayout
- BoxLayout
- GroupLayout
- SpringLayout

When you create an instance of a Container subclass that's provided with Java (JPanel, JFrame, JDialog, etc.), that object will automatically be assigned a layout manager. Table 6-1 lists some of the classes you might use and also identifies the default layout manager type for each one.

Table 6-1. *Layout Managers Used by Default for Various Component Subclasses*

Component	Default Layout Manager
JPanel	FlowLayout
JFrame (content pane)	BorderLayout
JDialog (content pane)	BorderLayout
JApplet (content pane)	BorderLayout
Box	BoxLayout

This chapter examines the capabilities of the layout managers that are provided with Java and specifically examines the following characteristics of each one:

- How a layout manager instance is constructed
- The constraints that can be specified when adding a child component
- How each child component's size is calculated
- How each child component's position is calculated
- What happens when the container has more or less space than it needs to display its child components
- How the values returned by a container's getMinimumSize(), getPreferredSize(), and getMaximumSize() methods are calculated by the layout manager

CardLayout

CardLayout allows you to add multiple components to a container, and each component is added and displayed in the same location. However, only one of the components is visible at any given time, and you can specify which one that should be by calling the first(), last(), next(), and previous() methods defined in CardLayout. Those methods refer to the components added to the container, and they display the component that was added in the order corresponding to the method name. For example, first() causes the component added first to appear, last() causes the most recently added one to appear, and next() and previous() allow you to iterate through the components in a forward or backward direction. In addition, the show() method allows you to specify that a particular component should be displayed, regardless of the order in which it was added to the container relative to the other components.

The CardLayout class is arguably the least useful of the layout managers included with Java. Prior to the introduction of Swing, CardLayout was envisioned as a way to create a tabbed user interface, but the JTabbedPane provides a much better mechanism for doing so. However, CardLayout may still be useful in some cases, such as when constructing a Windows-style "wizard" interface that displays a series of panels one at a time.

Constructing a CardLayout

You can specify horizontal and vertical gap values when you create a new instance of CardLayout, and these gaps will be placed around the edges of the component displayed in the container. Specifically, the horizontal gap appears on the left and right sides of the component, and the vertical gap appears at the top and bottom of the component to separate it from the edge of the container. Listing 6-1 shows a simple example of how to use CardLayout.

Listing 6-1. Simple CardLayout Test

```
import java.awt.*;
import javax.swing.*;

public class CardTest extends JFrame {

  private CardLayout layout;

  public static void main(String[] args) {
    CardTest ct = new CardTest();
    ct.setDefaultCloseOperation(JFrame.EXIT_ON_CLOSE);
    ct.displayTab("Green Tab");
    ct.setSize(400, 300);
    ct.setVisible(true);
  }

  public CardTest() {
    JPanel tab;
    Container pane = getContentPane();
    layout = new CardLayout();
    pane.setLayout(layout);
    tab = new JPanel();
    tab.setBackground(Color.red);
    pane.add(tab, "Red Tab");
    tab = new JPanel();
```

```
    tab.setBackground(Color.green);
    pane.add(tab, "Green Tab");
    tab = new JPanel();
    tab.setBackground(Color.blue);
    pane.add(tab, "Blue Tab");
  }
  public void displayTab(String name) {
    layout.show(this.getContentPane(), name);
  }

}
```

Child Component Sizes

Only a single child component is ever visible when a CardLayout is used, and that component's size is set to the container's available display area. The available display area is defined as the container's dimensions minus its insets and any horizontal and vertical gaps that should be placed around the edges of the child components.

Child Component Locations

The single visible child component always fills the entire available display area of the parent container, so its location is implicitly defined to be the upper-left corner of the parent.

Resizing Behavior

The size of the component displayed is set to the container's available display area. If the container's size increases or decreases, a corresponding change occurs to the size of the displayed component.

Container Size

CardLayout identifies the preferred size of its container as the largest preferred width and largest preferred height of any child component. Similarly, the minimum size is equal to the largest minimum width and height values returned by any of the container's child components. The maximum size is effectively set to infinity, since CardLayout's maximumLayoutSize() method returns Integer.MAX_VALUE for both the maximum width and maximum height, where Integer.MAX_VALUE is a constant that represents the largest possible integer (in other words, int or Integer) value.

FlowLayout

FlowLayout arranges the components in rows from left-to-right and top-to-bottom order based on the order in which they were added to the container, allowing each component to occupy as much or as little space as it needs. This layout manager is useful when you want to create a collection of adjacent components that are all allowed to be displayed using their default sizes.

Constructing a FlowLayout

When creating a new FlowLayout instance, you can specify the alignment that should be used when positioning the child components. The alignment value should correspond to one of the constants defined in FlowLayout; specifically, this is LEFT, CENTER, or RIGHT. As mentioned previously, FlowLayout arranges components in rows, and the alignment specifies the alignment of the rows. For example, if you create a FlowLayout that's left aligned, the components in each row will appear next to the left edge of the container.

The FlowLayout constructors allow you to specify the horizontal and vertical gaps that should appear between components, and if you use a constructor that doesn't accept these values, they both default to 5. Note that unlike the gaps used by some other layout managers, the gaps generated by a FlowLayout appear not only between adjacent components but also between components and the edge of the container.

To construct a FlowLayout that's right aligned and uses a horizontal gap of 10 pixels and vertical gap of 5 pixels between components, you can use the following code:

```
FlowLayout fl = new FlowLayout(FlowLayout.RIGHT, 10, 5);
```

Constraints

FlowLayout doesn't use any constraints to determine a component's location or size, and you should use the simple add(Component) method when adding components to a FlowLayout-managed container.

Child Component Sizes

Components managed by a FlowLayout are always set to their preferred size (both width and height), regardless of the size of the parent container.

Child Component Locations

Components added to a FlowLayout-managed container are displayed in rows in left-to-right and top-to-bottom order based on when each component was added to the container relative to the others. For example, the first component appears at the top of the container to the left of other components in the row.

A component's specific location depends upon three factors: the alignment value used by the FlowLayout, the size of the component, and the size of the other components that were added to the layout before it. A FlowLayout instance includes as many components as it can on each row until the width of the row would exceed the size of the container. In Figure 6-1, five components have been added to a container that uses a FlowLayout.

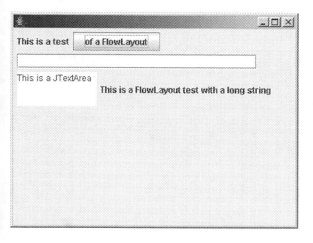

Figure 6-1. *An example of the default left alignment used by* FlowLayout

Listing 6-2 shows the code you can use to create this display.

Listing 6-2. FlowLayout Behavior

```
import java.awt.*;
import javax.swing.*;

public class FlowTest extends JFrame {

  public static void main(String[] args) {
    FlowTest ft = new FlowTest();
    ft.setDefaultCloseOperation(JFrame.EXIT_ON_CLOSE);
    ft.setSize(400, 300);
    ft.setVisible(true);
  }

  public FlowTest() {
    super();
    Container pane = getContentPane();
    pane.setLayout(new FlowLayout(FlowLayout.LEFT));
    pane.add(new JLabel("This is a test"));
    pane.add(new JButton("of a FlowLayout"));
    pane.add(new JTextField(30));
    pane.add(new JTextArea("This is a JTextArea", 3, 10));
    pane.add(new JLabel("This is a FlowLayout test with a long string"));
  }
}
```

In this case, the container is sufficiently wide to allow the first two components to be placed on the first row. However, the third component appears on the next row by itself, and the fourth and fifth components appear together on another row. The first row appears at the top of the container, and each subsequent row occurs immediately below the previous one, with the height of a row determined by the height of the tallest component in that row. Each component within a row is centered vertically within the row, as shown in Figure 6-1.

213

A component's horizontal position within a row is determined partly by when it was added to the container and is affected by the alignment value used by the FlowLayout instance. In Figure 6-1, the components are left aligned, but in Figure 6-2 and Figure 6-3 you can see the displays that are generated when the components are right aligned and center aligned, respectively.

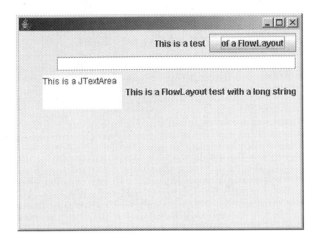

Figure 6-2. An example of how components appear when right aligned with FlowLayout

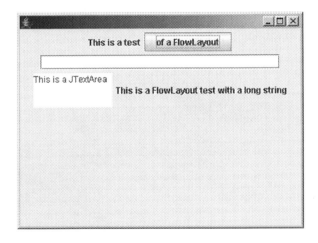

Figure 6-3. An example of how components appear when center aligned with FlowLayout

Resizing Behavior

Reducing the width of a container managed by a FlowLayout causes the rows to shrink in size, which may cause some components to be moved to a new or different row. If you reduce the width of the frame further, then portions of the wider components begin to disappear, as shown in Figure 6-4.

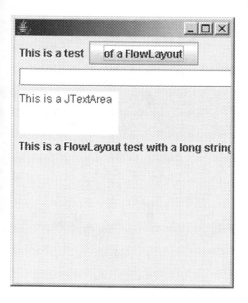

Figure 6-4. *FlowLayout uses components' preferred widths even when there isn't enough horizontal room to display the entire component*

Similarly, if you reduce the frame's vertical size so that there's not enough vertical space to display all rows, some of the components will become partially or completely inaccessible (see Figure 6-5).

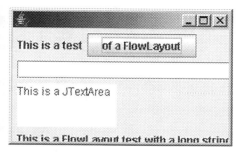

Figure 6-5. *FlowLayout uses components' preferred heights even when there isn't enough room to display the entire component*

Container Size

When calculating the preferred and minimum size values for a container, FlowLayout can't make any assumptions about the width of the container or about how many rows of components should be created. Instead, the size values are calculated so the container will be wide enough to contain all child components in a single row. For example, the preferred width value returned by a FlowLayout is determined by adding three values.

- The left and right inset values of the container

- The amount of space needed to provide horizontal gaps

- The sum of all child components' preferred widths

In other words, a FlowLayout's preferred width is the amount of horizontal space needed to display all its child components from end to end on a single row using their preferred sizes.

To determine the container's preferred height, FlowLayout first identifies the preferred height of the tallest component in the container. The container's preferred height is then calculated as the sum of the largest component height, the number of pixels needed to provide vertical gaps at the top and bottom edges of the container, and the container's top and bottom inset values.

The value returned for a container's minimum size by a FlowLayout is calculated in essentially the same way as the preferred size but by using the minimum sizes of the components in the container instead of their preferred sizes.

GridLayout

The GridLayout layout manager divides the available space into a grid of cells, evenly allocating the space among all the cells in the grid and placing one component in each cell. For example, in Listing 6-3, four buttons are added to a container that uses a GridLayout.

Listing 6-3. Sample GridLayout Application

```java
import java.awt.*;
import javax.swing.*;

public class GridSizeTest extends JFrame {

  public static void main(String[] args) {
    GridSizeTest gst = new GridSizeTest();
    gst.setDefaultCloseOperation(JFrame.EXIT_ON_CLOSE);
    gst.pack();
    gst.setVisible(true);
  }

  public GridSizeTest() {
    Container pane = getContentPane();
    pane.setLayout(new GridLayout(2, 2));
    JButton button = new JButton("First");
    pane.add(button);
    button = new JButton("Second with a very long name");
    pane.add(button);
    button = new JButton("Hi");
    button.setFont(new Font("Courier", Font.PLAIN, 36));
    pane.add(button);
    button = new JButton("There");
    pane.add(button);
  }

}
```

When this code is compiled and executed, it produces a display like the one shown in Figure 6-6. Notice that all the buttons are allocated the same amount of space, even though one button's label is wider than the others and another has a label that's much taller than the rest.

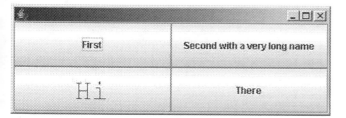

Figure 6-6. *GridLayout distributes both horizontal and vertical space evenly to the components regardless of their preferred sizes*

As this example illustrates, GridLayout is useful when some rectangular portion of your interface contains adjacent components that should all be assigned the same size and when the amount of space between those components is consistent. For instance, you might use a GridLayout to create a panel that contains a row of buttons that are all the same size and that have the same amount of space between one another.

Constructing a GridLayout

When you create an instance of GridLayout, you normally will specify the number of rows and columns that you want it to provide, and you may choose to specify the amount of horizontal and vertical space that should appear between adjacent components. However, you can choose to set any of these values after construction using the setRows(), setColumns(), setHgap(), and setVgap() methods. Listing 6-4 shows an example of creating a GridLayout and assigning it to a container. This application parses the command-line parameters to determine how many rows and columns should be available, creates 20 JButton instances, and adds each button to the container.

Listing 6-4. Creating Rows of Buttons

```
import java.awt.*;
import javax.swing.*;

public class GridTest extends JFrame {

  public static void main(String[] args) {
    if (args.length < 2) {
      System.out.println("You must enter a row count and a column count");
      return;
    }
    int rows = Integer.parseInt(args[0]);
    int cols = Integer.parseInt(args[1]);
    GridTest gt = new GridTest(rows, cols);
    gt.setDefaultCloseOperation(JFrame.EXIT_ON_CLOSE);
    gt.pack();
    gt.setVisible(true);
  }

  public GridTest(int rows, int cols) {
    Container pane = getContentPane();
    pane.setLayout(new GridLayout(rows, cols));
    for (int i = 0; i < 20; i++) {
```

```
        JButton button = new JButton(Integer.toString(i + 1));
        pane.add(button);
    }
  }

}
```

When you create a GridLayout, you can specify a value of 0 for either the row count or the column count, but not both. If you set the number of rows to 0, GridLayout creates as many rows as it needs to display all the components using the specified number of columns. For example, Figure 6-7 illustrates what will be displayed when 0 is specified for the number of rows and 3 for the number of columns.

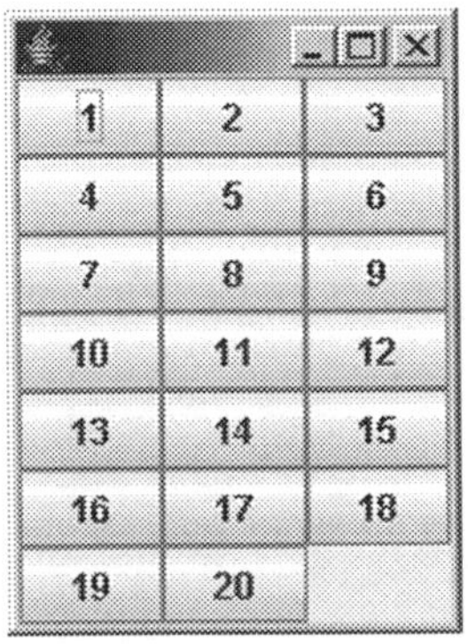

Figure 6-7. *You can force GridLayout to use a specific number of columns by specifying a column count but no row count*

Similarly, if you set the number of columns to 0, the layout manager creates as many columns as it needs to display the child components using the specified number of rows. In Figure 6-8, the column count was set to 0 and the row count to 3.

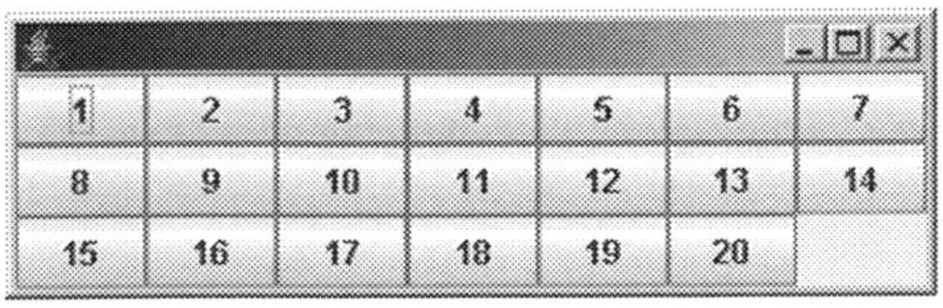

Figure 6-8. *You can force GridLayout to use a specific number of rows by specifying a row count but no column count*

It's important to understand that the row and column counts you specify are considered suggestions, and the GridLayout may not actually create the number you request. In most cases it will, but some exceptions exist. For example, if you specify a nonzero value for both the row and column count, the column count is effectively ignored, and the layout manager creates as many columns as it needs using the requested number of rows. In other words, specifying both a row and column count produces the same result as specifying 0 for the column count.

If you specify a value of 3 for the number of rows and 100 for the number of columns using the GridTest class, the result is the same as shown in Figure 6-8 for zero columns and three rows. This behavior might seem undesirable, but it happens this way for a reason. Specifically, it allows the layout manager to handle cases where the number of components in the container is greater than the product of the row count by the column count. For example, if you specify a row count of 2 and a column count of 2 but then proceed to add six components to the container, GridLayout simply adds another column to the grid so it can display all six components.

As you can see, the number of rows and columns created by a GridLayout isn't necessarily equal to the number you request. In fact, the number actually created is calculated with a simple formula that uses the number of child components in the container (which I'll call childComponentCount), the requested number of rows (requestedRows), and the requested number of columns (requestedColumns). If the requested number of rows is nonzero, the GridLayout determines the number of rows and columns using the following equations:

```
actualRows = requestedRows
actualColumns = (childComponentCount + requestedRows - 1) / requestedRows
```

Note that this formula can lead to a situation where more rows are created than are needed to display all the components. When that happens, an empty space will appear at the bottom of the container that represents the unused rows. Since that's not usually the desired behavior, you should be aware of this possibility when deciding how many rows to request when creating a GridLayout. On the other hand, if the requested number of rows (requestedRows) is zero, then GridLayout uses the following equations instead of the ones shown previously:

```
actualColumns = requestedColumns
actualRows = (childComponentCount + requestedColumns - 1) / requestedColumns
```

In most cases, these equations result in the GridLayout creating the number of rows and columns you specified, but as you've seen, that's not always the case.

Constraints

GridLayout doesn't use any constraints to determine a component's location or size, and you should use the add(Component) method when adding components to a GridLayout-managed container.

Child Component Sizes

Each cell in a GridLayout is assigned the same width and height, and each child component is compressed or stretched to fill a single cell. The specific height and width values for the cells are determined by calculating the available display area and dividing the width by the actual column count and the height by the actual row count. The available display area is defined as the dimensions of the container minus its insets and any space needed for the horizontal and vertical component gaps, as shown in the following equations:

```
availableWidth = totalWidth - leftInset -
                 rightInset - ((actualColumns - 1) * horizontalGap)
componentWidth = availableWidth / actualColumns
```

For example, if a component has a width of 400, has right and left insets of 5, has a horizontal gap value of 10 between the components in a row, and contains four columns, the width of each component will be the following:

```
availableWidth = 400 - 5 - 5 - ((4 - 1) * 10) = 400 - 10 - 30 = 360
componentWidth = 360 / 4 = 90 pixels
```

In this case, every component in the container will be 90 pixels wide, and a similar equation calculates the components' heights. Note that GridLayout doesn't respect the values returned by a component's getMinimumSize() and getMaximumSize() methods. In other words, a GridLayout may cause a component to be smaller than its "minimum" size or larger than its "maximum" size. You can see an example of this behavior by running the GridTest application defined earlier and resizing the frame that contains the buttons. As the frame's dimensions change, the button sizes will be increased or decreased to fill the available display area.

Child Component Locations

GridLayout divides the container into a grid using the actual number of rows and columns that it calculates is needed. As components are added to the container, they're placed in the grid from left to right and from top to bottom based on when they were added to the container relative to one another. For example, the first component added to the container appears in the upper-left corner of the screen, and the second one appears to the right of the first (if the grid provides at least two columns). That continues until an entire row in the grid has been filled. After that, adding another component will cause it to appear in the second row in the first column, the next one appears in the second row and second column, and so on.

Resizing Behavior

Since GridLayout forces all child components to fit within the container's display area, the component sizes may become very small if the container is allocated less space than it requests through its getPreferredSize() method. For example, Figure 6-9 illustrates what happens when the GridTest application runs and its window's height is reduced. In this case, the button labels have become vertically very small and are almost unreadable, illustrating the point made earlier that GridLayout doesn't respect a component's minimum size.

Figure 6-9. *GridLayout will shrink components if necessary to make them fit within the available space*

Similarly, if a GridLayout-managed container is made larger than its requested size, the components within the container will be made sufficiently large to fill the container, regardless of their maximum size.

Container Size

GridLayout calculates the size of its associated container by examining the dimensions of each child component within the container and recording the largest width and height values it finds. For example, when a GridLayout is asked for the container's preferred size, it calls getPreferredSize() for each child component and records the largest preferred height value returned by a component. That maximum preferred component height is then multiplied by the number of rows to be displayed and added to the container's top and bottom insets, along with the number of pixels needed to provide the vertical spacing between component rows. A similar calculation occurs for the container's width, as follows:

```
containerHeight = (largestComponentHeight * actualRows) +
                  ((actualRows - 1) * verticalGap) +
                  (containerTopInset + containerBottomInset)
```

```
containerWidth = (largestComponentWidth * actualColumns) +
                 ((actualColumns - 1) * horizontalGap) +
                 (containerLeftInset + containerRightInset)
```

The same equation calculates a container's minimum size, but the largestComponentWidth and largestComponentHeight values are obtained by calling getMinimumSize() instead of getPreferredSize().

BorderLayout

BorderLayout divides the container into five areas, and you can add a component to each area. The five regions correspond to the top, left, bottom, and right sides of the container, along with one in the center, as illustrated in Figure 6-10.

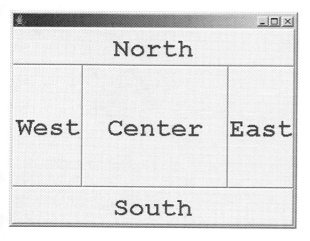

Figure 6-10. *BorderLayout divides the container into five areas: center, top ("north"), left ("west"), right ("east"), and bottom ("south")*

Listing 6-5 shows the code that produced this display. As the code and the button labels illustrate, each of the five areas is associated with a constant value defined in BorderLayout: NORTH, SOUTH, EAST, WEST, and CENTER for the top, bottom, right, left, and center regions, respectively.

Listing 6-5. A BorderLayout Example

```
import java.awt.*;
import javax.swing.*;
import javax.swing.border.BevelBorder;

public class BorderSample extends JFrame {

  public static void main(String[] args) {
    BorderSample bs = new BorderSample();
    bs.setDefaultCloseOperation(JFrame.EXIT_ON_CLOSE);
    Container pane = bs.getContentPane();
    pane.setLayout(new BorderLayout());
    Font f = new Font("Courier", Font.BOLD, 36);
```

```
    JLabel label = new JLabel("North", JLabel.CENTER);
    label.setFont(f);
    label.setBorder(BorderFactory.createBevelBorder(BevelBorder.RAISED));
    pane.add(label, BorderLayout.NORTH);
    label = new JLabel("South", JLabel.CENTER);
    label.setFont(f);
    label.setBorder(BorderFactory.createBevelBorder(BevelBorder.RAISED));
    pane.add(label, BorderLayout.SOUTH);
    label = new JLabel("East", JLabel.CENTER);
    label.setFont(f);
    label.setBorder(BorderFactory.createBevelBorder(BevelBorder.RAISED));
    pane.add(label, BorderLayout.EAST);
    label = new JLabel("West", JLabel.CENTER);
    label.setFont(f);
    label.setBorder(BorderFactory.createBevelBorder(BevelBorder.RAISED));
    pane.add(label, BorderLayout.WEST);
    label = new JLabel("Center", JLabel.CENTER);
    label.setFont(f);
    label.setBorder(BorderFactory.createBevelBorder(BevelBorder.RAISED));
    pane.add(label, BorderLayout.CENTER);
    bs.setSize(400, 300);
    bs.setVisible(true);
  }

}
```

Note that although five regions are available within a BorderLayout, it's not necessary to add a component to each one. Leaving an area empty doesn't affect the BorderLayout's behavior, but it may result in the CENTER component being made larger than it would have been otherwise.

Constructing a BorderLayout

The only parameters you're allowed to pass to a BorderLayout constructor are the horizontal and vertical gaps used to separate adjacent components. The vertical gap is inserted below the NORTH component and above the SOUTH component, and the horizontal gap appears to the right of the WEST component and to the left of the EAST component. If you use the constructor that doesn't accept any parameters, no gaps are inserted.

Constraints

When adding a component to a container that's using a BorderLayout, you should supply a constraint that identifies which area should contain the component. The constraint should be a reference to one of five constants defined in BorderLayout: NORTH, SOUTH, EAST, WEST, or CENTER. The following code is an example of adding a component to a container that uses a BorderLayout, where a JLabel instance is added to the NORTH (top) area of the container:

```
myContainer.add(new JLabel("Hello"), BorderLayout.NORTH);
```

You can use the simpler form of add() that accepts only a single Component parameter with no constraints, in which case the component will be added as if you had specified the CENTER area. However, since this form of add() doesn't explicitly identify which area the component is added to and may be confusing to someone reading your code, you should explicitly specify CENTER instead.

The last component you add to a region is the only one that will be displayed, so if you add a component and specify an area that's already occupied, the component that was previously added will not appear. However, you'll normally add a single component to a particular region, so you'll usually only encounter this behavior with code that was written incorrectly.

Child Component Sizes

The size assigned to a child component by BorderLayout depends upon a number of factors, including the following: the component's preferred size, the region of the container in which the component is displayed, the preferred size of the other components within the container, and the size of the container:

- **North component**: The component displayed in the NORTH area is assigned a height equal to its preferred height and a width equal to the available width of the container. The available width is defined as the container's total width minus its right and left inset values.

- **South component**: Like the NORTH component, the component displayed in the SOUTH area is assigned a height equal to its preferred height and a width equal to the available width of the container.

- **East component**: The component displayed in the EAST area is assigned a width equal to its preferred width and a height equal to the available height of the container minus the vertical space occupied by the NORTH and SOUTH components. The available height of the container is defined as the container's total height minus its top and bottom inset values.

- **West component**: Like the EAST component, the component displayed in the WEST area is assigned a width equal to its preferred width. Its height is set to the available height of the container minus the vertical space occupied by the NORTH and SOUTH components.

- **Center component**: The CENTER component is allocated any space that's left over inside the container after the other four components have been allocated space as described previously. As a result, the CENTER component shrinks and expands to fill the remaining area, so its size depends upon the size of the container and how much of that space is taken up by the other components in the container.

Child Component Locations

The location of each child component managed by BorderLayout is explicitly identified when it's added to the container. That is, the NORTH component appears at the top of the container, the SOUTH component at the bottom, the EAST component on the right, and the WEST component on the left. The CENTER component occupies any remaining area in the center of the container.

Resizing Behavior

When BorderLayout manages a container's components, reducing the container's vertical size causes the EAST, CENTER, and WEST components to become "shorter" (smaller vertically) until there's only enough vertical space to display the NORTH and SOUTH components. Reducing the container's height so that it's smaller than the combined height of the NORTH and SOUTH components (which are always displayed using their preferred height values) causes those two components to overlap one another, as shown in Figure 6-11.

Figure 6-11. *BorderLayout vertically resizes the NORTH and SOUTH components as the container height changes*

Reducing the width of a container managed by a BorderLayout initially causes the widths of the NORTH, CENTER, and SOUTH components to become smaller until the CENTER component eventually disappears completely. At that point, reducing the container's width further causes the EAST and WEST components to overlap, as shown in Figure 6-12.

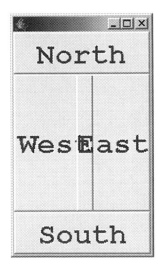

Figure 6-12. *BorderLayout horizontally resizes the EAST and WEST components as the container height changes*

Increasing the size of a BorderLayout-managed container causes the CENTER component to become larger and can increase the widths of the NORTH and SOUTH components and the heights of the EAST and WEST components.

Container Size

The minimum size defined for a container managed by a BorderLayout is calculated by calling the getMinimumSize() method for all components in the container. The minimum widths of the WEST, CENTER, and EAST components are added together (if they're present) along with the value needed to create a horizontal gap, and that sum is treated as a single value. The value is then compared to the minimum width of the NORTH component and the minimum width of the SOUTH component, and the largest value of the three is chosen as the container's minimum width. The minimum height of the container is selected using a similar approach, but the sequence of steps is slightly different. The minimum heights of the WEST, CENTER, and EAST components are compared, and the largest of those three values is selected. That value is then added to the minimum height of the NORTH and SOUTH components along with the space needed for vertical gaps, and that value is used as the container's minimum height.

The preferred size of a BorderLayout-managed container is calculated using the same approach described previously, except that the getPreferredSize() method is called for each component instead of getMinimumSize().

GridBagLayout

GridBagLayout is by far the most flexible layout manager that's included with Java, but it doesn't enjoy widespread popularity among Java programmers because of its complexity and its sometimes nonintuitive behavior. However, GridBagLayout is often the only layout manager flexible enough to arrange components in a particular manner and is used frequently in spite of the difficulty involved.

As its name implies, GridBagLayout bears some similarity to GridLayout but only at a superficial level. Both divide the container's available display area into a grid of cells, but beyond that, GridBagLayout and GridLayout don't have much in common. Some of the important differences between them include the following:

- When using a GridLayout, a component's position within the grid is determined by the order in which it's added to the container relative to other components. With a GridBagLayout, you can explicitly define the component's location within the grid.

- Each component in a GridLayout occupies exactly one cell in the grid, but components managed by a GridBagLayout can span multiple rows and/or columns within the grid.

- GridLayout assigns each row the same height and each column the same width, which causes every cell in the grid to have the same dimensions. In contrast, GridBagLayout allows each row to have a separate height and every column its own width, so every cell in the grid can theoretically have a unique size.

- GridLayout doesn't support any constraints, while GridBagLayout allows you to specify a different set of constraint values for each component; those constraints allow you to customize the component's size and position within the grid.

If you're not already familiar with it, you may be wondering why GridBagLayout is considered so difficult to use by many Java programmers. Some of the possible reasons are as follows:

- **The number of constraints and their interactions**: GridBagConstraints encapsulates 11 constraint values, and each child component is assigned its own instance of GridBagConstraints. Although no single constraint is particularly difficult to understand, the way in which the constraints interact with one another and with the constraints of other components is somewhat complex.

- **Row height and column width**: GridBagLayout's ability to provide a separate height for each row and width for each column is one of its primary advantages, but that capability also adds a great deal of complexity to its use. In some cases, especially with complex layouts containing many components, it can be difficult to predict what a component's size or position will be, and it's easy to make mistakes that produce results that are different from what you expected.

- **Component location**: When you see a component inside a GridLayout, it's usually easy to identify which cell the component occupies without examining the source code. That's because all cells (and components) are the same size and because the cells are aligned with one another. In the case of a GridBagLayout, identifying which cell or cells a component occupies can be difficult, since cell widths and heights can vary and since a component can span multiple cells.

- **Component size**: Most other layout managers have simple rules that determine the size that a component is set to, but GridBagLayout provides much greater flexibility in this area, as well as more complexity.

Figure 6-13 provides a simple example of the type of problem that can be difficult to diagnose when using GridBagLayout. In this case, a frame was created, and a JLabel and a JTextField were added to it. However, a large gap exists between the label and text field, and since JLabel instances are transparent by default, there's no indication of whether the gap is because of the label's size or exists for some other reason. Most of the time, a component includes a border that's drawn around its edges, and that border provides you with an easy way to estimate the component's size. However, some frequently used components such as JLabel and JPanel don't include a border by default, and it can be more difficult to determine their sizes visually.

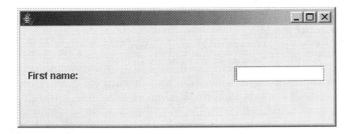

Figure 6-13. *Even if you're familiar with* GridBagLayout, *it's not always obvious why it doesn't produce the expected results*

When you're designing a user interface using a GridBagLayout, this type of problem can cause a great deal of frustration. However, you can modify your code in some simple ways so it provides you with visual feedback on the size of your components and/or the cells that they occupy. For example, when working with a JLabel or JPanel, it can be helpful to temporarily add a border or set the component's background color so you can easily identify its edges. The following code sets the background color for the JLabel used in the previous example, and Figure 6-14 shows how this is reflected in the interface:

```
label.setBackground(Color.pink);
label.setOpaque(true);
```

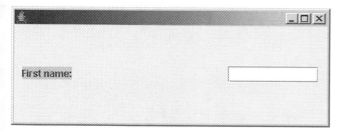

Figure 6-14. *Temporarily changing a component's background color is one way to determine what portion of a panel* GridBagLayout *has allocated to it*

In this case, the color was set to green, but you can use any color that contrasts with the background color of the parent container. Note also that it was necessary to call the setOpaque() method, since a JLabel normally has a transparent background. Although setting the label's background color did establish that the label itself doesn't occupy the space between its text and the JTextField, it's still not clear why such a large gap appears between the two components.

Another way to provide helpful visual information is to create a JPanel subclass that overrides the paintComponent() method and uses information provided by GridBagLayout to draw the borders of each cell within the grid. The getLayoutDimensions() method returns a two-dimensional array of integer values that identifies the height of each row and width of each column in the grid. Listing 6-6 shows how this affects the interface when this technique is used.

Listing 6-6. A Class That Puts Borders Around Layout Cells

```java
import java.awt.*;
import javax.swing.*;

public class GridBagCellPanel extends JPanel {

  public void paintComponent(Graphics g) {
    super.paintComponent(g);
    LayoutManager manager = getLayout();
    if ((manager != null) && (manager instanceof GridBagLayout)) {
      GridBagLayout layout = (GridBagLayout)manager;
      g.setColor(getForeground());
      Point p = layout.getLayoutOrigin();
      int[][] sizes = layout.getLayoutDimensions();
      int[] colWidths = sizes[0];
      int[] rowHeights = sizes[1];
      int width, height;
      int xpos = p.x;
      int ypos;
      for (int x = 0; x < colWidths.length; x++) {
        ypos = p.y;
        width = colWidths[x];
        for (int y = 0; y < rowHeights.length; y++) {
          height = rowHeights[y];
          g.drawRect(xpos, ypos, width - 1, height - 1);
          g.drawRect(xpos + 1, ypos + 1, width - 3,
              height - 3);
```

```
        ypos += height;
      }
      xpos += width;
    }
  }
}

}
```

If the user interface is added to an instance of the GridBagCellPanel class, a dark border appears around the edge of each cell in the grid, as shown in Figure 6-15. This illustrates that the column containing the label is very large, and the gap exists because the component is positioned on the left side of its cell.

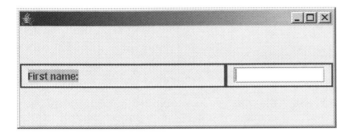

Figure 6-15. *Drawing borders around components makes it apparent how much space a GridBagLayout has allocated to a component's cell*

This example illustrates another important point related to GridBagLayout: a component doesn't necessarily expand to completely fill the cell or cells that it occupies. A component's size is normally set to its preferred or minimum size, and in this case, the component's preferred width is considerably smaller than the width of the cell it occupies. It's important to keep in mind this distinction between a component's actual size and its display area or the area of the container reserved for that component. A component's display area is the rectangular region defined by the cell or cells assigned to the component. In this case, only a single cell was assigned to each component, but as mentioned earlier, a cell can span multiple rows and/or columns.

Constructing a GridBagLayout

GridBagLayout provides only a single, no-argument constructor, so it's very simple to create one.

```
GridBagLayout gbl = new GridBagLayout();
```

Constraints

Each component that's added to a container managed by a GridBagLayout has an associated set of constraint values, and those values are encapsulated by an instance of the GridBagConstraints class.

GridBagConstraints provides two constructors: one that accepts no parameters and another that accepts the 11 constraint values that are supported. Although you can use either constructor, code that passes many parameter values to a constructor can be difficult to understand, even for someone who's familiar with GridBagLayout, so you should avoid using that form. GridBagConstraints represents one of the few cases in Java where it's acceptable to access the fields within an object without using accessor and mutator methods. In fact, because GridBagConstraints doesn't provide accessor or mutator methods for its properties, you must set those properties directly by assigning them values.

```
GridBagConstraints constraints = new GridBagConstraints();
constraints.gridx = 0;
constraints.gridy = 3;
```

When you add a component to a container managed by a GridBagLayout, you can use the add() method that accepts a Component and a constraint's Object, or you can use the simpler form that accepts only a Component reference. However, if you use the simpler form, you must call the setConstraints() method in GridBagLayout to associate the Component with a set of constraint values. For example, suppose you've created the following code:

```
GridBagLayout layout = new GridBagLayout();
setLayout(layout);
GridBagConstraints constraints = new GridBagConstraints();
JButton button = new JButton("Testing");
```

You can add the button to the container after first associating it with the set of constraints, as in the following code:

```
layout.setConstraints(button, constraints);
add(button);
```

Alternatively, you can use the form of the add() method that accepts a parameter representing constraint information:

```
add(button, constraints);
```

Both of these approaches are valid, but the second one is probably somewhat more intuitive for most people and requires slightly less code.

Although you'll typically add more than one component to a container and each component will usually have different constraint values from the others, you can use the same instance of GridBagConstraints for all components. That's because when you add a component to a container managed by a GridBagLayout, the layout manager uses the clone() method in GridBagConstraints to make a "deep copy" of the constraints. In other words, when you add a component, a copy is made of its associated GridBagConstraints object, and that copy is saved by the GridBagLayout for later reference. Therefore, you can use a single GridBagConstraints object repeatedly, since the layout manager uses it just long enough to create a copy of it.

Fields Defined in GridBagConstraints

The following fields are defined in GridBagConstraints, most of which are int values. However, the insets field is a reference to an instance of the java.awt.Insets class, and weightx and weighty are double (floating-point) values.

gridx

This constraint allows you to identify the first/leftmost column within the grid that should be assigned to the component's display area. The first column (the one at the left edge of the container) corresponds to a value of 0, the next column to a value of 1, and so on. For example, to specify that a component should begin in the first column, you can add the following code to your application:

```
GridBagConstraints constraints = new GridBagConstraints();
constraints.gridx = 0;
```

By default, the gridx constraint value is set to GridBagConstraints.RELATIVE, which is discussed in a moment.

gridy

This constraint allows you to identify the first/top row within the grid that should be assigned to the component's display area. The first row (the one at the top edge of the container) corresponds to a value of 0, the next row to a value of 1, and so on. For example, to specify that a component should begin in the third row, you can add the following code to your application:

```
GridBagConstraints constraints = new GridBagConstraints();
constraints.gridy = 2;
```

By default, the gridy constraint value is set to GridBagConstraints.RELATIVE.

Relative Positioning

The two examples shown previously both use absolute position values. However, you can set gridx and/or gridy to the value defined by the RELATIVE constant in GridBagConstraints to indicate that the component should be positioned relative to some other component. If you specify RELATIVE for gridx and an absolute value for gridy, the component you add will be placed at the end of the row identified by the gridy value. For example, Listing 6-7 will create five JButton instances, adding three of them to the second row using relative positioning.

Listing 6-7. Adding Components with a Relative X Position

```
import java.awt.*;
import javax.swing.*;

public class RelativeX {

    public static void main(String[] args) {
        JFrame f = new JFrame();
        f.setDefaultCloseOperation(JFrame.EXIT_ON_CLOSE);
        Container pane = f.getContentPane();
        pane.setLayout(new GridBagLayout());
        GridBagConstraints constraints = new GridBagConstraints();
        constraints.gridy = 0;
        pane.add(new JButton("First row"), constraints);
        constraints.gridx = GridBagConstraints.RELATIVE;
        constraints.gridy = 1;
```

```
    pane.add(new JButton("Second row, first column"), constraints);
    pane.add(new JButton("Second row, second column"), constraints);
    pane.add(new JButton("Second row, third column"), constraints);
    constraints.gridy = 2;
    pane.add(new JButton("Third row"), constraints);
    f.setSize(600, 300);
    f.setVisible(true);
  }

}
```

Figure 6-16 shows the display produced by this program.

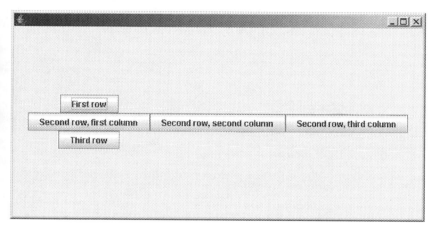

Figure 6-16. *Specifying an absolute Y position and a relative X position causes a component to appear to the right of the one most recently added for the same Y position*

Similarly, specifying an explicit column/gridx value and RELATIVE for the row/gridy value causes components to be added on a top-to-bottom basis to the specified column. For example, Listing 6-8 will create five JButton instances, adding three of them to the second column using relative positioning.

Listing 6-8. Adding Components with a Relative Y Positionimport java.awt.*;

```
import javax.swing.*;

public class RelativeY {

  public static void main(String[] args) {
    JFrame f = new JFrame();
    f.setDefaultCloseOperation(JFrame.EXIT_ON_CLOSE);
    Container pane = f.getContentPane();
    pane.setLayout(new GridBagLayout());
    GridBagConstraints constraints = new GridBagConstraints();
    constraints.gridx = 0;
    pane.add(new JButton("First column"), constraints);
    constraints.gridx = 1;
    constraints.gridy = GridBagConstraints.RELATIVE;
```

```
      pane.add(new JButton("Second column, first row"), constraints);
      pane.add(new JButton("Second column, second row"), constraints);
      pane.add(new JButton("Second column, third row"), constraints);
      constraints.gridx = 2;
      pane.add(new JButton("Third column"), constraints);
      f.setSize(500, 300);
      f.setVisible(true);
  }

}
```

This version produces the display shown in Figure 6-17.

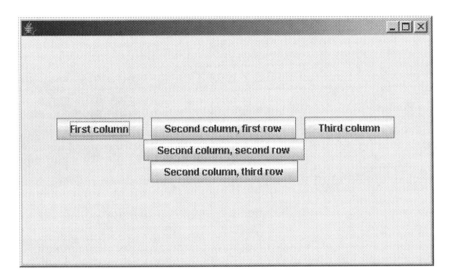

Figure 6-17. *Specifying an absolute X position and a relative Y position causes a component to appear below the one most recently added for the same X position*

You can also specify RELATIVE for both gridx and gridy when adding a component to a container. If you do so, the component will be added to the end of the top row (row 0) in the grid, as in Listing 6-9.

Listing 6-9. Adding Components with Relative X and Y Coordinatesimport java.awt.*;

```
import javax.swing.*;

public class RelativeXY {

  public static void main(String[] args) {
    JFrame f = new JFrame();
    f.setDefaultCloseOperation(JFrame.EXIT_ON_CLOSE);
    Container pane = f.getContentPane();
    pane.setLayout(new GridBagLayout());
    GridBagConstraints constraints = new GridBagConstraints();
    constraints.gridx = 1;
    constraints.gridy = GridBagConstraints.RELATIVE;
```

```
    pane.add(new JButton("First row, first column"), constraints);
    pane.add(new JButton("Second row"), constraints);
    pane.add(new JButton("Third row"), constraints);
    constraints.gridx = GridBagConstraints.RELATIVE;
    pane.add(new JButton("First row, second column"), constraints);
    f.setSize(500, 300);
    f.setVisible(true);
  }

}
```

That code results in the display shown in Figure 6-18.

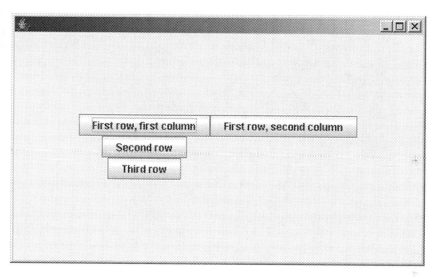

Figure 6-18. *Specifying RELATIVE for both the X and Y coordinates results in components being added to the end of the top row*

fill

By default, a component's size is set to either its preferred size or its minimum size, regardless of the size of the cell or cells reserved for it. At the beginning of this section on GridBagLayout, you saw a JLabel in a column that was much wider than the label's preferred width, so the label occupied only a small portion of its available display area. However, you can use the fill constraint to indicate that the component should be stretched to fill its available display area horizontally, vertically, or both. For example, Listing 6-10 creates three buttons, and the first two are displayed using their preferred sizes. However, the third button expands horizontally to fill the width of its column.

Listing 6-10. Effects of the `fill` Constraint

```java
import java.awt.*;
import javax.swing.*;

public class Fill {

  public static void main(String[] args) {
    JFrame f = new JFrame();
    f.setDefaultCloseOperation(JFrame.EXIT_ON_CLOSE);
    Container pane = f.getContentPane();
    pane.setLayout(new GridBagLayout());
    GridBagConstraints constraints = new GridBagConstraints();
    constraints.gridx = 0;
    constraints.gridy = GridBagConstraints.RELATIVE;
    pane.add(new JButton("This button's preferred width " +
      "is large because its text is long"),
      constraints);
    pane.add(new JButton("Small centered button"), constraints);
    constraints.fill = GridBagConstraints.HORIZONTAL;
    pane.add(new JButton("Expands to fill column width"), constraints);
    f.setSize(400, 300);
    f.setVisible(true);
  }

}
```

Figure 6-19 shows the display produced by this example.

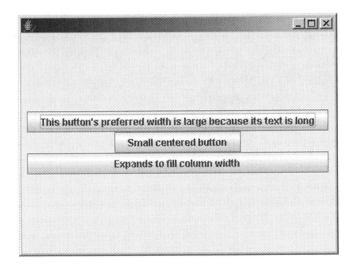

Figure 6-19. *You can make a component fill its entire cell vertically and/or horizontally*

GridBagConstraints has four constants that you can use to set the fill value.

- HORIZONTAL: this expands the component horizontally to fill its display area.

- VERTICAL: this expands the component vertically to fill its display area.

- BOTH: this expands the component both horizontally and vertically to fill its display area.

- NONE: the component should be allowed to remain at its natural (preferred or minimum) size; this is the default value.

gridwidth

This constraint identifies the number of columns that the component spans, and its default value is 1. For example, in Figure 6-20, the button in the third row spans both columns.

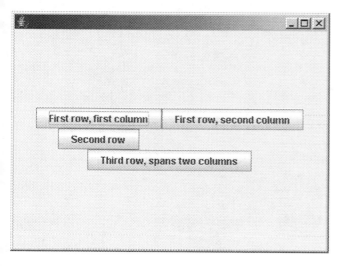

Figure 6-20. *Notice that the component in the third row spans two of the columns in the first row*

Listing 6-11 shows the code to create this display.

Listing 6-11. Effects of the gridwidth Constraint

```
import java.awt.*;
import javax.swing.*;

public class ColumnSpan {

    public static void main(String[] args) {
        JFrame f = new JFrame();
        f.setDefaultCloseOperation(JFrame.EXIT_ON_CLOSE);
        Container pane = f.getContentPane();
        pane.setLayout(new GridBagLayout());
        GridBagConstraints constraints = new GridBagConstraints();
        constraints.gridx = 1;
```

```
      constraints.gridy = GridBagConstraints.RELATIVE;
      pane.add(new JButton("First row, first column"), constraints);
      pane.add(new JButton("Second row"), constraints);
      constraints.gridwidth = 2;
      pane.add(new JButton("Third row, spans two columns"), constraints);
      constraints.gridwidth = 1;
      constraints.gridx = GridBagConstraints.RELATIVE;
      pane.add(new JButton("First row, second column"), constraints);
      f.setSize(400, 300);
      f.setVisible(true);
  }

}
```

In this case, the button's size is set to its preferred width, and the button is centered horizontally within its display area. However, you can make it fill both columns by setting the fill value, as shown in Listing 6-12.

Listing 6-12. Filling the Entire Column

```
import java.awt.*;
import javax.swing.*;

public class ColumnSpan {

  public static void main(String[] args) {
    JFrame f = new JFrame();
    f.setDefaultCloseOperation(JFrame.EXIT_ON_CLOSE);
    Container pane = f.getContentPane();
    pane.setLayout(new GridBagLayout());
    GridBagConstraints constraints = new GridBagConstraints();
    constraints.gridx = 1;
    constraints.gridy = GridBagConstraints.RELATIVE;
    pane.add(new JButton("First row, first column"), constraints);
    pane.add(new JButton("Second row"), constraints);
    constraints.gridwidth = 2;
    constraints.fill = GridBagConstraints.HORIZONTAL;
    pane.add(new JButton("Third row, spans two columns"), constraints);
    constraints.gridwidth = 1;
    constraints.fill = GridBagConstraints.NONE;
    constraints.gridx = GridBagConstraints.RELATIVE;
    pane.add(new JButton("First row, second column"), constraints);
    f.setSize(400, 300);
    f.setVisible(true);
  }

}
```

236

With these alterations, the display now looks like Figure 6-21.

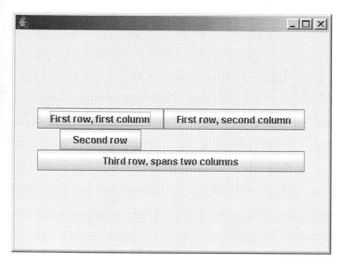

Figure 6-21. *The components in the top and bottom rows now expand to fill their entire cells*

In addition to specifying an explicit number of columns to span, you can use the REMAINDER constant defined in GridBagConstraints. This indicates that the component's display area should begin with the column specified by the gridx value and that it should fill all the remaining columns to the right of that column. Figure 6-22 shows an example.

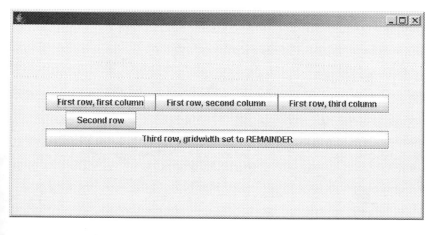

Figure 6-22. *Specifying REMAINDER for the width causes the cell's width to span the rest of the row*

Listing 6-13 shows the code to produce this display.

Listing 6-13. Using the REMAINDER Value for a Width

```
import java.awt.*;
import javax.swing.*;

public class Remainder {

  public static void main(String[] args) {
    JFrame f = new JFrame();
    f.setDefaultCloseOperation(JFrame.EXIT_ON_CLOSE);
    Container pane = f.getContentPane();
    pane.setLayout(new GridBagLayout());
    GridBagConstraints constraints = new GridBagConstraints();
    pane.add(new JButton("First row, first column"), constraints);
    pane.add(new JButton("First row, second column"), constraints);
    pane.add(new JButton("First row, third column"), constraints);
    constraints.gridx = 0;
    pane.add(new JButton("Second row"), constraints);
    constraints.gridwidth = GridBagConstraints.REMAINDER;
    constraints.fill = GridBagConstraints.HORIZONTAL;
    pane.add(new JButton(
      "Third row, gridwidth set to REMAINDER"), constraints);
    f.setSize(600, 300);
    f.setVisible(true);
  }

}
```

You can also set a gridwidth value to RELATIVE, which is similar to REMAINDER. However, RELATIVE causes the component to span all remaining columns except the last one in the grid. For example, you might make the following modifications to the Remainder class defined earlier:

```
pane.add(new JButton("Second row"), constraints);
constraints.gridwidth = GridBagConstraints.RELATIVE;
constraints.fill = GridBagConstraints.HORIZONTAL;
pane.add(new JButton("Third row, gridwidth set to RELATIVE"), constraints);
```

If you compile and execute the code, it will produce a display like the one shown in Figure 6-23.

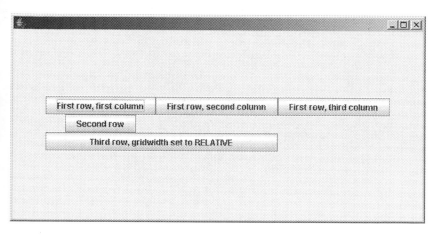

Figure 6-23. *Specifying RELATIVE for the width causes the cell's width to span the rest of the row except for the last column in the row*

gridheight

Just as gridwidth defines the number of columns that a component's display area spans, this constraint defines the number of rows allocated. As with gridwidth, you can specify RELATIVE, REMAINDER, or an absolute value. Listing 6-14 provides an example of this.

Listing 6-14. Effects of the gridheight Constraint

```java
import java.awt.*;
import javax.swing.*;

public class GridHeight {

  public static void main(String[] args) {
    JFrame f = new JFrame();
    f.setDefaultCloseOperation(JFrame.EXIT_ON_CLOSE);
    Container pane = f.getContentPane();
    pane.setLayout(new GridBagLayout());
    GridBagConstraints constraints = new GridBagConstraints();
    pane.add(new JButton("First row, first column"), constraints);
    pane.add(new JButton("First row, second column"), constraints);
    constraints.gridheight = GridBagConstraints.REMAINDER;
    constraints.fill = GridBagConstraints.VERTICAL;
    pane.add(new JButton("First row, third column"), constraints);
    constraints.gridx = 0;
    constraints.gridheight = 1;
    constraints.fill = GridBagConstraints.NONE;
    pane.add(new JButton("Second row"), constraints);
    pane.add(new JButton("Third row"), constraints);
    f.setSize(600, 300);
    f.setVisible(true);
  }

}
```

Figure 6-24 illustrates the behavior of this new class.

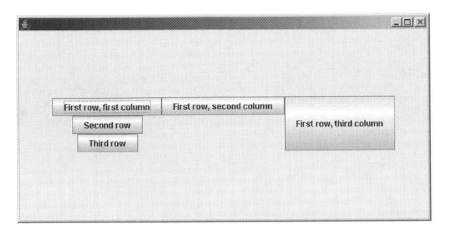

Figure 6-24. *Specifying REMAINDER for the height causes the cell to span the rest of the rows in the grid*

The default value for gridheight is 1, which causes the component to occupy a single row in the grid.

anchor

You can use this constraint to identify how a component should be positioned within its display area when its size is smaller than that area. The anchor constraint should be set to one of the following nine values: CENTER, NORTH, NORTHEAST, EAST, SOUTHEAST, SOUTH, SOUTHWEST, WEST, or NORTHWEST. The default value (CENTER) causes the component to be centered both vertically and horizontally within its display area, and the other values define a corner or side of the area. For example, NORTHEAST causes the component to be placed in the upper-right corner of its display area, EAST causes it to be centered vertically and placed against the right side of its display area, and so on. To illustrate an example of this behavior, suppose you make the following additions to the GridHeight class defined previously:

```
constraints.fill = GridBagConstraints.NONE;
constraints.anchor = GridBagConstraints.EAST;
pane.add(new JButton("Second row"), constraints);
constraints.anchor = GridBagConstraints.CENTER;
pane.add(new JButton("Third row"), constraints);
```

This modification causes the button in the second row to appear in the "east"/right side of its display area, as shown in Figure 6-25. However, once that button has been added to the panel, the anchor property changes back to CENTER (the default value), so the button in the third row appears centered.

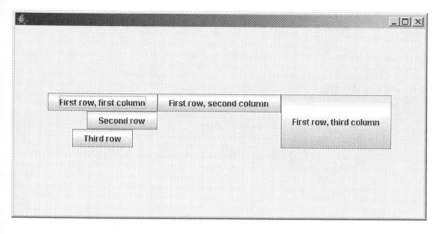

Figure 6-25. *The anchor constraint affects where and how components are aligned within their cells*

insets

The insets constraint is a reference to an instance of the Insets class and allows you to define some number of pixels that should be reserved around the four edges (top, left, bottom, and right) of the component's display area. You'll typically use this to provide whitespace between components in adjacent rows and columns, just as horizontal and vertical gap values are used by other layout managers. However, GridBagLayout's approach is much more flexible, because you can specify a different gap size for every component and also specify a unique size for each side of the component.

To set the inset values for a component, you can create an instance of Insets or modify the one that's created automatically when a GridBagConstraints object is created. The following code segment illustrates how to set these values:

```
GridBagConstraints constraints = new GridBagConstraints();
constraints.insets = new Insets(5, 10, 5, 10);
```

You can also use the following:

```
GridBagConstraints constraints = new GridBagConstraints();
constraints.insets.top = 5;
constraints.insets.left = 10;
constraints.insets.bottom = 5;
constraints.insets.right = 10;
```

If you insert one of these two code segments into the GridHeight class defined earlier, compile the code, and execute it, it will produce a display like the one shown in Figure 6-26.

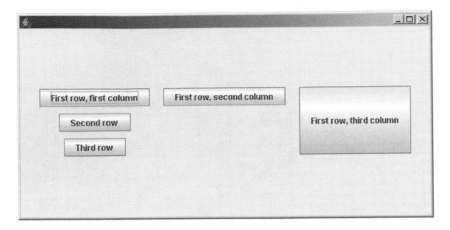

Figure 6-26. *Insets represent unused space between the outer edges of the components and their cells*

One final point worth noting relative to insets is that a component is never allowed to overlay the inset portions of its display area, even if the `fill` constraint causes the component be stretched.

ipadx

You can add this value to the component's preferred or minimum size to determine the width of the component, and the *i* refers to the fact that the pad value is added to the component's "internal" (in other words, preferred or minimum) width as opposed to its current (displayed) width. For example, if a component has a preferred width of 40 pixels and you specify a value of 10 for this constraint, the component will be 50 pixels wide when the components are displayed using preferred widths. You can also make components smaller than their preferred or minimum sizes by specifying negative pad values, so if you were to specify a value of -10 for this constraint in the previous example, the component would be assigned a width of 30 pixels instead of its preferred width of 40 pixels. The default value of this constraint is 0.

ipady

Just as `ipadx` represents some number that's added to a component's preferred or minimum width, this value is added to the component's height before it's displayed. The default value of this constraint is 0.

weightx

This value determines how to resize the columns in the grid when the container is either wider or narrower than the area needed to display the components at their preferred or minimum widths. If all components in a grid have a `weightx` value of 0.0 (the default), any extra horizontal space is divided evenly between the left and right edges of the container. I provide a detailed description of how weights are used and how they interact with other constraints later.

weighty

This value determines how to resize the rows within the grid when the container's height is larger or smaller than the size needed to display the components using their preferred or minimum heights. If all components in a grid have a `weighty` value of 0.0 (the default), any extra vertical space is divided evenly between the top and bottom edges of the container.

Calculating Row Heights and Column Widths

The initial calculation of the height of a row happens by determining the amount of space that's needed to display the tallest component in the row. The height of a particular component is the sum of its preferred or minimum height, the vertical pad value (ipady) specified for its constraints, and the top and bottom insets that should appear around the component.

Similarly, when calculating the width of a column, the width needed for each component is calculated, and the largest value is used as the column's width. A component's width is defined as the sum of its preferred or minimum width, its horizontal pad (ipadx) value, and its right and left inset values. For example, suppose you've created a container with nine child components, and those components have the width values specified in Table 6-2.

***Table 6-2.** Preferred Widths of the Components in a Table with Three Rows and Three Columns*

Column 1	Column 2	Column 3
35	50	32
47	25	10
28	30	28

Given these nine components and their preferred widths, the width of each of the three columns can easily be determined by selecting the largest preferred width from each column, as shown in Table 6-3. This assumes that the ipadx and left and right insets for all components are 0; otherwise, those values will be added to the appropriate component's width when determining the column width.

***Table 6-3.** Column Widths for the Three Columns in the Table*

Column 1 Width	Column 2 Width	Column 3 Width
47	50	32

Calculating Sizes When Components Span Multiple Cells

The process of calculating a row height or column width is slightly more complex when it involves a component that spans multiple rows or columns. When calculating row heights and column widths, GridBagLayout processes the components in order of their gridwidth (for column widths) and gridheight (for row heights) values. For example, to calculate column widths, the layout manager will first examine the components that have a gridwidth of 1, then those with a gridwidth of 2, and so on.

When GridBagLayout needs to determine the size of a column and it encounters a component that spans multiple columns, it attempts to distribute the component's preferred width across those columns. The distribution occurs in left-to-right order, and any remaining width is distributed to the last column that the component occupies. For example, suppose you have the same components described earlier, but with a component in the second row that has a gridwidth value of 2 (in other words, it fills the first two columns). In that case, the column widths will be calculated as shown in Table 6-4. In this example, the first component in the second row spans the first two columns (i.e., it has a grid width of 2).

Table 6-4. *A Component That Spans Multiple Columns*

Column 1	Column 2	Column 3
35	50	32
109		10
28	30	28

When the layout manager examines the components with a `gridwidth` value of 1, it establishes preliminary widths of 35, 50, and 32 for the three columns. However, when it examines components with a `gridwidth` of 2, it determines that the existing column widths aren't adequate to allow the components to be displayed properly. This is because of the component in the second row that spans the first two columns and has a width of 109 pixels. Since that component's width exceeds the sum of the preliminary widths for the columns it occupies (35 + 50 = 85), the width of the second column is increased to 74 (109 – 35 = 74) so that the component's size can be accommodated. As Table 6-5 shows, the second column's width is expanded to 74 to accommodate the wide component in the first row that spans the first and second columns.

Table 6-5. *Derived Column Widths*

Column 1 Width	Column 2 Width	Column 3 Width
35	74	44

Weight Values, Row Heights, and Column Widths

One of the more confusing aspects of `GridBagLayout` is how components' `weightx` values affect column widths and how `weighty` values affect row heights. When a `GridBagLayout` attempts to organize the components in its container, it compares the amount of space it needs to the actual size of the container. If the two sizes aren't the same, the layout manager must decide where and by how much to increase or reduce the size of rows and columns, and it uses weight values for this purpose. Stated simply, the weight values you specify through `GridBagConstraints` assign each row and column a weight, and the amount of space taken from or added to a row or column is determined by its weight value.

Distributing Extra Space

The following example illustrates how space is distributed, but for the sake of simplicity, it involves only `weightx` values and column width adjustments. However, the calculation of row heights using `weighty` values takes place in the same way, so the concepts are relevant to both column widths and row heights.

Let's assume you've created a container that uses a `GridBagLayout` to manage the size and position of its child components and that it needs a width of 400 pixels to display the components using their minimum sizes. However, let's also assume that when the layout manager prepares to arrange the components, it determines that the container is 600 pixels wide. In this case, the `GridBagLayout` must determine how to distribute the extra 200 pixels to its columns.

Calculating Column Weights

The first step that the `GridBagLayout` must take is to calculate a weight for each column, and that weight will determine how many of the extra 200 pixels are distributed to the column. In the simplest case where each component has a `gridwidth` value of 1 (in other words, no component spans multiple columns), the weight of a column is defined as the largest `weightx` value of any component within that column. For example, suppose that Table 6-6 represents the `weightx` values of components in a container.

Table 6-6. weightx *Settings for the Components in the Respective Cells*

Column 1	Column 2	Column 3
15	10	15
10	25	30
20	50	10

Since the weight of a column is defined as the maximum weightx value in that column, the weights of the three columns in this grid are 20, 50, and 30, respectively, as shown in Table 6-7. The weight of each column is equal to the largest weightx value selected from all the components in the column.

Table 6-7. *Weights of the Three Columns*

Column 1 Weight	Column 2 Weight	Column 3 Weight
20	50	30

Note that although this example has been deliberately designed so that the sum of the column weights is 100, there's no technical reason why this is necessary: it was simply done that way here to simplify the example. In fact, as you'll see shortly, neither the weights' absolute values nor their sum is particularly important, but you may find it easier to work with round numbers.

In the case where a component spans multiple columns, the calculation of a column's weight value is slightly more complex. Using a different set of components in some other container, let's suppose three rows of components appear in the grid and that the second row contains a component that spans the second and third columns, as shown in Table 6-8. It's easy to guess the weight of the first column, since it's simply the maximum weightx value found in that column (1.0). However, it's probably not as obvious how the weight values of the remaining two columns are calculated.

Table 6-8. *Calculating Weights When a Component Spans Two Columns*

Column 1	Column 2	Column 3
0.33	0.25	0.5
1.0	3.0	
0.66	0.15	0.5

Table 6-9 shows the weights calculated for the columns.

Table 6-9. *Derived Weight Values*

Column 1 Weight	Column 2 Weight	Column 3 Weight
1.0	1.0	2.0

To understand how the weight values were derived for the second and third columns, it's important to know that when GridBagLayout calculates column weights, it processes components in order based on their gridwidth values. In other words, GridBagLayout first examines the weightx values of all components that have a gridwidth value of 1, then those that have a value of 2, and so on. In this case, the layout manager's first iteration will process seven of the eight components in the container, initially ignoring the component in the second row that has a gridwidth of 2. In the process of doing so, it calculates a preliminary column weight of 0.25 for the second column and 0.5 for the third column.

On the GridBagLayout's next iteration, it processes the weightx of the component that spans the second and third columns and must distribute that value (3.0) across the two columns. It does this by distributing the amount proportionally based upon the preliminary weight values of the columns. Specifically, it adds the preliminary column weight values and divides the weight value of each column by that sum to determine a percentage of the spanning component's weightx value that should be distributed to the column.

For example, in this case, the preliminary weight values of the second and third columns are 0.25 and 0.5, respectively, and the sum of these two values is 0.75. Dividing the preliminary weight of the second column by 0.75 produces a value of 0.33, and dividing the third column's preliminary weight by the total produces a value of 0.67. These values represent the percentage of the spanning component's weightx value that will be distributed to each column. Specifically, one-third (33%) will be assigned to the second column, and the remaining two-thirds (67%) will be assigned to the third column. Since the weight of the component that spans the two columns is 3, it represents a weight of 1 (3.0 * 0.33 = 1.0) for the second column and 2 (3.0 * 0.67 = 2.0) for the third.

Since the component in the second row represents a weightx value of 1 for the second column and 2 for the third column, the second column's final weight value is 1 and the third column's final weight is 2.

Converting Weights to Percentages

Now that a weight value has been assigned to each column, those values can determine the amount of extra space that should be allocated to each column. This happens by first calculating the sum of all column weight values and dividing each column's weight by that sum. In this case, the sum of all the weights is 4 (1.0 + 1.0 + 2.0 = 4), and the first column is given one-fourth (25%) of the extra space. Similarly, the second column is allocated one-fourth (25%) of the space, and the third and final column receives the remaining two-fourths (50%).

Distributing the Extra Space

Having calculated the percentage of extra space that should be added to the width of each column, it's easy to determine the number of pixels that will be distributed in this example. Since there are 200 extra pixels, the first and second columns will be made wider by 50 pixels (200 * 0.25 = 50), and the third column becomes 100 pixels wider (200 * 0.5 = 100).

Although this example describes a situation where extra space was being added to columns, the same principles apply when you need to take away space. For example, if the container had been 200 pixels smaller than it needed to be instead of 200 larger, the three columns would have been reduced in size by 50, 50, and 100 pixels, respectively.

General Guidelines for Setting Weights

As you can see, GridBagLayout's behavior with respect to weight values is somewhat complex. However, you can reduce the complexity in some cases by assigning weightx values only to the components in a single row and weighty values to those in a particular column. If you do so, you're effectively setting the weight value for the entire row or column when you specify it for the component, which makes it easier to predict how space will be added or taken away.

In addition, you may find it easier to use weight values that add up to some round number such as 1.0 or 100.0, allowing you to easily associate a weight value with a percentage. For example, given the previous grid, you could specify the weightx values only on the components in the first row, as shown in Table 6-10. In this scenario, weights are specified only for the components in the first row, resulting in the columns' weights being assigned the corresponding values from those components.

Table 6-10. *Specifying Weights for Components in the First Row Only*

Column 1	Column 2	Column 3
25.0	25.0	50.0
0.0	0.0	
0.0	0.0	0.0

In this case, only the components in the first row were assigned weightx values, and the sum of those values is 100, making it much more obvious how space will be added or removed from the columns. Specifically, the first and second columns are allocated 25% of any extra space, and the third one is given the remaining 50%.

You may have noticed that in some examples, relatively large weight values (50, 10, 15, etc.) were used, while smaller ones were specified at other times. I did this deliberately to illustrate a point: the absolute size of weight values used is unimportant. What matters is how large those values are relative to one another. In other words, you can produce the same results using fractional values as you can by using very large numbers. For example, three columns with weights of 0.25, 0.25, and 0.50 have space distributed to them in the same amounts that they would if the columns had weights of 100, 100, and 200.

It's also important to remember that weights don't necessarily represent the relative sizes of the cells but rather the relative amount of space that will be added to or taken away from those cells. For example, if you create a grid with two columns and the second column is assigned a weight that's twice as large as the first, you shouldn't expect the second column to be twice as large. However, you can correctly assume that the second column will be given twice as much extra space as the first if excess space is distributed to them.

GridBagTester

Even with a good understanding of GridBagLayout, it can be difficult to assign constraint values so that your user interface is displayed correctly, and you may find it necessary to repeatedly modify, compile, and execute your code. However, you can use the GridBagTester utility provided in the Source Code/Download area of the Apress web site (www.apress.com) to test your user interface classes that use GridBagLayout and to modify the constraint values graphically until they produce the desired results.

To use GridBagTester, you simply create an instance of it by passing its constructor a Container that's managed by a GridBagLayout, and GridBagTester will create a JFrame that displays the container. In addition, it provides other information that describes the components, their constraint values, and the rows and columns defined in the container grid.

A table at the top of the frame displays the width and weight of each column in the grid. It also displays a value that identifies what percentage of space will be added to or taken away from the column's width if the container is made wider or narrower than its current width.

A table on the left side of the frame displays the height and weight of each row in the grid. It also displays a value that identifies what percentage of space will be added to or taken away from the row's height if the container is made taller or shorter than its current height.

A table at the bottom of the frame displays information about each component in the container. Specifically, that information includes the component's name, location within the container, actual/current size, preferred size, minimum size, and constraint values assigned to the component. With the exception of the preferred and minimum size values, all the cells in this table are editable. You can dynamically change a component's constraints and immediately see the effect of your change upon its size and position, as well as the weight and size of any rows and columns it occupies.

247

GridBagTester relies on a class called NumericTextField that's used to allow entry of numeric values; you can also download that class from the Source Code/Download area of the Apress web site (www.apress.com).

As an example of how GridBagTester may be useful, suppose you've created a layout similar to the one shown in Listing 6-15 that allows a first and last name to be entered, along with an address.

Listing 6-15. A Simple Application That Uses GridBagTester

```java
import java.awt.*;
import javax.swing.*;

public class SimplePanel extends JPanel {

  public static void main(String[] args) {
    JFrame f = new JFrame();
    f.setDefaultCloseOperation(JFrame.EXIT_ON_CLOSE);
    f.getContentPane().add(new SimplePanel());
    f.setSize(400, 300);
    f.setVisible(true);
  }

  public SimplePanel() {
    super();
    GridBagConstraints constraints = new GridBagConstraints();
    GridBagLayout layout = new GridBagLayout();
    setLayout(layout);

    constraints.anchor = GridBagConstraints.WEST;

    constraints.gridy = 0;
    JLabel label = new JLabel("First name:");
    add(label, constraints);

    JTextField tf = new JTextField(8);
    add(tf, constraints);

    label = new JLabel("Last name:");
    add(label, constraints);

    tf = new JTextField(8);
    add(tf, constraints);

    constraints.gridy = 1;
    label = new JLabel("Address:");
    add(label, constraints);

    tf = new JTextField(10);
    add(tf, constraints);
  }

}
```

Initially, it produces a display like the one shown in Figure 6-27.

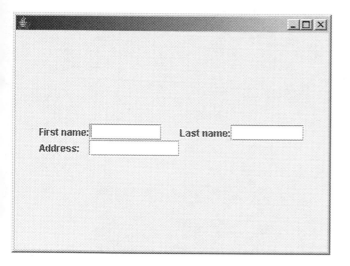

Figure 6-27. *Window that results from running the initial implementation of the* SimplePanel *class*

Although this display is functional, it's not very user-friendly. You can improve it by repeatedly modifying, compiling, and executing your code, but doing so is tedious and time-consuming. Alternatively, you can make a slight modification to the main() method that will allow you to view and modify the component's constraint information.

```
public static void main(String[] args) {
  // JFrame f = new JFrame();
  // f.setDefaultCloseOperation(JFrame.EXIT_ON_CLOSE);
  // f.getContentPane().add(new SimplePanel());
  // f.setSize(400, 300);
  // f.setVisible(true);
  GridBagTester gbt = new GridBagTester(new SimplePanel());
}
```

When the program runs now, the display is as shown in Figure 6-28.

GridBagLayout Tester

Column Widths and Weights

	0	1	2	3
Width	63	114	63	92
weightX	0.0	0.0	0.0	0.0
Percent	0	0	0	0

Row Heights and Weights

	Height	weightY	Percent
0	20	0.0	0
1	20	0.0	0

First name: Last name: Address:

Component Constraints

Name	X	Y	width	height	minSize	prefSize	gridx
JLabel	25	28	63	16	(63,16)	(63,16)	RELATI
JTextField	88	26	92	20	(4,20)	(92,20)	RELATI
JLabel	202	28	63	16	(63,16)	(63,16)	RELATI
JTextField	265	26	92	20	(4,20)	(92,20)	RELATI
JLabel	25	48	51	16	(51,16)	(51,16)	RELATI
JTextField	88	46	114	20	(4,20)	(114,20)	RELATI

Figure 6-28. *Window that results from running the initial implementation of the* SimplePanel *class*

To test the utility, you might change the gridwidth value of the JTextField on the second row to REMAINDER and its fill value to HORIZONTAL, which produces the display shown in Figure 6-29.

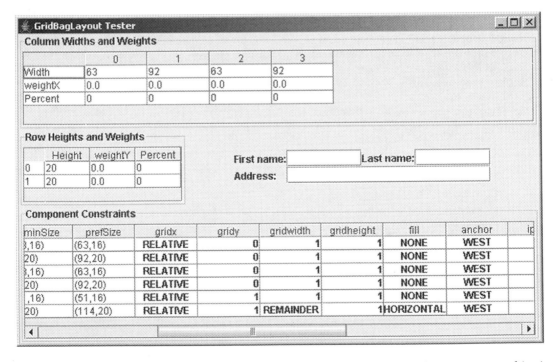

Figure 6-29. *Changing the grid width value causes the address text field to span the entire row, resulting in a more usable and appealing interface*

This improves the appearance of the display, but it still appears somewhat cluttered because no gaps appear between the components. To add space between them, you could change the inset values for all the components so there are 5 pixels above and below and 10 to the left and the right of each component, as shown in Figure 6-30.

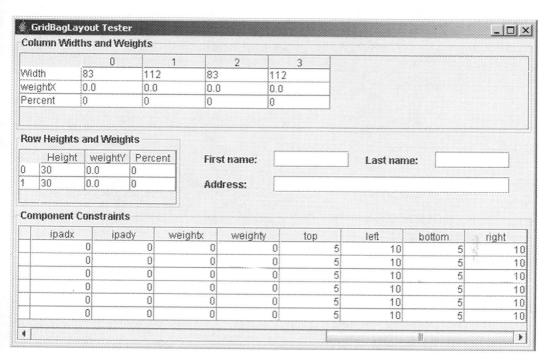

Figure 6-30. *Adding insets also improves the appearance of the container by adding whitespace between the child components*

You may also find it helpful to use GridBagTester in addition to the GridBagCellPanel class defined earlier so that you can easily identify the edges of a cell, as shown in Figure 6-31.

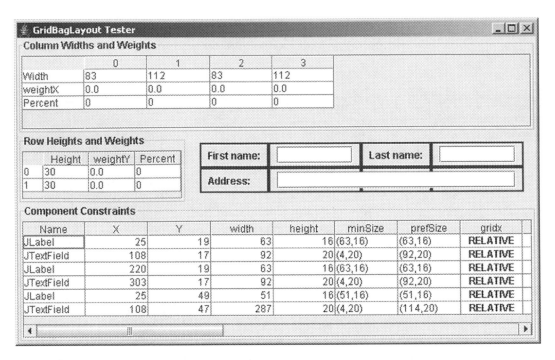

Figure 6-31. *Combining* GridBagTester *and* GridBagCellPanel *creates an interface that allows you to easily see the results of various constraint settings*

For example, changing the superclass of SimplePanel from JPanel to GridBagCellPanel causes a border to be drawn around each cell in the grid:

```
public class SimplePanel extends GridBagCellPanel {
```

Child Component Sizes

The size of a child component in a GridBagLayout depends upon the constraint values specified for the child component as well as the size of the parent container. Specifically, the ipadx and ipady values are added to the component's preferred or minimum width and height, respectively, and the fill constraint can cause the component to be expanded to fill its available display area.

I've stated a number of times that GridBagLayout uses a component's preferred size or its minimum size without explaining the circumstances in which one is used and the other isn't. Very simply, GridBagLayout attempts to use the preferred sizes of the child components, but it does so only if the container is large enough to display all the child components using their preferred sizes. Otherwise, the GridBagLayout reformats the display using the components' minimum sizes. However, GridBagLayout respects minimum sizes and will never make a component smaller than that size unless you specify a negative value for either the ipadx property or the ipady property. In addition, it always adds the ipadx and ipady values to either the preferred size or the minimum size, depending upon which one is being used.

To illustrate this behavior, let's first review the components' sizes in Figure 6-31, paying particular attention to the JTextField instances. Notice that with the exception of the JTextField in the second row, which has been stretched to fill three columns, each of the components is displayed using its preferred size. You should also note that although the JLabel instances have the same values for preferred and minimum sizes, the JTextField instances don't. The JTextField minimum width values are much smaller than the preferred widths (e.g., a minimum width of 4 pixels and a preferred width of 88 pixels). Since that's the case, you can expect that if the panel becomes too small to display the components using their preferred widths, the text fields will shrink to their minimum sizes. As shown in Figure 6-32, that's exactly what happens when the dialog is made slightly narrower, reducing the container's width as well. The second and fourth columns have been reallocated 24 pixels wide each, since they both contain a JTextField with a minimum width of 4 and left and right inset values of 10.

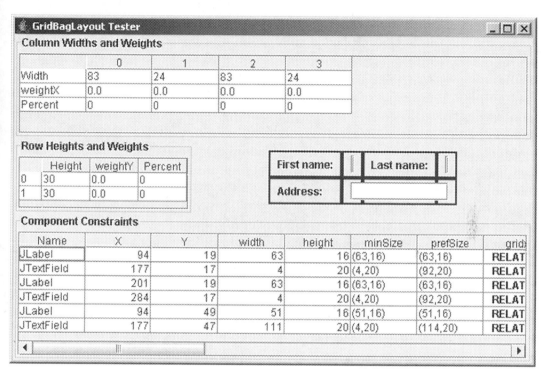

Figure 6-32. *Making the window narrower causes the text fields to "collapse" when they revert from their preferred widths to their minimum widths*

This behavior is somewhat undesirable, since the text fields can shrink dramatically in size to the point of being unusable. One solution to the problem is to set the weightx values of the text fields so they don't shrink as much. For example, if you set the weightx for both of the JTextField instances in the first row to 0.5 and set their fill values to HORIZONTAL, they'll grow and shrink as the width of the container changes (see Figure 6-33). You could also use the ipadx values to ensure that the JTextField instances don't become unusable when set to their minimum sizes. However, doing so would also result in the specified number of pixels being added to the JTextField widths when they're displayed using their preferred sizes, causing them to be larger than necessary in that case and wasting screen space.

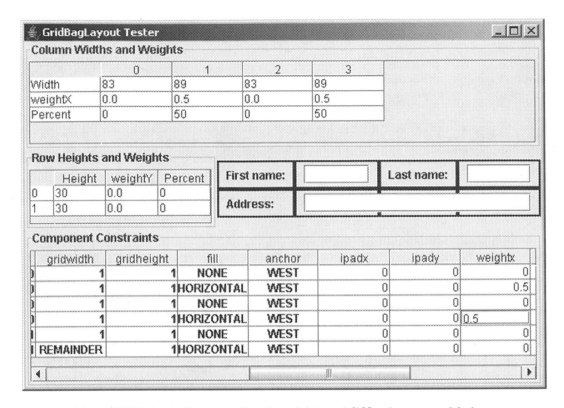

Figure 6-33. *Text field behavior improves when the* weightx *and* fill *values are modified*

The fill value also can affect a component's size, but it's applied only after the grid's row and column sizes have been calculated. In other words, the fill value can affect the size of a component within its display area, but unlike constraints such as ipadx, ipady, and insets, it's not used in calculating the size of that area. Similarly, the weight values are applicable only after the initial cell sizes have been calculated using the component sizes, pads, and inset values.

Child Component Locations

The location of each child component in a GridBagLayout-managed container is determined primarily by the component's display area, which is identified by its gridx, gridy, gridwidth, and gridheight values. Those values define the rectangular region within the grid that make up the component's display area, and the component will be displayed somewhere inside that area.

In addition to the number and location of cells that the component occupies, its anchor constraint affects where a component is located within those cells. By default, a component is centered both vertically and horizontally within its display area.

Resizing Behavior

If you shrink a container managed by a GridBagLayout so it can no longer display its components using their preferred sizes, it reformats the display using their minimum sizes. If the container continues to shrink until the components can't be displayed using their minimum sizes, then portions of the display will disappear from the panel, as shown in Figure 6-34.

Figure 6-34. *GridBagLayout uses preferred sizes if enough space is available but reverts to the minimum size if necessary*

Container Size

To calculate the preferred width of a container, GridBagLayout adds the widths of all grid columns in the container, and those widths are calculated using the preferred width of each component in the column. The sum of those width values is added to the container's left and right inset values to obtain the container's preferred width, and its preferred height is calculated in the same manner using the components' preferred heights.

The container's minimum size is calculated in the same manner, except that it uses the components' minimum size values instead of their preferred sizes. GridBagLayout doesn't impose any maximum size limit on the container.

BoxLayout

A BoxLayout allows you to create either a single row or a single column of components. In other words, the components you add to a BoxLayout are arranged vertically from top to bottom or horizontally from left to right.

BoxLayout is different from the other layout managers in a number of ways, and it uses some properties defined in Component that the other layout managers ignore. For example, BoxLayout respects a component's maximum size and will never make the component larger than the dimensions specified by that property. In addition, a BoxLayout that arranges its components vertically (or a "vertical BoxLayout") uses each component's alignment along the X axis, which is available through the getAlignmentX() method in Component. Similarly, BoxLayout uses the components' alignments along the Y axis (and the corresponding getAlignmentY() method) when it arranges them horizontally.

BoxLayout is different from the other layout managers in one other important way: it uses a component's maximum size to determine the amount of space that the component should occupy. In many cases, a component's maximum size is the same as or close to its preferred size. However, as you'll see later, some components have large maximum size values, which can produce unexpected or undesirable results when used with a BoxLayout.

Alignment Values, Ascents, and Descents

Component alignment values play a major role in determining how components are positioned within a BoxLayout-managed container, but before I can cover how alignment values are used, it's necessary to define some terms.

A component's *alignment* is represented by a float value that can range from 0.0 to 1.0, and you may find it helpful to think of this number as a percentage value, with 0.0 representing 0% and 1.0 representing 100%. By default, a component's X and Y alignment values are both set to 0.5. The component's *ascent* value is calculated by multiplying one of its dimensions by one of its alignment values. For example, if you're using a horizontal BoxLayout, you could calculate the preferred height ascent for a component by multiplying the component's preferred height by its Y alignment value, as in the following equation:

```
Dimension prefSize = comp.getPreferredSize();
int ascent = (int)(prefSize.height * comp.getAlignmentY());
```

Similarly, a component's *descent* value is calculated by subtracting the component's ascent value from the size that was used to calculate the ascent, as follows:

```
int descent = prefSize.height - ascent;
```

In other words, the sum of the ascent and descent values is equal to the dimension that was used to calculate them, and they represent the portions of the component that lie on either side of an imaginary line. For example, suppose that the previous code was executed for a component with a preferred height of 400 pixels and that the component's Y alignment value is 0.25. The ascent value would be 100 (400 * 0.25 = 100), and the descent value would be 300 (400 – 100 = 300).

Note that you can calculate ascent and descent values from a component's preferred, minimum, or maximum sizes, and as you'll see, each one plays a role in BoxLayout's behavior. In addition, the "ascent" and "descent" concepts apply to both a component's horizontal size as well as its vertical size, although only one (either vertical or horizontal) is used in a given BoxLayout. A component's horizontal ascent and descent are used when it's added to a vertical BoxLayout, while its vertical ascent and descent are used when it's in a horizontal BoxLayout. If this seems somewhat confusing, keep in mind that the horizontal placement of components in a horizontal box is simple—they appear next to one another from left to right. Similarly, for a vertical box, components are simply "stacked" from top to bottom. In either case, the alignment, ascent, and descent values calculate the component's position in the remaining dimension. You can see an example of this behavior by compiling Listing 6-16, which uses a vertical BoxLayout.

Listing 6-16. A Simple BoxLayout Test

```
import java.awt.*;
import javax.swing.*;

public class BoxTest {

  public static void main(String[] args) {
    JFrame f = new JFrame("Vertical BoxLayout-managed container");
    f.setDefaultCloseOperation(JFrame.EXIT_ON_CLOSE);
    Container pane = f.getContentPane();
    pane.setLayout(new BoxLayout(pane, BoxLayout.Y_AXIS));
    for (float align = 0.0f; align <= 1.0f; align += 0.25f) {
      JButton button = new JButton("X Alignment = " + align);
        button.setAlignmentX(align);
      pane.add(button);
```

```
    }
    f.setSize(400, 300);
    f.setVisible(true);
  }
}
```

When executed, this code produces a display like the one shown in Figure 6-35.

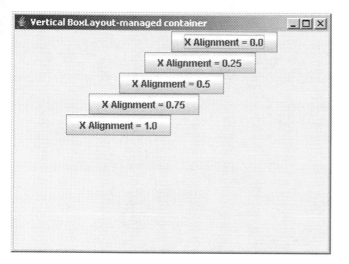

Figure 6-35. *An example of a component with varying alignment values arranged by a BoxLayout*

In addition to the alignment values assigned to each component, an alignment value is calculated for a container when it's managed by a BoxLayout. The container's horizontal alignment is calculated by a vertical BoxLayout, and the vertical alignment is used by a horizontal BoxLayout. These are accessible through LayoutManager2's getLayoutAlignmentX() and getLayoutAlignmentY() methods, although BoxLayout is currently the only layout manager that returns a meaningful value from those methods.

Layout Alignment Calculations

For a vertical BoxLayout, the container's X alignment is used to position components within the container, and its value is derived from the X alignment values of those components. The layout manager first examines each component and identifies the largest minimum width ascent and minimum width descent (in other words, ascent and descent values calculated using the components' minimum widths) of any component. Once it has identified those two values, it calculates their sum and divides the largest minimum width ascent by that sum, and the result of that calculation becomes the container's alignment.

For example, let's assume Table 6-11 describes the components in a container managed by a vertical BoxLayout. As mentioned, the ascent value is calculated by multiplying the dimension (in this case, the width) by the alignment value, and the descent is the dimension value minus the ascent.

Table 6-11. *Minimum Width, X Alignment, Ascent, and Descent Values for Five Components*

Minimum Width	X Alignment	Ascent	Descent
90	0.20	18	72
36	0.75	27	9
80	0.25	20	60
72	0.50	36	36
28	1.00	28	0

In this case, the largest ascent value is 36 and the largest descent is 72. Therefore, the container's alignment value is 0.33, as calculated using the following formula:

```
alignment = max(ascent) / ( max(ascent) + max(descent) )
```

or using this formula:

```
alignment = 36 / (36 + 72) = 0.33
```

Note that although this example examines the calculation of the X alignment for a vertical BoxLayout, the calculations are the same for a horizontal BoxLayout, although the components' Y alignments and height values are used instead.

Now that you've examined how a container's alignment is calculated, you may be wondering why it's important. Conceptually, you can think of the container's alignment as defining an imaginary line (or axis) inside the container around which the components are positioned. For example, for a vertical BoxLayout, a component with an X alignment of 0.0 will normally be placed completely to the right of the axis. Similarly, a component with an alignment of 1.0 appears entirely to the left, while a component with an alignment of 0.5 is centered on the axis. In other words, you can think of the component's alignment as a value that determines what portion of the component appears to the left of the container's axis.

To identify the location of a container's axis, you can multiply the appropriate alignment value by the corresponding dimension. For example, if you're using a horizontal container, you'd multiply the container's actual/current height by its Y alignment value. In Figure 6-36, the container's axis is represented graphically by a thick, dark-colored line (although you normally won't see such an indication of its location when using a BoxLayout).

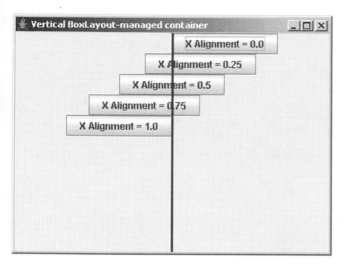

Figure 6-36. *The container's axis is displayed graphically to show an example of how BoxPanel can be used*

However, it's easy to implement this functionality, which serves a purpose similar to that of the GridBagCellPanel class defined earlier, as shown in Listing 6-17.

Listing 6-17. Drawing Borders Within a BoxLayout-Managed Container

```
import java.awt.*;
import javax.swing.*;

public class BoxPanel extends JPanel {

  public void paintChildren(Graphics g) {
    super.paintChildren(g);
    Dimension size = getSize();
    LayoutManager manager = getLayout();
    if ((manager != null) && (manager instanceof BoxLayout)) {
      BoxLayout layout = (BoxLayout)manager;
      //  There's currently no accessor method that allows
      //  us to determine the orientation (vertical or
      //  horizontal) used by a BoxLayout, so we'll hard-code
      //  this class to assume vertical orientation
      boolean vertical = true;
      if (vertical) {
        int axis = (int)(layout.getLayoutAlignmentX(this) * size.width);
        g.fillRect(axis - 1, 0, 3, size.height);
      }
```

```
    else {
      int axis = (int)(layout.getLayoutAlignmentY(this) * size.height);
      g.fillRect(0, axis - 1, size.width, 3);
    }
  }
}

}
```

Once you've compiled BoxPanel, you can easily modify the BoxTest application defined earlier so that it uses BoxTest (see Listing 6-18).

Listing 6-18. Incorporating the BoxPanel Class

```
public static void main(String[] args) {
  JFrame f = new JFrame("Vertical BoxLayout-managed container");
  f.setDefaultCloseOperation(JFrame.EXIT_ON_CLOSE);
  Container pane = new BoxPanel();
  f.setContentPane(pane);
  pane.setLayout(new BoxLayout(pane, BoxLayout.Y_AXIS));
  for (float align = 0.0f; align <= 1.0f; align += 0.25f) {
    JButton button = new JButton("X Alignment = " + align);
    button.setAlignmentX(align);
    pane.add(button);
  }
  f.setSize(400, 300);
  f.setVisible(true);
}
```

Constructing a BoxLayout

BoxLayout is somewhat different from the other layout managers in that its constructor must be passed a reference to the Container instance that uses it. In addition, you must specify how the BoxLayout should arrange its components: vertically (in a column) or horizontally (in a row), specifying either the BoxLayout.Y_AXIS constant or the BoxLayout.X_AXIS constant, respectively. For example, you can use the following code to create a BoxLayout that will display its components in a column:

```
JPanel panel = new JPanel();
BoxLayout bl = new BoxLayout(panel, BoxLayout.Y_AXIS);
panel.setLayout(bl);
```

In addition to creating a BoxLayout this way, the Box class provides an alternative. Specifically, it includes static getVerticalBox() and getHorizontalBox() factory methods that return an instance of Box that uses a BoxLayout to arrange its components. As you might expect, getVerticalBox() returns a container that arranges its components vertically, while getHorizontalBox() returns one that arranges its components horizontally. I discuss the Box class in more detail shortly.

Constraints

BoxLayout doesn't support constraints in the traditional sense, and you should use the simple form of add()
when adding a component to a parent container. However, a component's alignment values effectively act
as constraints by defining how the component should be placed within its parent container. In addition,
JComponent defines setAlignmentX() and setAlignmentY() mutator methods that allow you to set those
values instead of creating a subclass that overrides the accessor methods.

Child Component Sizes

Before setting the widths of components in a vertical box, BoxLayout calculates an ascent and a descent
value for the container using its current/actual width and its derived alignment value. In other words, the
BoxLayout determines how much space is available on each side of the container's axis.

When setting the size of a component in a vertical box, BoxLayout calculates the component's
maximum width ascent and maximum width descent. It then compares the component's ascent to the
container's ascent and compares the component's descent to the container's descent, selecting the smaller
value in each case. In other words, BoxLayout tries to use the component's maximum width, but if that width
exceeds the size available within the container, it uses the container's preferred width instead.

For many components, this behavior is acceptable because the maximum width is the same as or
close to the preferred width, but in some cases, the results may not be what you intended. For example, the
existing implementation of BoxTest displays buttons with different alignment values using the buttons'
preferred sizes. This behavior is consistent with the way that most other layout managers handle button
instances and is appropriate for most situations. However, suppose you modify the code so it creates
instances of JTextField instead of instances of JButton (see Listing 6-19).

Listing 6-19. BoxLayout with JTextField Instances

```
import java.awt.*;
import javax.swing.*;

public class BoxTest {

  public static void main(String[] args) {
    JFrame f = new JFrame("Vertical BoxLayout-managed container");
    f.setDefaultCloseOperation(JFrame.EXIT_ON_CLOSE);
    Container pane = new BoxPanel();
    f.setContentPane(pane);
    pane.setLayout(new BoxLayout(pane, BoxLayout.Y_AXIS));
    for (float align = 0.0f; align <= 1.0f; align += 0.25f) {
//    JButton button = new JButton("X Alignment = " + align);
//      button.setAlignmentX(align);
//      pane.add(button);
    JTextField tf = new JTextField("X Alignment = " + align, 10);
    tf.setAlignmentX(align);
    pane.add(tf);
    }
    f.setSize(400, 300);
    f.setVisible(true);
  }

}
```

As Figure 6-37 illustrates, making these changes to the code does indeed cause text fields to appear in place of the buttons, but unlike the buttons, the text fields are stretched to fill the parent container.

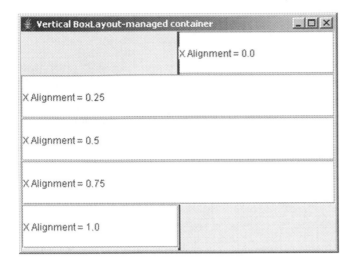

Figure 6-37. *Text field behavior with* BoxLayout *isn't always appropriate*

This occurs because unlike JButton, the JTextField class returns an extremely large value for its maximum width and height, and BoxLayout uses each component's maximum width to determine its size.

Notice that in this example, the container is also filled vertically. When managing a vertical box, BoxLayout attempts to stretch components to fill the container vertically, although it respects the components' maximum size values. If the components can't be stretched to fill the area vertically, then whitespace appears at the bottom (or at the right for a horizontal box), as shown earlier.

When components must be stretched vertically because the container is larger than their combined heights, BoxLayout first calculates how much space remains to be filled. It then stretches each component vertically by comparing the component's maximum height to its preferred height and allocates the extra space based on that difference. In other words, the closer a component's maximum size is to its preferred size, the less that component will be stretched. Components that have the same value for their maximum and preferred sizes will not be stretched at all, and no component is ever made larger than its maximum size by BoxLayout.

Although this discussion examines how a BoxLayout sets the sizes for child components in vertical boxes, the same concepts are applicable to horizontal boxes, but their width values are used instead of their heights.

Child Component Locations

The exact location of a child component within a BoxLayout is determined by a complex interaction between the child's size values, its alignment, and the size and alignment values of the other children in the container. In addition, the order in which a component is added to the container affects its location, since child components are displayed in top-to-bottom order for a vertical box and left-to-right order for a horizontal one.

In general, a child component's position is determined by its alignment values and the parent container's alignment value. If the child has an alignment value of 0.0, it appears to the right of or below the container's axis. Similarly, an alignment of 0.5 causes it to be centered on the axis, and a value of 1.0 causes it to appear left of or above the axis.

Resizing Behavior

Increasing and reducing the size of the parent container causes the absolute position of the container's axis to change, but the child components remain at the same position relative to the axis. If the child components were compressed, their sizes will increase as the container grows, or they may shrink if the container shrinks. For example, Figure 6-38 shows the results of running the modified BoxTest application and reducing the size of the frame.

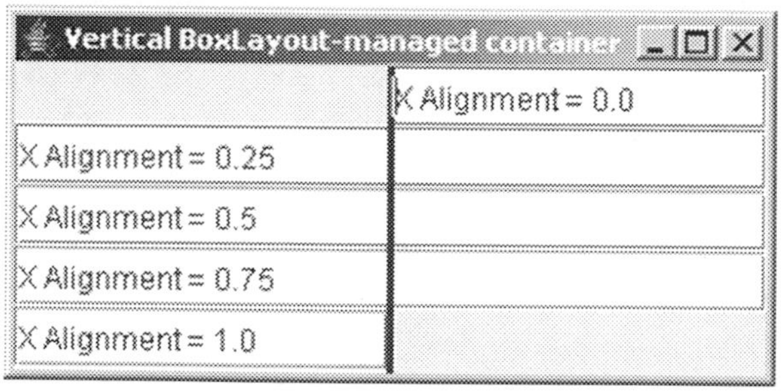

Figure 6-38. *The text fields become smaller as the size of the BoxLayout-controlled parent container decreases*

Container Size

The container's minimum, preferred, and maximum sizes returned by a BoxLayout are the sizes needed to display the components using their minimum, preferred, and maximum sizes, respectively. For example, when using a vertical box, each child component's size is calculated using the techniques described earlier; the height of the container will be the sum of the child components' heights, and the container's width will be equal to the width of the widest child component.

Swing's Box Class

In addition to BoxLayout, Swing includes the Box class, which provides functionality that's used to support BoxLayout. Box is a subclass of java.awt.Container, and you can use an instance of it as a visual component if it's convenient to do so. However, you should keep in mind that as a direct subclass of Container, Box doesn't inherit the functionality of JComponent, which you'll often need.

In addition to acting as a visual component, Box provides a number of static "factory methods" that can be used to create instances of components that make using BoxLayout easier. For example, the createHorizontalBox() and createVerticalBox() methods return instances of Box that use a horizontal and vertical BoxLayout, respectively.

Box also provides factory methods that create transparent components that you can add to a BoxLayout-managed container to provide space between the other components. The three types of components provided by Box are rigid areas, glue components, and struts.

Rigid Areas

A *rigid area* is simply a component with no visual representation that has the same dimensions for its minimum and maximum sizes. You must specify the dimensions to be used when you create a rigid area, which you can do by calling the static createRigidArea() method in the Box class. In Figure 6-39, a rigid area with a height of 15 has been added between each button in the original BoxTest class.

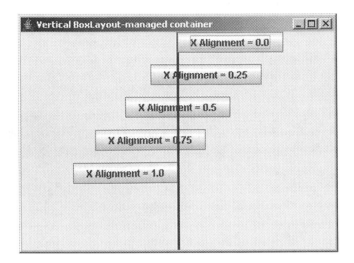

Figure 6-39. *Rigid areas with heights of 15 here generate whitespace between the components arranged by the* BoxLayout

You can achieve this by modifying the code as shown in Listing 6-20.

Listing 6-20. Incorporating Rigid Areas into a BoxLayout

```java
import java.awt.*;
import javax.swing.*;

public class BoxTest {

  public static void main(String[] args) {
    JFrame f = new JFrame("Vertical BoxLayout-managed container");
    f.setDefaultCloseOperation(JFrame.EXIT_ON_CLOSE);
    Container pane = new BoxPanel();
    f.setContentPane(pane);
    BoxLayout bl = new BoxLayout(pane, BoxLayout.Y_AXIS);
    pane.setLayout(bl);
    for (float align = 0.0f; align <= 1.0f; align += 0.25f) {
      JButton button = new JButton("X Alignment = " + align);
      button.setAlignmentX(align);
      pane.add(button);
      pane.add(Box.createRigidArea(new Dimension(0, 15)));
    }
    f.setSize(400, 300);
    f.setVisible(true);
  }
}
```

Glue

Like a rigid area, a *glue component* is simply a component with no visual representation, but unlike a rigid area, you're not allowed to specify a size when creating an instance of a glue component. That's because while rigid areas occupy some fixed amount of space within containers, glue components expand and contract based on the amount of space that's left unused by other (in other words, nonglue) components. If you think this brief description doesn't describe behavior that's conceptually similar to real-life glue, you're not alone. While "real" glue causes things to "stick together," Swing's glue components actually allow other components to be spread apart from one another. Regardless of whether the name is appropriate, *glue* is the term we're stuck with (pun intended).

Which method you call to create a glue object depends upon the orientation of the BoxLayout you're using. For a vertical box, you should call the static createVerticalGlue() method, while createHorizontalGlue() is intended to be used with a horizontal box.

Glue objects fill any extra vertical or horizontal space in a container so that the space won't appear at the bottom or right side of the container. Instead, the space is usually distributed evenly to the glue components. Note that unlike a rigid area, glue components expand and contract to fill the area between components when the container's size increases or decreases. Listing 6-21 shows an example of how to use glue, where the BoxTest application has been modified to add a glue component below each button.

Listing 6-21. Using "Glue" with a BoxLayoutimport java.awt.*;

```
import javax.swing.*;

public class BoxTest {

  public static void main(String[] args) {
    JFrame f = new JFrame("Vertical BoxLayout-managed container");
    f.setDefaultCloseOperation(JFrame.EXIT_ON_CLOSE);
    Container pane = new BoxPanel();
    f.setContentPane(pane);
    pane.setLayout(new BoxLayout(pane, BoxLayout.Y_AXIS));
    for (float align = 0.0f; align <= 1.0f; align += 0.25f) {
      JButton button = new JButton("X Alignment = " + align);
      button.setAlignmentX(align);
      pane.add(button);
      pane.add(Box.createVerticalGlue());
    }
    f.setSize(400, 300);
    f.setVisible(true);
  }

}
```

Executing this code produces results like those shown in Figure 6-40, where the extra vertical space is distributed evenly to each of the glue components.

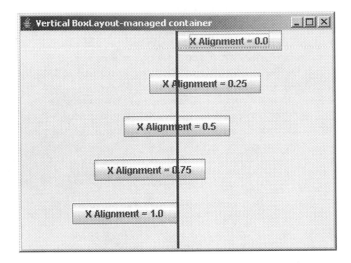

Figure 6-40. *These buttons are separated by "vertical glue"*

As mentioned earlier, extra vertical space is distributed by a vertical BoxLayout based on the difference between a component's maximum vertical size and its preferred vertical size. As you might guess, glue components are simply "dummy" components with a large maximum size and a minimum size of 0, so in many cases, all extra space will be assigned to them. However, as you saw earlier with JTextField instances, it's possible for other components with large maximum sizes to accidentally be made inappropriately large by a BoxLayout, and this can occur even when glue components are used.

Struts

One definition of the word *strut* in the dictionary is, "a brace fitted into a framework to resist pressure in the direction of its length." Unlike glue components, struts are appropriately named. Struts are similar to rigid areas but with an important difference: instead of specifying both the width and height of the component, you specify a strut's size in only one dimension. Specifically, you specify the width when you call createHorizontalStrut() and the height when calling createVerticalStrut(). The strut uses the value you specify for its minimum, preferred, and maximum sizes in that dimension and uses 0 for the other dimension when setting its minimum and preferred heights. However, when setting the maximum size, Box uses a very large value for the remaining dimension (width for a vertical box and height for a horizontal box), and this can cause undesirable results. Specifically, the presence of a very large strut component in the BoxLayout can result in its container being assigned a size that's larger than what was intended.

Because rigid areas can provide the same functionality and because there's a potential problem associated with the use of struts, you should avoid struts and use rigid areas instead.

Guidelines for Using Layout Managers

Now that I've covered the advantages and disadvantages of the layout managers included with Java, it's appropriate to discuss some general topics related to how to use layout managers.

Combining Layout Managers

In the previous discussions of layout managers, I treated each one independently of the other, but it's common practice for a user interface to use multiple layout managers. In fact, you'll often find it necessary or desirable to create a container that uses one type of layout manager and add child containers to that parent that use different types of layout managers. For example, suppose you want to create a user interface like the one shown in Figure 6-41. In this case, the component at the top is displayed using its preferred height and fills the width of the container. In addition, a row of buttons that are equal in size occupies the bottom, and a component in the center fills the remaining area.

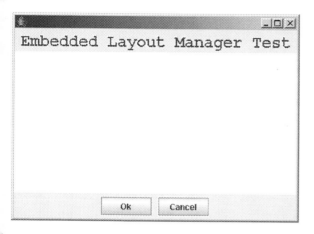

Figure 6-41. *Creating even a simple screen such as this one is difficult to do with a single layout manager*

To some extent, BorderLayout provides the functionality needed to create this component, but you can't use it directly to create the bottom row of buttons. That's because BorderLayout allows only a single component to be added to a location, such as the SOUTH portion of its container. You can resolve this problem by adding the two buttons to a container such as a JPanel and adding that panel to the parent managed by a BorderLayout. Since the buttons should be given the same size, GridLayout is the obvious choice for the container that the buttons will be added to; Listing 6-22 shows the code to implement this.

Listing 6-22. Combining Layout Managers

```java
import java.awt.*;
import javax.swing.*;

public class Embedded extends JFrame {

  public static void main(String[] args) {
    Embedded e = new Embedded();
    e.setDefaultCloseOperation(JFrame.EXIT_ON_CLOSE);
    e.setSize(400, 300);
    e.setVisible(true);
  }

  public Embedded() {
    Container pane = getContentPane();
    pane.setLayout(new BorderLayout());
```

```
    pane.add(getHeader(), BorderLayout.NORTH);
    pane.add(getTextArea(), BorderLayout.CENTER);
    pane.add(getButtonPanel(), BorderLayout.SOUTH);
  }

  private JComponent getHeader() {
    JLabel label = new JLabel("Embedded Layout Manager Test",
                              JLabel.CENTER);
    label.setFont(new Font("Courier", Font.BOLD, 24));
    return label;
  }

  private JComponent getTextArea() {
    return new JTextArea(10, 10);
  }

  private JComponent getButtonPanel() {
    JPanel inner = new JPanel();
    inner.setLayout(new GridLayout(1, 2, 10, 0));
    inner.add(new JButton("Ok"));
    inner.add(new JButton("Cancel"));
    return inner;
  }

}
```

As shown in Figure 6-42, this code doesn't quite achieve the desired results, since the buttons have been stretched to fill the width of the container.

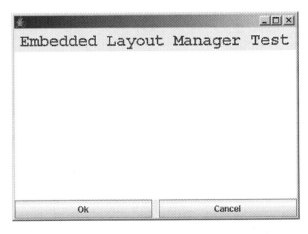

Figure 6-42. *The top portion of the window is correct, but the buttons at the bottom have expanded to fill the entire width of the container*

That's because the buttons' parent container was stretched by the BorderLayout so that its width is equal to the width of the frame, and that in turn causes the GridLayout to stretch the buttons to fill their parent container. To fix this problem, it's necessary to put the panel managed by the GridLayout into another container that won't stretch it. Since FlowLayout always displays components using their preferred size, you can use it to provide this behavior, so define an additional FlowLayout-managed JPanel, add the button panel to it, and add the button panel to the content pane.

```
private JComponent getButtonPanel() {
  JPanel inner = new JPanel();
  inner.setLayout(new GridLayout(1, 2, 10, 0));
  inner.add(new JButton("Ok"));
  inner.add(new JButton("Cancel"));
  JPanel outer = new JPanel();
  outer.setLayout(new FlowLayout());
  outer.add(inner);
  return outer;
  // return inner;
}
```

Finally, running this modified code produces the desired interface that was illustrated at the start of this section.

You'll often find it necessary to embed containers within other containers and to use different layout managers when doing so. If you're creating a complex user interface, it's often helpful to conceptually break the interface down into smaller, simpler portions that can be created using the existing layout managers. Those smaller pieces can then be created and combined into the large, complex interface instead of trying to produce the desired results with a single layout manager.

Absolute Positioning Without a Layout Manager

Although there's rarely a reason to do so, you can completely avoid using a layout manager when designing an interface. However, if you don't use a layout manager, you're responsible for explicitly setting the size and position of each component within a container using Component methods such as setSize(), setLocation(), and setBounds().

▓ **Note**   The approach described here—that is, using absolute positioning instead of a layout manager—is rarely desirable, because it usually results in an interface that must be revised to appropriately handle even minor changes.

If you want to remove the layout manager from a container and explicitly set the size and position of the components in that container, you can call the setLayout() method and specify a null value, as shown in the following code:

```
JPanel panel = new JPanel();
panel.setLayout(null);
```

When a container displays its child components, it does so using the position and size values assigned to those components, which are usually set by a layout manager. If you add a component to a container and don't set the component's location, it will appear at the container's origin (in other words, at coordinates 0, 0). However, if you add a component to a container and don't specify the component's size, it will not appear at all, because its width and height values will both be 0. The preferred, minimum, and maximum size values are used by layout managers to determine the size that should be used for a component, but components aren't automatically set to any of those three sizes when created.

Invisible Components

Components that have their visibility flag set to false don't appear when their parent container is displayed, and you can query and modify the visibility flag using Component's isVisible() and setVisible() methods. In general, layout managers ignore invisible components inside their layoutContainer() method, causing the container to be formatted as though the invisible components had not been added.

You'll most often use invisible components when some portion of your user interface shouldn't always be displayed. For example, your interface might have a menu item that allows the user to toggle the display status of some element such as a toolbar or status bar. In that case, you could add the element to the container when the container is being constructed but make it invisible until it should be displayed.

Depending upon the superclass of the component that's made visible or invisible, it may be necessary for you to use revalidate() to cause the layout manager to reposition and resize the components in the container. JComponent subclasses automatically trigger this behavior, but others don't.

Specifying an Index When Adding a Component

Earlier, you saw that each Container maintains a list of child components and that the components are listed in the order in which they were added to the container. Normally when a component is added to a container, that component is added to the end of the container's list. However, if you prefer to insert the component at a particular position within the list, you can use one of two additional forms of the add() method that weren't previously mentioned in this chapter:

- add(Component comp, int index)

- add(Component comp, Object constraints, int index)

As you've seen, some layout managers position child components within the container based on when they were added. In reality, that behavior is based on the component's index value (its position within the parent container's list), which is assumed to reflect the sequence in which the components were added to the container. In most cases where the index value is significant, you'll simply add components in the order you want them to appear. However, for various reasons, it's not always possible or desirable to do so, and you'll want to explicitly specify an index value when adding a child component.

A component's place in the list is sometimes significant for another reason as well, since its index value (also called its *Z-order*) defines its position on the Z axis. In other words, the order in which two components appear in their parent container's list determines which component appears "in front of" the other. When a container receives a paint() request, it paints its children in reverse order (from last to first), so the most recently added child appears "behind" the others, and the first one appears "in front."

Z-order isn't usually important because layout managers normally don't allow components to occupy the coordinates within their parent container. However, if you're not using a layout manager or if you're using one that allows components to overlap one another, Z-order can become significant. For example, the following application in Listing 6-23 defines two JButton instances that partially overlap:

Listing 6-23. How Z-order Affects Displaying Components

```java
import java.awt.*;
import javax.swing.*;

public class ZOrder extends JPanel {

  public static void main(String[] args) {
    JFrame f = new JFrame();
    f.setDefaultCloseOperation(JFrame.EXIT_ON_CLOSE);
    f.setContentPane(new ZOrder());
    f.setSize(400, 300);
    f.setVisible(true);
  }

  public ZOrder() {
    setLayout(null);
    JButton first = new JButton("This button is added first");
    first.setBounds(20, 50, 200, 30);
    add(first);
    JButton second = new JButton("This button is added second");
    second.setBounds(120, 65, 200, 30);
    add(second);
  }

}
```

If you compile and run this application, it displays the first button in front of the second one, as shown in Figure 6-43, which is the expected result based on the behavior described.

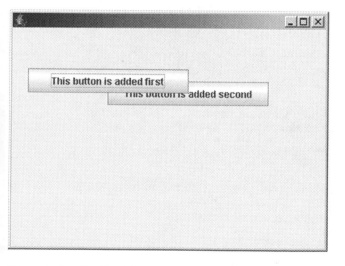

Figure 6-43. The "first" button appears on top of the "second" one, at least initially

271

However, if you move the cursor over the second button, that button will appear in front of the first one, which may seem to contradict the statements that have been made concerning Z-order (see Figure 6-44).

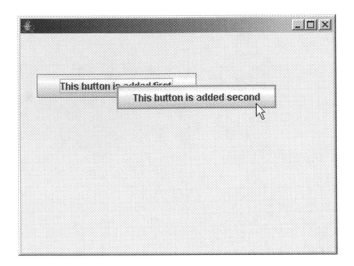

Figure 6-44. *Once the cursor is moved over the "second" button, it appears to be on top of the "first" one*

In reality, the second button is still behind the first one in those cases, but it has been repainted while the first one hasn't been, so the second one seems to be in front. Moving the mouse over a component causes the component to be repainted so that it will repair the "damage" done when the cursor painted over part of the component, which is why this behavior occurs. You can prove that the first button is still in front by moving the mouse over the portion of the interface where the two buttons overlap one another, at which time the first button will be repainted and again appear in front of the second one.

Note that unlike a component's X and Y coordinates, Z-order can be set only when a component is added to a container. Therefore, if you want to change a component's Z-order, you must remove it from the container and add it again, explicitly specifying the new index value when you call the add() method.

Creating Your Own Layout Manager

The layout managers you've examined so far are a standard part of Java and provide enough functionality to allow you to create very complex and flexible layouts. However, the existing layout managers are sometimes not capable of setting the size or position of components the way you'd like, and in that situation, you may choose to create your own layout manager.

For example, suppose you want to create a component that allows you to select items from a list like the one shown in Figure 6-45 and that you have the following requirements that must be met:

- The column of buttons in the middle of the component should always be displayed using its preferred size.

- The two JList components should both be the same size vertically and horizontally, and they should shrink or expand to fill the container's remaining horizontal space after the center component has been allocated its preferred size.

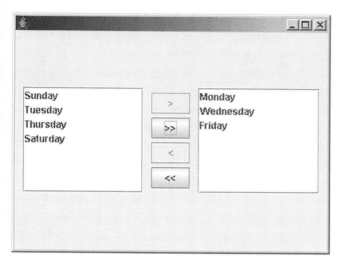

Figure 6-45. *Creating a panel like the one shown here can be difficult with Java's standard layout managers*

Given these requirements, none of the layout managers you've already seen is appropriate for this custom component, primarily because of the requirement that the two JList components be the same size. Only GridLayout allows you to ensure that two components have the same horizontal and vertical size, but using that layout manager would also cause the button column in the center to have the same size as the JList instances. GridBagLayout allows you to assign all components in a row the same height or all components in a column the same width, but it doesn't provide you with a way to make components the same size in both dimensions. In this case, it's necessary to create a layout manager to support this component; for this example, you'll name this new layout manager class DividerLayout.

As it turns out, creating a custom layout manager is simple. All you need to do is create a class that implements the LayoutManager2 interface defined in the java.awt package. You'll begin by examining the methods defined in LayoutManager2 that your custom layout manager class must implement, and then you'll examine those in the LayoutManager class, since it's the superclass of LayoutManager2.

When considering how you'll implement these methods, keep in mind that a layout manager instance is associated with and used by a Container and that these methods shouldn't normally be called directly by your application code.

With the exception of removeLayoutComponent() and the overloaded addLayoutComponent(), all methods defined in LayoutManager and LayoutManager2 are passed a reference to the parent container associated with the layout manager instance.

LayoutManager2 Methods

This interface defines five methods, three of which will normally contain little or no code. LayoutManager2 didn't exist in Java 1.0 but was added in 1.1 to provide support for new features such as alignment values, maximum sizes (Java 1.0 supported only minimum and preferred sizes), and a more generic add() method.

addLayoutComponent (Component, Object)

This method is called by the layout manager's container when its add() method is invoked, indicating that a component should be added to the container. The container passes the request along to the layout manager so that the manager can take whatever action is necessary, such as creating a copy of the constraint information and defining a relationship between the component and the constraint data. For example, GridBagLayout creates a clone of the GridBagConstraints object that's passed to it and associates that GridBagConstraints clone with the component by adding an entry to a Hashtable.

As mentioned earlier in this chapter, the layout manager isn't responsible for maintaining a list of the components that have been added to the container. That task is performed by the container itself, and the list of components maintained by the container is accessible through its getComponents() method. In fact, FlowLayout and GridLayout don't maintain references to the components added to the layout, since they don't support any constraint information. Instead, they position each component based on when it was added to the Container, and they're able to do this because the array returned by getComponents() lists the components in the order in which they were added to the container. Only when a layout manager needs to associate constraint information with a component will it normally maintain references to the components.

When you create a custom layout manager, you'll need to decide whether any constraint information should be specified when a component is added. If the layout manager doesn't need constraint information, then the application can simply call the add() method in Container that accepts a single component instance.

If your layout manager does need constraint information, you can create a custom class such as GridBagConstraints that encapsulates the information, or if the constraint information is simple, you can use an existing class. For example, the DividerLayout requires some type of constraint information that identifies which position (left, center, or right) the component should occupy. Since DividerLayout is somewhat similar to BorderLayout, for this example you'll define three String constants called WEST, CENTER, and EAST that correspond to the three positions available within the container:

```
import java.awt.*;

public class DividerLayout implements LayoutManager2 {

    public final static String WEST = "WEST";
    public final static String EAST = "EAST";
    public final static String CENTER = "CENTER";

    private Component westComponent;
    private Component centerComponent;
    private Component eastComponent;

    // Methods go here ...
}
```

In addition, DividerLayout needs to associate a component with its constraint value so that the component's position can be selected when the time comes to set the sizes and positions of the container's child components.

```
public void addLayoutComponent(Component comp, Object constraints) {
    if (WEST.equalsIgnoreCase((String)constraints)) {
        westComponent = comp;
    }
    else if (CENTER.equalsIgnoreCase((String)constraints)) {
        centerComponent = comp;
    }
    else if (EAST.equalsIgnoreCase((String)constraints)) {
        eastComponent = comp;
    }
}
```

maximumLayoutSize()

This method is called by a container when its getMaximumSize() method is called. The layout manager is responsible for calculating the amount of space that the container needs in order to display all its components using their maximum sizes.

In the case of DividerLayout, it identifies the largest height value from the three components and determines which of the two outer components has a larger width value. That width value is multiplied by 2 since there are two "outer" components that will be assigned identical widths, and the result is added to the width of the center component, as follows:

```
public Dimension maximumLayoutSize(Container target) {
  Dimension size;
  int width = 0;
  int height = 0;
  if ((westComponent != null) && (westComponent.isVisible())) {
    size = westComponent.getMaximumSize();
    width = Math.max(width, size.width);
    height = Math.max(height, size.height);
  }
  if ((eastComponent != null) && (eastComponent.isVisible())) {
    size = eastComponent.getMaximumSize();
    width = Math.max(width, size.width);
    height = Math.max(height, size.height);
  }
  width *= 2;
  if ((centerComponent != null) && (centerComponent.isVisible())) {
    size = centerComponent.getPreferredSize();
    width += size.width;
    height = Math.max(height, size.height);
  }
  return new Dimension(width, height);
}
```

getLayoutAlignmentX() and getLayoutAlignmentY()

These methods are provided for layout managers such as BoxLayout that use an alignment value to position the components within the container. Like most layout managers, however, DividerLayout doesn't use alignment values, so the value returned isn't important; the following code shows "dummy" implementations:

```
public float getLayoutAlignmentX(Container target) {
  return 0.0f;
}
public float getLayoutAlignmentY(Container target) {
  return 0.0f;
}
```

invalidateLayout()

This method is called to indicate to the layout manager that it should clear any cached information related to the size and position of the container's components. This is related only to information that has been derived by the layout manager itself, and a call to this method doesn't indicate that constraint information that was explicitly passed to the layout manager should be discarded. For example, if your layout manager performs computations that are slow and complex, it may be worthwhile to cache the results of those computations. Like most layout managers, no action needs to be taken in DividerLayout's implementation of this method.

```
public void invalidateLayout(Container target) {
}
```

LayoutManager Methods

This is the interface originally included in Java 1.0 for creating a layout manager. It defines basic methods related to managing the components added to a container.

addLayoutComponent (String, Component)

This is the method that was originally used for adding a child component to a parent container, but this method has effectively been deprecated. It's not marked as deprecated by a javadoc-style @deprecated tag, but it's deprecated conceptually, because another, more flexible method exists and should be used instead. In fact, as you'll see shortly, the implementation of this method in DividerLayout does nothing more than call its replacement, which is the addLayoutComponent() method defined in LayoutManager2.

This method was provided to allow String constraint values to be passed to CardLayout and BorderLayout instances. However, because this method accepts only a String value, you can't pass any other type of object to represent the constraints. For example, since an instance of GridBagConstraints isn't a subclass of String, you can't use it as an argument with the add() method in Java 1.0. Instead, it's necessary to call GridBagLayout's setConstraints() method to associate the GridBagConstraints with a component, as shown in the following code:

```
GridBagLayout gbl = new GridBagLayout();
setLayout(gbl);
GridBagConstraints constraints = new GridBagConstraints();
Button btn = new Button("Testing");
gbl.setConstraints(btn, constraints);
add(btn);
```

With the addition of the more generic addLayoutComponent() method in LayoutManager2, it's now possible to pass any type of Object to the layout manager when you call add(). In Java 1.1, GridBagLayout was modified to extend LayoutManager2, so you can now add a component to a container and specify that component's constraints at the same time, as follows:

```
GridBagLayout gbl = new GridBagLayout();
setLayout(gbl);
GridBagConstraints constraints = new GridBagConstraints();
Button btn = new Button("Testing");
// gbl.setConstraints(btn, constraints);
// add(btn);
add(btn, constraints);
```

As mentioned, you'll normally implement this method by delegating the call to the addLayoutComponent() method defined in LayoutManager2, which you can do by simply reversing the order of the parameter values as follows. Alternatively, you may simply choose to ignore a call to this method completely if your custom layout manager doesn't accept a String instance for a constraint parameter.

```java
public void addLayoutComponent(String name, Component comp) {
  // The following line can be commented out without
  // affecting this layout manager
  addLayoutComponent(comp, name);
}
```

removeLayoutComponent()

This method is called when a component is removed from the container. Your custom layout manager should remove any references to the component, as well as any data it maintains that's related to the component, such as constraint information. The following is the implementation of this method in DividerLayout:

```java
public void removeLayoutComponent(Component comp) {
  if (comp == westComponent) {
    westComponent = null;
  }
  else if (comp == centerComponent) {
    centerComponent = null;
  }
  else if (comp == eastComponent) {
    centerComponent = null;
  }
}
```

preferredLayoutSize() and minimumLayoutSize()

preferredLayoutSize() is similar to the maximumLayoutSize() method described earlier; in fact, its implementation will often differ only in that it calls the getPreferredSize() method for each component instead of getMaximumSize(). The purpose of this method is to calculate the preferred size of the Container instance associated with this layout manager. The following is the implementation of this method in DividerLayout:

```java
public Dimension preferredLayoutSize(Container parent) {
  Dimension size;
  int width = 0;
  int height = 0;
  if ((westComponent != null) && (westComponent.isVisible())) {
    size = westComponent.getPreferredSize();
    width = Math.max(width, size.width);
    height = Math.max(height, size.height);
  }
  if ((eastComponent != null) && (eastComponent.isVisible())) {
    size = eastComponent.getPreferredSize();
    width = Math.max(width, size.width);
    height = Math.max(height, size.height);
  }
```

```
  width *= 2;
  if ((centerComponent != null) && (centerComponent.isVisible())) {
    size = centerComponent.getPreferredSize();
    width += size.width;
    height = Math.max(height, size.height);
  }
  return new Dimension(width, height);
}
```

Similarly, `minimumLayoutSize()` differs only in that it calls the `getMinimumSize()` method instead of `getPreferredSize()` or `getMaximumSize()`; the purpose of this method is to calculate the minimum size of the `Container` instance associated with this layout manager.

```
public Dimension minimumLayoutSize(Container parent) {
  Dimension size;
  int width = 0;
  int height = 0;
  if ((westComponent != null) && (westComponent.isVisible())) {
    size = westComponent.getMinimumSize();
    width = Math.max(width, size.width);
    height = Math.max(height, size.height);
  }
  if ((eastComponent != null) && (eastComponent.isVisible())) {
    size = eastComponent.getMinimumSize();
    width = Math.max(width, size.width);
    height = Math.max(height, size.height);
  }
  width *= 2;
  if ((centerComponent != null) && (centerComponent.isVisible())) {
    size = centerComponent.getPreferredSize();
    width += size.width;
    height += Math.max(height, size.height);
  }
  return new Dimension(width, height);
}
```

layoutContainer()

This is the method that's responsible for setting the size and position of the child components within a container and is called when the container's `doLayout()` method is invoked.

Within this method, you'll typically use the preferred, minimum, or maximum component sizes, or some combination of those, and you should use methods defined in `Component` such as `setSize()`, `setLocation()`, and `setBounds()` to modify each component's size and/or position.

When implementing `layoutContainer()`, you should keep in mind that the size of the container may or may not be the same size that your class returned from `minimumLayoutSize()`, `preferredLayoutSize()`, or `maximumLayoutSize()`. In other words, you may have to allocate excess space or shrink your components, depending upon what you decide is appropriate for your layout manager. For example, in the case of `DividerLayout`, the two outer components are expected to shrink or expand to fill the space that remains after the middle component is allocated its preferred size.

Finally, you should be aware that it's standard practice to ignore components that are invisible, which can be determined by calling the isVisible() method. I discuss the reasons for making components invisible in more detail later, but you should keep this guideline in mind when designing a custom layout manager. Listing 6-24 shows the implementation of layoutContainer() and includes logic that will ignore components that are invisible.

Listing 6-24. Implementing layoutContainer()

```java
public void layoutContainer(Container container) {
  Insets insets = container.getInsets();
  Dimension westSize = new Dimension(0, 0);
  Dimension centerSize = new Dimension(0, 0);
  Dimension eastSize = new Dimension(0, 0);
  Rectangle centerBounds = new Rectangle(0, 0, 0, 0);
  Dimension containerSize = container.getSize();
  int centerX = containerSize.width / 2;
  int centerY = containerSize.height / 2;
  if ((centerComponent != null) &&
      (centerComponent.isVisible())) {
    centerSize = centerComponent.getPreferredSize();
    centerSize.width = Math.min(centerSize.width,
      containerSize.width - insets.left -
      insets.right);
    centerSize.height = Math.min(centerSize.height,
      containerSize.height - insets.top -
      insets.bottom);
    centerComponent.setBounds(centerX -
      (centerSize.width / 2),
      centerY - (centerSize.height / 2),
      centerSize.width, centerSize.height);
    centerBounds = centerComponent.getBounds();
  }
  if ((westComponent != null) && (westComponent.isVisible())) {
    westSize = westComponent.getPreferredSize();
  }
  if ((eastComponent != null) && (eastComponent.isVisible())) {
    eastSize = eastComponent.getPreferredSize();
  } int maxWidth = Math.min(westSize.width, eastSize.width);
maxWidth = Math.max(maxWidth, (containerSize.width -
    centerBounds.width - insets.left -
    insets.right) / 2);
  int maxHeight = Math.min(westSize.height, eastSize.height);
maxHeight = Math.min(maxHeight, containerSize.height -
    insets.top - insets.bottom);
  if (westComponent != null) {
    westComponent.setBounds(centerBounds.x - maxWidth,
        centerY - (maxHeight / 2),
        maxWidth, maxHeight);
  }
  if (eastComponent != null) {
    eastComponent.setBounds(centerBounds.x +
        centerBounds.width,
```

```
        centerY - (maxHeight / 2),
        maxWidth, maxHeight);
  }
}
```

Using a Custom Layout Manager

You've now examined each of the methods you must implement to create a custom layout manager, and you can download the completed DividerLayout from the Source Code/Download area of the Apress web site (www.apress.com). To see how it's used, you can also download, compile, and run the SelectorPanel class stored there as well.

Finally, you can easily test this new class by compiling and executing the following code, shown in Listing 6-25:

Listing 6-25. Simple Class That Uses a Custom Layout Manager

```java
import java.awt.*;
import javax.swing.*;

public class SelectorTest extends JPanel {

  public static void main(String[] args) {
    JFrame f = new JFrame();
    f.setDefaultCloseOperation(JFrame.EXIT_ON_CLOSE);
    Container pane = f.getContentPane();
    pane.setLayout(new BorderLayout());
    Object[] values = {"Sunday", "Monday", "Tuesday", "Wednesday",
                       "Thursday", "Friday", "Saturday"};
    SelectorPanel sp = new SelectorPanel(values);
    sp.setBorder(BorderFactory.createEmptyBorder(5, 10, 5, 10));
    pane.add(sp);
    f.setSize(400, 300);
    f.setVisible(true);
  }

}
```

Summary

In this chapter, I covered the following topics related to layout managers:

- The layout managers provided with the Java core classes and how they work

- How and when to create a custom layout manager class

- How to use layout managers together to build complex user interfaces

- How and when to use absolute positioning instead of a layout manager

- The behavior of layout managers with respect to invisible components

- The importance of Z-order and how to control it

CHAPTER 7

■ ■ ■

Using Swing's JTable

Many applications need to display data in a tabular form, and Swing provides a table component (also sometimes called a *grid*) that allows you to do so. The JTable class, defined in the javax.swing package, provides a great deal of functionality that you can use to create a user interface for viewing and updating data. This chapter covers some of the functionality that's commonly needed when using a table component and illustrates how to implement it using JTable. In the process, you'll learn a great deal about how JTable works, how to use its existing capabilities, and how to extend its capabilities.

In this chapter, I'll cover a variety of topics related to JTable, including the following:

- Creating a data model for a table

- Assigning column widths

- Using different data models

- Cell rendering and editing

- Handling cell selections

- Working with table headers

- Implementing sort functionality for table rows

Figure 7-1 shows an example of how a JTable component appears.

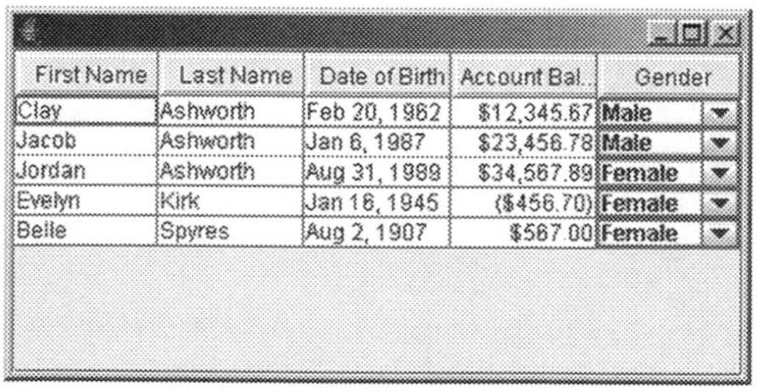

First Name	Last Name	Date of Birth	Account Bal..	Gender
Clay	Ashworth	Feb 20, 1962	$12,345.67	Male
Jacob	Ashworth	Jan 6, 1987	$23,456.78	Male
Jordan	Ashworth	Aug 31, 1989	$34,567.89	Female
Evelyn	Kirk	Jan 16, 1945	($456.70)	Female
Belle	Spyres	Aug 2, 1907	$567.00	Female

Figure 7-1. *An example of how a JTable might be used*

Besides the obvious ability to display information, JTable also allows you to easily edit the information, set column headers and widths, and control how information is displayed within the table. However, the most basic function is that of displaying the data, and before you can display information in a JTable, you must encapsulate the data in a data model and make the model available to the table.

The Data Model

In addition to the JTable class, which represents the visual table component, Swing provides a number of support classes that are used by JTable, and they're defined in the javax.swing.table package. Perhaps the most important support class is TableModel, which defines the interface between a JTable and its data model. Like other Swing components, JTable uses a model/view/controller design that separates the visual component (a JTable instance) from its data (a TableModel implementation). This provides greater flexibility and reusability but can also make JTable more complex to use. Fortunately, programmers can insulate themselves from much of the complexity by using some of the default implementations provided with Swing.

As you might expect, the TableModel associated with a JTable is responsible for providing the table with the data that it displays, but the model is also responsible for providing some information that may not be as obvious, including the following:

- The dimensions of the table (in other words, the number of rows and the number of columns in the table)

- The type of data contained within each column within the table

- The column headers that should be displayed

- Whether the value in a given cell can be edited

Although this example is somewhat contrived, you'll use the data that's hard-coded in Listing 7-1 for most of the chapter. In reality, the data displayed in a JTable is usually retrieved from some external source such as a relational database table. However, the TableValues class is convenient because it can be created easily and allows you to create sample JTable code without also writing JDBC code, which makes the examples easier to follow.

Listing 7-1. A Class That Contains Table Data

```java
import java.util.Calendar;
import java.util.GregorianCalendar;

public class TableValues {

    public final static int FIRST_NAME = 0;
    public final static int LAST_NAME = 1;
    public final static int DATE_OF_BIRTH = 2;
    public final static int ACCOUNT_BALANCE = 3;
    public final static int GENDER = 4;
    public final static boolean GENDER_MALE = true;
    public final static boolean GENDER_FEMALE = false;

    public Object[][] values = {
      {
      "Clay", "Ashworth",
      new GregorianCalendar(1962, Calendar.FEBRUARY, 20).getTime(),
      new Float(12345.67), new Boolean(GENDER_MALE)
    }, {
      "Jacob", "Ashworth",
      new GregorianCalendar(1987, Calendar.JANUARY, 6).getTime(),
      new Float(23456.78), new Boolean(GENDER_MALE)
```

```
    }, {
        "Jordan", "Ashworth",
        new GregorianCalendar(1989, Calendar.AUGUST, 31).getTime(),
        new Float(34567.89), new Boolean(GENDER_FEMALE)
    }, {
        "Evelyn", "Kirk",
        new GregorianCalendar(1945, Calendar.JANUARY, 16).getTime(),
        new Float(-456.70), new Boolean(GENDER_FEMALE)
    }, {
        "Belle", "Spyres",
        new GregorianCalendar(1907, Calendar.AUGUST, 2).getTime(),
        new Float(567.00), new Boolean(GENDER_FEMALE)
    }
    };

}
```

At this point, the class contains only data and no executable code, but as you'll see shortly, you can easily transform it into a `TableModel` implementation that can expose the data to a `JTable`. Before doing so, you may want to briefly study the class diagram shown in Figure 7-2, which describes the `TableModel` interface and its methods.

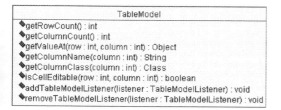

Figure 7-2. *A simple class diagram showing the methods defined in* `TableModel`

With nine methods to implement, the interface might appear complex and tedious to implement to someone who wants to create a table quickly. However, Java also provides the `AbstractTableModel` and `DefaultTableModel` classes, which both implement the `TableModel` interface and which can be used with minimal effort. In fact, you can extend the `AbstractTableModel` by implementing three simple methods.

- One that returns the row count

- Another that returns the column count

- A third that returns the value associated with a particular cell

Listing 7-2 shows an example of how to implement this; the code modifies the `TableValues` class to extend `AbstractTableModel` and implements its three abstract methods.

Listing 7-2. Extending AbstractTableModel

```java
import java.util.Calendar;
import java.util.GregorianCalendar;
import javax.swing.table.AbstractTableModel;

public class TableValues extends AbstractTableModel {

  public final static int FIRST_NAME = 0;
  public final static int LAST_NAME = 1;
  public final static int DATE_OF_BIRTH = 2;
  public final static int ACCOUNT_BALANCE = 3;
  public final static int GENDER = 4;

  public final static boolean GENDER_MALE = true;
  public final static boolean GENDER_FEMALE = false;

  public Object[][] values = {
    {
    "Clay", "Ashworth",
    new GregorianCalendar(1962, Calendar.FEBRUARY, 20).getTime(),
    new Float(12345.67), new Boolean(GENDER_MALE)
  }, {
    "Jacob", "Ashworth",
    new GregorianCalendar(1987, Calendar.JANUARY, 6).getTime(),
    new Float(23456.78), new Boolean(GENDER_MALE)
  }, {
    "Jordan", "Ashworth",
    new GregorianCalendar(1989, Calendar.AUGUST, 31).getTime(),
    new Float(34567.89), new Boolean(GENDER_FEMALE)
  }, {
    "Evelyn", "Kirk",
    new GregorianCalendar(1945, Calendar.JANUARY, 16).getTime(),
    new Float(-456.70), new Boolean(GENDER_FEMALE)
  }, {
    "Belle", "Spyres",
    new GregorianCalendar(1907, Calendar.AUGUST, 2).getTime(),
    new Float(567.00), new Boolean(GENDER_FEMALE)
  }
  };

  public int getRowCount() {
    return values.length;
  }

  public int getColumnCount() {
    return values[0].length;
  }

  public Object getValueAt(int row, int column) {
    return values[row][column];
  }

}
```

Creating a TableModel implementation is a trivial matter when using AbstractTableModel, and in this case, it requires just a single line for each of the three methods implemented. Although the DefaultTableModel provides a way to create a TableModel that's sometimes even easier, its use isn't recommended, primarily because it creates its own references to the cell data. Besides being less scalable and less flexible, that approach complicates the issue of editing, which I'll cover later. To understand why DefaultTableModel isn't scalable, it's necessary to have some understanding of how JTable works.

As you've seen, the TableModel is responsible for indicating how many rows and columns the table contains, and getRowCount() and getColumnCount() are called immediately when a table is created and displayed. However, the table never maintains references to the data from the TableModel but simply accesses the information long enough to render it when needed. For example, suppose you create a model that returns a value of 100 from getRowCount(), but your table is inside a JScrollPane and the display area is large enough to display only ten rows at once. When the table is displayed, it will initially access the first ten rows of data in the TableModel and will access the data for the other rows only when (or if) you scroll down so that they're displayed within the JScrollPane's viewport. Why is this behavior important? It allows you to display extremely large amounts of data within a JTable without having all the data loaded into memory simultaneously. Instead, your TableModel can load the data it needs in an "on-demand" (or if you prefer, "just-in-time") fashion, which allows you to minimize the amount of memory used.

With this point in mind, let's return to the discussion of DefaultTableModel and consider the implications of it creating a reference to each of the data items it encapsulates. Since it requires a reference to each item, all its data must be in memory for as long as the model is in use; it can't respond to data retrieval requests on an "as-needed" basis. Therefore, since DefaultTableModel has potentially serious drawbacks and is only slightly easier to use, you should generally use AbstractTableModel instead. You may still choose to use DefaultTableModel if your table will contain only a small amount of data, since it's always faster to have data cached in memory. However, if your table will contain a large amount of data and memory utilization is a concern, you'll want to use AbstractTableModel. When you create a subclass of AbstractTableModel, that class is completely responsible for accessing the data that's needed by the table. Your implementation might cache data in memory the way DefaultTableModel does, or you might leave the data in some external location such as a relational database and access it only when it's needed. In the case of the TableValues class, you hard-coded data into a class for the sake of convenience, but a more realistic scenario would be to have the data retrieved from a database or a disk file.

Now that you've created a TableModel implementation, it's possible to create a JTable and populate it with the data stored in the TableValues class, as shown in Listing 7-3.

Listing 7-3. Using the Table Model

```java
import java.awt.*;
import javax.swing.*;

public class SimpleTableTest extends JFrame {

  private JTable table;

  public static void main(String[] args) {
    SimpleTableTest stt = new SimpleTableTest();
    stt.setDefaultCloseOperation(JFrame.EXIT_ON_CLOSE);
    stt.setSize(400, 200);
    stt.setVisible(true);
  }
```

```
public SimpleTableTest() {
  Container pane = getContentPane();
  pane.setLayout(new BorderLayout());
  TableValues tv = new TableValues();
  table = new JTable(tv);
  pane.add(table, BorderLayout.CENTER);
}

}
```

This application provides a simple table that displays the `TableValues` data, as shown in Figure 7-3.

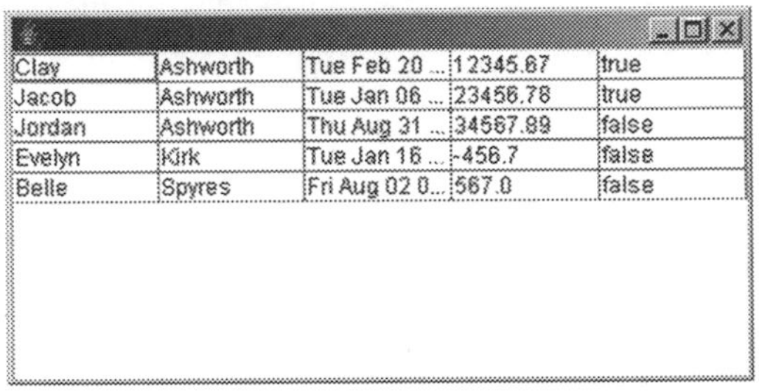

Figure 7-3. *The initial display produced by the* `SimpleTableTest` *class*

However, this has several problems. For example, if the frame is resized so that it's smaller than the table, portions of the data are invisible and inaccessible, as shown in Figure 7-4.

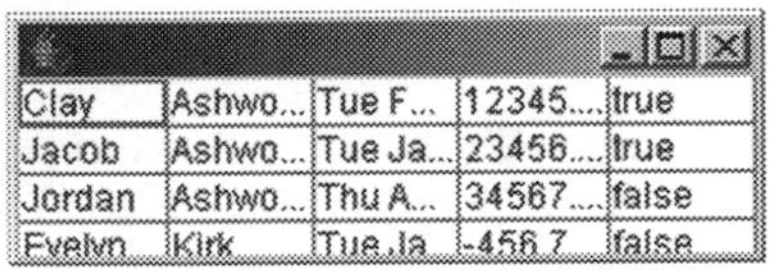

Figure 7-4. *Making the frame smaller causes the cells to partially conceal their contents*

In addition, several of the columns format their data in a way that's not appropriate or not ideal. For example, the Gender column displays "true" or "false" instead of "Male" or "Female," and the Account Balance column correctly displays the numeric value but doesn't use currency conventions.

Using JScrollPane with JTable

As in any case where there may be too much information to display at one time, you can use the `JScrollPane` class to allow large amounts of data to be viewed. In fact, instances of `JTable` should almost always be displayed inside a `JScrollPane`, because as well as allowing you to view large tables, `JScrollPane` also provides support for column headers.

You can supply the column headers by implementing the `getColumnName()` method in your `TableModel`, or they will default to a letter of the alphabet, with a header of *A* for the first column, *B* for the second, and so on. Listing 7-4 shows a modified version of `TableValues` that returns the column names.

Listing 7-4. Specifying Column Names

```java
import java.util.Calendar;
import java.util.GregorianCalendar;
import javax.swing.table.AbstractTableModel;

public class TableValues extends AbstractTableModel {

  public final static int FIRST_NAME = 0;
  public final static int LAST_NAME = 1;
  public final static int DATE_OF_BIRTH = 2;
  public final static int ACCOUNT_BALANCE = 3;
  public final static int GENDER = 4;

  public final static boolean GENDER_MALE = true;
  public final static boolean GENDER_FEMALE = false;

  public final static String[] COLUMN_NAMES = {
    "First Name", "Last Name", "Date of Birth", "Account Balance",
    "Gender"
  };

  public Object[][] values = {
    {
    "Clay", "Ashworth",
    new GregorianCalendar(1962, Calendar.FEBRUARY, 20).getTime(),
    new Float(12345.67), new Boolean(GENDER_MALE)
  }, {
    "Jacob", "Ashworth",
    new GregorianCalendar(1987, Calendar.JANUARY, 6).getTime(),
    new Float(23456.78), new Boolean(GENDER_MALE)
  }, {
    "Jordan", "Ashworth",
    new GregorianCalendar(1989, Calendar.AUGUST, 31).getTime(),
    new Float(34567.89), new Boolean(GENDER_FEMALE)
  }, {
    "Evelyn", "Kirk",
    new GregorianCalendar(1945, Calendar.JANUARY, 16).getTime(),
    new Float(-456.70), new Boolean(GENDER_FEMALE)
  }, {
    "Belle", "Spyres",
    new GregorianCalendar(1907, Calendar.AUGUST, 2).getTime(),
    new Float(567.00), new Boolean(GENDER_FEMALE)
  }
};

  public int getRowCount() {
    return values.length;
  }

  public int getColumnCount() {
    return values[0].length;
  }
```

```
  public Object getValueAt(int row, int column) {
    return values[row][column];
  }

  public String getColumnName(int column) {
    return COLUMN_NAMES[column];
  }

}
```

You'll now modify the `SimpleTableTest` constructor so that it encloses the table within a `JScrollPane`.

```
public SimpleTableTest() {
  Container pane = getContentPane();
  pane.setLayout(new BorderLayout());
  TableValues tv = new TableValues();
  table = new JTable(tv);
  // pane.add(table, BorderLayout.CENTER);
  JScrollPane jsp = new JScrollPane(table);
  pane.add(jsp, BorderLayout.CENTER);
}
```

Now that the table is displayed inside a `JScrollPane`, the column headers appear, as shown in Figure 7-5.

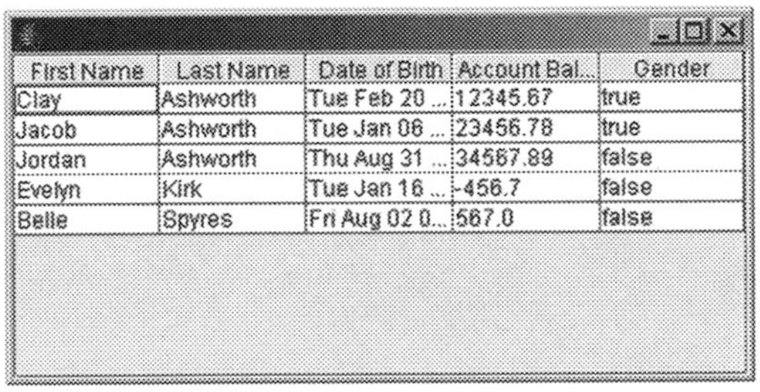

Figure 7-5. *Tables are normally displayed within a `JScrollPane`, which allows the headers to appear and results in vertical scrollbars appearing when needed*

You might also expect that resizing the frame (and as a result, the table) will cause scrollbars to appear when there's not enough space to display all the data. As Figure 7-6 shows, a vertical scrollbar does appear when the table is reduced in size, but instead of a horizontal scrollbar appearing, each column shrinks and expands along with the table.

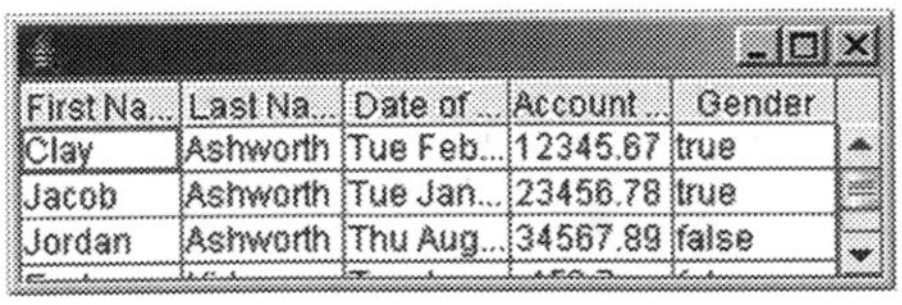

Figure 7-6. *Instead of a horizontal scrollbar appearing when the table is too narrow to completely display its contents, the cells become smaller*

288

To understand why this occurs, it's necessary to examine the design of JTable and how some of its support classes function.

JTable's Column-Oriented Design

The design of the JTable component is very much column-oriented, and each JTable contains a reference to an implementation of the TableColumnModel interface. A TableColumnModel, such as DefaultTableColumnModel defined in javax.swing.table, describes a set of columns displayed by a JTable and represents each column with an instance of the TableColumn class. For example, suppose you define a TableModel that contains five columns of data. If you then create an instance of JTable using that model, the table creates an instance of DefaultTableColumnModel, retrieves the column count from the TableModel, and creates and adds five TableColumn instances to the DefaultTableColumnModel.

Each instance of TableColumn contains information such as the column header; the current, minimum, maximum, and preferred width values for the column; and a flag that indicates whether the column can be resized. When created, a column's current and preferred width values are initially set to 75, the minimum is set to 15, and the maximum width is effectively set to infinity (Integer.MAX_VALUE).

After you create a column, you can change its width values explicitly by using the setWidth(), setMinWidth(), setMaxWidth(), and setPreferredWidth() methods for the current, minimum, maximum, and preferred widths, respectively. In addition, you can modify a column's current width if the size of the table that it's a part of changes.

Each JTable instance has an auto resize mode setting, which can be one of five values that correspond to constants defined in JTable.

- AUTO_RESIZE_ALL_COLUMNS
- AUTO_RESIZE_LAST_COLUMN
- AUTO_RESIZE_NEXT_COLUMN
- AUTO_RESIZE_OFF
- AUTO_RESIZE_SUBSEQUENT_COLUMNS

The value of this setting determines how or if the table's columns are resized when the width of the table or one of the columns changes.

Table Resizing

If the table's auto resize mode is set to AUTO_RESIZE_OFF, changing the size of the table doesn't affect the current size of the columns within the table. When it's set to any of the other four values, however, a change to the table's width is distributed among all the columns in the table proportionally based on their preferred sizes. For example, suppose that a table contains two columns and that one of the columns has a preferred width of 200 and the other a preferred width of 100. In that case, the first column occupies two-thirds of the table's horizontal space, and the second column occupies the remaining one-third. If the table is then made 30 pixels wider, 20 of the additional pixels will be distributed to the first column, and 10 to the second one. This allows the column sizes to remain proportionally the same relative to one another, regardless of changes to the table's actual size.

If a table's mode is AUTO_RESIZE_OFF and the sum of all the column widths is greater than the table's width, then a horizontal scrollbar appears. To see this behavior, let's make another minor change to the SimpleTableTest constructor.

```
public SimpleTableTest() {
  Container pane = getContentPane();
  pane.setLayout(new BorderLayout());
  TableValues tv = new TableValues();
  table = new JTable(tv);
  table.setAutoResizeMode(JTable.AUTO_RESIZE_OFF);
  // pane.add(table, BorderLayout.CENTER);
  JScrollPane jsp = new JScrollPane(table);
  pane.add(jsp, BorderLayout.CENTER);
}
```

Each column maintains its default width (75), and when the table is made too narrow to display all the columns, a horizontal scrollbar appears. Any other auto resize mode causes the columns to expand or contract when the table is resized, as shown in Figure 7-7.

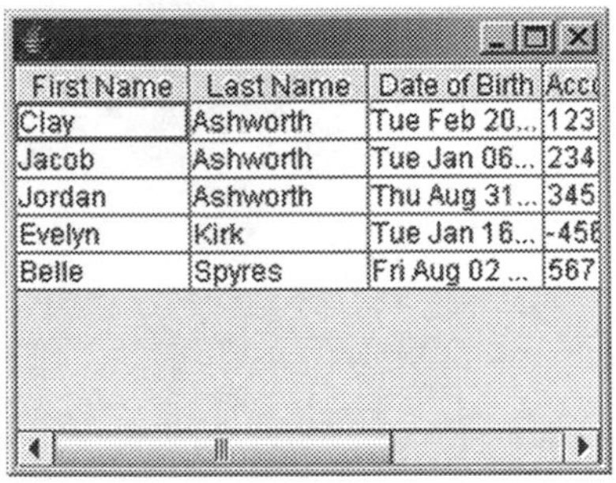

Figure 7-7. *Changing the auto resize mode results in a scrollbar appearing when the table isn't wide enough to display the contents of all its columns*

Column Resizing

Now that you've seen how changing the width of a table can affect the width of the columns within that table, it's also important to examine how changing the width of one column can change the widths of the others. You can change a column's width programmatically via the mutator methods for the four width values (current, minimum, maximum, and preferred), or you can modify it through the user interface provided by JTable. Specifically, to resize a column you must move the pointer to the right side of the header above the column you want to resize. For example, to resize the "First Name" column in the test table you should move the pointer so that it's over the vertical line that separates that column from the next one ("Last Name"). The cursor will change to a left/right resize cursor and at that point you can begin a drag operation by pressing the left mouse button and moving it to the left to make the "First Name" column narrower or to the right to make it wider.

When one column's size is changed, its effect on the widths of the other columns depends upon the table's auto resize mode setting; I describe the behavior associated with each setting next.

AUTO_RESIZE_OFF

When auto resizing is disabled, changing the width of one column has no effect on the size of the other columns in the table. This may result in the table being too small to display all the columns, in which case a horizontal scrollbar appears (if the table is contained within a JScrollPane). Alternatively, resizing a column may result in the table being larger than the combined width of all the columns, in which case some amount of whitespace appears inside the table.

AUTO_RESIZE_NEXT_COLUMN

With this setting, when a change is made to the width of a column, the column to the right of that column (in other words, the next column) gains or loses horizontal space. In Figure 7-8, the Date of Birth column has been increased in size, which results in the column to its right (Account Balance) becoming narrower.

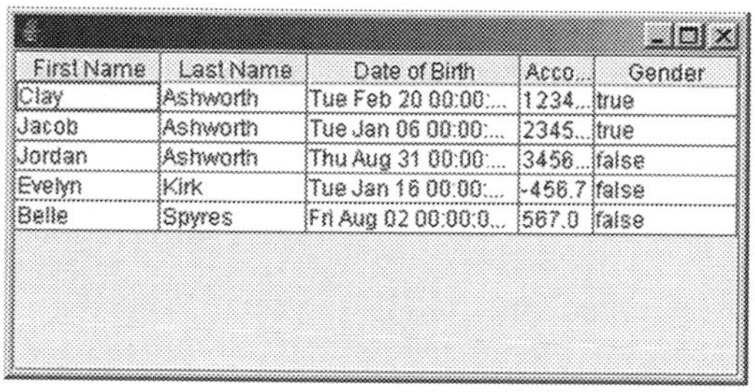

Figure 7-8. An example of AUTO_RESIZE_NEXT_COLUMN

AUTO_RESIZE_SUBSEQUENT_COLUMNS

This setting is similar to AUTO_RESIZE_NEXT_COLUMN, except that when a column is resized, all the other columns to its right gain or lose width. In Figure 7-9, the Date of Birth column has been made wider, which causes the two columns that follow it (Account Balance and Gender) to become narrower.

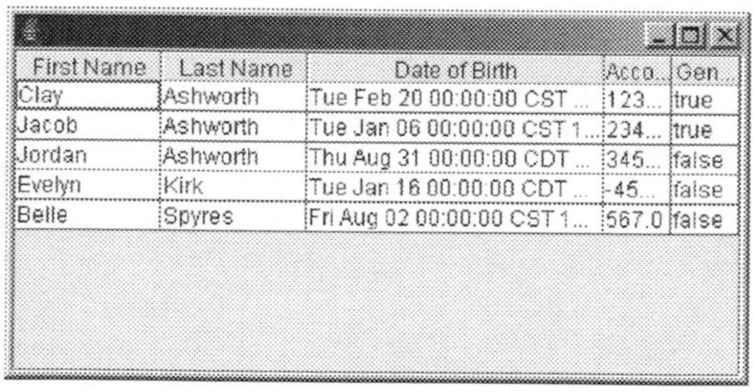

Figure 7-9. As the Date of Birth column is made wider, the columns to its right become narrower

The difference between the original width of the resized column and its new width is referred to as the *delta value*, and this amount is distributed proportionally among the columns to the right of the resized column.

AUTO_RESIZE_LAST_COLUMN

When this setting is used and a column is resized, the delta value is applied to the last column in the table to make it wider or narrower than it was. In Figure 7-10, the Date of Birth column has been made wider, causing the Gender column to become narrower by the same amount.

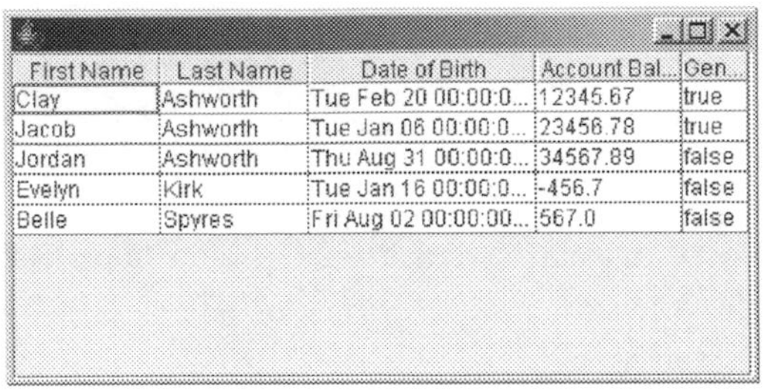

Figure 7-10. *With* AUTO_RESIZE_LAST_COLUMN, *the last column's size changes to accommodate changes to the other columns' sizes*

AUTO_RESIZE_ALL_COLUMNS

This is the default setting for a new instance of JTable, and it causes any changes to one column's width to be proportionally distributed among all other columns in the table. When the Date of Birth column becomes larger, the delta value is divided among the other columns in the table, causing them to become narrower, as shown in Figure 7-11.

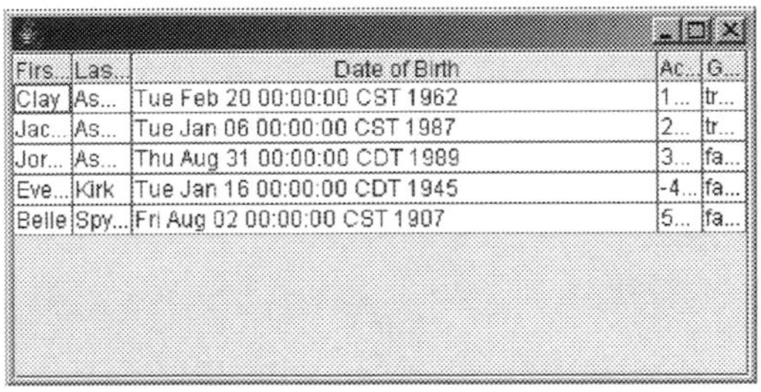

Figure 7-11. *With* AUTO_RESIZE_ALL_COLUMNS, *resizing one column causes all the others to increase or decrease in size accordingly*

Cell Rendering

As mentioned earlier, the data in several of the columns isn't displayed in an ideal fashion. Specifically, you can improve three things.

- The Date of Birth column displays both a date and time but should display only a date, and that date should be in a format that doesn't include the day of the week.

- The Account Balance column displays a simple numeric value but should use currency-formatting conventions.

- The Gender column displays a somewhat nonintuitive value of "true" or "false" instead of "Male" or "Female."

JTable cells are drawn by *cell renderers*, which are classes that implement the TableCellRenderer interface. That interface defines a single getTableCellRendererComponent() method that returns a reference to the Component that will perform the drawing operation. However, since it's often convenient to define a single class that implements TableCellRenderer and can perform the rendering, a TableCellRenderer will often simply return a reference to itself. Following are the parameters passed to getTableCellRendererComponent():

- A reference to the JTable that contains the cell being drawn
- A reference to the cell's value
- A Boolean flag that indicates whether the cell is selected
- A Boolean flag that indicates whether the cell has the input focus
- The row index of the cell being drawn
- The column index of the cell being drawn

In addition to returning a reference to the rendering component, getTableCellRenderer ➤ Component() is responsible for initializing the component's state. Notice that one of the parameters listed previously is a reference to the value stored in the cell that's about to be rendered, and some representation of that value is usually stored in the rendering component before a reference to it is returned.

As you'll see shortly, JTable provides predefined renderers that you can use to have your data displayed properly, but first you'll look at how easily you can define custom renderer classes.

Creating Custom Renderers

The class in Listing 7-5 provides an example of a custom renderer, and it will be used to display the values in the Gender field in the sample application's table. Those values currently appear as a text string of "true" or "false" depending upon the cell's value, but this renderer will cause them to be drawn by a JComboBox.

Listing 7-5. Cell Renderer for the Gender Column

```
import java.awt.Component;
import javax.swing.JComboBox;
import javax.swing.JTable;
import javax.swing.table.TableCellRenderer;

public class GenderRenderer extends JComboBox implements TableCellRenderer {

  public GenderRenderer() {
    super();
    addItem("Male");
    addItem("Female");
  }

  public Component getTableCellRendererComponent(JTable table,
          Object value, boolean isSelected, boolean hasFocus,
          int row, int column) {
```

```
    if (isSelected) {
      setForeground(table.getSelectionForeground());
      super.setBackground(table.getSelectionBackground());
    } else {
      setForeground(table.getForeground());
      setBackground(table.getBackground());
    }

    boolean isMale = ((Boolean)value).booleanValue();
    setSelectedIndex(isMale ? 0 : 1);
    return this;
    }

}
```

When an instance of this class is created, it adds two items to its list: a Male selection and a Female selection. The getTableCellRendererComponent() performs some simple color selection for the foreground and background and then selects the appropriate gender based on the cell's value (Male for true and Female for false). Once this renderer class has been created, you can specify that it should be used for the Gender column by making the following changes (see Listing 7-6) to SimpleTableTest:

Listing 7-6. Assigning a Renderer to a Column

```
import java.awt.*;
import javax.swing.*;
import javax.swing.table.*;

public class SimpleTableTest extends JFrame {

  private JTable table;

  public static void main(String[] args) {
    SimpleTableTest stt = new SimpleTableTest();
    stt.setDefaultCloseOperation(JFrame.EXIT_ON_CLOSE);
    stt.setSize(400, 200);
    stt.setVisible(true);
  }

  public SimpleTableTest() {
    Container pane = getContentPane();
    pane.setLayout(new BorderLayout());
    TableValues tv = new TableValues();
    table = new JTable(tv);
    TableColumnModel tcm = table.getColumnModel();
    TableColumn tc = tcm.getColumn(TableValues.GENDER);
    tc.setCellRenderer(new GenderRenderer());
    JScrollPane jsp = new JScrollPane(table);
    pane.add(jsp, BorderLayout.CENTER);
  }

}
```

When you compile and execute the modified version of the application, it produces a display like the one shown in Figure 7-12. Notice that the "true" and "false" strings that previously appeared in the Gender column now seem to have been replaced by instances of JCheckBox.

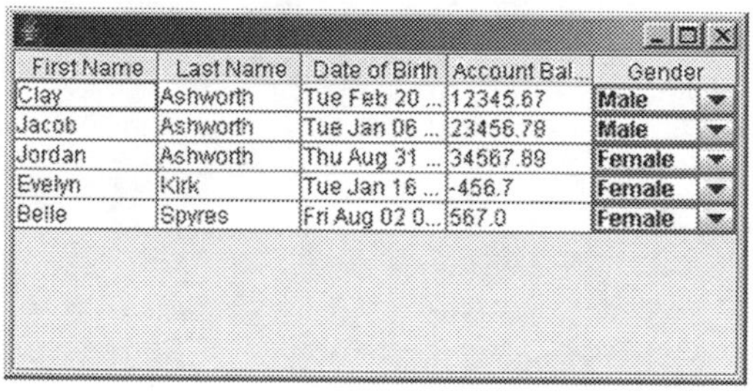

Figure 7-12. *With a custom renderer, the Gender column's contents appear as JCheckBox components instead of text*

It's important to realize that renderers aren't really added to JTable instances the way that visual components are added to a Container, which in this case means that the table doesn't contain any instances of JCheckBox. Instead, when the table is painted, each cell delegates responsibility for drawing its contents, which is done by passing a Graphics object to a renderer component's paint() method, and the drawing region is set to correspond to the area occupied by the cell. In other words, no instances of JCheckBox were added to the JTable in this example, but rather a single instance of JCheckBox drew itself onto the area occupied by each cell in the Gender column. This approach may seem unnecessarily complex, but it allows a single component to draw most or all of a table's cells instead of requiring the table to allocate a component for each cell, which would consume far more memory.

In many cases, the easiest way to define a custom cell renderer is to extend Swing's DefaultTableCellRenderer, which as its name implies is the default renderer for cells in a JTable. DefaultTableCellRenderer extends JLabel, and it displays cell values using their String representations. An object's String representation is obtained by calling its toString() method, and DefaultTableCellRenderer passes that representation to the setText() method it inherits from JLabel. This behavior is implemented in the setValue() method, which is passed a reference to the value of the cell that's about to be rendered.

```
private void setValue(Object value) {
  setText((value == null) ? "" : value.toString());
}
```

In effect, DefaultTableCellRenderer is simply a JLabel that sets its own text based on the value of the cell being rendered.

In many cases, calling toString() isn't an appropriate way to obtain a representation of the cell's value, and an example of this is the Account Balance column in the sample application. The values displayed in that column are technically correct, but they're not formatted in a manner that makes it obvious that they represent currency values. However, you can easily address this by creating a custom TableCellRenderer and assigning it responsibility for drawing the cells in that column (see Listing 7-7).

Listing 7-7. Defining a Currency Renderer

```
import java.text.NumberFormat;
import javax.swing.table.DefaultTableCellRenderer;

public class CurrencyRenderer extends DefaultTableCellRenderer {

  public CurrencyRenderer() {
    super();
    setHorizontalAlignment(javax.swing.SwingConstants.RIGHT);
}

  public void setValue(Object value) {
    if ((value != null) && (value instanceof Number)) {
      Number numberValue = (Number)value;
      NumberFormat formatter = NumberFormat.getCurrencyInstance();
      value = formatter.format(numberValue.doubleValue());
    }
    super.setValue(value);
  }

}
```

This simple class does just two things: it changes the label's horizontal alignment during construction, and it overrides the setValue() method defined in DefaultTableCellRenderer. Since you know that this renderer class will be used only to render the cells containing numeric values, you can cast the cell's value to a Number and then format the value as a currency using Java's NumberFormat class.

Now that you've created a custom renderer for the Account Balance column, you need to have the table use the renderer when drawing the cells in that column, which you can do by explicitly assigning it to the TableColumn as you did in the previous example. However, there's another way to accomplish this that's worth mentioning and that's more appropriate in many cases. Besides associating a renderer with a particular column, you can also associate it with a particular type of data, and the renderer will then be used to draw all cells in columns that contain that type of data.

When a JTable is initialized, it creates a map that defines associations between classes and renderers, and it uses that map to select a cell renderer when drawing cells in columns for which no renderer was explicitly set. In other words, if you haven't explicitly assigned a renderer to a column as you did earlier, JTable will select a renderer based upon the type of data stored in that column. It determines the column's data type by calling the getColumnClass() method in the TableModel, and that method returns an instance of Class. However, the implementation of getColumnClass() in AbstractTableModel simply indicates that all its columns contain instances of Object.

```
public Class<?> getColumnClass(int columnIndex) {
  return Object.class;
}
```

Since AbstractTableModel can't know what kind of data its subclasses will contain, the only assumption it can safely make is that each cell contains an instance of Object; however, in practice, the cells will almost certainly contain instances of some subclass of Object such as Float, Date, and so on. Therefore, if you want the table to be able to determine the specific type of data its columns contain, you must override getColumnClass() in your TableModel class. For example, since all the values in the Account Balance column are instances of Float, you could add the following getColumnClass() implementation to the TableValues class:

```
public Class<?> getColumnClass(int  column) {
  Class<?> dataType = super.getColumnClass(column);
  if (column == ACCOUNT_BALANCE)  {
    dataType = Float.class;
  }
  return  dataType;
}
```

Now that the JTable is able to determine that the Account Balance column contains Float data, you need to associate the CurrencyRenderer class with that data type, which you can easily do by calling setDefaultRenderer().

```
public SimpleTableTest() {
  Container pane = getContentPane();
  pane.setLayout(new BorderLayout());
  TableValues tv = new TableValues();
  table = new JTable(tv);
  TableColumnModel tcm = table.getColumnModel();
  TableColumn tc = tcm.getColumn(TableValues.GENDER);

  tc.setCellRenderer(new GenderRenderer());
  table.setDefaultRenderer(Float.class, new CurrencyRenderer());
  JScrollPane jsp = new JScrollPane(table);
  pane.add(jsp, BorderLayout.CENTER);
}
```

This new addition to SimpleTableTest causes CurrencyRenderer to become the default renderer for all columns containing Float data. Therefore, CurrencyRenderer will be used to draw the cells in the Account Balance column because no renderer was assigned to the column and because getColumnClass() now indicates that the column contains Float data. Figure 7-13 shows an example of how the interface will appear when the program is executed with these modifications.

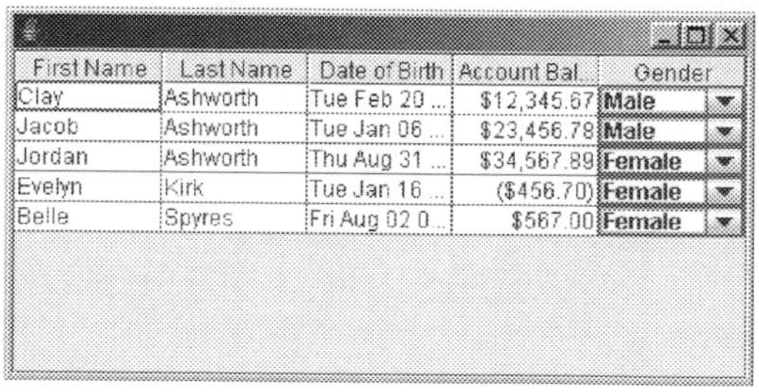

First Name	Last Name	Date of Birth	Account Bal.	Gender	
Clay	Ashworth	Tue Feb 20 ...	$12,345.67	Male	▼
Jacob	Ashworth	Tue Jan 06 ...	$23,456.78	Male	▼
Jordan	Ashworth	Thu Aug 31 ...	$34,567.89	Female	▼
Evelyn	Kirk	Tue Jan 16 ...	($456.70)	Female	▼
Belle	Spyres	Fri Aug 02 0 ...	$567.00	Female	▼

Figure 7-13. CurrencyRenderer has been associated with columns containing floating-point data

At this point, you may be wondering what happens when no renderer has been explicitly assigned to a column and no entry in the table's class-to-renderer map matches the column's data type. You're correct if you guessed that the rendering is handled by DefaultTableCellRenderer, but it's important to understand exactly how that occurs.

When no renderer has been explicitly assigned to a column and no entry for the column's Class is found in the table's class-to-renderer map, JTable traverses the inheritance hierarchy of the column's Class, searching the class-to-renderer map for an entry corresponding to each superclass until it locates one. For example, if getColumnClass() indicates that the column contains Float data but no entry for Float is found in the class-to-renderer map, JTable next attempts to locate a map entry that corresponds to Float's immediate superclass, which is Number. If it also doesn't find an entry for Number, it will attempt to retrieve an entry for Object (Number's immediate superclass), which will always succeed because the map automatically contains an entry that associates Object columns with DefaultTableCellRenderer.

To summarize JTable's behavior, the steps for locating a renderer are as follows:

1. If a renderer has been set for the cell's TableColumn, use that renderer.

2. Obtain a reference to a Class instance by calling the TableModel's getColumnClass() method.

3. If a renderer has been mapped to that Class, use that renderer.

4. Obtain a reference to the Class instance of the type's superclass, and repeat the previous step until a match is found.

This approach provides a great deal of flexibility in assigning renderers to table cells, since it allows you to create a renderer and have it handle rendering for columns with a specific data type, along with any subclasses of that type.

JTable's Default Renderers

You've now seen how to create custom renderers and how to associate a renderer with a given type of data. However, it's often not necessary to do either one, since JTable includes a number of predefined renderers for commonly used data types, and entries for those renderers are automatically included in its class-to-renderer map. For example, I already mentioned that an entry exists in the map that associates Object columns with DefaultTableCellRenderer, but other, more sophisticated renderers are provided as well. This means that if one of the predefined renderers is appropriate for your application, the only coding you need to do is to identify your columns' data types in an implementation of getColumnClass() so that JTable will use the appropriate renderers. To put this to use, you'll use JTable's predefined renderer for instances of java.util.Date by simply modifying TableValues so it indicates that the Date of Birth column contains instances of Date.

```
public Class<?> getColumnClass(int column) {
  Class<?> dataType = super.getColumnClass(column);
  if (column == ACCOUNT_BALANCE) {
    dataType = Float.class;
  }
  else if (column == DATE_OF_BIRTH) {
    dataType = java.util.Date.class;
  }
  return dataType;
}
```

As you saw earlier, the date values displayed by DefaultTableCellRenderer were lengthy and included a time (since Java's Date class represents both a date and a time). However, JTable's predefined date renderer produces a shorter, more appropriate representation of each date value, as shown in Figure 7-14.

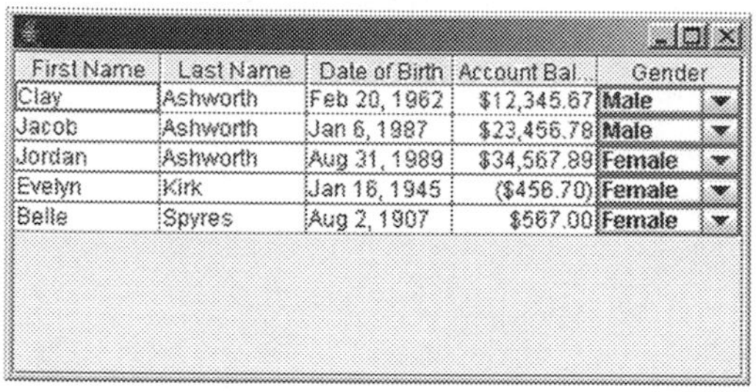

Figure 7-14. JTable's *default date renderer produces an abbreviated month*

In addition to java.util.Date, JTable includes predefined renderers for a number of other classes, including the following.

java.lang.Number

This is the superclass of the numeric wrappers such as Integer, Float, Long, and so on. The renderer that's defined for Number is a subclass of DefaultTableCellRenderer that simply sets its alignment value to RIGHT as you did in CurrencyRenderer. In other words, the Number renderer displays the toString() representation of the cell values, but it displays the text adjacent to the right side of the cell instead of the left (the default). Figure 7-15 shows an example of how this would appear if used with the Account Balance column in the SampleTableTest class.

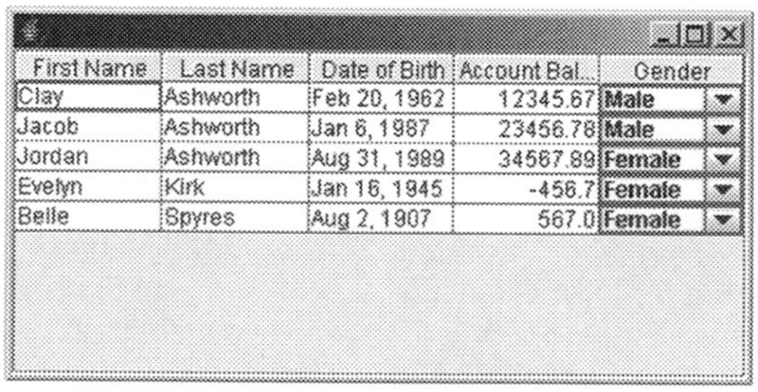

Figure 7-15. *The default formatter for* Number *instances right-aligns the displayed values*

javax.swing.ImageIcon

The renderer associated with this class allows you to display instances of ImageIcon within a table. The renderer is simply an instance of DefaultTableCellRenderer that takes advantage of the fact that a JLabel can contain both text and an icon. Instead of rendering the cell by setting its text value, this renderer sets its icon instead.

java.lang.Boolean

When this renderer is used, it displays the value for the cell as a JCheckBox that's either checked (when the cell's value is true) or unchecked (when the value is false). Figure 7-16 shows an example of how it would appear if used with the Gender column SimpleTableTest.

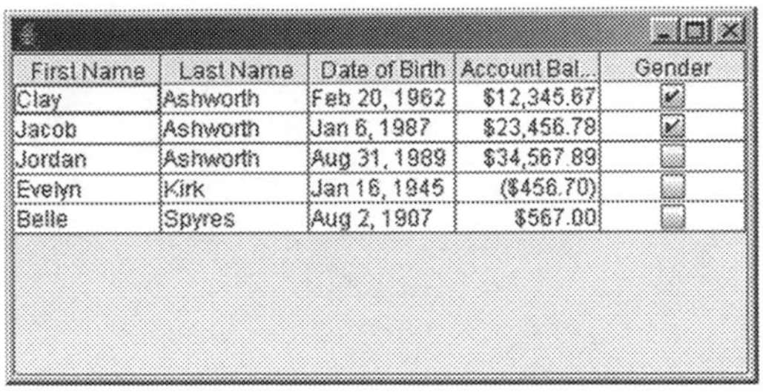

Figure 7-16. *Boolean values are rendered using check boxes*

Editing Table Cells

Although each cell in the Gender column now appears to be a JComboBox, it's not possible to change the gender that's selected. In fact, none of the cells in the table is editable, and clicking them merely causes the row to be selected. To change this behavior, you must override the isCellEditable() method, because the implementation in DefaultTableModel always returns false. However, you can change this easily by adding the following code to TableValues:

```java
public boolean isCellEditable(int row, int column) {
  if (column == GENDER) {
    return true;
  }
  return false;
}
```

This indicates that the cells in the Gender column are now editable. However, if you click a cell in that column intending to select a gender from a JComboBox, you may be surprised to find that nothing happens except that the row you clicked becomes selected. If you double-click the cell, a JTextField appears that's initialized with the string equivalent of the cell's Boolean value (true or false), and you can edit the data in the text field, as shown in Figure 7-17.

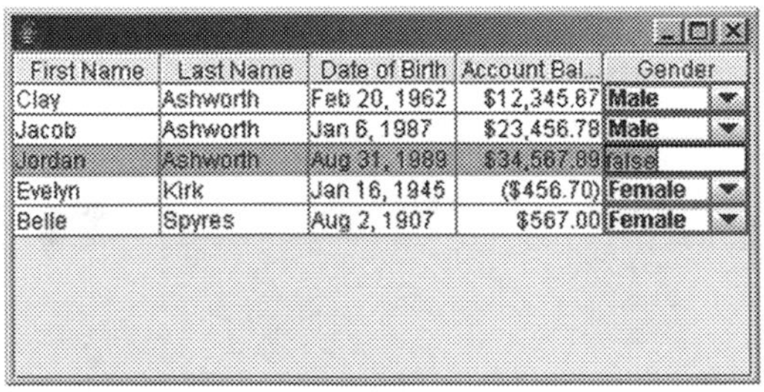

Figure 7-17. *Double-clicking a cell causes a text field to appear*

You may be surprised that a text field appears when you edit the cell, because the cell seems to contain a JComboBox, but remember that table cells don't actually contain any components. The cells are simply drawn by components (in other words, the renderers), and in this case, the component happens to be a JComboBox. However, editing is a completely separate process that may or may not be handled by the same type of component that performed the rendering. For example, the default rendering component used by JTable is a JLabel, while the default editing component is a JTextField, which is why a text field appeared in this case.

Regardless of which type of component is used, it may seem that the cells are finally editable, which is partly true, but if you enter a value into one of these cells, the value you type is discarded once you complete the editing. To understand why this occurs and what to do about it, you should be familiar with cell editors and how JTable handles the editing of its cells.

Cell Editors

Just as cell renderers control the way that cells' values are drawn, cell editors handle cell value editing. Editors are slightly more complex than renderers but have many similarities to renderers.

- An editor can be assigned to one or more TableColumn instances.

- An editor can be associated with one or more data types (classes) and will be used to display that type of data when no editor is associated with a cell's column.

- Existing visual components are used to provide editing capabilities, just as they're used by renderers to draw cell values. In fact, the same type of visual component that's used as a cell's renderer is often used for its editor as well. For example, a cell might be assigned a renderer that uses a JComboBox and an editor that uses the same component.

You can assign an editor to one or more TableColumn instances or object types using the setCellEditor() method in TableColumn and setDefaultEditor() in JTable, respectively. However, the implementation of the TableCellEditor interface is more complex than TableCellRenderer, and to understand the methods defined in TableCellEditor, it's useful to examine how editors interact with JTable instances.

When a JTable detects a mouse click over one of its cells, it calls the isCellEditable() method in the TableModel. That method returns a value of false if the cell shouldn't be editable, in which case processing terminates, and no further action is taken. However, if the method returns true, then the table identifies the cell editor for that cell and calls the editor's isCellEditable() method as well. Although TableModel and CellEditor both define methods called isCellEditable(), an important difference exists between the two. Specifically, the TableModel method is passed only row and column index values, while the CellEditor method is also passed the EventObject representing the mouse click. You can use this, for example, to check the "click count" stored in the event. A cell must be double-clicked before it's edited, which is exactly the behavior observed earlier when editing the Gender column values. In other words, the isCellEditable() method returns a value of false when the click count is 1, while it returns true if the count is greater than 1. This behavior allows the cell editor to distinguish between a request to select the cell (a single click) and a request to edit the cell (a double click).

The edit operation is allowed to proceed only if both isCellEditable() methods return a value of true. When that's the case, the editing is initiated by calling the getTableCell ➤ EditorComponent() method, which is passed the following parameters:

- A reference to the JTable that contains the cell being edited

- A reference to the cell's current value

- A Boolean flag that indicates whether the cell is selected

- The row index of the cell being edited

- The column index of the cell being edited

If these parameters look familiar, it's because they're almost identical to those passed to the getTableCellRendererComponent() method in TableCellRenderer. The only difference is that this method isn't passed a Boolean value indicating whether the cell has the input focus, since that's implied because the cell is being edited.

Before returning a reference to the component that's responsible for handling editing, the getTableCellEditorComponent() should prepare the editor by initializing its value appropriately so that it matches the current cell value. For example, let's assume you're creating an editor that allows users to select either Male or Female from a JComboBox that represents the Gender column value in TableValues. In that case, you should prepare the JComboBox that performs the editing by selecting the item it contains that corresponds to the cell's gender value: Male if the cell's value is true and Female if the value is false.

Once the editing component has been prepared and returned from the getTableCellEditorComponent() method, the JTable sets the size and location of that component so it's directly "over" the cell being edited. This makes it appear that the cell is edited in place, when in fact, a component that supports editing (such as a JTextField or in this case, a JComboBox) has been superimposed over the cell.

With the editing component positioned over the cell being edited, the event that originally triggered the edit processing is posted to the editing component. For example, in the case of a JComboBox-based editor, the same mouse event that initiated the editing is passed to the combo box, possibly causing it to display its drop-down menu when editing starts. Finally, the CellEditor's shouldSelectCell() method is passed the same mouse event object, and if it returns true, the cell (and possibly others, depending upon the table's selection settings) is selected.

Each CellEditor is required to implement the addCellEditorListener() and removeCellEditorListener() methods, and the CellEditorListener interface defines two methods: editingStopped() and editingCanceled(). In practice, the only listener is usually the JTable itself, which is notified when editing is stopped or canceled. In addition, the CellEditor must implement the cancelCellEditing() and stopCellEditing() methods, which call the editingStopped() and editingCanceled() methods of registered listeners.

A request to end editing can come either from the JTable that contains the cell or from the editor component itself. For example, suppose you click one cell and begin editing its value. If you then click a different cell, the JTable calls the stopCellEditing() method of the first cell's editor before it initiates editing the second cell. Alternatively, the editor component may stop the editing when some event occurs that implies that editing is complete. For example, when using a JComboBox as an editor, if it receives an ActionEvent message indicating that a selection was made, then it's appropriate to terminate the edit. Similarly, a JTextField might signal that editing has ended when it detects that the Return key was pressed.

Regardless of where the request originates to end editing, the JTable's editingStopped() method is called since it's a registered CellEditorListener. Inside this method, the table calls the editor's getCellEditorValue() method to retrieve the cell's new value and passes that value to the setValueAt() method in the JTable's TableModel. That is, it retrieves the cell's new value from the editor and sends it to the data model so it can be stored "permanently."

The class in Listing 7-8 defines a component you can use to provide editing of the rows in the Gender column defined in TableValues. It defines a subclass of JComboBox that initializes itself with Male and Female entries and listens for changes to its state (in other words, waits for a selection to be made).

When editing is initiated for one of the cells in the Gender column, the getTableCellEditorComponent() method is called, giving the editor a chance to initialize its state before it's made visible. In this case, the editor simply makes either Male or Female the selected entry based on the value stored in the cell being edited. When the user selects an item in the JComboBox, fireEditingStopped() is called, which signals to the table that the edit session has ended. The table will then call getCellEditorValue() to retrieve the new value that should be stored in the cell and will pass that value to the TableModel's setValueAt() method.

Listing 7-8. An Editor for the Gender Column

```java
import java.awt.Component;
import java.util.EventObject;
import java.awt.event.*;
import javax.swing.*;
import javax.swing.event.*;
import javax.swing.table.*;

public class GenderEditor extends JComboBox implements TableCellEditor {

  protected EventListenerList listenerList = new EventListenerList();
  protected ChangeEvent changeEvent = new ChangeEvent(this);

  public GenderEditor() {
    super();
    addItem("Male");
    addItem("Female");
    addActionListener(new ActionListener() {
        public void actionPerformed(ActionEvent event) {
          fireEditingStopped();
        }
    });
  }

  public void addCellEditorListener(CellEditorListener listener) {
    listenerList.add(CellEditorListener.class, listener);
  }

  public void removeCellEditorListener(CellEditorListener listener) {
    listenerList.remove(CellEditorListener.class, listener);
  }

  protected void fireEditingStopped() {
    CellEditorListener listener;
    Object[] listeners = listenerList.getListenerList();
    for (int i = 0; i < listeners.length; i++) {
      if (listeners[i] == CellEditorListener.class) {
          listener = (CellEditorListener)listeners[i + 1];
          listener.editingStopped(changeEvent);
      }
    }
  }

  protected void fireEditingCanceled() {
    CellEditorListener listener;
    Object[] listeners = listenerList.getListenerList();
    for (int i = 0; i < listeners.length; i++) {
      if (listeners[i] == CellEditorListener.class) {
        listener = (CellEditorListener)listeners[i + 1];
        listener.editingCanceled(changeEvent);
      }
    }
  }
}
```

```java
  public void cancelCellEditing() {
    fireEditingCanceled();
  }

  public boolean stopCellEditing() {
    fireEditingStopped();
    return true;
  }

  public boolean isCellEditable(EventObject event) {
    return true;
  }

  public boolean shouldSelectCell(EventObject event) {
    return true;
  }

  public Object getCellEditorValue() {
    return new Boolean(getSelectedIndex() == 0 ? true : false);
  }

  public Component getTableCellEditorComponent(
      JTable table, Object value, boolean isSelected, int row, int column) {
    boolean isMale = ((Boolean)value).booleanValue();
    setSelectedIndex(isMale ? 0 : 1);
    return this;
  }

}
```

Now that you've defined the editor component, you need to associate it with the Gender column, as shown in the following code:

```java
public SimpleTableTest() {
  Container pane = getContentPane();
  pane.setLayout(new BorderLayout());
  TableValues tv = new TableValues();
  table = new JTable(tv);
  TableColumnModel tcm = table.getColumnModel();
  TableColumn tc = tcm.getColumn(TableValues.GENDER);
  tc.setCellRenderer(new GenderRenderer());
  tc.setCellEditor(new GenderEditor());
  table.setDefaultRenderer(Float.class, new CurrencyRenderer());
  JScrollPane jsp = new JScrollPane(table);
  pane.add(jsp, BorderLayout.CENTER);
}
```

When this code is compiled and run, a JComboBox correctly appears, is initialized with the appropriate gender value, and allows you to select either Male or Female, as shown in Figure 7-18.

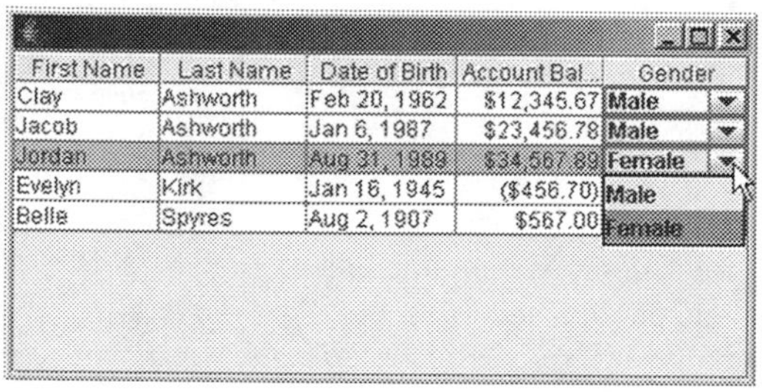

Figure 7-18. *Changing the cell editor causes a JComboBox to appear when the cell is edited*

However, selecting a different value from the one already stored in the cell doesn't result in the cell's value being modified. That's because the value is never changed in the TableModel; you can do this by implementing the setValueAt() method in the TableValues class.

```
public void setValueAt(Object value, int row, int column) {
  values[row][column] = value;
}
```

DefaultCellEditor

It's not necessary in every case to build a completely new cell editor. In fact, the DefaultCellEditor class allows you to easily create editor components using a JCheckBox, JComboBox, or JTextField. All that's necessary is to create an instance of DefaultCellEditor and pass it an instance of one of these three components. However, the DefaultCellEditor isn't very flexible, and you'll often need to create your own editor as in this case.

Table Selection Settings

From a selection perspective, JTable is a two-dimensional component: each selected cell has both a row and a column index. In contrast, JList selections are one-dimensional, since only a row index value is associated with each cell. Because of its two-dimensional nature, a JTable's selection information can't be maintained by a single ListSelectionModel, because that interface supports only one-dimensional selection information. To address this issue, JTable uses two DefaultListSelectionModel instances.

- One that's maintained directly by the JTable itself for row selection information

- Another that's maintained through the TableColumnModel for column selections

I mentioned earlier that when a cell is selected, other cells might also become selected, depending upon the table's selection settings. In fact, the JTable component is flexible in terms of the types of selections that can be made and supports a number of different settings related to selection behavior. To manage its selection behavior, JTable uses the ListSelectionModel interface and its DefaultListSelectionModel implementation.

> **Row selections**: If enabled, row selection mode indicates that when a cell is selected, all other cells in its row should become selected as well. This is the default behavior for a JTable, where an entire row is selected when a single cell in that row was clicked. JTable provides accessor and mutator methods called getRowSelectionAllowed() and setRowSelectionAllowed(), respectively, and these methods allow you to query and enable or disable row selection mode.

Column selections: Just as JTable supports a row selection mode, it also supports a column selection mode, where selecting one cell causes all cells in its column to become selected. The getColumnSelectionAllowed() and setColumnSelectionAllowed() accessor and mutator methods allow you to query and modify this mode.

Cell selections: In cell selection mode, selecting a cell doesn't cause any other cells in the table to become selected. The getCellSelectionEnabled() and setCellSelectionEnabled() methods query and modify the cell selection mode for a JTable. Enabling cell selection mode effectively disables the row and column selection modes.

Combining Row, Column, and Cell Selection Modes

You can use the row and column selection modes together so that clicking a cell causes all other cells in the same row or column to be selected. However, enabling cell selection mode overrides the row and column selection modes, causing them to be ignored as if they were both disabled. For example, suppose you create the following code segment:

```
JTable table;
.
.
.
table.setRowSelectionAllowed(true);
table.setColumnSelectionAllowed(true);
table.setCellSelectionEnabled(true);
```

As long as cell selection mode is enabled, the row and column selection modes are effectively disabled, and only cell selections are allowed. Therefore, although there are three selection settings, there are only four meaningful combinations of those three settings.

- Only row selection mode is enabled.
- Only column selection mode is enabled.
- Cell selection mode is enabled (the other two are ignored).
- All three (row, column, and cell) selection modes are disabled.

In this last case, the behavior is what you'd probably expect; with all three modes disabled, no cells can be selected.

List Selection Modes

When some type of cell selection occurs, one or both of the ListSelectionModel instances are updated to reflect the selection(s) made (the specific changes to those models will depend on the selection mode or modes enabled). By default, each model can maintain multiple value ranges (or intervals). For example, given the selections shown in Figure 7-19, the selection model that's responsible for recording row selections might record that items 0 through 1 and items 3 through 4 are selected (a total of four rows).

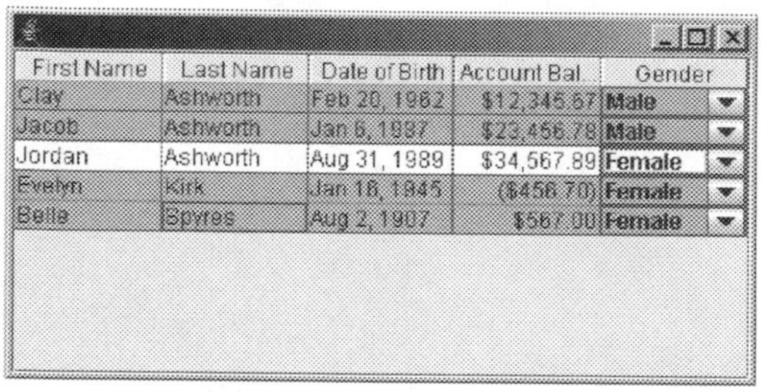

Figure 7-19. *In this example, two sets of rows are selected: the two top and the two bottom rows*

To select two intervals like this, perform the following steps:

1. Click the top row.

2. Press and hold down the Shift key, and click the second row. At this point, the first range (0 through 1) of rows has been selected.

3. Release the Shift key, press and hold down the Ctrl key, and click the fourth row.

4. Release the Ctrl key, press and hold down the Shift key, and click the last row—the second range of rows (3 through 4) has now been selected.

As you can see, holding down the Shift key while making a selection indicates you want to select the second in a pair of values that defines a range of values (e.g., a set of consecutive rows). Holding down the Ctrl key while making a selection indicates that any previous selections shouldn't be cleared before making another selection. An alternative approach to using the Shift key to select a range of values is to drag the mouse (in other words, press and hold down the left mouse button while moving the cursor) from one cell to another. For example, in this case, you could click a cell in the top row and drag the mouse to the second row to select the first range of rows.

This example illustrates the default mode, known as *multiple-interval selection*, which is one of three modes that the ListSelectionModel supports. The other two modes are *single-interval selection* and *single selection*.

As its name implies, single-interval selection mode allows a model to maintain a single interval instead of multiple intervals. For example, if you repeat the previous steps with single-interval selection, the first range of values (rows 0 through 1) becomes deselected when you attempt to select the second interval (rows 3 through 4).

In single-selection mode, a ListSelectionModel allows only a single item to be selected, and no range of items is allowed. Any attempt to select another item will cause the previously selected item to be deselected. For example, when you enable column selection mode in conjunction with single-selection mode, you can select only a single column at a time.

As mentioned earlier, each JTable maintains two ListSelectionModel instances and provides a setSelectionMode() method that sets the selection mode for both instances. Each selection mode is represented by a constant value defined in ListSelectionModel.

- MULTIPLE_INTERVAL_SELECTION

- SINGLE_INTERVAL_SELECTION

- SINGLE_SELECTION

Note, however, that JTable doesn't provide a getSelectionMode() method; to determine the current mode, you must retrieve that information from one of the ListSelectionModel instances, as illustrated in the following code:

```
JTable table;
.
.
.
int oldSelectionMode = table.getSelectionModel().getSelectionMode();
table.setSelectionMode(ListSelectionModel.SINGLE_INTERVAL_SELECT);
```

Selection Mode Combinations

As mentioned earlier, five combinations of row, column, and cell selection modes are available. In addition, three ListSelectionModel modes are available, which results in 15 combinations. Although this provides you with a great deal of flexibility in how table cells are selected, it also results in a somewhat confusing array of choices. However, by temporarily making the following modifications to SimpleTableTest, you can select the table and list selection modes used, which allows you to experiment with the behavior of different combinations, as shown in Listing 7-9.

Listing 7-9. Selection Mode Testing

```
import java.awt.*;
import java.awt.event.*;
import javax.swing.*;
import javax.swing.table.*;
import javax.swing.border.*;

public class SimpleTableTest extends JFrame {

  private JTable table;

  public static void main(String[] args) {
    SimpleTableTest stt = new SimpleTableTest();
    stt.setDefaultCloseOperation(JFrame.EXIT_ON_CLOSE);
    stt.setSize(400, 200);
    stt.setVisible(true);
  }

  public SimpleTableTest() {
    Container pane = getContentPane();
    pane.setLayout(new BorderLayout());
    TableValues tv = new TableValues();
    table = new JTable(tv);
    TableColumnModel tcm = table.getColumnModel();
    TableColumn tc = tcm.getColumn(TableValues.GENDER);
    tc.setCellRenderer(new GenderRenderer());
    tc.setCellEditor(new GenderEditor());
    table.setDefaultRenderer(Float.class, new CurrencyRenderer());
    JScrollPane jsp = new JScrollPane(table);
    pane.add(jsp, BorderLayout.CENTER);
```

```java
JPanel outerPanel = new JPanel();
outerPanel.setLayout(new GridLayout(1, 2, 0, 0));
JPanel innerPanel = new JPanel();
innerPanel.setLayout(new FlowLayout());
JCheckBox modeBox = new JCheckBox("Row", true);
modeBox.addItemListener(new ItemListener() {
  public void itemStateChanged(ItemEvent event) {
    JCheckBox box = (JCheckBox)(event.getSource());
    table.setRowSelectionAllowed(box.isSelected());
  }
});
innerPanel.add(modeBox);
modeBox = new JCheckBox("Column");
modeBox.addItemListener(new ItemListener() {
  public void itemStateChanged(ItemEvent event) {
    JCheckBox box = (JCheckBox)(event.getSource());
    table.setColumnSelectionAllowed(box.isSelected());
  }
});
innerPanel.add(modeBox);
modeBox = new JCheckBox("Cell");
modeBox.addItemListener(new ItemListener() {
  public void itemStateChanged(ItemEvent event) {
    JCheckBox box = (JCheckBox)(event.getSource());
    table.setCellSelectionEnabled(box.isSelected());
  }
});
innerPanel.add(modeBox);

BevelBorder bb = new BevelBorder(BevelBorder.RAISED);
TitledBorder tb = new TitledBorder(bb, "Table Selection Types");
innerPanel.setBorder(tb);
outerPanel.add(innerPanel);
innerPanel = new JPanel();
innerPanel.setLayout(new FlowLayout());
JComboBox listModes = new JComboBox();
listModes.addItem("Single Selection");
listModes.addItem("Single Interval Selection");
listModes.addItem("Multiple Interval Selections");
listModes.setSelectedIndex(2);
listModes.addItemListener(new ItemListener() {
  public void itemStateChanged(ItemEvent event) {
    JComboBox box = (JComboBox)(event.getSource());
    int index = box.getSelectedIndex();
    switch (index) {
    case 0:
      table.setSelectionMode(ListSelectionModel.SINGLE_SELECTION);
      break;
    case 1:
      table.setSelectionMode(ListSelectionModel.SINGLE_INTERVAL_SELECTION);
      break;
```

```
      case 2:
        table.setSelectionMode(ListSelectionModel.MULTIPLE_INTERVAL_SELECTION);
        break;
      }
    }
});
innerPanel.add(listModes);
bb = new BevelBorder(BevelBorder.RAISED);
tb = new TitledBorder(bb, "List Selection Modes");
innerPanel.setBorder(tb);
outerPanel.add(innerPanel);

    pane.add(outerPanel, BorderLayout.SOUTH);
  }
}
```

As shown in Figure 7-20, this code adds a pair of panels to the bottom of the SimpleTableTest interface. The panel on the left allows you to enable and disable row, column, and cell selections, while the panel on the right contains a JComboBox that allows you to choose a selection mode. The selections you make in the check boxes and the combo box are detected and used to update the selection state of the JTable, which provides you with the ability to experiment with different selection modes.

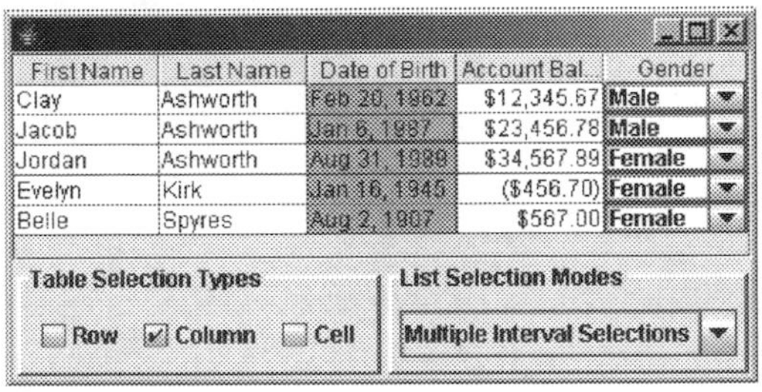

Figure 7-20. *This testing utility allows you to graphically control the selection settings in a table to see how those changes affect its appearance*

Setting Selections Programmatically

In addition to user-generated events that change which cells are selected within a table, it's also possible to set and query a JTable's selections programmatically; Table 7-1 describes the methods available for doing so.

Table 7-1. *Cell Selection Methods*

Method	Behavior
getSelectedRowCount()	Returns the number of rows in the table that are currently selected.
getSelectedRows()	Returns an array of integers, each one representing the index value of a currently selected row in the table.
getSelectedRow()	Returns an integer index value that identifies the first row (the row closest to the top of the table) that's selected. This is useful when only a single row can be selected.
setRowSelectionInterval (int index0, int index1)	Each row within the range of values (inclusive) is selected. Any rows not in that range that were selected prior to this method call are deselected.
addRowSelectionInterval (int index0, int index1)	Each row within the range of values (inclusive) is selected.
getSelectedColumnCount()	Returns the number of columns in the table that are currently selected.
getSelectedColumns()	Returns an array of integers, each one representing the index value of a currently selected column in the table.
getSelectedColumn()	Returns an integer index value that identifies the first column (the row closest to the left side of the table) that's selected. This is useful only when a single column can be selected.
setColumnSelectionInterval (int index0, int index1)	Each column within the range of values (inclusive) is selected. Any columns not in that range that were selected prior to this method call are deselected.
addColumnSelectionInterval()	Two integer values are passed to this method, and each column within the range of values (inclusive) is selected.

All these methods are defined in JTable, but each of them delegates the request to a ListSelectionModel. Specifically, the row selection method calls are delegated to the model maintained by the JTable itself (the row model), while the column selection calls are handled by the selection model maintained by the table's TableColumnModel implementation.

Table Headers

Early in the chapter we saw that adding a JTable to a JScrollPane results in the appearance of a header above each column and that a user can dynamically resize columns using mouse drags that begin at the right edge of the header of the column to be sorted. In fact, that ability to resize columns dynamically is only part of the functionality supported by JTable headers. For example, you can dynamically change the order of the columns within a JTable by dragging the column's header left or right to reposition the column.

In reality, the functions just described aren't provided by the JTable class itself but by a support class defined in the javax.swing.table package created for the purpose of providing a robust table header—specifically, the JTableHeader class. The table header is created for you automatically when the table is added to a scroll pane and it's rarely necessary for you to access the header directly, but it is accessible through the getTableHeader() method defined in JTable.

In some ways the design of JTableHeader is similar to that of JTable. For example, the header above each column in the table is considered a "cell" that's drawn by a TableCellRenderer and just as with the data cells within the table you can customize the appearance of header cells by creating and using a custom renderer. You can assign a header renderer to a single column by using the setHeaderRenderer() method in TableColumn, but if no renderer has been explicitly assigned to the column using that method the JTableHeader's default renderer will be used, which can also be set and retrieved using the setDefaultRenderer() and getDefaultRenderer() methods, respectively. We won't cover an example of how to do so because the technique is identical to the one we already examined that's used for data cells.

Multiline Column Headers

Notice that the "Account Balance" column header doesn't quite fit within the space provided for the column and is truncated with ellipses (...) to indicate that the entire text is not displayed. This is a fairly common problem, especially when the column header is long or the data within the column doesn't require much space and as a consequence you decide to make the column narrow.

An easy solution to this problem is to use a multiline column header, which can be done by wrapping the column name into HTML elements and inserting a break (<br>) element where you'd like a line break to occur. Following is an example of how this would appear in the code:

```
public final static String[] columnNames = {
  "First Name", "Last Name", "Date of Birth", "<html>Account<br>Balance</html>",
  "Gender"
};
```

By default the table header is only tall enough to display one line of text, so to ensure that it can display two lines you should also include code like the following that increases the header's preferred height:

```
JTableHeader header = table.getTableHeader();
header.setPreferredSize(new Dimension(
    header.getPreferredSize().width, header.getPreferredSize().height * 2));
```

With these two changes made, running the sample application produces a window like the one shown in Figure 7-21.

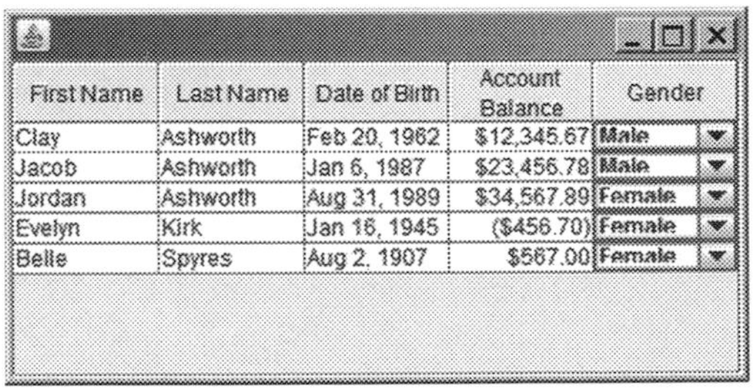

Figure 7-21. *An example of a multiline table header*

Adding Table Header Tool Tips

Assuming that we want to define a custom JTable subclass that can display a different tool tip for each column we can begin by defining a class like the one shown in Listing 7-10.

Listing 7-10. A JTable Subclass That Maintains a Mapping of Column Names to Tool Tips

```java
import java.util.*;
import javax.swing.*;

public class ToolTipTable extends JTable {

  private final Map<String, String> columnTips = new HashMap<String, String>();

  public ToolTipTable(TableValues model) {
    super(model);
  }

  public void setColumnToolTip(String columnName, String toolTipText) {
    columnTips.put(columnName, toolTipText);
  }

  public String getColumnToolTip(String columnName) {
    return columnTips.get(columnName);
  }

}
```

This table defines a collection in which it stores a mapping between column names and tool tips. Now what's needed is to create the code that will actually cause a tool tip to be displayed. Because the table header is a separate component we can simply create a MouseListener that is notified whenever mouse movement occurs over the header. That listener will need to determine which column the cursor is over, retrieve the appropriate tool tip for that column, and set the header's tool tip text to that value as shown in Listing 7-11.

Listing 7-11. Selecting and Assigning a Tool Tip

```java
import java.awt.event.*;
import java.util.*;
import javax.swing.*;
import javax.swing.table.*;

public class ToolTipTable extends JTable {

  private final Map<String, String> columnTips = new HashMap<String, String>();

  public ToolTipTable(TableValues model) {
    super(model);
    createToolTipListener();
  }
```

313

```
  private void createToolTipListener() {
    JTableHeader header = getTableHeader();
    header.addMouseMotionListener(new MouseAdapter() {
      public void mouseMoved(MouseEvent event) {
          JTableHeader source = (JTableHeader)(event.getSource());
          int viewIndex = source.columnAtPoint(event.getPoint());
          String columnName = getColumnName(viewIndex);
          String toolTipText = getColumnToolTip(columnName);
          source.setToolTipText(toolTipText);
      }
    });
  }

  public void setColumnToolTip(String columnName, String toolTipText) {
    columnTips.put(columnName, toolTipText);
  }

  public String getColumnToolTip(String columnName) {
    return columnTips.get(columnName);
  }

}
```

Finally, we'll need to update our program to specify the name of the column or columns for which we want a tool tip displayed. For this example we'll just assign a tool tip to the "Date of Birth" column as shown in Listing 7-12.

Listing 7-12. Setting the Tool Tip Text for one of the Table's Columns

```
public class SimpleTableTest extends JFrame {

  private ToolTipTable table;

  public static void main(String[] args) {
    SimpleTableTest stt = new SimpleTableTest();
    stt.setDefaultCloseOperation(JFrame.EXIT_ON_CLOSE);
    stt.setSize(400, 200);
    stt.setVisible(true);
  }

  public SimpleTableTest() {
    Container pane = getContentPane();
    pane.setLayout(new BorderLayout());
    TableValues tv = new TableValues();
    table = new ToolTipTable(tv);
    table.setColumnToolTip("Date of Birth", "Date on which the person was born");
```

If you compile and run this code, you'll find that it displays the tool tip only when the cursor hovers over the "Account Balance" column as illustrated in Figure 7-22.

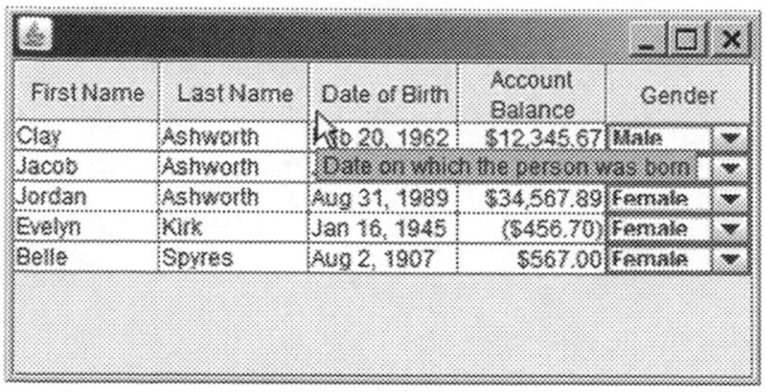

Figure 7-22. *Displaying a tool tip for a table header column*

Creating Row Headers

For many displays, column headers are sufficient, but you'll sometimes want to create row headers for the data in a JTable. As it turns out, this is easy to do, since the JScrollPane provides not only a viewport for column headers but also one for row headers. Unlike the column header viewport, the row viewport is empty by default, but it's trivial to create your own header and have it displayed.

You can use the class in Listing 7-13 as a row header; it's simply a JTable that displays a single column with the index value (starting at 1 instead of 0) of each row displayed in that column. The class is very simple, and in fact, much of its code exists simply to make minor adjustments to its appearance and behavior, such as preventing its cells from being selected.

Listing 7-13. Row Header Component

```java
import javax.swing.*;
import javax.swing.table.*;

public class RowNumberHeader extends JTable {

  private JTable mainTable;

  public RowNumberHeader(JTable table) {
    super();
    mainTable = table;
    setModel(new RowNumberTableModel());
    setPreferredScrollableViewportSize(getMinimumSize());
    setRowSelectionAllowed(false);
    JComponent renderer = (JComponent)getDefaultRenderer(Object.class);
    LookAndFeel.installColorsAndFont(renderer,
                                    "TableHeader.background",
                                    "TableHeader.foreground",
                                    "TableHeader.font");
    LookAndFeel.installBorder(this, "TableHeader.cellBorder");
  }

  public int getRowHeight(int row) {
    return mainTable.getRowHeight();
  }
```

315

```
class RowNumberTableModel extends AbstractTableModel {

  public int getRowCount() {
    return mainTable.getModel().getRowCount();
  }

  public int getColumnCount() {
    return 1;
  }

  public Object getValueAt(int row, int column) {
    return new Integer(row + 1);
  }

}

}
```

After defining this class, you can use it by making a temporary change to the SimpleTableTest class (see Listing 7-14).

Listing 7-14. Using the Row Header Component

```
public SimpleTableTest() {
  Container pane = getContentPane();
  pane.setLayout(new BorderLayout());
  TableValues tv = new TableValues();
  table = new JTable(tv);
  table.setRowSelectionAllowed(false);
  table.setColumnSelectionAllowed(true);
  TableColumnModel tcm = table.getColumnModel();
  TableColumn tc = tcm.getColumn(TableValues.GENDER);
  tc.setCellRenderer(new GenderRenderer());
  tc.setCellEditor(new GenderEditor());
  MultiLineHeaderRenderer mlhr = new MultiLineHeaderRenderer();
  tc = tcm.getColumn(TableValues.ACCOUNT_BALANCE);
  tc.setHeaderRenderer(mlhr);
  JTableHeaderToolTips jthtt =
      new JTableHeaderToolTips(table.getColumnModel());
  jthtt.setToolTips(new String[] {"Customer's First Name",
      "Customer's Last Name", "Customer's Date of Birth",
      "Customer's Account Balance", "Customer's Gender"});
  table.setTableHeader(jthtt);
  table.setDefaultRenderer(Float.class, new CurrencyRenderer());
  JScrollPane jsp = new JScrollPane(table);
  JViewport jvp = new JViewport();
  jvp.setView(new RowNumberHeader(table));
  jsp.setRowHeader(jvp);
  pane.add(jsp, BorderLayout.CENTER);
  addHeaderListener();
}
```

When executed, each table row includes a number on the left side, as shown in Figure 7-23.

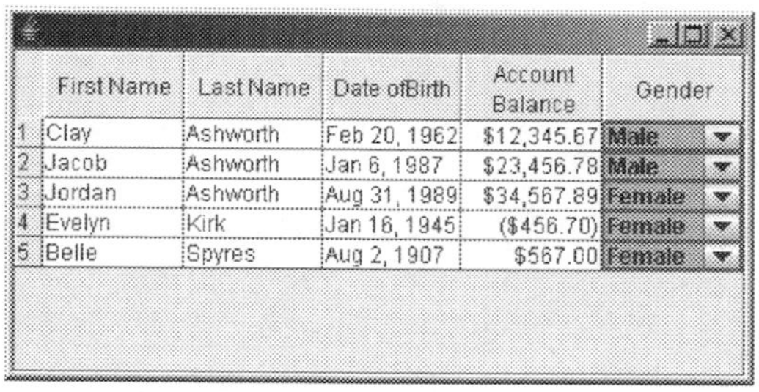

	First Name	Last Name	Date ofBirth	Account Balance	Gender	
1	Clay	Ashworth	Feb 20, 1962	$12,345.67	Male	▼
2	Jacob	Ashworth	Jan 6, 1987	$23,456.78	Male	▼
3	Jordan	Ashworth	Aug 31, 1989	$34,567.89	Female	▼
4	Evelyn	Kirk	Jan 16, 1945	($456.70)	Female	▼
5	Belle	Spyres	Aug 2, 1907	$567.00	Female	▼

Figure 7-23. *Although column headers are used more frequently, it's sometimes also helpful to use row headers, such as in this case where each row is numbered*

Frozen Columns

In addition to displaying row headers, it's sometimes desirable to "freeze" one or more columns in the table so they're visible even when the user scrolls right or left horizontally. For example, in the case of this data, it might be desirable to freeze the first column (First Name) so it's always visible. You can do this, but it's slightly more complex than creating simple row labels.

The steps are as follows:

1. Create a JTable that you'll call the main table, and enclose it in a JScrollPane. This table will display the nonfrozen data.

2. Create a second JTable that you'll call the header table, and add it to a JScrollPane as well. This table should use the same TableModel as the main table but will display the frozen column(s).

3. Create an empty TableColumnModel that will later be assigned to the header table.

4. Remove the TableColumn instances from the main table's TableColumnModel for each column to be frozen, and add them to the column model created in the previous step.

5. Assign the column model that now contains the frozen TableColumn instances to the header table using setColumnModel().

6. The JScrollPane that contains the header table should now also contain a JTableHeader in its column header viewport. Obtain a reference to it, and move it to the upper-left corner of the JScrollPane that contains the main table. You can do this using the scroll pane's setCorner() method.

7. Set the header table's preferred scrollable viewport width so it's just large enough to display the frozen columns. Its default width is 450, which is usually larger than necessary.

In effect, to freeze columns, you split the JTable into two separate tables, display the table containing the frozen columns as the JScrollPane's row header, and move that table's column headers to the upper-left corner of the outer scroll pane. Listing 7-15 shows how to implement this behavior.

Listing 7-15. A Frozen Column Header Component

```
import java.awt.*;
import javax.swing.*;
import javax.swing.table.*;

public class FrozenColumnHeader extends JScrollPane {

  private JTable mainTable;
  private JTable headerTable;
  private int columnCount;

  public FrozenColumnHeader(JTable table, int columns) {
    super();
    mainTable = table;
    headerTable = new JTable(mainTable.getModel());
    getViewport().setView(headerTable);
    columnCount = columns;
  }

  public void addNotify() {
    TableColumn column;
    super.addNotify();
    TableColumnModel mainModel = mainTable.getColumnModel();
    TableColumnModel headerModel = new DefaultTableColumnModel();
    int frozenWidth = 0;
    for (int i = 0; i < columnCount; i++) {
      column = mainModel.getColumn(0);
      mainModel.removeColumn(column);
      headerModel.addColumn(column);
      frozenWidth += column.getPreferredWidth() + headerModel.getColumnMargin();
  }
  headerTable.setColumnModel(headerModel);
  Component columnHeader = getColumnHeader().getView();
  getColumnHeader().setView(null);
  JScrollPane mainScrollPane = (JScrollPane)SwingUtilities.getAncestorOfClass(
    JScrollPane.class, mainTable);
  mainScrollPane.setCorner(JScrollPane.UPPER_LEFT_CORNER, columnHeader);
  headerTable.setPreferredScrollableViewportSize(
    new Dimension(frozenWidth, 0));
 }
}
```

You can use this class by creating an instance of it and passing a reference to a JTable to the constructor, along with the number of columns from that table to freeze. For example, the following modification to SimpleTableTest causes the First Name column to be frozen (see Listing 7-16):

Listing 7-16. Integrating the Frozen Column Header into a Table

```
public SimpleTableTest() {
  Container pane = getContentPane();
  pane.setLayout(new BorderLayout());
  TableValues tv = new TableValues();
  table = new JTable(tv);
  table.setRowSelectionAllowed(false);
  table.setColumnSelectionAllowed(true);
  TableColumnModel tcm = table.getColumnModel();
  TableColumn tc = tcm.getColumn(TableValues.GENDER);
  tc.setCellRenderer(new GenderRenderer());
  tc.setCellEditor(new GenderEditor());
  MultiLineHeaderRenderer mlhr = new MultiLineHeaderRenderer();
  tc = tcm.getColumn(TableValues.ACCOUNT_BALANCE);
  tc.setHeaderRenderer(mlhr);
  JTableHeaderToolTips jthtt =
    new JTableHeaderToolTips(table.getColumnModel());
  jthtt.setToolTips(new String[] {"Customer's First Name",
    "Customer's Last Name", "Customer's Date of Birth",
    "Customer's Account Balance", "Customer's Gender"});
  table.setTableHeader(jthtt);
  table.setDefaultRenderer(Float.class, new CurrencyRenderer());
  JScrollPane jsp = new JScrollPane(table);
  JViewport jvp = new JViewport();
  jvp.setView(new FrozenColumnHeader(table, 1));
  //  The following line isn't necessary but is done
  //  to illustrate that the "frozen" columns remain
  //  visible even when the main table is scrolled
  table.setAutoResizeMode(JTable.AUTO_RESIZE_OFF);
  jsp.setRowHeader(jvp);
  pane.add(jsp, BorderLayout.CENTER);
  addHeaderListener();
}
```

When you execute this code, you can resize the frame so it's too narrow to display all the columns in the table. However, regardless of which portion of the table is displayed, the "frozen" column on the left will remain visible, as shown in Figure 7-24.

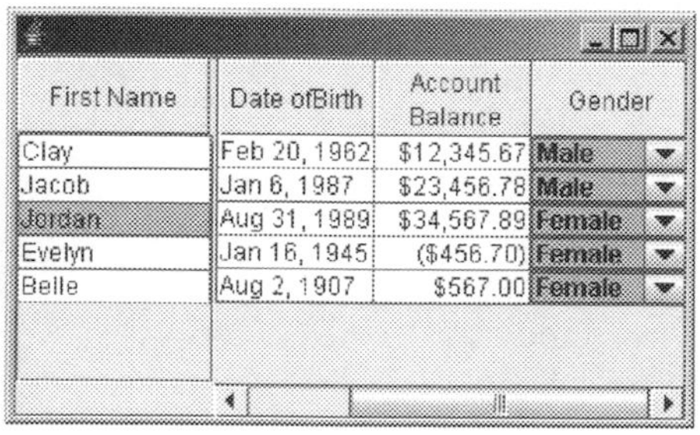

Figure 7-24. *Frozen column headers are useful when the table data is wider than can be displayed*

319

Although this example illustrates how to freeze a single column, you can apply this same technique if you want to freeze multiple columns. You can also use this approach to freeze rows of data simply by adding a table containing the rows to the JScrollPane's column header viewport.

Sorting Table Rows

When displaying information in a JTable, you'll sometimes want to sort the rows in the table based on the values in one or more of the columns. Since sorting is a slow and potentially complex task, it's best to have the data sorted by some external application. For example, if you're displaying data from a relational database, you can have the database present the rows to you in sorted order by indicating that fact in the SELECT statement you issue. However, you'll often want to allow the user to determine which column should be used for sorting and whether to sort in ascending or descending order, and since Java 6 the JTable class has included built-in support for sorting.

To enable table sorting you can simply add the following line of code to your class that creates the table:

```
table.setAutoCreateRowSorter(true);
```

As its name implies, this method tells the table to create a row sorter that will cause the rows to be sorted. You can see the results of this by clicking one of the columns in the test application, which will result in the appearance of an arrow button in the header cell you clicked as shown in Figure 7-25.

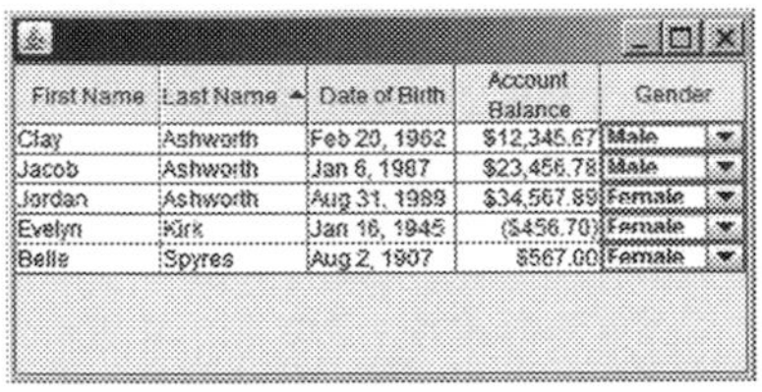

Figure 7-25. *An arrow appears to indicate the sort order; an up arrow indicates an ascending sort*

Clicking the same column header a second time will toggle the sort order so that it changes to a descending sort, and clicking a different header cell will cause the table data to be re-sorted using an ascending sort of that column's data, and so on.

This approach works fine when you want the user to select a single column, but what about the case where you want to have the table sorted by default without any action on the part of the user? The column header clicking is supported by a programmatic interface included in the JTable class that allows the caller to specify which column(s) should be used for sorting and, for each one of the columns, the sort order (ascending or descending). Specifically, the TableRowSorter class defined in the javax.swing.table package encapsulates the sorting preferences. TableRowSorter is a generic type that expects you to indicate the TableModel implementation that you intend to use it with, though you can usually just specify TableModel itself. It does require you to provide, either on construction or later via its setModel() method, a reference to the model containing the data to be sorted. In this case we'll provide a reference to our TableValues model and specify that as the model class.

```
TableRowSorter<TableValues> sorter = new TableRowSorter<TableValues>(tv);
```

320

The next step is to indicate the columns on which to sort and, for each one, the sort order. This is done using the column's index along with an instance of the SortOrder enumeration defined in javax.swing, with the column index/sort order pair stored in an instance of SortKey, which is an inner class defined in the RowSorter class. In the following code we indicate that sorting should be done using the values in the second column in descending order and when two rows in that column contain the same value they should be further sorted in descending order based on the third column's value:

```
RowSorter.SortKey key1 = new RowSorter.SortKey(1, SortOrder.DESCENDING);
RowSorter.SortKey key2 = new RowSorter.SortKey(2, SortOrder.DESCENDING);
java.util.List<RowSorter.SortKey> sortKeys = java.util.Arrays.asList(key1, key2);
```

Now that we've created our instance of TableRowSorter and created a list containing the sort keys, we can set that list of keys in the sorter object and tell the table to use that sorter to determine the order of its rows. The complete code is shown next and should replace the previously described call to setAutoCreateRowSorter().

```
TableRowSorter<TableValues> sorter = new TableRowSorter<TableValues>(tv);
TableRowSorter.SortKey key1 = new TableRowSorter.SortKey(1, SortOrder.DESCENDING);
TableRowSorter.SortKey key2 = new TableRowSorter.SortKey(2, SortOrder.DESCENDING);
java.util.List<RowSorter.SortKey> sortKeys = java.util.Arrays.asList(key1, key2);
sorter.setSortKeys(sortKeys);
table.setRowSorter(sorter);
```

Once these changes are made and the sample program run, it displays the table with its data sorted using the second and third column values as shown in Figure 7-26.

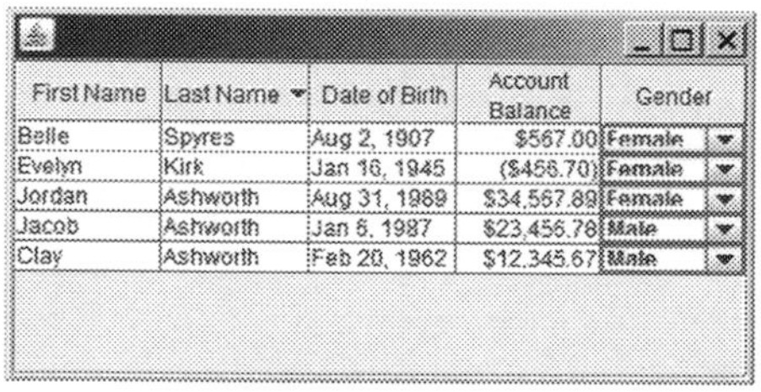

Figure 7-26. *A table with its rows sorted programmatically*

Adding and Removing Table Rows

In all the examples you've seen so far, no JTable data was changed, added, or removed programmatically. However, you'll sometimes want to dynamically change the data in a JTable after it's displayed, and all that's necessary is to make the changes to your TableModel and then notify its listeners (in other words, the JTable instance) that the data was modified.

For example, Listing 7-17 provides a simple one-column table and a text field that allows you to add lines of text to the table.

Listing 7-17. Adding Table Rows

```java
import java.awt.*;
import java.awt.event.*;
import javax.swing.*;
import javax.swing.event.*;
import javax.swing.table.*;
import java.util.Vector;

public class RowAdder extends JFrame {

  private SimpleModel tableData;
  private JTable table;
  private JTextField textField;

  public static void main(String[] args) {
    RowAdder ra = new RowAdder();
    ra.setDefaultCloseOperation(JFrame.EXIT_ON_CLOSE);
    ra.setSize(400, 300);
    ra.setVisible(true);
  }

  public RowAdder() {
    Container pane = getContentPane();
    pane.setLayout(new BorderLayout());
    tableData = new SimpleModel();
    table = new JTable(tableData);
    table.getColumnModel().getColumn(0).setPreferredWidth(300);
    JScrollPane jsp = new JScrollPane(table);
    pane.add(jsp, BorderLayout.CENTER);
    textField = new JTextField();
    textField.addActionListener(new ActionListener() {
      public void actionPerformed(ActionEvent event) {
        addLineToTable();
      }
    });
    pane.add(textField, BorderLayout.SOUTH);
  }

  private void addLineToTable() {
    tableData.addText(textField.getText());
    textField.setText("");
  }

  class SimpleModel extends AbstractTableModel {

    private Vector textData = new Vector();

    public void addText(String text) {
      textData.addElement(text);
      fireTableDataChanged();
    }
```

```
    public int getRowCount() {
      return textData.size();
    }

    public int getColumnCount() {
      return 1;
    }

    public Object getValueAt(int row, int column) {
      return textData.elementAt(row);
    }

  }

}
```

This code creates a JTable and allows you to enter text in a text field and press the Return key to add that text to the table, as shown in Figure 7-27.

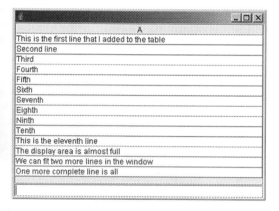

Figure 7-27. *This simplistic interface illustrates how rows can be added to a table dynamically*

When that occurs, the data is added to the TableModel, and the fireTableDataChanged() method is called. That method is provided by AbstractTableModel as a convenience, but even if your TableModel isn't a subclass of AbstractTableModel, it's still trivial to refresh the table display when your data changes. All that's necessary is to construct an instance of TableModelEvent and pass it as the parameter to the tableChanged() method of all listeners that registered with the TableModel through its addTableModelListener() method. The following code segment illustrates how to do this:

```
private EventListenerList listenerList = new EventListenerList();
.
.
.
public void notifyListenersOfDataChange() {
  TableModelEvent event = new TableModelEvent(this);
  Object[] listeners = listenerList.getListenerList();
```

```
    for (int i = 0; i < listeners.length; i++) {
    if (listeners[i] == TableModelListener.class) {
      TableModelListener listener = (TableModelListener)(listeners[i + 1]);
      listener.tableChanged(event);
      }
    }
}
```

This code illustrates how easily you can notify listeners (in practice, usually a single JTable instance) of a change to a TableModel's data. However, as mentioned, AbstractTableModel implements this functionality for you. It also includes a number of fireTable() methods that create a TableModelEvent containing information about specifically what type of change (insert, update, or delete) occurred, along with the rows and columns that were affected by the change. You can use those methods to cause your table to be refreshed when you have made insertions, updates, or deletions to the data in the table's model.

Displaying a Particular Table Row

In the RowAdder class just defined, a row is added to the table each time the Return key is pressed in a text field. The first dozen or so rows appear immediately in the table, but eventually, there's not enough room to display all the table rows, and a vertical scrollbar appears. At that point, since new rows are added to the end of the table, they won't be visible unless you manually scroll to the bottom of the table. However, when you're adding data to a table like this, it's often helpful to scroll the table automatically so that it always shows the most recently added row. You can do this by accessing the JViewport instance that's associated with the table's scroll pane and changing the view position so that the bottom row appears at the scroll pane. You can easily modify the RowAdder class previously defined to perform this operation, as shown in Listing 7-18.

Listing 7-18. Scrolling to a Particular Row

```
public RowAdder() {
  Container pane = getContentPane();
  pane.setLayout(new BorderLayout());
  tableData = new SimpleModel();
  table = new JTable(tableData);
  table.getColumnModel().getColumn(0).setPreferredWidth(300);
  table.addComponentListener(new TableScroller());
  JScrollPane jsp = new JScrollPane(table);
  pane.add(jsp, BorderLayout.CENTER);
  textField = new JTextField();
  textField.addActionListener(new ActionListener() {
    public void actionPerformed(ActionEvent event) {
      addLineToTable();
    }
  });
  pane.add(textField, BorderLayout.SOUTH);
}
class TableScroller extends ComponentAdapter {

  public void componentResized(ComponentEvent event) {
    int lastRow = tableData.getRowCount() - 1;
    int cellTop = table.getCellRect(lastRow, 0, true).y;
```

```
JScrollPane jsp = (JScrollPane)SwingUtilities.getAncestorOfClass(
    JScrollPane.class, table);
JViewport jvp = jsp.getViewport();
int portHeight = jvp.getSize().height;
int position = cellTop - (portHeight - table.getRowHeight() -
    table.getRowMargin());
if (position >= 0) {
    jvp.setViewPosition(new Point(0, position));
    }
  }
}
```

The componentResized() method obtains the last row's size and coordinates by calling the table's getCellRect() method. It then uses the row's vertical position, the size of the viewport, and the height of the row to adjust the view position so the last row is displayed at the bottom of the table. By using functionality similar to this, you can ensure that any given table row is visible, such as in this case where a new row was added to the table and should be displayed.

Summary

In this chapter, you examined the functionality provided by JTable and how it provides those capabilities. Specifically, I discussed the following:

- How to create a TableModel

- Column resizing modes

- How to render and edit table cells

- Selection modes

- JTableHeader and how it can provide an improved user interface

- How to create numbered rows and frozen columns

- How to implement sorting

- How to handle dynamic updates to the table data

CHAPTER 8

■ ■ ■ ■

Using Swing's JTree

The JTree component defined in the javax.swing package is commonly used to display hierarchical data such as the contents of a file system. Even if you've never used JTree before, you've almost certainly seen a component like the one that appears on the left side of the Windows Explorer application (see Figure 8-1).

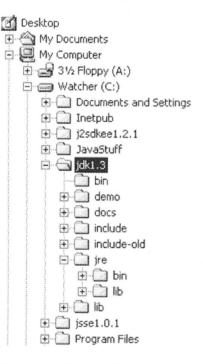

Figure 8-1. *Windows Explorer represents the relationships between a set of disks and directories*

This chapter describes how to use JTree and illustrates how to provide some functionality that's often needed. Specifically, in this chapter I'll cover the following:

- Understanding the terminology related to tree structures and the data they display

- Using JTree's support classes and interfaces

- Constructing and manipulating the data model associated with a tree

- Controlling how the items in a tree are drawn (rendered) and edited

- Selecting items in a tree and detecting when selections change

- Controlling which portions of a tree's data are displayed (expanded) or concealed (collapsed)

JTree Terminology

Before discussing how to use JTree, I'll define the terminology that describes the different parts of a tree and its behavior. Each item that's displayed in the tree is referred to as a *node*, and every JTree contains a single *root* node that resides at the top of the node hierarchy (see Figure 8-2).

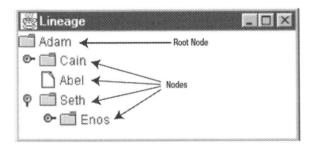

Figure 8-2. *Each row of the tree is referred to as a node, and a tree typically displays a top root node*

Each node is either a branch node or a leaf node, although the exact meanings of those terms can vary. Leaf node can refer to a node that doesn't contain other nodes, or it can refer to a node that can't contain other nodes. Branch node similarly can mean a node that does contain other nodes or one that can contain other nodes. In other words, a node that doesn't contain other nodes can be described as either a leaf node or a branch node; I discuss the variation in meaning in more detail later.

When a branch node does contain other nodes, it's said to be the parent of those nodes, and they're referred to as children of that branch and siblings of one another. In Figure 8-2, the Adam node is the parent of Cain, Abel, and Seth, and those three are likewise children of Adam and siblings of one another. Since the parent-child relationship is relative (it describes one node's relationship to another), a single node can be both a parent and a child. For example, Seth is both a parent (relative to Enos) and a child (relative to Adam).

All nodes that are contained by a branch node either directly or indirectly are referred to as the branch's descendents, and the branch itself is likewise referred to as an ancestor of its descendents. In Figure 8-2, the Adam node is the ancestor of all other nodes in the tree, and those nodes are all descendents of Adam. A closely related concept is that of a subtree, which is simply a tree node and all of its descendents, since that collection of nodes effectively forms a separate "tree within the tree."

The JTree component normally allows a parent node to be displayed in one of two states: with its children visible or with its children concealed. When a node's children are visible, that node is expanded; a collapsed node is one for which its descendents are concealed. It's normally possible for you to toggle this state by clicking the node's handle, which is a small image that appears to the left of the node. Figure 8-3 shows two instances of JTree that contain the same data, but two of the three nonroot nodes (colors and food) in the left tree are expanded, while all three of those in the right tree are collapsed. Note that the appearance of the handle varies slightly based upon the state (expanded or collapsed) of the node with which it's associated.

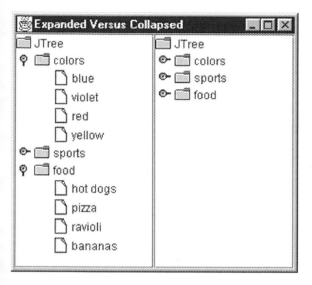

Figure 8-3. *A collapsed tree node is one that has descendents that aren't displayed, and the appearance of the node's handle indicates when it's collapsed*

When a node is collapsed, all of its descendents are hidden, because those nodes can't be seen, while a node for which all ancestors are expanded is considered *viewable*. The term *viewable* correctly implies that a node is eligible to be seen but not that it's currently visible. The reason for this distinction is that like JTable components, JTree instances often contain too much data to be able to display all of their nodes simultaneously, and for that reason, trees are often contained inside instances of JScrollPane. Only when a node is actually visible is it considered displayed, which means the node lies within the portion of the tree that's currently visible in the JScrollPane.

Creating a JTree

Creating a JTree instance is easy to do (see Listing 8-1), and many different constructors are provided, although the no-argument constructor populates the tree with dummy data like that shown in Figure 8-3. Several others accept a list of items in the form of an object array, Vector, or Hashtable.

Listing 8-1. Creating a New JTree

```
import javax.swing.*;

public class SimpleTreeTest extends JFrame {

  public static void main(String[] args) {
    SimpleTreeTest stt = new SimpleTreeTest();
    stt.setDefaultCloseOperation(JFrame.EXIT_ON_CLOSE);
    stt.setSize(250, 250);
    stt.setVisible(true);
  }
  public SimpleTreeTest() {
    Object[] genealogy = {"Jeff", "Joseph", "Pearl", "Owen", "Sarah",
        "John"};
```

```
    JTree tree = new JTree(genealogy);
    JScrollPane jsp = new JScrollPane(tree);
    getContentPane().add(jsp);
  }


}
```

This results in a display like the one shown in Figure 8-4.

Figure 8-4. *A simple tree with six sibling nodes visible*

It may appear at first glance that there's no root node or that each of the six nodes in the array passed to the JTree constructor is somehow a root node. In reality, this constructor produces a JTree instance that has a concealed root node, and each of the objects in the array parameter is made a child of that invisible root. To view the root node, add a line of code that calls the setRootVisible() method.

```
public SimpleTreeTest() {
  Object[] genealogy = {"Jeff", "Joseph", "Pearl", "Owen", "Sarah",
      "John"};
  JTree tree = new JTree(genealogy);
  tree.setRootVisible(true);
  JScrollPane jsp = new JScrollPane(tree);
  getContentPane().add(jsp);
}
```

This results in a display like the one shown in Figure 8-5.

Figure 8-5. *In this example, the root node appears because you've explicitly indicated it should be displayed*

Here the node values are all instances of the String class, but you can use any type of object as a node. JTree's default behavior is to display the value returned by each object's toString() method, which in this case is simply the String value itself.

330

In this example, each of the six nodes is assumed to be a leaf node since there are no children defined, but it's possible to use this technique to create more complex tree structures. For example, you could add a second level of nodes by modifying the following code:

```
public SimpleTreeTest() {
  Object[] genealogy = {"Jeff", "Joseph", "Pearl", "Owen", "Sarah",
      "John"};
  genealogy[0] = new Object[] {"Jerry", "Selma", "Joe", "Evelyn"};
  JTree tree = new JTree(genealogy);
  tree.setRootVisible(true);
  JScrollPane jsp = new JScrollPane(tree);
  getContentPane().add(jsp);
}
```

This modification changed the first element in the genealogy array from a String into another array, and when this code is compiled and executed, it produces a tree like the one shown in Figure 8-6.

Figure 8-6. *Defining a node as an array results in the array elements being represented as children within the tree*

Although this figure displays the data in a way that's largely appropriate, the toString() method of the second object array returns a value ([Ljava.lang.Object;@2701e) that's not meaningful. You can address this problem in several ways, but one easy way is to use either Vector or Hashtable instead of an array and override the object's toString() method so it returns the desired value. The following code segment illustrates how you can do this:

```
public SimpleTreeTest() {
  Object[] genealogy = {"Jeff", "Joseph", "Pearl", "Owen", "Sarah",
      "John"};
  java.util.Vector v = new java.util.Vector() {
    public String toString() {
      return "Jeff";
    }
  };
  v.addElement("Jerry");
  v.addElement("Selma");
  v.addElement("Joe");
  v.addElement("Evelyn");
  genealogy[0] = v;
```

```
    JTree tree = new JTree(genealogy);
    tree.setRootVisible(true);
    JScrollPane jsp = new JScrollPane(tree);
    getContentPane().add(jsp);
}
```

▓ **Note**   Overriding the `toString()` method of a collection like `Vector` is generally a very poor programming practice and isn't really a good solution to this problem. A better approach to this type of problem is provided by using the classes defined in Swing for representing tree nodes that we'll examine shortly.

As expected, this modified version of the code displays the name Jeff for the first child node's label instead of the cryptic value returned by the `Object` array (see Figure 8-7).

Figure 8-7. *By changing the value returned by an object's* `toString()` *method, you can control what's displayed for that object when it's part of a tree*

However, this approach is less than ideal, and as you'll see later in this chapter, the classes and interfaces in the `javax.swing.tree` package provide a better way to define the nodes in a tree and their parent-child relationships. Prior to that discussion, it's useful to examine the `TreeModel` interface, which defines the methods that are invoked by `JTree` to retrieve the data it displays.

TreeModel

Like other Swing components, an instance of the `JTree` class defined in `javax.swing` represents the component view, and some other object represents the model. In other words, the *model* is the object that encapsulates the data to be displayed, and the *view* (a `JTree` instance) is the visual representation of that data. For a class to serve as a `JTree` model, it must implement `TreeModel`, an interface that's defined in the `javax.swing.tree` package. I describe each of the methods defined in `TreeModel` next, although you won't normally call these methods yourself. Instead, an instance of `JTree` typically uses them to obtain the data it displays.

addTreeModelListener( ), removeTreeModelListener( )

An instance of a `TreeModelListener` implementation is passed to these methods, which are used to add and remove listeners to and from a list of objects that want to be notified of changes to the tree data. Each listener is notified when a node is added or removed from the tree and when the tree's structure otherwise changes. In practice, the only registered listener of a given `TreeModel` instance will be the `JTree` instance associated with the model, and by registering as a listener, the tree can be notified of changes to the data it displays.

getRoot( )

This method returns the object representing the tree's root node. In the previous examples, a root node was constructed automatically, and the objects in the array or `Vector` passed to the `JTree` constructor were made children of that root node. In most cases, however, you'll construct your own root node, add children to it, and pass it to a `JTree` constructor.

getChildCount( )

An object representing one of the previously identified tree nodes (the root node or one of its descendents) is passed to this method, which returns an integer value that identifies the number of children associated with that node.

getChild( )

An object representing one of the previously identified tree nodes is passed to this method along with an integer index value, and a reference to the appropriate child node is returned. The specific node returned is based on the value of the index parameter and corresponds to the child's position within its parent's list of children. For example, if the index value is 0, the first child node (the one that appears directly below its parent) is returned, and a value of 1 returns the second child node, and so on. In the following code segment, the third child of the node represented by parent is returned:

```
TreeModel model;
Object childNode, parentNode;
.
.
.
Object childNode = model.getChild(parentNode, 2);
```

getIndexOfChild( )

This method provides functionality that's essentially the opposite of that provided by `getChild()`. While `getChild()` returns a child node given an index, `getIndexOfChild()` returns the index associated with a specific child node. Two parameters representing tree nodes are passed to this method: one that's a parent and another representing one of that parent's children; `getIndexOfChild()` returns an integer that identifies the child's position within the parent's list of children. For example, if `getIndexOfChild()` is called and passed a reference to a node that's the third child of the specified parent node, it returns a value of 2. If a parent-child relationship doesn't exist between the two nodes, a value of -1 is returned.

isLeaf( )

This method is passed an object that has previously been identified by the TreeModel as one of the nodes in the tree, and it should return a Boolean value of true if that object represents a leaf node. As mentioned earlier, it's possible for *leaf node* to refer either to a node that can't have children or to one that simply doesn't currently have children, which is why it's necessary to define both this method and getChildCount( ). Depending upon which definition of *leaf node* is applied, it may or may not be possible to identify leaf nodes based solely upon a node's child count.

valueForPathChanged( )

This method is passed an instance of TreePath and an Object representing the new value that's to be associated with the node identified by the TreePath and is called when the node's value has changed. For example, when the editing of a tree node is completed and the new value should be saved, this method is called to cause the TreeModel to update its data accordingly. I discuss TreePath, which identifies a specific node within the tree, in the section "TreePath," later in this chapter.

Creating Tree Nodes

Now that you've seen how TreeModel encapsulates the data displayed in a JTree, you'll examine the interfaces and class provided in the javax.swing.tree package that allow you to easily create and manipulate tree nodes. The class most commonly used to represent a tree node is DefaultMutableTree, an implementation of the MutableTreeNode interface, which is in turn a subinterface of TreeNode. Although you won't often find it necessary to create your own TreeNode or MutableTreeNode implementations, a familiarity with those interfaces and some knowledge of how they can be implemented is helpful when using JTree.

TreeNode

One point that should be apparent from the description of TreeModel is that a model is responsible for providing information, such as whether a given node is a leaf or a branch and such as a list of each node's children. Although it might be technically possible to store that information in the TreeModel itself, doing so is difficult and complex at best. A better approach is to allow each node to maintain its own information, and TreeNode provides an interface that a TreeModel can use to retrieve the data from the node. In fact, of the seven TreeNode methods, four of them map directly to methods in TreeModel. The DefaultTreeModel class described in the section of that name, later in this chapter, takes advantage of that by supporting only objects that implement TreeNode, allowing it to delegate responsibility for the four methods listed in Table 8-1 to the nodes themselves.

Table 8-1. *TreeNode Methods*

TreeModel Method	Corresponding Method in TreeNode
getChild( )	getChildAt( )
getChildCount( )	getChildCount( )
getIndexOfChild( )	getIndex( )
isLeaf( )	isLeaf( )

Although the names vary slightly in two cases, the only difference between the parameter lists of the methods in a pair is the presence or absence of an Object that represents the node for which the information should be provided. For example, the TreeModel's getChildCount() method accepts a single Object parameter that identifies the parent node for which the child count should be returned.

```
public int getChildCount(Object parent);
```

In contrast, the getChildCount() method in TreeNode is defined to return the child count of the object for which the method is called (the this object), so no identifying node parameter is required.

```
public int getChildCount();
```

Since all nodes in a DefaultTreeModel must be instances of TreeNode, the implementation of getChildCount() in that model implementation is trivial.

```
public class DefaultTreeModel implements TreeModel {

  public int getChildCount(Object parent) {
    return ((TreeNode)parent).getChildCount();
  }
  // ...
```

getChildCount()

This method returns an integer value that identifies the number of children that the node has, and it's called by the method of the same name in TreeModel.

getChildAt()

A single integer index value is passed to getChildAt(), and it returns the TreeNode corresponding to the child node at the specified index. For example, a parent's first child corresponds to a value of 0, the second to a value of 1, and so on. A TreeModel can use this method to delegate responsibility for identifying a child's index by calling getChildAt() from the getChild() method in the TreeModel implementation.

getIndex()

The functionality of this method is essentially the opposite of that found in getChildAt(), and although getChildAt() returns a TreeNode given an index, this method is passed a TreeNode and returns that node's index. By calling this method from the getIndexOfChild() method in TreeModel, a model can delegate responsibility for that function to the node itself.

children()

This method returns an instance of java.util.Enumeration containing the TreeNode objects that are the children of this node.

getParent()

This method returns a reference to the TreeNode that's the parent of this node, unless this node represents the root node, in which case getParent() returns a value of null.

isLeaf()

This method should return a value of true if the node represents a leaf node or false if it represents a branch node. JTree's normal behavior is to display an icon for leaf nodes that's different from the one it displays for branch nodes, and this method determines which icon is associated with the node.

getAllowsChildren()

As its name implies, this method returns a Boolean value that indicates whether the node is eligible to have children. If the node supports children, it should return a value of true, while nodes that don't support children should return false.

Nodes Without Children: Leaf or Branch?

As previously mentioned, you can use the terms *leaf* and *branch* in one of the following two ways:

- Leaf nodes are those that don't have any children, while branch nodes are those that do have children.

- Alternatively, leaf nodes are those that can't have children, while branch nodes are those that can, which may include some nodes without children.

This ambiguity can be confusing, and it may seem unnecessarily so, but the reason for this vagueness is that you may want the first meaning to apply in some cases and the second to apply in others. For example, suppose you're using JTree to display genealogy/lineage information (a "family tree"). In that situation, it's probably reasonable to apply the first set of definitions to the JTree: leaf nodes represent individuals who don't (or didn't) have any children, while branch nodes are people who do (or did) have children. However, let's also consider the case where you're using a JTree to represent the contents of a file system. In that case, you'd probably want each directory displayed as a branch node, even if the directory doesn't contain any children (files or other directories). In other words, empty directories should be represented by the same icon as those that aren't empty, meaning that the node type (leaf or branch) should be determined by a node's ability to contain children instead of whether it actually does.

You've probably guessed that JTree supports both sets of definitions, which is indeed the case, but you may be wondering how to control which one is used. It's ultimately the responsibility of the TreeModel to make that determination, since its isLeaf() method is responsible for classifying a node as a leaf or branch. The TreeModel can determine which value should be returned from that method, or it can delegate responsibility to the node itself. For example, if you've created a TreeModel implementation that contains a set of objects that all implement TreeNode, you could implement the model's isLeaf() method in many ways. For example, the following implementation simply leaves it up to each node to determine whether the node is a branch of a leaf node:

```
public class MyTreeModel implements TreeModel {

  public boolean isLeaf(Object node) {
    return ((TreeNode)node).isLeaf();
  }
  // ...
```

You'll more commonly want the model itself to determine whether a node is a leaf or a branch so all the nodes in the tree are classified consistently. The following implementation uses the first definition given earlier, returning `true` from `isLeaf()` if the node doesn't have any children or `false` if it does have children:

```
public boolean isLeaf(Object node) {
  return ((TreeNode)node).getChildCount() == 0;
}
```

Similarly, the following implementation uses the second definition of a leaf node, returning `true` from `isLeaf()` if the node is capable of having children (regardless of whether it currently does have children):

```
public boolean isLeaf(Object node) {
  return ((TreeNode)node).getAllowsChildren();
}
```

Another approach is to create a `TreeModel` that can use either definition. For example, you might create an implementation such as the following one that allows you to set a Boolean value called `asksAllowsChildren`. When that value is `true`, the node's `getAllowsChildren()` method determines whether the node is a leaf or branch node (using the second definition). However, when the value of `asksAllowsChildren` is `false`, the node's type (leaf or branch) is determined by the presence or absence of children (the first definition).

```
public class MyTreeModel implements TreeModel {

  private boolean asksAllowsChildren;

  public void setAsksAllowsChildren(boolean asks) {

    asksAllowsChildren = asks;
  }

  public boolean isLeaf(Object node) {
    boolean result;
    TreeNode treenode = (TreeNode)node;
    if (asksAllowsChildren) {
      result = treenode.getAllowsChildren();
    }
    else {
      result = (treenode.getChildCount() == 0);
    }
    return result;
  }

  // ...
```

The previous approach is similar to that used by `DefaultTreeModel`, which is the only `TreeModel` implementation supplied with Swing. In fact, the only difference is that instead of calling the `TreeNode`'s `getChildCount()` method if `asksAllowChildren` is `false`, `DefaultTreeModel` calls the node's `isLeaf()` method. When using `DefaultTreeModel`, therefore, choosing a definition of *leaf* and *branch* is as easy as calling `setAsksAllowsChildren()`. The default behavior is to classify all nodes without children as leaf nodes, but by passing a value of `true` to `setAsksAllowsChildren()`, you can cause the alternate definition to be used instead.

MutableTreeNode

I gave some examples at the beginning of this chapter to show how to create a JTree, and in those cases, a single object instance (a String) represented both a node and the value associated with that node. As you've seen, however, it can be helpful to create a class that implements TreeNode, in which case it's necessary to separate the value associated with a node from the class that implements TreeNode.

For example, you couldn't create a subclass of java.lang.String that implements TreeNode because String is a final class, and even if possible, it wouldn't be desirable from an object-oriented design standpoint. A better solution is to create an interface that extends TreeNode and adds support for a user object, which is simply a value that's associated with the node, and MutableTreeNode does just that. The Mutable portion of this interface's name indicates it defines methods that can be called to modify the state of the node, specifically its parent, its list of child nodes, and the associated user object value. The following sections describe the methods defined in MutableTreeNode; I give examples in each case of how you might implement the method.

setUserObject()

Use setUserObject() to specify the value of the user object for this node. A single Object parameter is passed to this method, and a class that implements this interface should normally save a reference to that object. You can do this with a simple mutator method, as follows:

```
public class MyMutableTreeNode implements MutableTreeNode {

  private Object userObject;

  public void setUserObject(Object value) {
    userObject = value;
  }
}
```

setParent()

You should use setParent() to store a reference to the node's parent, passing it a reference to a MutableTreeNode. A class that implements this interface will typically choose to save a reference to the parent node, as in the following code:

```
public class MyMutableTreeNode implements MutableTreeNode {

  private MutableTreeNode parent;

  public void setParent(MutableTreeNode newParent) {
    parent = newParent;
  }
}
```

remove()

This overloaded method has two versions: one that's passed an integer index value that identifies the child to be removed and another that's passed a reference to the MutableTreeNode to be removed. When called, remove() should set the child node's parent to null and remove the child from this parent node's list of child nodes, as in the following code:

```
public class MyMutableTreeNode implements MutableTreeNode {

  private java.util.Vector children = new java.util.Vector();

  public void remove(MutableTreeNode child) {
    remove(children.indexOf(child));
  }

  public void remove(int index) {
    MutableTreeNode child = (MutableTreeNode)(children.remove(
                index));
    child.setParent(null);
  }
```

removeFromParent()

As its name suggests, this method is responsible for removing the node from its parent; the following is an example of how you can implement this:

```
public class MyMutableTreeNode implements MutableTreeNode {

  private java.util.Vector children = new java.util.Vector();

  public void removeFromParent() {
    // Obtain a reference to this node's parent
    MutableTreeNode parent = (MutableTreeNode)getParent();
    // If it has a parent, remove it from that parent node first
    if (parent != null) {
      parent.remove(child);
    }
  }
}
```

insert()

Two parameters are passed to this method: a reference to an instance of MutableTreeNode and an index value that identifies where the node should be inserted relative to the parent node's existing children. For example, if the index value is 0, the node being inserted is made the first child of this node, and the index values of the other children are incremented by 1.

If you create your own implementation of MutableTreeNode, you should ensure that the setParent() method of the node being inserted is called and passed a reference to this node, as shown in the following sample code. You should also ensure that the node being added is removed from any parent to which it had previously been assigned so that the child isn't referenced by more than one parent. The following is an example of how you can implement this:

```
public class MyMutableTreeNode implements MutableTreeNode {

  private java.util.Vector children = new java.util.Vector();

  public void insert(MutableTreeNode child, int index) {
    // If node has a parent, remove it from that parent first
    child.removeFromParent();
    // Insert the child into the list at the specified location
    children.insertElementAt(child, index);
    // Now set its parent to this node
    child.setParent(this);
  }
}
```

DefaultMutableTreeNode

It should be obvious from the descriptions of the methods in TreeNode and MutableTreeNode that it's easy to create your own implementations of those interfaces. As mentioned earlier, however, it's rarely necessary to do so because the javax.swing.tree package also includes DefaultMutableTreeNode, and the behavior of this class is appropriate for most applications. In addition to its many methods, DefaultMutableTreeNode contains four fields, although each of them exists solely to support the implementation of the TreeNode and MutableTreeNode methods.

- A reference to a parent MutableTreeNode, the value of which is returned by getParent().

- A collection of child nodes that are all instances of MutableTreeNode. The child nodes are accessible through a variety of methods, including children(), getChildAt(), and many others.

- A reference to a user object that's accessible through the getUserObject() and setUserObject() accessor and mutator methods. As mentioned earlier, the user object allows you to associate a value with a node, and you can use any type of Object; note, however, that the reference to the user object is transient, which means the user object will not be marshaled along with the node that references whether the node is serialized.

- A flag named allowsChildren that you can use to specify whether this node is allowed to have children. That flag is accessible through the getAllowsChildren() and setAllowsChildren() methods.

Creating DefaultMutableTreeNode Instances

You can create and use instances of DefaultMutableTreeNode easily, and only three constructors are defined. One constructor accepts no parameters, another expects a user object (Object) value, and the third allows you to specify a user object and a Boolean value that indicates whether the node allows children to be added. The first two constructors result in an instance that allows children, so to create a node with an initial user object value of "Hello" that accepts children, you could use the following code:

```
DefaultMutableTreeNode node = new DefaultMutableTreeNode("Hello");
```

It's equally simple to add children to a node, since in addition to the insert() method defined in MutableTreeNode, DefaultMutableTreeNode also includes a method called add(), which appends the specified node to the end of the list of children.

```
DefaultMutableTreeNode parent = new DefaultMutableTreeNode("Adam");
DefaultMutableTreeNode child = new DefaultMutableTreeNode("Cain");
parent.add(child);
```

Note that before a node is added as a child of some other node, it's first removed from the child list of any existing parent it may have. For example, suppose you execute the following code:

```
DefaultMutableTreeNode parent = new DefaultMutableTreeNode("Adam");
DefaultMutableTreeNode child = new DefaultMutableTreeNode("Cain");
parent.add(child);
DefaultMutableTreeNode otherParent = new DefaultMutableTreeNode("Eve");
otherParent.add(child);
```

The first three lines shown are identical to those of the previous code segment, so they obviously will produce the same results. However, when otherParent's add() method is called, the child node will first be removed from its existing parent (in other words, Adam), and only then will it be added to otherParent's list of children. This behavior ensures that a child node only ever has a single parent and that no parent node has references to children that have been added to some other parent.

Using DefaultMutableTreeNode

DefaultMutableTreeNode contains many methods in addition to those needed to implement the TreeNode and MutableTreeNode interfaces, and most of the methods have names that should be self-explanatory. For example, getFirstChild() and getLastChild() return references to the node's first and last child nodes, respectively. In fact, most methods in DefaultMutableTreeNode retrieve some node or group of nodes that has some relationship to the node for which the method is called. Some of the remaining methods (such as isNodeXXX()) determine whether some specific type of relationship exists between this node and another. For example, isNodeRelated() is passed a reference to a TreeNode and returns a value of true if any type of relationship exists between that node and the one for which the method is called. In other words, it returns true if the two nodes are contained within the same tree.

Although the purpose of most of the methods should be obvious from their names, others may be less intuitive; in the following sections, I describe some of the methods likely to fall into the latter category.

getLevel(), getDepth()

A node's *level* refers to the number of parent nodes that must be traversed to reach the root node, and a node's *depth* represents the maximum number of levels that currently exist below the node. In other words, the level value is derived by counting the number of levels that must be traveled "up" the tree until the root node is reached. In contrast, the depth is the maximum number of levels that can be traversed "down" the tree from that node.

For each node in the fully expanded tree in Figure 8-8, the level and depth of each node in the tree are shown in Table 8-2.

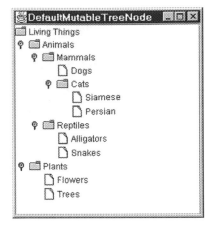

Figure 8-8. *A sample tree that's used to illustrate levels and depths within a tree's nodes*

Table 8-2. *Levels and Depths in Figure 8-8*

Node Name	Level	Depth
Living Things	0	4
Animals	1	3
Mammals	2	2
Dogs	3	0
Cats	3	1
Siamese	4	0
Persian	4	0
Reptiles	2	1
Alligators	3	0
Snakes	3	0
Plants	1	1
Flowers	2	0
Trees	2	0

getSharedAncestor()

To use this method, you must pass a reference to another DefaultMutableTreeNode, and getSharedAncestor() returns a reference to the first node that's a common ancestor of that parameter node and the one for which this method was called. For example, if a reference to the Persian node in the previous tree is passed to the getSharedAncestor() method of the Alligators node (or vice versa), a reference to the Animals node is returned.

getPath( ), getUserObjectPath( )

When you call the getPath( ) method, it returns an array of TreeNode objects that represent the nodes that must be traversed from the root node to reach the node for which the method is called. For example, if this method is called for the Reptiles node in the previous tree, it will return references to three nodes: Living Things, Animals, and Reptiles. Note that the first entry in the array is always the root node, and the last is always the node for which this method was called.

The getUserObjectPath( ) method is similar to getPath( ), but instead of returning references to the TreeNode objects, it instead returns an Object array representing the user object associated with each node in the path. If the path includes nodes that haven't been assigned user object values, null values will appear in the appropriate places within the array returned by getUserObjectPath( ).

pathFromAncestorEnumeration( )

To use this method, you must pass it a TreeNode representing an ancestor of the node for which the method is called. Like getPath( ), this method returns a list of nodes, but it has two differences. First, pathsFromAncestorEnumeration( ) returns an Enumeration instead of an array; second, the list of nodes begins with the ancestor you identified instead of the tree's root node. Therefore, the first node in the list will always be the ancestor node parameter, and the last node will (as in the case of getPath( )) always be the node against which the method was invoked.

For example, if you call pathFromAncestorEnumeration( ) for the Siamese node in the previous tree and pass it a reference to the Mammals node, it will return an enumeration containing references to three nodes: Mammals, Cats, and Siamese (in that order).

This method throws an IllegalArgumentException if the node passed to it isn't an ancestor of the node against which the method is invoked. Therefore, you should be prepared to handle the exception, or you should ensure that the argument node is indeed an ancestor before calling this method.

Obtaining a List of Nodes

The last four DefaultMutableTreeNode methods you'll examine all obtain a list of the nodes in a tree or the subtree defined by the node for which the method is invoked. For example, if you call one of these methods for the root node shown in the previous tree, it will return a list that contains an entry for each of the nodes in the tree. However, if you call the method for the Reptiles node, the list will contain entries only for the Reptiles, Alligators, and Snakes nodes.

Since these four methods all return an Enumeration containing a node and all its descendent nodes, the obvious question is, how do these methods differ? As you might expect, the difference is in the order in which the nodes occur in the list that's returned.

depthFirstEnumeration( ), postorderEnumeration( )

These two methods are effectively synonyms for one another, since they both produce the same results, returning a list generated using a *depth-first*, or *postorder*, traversal of the appropriate tree nodes. When a node is being processed using this approach, it's first examined to determine whether it has any children. If it does, each child is processed before the parent node is added to the list, and this behavior is repeated recursively until a node is reached that doesn't have children. A parent is added to the list that's being built only after any child nodes have been processed, and it's that behavior that gives postorder traversal its name. Since children are added before their parents, the node for which this method is called is always the last node in the list returned.

To illustrate this technique, let's assume you call depthFirstEnumeration() or postorderEnumeration() for the Cats node shown in the previous tree. Since that node has two children, they will be processed before the Cats node is added to the list, and since those two children don't have any descendents, they're simply added to the list without additional recursive calls. Once the two child nodes have been processed, the parent Cats node is added to the list, and an Enumeration is returned that contains references to the three nodes in the following order:

- Siamese

- Persian

- Cats

Figure 8-9 shows the sequence in which the nodes are traversed.

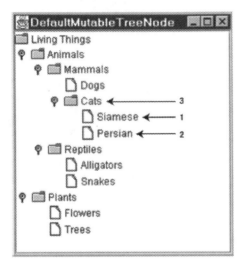

Figure 8-9. *With depth-first enumeration, the children are processed before their parents*

Similarly, if one of these methods is called for the Mammals node, the Dog node will be the first in the list, because it's the first node found that doesn't have any children. After that, the next three nodes processed will be the same ones added to the list in the previous example, and finally the Mammals node itself is added, resulting in the following entries in the list returned:

- Dogs

- Siamese

- Persian

- Cats

- Mammals

Figure 8-10 represents the sequence graphically.

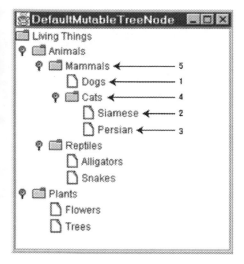

Figure 8-10. *A more complex example of how depth-first enumeration works*

Since these two methods (depthFirstEnumeration() and postorderEnumeration()) produce the same results, which one you should use is largely a matter of personal preference. For instance, you may find it easier to remember that this technique involves processing nodes in a depth-first order, in which case you might be more inclined to use depthFirstEnumeration().

breadthFirstEnumeration()

This type of enumeration is easier to visualize, since it traverses the nodes in order of their level, and nodes that are at the same level are listed in order from top to bottom. For example, if you call this method for the Animals node of the previous tree, it first adds that node to the list, since it's the top node. The next two nodes added are Mammals and Reptiles (which are both children of Animals) followed by Dogs, Cats, Alligators, Snakes, and finally Siamese and Persian. In other words, this method starts with the node specified and works its way through the tree from the closest descendents to the most distant ones. The name is derived from the fact that this technique results in the tree's breadth/width being traversed before its depth when the tree is visualized with the root node at the top and the most distant descendents at the bottom. Figure 8-11 shows a visual representation of this sequence.

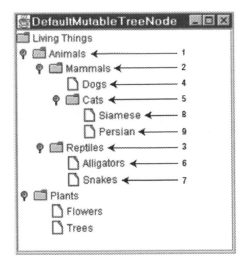

Figure 8-11. *Breadth-first enumeration traverses a set of nodes based on their level*

preorderEnumeration()

This technique most closely resembles the depthFirstEnumeration()/postorderEnumeration() methods described previously, but each parent is added to the list before its children are processed recursively instead of afterward. The resulting order of the nodes is the same order that they appear from top to bottom in the JTree. In the case of the previous tree, calling preorderEnumeration() for the root node causes the nodes to appear in the list in the following order:

- Living Things
- Animals
- Mammals
- Dogs
- Cats
- Siamese
- Persian
- Reptiles
- Alligators
- Snakes
- Plants
- Flowers
- Trees

TreePath

When working with a Vector or an array of values, you can reference each value by using its index, as illustrated in the following code segment where the second value in a Vector and third value in an array are printed:

```
Vector v;
Object[] array;
// ...

System.out.println(v.elementAt(1));
System.out.println(array[2]);
```

You can use this simple index approach for an array or Vector, because those objects represent linear (one-dimensional) data structures. In other words, each value is assigned a position that can be uniquely identified by a simple whole number (0, 1, 2, 3, etc.). However, the hierarchical structure of nodes in a JTree makes it somewhat more difficult to define a technique for identifying a particular node within the tree.

JTree does use index values to identify visible nodes within a tree, assigning each node a value based on its vertical position within the tree. The root node is always at the top of the tree, so its position (when it's visible) corresponds to an index value of 0, and each node below it is assigned a unique value, as shown in Figure 8-12.

Figure 8-12. *A node's index corresponds to its vertical location within the tree given the current state (collapsed or expanded) of the tree's nodes*

Although some of the methods in JTree allow you to reference nodes in this manner, you should keep in mind that a node's index value depends upon the state of the tree.

To illustrate this point, suppose that the previous tree is partially collapsed so the children of the Jeff node aren't visible. As Figure 8-13 shows, most of the visible rows' index values have changed, which shows that a given index can't be relied upon to consistently identify a particular node.

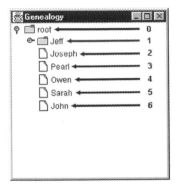

Figure 8-13. *Note that the index value for each child of the Jeff node has changed as a result of the parent being collapsed*

In addition, adding or deleting nodes or even changing the position of a node within the tree can cause a node's index value to change. Therefore, you should use index values only to refer to the node at a given vertical position within the tree, not as a means of identifying a specific node. For that purpose, you should use an instance of TreePath, which is a class defined in the javax.swing.tree package.

As its name implies, a TreePath encapsulates a node's path, which is simply a list of nodes that must be traversed (usually starting from the root node) to reach the node identified by the path. For example, you could construct the TreePath associated with the soccer node in Figure 8-14 by creating a three-element array containing references to the JTree, sports, and soccer nodes, in that order.

Figure 8-14. *To reach the soccer node shown in this tree, you'd need to traverse the JTree, sports, and soccer nodes*

As you saw earlier, you can use the getPath() method in DefaultMutableTreeNode to obtain such an array, and you can use it to create an instance of TreePath using the following code:

```
DefaultMutableTreeNode myNode;
// ...

// This code assumes that the node has been added to the tree
TreePath path = new TreePath(myNode.getPath());
```

Unlike an index value, a path can always be used to identify a specific node regardless of which portions of a tree are collapsed or expanded. For that reason, most of the methods in JTree that perform some operation related to a specific node allow you to identify that node through a TreePath. Some JTree methods are overloaded, providing one implementation that allows you to specify a TreePath and another that allows you to specify an index value that identifies a visible node based on its vertical position (as described previously). In general, you should use the TreePath implementation instead of the index implementation, since TreePath values are less sensitive to changes in the tree's state.

TreeModelListener

TreeModelListener is an interface that can be implemented by classes that will register as listeners of TreeModel events, such as the addition, deletion, or modification of nodes in the model. In practice, the only listener registered with a model is usually the JTree that uses the model, and it uses this interface to receive notification of changes to the data it displays. Only four methods are defined in TreeModelListener; I describe them in the next sections.

treeNodesChanged()

This method is called when one or more of the nodes within the model have experienced a state change (e.g., the user object value associated with the node changes). Note that this method shouldn't be called to notify listeners of structural changes to the tree (an insertion, deletion, or change in the position of nodes) because other TreeModelListener methods offer that functionality.

treeNodesInserted()

The treeNodesInserted() method is called for each registered listener after nodes have been inserted into the tree.

treeNodesRemoved()

Just as treeNodesInserted() is called after nodes have been added to the model/tree, this method is called after nodes have been removed. This method is called only one time for each removal, even if a node with descendents is removed, which effectively means multiple nodes have been eliminated from the tree.

treeStructureChanged()

When this method is called, it indicates that a significant change (in other words, something more complex than the simple addition, modification, or deletion of nodes) was made to the tree or to some portion of the tree below a particular node. For example, treeStructureChanged() may be called if the current root node is replaced with a different one, which results in the entire tree structure being replaced.

TreeModelEvent

Each of the methods defined in TreeModelListener is passed a reference to a TreeModelEvent object that can be used to obtain information about the source and nature of the event that occurred. The following sections describe the methods defined in TreeModelEvent, and each one includes an explanation of when and how to use the methods.

getTreePath(), getPath()

These methods identify the parent node of the nodes that have been modified, inserted, or deleted. When getTreePath() is called, it returns an instance of TreePath that identifies the parent of the affected nodes, while getPath() returns the array of Object values that are encapsulated by the TreePath. In other words, these methods provide essentially the same information in two different forms.

getChildren()

Just as getPath() and getTreePath() identify the parent of the nodes that were inserted, updated, or deleted, this method can obtain references to the specific nodes that triggered the event. It returns an array of Object values, and each entry in the array represents one of the nodes that was modified, added, or removed.

getChildIndices()

You can use this method within calls to treeNodesChanged(), treeNodesRemoved(), and treeNodesInserted() to identify the nodes that were changed, removed, or inserted. An array of integer values is returned, and each integer represents the index into a parent's list of children. In the case of a deletion, the index identifies the position that the node held in the parent's list before the node was deleted; when an update or insertion has occurred, the index represents the node's current position. For example, if the second and fourth children of some node are modified, this method returns an int array with two elements: the first with a value of 1 and the second entry with a value of 3.

DefaultTreeModel

The DefaultTreeModel class defined in javax.swing.tree is the only TreeModel implementation supplied with Java, but it's easy to use and is appropriate for most applications. However, it supports only those nodes that are instances of DefaultMutableTreeNode, so you must ensure your nodes are all instances of that class or create your own TreeModel implementation.

It's easy to create an instance of DefaultTreeModel, although you won't normally do so explicitly but will instead allow a JTree to create one automatically. For example, the code segments at the beginning of this chapter that created String arrays and passed them to a JTree constructor resulted in the creation of a DefaultTreeModel. To access a JTree's existing model, simply call its getModel() method, which returns an instance of TreeModel that you can cast to DefaultTreeModel (or some other class) if you know which type of model is being used.

If you want to create a model, simply use the constructor that accepts an instance of a TreeNode as in the following example, and that node will be used as the root node of your tree. Once the model has been created, it can be passed to a JTree constructor or specified as the model of an existing tree by calling the JTree's setModel() method.

```
TreeNode myRoot;
JTree myTree;
// ...

DefaultTreeModel myModel = new DefaultTreeModel(myRoot);
myTree = new JTree(myModel);
```

Alternatively, the following JTree setModel() works:

```
TreeNode myRoot;
JTree myTree = new JTree();
// ...

DefaultTreeModel myModel = new DefaultTreeModel(myRoot);
myTree.setModel(myModel);
```

In addition to implementing the TreeModel methods, DefaultTreeModel also provides pairs of methods that make it easy for you to modify the structure of the tree and to notify listeners of changes. Each pair consists of a method that performs the modification (e.g., inserting a node) and another method that creates an appropriate TreeModelEvent and notifies any registered listeners of the modification. Table 8-3 describes those methods.

Table 8-3. *TreeModel Methods*

Update Method	Notification Method	Typical Use
setRoot()	nodeStructureChanged()	Setting a new root node
valueForPathChanged()	nodesChanged()	Modifying a node's value
insertNodeInto()	nodesWereInserted()	Inserting a node
removeNodeFromParent()	nodesWereRemoved()	Deleting a node

It's not necessary for you to invoke both methods when you make a change to the tree's structure, since each of the update methods listed in Table 8-3 will call the corresponding notification method for you. However, if you make changes to a node (modify its value, insert or delete children, etc.) directly instead of through the model's update method, you should call the appropriate notification method. For example, suppose you want to insert several nodes into the tree and you have a reference to the parent to which they should be added. You can use the insertNodeInto() method (which is the preferred approach), or you can perform the insertion "manually" and then call the notification method. The following example illustrates how to use insertNodeInto() given an array of nodes to be inserted:

```
MutableTreeNode parentNode;
MutableTreeNode[] childrenToAdd;
JTree tree;
// ...

DefaultTreeModel model = (DefaultTreeModel)(tree.getModel());
for (int i = 0; i < childrenToAdd.length; i++) {
  model.insertNodeInto(childrenToAdd[i], parentNode, i);
}
```

This is a convenient approach because it prevents you from having to construct your own TreeModelEvent object and explicitly request that registered listeners be notified. However, one problem with this approach is that it will generate a separate TreeModelListener notification for each node inserted, which can be undesirable from a performance standpoint if you're inserting a larger number of nodes. In that case, it may be preferable to perform the insertions directly and then request that a notification be sent, as in the following segment:

```
MutableTreeNode parentNode;
MutableTreeNode[] childrenToAdd;
JTree tree;
// ...

DefaultTreeModel model = (DefaultTreeModel)(tree.getModel());
int[] indices = new int[childrenToAdd.length];
for (int i = 0; i < childrenToAdd.length; i++) {
  parentNode.insert(childrenToAdd[i], i);
  indices[i] = i;
}
model.nodesWereInserted(parentNode, indices);
```

Although this example illustrates only how insertNodeInto() and nodesWereInserted() are used, the other methods function essentially the same way. For example, valueForPathChanged() simply sets the user object of the node you identify with a TreePath and then calls the nodeChanged() method (which in turn calls nodesChanged() to notify listeners that the node changed). In most cases, these notification methods will simply cause the JTree to refresh its appearance so it reflects the modified state of its TreeModel.

Another DefaultTreeModel method worth mentioning is reload(), which is overloaded with two implementations: one that doesn't accept any parameters and another that accepts a single TreeNode reference. Like setRoot(), the reload() methods call nodeStructureChanged(), and these methods are useful when the tree or some portion of it has changed significantly. However, reload() also causes all nodes with children to be collapsed, so you shouldn't call it if you want to maintain the visual state of your JTree.

Rendering Tree Nodes

Responsibility for drawing the nodes within a tree (also sometimes called *cells*) is assigned to an implementation of TreeCellRenderer, an interface defined in javax.swing.tree. That interface defines a single getTreeCellRendererComponent() method, which is responsible for preparing and returning a Component that's used to draw the cell. In other words, for each visible node in a JTree, the paint() method of the renderer associated with the tree is used to draw the node. TreeCellRenderer implementations often extend an existing visual component (e.g., JLabel), which allows the renderer to be created easily. For example, a renderer is easy to create by extending JLabel because that class already contains painting/ rendering logic that's appropriate in many cases for displaying tree nodes.

When called, the getTreeCellRendererComponent() method is passed the following parameters:

- A reference to the JTree with which the node is associated
- An Object representing the node's value
- A Boolean value that indicates whether the node is currently selected
- A Boolean value that indicates whether the node is currently expanded
- A Boolean value that indicates whether the node is a leaf
- An integer that identifies the node's vertical position within the tree
- A Boolean value that indicates whether the node currently has the input focus

Before getTreeCellRendererComponent() returns a reference to the renderer, it should first use the previous parameter values to modify the state of the component appropriately. At a minimum, you should use the parameter representing the node's value to initialize the renderer component so it displays that value when its paint() method is called. You'll also typically want to initialize the component based on the state of the node being rendered, such as using different background colors to identify selected nodes as opposed to those that aren't selected.

By default, JTree instances create and use an instance of DefaultTreeCellRenderer, which is a subclass of JLabel. When its getTreeCellRendererComponent() method is called, this class first converts the node's value into a String by passing a reference to the value to the tree's convertValueToText() method. That method simply calls the value object's toString() method and returns the result (see Figure 8-15), although you can modify that behavior by creating your own JTree subclass and overriding convertValueToText().

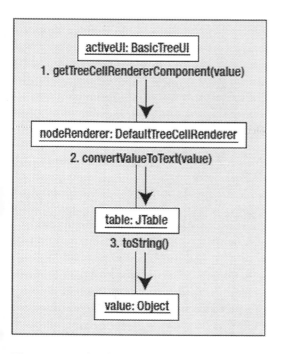

Figure 8-15. *The classes and methods used by default to render the nodes in a tree*

Once the DefaultTreeCellRender has obtained a text representation of the node's value, it sets foreground and background colors appropriately based upon whether the node is selected and then obtains an icon. The specific icon displayed is based upon whether the node is a leaf or a branch and, if a branch, whether it's currently expanded or contracted. If you prefer to use icons other than those provided with the active look and feel, you can modify the appropriate properties in a DefaultTreeCellRenderer. Accessor and mutator methods are provided for each of the properties listed in Table 8-4, and you can easily customize a JTree's appearance through these methods.

Table 8-4. `JTree` *Appearance Methods*

DefaultTreeCellRenderer	Property Description
backgroundNonSelectionColor	Background color used when node not selected
backgroundSelectionColor	Background color used when node is selected
borderSelectionColor	Color used to draw the component's border
leafIcon	Icon used for leaf nodes
closedIcon	Icon used for collapsed branch nodes
openIcon	Icon used for expanded branch nodes
textNonSelectionColor	Text color used when node not selected
textSelectionColor	Text color used when node is selected

For example, suppose you want to use your own icon for leaf nodes instead of the default icon. To do so, you simply need to obtain a reference to the DefaultTreeCellRenderer and call the appropriate mutator method, as shown in the following code:

```
javax.swing.JTree myTree;
javax.swing.Icon myCustomLeafIcon =
    new ImageIcon("D:/brett/temp/myicon.gif");
// ...

DefaultTreeCellRenderer renderer =
    (DefaultTreeCellRenderer)(myTree.getCellRenderer());
renderer.setLeafIcon(myCustomLeafIcon);
```

Creating a Custom Renderer

Although the DefaultTreeCellRenderer class is appropriate in many cases, you'll sometimes need to create a custom renderer when you want to display node(s) in a manner that's not possible when using the default renderer. Creating a custom renderer for use with a JTree is easy to do, and the process is almost identical to that used for creating renderers for JTable cells. Simply create an implementation of TreeCellRenderer, and specify that the JTree should use that renderer to draw its nodes. For example, let's suppose you've defined a class similar to the one in Listing 8-2 that encapsulates a true/false test question and the answer given to it.

Listing 8-2. True and False Q&A

```
public class TrueFalseQuestion {

  private final String question;
  private boolean answer;

  public TrueFalseQuestion(String quest) {
    question = quest;
  }
```

```
  public String getQuestion() {
    return question;
  }

  public boolean getAnswer() {
    return answer;
  }

  public void setAnswer(boolean ans) {
    answer = ans;
  }

  public String toString() {
    return question + " = " + answer;
  }

}
```

Since this class encapsulates a single immutable (unchangeable) String value and a mutable Boolean value, it's an ideal candidate to be rendered by a JCheckBox. Let's further assume you want to create a user interface that displays a group of these objects in a JTree. You could attempt to do so using the default renderer with code like that shown in Listing 8-3.

Listing 8-3. Using the Default Renderer in a Sample Final Exam

```
import javax.swing.*;
import javax.swing.tree.*;

public class TreeTest extends JFrame {

  private final static String[] questions = {
      "Green Kryptonite is only deadly " +
      "to beings from Krypton with superpowers",
      "Red Kryptonite's effects are permanent",
      "Gold Kryptonite permanently enhances superpowers",
      "Blue Kryptonite affects only Bizarros",
      "White Kryptonite affects only marine life",
      "Jewel Kryptonite was formed from Krypton's " +
      "Jewel Mountains"};

  public static void main(String[] args) {
    TreeTest tt = new TreeTest();
    tt.setDefaultCloseOperation(JFrame.EXIT_ON_CLOSE);
    tt.setSize(500, 200);
    tt.setVisible(true);
  }

  public TreeTest() {
    super("Smallville University Final Exam");
    JTree tree = new JTree(getRootNode());
    JScrollPane jsp = new JScrollPane(tree);
    getContentPane().add(jsp);
  }
```

```
private MutableTreeNode getRootNode() {
  DefaultMutableTreeNode root, child;
  TrueFalseQuestion question;
  root = new DefaultMutableTreeNode(
    "Kryptonite Questions -- Check all " +
    "of the following that are true " +
    "statements");
  for (int i = 0; i < questions.length; i++) {
    question = new TrueFalseQuestion(questions[i]);
    child = new DefaultMutableTreeNode(question);
    root.add(child);
  }
  return root;
}
}
```

In this case, however, the display won't produce the desired results (see Figure 8-16).

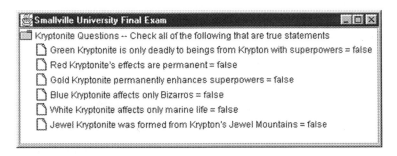

Figure 8-16. *The instances of TrueFalseQuestion are represented visually using their toString() values*

As described earlier, the default renderer is a JLabel that renders a node's value by displaying its text representation (the String returned by the object's toString() method) and an appropriate icon. In this case, the test questions should be represented by instances of JCheckBox, and no icons should appear. You can accomplish this by simply creating a TreeCellRenderer implementation that extends JCheckBox, but you'll instead extend the existing DefaultTreeCellRenderer. The reason for this is that it's not appropriate to render all tree nodes as check boxes, only those that are instances of TrueFalseQuestion. For example, the Kryptonite Questions branch node should continue to be rendered as a label, but its children (which are instances of TrueFalseQuestion) should be rendered as check boxes. By extending DefaultTreeCellRenderer, you can create a class that handles TrueFalseQuestion nodes but delegates rendering responsibilities to its superclass for other node types.

Listing 8-4 does just that: it examines the value parameter passed to getTreeCell➥RendererComponent(), and if that value doesn't encapsulate a TrueFalseQuestion instance, it allows the superclass code to render the node. If, on the other hand, the node is a TrueFalseQuestion, the text and selection status of a JCheckBox are updated appropriately, and that component is allowed to perform the rendering operation.

Listing 8-4. JTree Example Rendering Operation

```java
import java.awt.*;
import javax.swing.*;
import javax.swing.tree.*;

public class QuestionCellRenderer extends DefaultTreeCellRenderer {

  private JCheckBox questionRenderer = new JCheckBox();

  public Component getTreeCellRendererComponent(JTree tree,
      Object value, boolean selected, boolean expanded,
      boolean leaf, int row, boolean hasFocus) {
    if (value instanceof DefaultMutableTreeNode) {
      DefaultMutableTreeNode node =
          (DefaultMutableTreeNode)value;
      Object userObject = node.getUserObject();
      if (userObject instanceof TrueFalseQuestion) {
        TrueFalseQuestion question =
            (TrueFalseQuestion)userObject;
        prepareQuestionRenderer(question, selected);
        return questionRenderer;
        }
    }
    return super.getTreeCellRendererComponent(tree, value,
        selected, expanded, leaf, row, hasFocus);
  }

  private void prepareQuestionRenderer(TrueFalseQuestion tfq,
      boolean selected) {
    questionRenderer.setText(tfq.getQuestion());
    questionRenderer.setSelected(tfq.getAnswer());
    if (selected) {
      questionRenderer.setForeground(
          getTextSelectionColor());
      questionRenderer.setBackground(
          getBackgroundSelectionColor());
    }
    else {
      questionRenderer.setForeground(
          getTextNonSelectionColor());
      questionRenderer.setBackground(
          getBackgroundNonSelectionColor());
    }
  }

}
```

To use this renderer, simply create an instance of it and assign that object to the JTree. The following is an example of how to do this, showing a modified version of the TreeTest constructor defined earlier:

```
public TreeTest() {
  super("Smallville University Final Exam");
  JTree tree = new JTree(getRootNode());
  QuestionCellRenderer renderer = new QuestionCellRenderer();
  tree.setCellRenderer(renderer);
  JScrollPane jsp = new JScrollPane(tree);
  getContentPane().add(jsp);
}
```

When this code is compiled and executed, it renders the TrueFalseQuestion objects as instances of JCheckBox, as illustrated in Figure 8-17.

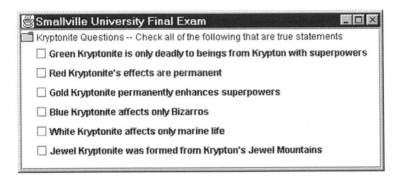

Figure 8-17. *Displaying the questions next to check boxes that indicate the user's answer is much more appealing and intuitive*

At this point, the tree's appearance is appropriate, but its behavior isn't. If you attempt to check one of the boxes that appear in the frame, nothing will happen, which is because JTree doesn't allow you to edit its cells by default. However, you can control that behavior by calling the tree's setEditable() method.

```
public TreeTest() {
  super("Smallville University Final Exam");
  JTree tree = new JTree(getRootNode());
  QuestionCellRenderer renderer = new QuestionCellRenderer();
  tree.setCellRenderer(renderer);
  tree.setEditable(true);
  JScrollPane jsp = new JScrollPane(tree);
  getContentPane().add(jsp);
}
```

After making this change, you'll be able to initiate editing of a node's value by clicking the node three times or by clicking, once, a node that's already selected. However, when you attempt to edit a node, the results will probably not be what you expect. Instead of the JCheckBox's state changing, a text representation of the TrueFalseQuestion appears in a JTextBox; it will remain there until you press Enter to complete the edit. To understand why this occurs and how to provide more appropriate behavior, it's necessary to understand the editing mechanism used by instances of JTree.

Editing Tree Nodes

Tree cell editing is conceptually similar to rendering, although some important differences exist. Just as a renderer is associated with each JTree, a TreeCellEditor is also assigned to every tree. TreeCellEditor is an interface defined in javax.swing.tree and is a subclass of the CellEditor interface (which is also the superinterface of the TableCellEditor interface used by JTable instances). Figure 8-18 illustrates the relationships between these interfaces and classes, as well as the DefaultCellEditor class discussed in a moment.

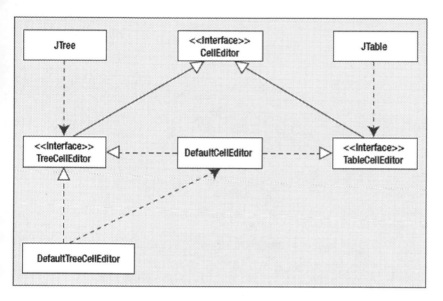

Figure 8-18. *The relationships between the classes and interfaces involved in editing tree and table cells*

By default, each JTree creates and uses an instance of DefaultTreeCellEditor to manage the editing of its nodes, although you can create your own TreeCellEditor implementation or create a subclass of DefaultTreeCellEditor. Just as a tree's renderer provides a method that returns a rendering component, each TreeCellEditor provides a getTreeCellEditorComponent() method that returns an editing component. In addition, just as the DefaultTreeCellRenderer is a JLabel subclass that displays each node's value as a text string, the DefaultTreeCellEditor uses a JTextField to allow editing of those values. Before describing the behavior of the DefaultTreeCellEditor class, it's helpful to understand how a determination is made that a tree node/cell should be edited.

When a JTree is created, it uses a subclass of BasicTreeUI (defined in javax.swing. plaf.basic) to provide the tree's appearance. The BasicTreeUI creates listeners that will be notified of events that occur such as mouse clicks, since those events can trigger behavior such as the selection or editing of a tree node. When a mouse click event is detected by the listener and the click occurred over a node, the BasicTreeUI's startEditing() method is called, which is responsible for determining whether the mouse click should cause editing to begin. If so, editing is initiated, and startEditing() returns a value of true. On the other hand, if startEditing() determines that the mouse event shouldn't cause an edit to be performed, it returns a value of false, which will cause the BasicTreeUI's selectPathForEvent() to be invoked, allowing the mouse event to be interpreted as a request to select the node instead of a request to begin editing it. In other words, the tree first attempts to interpret a mouse click as an attempt to edit a node and then as an attempt to select the node.

When deciding whether the mouse event should cause an edit operation to occur, BasicTreeUI's startEditing() method first determines whether the tree considers the cell eligible for editing by calling the JTree's isPathEditable() method. That method returns the value of the Boolean flag called editable, which is controlled by the setEditable() method in JTree that you used earlier to allow tree nodes to be edited. As you'll see later, you can control whether individual nodes are editable by creating a JTree subclass that overrides isPathEditable(). You can use this approach when you want to allow only some of the tree's nodes to be edited, as opposed to the previous technique, which makes all nodes eligible for editing.

Assuming that the JTree allows its nodes to be edited, the startEditing() method in BasicTreeUI next calls the cell editor's getTreeCellEditorComponent() method and then its isCellEditable() method. If the cell editor also gives its permission to initiate editing (in other words, its isCellEditable() method returns true), the editor component is added to the JTree at the position of the node being edited, and editing is allowed to begin. Figure 8-19 shows most of the behavior just described.

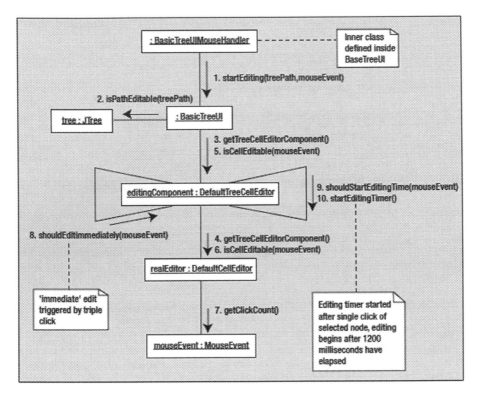

Figure 8-19. *Editing a tree cell involves a somewhat complex sequence of events*

When it's determined that the editing of a cell should end, the CellEditor's stopCellEditing() or cancelCellEditing() method is called. For editing to be *stopped* means that changes made during the edit session should be saved; *canceling* an edit means to discard any changes and restore the node's value to its original state. In the case of a JTextField-based editor, for example, editing ends when the Enter key is pressed (which generates an ActionEvent for the text field), when a node other than the one being edited is selected with the mouse, or when the Escape key is pressed. The first scenario described (when the Enter key is pressed) causes editing to be stopped, and the other two are examples of how editing can be canceled. In other words, pressing the Enter key causes your changes to be saved, while selecting a different node or pressing Escape causes them to be discarded.

When editing ends (in other words, is stopped or canceled), the editor component is removed from the JTree and the editor's getCellEditorValue() method is called to retrieve the node's new value. That value is then passed to the valueForPathChanged() method of the TreeModel associated with the JTree, causing the value returned by the editor to be propagated to the model (in other words, the modified value is saved in the tree's data model).

Now that you understand how cell editing occurs, I can return to the topic of the DefaultTreeCellEditor class mentioned earlier.

DefaultTreeCellEditor and DefaultCellEditor

Previously you saw that the DefaultTreeCellRenderer class serves as both the TreeCellRenderer implementation and the renderer component, which it does by implementing TreeCellRenderer and by extending JLabel, respectively. In contrast, although DefaultTreeCellEditor does implement TreeCellEditor, it's not the editing component. (It doesn't extend JTextField.) Instead, it maintains a reference to another object that handles the editing, specifically an instance of DefaultCellEditor. DefaultCellEditor implements both TreeCellEditor and TableCellEditor, and it's used by JTable in addition to JTree as the default cell editor component.

In fact, you can use DefaultCellEditor by itself to perform tree cell editing without any involvement from DefaultTreeCellEditor. To illustrate this, simply compile and execute code like the following segment that creates a new tree and sets its editor to a new instance of DefaultCellEditor that uses a JTextField for editing:

```
JTree tree = new JTree();
// ...

tree.setCellEditor(new DefaultCellEditor(new JTextField()));
tree.setEditable(true);
```

When this code executes, you can edit a tree node by double-clicking it, which causes the JTextField to appear in the node's location (see Figure 8-20).

Figure 8-20. *Double-clicking a tree cell with editing enabled causes a text field to appear in which the cell's text representation is displayed and can be edited*

The problem with this behavior that DefaultTreeCellEditor is designed to address is that the editing component (in this case, the JTextField) covers all the node's display area including its icon. Notice, for example, that no icon is displayed for the node being edited (baseball). Recall that by default nodes are rendered by a JLabel (which includes both an icon and a text area) but are edited by a JTextField (which doesn't support icons). DefaultTreeCellEditor overcomes this problem by creating an editing container that consists of an icon extracted from the TreeCellRenderer and the editing component itself (e.g., a JTextField).

In addition to providing a single class that can be used for both table and tree editing, DefaultCellEditor allows you to perform the editing with a JTextField, JComboBox, or JCheckBox. In addition, since mouse clicks are the traditional way of initiating the edit of a cell, DefaultCellEditor maintains a value that you can set to control the number of clicks required to begin an edit operation. For example, setting the value to 2 makes it necessary for the user to double-click a cell to initiate an edit session. This allows you to easily distinguish between a request to select a cell (in other words, a single click) and a request to edit (a double click).

DefaultTreeCellEditor Behavior

Continuing the discussion of DefaultTreeCellEditor, recall that its isCellEditable() method is called by the BasicTreeUI to determine whether editing should begin. When DefaultTreeCellEditor's isCellEditable() method is called, it in turn calls the implementation of isCellEditable() in the DefaultCellEditor to which it maintains a reference. The DefaultCellEditor will return a value of true if the click count associated with the mouse event is at least as great as the number of clicks it has been programmed to require and will return false otherwise. If it does return false, the DefaultTreeCellEditor will likewise return that value, and editing won't be started, although the JTree sets the click count to 1, so this method will normally always return true.

Once the DefaultTreeCellEditor has queried the DefaultCellEditor to determine whether editing should be started, it next checks for a special case: three or more mouse clicks. When this occurs, it triggers an "immediate edit" that causes editing of the node to begin immediately. Finally, if you single-click a node that's already selected, a timer is started, and a "delayed edit" will occur 1.2 seconds later as long as you don't select a different node before that time elapses. Stated simply, the behavior of a DefaultTreeCellEditor is such that a "triple click" (three quick, successive mouse clicks) causes editing to begin immediately, while a single click of an already selected node causes editing to begin 1.2 seconds later.

Creating a Custom Editor

You'll now create a custom editor that you can use to edit TrueFalseQuestion nodes that are rendered by the QuestionCellRenderer class defined earlier. It's appropriate in some cases to use one type of component for drawing nodes and a different type for editing their values (e.g., a JLabel for rendering and a JTextField for editing). In this case, however, JCheckBox is an appropriate choice for both rendering and editing, so this custom editor class will use a JCheckBox just as the previously defined custom renderer class did.

Before creating the custom editor, an obvious question that must be answered is which existing class (if any) should be used as the superclass. Although DefaultTreeCellEditor might seem like an obvious choice, it's moderately complex and is somewhat coupled to the use of a JTextField for editing. In contrast, DefaultCellEditor is more generic and includes a constructor that accepts a single parameter representing the JCheckBox to be used for editing. Therefore, you can begin the implementation of the custom editor class by extending DefaultCellEditor and providing a no-argument constructor that creates a new JCheckBox and passes it to the superclass constructor:

```
import java.awt.*;
import javax.swing.*;
import javax.swing.tree.*;

public class QuestionCellEditor extends DefaultCellEditor {

  public QuestionCellEditor() {
    super(new JCheckBox());
  }

  // More methods and member variables here ...
}
```

Since DefaultCellEditor already implements TreeCellEditor, it's not necessary to explicitly specify that interface in QuestionCellEditor, but it's necessary to override the getTreeCellEditorComponent() method. Although DefaultCellEditor already supports the use of a JCheckBox instance for editing, it assumes that the value being edited is a Boolean value. In this case, however, the value being edited is an instance of TrueFalseQuestion, and getTreeCellEditorComponent() must be implemented accordingly. Doing so is very much like implementing getTreeCellRendererComponent() in a renderer class. Specifically, all you must do is initialize the component used for editing so it will contain the appropriate initial value when it's made visible to the user. For the QuestionCellEditor class, this means setting the JCheckBox's text and selection state values to match the question and answer values encapsulated by the TrueFalseQuestion object. Note that the TrueFalseQuestion instance is encapsulated within an instance of DefaultMutableTreeNode when it's passed to getTreeCellEditorComponent(), and it's the responsibility of getQuestionFromValue() to extract it.

```
private TrueFalseQuestion question;

public Component getTreeCellEditorComponent(JTree tree, Object value,
    boolean selected, boolean expanded, boolean leaf,
    int row) {
  JCheckBox editor = null;
  question = getQuestionFromValue(value);
  if (question != null) {
    editor = (JCheckBox)(super.getComponent());
    editor.setText(question.getQuestion());
    editor.setSelected(question.getAnswer());
  }
  return editor;
}
```

```
public static TrueFalseQuestion getQuestionFromValue(
    Object value) {
  if (value instanceof DefaultMutableTreeNode) {
    DefaultMutableTreeNode node =
        (DefaultMutableTreeNode)value;
    Object userObject = node.getUserObject();
    if (userObject instanceof TrueFalseQuestion) {
      return (TrueFalseQuestion)userObject;
    }
  }
  return null;
}
```

The only other change you must make to this class is to override the getCellEditorValue()
method. That method is called when editing is completed so that the modified value can be stored in the
TreeModel associated with the tree. In this case, the object being edited was a TrueFalseQuestion, so
getCellEditorValue() should return an instance of that class. Since a reference to the object being edited
is maintained in QuestionCellEditor, it can simply update that object based on the results of the edit and
return a reference to it from getCellEditorValue(). However, it would be equally valid to create a new
instance of TrueFalseQuestion and return a reference to that object instead.

```
public Object getCellEditorValue() {
  JCheckBox editor = (JCheckBox)(super.getComponent());
  question.setAnswer(editor.isSelected());
  return question;
}
```

Since the TrueFalseQuestion object passed to getTreeCellEditorComponent() is encapsulated
within a DefaultMutableTreeNode, you might have expected it to also be necessary to return a
DefaultMutableTreeNode from getCellEditorValue(). However, this isn't required because the
DefaultTreeModel class automatically encapsulates the objects passed to its valueForPathChanged()
method inside instances of DefaultMutableTreeNode. In other words, the value object passed to
getTreeCellEditorComponent() is normally a DefaultMutableTreeNode that encapsulates the "real"
data (the user object), but you shouldn't wrap data in a DefaultMutableTreeNode before returning it from
getCellEditorValue().

Finally, with the editor class defined, you can create an instance of it, assign that object responsibility
for the editing of a JTree's nodes, and enable the nodes for editing:

```
public TreeTest() {
  super("Smallville University Final Exam");
  JTree tree = new JTree(getRootNode());
  QuestionCellRenderer renderer = new QuestionCellRenderer();
  tree.setCellRenderer(renderer);
  QuestionCellEditor editor = new QuestionCellEditor();
  tree.setCellEditor(editor);
  tree.setEditable(true);
  JScrollPane jsp = new JScrollPane(tree);
  getContentPane().add(jsp);
}
```

Unfortunately, a problem exists with this code: because it enables editing for all cells and because the root node doesn't represent a TrueFalseQuestion, an exception will occur if you attempt to edit that node.

Limiting Edits to Certain Nodes

To complete this application, you may want to allow some nodes to be edited while preventing others from being modified. In the case of the TreeTest application, simply setting the JTree's editable property to true will allow all nodes to be edited, including the header/root node that's simply a String instead of TrueFalseQuestion. As mentioned earlier, a node's ability to be edited is controlled by the isPathEditable() method in JTree, and by creating a subclass and overriding that method, you can modify the default behavior. The following code segment does just that, returning a value of true for nodes that represent TrueFalseQuestion instances and false for all other nodes:

```
public TreeTest() {
  super("Smallville University Final Exam");
  JTree tree = new JTree(getRootNode()) {
    public boolean isPathEditable(TreePath path) {
      Object comp = path.getLastPathComponent();
      if (comp instanceof DefaultMutableTreeNode) {
        DefaultMutableTreeNode node =
            (DefaultMutableTreeNode)comp;
        Object userObject = node.getUserObject();
        if (userObject instanceof TrueFalseQuestion) {
          return true;
        }
      }
      return false;
    }
  };
  QuestionCellRenderer renderer = new QuestionCellRenderer();
  tree.setCellRenderer(renderer);
  QuestionCellEditor editor = new QuestionCellEditor();
  tree.setCellEditor(editor);
  tree.setEditable(true);
  JScrollPane jsp = new JScrollPane(tree);
  getContentPane().add(jsp);
}
```

Customizing Branch Node Handles

When customizing the nodes' appearance earlier, you may have noticed that creating a custom renderer had no effect upon the handle icons used to indicate whether branch nodes are expanded or collapsed. That's because the handle icon is drawn by the tree's user interface (UI) object instead of the cell renderer. For a JTree, that object is a subclass of BasicTreeUI (such as the MetalTreeUI class, which is used when the Java or Metal look and feel is active), and BasicTreeUI maintains two icons: one for collapsed branch nodes and another for expanded nodes.

You have two ways to modify these icons; the approach you take will depend upon whether you want to modify them for all JTree instances or for a single instance. To modify them for a single JTree instance, obtain a reference to the instance of BasicTreeUI that's associated with the tree and call its setCollapsedIcon() and setExpandedIcon() methods as follows:

```
import javax.swing.plaf.basic.*;
// ...
javax.swing.Icon customExpandedIcon;
javax.swing.Icon customCollapsedIcon;
// ...

JTree myTree = new JTree();
// Obtain a reference to the BasicTreeUI used by this tree
BasicTreeUI ui = (BasicTreeUI)(myTree.getUI());
// Now set the icons it uses for branch node handles
ui.setExpandedIcon(customExpandedIcon);
ui.setCollapsedIcon(customCollapsedIcon);
```

If, on the other hand, you want to change the icons for all instances of JTree, you can use the UIManager's put() method. When a new BasicTreeUI is created, it retrieves the pair of icons maintained by the UIManager, so by changing those two icons, you'll effectively be changing the icons used by each new JTree instance that's created. The following code illustrates how you can do this:

```
javax.swing.Icon customExpandedIcon;
javax.swing.Icon customCollapsedIcon;
// ...

UIManager.put("Tree.expandedIcon", customExpandedIcon);
UIManager.put("Tree.collapsedIcon", customCollapsedIcon);
```

It's also possible to eliminate the handle icons completely by creating a BasicTreeUI subclass that returns false from its shouldPaintExpandControlMethod(). As its name implies, that method's purpose is to determine whether a handle icon should be displayed at all. It's normally used to prevent handles from being displayed next to leaf nodes and the root node, which doesn't display a handle unless you call the JTree's setShowsRootHandles() method and pass it a value of true. Here, however, you can create an implementation of shouldPaintExpandControlMethod() that always returns false, which prevents handles from appearing next to any of the nodes. The easiest way to override the method is to create an anonymous inner class as follows, where the appropriate BasicTreeUIClass is extended:

```
JTree myTree = new JTree();
javax.swing.plaf.metal.MetalTreeUI customUI =
    new javax.swing.plaf.metal.MetalTreeUI() {
  private boolean shouldPaintExpandControl(TreePath path, int row,
      boolean isExpanded, boolean wasExpanded, boolean leaf) {
    return false;
  }
};
myTree.setUI(customUI);
```

As Figure 8-21 shows, this code causes the branch nodes within the tree to be drawn without handles, although the nodes can still be expanded and collapsed by double-clicking them (if editing isn't enabled) or by using the right and left arrow keys.

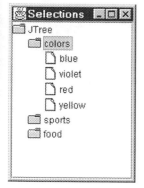

Figure 8-21. *It's possible and occasionally desirable to eliminate the node handles completely*

Line Style with the Java/Metal Look and Feel

All the examples shown in this chapter so far have used the Java (or Metal) look and feel, but Figure 8-22 and Figure 8-23 illustrate how JTree instances are drawn when using the Motif and Windows look and feels, respectively.

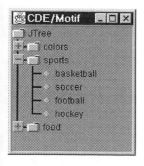

Figure 8-22. *A JTree drawn using the Motif look and feel*

Figure 8-23. *A JTree drawn using the Windows look and feel*

367

As these figures show, the Java look and feel is the only one that doesn't draw lines between the nodes in a JTree, although it's possible to modify this behavior. To do so, call the JTree's putClientProperty() method to modify the JTree.lineStyle property as follows, specifying one of three line styles: None (the default), Angled, or Horizontal:

```
JTree myTree = new JTree();
myTree.putClientProperty("JTree.lineStyle", "Angled");
```

The Angled style draws lines between the parent nodes and their children, and the Horizontal style results in a line being drawn above each node that has children. Figure 8-24 and Figure 8-25 illustrate the Angled and Horizontal styles, respectively.

Figure 8-24. *An example of the Angled line style*

Figure 8-25. *An example of the Horizontal line style*

Note that this technique works only with the Java/Metal look and feel, and you can't use it to modify the lines drawn between nodes with the Motif or Windows look and feels.

Node Selection

Many applications allow users to select one or more nodes within a JTree for some purpose. For example, suppose you want users to be able to select nodes graphically using only a mouse so that they can perform some operation (such as deletion from the tree) on the selected nodes. It's easy to make selections when using JTree; you can do this by simply moving the cursor over the node you want to select and pressing the left mouse button. As illustrated in Figure 8-26, DefaultTreeCellRenderer highlights selected nodes by rendering them with colors that are different from those used for unselected nodes.

Figure 8-26. *How a* JTree *appears when the basketball and soccer nodes are highlighted*

The selection of a JTree's nodes is controlled by an implementation of TreeSelectionModel, and the DefaultTreeSelectionModel class is used by default. Although it's possible to create your own selection model implementation, you'll rarely have any reason to do so, since DefaultTreeSelectionModel is flexible. In any case, you can specify which model should be used or retrieve a reference to the existing model using the setSelectionModel() and getSelectionModel() methods defined in JTree. If you want to prevent any tree nodes from being selected, simply pass a null value to setSelectionModel(), as shown in the following code segment:

```
JTree myTree = new JTree();
// The following code will prevent the user from selecting nodes in the tree
myTree.setSelectionModel(null);
```

Selection Modes

TreeSelectionModel supports three selection modes, each of which is represented by a constant value defined in that interface. The following are those constants and the behavior associated with each one:

- SINGLE_TREE_SELECTION: When this selection mode is active, only a single node can be selected at any given time. Each time you select a node, any node that was previously selected becomes deselected.

- CONTIGUOUS_TREE_SELECTION: This mode allows you to define a single range of nodes (a set of "contiguous" nodes), and all the nodes within that range become selected.

- DISCONTIGUOUS_TREE_SELECTION: With this selection mode, which is the default, no restrictions exist on how many nodes can be selected or on where the nodes that are selected must be positioned relative to one another. Any group of nodes within the tree can be selected at any time.

To set the selection mode, simply call the TreeSelectionModel's setSelectionMode() method, passing it the value of one of the three constants defined previously. For example, to set the selection mode for a given JTree, you could use code such as the following:

```
JTree myTree = new JTree();
TreeSelectionModel model = myTree.getSelectionModel();
model.setSelectionMode(TreeSelectionModel.CONTIGUOUS_TREE_SELECTION);
```

For the most part, the selection modes are simple and easy to understand, but I'll briefly illustrate how contiguous selections work. As mentioned, a *contiguous* selection is simply a group of adjacent (or contiguous) nodes. Given the tree shown in Figure 8-27, suppose you want to select all the nodes in the tree beginning with February and ending with October.

Figure 8-27. *You'll often want to select a range of nodes*

One way of doing this is to press and hold down the Ctrl key while clicking each node separately, but a quicker way is to select the appropriate range of nodes. For example, you might first click the February node and then press and hold down the Shift key while clicking the October node, resulting in the desired range of nodes being selected, as shown in Figure 8-28. In this case, the February node is referred to as the *anchor selection*, since it's the first node used to define the range of contiguous nodes, and the October node is referred to as the *lead selection*.

Figure 8-28. *The anchor selection (February in this case) is the first node in a range selected, and the lead selection (October) is the node at the opposite end of the selection range*

I should make two important points concerning the behavior of JTree and DefaultSelectionModel and which nodes are selected when you use the mouse in this manner. First, selecting a branch node such as the colors, sports, or food nodes in Figure 8-29 won't cause that node's children to be selected.

Figure 8-29. *Selecting a node with children doesn't cause those child nodes to also be selected*

Second, be aware that mouse-initiated selections apply only to viewable nodes, recalling that a *viewable* node is one for which all ancestors are expanded. To illustrate this point, suppose you select a range of nodes displayed by the tree in Figure 8-30 by first selecting yellow and then hot dogs. This will result in exactly four nodes being selected: yellow, sports, food, and hot dogs. Note that although the sports node is selected, its children remain unselected, which you can see by expanding that node (see Figure 8-31) and noting that its children aren't selected.

Figure 8-30. *In this example, the children of the sports node aren't considered to be selected because their parent is collapsed*

Figure 8-31. *Expanding the selected node reveals that its children weren't selected as part of the range selection*

TreeSelectionListener

You'll sometimes want to be notified when tree selection changes have been made, and by creating an instance of TreeSelectionListener and registering it with the JTree, you can receive such notification. This interface defines a single valueChanged() method that's called when the selection state of one or more nodes has changed. In other words, registered listeners are notified when unselected nodes become selected, as well as when selected nodes become unselected. For example, to create a listener using an anonymous inner class, you could write code similar to the following:

```
import javax.swing.event.*;
// ...
JTree myTree = new JTree();
myTree.addTreeSelectionListener(new TreeSelectionListener() {
  public void valueChanged(TreeSelectionEvent event) {
    // Add code here to handle selection changes
  }
});
```

TreeSelectionEvent

As the previous code segment illustrates, the valueChanged() method defined in TreeSelectionListener is passed an instance of TreeSelectionEvent. You can use the following methods in TreeSelectionEvent to obtain information that describes the type of selection change that occurred and to determine which nodes were involved in the change.

getPaths(), getPath()

You can use these methods to determine which path or paths were involved in the selection change that occurred. The getPaths() method returns an array of TreePath objects, each of which identifies a node that experienced a selection state change. The getPath() method returns a single TreePath object and is provided as a convenience for those times when you're using SINGLE_TREE_SELECTION mode and need to obtain a reference only to a single TreePath object. If you're using either of the other selection modes, getPath() returns the first path in the array that's provided by getPaths().

isAddedPath()

This overloaded method has three implementations, each of which returns a Boolean value that indicates whether some specific node/path became selected (as opposed to deselected). One implementation accepts a TreePath that should be equal to one of those returned by getPaths(), and another accepts an integer index value that should be greater than zero and less than the number of paths returned by getPaths(). In both cases, the parameter value identifies a specific node/path for which the selection state changed, and this method returns a value of true if the node was selected or false if it was deselected. The third implementation of isAddedPath() doesn't accept parameters, and like getPath(), it's provided as a convenience for cases where only a single path can be selected at any given time.

getNewLeadSelectionPath(), getOldLeadSelectionPath()

Each of these methods returns a reference to a TreeNode representing the new (after the selection state change occurs) and old (before the change occurs) lead selection paths. In most cases, your application won't need to be concerned with lead (or anchor) paths, so these methods aren't normally used.

Selection Methods in JTree

While the methods defined in TreeSelectionEvent are useful for identifying nodes that are newly selected or deselected, you'll often want to retrieve a list of all selected nodes. In addition, it's often desirable to select nodes programmatically, and JTree contains methods that allow you to do all these things. For example, getSelectionPaths() returns an array of TreePath objects that identifies all paths/nodes that are currently selected, and setSelectionPaths() allows your code to specify which paths should be selected. If you want to identify paths using their index (vertical position) values instead of TreeNode instances, you can use the getSelectionRows() and setSelectionInterval() methods instead.

Listing 8-5 provides an example of how you can use getSelectionPaths() to create an application that displays a pop-up menu that can be used to delete the currently selected nodes, as illustrated in Figure 8-32.

This application displays a JTree and adds a MouseListener that will cause a JPopupMenu to appear when a right mouse click occurs. If the user activates the Delete menu item in that pop-up menu, the deleteSelectedItems() method is called, which deletes the currently selected nodes from the tree.

Listing 8-5. JTree Pop-up Menu: Delete Select/Use Example

```
import java.awt.event.*;
import javax.swing.*;
import javax.swing.tree.*;

public class DeleteNodes extends JFrame {

  private JTree tree;
```

```java
  public static void main(String[] args) {
    DeleteNodes dn = new DeleteNodes(new JTree());
    dn.setDefaultCloseOperation(JFrame.EXIT_ON_CLOSE);
    dn.setSize(400, 300);
    dn.setVisible(true);
  }

  public DeleteNodes(JTree jt) {
    super("Node Selection");
    tree = jt;
    getContentPane().add(tree);
    tree.addMouseListener(new MouseAdapter() {
      public void mousePressed(MouseEvent event) {
        if (((event.getModifiers() &
            InputEvent.BUTTON3_MASK)
            != 0) &&
            (tree.getSelectionCount() > 0)) {
          showMenu(event.getX(), event.getY());
        }
      }
    });
  }

  private void showMenu(int x, int y) {
    JPopupMenu popup = new JPopupMenu();
    JMenuItem mi = new JMenuItem("Delete");
    TreePath path = tree.getSelectionPath();
    Object node = path.getLastPathComponent();
    if (node == tree.getModel().getRoot()) {
      mi.setEnabled(false);
    }
    popup.add(mi);
    mi.addActionListener(new ActionListener() {
      public void actionPerformed(ActionEvent event) {
        deleteSelectedItems();
      }
    });
    popup.show(tree, x, y);
  }

  private void deleteSelectedItems() {
    DefaultMutableTreeNode node;
    DefaultTreeModel model =
        (DefaultTreeModel)(tree.getModel());
    TreePath[] paths = tree.getSelectionPaths();
    for (int i = 0; i < paths.length; i++) {
      node = (DefaultMutableTreeNode)(
          paths[i].getLastPathComponent());
      model.removeNodeFromParent(node);
    }
  }
}
```

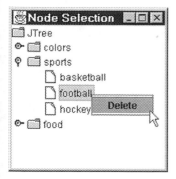

Figure 8-32. *You'll often want to allow users to perform operations on the selected node(s) in a tree, and* getSelectionPaths() *can be helpful when doing this*

Notice that this application is designed to allow you to perform the deletion only when the root node is not one of the nodes selected, which is necessary because DefaultTreeModel requires the presence of a root node. If you select the root node and then press the right mouse button, the pop-up menu will still appear, but the Delete menu item will be disabled, preventing you from performing the operation.

Collapsing and Expanding Nodes

In most cases, you'll leave the responsibility for collapsing and expanding nodes to the user, who will do so graphically with the mouse. However, sometimes it's convenient or necessary to expand or collapse nodes programmatically, which you can do easily. To do so, use the expandPath() and collapsePath() methods or the expandRow() and collapseRow() methods defined in JTree. As their names imply, the first pair of methods requires that you specify a TreePath parameter that identifies the node to be expanded or collapsed. In contrast, the second pair allows you to identify the node by specifying its position index (an integer value representing its vertical position within the tree).

For example, say you have the tree shown in Figure 8-33.

Figure 8-33. *You can collapse and expand tree nodes programatically easily using the methods provided in* JTree

To collapse the sports node, you can execute the following code:

```
JTree myTree = new JTree();
// ...
myTree.collapseRow(2);
```

Similarly, to expand the food node, you can execute the following statement:

```
myTree.expandRow(7);
```

Detecting Collapses and Expansions

In addition to being able to expand and collapse nodes programmatically, it's also sometimes useful to be notified when those operations occur. Fortunately, JTree supports two types of listeners that allow you to receive such notifications, one of which notifies you before the operation occurs and another that notifies listeners after the change has occurred.

TreeExpansionListener

By implementing this interface, you can create an object that can register with a JTree to receive notifications after one of the tree's nodes has been expanded or collapsed. TreeExpansionListener defines two methods, both of which are passed instances of TreeExpansionEvent. That event class provides a single getPath() method that returns an instance of TreePath to identify the node that was expanded or collapsed.

To register an object so it will receive these notifications, simply call JTree's addTreeExpansionListener() method, passing a reference to the object that implements TreeExpansionListener. You can also use the tree's removeTreeExpansionListener() to prevent the listener from receiving further notifications.

treeCollapsed()

This method is called for all registered listeners after one of the tree's nodes has been collapsed. You can use the TreeExpansionEvent parameter's getPath() method to obtain access to a TreePath object that identifies the node that was collapsed.

treeExpanded()

This method is called for all registered listeners after one of the tree's nodes has been expanded. You can use the TreeExpansionEvent parameter's getPath() method to obtain access to a TreePath object that identifies the node that was expanded.

TreeWillExpandListener

Like TreeExpansionListener, this interface creates listeners that will be notified of requests to collapse and expand nodes. However, as its name implies, this interface identifies listeners that are notified of those operations before they occur instead of afterward. This allows you to populate a tree's data in an "on-demand" fashion, creating a node's children (and loading the data associated with those children) only when the node is about to be expanded and its children displayed. In addition, this interface allows you to actually prevent (or "veto") the pending operation by throwing an exception from the notification method. To do so, create and throw an instance of the ExpandVetoException class defined in the javax.swing.tree package. That class provides two constructors, both of which require that you pass a reference to a TreeExpansionEvent object. One of the two constructors also allows you to specify an error message that will be passed to the exception object's constructor and used as its message text.

The following code illustrates how you can implement a TreeWillExpandListener using an anonymous inner class, and this listener will allow all expansions but prevent/veto all attempts to collapse the tree's nodes.

```
import javax.swing.event.*;
// ...
JTree myTree = new JTree();
myTree.addTreeWillExpandListener(new TreeWillExpandListener() {
  public void treeWillExpand(TreeExpansionEvent event)
      throws ExpandVetoException {
    System.out.println("Expanding path " + event.getPath());
  }

  public void treeWillCollapse(TreeExpansionEvent event)
      throws ExpandVetoException {
    throw new ExpandVetoException(event, "Collapses not allowed");
  }
});
```

Note that it's never necessary for you to handle an ExpandVetoException, even if an expansion or collapse operation you initiate programmatically (through JTree's collapseXXX() and expandXXX() methods) is vetoed. However, if you want your code to determine whether the operation was successful, the expandXXX() or collapseXXX() call can be followed by a call to JTree's isExpanded() or isCollapsed() methods. Those return Boolean values that will allow you to determine whether the node's expansion state matches what it should be if the requested operation succeeded; following is an example of how you can use them:

```
JTree myTree;
TreePath somePath;
// ...

myTree.expandPath(somePath);
if (myTree.isExpanded(somePath)) {
  System.out.println("Expansion succeeded");
}
else {
  System.out.println("Expansion failed");
}
```

treeWillExpand()

This method is called for all registered listeners before one of the tree's nodes is expanded. You can use the TreeExpansionEvent parameter's getPath() method to obtain access to a TreePath object that identifies the node that will be expanded, and throwing an ExpandVetoException from this method will prevent the expansion from occurring.

treeWillCollapse( )

This method is called for all registered listeners before one of the tree's nodes is collapsed. You can use the `TreeExpansionEvent` parameter's `getPath( )` method to obtain access to a `TreePath` object that identifies the node that will be collapsed, and throwing an `ExpandVetoException` from this method will prevent the collapse from occurring.

Summary

I covered the following in this chapter:

- Terminology related to tree structures and the data they display
- `JTree`'s support classes and interfaces
- How to construct and manipulate the data model associated with a tree
- How to control how the items in a tree are drawn (rendered) and edited
- How to select items in a tree and detect when selections change
- How to control which portions of a tree's data are displayed (expanded) or concealed (collapsed)

CHAPTER 9

■ ■ ■

Adding Cut-and-Paste Functionality

Cut-and-paste functionality is extremely useful because it allows you to transfer data between user interface components and even between different applications. In general, cut-and-paste operations are performed on components that support the concept of a selection, and the operations are initiated by the keyboard and performed for the component that currently has the input focus.

Some Swing components include built-in support for cut-and-paste and as a result you'll often be able to use cut-and-paste operations within your application without writing any extra code. However, it's still helpful to be familiar with the API (application programming interface) for situations where it's needed, such as when you need to create a custom Swing component. For example, in this chapter you'll see how to create a component that can edit images; cut, copy, and paste operations are essential in such an application. Although the data transfer API simplifies implementing this as much as possible; adding cut-and-paste support to a component that doesn't already support it is a nontrivial exercise and isn't well-documented. To understand how to perform cut-and-paste operations, you'll examine the following topics:

- Clipboards and their relevance to cut-and-paste operations

- The classes and interfaces Java provides that support these operations

- How to cut, copy, and paste various data types

Even if you don't intend to provide cut-and-paste functions, it's still a good idea to understand how to implement them, particularly if your application needs to support drag-and-drop operations. Chapter 10 covers Java's drag-and-drop capabilities, but much of the information covered here is relevant to that discussion as well.

The package containing the classes and interfaces related to cut-and-paste operations is fairly small, and the number of classes and interfaces that are really important is even smaller. In fact, the ones shown in Figure 9-1 are the ones you'll primarily need to be concerned with if you implement cut-and-paste support.

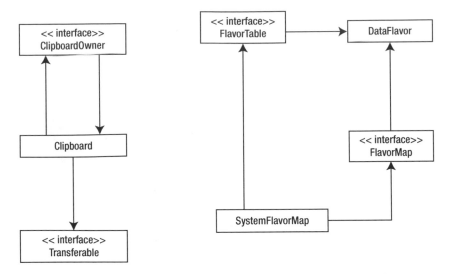

Figure 9-1. *The classes and interfaces relevant to implementing cut-and-paste support in Java*

Clipboards: Where Cut and Copied Data Is Stored

Usually when you cut or copy data from an application and then terminate the application, the data you extracted can still be pasted to some other location. For example, if you copy text from a word processor, you'll be able to paste that text to another application even after the word processor is no longer running. As you might expect, that's possible because the data is copied to a location outside the application from which it was extracted. The resource provided for that purpose is called a *clipboard*, and in Java, a clipboard is represented by an instance of the Clipboard class defined in java.awt.datatransfer. Although you can create your own instances of Clipboard in Java, you won't usually need or want to do so. Instead, you'll use the system clipboard that represents the underlying operating system's clipboard, and you can obtain a reference to it through an instance of Toolkit.

The Toolkit class defined in java.awt provides a variety of utility functions related to user interface behavior. You can access an instance of Toolkit by calling the getToolkit() method in Component, as follows:

```
JButton btn = new JButton("Hello");
Toolkit tk = btn.getToolkit();
```

or by using the static getDefaultToolkit() method defined in Toolkit.

```
Toolkit tk = Toolkit.getDefaultToolkit();.
```

Once you've obtained a reference to a Toolkit, you can access the system clipboard by calling getSystemClipboard().

```
Clipboard scb = Toolkit.getDefaultToolkit().getSystemClipboard();
```

Using the System Clipboard

The system clipboard should theoretically allow you to cut or copy data from a Java application and paste that data into a Java or non-Java application, but, unfortunately, it isn't that simple. The way in which data is stored often isn't as simple as you might expect it to be based upon its visual representation. For example, documents created by an application such as Microsoft Word may appear to contain simple text information that can be easily transferred from that application to, for example, a Swing component such as JTextField. In reality, though, the document probably contains formatting and other information that's not visible and that may not be transferable in any meaningful way to another application. In addition, an application such as Microsoft Word can take advantage of operating system–specific features that aren't supported in a Java application that's supposed to run correctly on any platform that supports Java. Finally, clipboard transfers are also complicated by the numerous character sets that are available and used. (However, this limitation at least is usually reasonably simple to overcome.)

The main point to keep in mind is simply that not every data type can be transferred between Java and native applications. Some of the most important types can be transferred, though, and later in this chapter you'll see what kinds of data you can safely store in the clipboard from a Java application. First, however, you'll examine Clipboard and the classes associated with it.

Using Clipboard

The Clipboard class includes three methods: getContents(), setContents(), and getName(). You'll rarely have any reason to access the clipboard's name, so the only two methods of interest are setContents() and getContents(). As their names imply, those methods set and retrieve the clipboard's contents, so you'll use setContents() for cut/copy operations and getContents() when pasting data.

setContents()

The setContents() method is passed two parameters:

- A reference to an implementation of the Transferable interface
- A reference to an implementation of the ClipboardOwner interface

The Transferable parameter represents the data you want to store in the clipboard, while the ClipboardOwner is an object that should be notified when the data being stored is later overwritten.

getContents()

This method returns an instance of Transferable to the caller, and that object represents the contents of the clipboard. If the clipboard is empty or contains a type of data that Java can't process, getContents() returns a null value.

Using Transferable

To store data in the clipboard, you must wrap it in an instance of a Transferable implementation, and data is similarly encapsulated when you read it from the clipboard. In addition to serving as a container for clipboard data, a Transferable implementation provides methods that allow you to determine the type of data it contains.

Many different applications can store data in the clipboard, and these applications use many different data formats. For example, information cut or copied from a text editor is very different from data stored by an application that allows you to edit image files. In addition, the image editor's data is probably not meaningful to the text editor, and vice versa. As you might expect, when information is stored in the clipboard, the type of data it represents is recorded as well. This allows an application to determine whether the data represents a type that it's able to process, and if so, the user may be able to paste the data into that application.

In many cases, it's oversimplifying matters to associate data with a single, specific type, because information can often be represented in more than one way. If you create an instance of Java's Integer wrapper class, you'll normally think of it as an Integer object, and rightly so. However, if you examine the API documentation for Integer, you'll see it has a large number of methods that allow you to extract the value it encapsulates in many different forms. For example, you can call the intValue(), longValue(), and floatValue() methods to obtain a reference to an int, long, or float primitive instead of an Integer. In addition, you can call toString() to obtain a String representation of the numeric value, as well as toBinaryString(), toHexString(), and so on. The point is that even this simple piece of information can be retrieved in many different (but equally valid) forms, and that's often true of data in the clipboard as well.

This is why one of the responsibilities of a Transferable implementation is to identify the different formats in which the data it encapsulates can be retrieved. Each type is represented by an instance of DataFlavor, which you'll examine in detail shortly. First, however, you'll look at Transferable's methods and then at the ClipboardOwner interface.

getTransferDataFlavors()

This method returns an array of DataFlavor objects that identify the different data formats ("flavors") that are supported by Transferable. For example, if you cut or copy text from a StyledDocument in Java, it may be possible to read the clipboard contents in more than one format. One flavor could represent text with its style information (colors, fonts, etc.) intact, and that representation might be used to insert the text into a StyledDocument. However, to allow the text to be pasted into a JTextField, you'd use a flavor that represents the text data stripped of its style information.

The DataFlavor instances returned by getTransferDataFlavors() are ordered based on which format provides the most detailed (or "richest") version of the data. This allows an application to select the best flavor by identifying the first one in the list that it can accept. In the previous example, the flavor representing styled text would appear first in the list, since it provides the most detailed representation of the data in the clipboard.

isDataFlavorSupported()

You can use this method to determine whether a specific DataFlavor is supported by Transferable. It accepts a DataFlavor as a parameter and returns a boolean value of true if the specified flavor is supported.

When isDataFlavorSupported() is called, it should compare the DataFlavor that was passed as a parameter to the flavors in the list of those it supports. In other words, if the DataFlavor parameter is equal to one of the flavors that would be returned by getTransferDataFlavors(), this method should return true.

Note that when comparing DataFlavor instances, you should be sure to use the equals() method instead of the equality (==) operator. It's usually not important whether two DataFlavor references point to the same object instance. Instead, your code should establish whether two instances describe the same type of data, and you can determine that using DataFlavor's implementation of the equals() method.

getTransferData()

This method returns the data encapsulated by Transferable, and as you might expect, an instance of DataFlavor must be specified as a parameter. If that parameter represents a flavor that's not supported, an UnsupportedFlavorException is thrown. Otherwise, the data is returned to the caller in the requested format.

Note that you must also declare java.io.IOException as a checked exception that can be thrown by this method.

Using ClipboardOwner

In addition to Transferable, an instance of a ClipboardOwner implementation is passed as a parameter to the setContents() method. The ClipboardOwner interface defines a single lostOwnership() method that's called when the data being stored in the clipboard is later overwritten by another call to setContents(). In other words, the ClipboardOwner object is temporarily registered as a listener of the clipboard data, and that owner will receive a notification when the clipboard is next modified.

You're free to use the ClipboardOwner in any way that's helpful, but you often won't need to take any action when data you stored in the clipboard has been overwritten. When that's the case, you can pass a null value to setContents() for the ClipboardOwner, or you can implement a "dummy" lostOwnership() method that contains no code. However, as you'll see, ClipboardOwner can sometimes play an important role in maintaining clipboard data.

The StringSelection class defined in java.awt.datatransfer implements both Transferable and ClipboardOwner, and it allows you to store and retrieve text data. Although Java's data transfer API may appear somewhat complex, it's easy to cut and paste text. For example, the following code segment stores "Hello" in the clipboard using the StringSelection class:

```
Clipboard cb = Toolkit.getDefaultToolkit().getSystemClipboard();
StringSelection ss = new StringSelection("Hello");
cb.setContents(ss, ss);
```

Note that in this case, the StringSelection instance was used for both parameter values passed to the setContents() method. That's possible because StringSelection implements both the Transferable and ClipboardOwner interfaces (although its lostOwnership() method currently doesn't contain any code).

When you encapsulate data in Transferable and store that Transferable in the clipboard, you shouldn't modify the data until after lostOwnership() is called. Java's data transfer specification allows a "lazy data model" to be used, which means that calling setContents() may or may not result in the data being copied from Transferable into the clipboard. In some cases, the data isn't retrieved until a request is made to read the contents of the clipboard, so you should leave the data intact, at least until lostOwnership() is called.

For example, suppose your application uses a Transferable interface that encapsulates an array of integer values, and an instance of that class is stored in the clipboard. For the original data to be accessible, the values in the array must remain unchanged even after you call the setContents() method. Only when the ClipboardOwner's lostOwnership() notification occurs can your application safely make changes to the array. Later in the chapter, you'll see how you can design your code with this behavior in mind. However, you should be aware that if your application terminates before you retrieve the data it stored in the clipboard, the information won't be available to other applications via the clipboard.

Using DataFlavor

As mentioned earlier, an instance of DataFlavor identifies a specific type of data supported by a Transferable implementation. DataFlavor defines three properties that are used to describe the data type:

- **A human-readable name**: The human-readable name is provided as a convenience, and its use is optional. It does allow you to associate a user-friendly name with a data flavor, so you may choose to use it in your application.

- **A representation class**: A DataFlavor's representation class identifies the type of Java object returned from Transferable when its getContents() method is passed a reference to that DataFlavor. The representation class is maintained in DataFlavor as an instance of java.lang.Class.

- **A Multipurpose Internet Mail Extensions (MIME) type**: The third property stored in a DataFlavor is a MIME type, which is represented as a String value.

Introducing MIME Types

If you only ever needed to transfer data between Java applications, then the representation class maintained in DataFlavor would be sufficient to describe the type of data in the clipboard. For example, if you were to store text information in the clipboard, you could associate the data with the java.lang.String class, but that association would be meaningful only to Java programs.

However, to transfer data between Java and non-Java applications, it's necessary to assign each data type a name that's not specific to Java. In addition, since Java applications can run on many platforms, the data type's name shouldn't be tied to a particular application or platform. In other words, what's needed is a set of platform-independent, language-neutral names that are associated with different types of data (text, graphics, audio, etc.). Fortunately, such names have already been defined and are used by DataFlavor.

MIME is an Internet standard that allows different types of data to be embedded within electronic mail documents. This is accomplished partly through the definition of content types (or simply, MIME types), which are names associated with commonly used data types.

A MIME type consists of a top-level media type that describes the general category of the data and a subtype that defines a more specific type of data, with the two types separated by a forward slash (/). For example, simple character data with no attributes (such as font, color, or formatting information) is defined as text/plain. Other top-level types include image, audio, video, and application, so some examples of other MIME types are image/gif, image/jpeg, text/html, and video/mpeg. A large number of data types are registered with the Internet Assigned Numbers Authority (IANA), including those just mentioned. Applications that read and write those data types are encouraged to use and recognize the MIME types, and a process exists for registering a new MIME type when one doesn't already exist.

You can also define custom MIME types for your application to use, in which case you should use a top-level type of application. You can use any subtype name you'd like, but it should begin with "x-" to indicate that it's an unregistered type. Finally, application/octet-stream is a generic type to describe binary data of an unknown format.

In addition to the type and subtype, a MIME type can include additional parameters that describe the data. For example, while text/plain might seem adequate to identify simple text data, the issue is complicated by the existence of a large number of different character sets. To address this, you can use parameters to provide an even more detailed description of the type of data a MIME type represents. A parameter consists of a type/value pair separated by an equal (=) sign, and parameters are delimited by semicolon (;) characters. For example, the following MIME types describe three varieties of text data:

- text/plain; charset=unicode
- text/plain; charset=ascii
- text/plain; charset=iso-8859-1

Creating an Instance of DataFlavor

You can create a new DataFlavor using the constructor that takes a single String parameter representing a MIME type. For example, the following creates an instance of DataFlavor that represents Rich Text Format (RTF) data:

```
DataFlavor rtfFlavor = new DataFlavor("text/rtf; charset=ascii");
```

When you use this constructor, the representation class for the DataFlavor is set to java.io.InputStream, which has a special significance with respect to transferable data. A variation of this constructor is also provided that allows you to specify the human-readable name that should be assigned to the DataFlavor. If you want to assign the name, you can use that constructor, or you can call the setHumanPresentableName() method after the DataFlavor has been created.

Depending upon the type of data contained within your application, you may sometimes want to store an instance of a serializable Java object in the clipboard instead of raw data, and a different constructor is provided for that purpose. It requires you to pass an instance of java.lang.Class that identifies the representation class and a String that identifies the human-readable name, as follows:

```
DataFlavor myFlavor = new DataFlavor(MySerial.class, "A class I created");
```

When you use this constructor, the MIME type for the DataFlavor is set to application/x-java-serialized-object. Since a serialized Java object is meaningful only to a Java Virtual Machine (JVM), this type of DataFlavor is useful only when transferring information between Java applications.

You've now looked at the two categories of DataFlavor instances: those that are associated with a particular MIME type and those that are related to a particular Java class. When creating your own DataFlavor, the type of flavor you create will depend on the type of data being cut and pasted, as well as the type of applications involved in the transfer. For example, if you intend to cut and paste data only between Java applications, you should define flavors that are class-based and use serialized object instances. However, if you intend to transfer between Java and non-Java (or "native") applications, you should use a MIME-based DataFlavor that has a representation class of InputStream. Doing so allows the JVM to transfer the clipboard data to a native application as a stream of binary data that conforms to some agreed-upon protocol (in other words, a MIME type).

Storing and Retrieving Serialized Java Objects

To illustrate how to store and retrieve serialized Java objects, I'll now show you how to create a crude image-editing application. The application will allow you to select portions of an image and cut, copy, or paste selections to and from the clipboard.

The ImageEditor class displays the contents of an image file in a JFrame and allows you to select a rectangular portion of the image by dragging the mouse. The selected area is identified by a brightly colored rectangle that's drawn as the mouse is dragged.

Once you've selected a portion of the image, you can right-click to display a pop-up menu that allows you to cut or copy the selection (see Figure 9-2).

Figure 9-2. *Image-editing applications typically allow you to cut or copy one portion of an image and paste it somewhere else*

Listing 9-1 provides this functionality (although the performCut(), performCopy(), and performPaste() methods aren't complete yet). Specifically, this application uses an ImageIcon and a JLabel to display the contents of an image file, and it listens for mouse events, drawing a selection square around the selected area as the mouse is dragged. In addition, it creates a pop-up menu that's displayed when the right mouse button is pressed.

Listing 9-1. Cut/Copy Functionality

```java
import java.awt.*;
import java.awt.datatransfer.*;
import java.awt.event.*;
import java.awt.image.*;
import javax.swing.*;

public class ImageEditor extends JPanel {

  public final static int LINE_WIDTH = 2;

  private ImageIcon icon;
  private Point start = new Point(0, 0);
  private Point finish = new Point(0, 0);
  private Point pastePoint;

  private JPopupMenu popupMenu;
  private AbstractAction cutAction;
  private AbstractAction copyAction;
  private AbstractAction pasteAction;
```

```java
public static void main(String[] args) {
  if (args.length == 0) {
    System.out.println("You must specify the name of an image file");
    return;
  }
  ImageEditor editor = new ImageEditor(args[0]);
  JFrame f = new JFrame(args[0]);
  f.setDefaultCloseOperation(JFrame.EXIT_ON_CLOSE);
  f.setContentPane(editor);
  f.setSize(400, 300);
  f.setVisible(true);
}

public ImageEditor(String name) {
  super();
  buildPopupMenu();
  setBackground(Color.black);
  setLayout(new GridLayout(1, 1, 0, 0));
  icon = new ImageIcon(name);
  JLabel label = new JLabel(icon);
  label.setHorizontalAlignment(SwingConstants.LEFT);
  label.setVerticalAlignment(SwingConstants.TOP);
  label.addMouseListener(new MouseAdapter() {
    public void mousePressed(MouseEvent event) {
      handleMouseDown(event);
    }
  });
  label.addMouseMotionListener(new MouseMotionAdapter() {
    public void mouseDragged(MouseEvent event) {
      handleMouseDrag(event);
    }
  });
  JScrollPane jsp = new JScrollPane(label);
  add(jsp);
}

private void handleMouseDown(MouseEvent event) {
  if ((event.getModifiers() & InputEvent.BUTTON1_MASK) != 0) {
    start = event.getPoint();
    finish = event.getPoint();
  }
  else if ((event.getModifiers() & InputEvent.BUTTON3_MASK) != 0) {
    displayPopupMenu(event.getPoint());
    pastePoint = event.getPoint();
  }
}

private void handleMouseDrag(MouseEvent event) {
  finish = event.getPoint();
  repaint();
}
```

```java
  private void buildPopupMenu() {
    popupMenu = new JPopupMenu();
    copyAction = new AbstractAction("Copy") {
      public void actionPerformed(ActionEvent event) {
        performCopy();
      }
    };
    popupMenu.add(copyAction);
    cutAction = new AbstractAction("Cut") {
      public void actionPerformed(ActionEvent event) {
        performCut();
      }
    };
    popupMenu.add(cutAction);
    pasteAction = new AbstractAction("Paste") {
      public void actionPerformed(ActionEvent event) {
        performPaste();
      }
    };
    popupMenu.add(pasteAction);
  }

  private void displayPopupMenu(Point p) {
    Clipboard cb = getToolkit().getSystemClipboard();
    Transferable t = cb.getContents(this);
    boolean isSelected = !(start.equals(finish));
    cutAction.setEnabled(isSelected);
    copyAction.setEnabled(isSelected);
    popupMenu.show(this, p.x, p.y);
  }

  private void performCopy() {
  }

  private void performCut() {
  }

  private void performPaste() {
  }

  private Rectangle getSelectedArea() {
    int width = finish.x - start.x;
    int height = finish.y - start.y;
    return new Rectangle(start.x, start.y, width, height);
  }

  private int[] getPixels(Rectangle area) {
    int[] pixels = new int[area.width * area.height];
    PixelGrabber pg = new PixelGrabber(icon.getImage(), area.x,
                                       area.y, area.width,
                                       area.height, pixels, 0,
                                       area.width);
```

```
      try {
        pg.grabPixels();
      } catch (Exception e) {};
      return pixels;
  }

  private void setPixels(int[] newPixels, Rectangle area) {
    int pixel;
    Image image = icon.getImage();
    int imageWidth = icon.getIconWidth();
    int imageHeight = icon.getIconHeight();
    int[] oldPixels = new int[imageWidth * imageHeight];
    PixelGrabber pg = new PixelGrabber(image, 0, 0, imageWidth,
                                       imageHeight, oldPixels, 0,
                                       imageWidth);
    try {
      pg.grabPixels();
    } catch (Exception e) {};
    for (int y = 0; y < area.height; y++) {
      if (imageHeight <= area.y + y) {
        break;
      }
      for (int x = 0; x < area.width; x++) {
        if (imageWidth <= area.x + x) {
          break;
        }
        oldPixels[((area.y + y) * imageWidth) + area.x + x] =
          newPixels[(area.width * y) + x];
      }
    }
    MemoryImageSource mis = new MemoryImageSource(imageWidth,
            imageHeight, oldPixels, 0, imageWidth);
    icon.setImage(createImage(mis));
    repaint();
  }

  public void paint(Graphics g) {
    super.paint(g);
    int width = finish.x - start.x;
    int height = finish.y - start.y;
    if ((width > 0) && (height > 0)) {
      g.setColor(Color.blue);
      for (int i = 0; i < LINE_WIDTH; i++) {
        g.drawRect(start.x + i, start.y + i, width, height);
      }
    }
  }
}
```

To support the cut-and-paste operations, you must define a Java class that can be used to encapsulate a portion of the image that's cut or copied. In addition, it's necessary to define an implementation of Transferable that can be stored in and retrieved from the clipboard. Although these two functions could easily be combined in a single class, we'll implement them separately to provide a more cohesive design for the application.

The ImageData class defined in Listing 9-2 can store part of an image that's cut or copied, along with the width and height of that area. Note that it implements the Serializable interface, which allows instances of ImageData to be serialized.

Listing 9-2. ImageData

```java
public class ImageData implements java.io.Serializable {

  private int width;
  private int height;
  private int[] pixelData;

  public ImageData(int width, int height, int[] pixels) {
    this.width = width;
    this.height = height;
    pixelData = pixels;
  }

  public int getWidth() {
    return width;
  }

  public int getHeight() {
    return height;
  }

  public int[] getPixelData() {
    return pixelData;
  }

}
```

The next task is to define the Transferable implementation that can store image data in the clipboard. You'll also have this class implement ClipboardOwner so it can be notified when its data is no longer stored in the clipboard. In this case, however, the lostOwnership() implementation doesn't do anything when that occurs.

```java
import java.awt.datatransfer.*;

public class ImageSelection implements Transferable, ClipboardOwner {

  public void lostOwnership(Clipboard cb, Transferable t) {}

}
```

Since ImageSelection encapsulates an instance of ImageData, a constructor should be defined that accepts an ImageData object and stores a reference to the object.

```
import java.awt.datatransfer.*;

public class ImageSelection implements Transferable, ClipboardOwner {

    private ImageData imageData;

    public ImageSelection(ImageData data) {
        imageData = data;
    }

    public void lostOwnership(Clipboard cb, Transferable t) {
    }

}
```

In addition, it's necessary for ImageSelection to identify the data formats it supports. To provide that capability, define a single DataFlavor with a representation class of ImageData and a MIME type of application/x-java-serialized-object. In other words, this flavor represents serialized ImageData instances.

```
import java.awt.datatransfer.*;

public class ImageSelection implements Transferable, ClipboardOwner {

  private ImageData imageData;

  public final static DataFlavor IMAGE_DATA_FLAVOR =
      new DataFlavor (ImageData.class, "Image Data");

  public ImageSelection(ImageData data) {
    imageData = data;
  }

  public void lostOwnership(Clipboard cb, Transferable t) {
  }

}
```

Although the DataFlavor was defined inside the Transferable class in this case, you may or may not choose to use this approach when creating your own Transferable implementations. The issue of where to define a DataFlavor is strictly one of good object-oriented design and has no effect on the flavor's usability.

To complete the ImageSelection class, you must implement the Transferable methods. First write the code for getTransferDataFlavors(), which you can do by defining a static array of DataFlavor objects and returning a reference to that array.

```
import java.awt.datatransfer.*;

public class ImageSelection implements Transferable, ClipboardOwner {

  private ImageData imageData;

  public final static DataFlavor IMAGE_DATA_FLAVOR =
      new DataFlavor (ImageData.class, "Image Data");
```

```
  private final static DataFlavor [] flavors = {
    IMAGE_DATA_FLAVOR
  };

  public ImageSelection(ImageData data) {
    imageData = data;
  }

  public DataFlavor [] getTransferDataFlavors() {
    return flavors;
  }

  public void lostOwnership(Clipboard cb, Transferable t) {
  }

}
```

The isDataFlavorSupported() method is equally simple, and all that's necessary is to loop through the flavors in the array and compare each one to the parameter value.

```
import java.awt.datatransfer.*;

public class ImageSelection implements Transferable, ClipboardOwner {

  private ImageData imageData;

  public final static DataFlavor IMAGE_DATA_FLAVOR =
    new DataFlavor (ImageData.class, "Image Data");

  private final static DataFlavor [] flavors = {
    IMAGE_DATA_FLAVOR
  };

  public ImageSelection(ImageData data) {
    imageData = data;
  }

  public DataFlavor [] getTransferDataFlavors() {
    return flavors;
  }

  public boolean isDataFlavorSupported(DataFlavor flavor) {
    for (int i = 0; i < flavors.length; i++) {
      if (flavor.equals(flavors[i])) {
        return true;
      }
    }
    return false;
  }

  public void lostOwnership(Clipboard cb, Transferable t) {}

}
```

Finally, getTransferData() must be implemented, which is responsible for returning data in the requested flavor. In this case, only IMAGE_DATA_FLAVOR is supported, and that flavor can be provided simply by returning a reference to the encapsulated data object.

```
import java.awt.datatransfer.*;

public class ImageSelection implements Transferable, ClipboardOwner {

  private ImageData imageData;

  public final static DataFlavor IMAGE_DATA_FLAVOR =
    new DataFlavor (ImageData.class, "Image Data");

  private final static DataFlavor [] flavors = {
    IMAGE_DATA_FLAVOR
  };

  public ImageSelection(ImageData data) {
    imageData = data;
  }

  public Object getTransferData(DataFlavor flavor)
        throws java.io.IOException, UnsupportedFlavorException {
    if (flavor.equals(IMAGE_DATA_FLAVOR)) {
     return imageData;
    }
    throw new UnsupportedFlavorException(flavor);
  }

  public DataFlavor [] getTransferDataFlavors() {
    return flavors;
  }

  public boolean isDataFlavorSupported(DataFlavor flavor) {
    for (int i = 0; i < flavors.length; i++) {
      if (flavor.equals(flavors[i])) {
        return true;
      }
    }
    return false;
  }

  public void lostOwnership(Clipboard cb, Transferable t) {}

}
```

Now that the Transferable implementation is complete, all that's left is to write the code in ImageEditor to perform the cut, copy, and paste operations. Since most of the needed functionality is already present, you have very little work to do.

In the case of the performCopy() method, you can create an instance of ImageSelection and store it in the clipboard using the setContents() method, as follows:

```
private void performCopy() {
  Rectangle r = getSelectedArea();
  int[] pixels = getPixels(r);
  ImageData data = new ImageData(r.width, r.height, pixels);
  ImageSelection selection = new ImageSelection(data);
  Clipboard cb = getToolkit().getSystemClipboard();
  cb.setContents(selection, selection);
}
```

The cut operation is almost identical but has one additional step. After the image data is copied to the clipboard, the pixels that were copied are set to zero in the original image (in other words, they're "removed" from the image).

```
private void performCut() {
  Rectangle r = getSelectedArea();
  int[] pixels = getPixels(r);
  ImageData data = new ImageData(r.width, r.height, pixels);
  ImageSelection selection = new ImageSelection(data);
  Clipboard cb = getToolkit().getSystemClipboard();
  cb.setContents(selection, selection);
  for (int i = 0; i < pixels.length; i++) {
    pixels[i] = 0;
  }
  setPixels(pixels, r);
}
```

Finally, you can complete the performPaste() method. It must obtain a reference to the Transferable implementation stored in the clipboard (if any), ensure that the data can be retrieved in the supported format, and overwrite a portion of the image with that data.

```
private void performPaste() {
  Clipboard cb = getToolkit().getSystemClipboard();
  try {
    Transferable t = cb.getContents(this);
    if (t.isDataFlavorSupported(
        ImageSelection.IMAGE_DATA_FLAVOR)) {
      ImageData data = (ImageData)(t.getTransferData(
        ImageSelection.IMAGE_DATA_FLAVOR));
      Rectangle area = new Rectangle(start.x, start.y,
        data.getWidth(), data.getHeight());
      int[] pixels = data.getPixelData();
      setPixels(pixels, area);
    }
  }
  catch (Exception e) {
    JOptionPane.showMessageDialog(this,
        "Unable to paste clipboard data");
  }
}
```

Finally, you can also make a minor change to `ImageEditor` that causes the Paste menu item to be disabled when the clipboard doesn't contain the supported data flavor.

```
private void displayPopupMenu(Point p) {
  Clipboard cb = getToolkit().getSystemClipboard();
  Transferable t = cb.getContents(this);
  boolean isSelected = !(start.equals(finish));
  cutAction.setEnabled(isSelected);
  copyAction.setEnabled(isSelected);
  boolean canPaste = ((t != null) &&
     (t.isDataFlavorSupported(
      ImageSelection.IMAGE_DATA_FLAVOR)));
  pasteAction.setEnabled(canPaste);
  popupMenu.show(this, p.x, p.y);
}
```

To execute this application, compile and run it, specifying the name of a GIF or JPEG file as the first command-line parameter. For example,

```
java ImageEditor ProJava3.gif
```

To select an area of the image to cut or paste, move the mouse to the upper-left corner of the region, and press and hold the left mouse button. As you drag the cursor, a brightly colored rectangle appears that identifies the selected area. Once you make a selection, you can right-click to access a `JPopupMenu` with Cut, Copy, and Paste menu items as shown in Figure 9-3.

Figure 9-3. *Once you've cut or copied a selection onto the clipboard you'll be able to paste it back using the sample application*

The pasted selection will overwrite a rectangular section of the image corresponding to the pointer location as illustrated in Figure 9-4.

Figure 9-4. *Pasting overwrites a portion of the image with the data copied to the clipboard*

Although we only created a very crude application, it does illustrate that Java's cut-and-paste facility is capable of performing the same operations as a native program.

Transferring Between Java and Native Applications

So far, you've looked only at storing Java objects in the clipboard. However, in some cases, it's useful to be able to transfer data between Java and non-Java applications.

It might seem that Java's MIME-based approach to identifying the content type of a Transferable's data would make it easy to transfer data between Java and non-Java applications. However, this isn't the case, primarily because each operating system's clipboard supports its own proprietary data types instead of standard MIME types. For example, Windows defines the CF_TEXT, CF_DIB, and CF_HDROP clipboard types for text, bitmap (image), and file selection data, respectively.

Although native clipboards don't use MIME types, it's possible in some cases to define a mapping between a native platform's clipboard type and a MIME type. In fact, that's exactly what occurs when you use the StringSelection class provided with Java. When you call the setContents() method to store a StringSelection in the clipboard, the text is automatically converted to an appropriate native clipboard format (e.g., CF_TEXT) so that it's readable by non-Java applications. Similarly, when getContents() is called, the data is translated from the native format, such as CF_TEXT, into a String encapsulated by an instance of StringSelection. In the future, other Transferable types may exist that are translated automatically for you this way, but text data is the only type currently supported for clipboard operations.

In Java 1.2, StringSelection supported two flavors, both of which are represented by constants defined in DataFlavor: stringFlavor and plainTextFlavor. While stringFlavor is used to transfer serialized String instances between Java programs, plainTextFlavor was created for text transfers between Java and non-Java applications. However, because of problems in the design and implementation of StringSelection, plainTextFlavor was deprecated in Java 1.3, so you should avoid using it.

Writing Arbitrary Binary Data

To store binary data in the clipboard, you must define a DataFlavor that represents the MIME type associated with the data and that has a representation class of InputStream. A Transferable that supports the flavor should provide an InputStream that returns a stream of bytes in the appropriate format for the MIME type.

Normally when you write binary data to the clipboard, it will be necessary to write it using a format that one or more other applications are able to interpret. In some cases, you can do this through a codec, which is software that performs data conversions between two or more formats. For example, Sun provides a codec with the Java 2D API that allows you to convert data representing a JPEG image to and from an instance of Java's BufferedImage class.

I'll now show how to modify the ImageSelection class so that it supports an additional DataFlavor representing the image/jpeg MIME type (see Listing 9-3). When that flavor is requested on a call to getTransferData(), an InputStream is returned that can be used to read a stream of bytes in JPEG format.

Listing 9-3. Enhancing ImageSelection

```java
import java.awt.*;
import java.awt.datatransfer.*;
import java.awt.image.*;
import java.io.*;
import com.sun.image.codec.jpeg.*;

public class ImageSelection implements Transferable, ClipboardOwner{

  private ImageData imageData;

  public final static DataFlavor IMAGE_DATA_FLAVOR =
    new DataFlavor (ImageData.class, "Image Data");

  public final static DataFlavor JPEG_MIME_FLAVOR =
    new DataFlavor ("image/jpeg", "JPEG Image Data");

  private final static DataFlavor [] flavors = {
    JPEG_MIME_FLAVOR, IMAGE_DATA_FLAVOR
  };

  public ImageSelection(ImageData data) {
    imageData = data;
  }

  public Object getTransferData(DataFlavor flavor)
         throws java.io.IOException, UnsupportedFlavorException {
    if (flavor.equals(IMAGE_DATA_FLAVOR)) {
      return imageData;
    } else if (flavor.equals(JPEG_MIME_FLAVOR)) {
      return getJPEGInputStream();
    }
    throw new UnsupportedFlavorException(flavor);
  }
```

```java
    private InputStream getJPEGInputStream() throws IOException {
      int width = imageData.getWidth();
      int height = imageData.getHeight();
      MemoryImageSource mis = new MemoryImageSource(width, height,
              imageData.getPixelData(), 0, width);
      BufferedImage bi =
        new BufferedImage(width, height, BufferedImage.TYPE_3BYTE_BGR);
      Graphics2D g2d = bi.createGraphics();
      Image img = Toolkit.getDefaultToolkit().createImage(mis);
      g2d.drawImage(img, 0, 0, null);
      ByteArrayOutputStream baos = new ByteArrayOutputStream();
      JPEGImageEncoder jie = JPEGCodec.createJPEGEncoder(baos);
      jie.encode(bi);
      baos.close();
      return new ByteArrayInputStream(baos.toByteArray());
    }

  public DataFlavor [] getTransferDataFlavors() {
    return flavors;
  }

  public boolean isDataFlavorSupported(DataFlavor flavor) {
    for (int i = 0; i < flavors.length; i++) {
      if (flavor.equals(flavors[i])) {
        return true;
      }
    }
    return false;
  }

  public void lostOwnership(Clipboard cb, Transferable t) {}

}
```

Note that, in this example, the binary data corresponds to a specific MIME format, that of a JPEG image. If you want to write binary data that doesn't correspond to an existing MIME type, you can create a custom type (e.g., application/x-mybinary) or simply use the generic application/octet-stream type.

Once the problems with Java's data transfer API have been resolved, you'll be able to transfer data between Java and non-Java applications by storing the data as a stream of binary data as I did in this example. In the meantime, however, you can test the functionality added to ImageSelection by adding a pop-up menu item to ImageEditor. That menu item should allow you to retrieve the contents of the clipboard as a stream of JPEG data and save the data to a disk file. In other words, you can cut or copy a portion of an image and save the selection to disk as a new JPEG file by making the following changes. To do this, first define an AbstractAction that corresponds to the new menu item.

```java
private JPopupMenu popupMenu;
private AbstractAction cutAction;
private AbstractAction copyAction;
private AbstractAction pasteAction;
private AbstractAction saveAction;
```

Next, add a new menu item to the pop-up menu.

```
private void buildPopupMenu() {
  popupMenu = new JPopupMenu();
  copyAction = new AbstractAction("Copy") {
    public void actionPerformed(ActionEvent event) {
      performCopy();
    }
  };
  popupMenu.add(copyAction);
  cutAction = new AbstractAction("Cut") {
    public void actionPerformed(ActionEvent event) {
      performCut();
    }
  };
  popupMenu.add(cutAction);
  pasteAction = new AbstractAction("Paste") {
    public void actionPerformed(ActionEvent event) {
      performPaste();
    }
  };
  popupMenu.add(pasteAction);
  saveAction = new AbstractAction("Save") {
    public void actionPerformed(ActionEvent event) {
      performSave();
    }
  };
  popupMenu.add(saveAction);
}
```

Finally, implement the method that will perform the save operation, and update the code that sets the state of the menu items so the Save menu item is enabled only when there's data in the clipboard.

```
private void displayPopupMenu(Point p) {
  Clipboard cb = getToolkit().getSystemClipboard();
  Transferable t = cb.getContents(this);
  boolean isSelected = !(start.equals(finish));
  cutAction.setEnabled(isSelected);
  copyAction.setEnabled(isSelected);
  boolean canPaste = ((t != null) &&
      (t.isDataFlavorSupported(
      ImageSelection.IMAGE_DATA_FLAVOR)));
  pasteAction.setEnabled(canPaste);
  saveAction.setEnabled(canPaste);
  popupMenu.show(this, p.x, p.y);
}
```

```
private void performSave() {
  JFileChooser jfc = new JFileChooser();
  jfc.showSaveDialog(this);
  java.io.File f = jfc.getSelectedFile();
  Clipboard cb = getToolkit().getSystemClipboard();
  Transferable t = cb.getContents(this);
  DataFlavor flavor = ImageSelection.JPEG_MIME_FLAVOR;
  if ((!(f == null)) && (!(t == null))
        && (t.isDataFlavorSupported(flavor))) {
    try {
      java.io.FileOutputStream fos =
        new java.io.FileOutputStream(f);
      java.io.InputStream is =
        (java.io.InputStream) (t.getTransferData(flavor));
      int value = is.read();
      while (value != -1) {
        fos.write((byte) value);
        value = is.read();
      }
      fos.close();
      is.close();
    } catch (Exception e) {}
  }
}
```

Add a new menu item to the pop-up menu.

```
private void displayPopupMenu(Point p) {
  JPopupMenu jpm = new JPopupMenu();
  jpm.add(new AbstractAction("Copy") {
    public void actionPerformed(ActionEvent event) {
      performCopy();
    }
  });
  jpm.add(new AbstractAction("Cut") {
    public void actionPerformed(ActionEvent event) {
      performCut();
    }
  });
  jpm.add(new AbstractAction("Paste") {
    public void actionPerformed(ActionEvent event) {
      performPaste();
    }
  });
  jpm.add(new AbstractAction("Save") {
    public void actionPerformed(ActionEvent event) {
      performSave();
    }
  });
  jpm.show(this, p.x, p.y);
}
```

And add the code to actually perform the operation.

```
private void performSave() {
    JFileChooser jfc = new JFileChooser();
    jfc.showSaveDialog(this);
    java.io.File f = jfc.getSelectedFile();
    Clipboard cb = getToolkit().getSystemClipboard();
    Transferable t = cb.getContents(this);
    DataFlavor flavor = ImageSelection.JPEG_MIME_FLAVOR;
    if ((!(f == null)) && (!(t == null))
            && (t.isDataFlavorSupported(flavor))) {
        try {
            java.io.FileOutputStream fos =
                new java.io.FileOutputStream(f);
            java.io.InputStream is =
                (java.io.InputStream) (t.getTransferData(flavor));
            int value = is.read();
            while (value != -1) {
                fos.write((byte) value);
                value = is.read();
            }
            fos.close();
            is.close();
        } catch (Exception e) {}
    }
}
```

Summary

In this chapter, you examined Java's cut-and-paste capabilities and learned how to use them in conjunction with the clipboard.

■ ■ ■

CHAPTER 10

Adding Drag-and-Drop Functionality

In a drag-and-drop operation, data is moved (*dragged*) from one location and stored (*dropped*) in another. For example, most operating systems provide a utility similar to Windows Explorer, which allows you to perform drag-and-drop operations on a list of available files. Drag-and-drop functionality provides an intuitive visual representation of moving or copying data from one location to another and is an important part of most modern operating systems. Many applications use it in a variety of ways, so it's helpful to be familiar with the functionality that's available in Java.

The standard Swing components come with drag-and-drop support already built in, and, in most cases, it's completely functional and behaves in a way that's intuitive and consistent with what you'd expect. As we'll see in the section "TransferHandler," though, the nature of some components makes it impossible to define and implement behavior that's appropriate for all or even most applications. As a result, those few Swing components where this is the case—specifically, JList, JTable, and JTree—provide only partial support for drag-and-drop, but you have the option of extending that support and tailoring the additional functionality to the needs of your application. The majority of this chapter describes how to provide drag-and-drop support for a custom component that initially doesn't support it at all, and an understanding of how to implement that support is helpful if you do need to provide extended capabilities for one of the three components just mentioned.

Most of the classes associated with drag-and-drop functionality are defined in the java.awt.dnd package, but some parts of the data transfer API defined in java.awt.datatransfer are also used. The classes defined in java.awt.dnd may seem complex and confusing, but the truth is that it's not difficult to add drag-and-drop capabilities to your applications. In fact, once the data to be dragged is wrapped in a Transferable, you usually won't have much more code to write.

The Transferable interface in the java.awt.datatransfer package serves the same purpose in a drag-and-drop operation that it does when used to cut and paste. Specifically, a Transferable encapsulates the data that's dragged and provides DataFlavor instances that identify the formats in which the data can be retrieved.

In this chapter, you'll examine the following issues:

- The fundamental concepts associated with drag-and-drop operations

- How to add drag support to components so they can be used to initiate drag-and-drop operations

- How to add drop support to components so they can be used to terminate drag-and-drop operations

- Issues related to different types of transfers (e.g., those between Java and native applications, as opposed to transferring within a single Java Virtual Machine, or JVM)

- How to implement autoscroll support for drop targets contained within a scroll pane

- Issues related to transferring text data between Java and native applications

Introducing Drag-and-Drop Operation Types

Just as cut, copy, and paste functions are collectively referred to as *cut and paste*, the phrase *drag and drop* refers to several different operations. In a move operation, the data that's dragged is removed from its original location and stored in some other location. A copy operation is similar to a move, except that the original data remains intact and a copy of it is created and stored in the drop location. Finally, a link or reference operation results in the creation of a representation of or a reference to the original data. For example, the terminology varies across platforms, but most operating systems allow you to create file *shortcuts* or *aliases*.

The way in which drag-and-drop operations start and end varies from one operating system to the next, because each platform defines its own set of gestures for those purposes. Those gestures are usually a combination of mouse button and key presses, and the buttons and keys involved are referred to as *modifiers*.

For example, on Windows, you can initiate a move operation by clicking and then dragging the cursor (in other words, moving the mouse with the left button still pressed). You initiate a copy operation by performing the same steps while also holding down the Ctrl key. Finally, a link operation requires you to press and hold down both the Shift and Ctrl keys while dragging the mouse. In each case, the object that's dragged is usually either the component that was underneath the cursor when the left button was initially pressed or some data item that the component represents.

When the appropriate drag gestures have been performed, the drag operation is initiated by an object called a *drag source*, and the drop is handled by an object called a *drop target*. You'll write code to control the behavior of the drag source and drop target, and that code can take any action that's appropriate for the application. In some cases, your code may choose to perform an operation (copy, move, or link) other than the one associated with the user's gestures. For example, if a Windows user requests a copy operation by pressing the Ctrl key while dragging, your application might choose to perform a move instead if the copy operation isn't appropriate in the context of that application.

The individual drag-and-drop operations (and some combinations) are represented by int values defined in the DnDConstants class. Specifically, those constants are as follows:

- ACTION_MOVE

- ACTION_COPY

- ACTION_REFERENCE

- ACTION_LINK

- ACTION_COPY_OR_MOVE

Reference and *link* are synonyms for the same operation, so their associated constants are assigned the same value. The ACTION_COPY_OR_MOVE constant is provided as a convenience since it represents a commonly used combination.

Using the Predefined Cursors

During drag-and-drop operations, it's common practice to provide visual feedback to the user concerning the state of the operation, and one way you can do this is through the cursor that's displayed. A pair of cursors exists for each of the three operation types, and those cursors are accessible through constants defined in DragSource. Each pair includes a drop cursor that's normally displayed when the cursor is over a component that can accept a drop and a no-drop cursor when the cursor is over components that can't accept a drop (see Table 10-1).

Table 10-1. *Cursor Constants Defined in DragSource*

Action	Drop Cursor	No-Drop Cursor
Move	DefaultMoveDrop	DefaultMoveNoDrop
Copy	DefaultCopyDrop	DefaultCopyNoDrop
Link	DefaultLinkDrop	DefaultLinkNoDrop

You won't normally find it necessary to use these constants, because in most cases, Java's drag-and-drop facility will change the cursor for you automatically to reflect the status of the drag-and-drop operation. In general, the only time you need to select one of these cursors is when initiating a drag event, in which case you'll specify the initial cursor that should be displayed.

Performing File Selection Drops from Native Applications

In Chapter 9, you saw that each DataFlavor contains a MIME type used to identify the specific data format the flavor represents. However, each operating system defines its own proprietary data types, and to transfer data between a Java and native application, a DataFlavor's MIME type must be mapped to an equivalent native type. For example, to transfer text information between Java and native Windows applications, Java automatically converts a StringSelection in the clipboard to the CF_TEXT type, and vice versa.

While text information is the type of data most commonly involved in cut-and-paste operations, file selections represent the most frequently used data type in drag-and-drop operations.

In the same way that Java provides an automatic conversion of clipboard text data, it also performs a translation that allows you to drag and drop file selections between Java and native applications. Those selections are represented by a Transferable that supports a DataFlavor with a MIME type of application/x-java-file-list and a representation class of java.util.List. The List object returned by this type of Transferable contains a collection of java.io.File objects that identify the files selected. If you drop files from a native application onto a Java program, Java automatically creates an instance of java.util.List containing File objects and wraps that list in a Transferable.

Adding Drop Support

Although it might seem more logical to begin with support for dragging, we'll first cover how to handle drops in Java. Drop support is somewhat easier to implement, and this approach provides a good opportunity to illustrate how Java can accept data that's dropped from a native application, such as Windows Explorer.

To demonstrate how to implement drop support we'll show how to create a subclass of JPanel called ImageViewer that accepts image file selection drops (see Figure 10-1). For each file that's dropped, ImageViewer creates an ImageIcon and displays the icon in a JLabel.

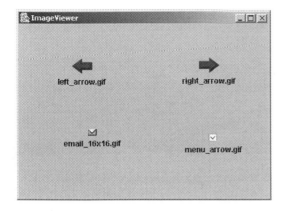

Figure 10-1. *The ImageViewer application*

Listing 10-1 represents the initial implementation of ImageViewer. The getLabelFromFile() method is passed an instance of File and attempts to use that file to create and return a JLabel. Since you want to be able to add JLabel instances to any point in the container, ImageViewer doesn't use a layout manager. Therefore, it's necessary to explicitly set the size and position of each component added, and addNewComponent() provides that.

Listing 10-1. ImageViewer

```java
import java.awt.*;
import java.awt.datatransfer.*;
import java.awt.dnd.*;
import java.io.*;
import javax.swing.*;

public class ImageViewer extends JPanel {

  public static void main(String[] args) {
    JFrame f = new JFrame("ImageViewer");
    f.setDefaultCloseOperation(JFrame.EXIT_ON_CLOSE);
    f.setContentPane(new ImageViewer());
    f.setSize(400, 300);
    f.setVisible(true);
  }

  public ImageViewer() {
    super();
    setLayout(null);
  }

  private JLabel getLabelFromFile(File f) {
    ImageIcon icon = new ImageIcon(f.getAbsolutePath());
    JLabel label = new JLabel(icon);
    label.setText(f.getName());
```

```
    label.setHorizontalTextPosition(JLabel.CENTER);
    label.setVerticalTextPosition(JLabel.BOTTOM);
    return label;
  }

  private void addNewComponent(Component comp, Point location) {
    comp.setLocation(location);
    comp.setSize(comp.getPreferredSize());
    add(comp);
    repaint();
  }

}
```

With the basic functionality implemented, you can begin to add drop support to the custom component, and the first step in doing so is to associate it with a drop target.

DropTarget

Before you can perform drops on a Component, you must create an instance of DropTarget and associate it with the component, which can be done in several different ways. However, the easiest approach in most cases is to provide a reference to the component when you create the DropTarget. Once it has been created, you can enable and disable a DropTarget by calling its setActive() method, and its state can be queried using isActive().

The DropTarget receives notification of events related to the drag-and-drop operation and provides support for a single listener that's also notified of those events. To handle drops, you must define a DropTargetListener implementation and associate it with a DropTarget just as you did for the drop component.

DropTargetListener

A DropTargetListener has two primary responsibilities: providing drag-under effects during a drag-and-drop operation and handling the recipient's side of a drop when it occurs. *Drag-under effects* are changes made to the drop component's appearance that provide feedback to the user during the drag operation. For example, if you create a DropTargetListener for use with a JTable, you might implement code that highlights the cell underneath the cursor as it moves across the table. We'll see an example of this later in the chapter, but for now, drag-under effects are an advanced topic and in practice are often not needed.

In addition to the drag-under effects, a DropTargetListener is responsible for handling the drop operation, which typically involves storing a copy of or a reference to the data that's dropped. How and where the data is stored is application-specific and usually depends on the operation type (move, copy, or link), the type of data dropped, and the type of component onto which it's dropped. In the case of ImageViewer, the DropTargetListener uses the file selections to create JLabel instances, and the labels are added to the panel at the drop location.

ImageViewer contains an inner class, shown in Listing 10-2, which provides an implementation of DropTargetListener. We'll cover each of the five methods defined in DropTargetListener in detail in this chapter, but in many cases, you'll need to write code only for drop(), which (as its name implies) is called when a drop occurs. To use this inner class, insert it into the ImageViewer class after the addNewComponent() method.

Listing 10-2. Providing an Implementation of DropTargetListener

```
class MyDropListener implements DropTargetListener {

  public void dragEnter(DropTargetDragEvent event) {
  }

  public void dragExit(DropTargetEvent event) {
  }

  public void dragOver(DropTargetDragEvent event) {
  }

  public void dropActionChanged(DropTargetDragEvent event) {
  }

  public void drop(DropTargetDropEvent event) {
  }

}
```

It's now possible to create a DropTarget, which you'll do using a constructor that's passed a reference to the drop component (in other words, the ImageViewer instance), the operations the target supports, and a reference to a DropTargetListener.

```
public ImageViewer() {
  super();
  setLayout(null);
  DropTarget dt = new DropTarget(this,
      DnDConstants.ACTION_COPY_OR_MOVE,
      new MyDropListener());
}
```

Events Passed to DropTargetListener Methods

Now that you've created the DropTarget, it's necessary to complete the implementation of the methods within MyDropListener. To better understand how those methods are used, you need to examine the event objects that are passed to them.

DropTargetEvent

This is the superclass of the DropTargetDragEvent and DropTargetDropEvent classes discussed next, and an instance of this class is passed to dragExit(). However, DropTargetEvent doesn't define any methods or properties you'll normally use.

DropTargetDragEvent

An instance of DropTargetDragEvent is passed to the dragEnter(), dragOver(), and dropActionChanged() methods. DropTargetDragEvent allows those methods to identify the type of data being dragged, as well as the specific location of the cursor and other information regarding the current operation. In addition, this event object provides methods that allow the drag operation to be accepted or rejected, and I discuss the reasons for doing so and consequences of those actions later.

getCurrentDataFlavors( ), getCurrentDataFlavorsAsList( ), isDataFlavorSupported( )

These methods allow you to determine which DataFlavor(s) can be used to transfer data if a drop occurs. While getCurrentDataFlavors() returns an array of DataFlavor instances, getCurrentDataFlavorsAsList() returns a java.util.List containing the valid flavors. When you need to determine whether the data can be retrieved using a specific flavor, you should use isDataFlavorSupported(). That method returns a boolean value of true if the flavor you pass to it as a parameter is supported.

These methods are often used by a DropTargetListener to determine whether the data being dragged can be represented in a form that the drop target can process. If not, it's common for the drop target to reject the drag operation, the implications of which are discussed later.

getLocation( )

You can use this method to determine where the cursor was located when the event occurred. An instance of java.awt.Point is returned that identifies the cursor's position within the component across which it's being dragged, and the position is relative to the component's origin (coordinates 0, 0).

This method is most commonly used to provide drag-under effects. For example, if data is dragged across a JTable, the drop target may use the cursor's location to determine which table cell is underneath the cursor and select or highlight that cell appropriately.

getSourceActions( )

A drop target may need to determine what operations are supported by the drag source, and this method makes it possible to obtain that information.

acceptDrag( )

This method indicates that the drop target is prepared to accept a drop, and you should specify the operation type that the target will perform if a drop does occur. That type should be one of the types supported by the drag source, which can be identified by calling getSourceActions().

You're not required to call this method within the DropTargetListener methods. However, you should call acceptDrag() if your drop target wants to perform an operation other than the one selected by the user.

rejectDrag( )

A call to rejectDrag() indicates that your drop target isn't prepared to accept a drop, and the reasons for that can vary from one application to the next. A drag is often rejected when the type of data being dragged can't be processed by the drop target or when the cursor is over an area of the component that can't accept drops. For example, ImageViewer rejects drags when the data being dragged can't be retrieved using the javaFileListFlavor data flavor.

getDropAction( )

This method identifies the operation type that the user currently has selected and returns an int value that corresponds to one of the action constants defined in DragSource: ACTION_MOVE, ACTION_COPY, or ACTION_LINK/ACTION_REFERENCE.

If your drop target can support more than one type of operation, it normally should use this method to select the operation that the user requested.

DropTargetDropEvent

An instance of `DropTargetDropEvent` is passed to the `drop()` method when a drop occurs. Many of the methods in this class are identical in name and function to those in `DropTargetDragEvent`, so I'll discuss only those that are unique to `DropTargetDropEvent`.

acceptDrop( )

This method is essentially the same as `acceptDrag()` and indicates to the caller which operation is to be performed on the data that's transferred. This method should be called before the data is accessed using `getTransferable()`, or that call may fail.

rejectDrop( )

You should call this method if your drop target can't perform the requested operation.

getTransferable( )

This method can be called to retrieve a `Transferable` that encapsulates the data that was dropped. Note that it should be called only after your drop target has invoked `acceptDrop()`.

isLocalTransfer( )

Use this method to find out if the drag-and-drop operation has taken place within a single JVM (in other words, when this is a local transfer). It's sometimes important to distinguish local from remote transfers, and I describe the reasons for doing so in detail later in this chapter.

dropComplete( )

Once your drop processing is finished, you should call the `dropComplete()` method to signal the completion of the drop operation. A parameter value of true indicates that the transfer was successful; false indicates it wasn't.

Drag Sessions

Several of the methods in `DropTargetListener` are called as a result of cursor movement, and to accurately determine when they're invoked, it's necessary to identify what we'll call a *drag session*. A drag session begins when the cursor enters the component's display area and ends when it exits the display area or when a drop occurs. In most cases, only one drag session occurs per component in a single drag-and-drop operation. However, the user may choose to repeatedly move the cursor over a component and then away from it for some reason. In general, you won't need to concern yourself with drag sessions, but the concept is relevant to some of the `DropTargetListener` behavior described next.

Rejecting Drags and Drops

When your drop target wants to indicate that it won't accept a drop, it can call `rejectDrag()` from within the `dragEnter()`, `dragOver()`, and `dropActionChanged()` methods. When a drag is rejected, the cursor changes to a no-drop cursor, and if a drop occurs during that drag session, it's ignored (in other words, the `drop()` method isn't called).

Note that a drag rejection is effective only for the current drag session, and if the cursor exits and reenters the component's display area, any previous rejection is effectively canceled. This isn't a problem in most cases, because the same conditions that caused your code to reject the drag in one drag session normally will still exist in another. However, you should realize that rejecting a drag doesn't permanently prevent the drop from completing.

It's also important to know that rejecting a drag doesn't prevent further DropTargetListener notifications. For example, if you reject a drag operation from the dragEnter() method, dragOver() will still be called as the cursor moves over the component, and dragExit() will be called when the cursor exits the component area. As you'll see later, it's even possible to accept a drag after you've rejected a previous one in the same drag session.

Given the choice between rejecting a drop request or rejecting a drag operation and preventing the drop request from occurring, you may be wondering which you should choose. In most cases, it's appropriate to reject the drag operation, because you'll usually know at that time (in other words, before the drop actually occurs) whether you intend to allow the drop to take place. However, sometimes the state of the drop target may change while the drag is taking place, which in turn may affect its ability to accept the drop. In other words, if you can't be certain whether a drop target will accept the drop until it actually occurs, you should accept the drag requests and reject the drop if necessary.

DropTargetListener Methods

Now that you've examined the event objects that are passed to the DropTargetListener methods, you'll see when those methods are called and how you should use them.

dragEnter()

During a drag-and-drop operation, this method is called when the cursor enters the display area of the component associated with the DropTarget. You may want to use this method to initiate drag-under effects for the component, or you may choose to accept or reject the drag operation. ImageViewer uses dragEnter() to reject the drag operation when the data being dragged isn't a list of files.

```
public void dragEnter(DropTargetDragEvent event) {
  if (event.isDataFlavorSupported(
      DataFlavor.javaFileListFlavor)) {
    return;
  }
  event.rejectDrag();
}
```

dragOver()

This method is passed an instance of DropTargetDragEvent and is called when the cursor moves after it has previously entered the display area of the drop component. If you're providing drag-under effects, you may need to update them each time dragOver() is called. However, if you're not providing drag-under effects, you won't need to implement this method, which is the case with the ImageViewer application.

dragExit()

An instance of DropTargetEvent is passed to this method, which is called when the cursor exits the display area of the drop component. If you're providing drag-under effects, you normally should discontinue them when dragExit() is invoked. As with dragOver(), you won't normally implement this method if you're not providing drag-under support.

drop( )

This method is called when a drop occurs, and it's responsible for accepting or rejecting the drop and for processing the dropped data. When a drop takes place over an instance of ImageViewer, for example, the file selections that were dropped must be converted into JLabel instances and added to the container, as shown in Listing 10-3.

Listing 10-3. Handling Drop Operations

```
import java.awt.*;
import java.awt.datatransfer.*;
import java.awt.dnd.*;
import java.io.*;
import javax.swing.*;

public class ImageViewer extends JPanel {

  public static void main(String[] args) {
    JFrame f = new JFrame("ImageViewer");
    f.setDefaultCloseOperation(JFrame.EXIT_ON_CLOSE);
    f.setContentPane(new ImageViewer());
    f.setSize(400, 300);
    f.setVisible(true);
  }

  public ImageViewer() {
    super();
    setLayout(null);
    DropTarget dt = new DropTarget(this,
        DnDConstants.ACTION_COPY_OR_MOVE,
        new MyDropListener());
  }

  private JLabel getLabelFromFile(File f) {
    ImageIcon icon = new ImageIcon(f.getAbsolutePath());
    JLabel label = new JLabel(icon);
    label.setText(f.getName());
    label.setHorizontalTextPosition(JLabel.CENTER);
    label.setVerticalTextPosition(JLabel.BOTTOM);
    return label;
  }

  private void addNewComponent(Component comp, Point location) {
    comp.setLocation(location);
    comp.setSize(comp.getPreferredSize());
    add(comp);
    repaint();
  }
```

```
class MyDropListener implements DropTargetListener {

  public void dragEnter(DropTargetDragEvent event) {
    if (event.isDataFlavorSupported(
        DataFlavor.javaFileListFlavor)) {
      return;
    }
    event.rejectDrag();
  }

  public void dragExit(DropTargetEvent event) {
  }

  public void dragOver(DropTargetDragEvent event) {
  }

  public void dropActionChanged(DropTargetDragEvent event) {
  }

  public void drop(DropTargetDropEvent event) {
    if (event.isDataFlavorSupported(
        DataFlavor.javaFileListFlavor)) try {
      event.acceptDrop(DnDConstants.ACTION_COPY);
      Transferable t = event.getTransferable();
      java.util.List list = (java.util.List)(
          t.getTransferData(
          DataFlavor.javaFileListFlavor));
      java.util.Iterator i = list.iterator();
      while (i.hasNext()) {
        JLabel label = getLabelFromFile(
            (File)(i.next()));
        addNewComponent(label, event.getLocation());
      }
      event.dropComplete(true);
    } catch (Exception e) {
      event.dropComplete(false);
    }
  }

}

}
```

The first action this drop() implementation takes is to determine whether javaFileListFlavor can be used to retrieve the data. That test isn't really needed because a similar test was already performed in dragEnter(), and drop() won't be called if the drag was rejected. However, I'll leave the code in place because I'll later show how to modify ImageViewer to accept an additional DataFlavor. When you make that change, the drop() method must distinguish between the two flavors so that it can handle each of them differently.

After the data type has been verified, acceptDrop() is called and is passed the type of operation to be performed. As you may recall, the drop target is able to support both move and copy (ACTION_COPY_OR_MOVE) operations, but a single operation should be specified when calling acceptDrop(). In many cases, the copy and move operations are handled the same way by a drop target, but it's still important to select the appropriate operation. That's because the drag source is notified of which operation was selected, and the drag source processing often varies based on that selection.

After accepting the drop operation, the method shown in Listing 10-3 retrieves the Transferable data, extracts the file list from it, creates a JLabel for each file, and adds the labels to the container. Once the data has been successfully retrieved and processed, dropComplete() is called and is passed a parameter value of true, indicating that the drop was successful.

In addition to identifying the type of operation accepted by the drop target, a drag source is also able to determine whether the drop operation completed successfully. That information is needed so that the drag source can take appropriate action based on the outcome of the drop. For example, if a move operation was requested and the drop was successful, the drag source often must remove the dragged data from its original location.

dropActionChanged( )

Earlier you saw that the type of operation to perform is determined by the status of keyboard and mouse modifier buttons. However, it's possible for the user to change the selected drop action after a drag has been initiated by changing the state of those modifiers. For example, if you begin a copy operation on Windows and then release the Ctrl key while dragging the data, you've effectively changed the requested drop action. When such a change does occur, this method is called to notify the DropTargetListener of the modification. You'll need to implement this method only if your application needs to take some action when the drop action changes, which isn't the case with ImageViewer.

Drop Enabling ImageViewer

You've now created all the code that's necessary to allow ImageViewer to display image files that are dropped on it. If you compile and run this application, you'll be able to drop image file selections onto the window. For example, once this application's user interface appears, you should start Windows Explorer (or a similar application) and use that application to drag GIF and JPEG files and drop them into the frame created by ImageViewer, as shown in Figure 10-2.

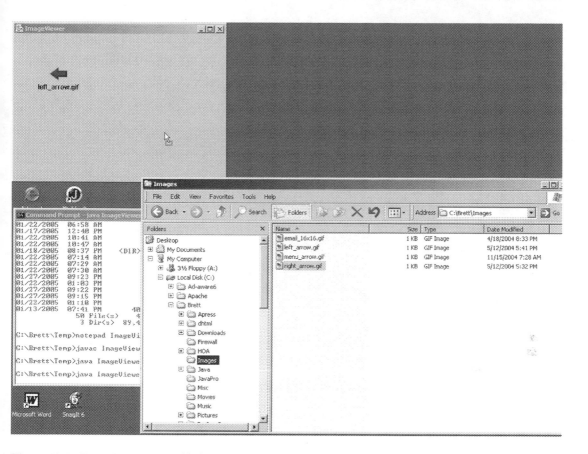

Figure 10-2. *Dragging an image file from a native window and dropping it onto the application to display it*

Adding Drag Support

Now that ImageViewer is able to process file selection drops, we'll see how to add drag support so that it's possible to drag and drop the JLabel objects that were created. Once that's done, it will be possible to move the labels around within a single ImageViewer and to move a label from one instance of ImageViewer to another.

Defining a Transferable

Before data can be dragged, it must be wrapped in a Transferable implementation, just as you did in the previous chapter for cut-and-paste operations. To support the Transferable implementation for JLabel instances, you'll first define a DataFlavor that describes the type of data encapsulated by the Transferable.

```
public class ImageViewer extends JPanel {

    public final static DataFlavor LABEL_FLAVOR =
        new DataFlavor(JLabel.class, "Label Instances");
```

The DataFlavor constructor used here allows you to create flavors that describe serialized Java objects, and this data flavor's MIME type is set to application/x-java-serialized-object accordingly. JLabel instances are serializable because Component (which JLabel inherits from) implements the Serializable interface.

With the DataFlavor defined, you can create a Transferable implementation, which in this case is defined as an inner class of ImageViewer named LabelSelection, as shown in Listing 10-4.

Listing 10-4. LabelSelection

```java
class LabelSelection implements Transferable {

  private DataFlavor[] flavors = {
    LABEL_FLAVOR
  };

  private JLabel label;

  public LabelSelection(JLabel lbl) {
    label = lbl;
  }

  public DataFlavor[] getTransferDataFlavors() {
    return flavors;
  }

  public boolean isDataFlavorSupported(DataFlavor flavor) {
    for (int i = 0; i < flavors.length; i++) {
      if (flavors[i].equals(flavor)) {
        return true;
      }
    }
    return false;
  }

  public Object getTransferData(DataFlavor flavor)
        throws UnsupportedFlavorException, IOException {
    if (flavor.equals(LABEL_FLAVOR)) {
      return label;
    }
    throw new UnsupportedFlavorException(flavor);
  }

}
```

Now that you've created a Transferable that encapsulates a JLabel, you can write the code that initiates a drag operation.

Obtaining a Drag Source

Earlier you saw that an instance of DropTarget is created for each component that should be able to receive drops. In contrast, an application normally has only one drag source. That's because although many drop targets can exist simultaneously, only one drag operation can be in progress at any given time since you have only one mouse with which to control an operation.

As you might expect, a drag source in Java is represented by an instance of the DragSource class, and a singleton instance of that class is accessible through the static getDefaultDragSource() method.

```
DragSource source = DragSource.getDefaultDragSource();
```

As you'll see, DragSource and DropTarget have many similarities, and one of those similarities is that, like DropTarget, a DragSource can support a listener.

In the case of ImageViewer, you want to be able to drag each JLabel that's added to the container. To accomplish this, you'll first modify the addNewComponent() method so that the default drag source is accessed each time a JLabel is added.

```
private void addNewComponent(Component comp, Point location) {
    DragSource source = DragSource.getDefaultDragSource();
    comp.setLocation(location);
    comp.setSize(comp.getPreferredSize());
    add(comp);
    repaint();
}
```

At this point, it may not be obvious what to do with the DragSource. No DragSource constructor exists to which you can pass a reference to the label being added, and an addDragSourceListener() method isn't available. Instead, your application should register a listener indirectly by creating a DragGestureRecognizer.

Drag Gesture Recognizers

The gestures used to initiate drag-and-drop operations can vary from one operating system to the next. For example, a move operation is initiated on Windows by clicking and then dragging the cursor. However, other operating systems may use different key/button combinations to initiate the same operation.

Ideally, a Java application should be able to recognize the gestures that are appropriate for the platform on which it's running, but at the same time, an application shouldn't contain code that's specific to any one platform. DragGestureRecognizer allows you to satisfy both requirements by providing a level of abstraction between your application and the recognition of gestures that should initiate a drag-and-drop operation.

Just as you create a DropTarget for each component that can accept drops, it's necessary to create a DragGestureRecognizer for each component that can be used to initiate a drag. The parameters passed to the DragGestureRecognizer constructor are similar to those passed to a DropTarget: a Component instance, the operations supported, and a listener. In this case, however, the listener is an implementation of DragGestureListener.

```
private void addNewComponent(Component comp, Point location) {
    DragSource source = DragSource.getDefaultDragSource();
    source.createDefaultDragGestureRecognizer(comp,
        DnDConstants.ACTION_COPY_OR_MOVE,
        new MyGestureListener());
```

```
    comp.setLocation(location);
    comp.setSize(comp.getPreferredSize());
    add(comp);
    repaint();
}

class MyGestureListener implements DragGestureListener {

    public void dragGestureRecognized(DragGestureEvent event) {}

}
```

Although you can create your own DragGestureRecognizer class, you'll rarely have a reason to do so. Instead, you'll normally obtain an instance of the default DragGestureRecognizer class that's provided by the singleton DragSource. When you do so, the DragGestureRecognizer registers itself as a listener of the component's events so that it can determine when a drag operation should be started. It accomplishes this by monitoring the component events, and when it detects that the user has taken the appropriate action(s) to begin dragging, it sends a notification to the DragGestureListener by calling its dragGestureRecognized() method.

DragGestureListener

The DragGestureListener interface defines a single method that's called when a DragGestureRecognizer determines that a drag operation has been requested.

dragGestureRecognized()

This method is called when a DragGestureRecognizer determines that the user has requested a drag operation using the standard gestures for the current platform. It's the responsibility of dragGestureRecognized() to initiate the drag operation once it has determined that the drag should be allowed to take place.

Many times, such as in the ImageViewer application, the drag can be allowed to start unconditionally when dragGestureRecognized() is called. However, if the drag component is a more sophisticated control such as a JTable or JTree, you may want to be more selective. In the case of a JTree, you might allow the user to drag nodes around within the tree but allow only certain nodes to be dragged (e.g., only leaf nodes). In that case, you might ignore gestures that occur over nodes that can't be dragged, or you may display an error message when the user attempts to drag an ineligible node.

DragGestureEvent

Among other things, an instance of DragGestureEvent describes the events that were detected by the DragGestureRecognizer. A number of methods within DragGestureEvent allow you to access the InputEvent objects that describe those events, although there's almost never a reason for you to do so. In fact, if you create code that's dependent upon platform-specific event information, you'll have defeated the purpose of using a DragGestureRecognizer.

In many cases, the only method you'll use in DragGestureEvent is startDrag(). However, some other methods can be helpful, and I'll cover each of them briefly.

getComponent()

This method returns a reference to the component associated with the DragGestureRecognizer. In the case of ImageViewer, this is an instance of JLabel.

getDragAction()

The specific operation type requested (move, copy, or link/reference) is returned by this method. It's represented as an int value and will be one of the following: ACTION_MOVE, ACTION_COPY, or ACTION_LINK (which is equivalent to ACTION_REFERENCE).

getDragOrigin()

You can use this method to determine where the cursor was located when the drag was started. It returns an instance of java.awt.Point that identifies the cursor's position relative to the component origin (in other words, coordinates 0, 0).

getDragSource()

This returns a reference to the DragSource that created the DragGestureRecognizer.

getSourceAsDragGestureRecognizer()

This method returns a reference to the DragGestureRecognizer.

startDrag()

In many cases, startDrag() is the only method you'll call from your dragGestureRecognized() implementation, and as its name implies, it initiates the drag operation. The parameters you can specify when calling startDrag() are as follows:

- The initial Cursor to display during the operation.

- An image used to visually represent the data while it's being dragged. Some operating systems (including Windows) don't support drag images and will ignore this parameter value. To determine whether drag image support is available, your application can call the static isDragImageSupported() method in DragSource.

- The location (represented by an instance of java.awt.Point) relative to the cursor's "hotspot" where the drag image will be displayed if it's supported.

- A Transferable that encapsulates the data to be moved, copied, or linked.

- An instance of a DragSourceListener implementation that's used to track the progress of the operation and to perform tasks that are the responsibility of the initiator of the operation.

The startDrag() method has two implementations, one of which accepts all five of the parameters just described. However, you'll use the simpler version that allows the drag image and coordinate parameters to be omitted. Listing 10-5 is a partial listing of the modified ImageViewer class.

Listing 10-5. Modified ImageViewer Class (Partial Listing)

```
public class ImageViewer extends JPanel {

  public final static DataFlavor LABEL_FLAVOR =
      new DataFlavor(JLabel.class, "Label Instances");

  private DragSourceListener sourceListener;
  private JLabel draggedComponent;

  public static void main(String[] args) {
    JFrame f = new JFrame("ImageViewer");
    f.setDefaultCloseOperation(JFrame.EXIT_ON_CLOSE);
    f.setContentPane(new ImageViewer());
    f.setSize(400, 300);
    f.setVisible(true);
  }

  public ImageViewer() {
    super();
    setLayout(null);
    DropTarget dt = new DropTarget(this,
        DnDConstants.ACTION_COPY_OR_MOVE,
        new MyDropListener());
    sourceListener = new MySourceListener();
  }

  private JLabel getLabelFromFile(File f) {
    ImageIcon icon = new ImageIcon(f.getAbsolutePath());
    JLabel label = new JLabel(icon);
    label.setText(f.getName());
    label.setHorizontalTextPosition(JLabel.CENTER);
    label.setVerticalTextPosition(JLabel.BOTTOM);
    return label;
  }

  private void addNewComponent(Component comp, Point location) {
    DragSource source = DragSource.getDefaultDragSource();
    source.createDefaultDragGestureRecognizer(comp,
        DnDConstants.ACTION_COPY_OR_MOVE,
        new MyGestureListener());
    comp.setLocation(location);
    comp.setSize(comp.getPreferredSize());
    add(comp);
    repaint();
  }

class MyGestureListener implements DragGestureListener {

  public void dragGestureRecognized(DragGestureEvent event) {
    Cursor cursor = null;
    draggedComponent = (JLabel)(event.getComponent());
```

```
    switch (event.getDragAction()) {
      case DnDConstants.ACTION_MOVE:
        cursor = DragSource.DefaultMoveDrop;
        break;
      case DnDConstants.ACTION_COPY:
        cursor = DragSource.DefaultCopyDrop;
        break;
      case DnDConstants.ACTION_LINK:
        cursor = DragSource.DefaultLinkDrop;
        break;
    }
    event.startDrag(cursor,
        new LabelSelection(draggedComponent),
        sourceListener);
  }
}

class MySourceListener implements DragSourceListener {

  public void dragEnter(DragSourceDragEvent event) {};
  public void dragExit(DragSourceEvent event) {};
  public void dragOver(DragSourceDragEvent event) {};
  public void dropActionChanged(DragSourceDragEvent event) {};
  public void dragDropEnd(DragSourceDropEvent event) {};
}
```

The dragGestureRecognized() method defined here selects an appropriate cursor based on the operation type. The cursor types defined here have "no-drop" counterparts that you can use instead if you want to indicate that a drop is not allowed to occur over the source component, which is often the case.

The second parameter passed to startDrag() in Listing 10-5 is an instance of the LabelSelection class that was defined earlier. That class implements Transferable and maintains a reference to the JLabel that will be dragged.

Finally, startDrag() is passed as a reference to a DragSourceListener that can be used to track the drag operation. In most cases, it's possible to use a single DragSourceListener for all the DragGestureRecognizers since only a single drag-and-drop operation can be in progress at any given time. Note that in this case we provided an implementation for each of the methods defined in DragSourceListener. A better option—and one that we'll use in the remainder of the chapter—is to extend DragSourceAdapter and implement only the methods where some custom logic is needed. That adapter class, like the others defined in Swing, is provided as a convenience and includes "stub" implementations of each of the methods defined in the interface. Those implementations are essentially just empty methods and the sole purpose of the adapter class is to allow you to create simpler implementations of the interface.

You've now done everything that's necessary to begin the drag operation. At this point, all that's left is to handle the drop, and most of the code necessary to do so is similar to code you've already written. In fact, simply add another block of code, shown in Listing 10-6, to the existing drop() method so that it can process Transferable instances that encapsulate labels.

Listing 10-6. Handling the Drop Operation

```
public void drop(DropTargetDropEvent event) {
  if (event.isDataFlavorSupported(DataFlavor.javaFileListFlavor)) {
    try {
      event.acceptDrop(DnDConstants.ACTION_COPY);
      Transferable t = event.getTransferable();
      java.util.List list = (java.util.List)
            (t.getTransferData(DataFlavor.javaFileListFlavor));
      java.util.Iterator i = list.iterator();
      while (i.hasNext()) {
        JLabel label = getLabelFromFile((File)(i.next()));
        addNewComponent(label, event.getLocation());
      }
      event.dropComplete(true);
    } catch (Exception e) {
      event.dropComplete(false);
    }
  } else if (event.isDataFlavorSupported(LABEL_FLAVOR)) {
    try {
      event.acceptDrop(DnDConstants.ACTION_MOVE);
      Transferable t = event.getTransferable();
      JLabel label = (JLabel)(t.getTransferData(LABEL_FLAVOR));
      addNewComponent(label, event.getLocation());
      event.dropComplete(true);
    } catch (Exception e) {
      event.dropComplete(false);
    }
  }
}
```

As you may recall, the original implementation of MyDropListener's dragEnter() method rejects drags when the data can't be accessed using javaFileListFlavor. However, since you now also provide support for LABEL_FLAVOR, you should modify the dragEnter() method to allow that flavor as well.

```
class MyDropListener implements DropTargetListener {

  public void dragEnter(DropTargetDragEvent event) {
    if ((event.isDataFlavorSupported(
      DataFlavor.javaFileListFlavor)) ||
      (event.isDataFlavorSupported(
      LABEL_FLAVOR))) {
      return;
    }
    event.rejectDrag();
  }
}
```

At this point, ImageViewer supports both drag-and-drop operations; however, if you execute the application in its current state, you'll see that something is still missing. Each time you drag and drop a JLabel, the original remains intact, and a duplicate of it appears at the drop location, as shown in Figure 10-3.

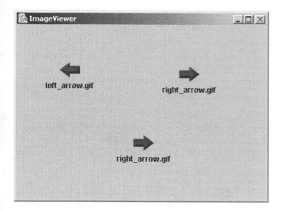

Figure 10-3. *Incomplete drag-and-drop implementation*

This occurs despite the fact that the move operation is selected by the drop target. To understand why this happens, it's necessary to understand why the object serialization facility is used to transfer Java objects.

An object reference is meaningful only within the JVM in which it exists, so an object can't really be moved when data is dragged from one JVM instance and dropped onto another. However, it's possible to create a copy of an object by sending a representation of it to the target JVM, which can then create a duplicate. That's exactly what Java's object serialization provides and is the reason why it's necessary for the drag source to delete the original JLabel. Serialized objects are never really moved but are copied, so to simulate a move in a drag-and-drop operation, the original object must be deleted after its copy is created.

Later you'll see how you can transfer an object reference when a drag-and-drop operation occurs within a single JVM instance. However, any time you use a DataFlavor with a MIME type of application/x-java-serialized-object, your drop target receives a copy of the original object instead of a reference to it.

We've now established why the drag source in ImageViewer must delete the original label after it's dropped, but you haven't yet implemented any code to do so. To identify the appropriate place for that logic, it's necessary to be familiar with the DragSourceListener interface, its methods, and the event objects passed to those methods.

DragSourceListener

The drag source has two primary responsibilities: removing the source data from its previous location in a move operation and providing drag-over effects. As you may recall, drag-under effects are provided by the drop target and are used to modify the appearance of the drop component. In contrast, *drag-over effects* are related to the cursor's appearance and are provided by the drag source. For example, when a drag occurs over a component that can't accept a drop, the drag source is responsible for displaying a no-drop cursor.

You won't normally find it necessary to provide drag-over effects because in most cases the appropriate cursor appears automatically. If you move the cursor over a component that's not able to accept the drop or if a drag is rejected, a no-drop cursor appears. However, sometimes you may want to customize the appearance of the cursor so that it's different from what's displayed by default.

To change the cursor, you must obtain a reference to the DragSourceContext using the getDragSourceContext() defined in DragSourceEvent and inherited by its subclasses. Once you have a DragSourceContext reference, you can call the setCursor() method as follows:

```
public void dragOver(DragSourceDragEvent event) {
  // Normally some condition logic would go here
  DragSourceContext dsc = event.getDragSourceContext();
  dsc.setCursor(DragSource.DefaultCopyNoDrop);
}
```

Now that you've seen what the `DragSourceListener` interface is responsible for, you'll examine each of the methods it defines.

dragEnter()

This method is called when the cursor enters the display area of a drop component, and you may remember that a method by this same name is defined in the `DropTargetListener` interface. When the cursor enters a drop component's display area, the drop target's `dragEnter()` method is called first, followed by that of the drag source. However, that latter call occurs only if the first drop target's `dragEnter()` method doesn't reject the drag operation.

dragOver()

This method is called when the cursor is moved after it has previously entered the drop component's display area. A method by the same name is defined in `DropTargetListener`, and this one is called only after that one has executed. In other words, `dragOver()` is first called for the drop target and then called for the drag source. However, if the drop target rejects the operation, the drag source's method isn't called.

dragExit()

This method is called when the cursor exits the display area of a drop component.

dropActionChanged()

A call to `dropActionChanged()` indicates that the status of a modifier used to select the drop action (e.g., the Ctrl or Shift key) has changed. A method with the same name as this one is defined in `DropTargetListener`, and this one is called only after that one has executed. In other words, `dropActionChanged()` is first called for the drop target and then called for the drag source. However, if the drop target rejects the operation, the drag source's method isn't called.

dragDropEnd()

After a drop has occurred and the `DropTargetListener`'s `drop()` method is invoked, `dragDropEnd()` is called to notify the drag source that the drop has completed. As you'll see shortly, the event object passed to this method allows it to determine the type of operation selected by the drop target and to determine the value specified when the drop target called `dropComplete()`. In other words, this method can determine whether the drop completed successfully.

Since this method is called once the drop has completed and because it allows you to determine the final status of the operation, you should use `dragDropEnd()` to perform the `DragSourceListener`'s cleanup-related tasks.

Event Objects Passed to DragSourceListener Methods

Now that you've learned about the methods defined by DragSourceListener, it's appropriate to examine the event objects passed to those methods.

DragSourceEvent

This is the superclass of the DragSourceDragEvent and DragSourceDropEvent classes defined next. However, DragSourceEvent doesn't provide any methods you'll use.

DragSourceDragEvent

An instance of DragSourceDragEvent class is passed to the dragEnter(), dragOver(), and dropActionChanged() methods. Unlike a drop target, a drag source can't accept or reject a drag, so the methods provided by this event object are purely informational.

getTargetActions( )

This method identifies the intersection of the actions supported by the drag source and those supported by the drop target. For example, suppose that the drag source supports move, copy, and link operations, but the drop target supports only move and link. In that case, the value returned by getTargetActions() would equal the combined values of the ACTION_MOVE and ACTION_LINK constants. In other words, this method identifies the operations that both the drag source and the drop target support.

getUserAction( )

The operation requested by the user is identified by this method and is based on the current state of the modifier keys and buttons.

getDropAction( )

This identifies the effective drop action, which is defined as the intersection of the target actions and the current user action. If the user has selected an action that the drag source or the drop target doesn't support, this value will be equal to the ACTION_NONE constant defined in DnDConstants.

getGestureModifiers( )

You can use this method to determine the state of the modifiers that determine the type of operation requested. For example, this value identifies the state of the mouse buttons and the Shift, Alt, and Ctrl keys. For more information on how to interpret the value returned by this method, see the modifier constants defined in java.awt.event.InputEvent.

DragSourceDropEvent

An instance of this class is passed to dragDropEnd(), which is called after the drop has been processed by the drop target.

getDropAction( )

You can use this method to determine which operation the drop target selected. In other words, this identifies the action specified when the DropTargetListener's drop() method called acceptDrop().

You'll normally use this value to determine what action your DragSourceListener should take. If a move operation was selected, the data that was dropped usually must be removed from its original location by the drag source.

getDropSuccess()

While the getDropAction() method identifies the action selected by the drop target, this method provides an indication of the value specified by the target when dropComplete() was called. In other words, this method returns a value of true if the drop completed successfully or false otherwise.

Drag Source Handling of Drop Completion

Now that we've reviewed the events and methods associated with DragSourceListener, it should be obvious how to fix the problem with ImageViewer that was identified earlier. When a JLabel is moved, the drag source is responsible for removing the label from its original location, and that should be done in the dragDropEnd() method.

Listing 10-7 highlights the modifications to dragDropEnd(). Note that most of the cleanup performed in that method depends upon both the successful completion of the drop and the type of operation selected by the drop target. If the target selects an operation other than ACTION_MOVE, the original JLabel component won't be removed. Also note that as mentioned earlier this implementation extends DragSourceAdapter instead of simply implementing DragSourceListener and creating an implementation for every one of its methods.

Listing 10-7. Updating the dragDropEnd() Method

```
class MySourceListener extends DragSourceAdapter {

  public void dragDropEnd(DragSourceDropEvent event) {
    if ((event.getDropSuccess())
            && (event.getDropAction() == DnDConstants.ACTION_MOVE)) {
      remove(draggedComponent);
      repaint();
    }
    draggedComponent = null;
  }
}
```

Performing Local Transfers

When dragging and dropping Java objects, as ImageViewer now allows you to do, you'll encounter two categories of transfer operations. In a local transfer, the drag source and drop target (and the data transferred) reside in a single JVM instance, while a remote transfer involves moving data from one JVM instance to a different one.

The DataFlavor used by ImageViewer has a representation class of JLabel, and its MIME type defaults to application/x-java-serialized-object. As mentioned earlier, using that MIME type always results in the drop target receiving a copy of the original object instead of a reference to it, even in a local transfer. However, it's sometimes desirable in local transfers to pass a reference to the original data instead of a copy. For example, you might want to do so if the data can't be serialized or if you want to improve the performance of local transfers, since serialization can be relatively slow. To illustrate how to pass object references, you'll now see how to modify ImageViewer to do so when a local transfer takes place.

Introducing Local Object Data Flavors

To perform reference transfers, you must define a DataFlavor that has a representation class corresponding to the type of object to be transferred, which in this case is JLabel. In addition, the flavor's MIME type should be set to the javaJVMLocalObjectMimeType string constant defined in DataFlavor. However, it may not be immediately obvious how to create a flavor that fulfills these two requirements.

You saw earlier that DataFlavor provides two types of constructors: one that allows you to specify the flavor's MIME type and another that allows you to identify its representation class. In this case, you want to specify both items, but there doesn't appear to be a constructor that allows you to do so. In addition, there are no mutator methods for either the MIME type or the representation class, so it's not possible to modify those values after construction.

In fact, it's possible to specify both values using the DataFlavor constructor that accepts a MIME type String. You can do this by specifying the representation class as a parameter that's appended to the MIME type, as follows:

```
public class ImageViewer extends JPanel {

  public final static DataFlavor LABEL_FLAVOR =
      new DataFlavor(JLabel.class, "Label Instances");

  public final static DataFlavor LOCAL_LABEL_FLAVOR = new DataFlavor(
      DataFlavor.javaJVMLocalObjectMimeType +
      "; class=javax.swing.JLabel", "Local Label");
```

The LOCAL_LABEL_FLAVOR will be created with a MIME type of application/x-java-jvm-local-objectref (the value stored in javaJVMLocalObjectMimeType), a representation class of JLabel, and a human-readable name of "Local Label."

Since this new DataFlavor will be used with LabelSelection to transfer JLabel references, it's necessary to update LabelSelection appropriately. In addition to adding LOCAL_LABEL_FLAVOR to the list of flavors supported by LabelSelection, you must create a block of code in getTransferData(), as shown in Listing 10-8.

Listing 10-8. Supporting the Local Label Flavor

```
class LabelSelection implements Transferable {

  private DataFlavor[] flavors = {LABEL_FLAVOR, LOCAL_LABEL_FLAVOR};

  private JLabel label;

  public LabelSelection(JLabel lbl) {
    label = lbl;
  }

  public DataFlavor[] getTransferDataFlavors() {
    return flavors;
  }

  public boolean isDataFlavorSupported(DataFlavor flavor) {
    for (int i = 0; i < flavors.length; i++) {
      if (flavors[i].equals(flavor)) return true;
    }
    return false;
  }
```

```
  public Object getTransferData(DataFlavor flavor) throws
      UnsupportedFlavorException, IOException {
    if (flavor.equals(LABEL_FLAVOR)) {
      return label;
    }
    else if (flavor.equals(LOCAL_LABEL_FLAVOR)) {
      return label;
    }
    throw new UnsupportedFlavorException(flavor);
  }

}
```

It may seem strange that the code in getTransferData() is the same for LABEL_FLAVOR and LOCAL_
LABEL_FLAVOR. After all, LABEL_FLAVOR is used to retrieve a serialized copy of the object, while LOCAL_
LABEL_FLAVOR is intended to provide a reference to the original object. The reason that this code will work
as expected is that Java's drag-and-drop facility treats the application/x-java-serialized-object MIME
type used by LABEL_FLAVOR as a special case. When data is retrieved using that type, the drag-and-drop
facility ensures that a serialized copy of the object is returned, even in a local transfer. In other words, if you
use application/x-java-serialized-object, you always get a copy of the data and never a reference to
the original when calling getTransferData(). In contrast, when other MIME types are used (e.g., LOCAL_
LABEL_FLAVOR), no special processing occurs, and getTransferData() is allowed to return a reference to the
original object.

Handling the Reference Transfer

Now that we've defined a DataFlavor for transferring object references and added support for it to the
Transferable implementation, it's easy to modify ImageViewer to support reference transfers. All that's needed
is a change to the drop() method so that it uses the new LOCAL_LABEL_FLAVOR when possible (see Listing 10-9).

Listing 10-9. Reference Transfer Support

```
public void drop(DropTargetDropEvent event) {
  if (event.isDataFlavorSupported(DataFlavor.javaFileListFlavor)) {
    try {
      event.acceptDrop(DnDConstants.ACTION_COPY);
      Transferable t = event.getTransferable();
      java.util.List list = (java.util.List)
            (t.getTransferData(DataFlavor.javaFileListFlavor));
      java.util.Iterator i = list.iterator();
      while (i.hasNext()) {
        JLabel label = getLabelFromFile((File)(i.next()));
        addNewComponent(label, event.getLocation());
      }
      event.dropComplete(true);
    } catch (Exception e) {
      event.dropComplete(false);
    }
  } else if (event.isDataFlavorSupported(LABEL_FLAVOR)) {
    try {
      event.acceptDrop(DnDConstants.ACTION_MOVE);
```

```
      Transferable t = event.getTransferable();
      boolean doLocal = (event.isLocalTransfer() &&
          (t.isDataFlavorSupported(LOCAL_LABEL_FLAVOR)));
      DataFlavor flavor = (doLocal ? LOCAL_LABEL_FLAVOR : LABEL_FLAVOR);
      JLabel label = (JLabel)(t.getTransferData(flavor));
      addNewComponent(label, event.getLocation());
      event.dropComplete(true);
    } catch (Exception e) {
      event.dropComplete(false);
    }
  }
}
```

You've now made several changes to ImageViewer that should allow it to correctly process reference transfers. However, if you run the application and try to drag and drop JLabel instances within a single ImageViewer application, you may be surprised by the results. Instead of moving to the drop location, the labels disappear from the panel when they're dropped.

You may recall that the DropTargetListener's drop() method is called when the drop occurs, and that method adds the label that's dropped to the ImageViewer container. Once drop() has executed, the DragSourceListener's dragDropEnd() method is called to allow the drag source to remove the original data, as follows:

```
public void dragDropEnd(DragSourceDropEvent event) {
  if ((event.getDropSuccess()) &&
      (event.getDropAction() ==
      DnDConstants.ACTION_MOVE)) {
    remove(draggedComponent);
    repaint();
  }
  draggedComponent = null;
}
```

In this case, the drop target adds the dropped label to its new container, and the drag source removes it from its old container. In a local transfer using ImageViewer, the "old" and "new" containers are actually the same object, but that fact isn't relevant to the problem. What is important, however, is the order in which the drag source and drop target processing takes place.

Since drop() is called before dragDropEnd(), the component is added to its new container before being removed from the old one. When it's added, logic in the java.awt.Container class causes the label to be removed from its old container, which is done to ensure that a Component can only ever reside within a single parent container at any given time. After drop() completes, dragDropEnd() is called and, being unaware that the label was already removed from its old container, proceeds to remove the component from its container. The result of this second removal is the effective deletion of the label, since no more references to it exist.

It might seem that one way to address this problem is to have the drag source determine the type of transfer (local or remote) and handle the drop differently for each type. For example, the drag source could be designed so that it doesn't remove the JLabel from its parent container when a local transfer takes place. Unfortunately, the DragSourceDropEvent object passed to dragDropEnd() provides just two items of information: the type of operation selected by the drop target and an indication of the success or failure of the transfer. Therefore, a drag source can't distinguish local transfers from remote transfers.

On the other hand, the drop target can distinguish between local and remote transfers, and that capability provides a solution to this problem. Since the drag source removes only the label from its old container when a move occurs, you can address the problem by changing the drop target so that it selects an operation other than move.

Performing Link/Reference Operations

It has been mentioned that Java's drag-and-drop support defines a link or reference operation in addition to move and copy. However, the purpose of the link/reference operation may not be obvious, since there's no consistent meaning associated with the terms *link* or *reference*. Although *move* and *copy* mean the same thing on all platforms, Windows may define a *reference* operation that's completely different from the Solaris *reference* operation.

Since the meaning of the reference operation is vague, you shouldn't use it to drag and drop data between Java and native applications; however, when transferring data between Java applications, the link/reference operation has been assigned a specific meaning. In the context of a local transfer, the reference operation is used to transfer a reference to some object, just as ImageViewer is now capable of doing. Similarly, when you're performing remote transfers between Java applications, the data that's transferred should be some representation of the original object but not a copy of it. For example, you might pass a reference to a remote object defined using Java's Remote Method Invocation (RMI) facilities if the data that's being dragged represents some remote resource.

Given this definition of the reference operation, you can make a small change to ImageViewer that accomplishes two things. First, it correctly identifies a local transfer within ImageViewer as a reference operation instead of a move. Second, it prevents the drag source from incorrectly deleting the component that's dragged in a local transfer, as shown in Listing 10-10.

Listing 10-10. Handling Local Transfers

```
public void drop(DropTargetDropEvent event) {
  if (event.isDataFlavorSupported(DataFlavor.javaFileListFlavor)) {
    try {
      event.acceptDrop(DnDConstants.ACTION_COPY);
      Transferable t = event.getTransferable();
      java.util.List list = (java.util.List)
              (t.getTransferData(DataFlavor.javaFileListFlavor));
      java.util.Iterator i = list.iterator();
      while (i.hasNext()) {
        JLabel label = getLabelFromFile((File)(i.next()));
        addNewComponent(label, event.getLocation());
      }
      event.dropComplete(true);
    } catch (Exception e) {
      event.dropComplete(false);
    }
  } else if (event.isDataFlavorSupported(LABEL_FLAVOR)) {
    try {
      int operation = (event.isLocalTransfer()
                        ? DnDConstants.ACTION_REFERENCE
                        : DnDConstants.ACTION_MOVE);
      event.acceptDrop(operation);
      Transferable t = event.getTransferable();
      boolean doLocal = (event.isLocalTransfer() &&
          (t.isDataFlavorSupported(LOCAL_LABEL_FLAVOR)));
      DataFlavor flavor = (doLocal ? LOCAL_LABEL_FLAVOR : LABEL_FLAVOR);
      JLabel label = (JLabel)(t.getTransferData(flavor));
```

```
        addNewComponent(label, event.getLocation());
        event.dropComplete(true);
      } catch (Exception e) {
        event.dropComplete(false);
      }
    }
  }
}
```

Local transfers have other implications that you must consider as well, including how to support the copy operation. That operation is easy to support in a remote transfer because the drop target always receives a copy of the data, but for local transfers, you need some way to create a copy of the data that's dropped. Some classes simplify this for you by overriding the clone() method defined in java.lang.Object, but many (including JLabel) don't.

Transferring Between Java and Native Applications

You've already seen that it's possible to drop file selections made from a native application into a Java application. Those selections are represented by a Transferable that returns an instance of java.util. List, and that list contains java.io.File objects that identify the files selected. In reality, of course, the native platform doesn't use any Java classes when it allows users to make file selections. However, Java's drag-and-drop facility automatically converts the native type (e.g., CF_HDROP on Windows) into a form that your Java application can use easily, just as the clipboard facility does with text data.

In some cases, you may want to transfer data between a Java application and a native application in a format that isn't converted automatically (e.g., image data). However, for your application to perform some sort of processing of data dropped from a native application, it usually must convert the information into a more convenient format. For example, if Device Independent Bitmap (DIB) data is dragged from a native Windows application and dropped onto your Java program, you'll probably want to convert the information to a more usable format such as an instance of java.awt.Image. Similarly, when dragging data from a Java application and dropping onto a native application, it's necessary to provide the information in a format that the native program can process (e.g., DIB). In Chapter 9, an application was created that could convert pixel data from an instance of Image into a JPEG-compatible byte string using a codec that's provided with the Java 2D API.

Once you're able to perform data conversions, you must complete one other task before you can drag and drop that type of data between Java and native applications. Specifically, you must define the mapping between the MIME type you'll use and the corresponding platform-specific data type; you define the mapping by adding an entry to the flavormap.properties file. That file is located in the /jre/lib/ subdirectory of your JDK/JRE (Java Development Kit/Java Runtime Environment) installation.

If you edit the file, you'll see entries for some of the data types that can already be transferred between Java and native applications, such as file selections (HDROP on Windows) and text. The format for entries in flavormap.properties is as follows:

```
NATIVE=MIME Type
```

NATIVE is the name of the native data type you intend to use (e.g., HDROP), and MIME Type is the MIME type that a compatible DataFlavor encapsulates. For example, to add an entry for DIB data, you could specify the following entry:

```
DIB=image/x-win-bmp; class=java.io.InputStream
```

With this entry added to the file, you'll be able to drag and drop DIB information between Java and non-Java applications. When you drop DIB information onto a Java application, it's automatically wrapped in a `Transferable` that returns an `InputStream`, and you can use that stream to read the raw DIB data. To support the dragging of DIB data from a Java application to a Windows program, you must first define a `DataFlavor` that uses the previous MIME type, as in the following example:

```
DataFlavor DIBFlavor = new DataFlavor("image/x-win-bmp", "DIB Data");
```

Note that it's not necessary to identify the representation class as `InputStream`, since the `DataFlavor` constructor used here selects that value by default.

The next step is to create a `Transferable` that supports this flavor by returning an `InputStream` that produces a sequence of bytes conforming to the DIB format. Converting data between the DIB and Java image formats is a nontrivial exercise and is beyond the scope of this book.

The `FlavorMap` interface in `java.awt.datatransfer` defines a mapping between native data types and MIME types. A default map is created using the entries in `flavormap.properties`, and that map is accessible through the `SystemFlavorMap` class. When performing drag-and-drop operations, you can specify the map that should be used to translate data types, but if you don't do so, the default map is used instead.

When you drag `Transferable` data from a Java application and drop it onto a native program, the MIME types that the `Transferable` supports are extracted from its `DataFlavor` list. For each MIME type that has a matching entry in the `FlavorMap`, a corresponding native type is identified to the native application, which uses that information to process the data that's dropped.

A similar conversion takes place when you drag data from a native application and drop it onto a Java program. In that case, Java's drag-and-drop facility wraps the data from the native application in a `Transferable` and provides a `DataFlavor` for each native type corresponding to a MIME type in the `FlavorMap`.

Transferring Text Data

In Chapter 9, on cut-and-paste operations, you saw that text information can be transferred with minimal effort using the clipboard facility and the `StringSelection` class that implements `Transferable`. Unfortunately, dragging and dropping text information is somewhat more complex.

Before exploring the issues involved in the transfer of text information, let's briefly review `StringSelection`. You may recall that it encapsulates a `String` and is able to return the text in one of two flavors, each of which is represented by a constant in `DataFlavor`. The `stringFlavor` constant has a representation class of `java.lang.String`, has a MIME type of `application/x-java-serialized-object`, and represents a serialized `String` object. That flavor can be used to transfer text between only Java applications since a serialized Java object isn't meaningful to a native application.

In contrast, the `plainTextFlavor` was specifically intended to provide the ability to transfer text data between Java and native applications and has a representation class of `java.io.InputStream` and a MIME type of text/plain. In other words, passing this flavor to a `StringSelection`'s `getTransferData()` method should return an `InputStream` that produces a stream of text data.

Transferring Text Between Java and Native Applications

Transferring text data between Java and native applications is more complicated than transfers within Java, mostly because no single character set is used on all platforms, or even by all applications on a single platform. For example, Java applications maintain text information using Unicode, but native applications can and frequently do use other character sets, such as ASCII and ISO 8859-1. Therefore, it's often necessary to perform conversions when transferring text data between Java and native applications.

In Chapter 9, you saw that it's possible to transfer text data between Java and native applications using the clipboard (in other words, cutting and pasting), and it wasn't necessary to perform any sort of character set conversions. In reality, they're performed but are handled automatically and transparently by Java's clipboard facility. In contrast, you're responsible for performing such conversions when transferring text using drag-and-drop operations.

Transferring Text from Java to Native Applications

If you wrap text data in a `StringSelection` and drag it over a native application, the application will probably not accept a drop of that data. That's because most applications can't process either of the two flavors supported by `StringSelection` (in other words, `stringFlavor` and `plainTextFlavor`). It shouldn't be surprising that native applications can't accept `stringFlavor` data, because that flavor represents an instance of a serialized Java object. However, you might expect that `plainTextFlavor` could be used since it has a MIME type of text/plain.

To understand why `plainTextFlavor` can't be used in a Java-to-native transfer of text information, it's necessary to review the definition of that flavor, which is as follows:

```
text/plain; class=java.io.InputStream; charset=unicode
```

As you can see, `plainTextFlavor` represents an `InputStream` that returns a sequence of bytes representing Unicode character data. Unfortunately, this prevents it from being used by programs that can't process Unicode data and is the reason most native applications won't allow you to drop text that's encapsulated in an instance of `StringSelection`.

Note that because it fails when used with `StringSelection` and since it can't be used to transfer data from Java to native applications, the `plainTextFlavor` constant defined in `DataFlavor` is deprecated, so you should avoid using it.

Transferring Text from Native Applications to Java

As mentioned earlier, dragging data from a native program and dropping it onto a Java application causes the data to be wrapped in a generic `Transferable` object. That object will also contain a list of `DataFlavor` instances that were created by mapping native types to MIME types using the entries in a `FlavorMap`.

In the case of text data transfers, the `DataFlavor` will normally have a MIME type of text/plain and includes a parameter that identifies the character set associated with the data. For example:

```
text/plain; charset=ascii
text/plain; charset=iso-8859-1
```

As these definitions imply, the `InputStream` provided by the `Transferable` will produce a stream of bytes representing the text information as it was stored by the native application. For example, in the case of the first definition listed previously, the `InputStream` would return a sequence of ASCII characters. Therefore, if your application needs to process the information as an instance of `String`, the data must first be converted from ASCII to Unicode.

The `DataFlavor` class includes a method that makes it easy for you to perform character set conversions. The `getReaderForText()` method requires that you pass a `Transferable` instance as a parameter, and it returns an appropriate subclass of `java.io.Reader` that will convert the native character data into Unicode.

When handling text data that was dropped from a native application, you can use getReaderForText() to convert the data into a String using code similar to that shown in Listing 10-11.

Listing 10-11. Using getReaderForText()

```java
public void drop(DropTargetDropEvent event) {
  StringBuffer result = new StringBuffer();
  event.acceptDrop(DnDConstants.ACTION_COPY);
  DataFlavor[] flavors = event.getCurrentDataFlavors();
  Transferable t = event.getTransferable();
  try {
    Reader r = flavors[0].getReaderForText(t);
    int nextChar = r.read();
    while (nextChar != -1) {
      result.append((char)nextChar);
      nextChar = r.read();
    }
    event.dropComplete(true);
  } catch (Exception e) {
    event.dropComplete(false);
  }
  System.out.println("String '" + result + "' was dropped");
}
```

Creating a New Transferable for Text Data

As you've seen, StringSelection has some significant limitations when used in drag-and-drop operations. Specifically, it often can't be used to transfer text data from Java to non-Java applications because it can provide the data only as a stream of Unicode characters. In addition, transfers from one Java application to another fail if the recipient attempts to use plainTextFlavor, which StringSelection claims to support.

The easiest way to address these problems is to create a new Transferable that provides the ability to transfer text data but that doesn't have the limitations of StringSelection. The TextSelection class shown in Listing 10-12 fulfills those requirements.

Listing 10-12. TextSelection Source Code

```java
import java.awt.datatransfer.*;
import java.io.*;

public class TextSelection implements Transferable {

  private String text;

  public final static DataFlavor UNICODE_FLAVOR = new DataFlavor(
      "text/plain; charset=unicode; " +
      "class=java.io.InputStream", "Unicode Text");
  public final static DataFlavor LATIN1_FLAVOR = new DataFlavor(
      "text/plain; charset=iso-8859-1; " +
      "class=java.io.InputStream", "Latin-1 Text");
```

```java
  public final static DataFlavor ASCII_FLAVOR = new DataFlavor(
      "text/plain; charset=ascii; " +
      "class=java.io.InputStream", "ASCII Text");

  public static DataFlavor[] SUPPORTED_FLAVORS = {DataFlavor.stringFlavor,
      UNICODE_FLAVOR, LATIN1_FLAVOR, ASCII_FLAVOR};

  public TextSelection(String selection) {
    text = selection;
  }

  public DataFlavor[] getTransferDataFlavors() {
    return SUPPORTED_FLAVORS;
  }

  public boolean isDataFlavorSupported(DataFlavor flavor) {
    for (int i = 0; i < SUPPORTED_FLAVORS.length; i++) {
      if (SUPPORTED_FLAVORS[i].equals(flavor)) return true;
    }
    return false;
  }
  public Object getTransferData(DataFlavor flavor) throws
      IOException, UnsupportedFlavorException {
    if (flavor.equals(DataFlavor.stringFlavor)) {
      return text;
    }
    else if ((flavor.isMimeTypeEqual("text/plain")) &&
        (flavor.getRepresentationClass().equals(
        java.io.InputStream.class))) try {
      String encoding = flavor.getParameter("charset");
      if ((encoding != null) && (encoding.length() > 0)) {
        return new ByteArrayInputStream(
          text.getBytes(encoding));
      }
      return new ByteArrayInputStream(text.getBytes());
    } catch (Exception e) {};
    throw new UnsupportedFlavorException(flavor);
  }

}
```

You can use this class when you want to drag text from a Java application to a native application; to do so, simply encapsulate the String in an instance of TextSelection by passing it to the constructor as follows:

```java
String transferText;
.
.
.
TextSelection ts = new TextSelection(transferText);
```

In other words, you can use this class in the same way you'd use Java's `StringSelection`, but it doesn't have the limitations that exist with that class.

The only part of this class that might require explanation is the `getTransferData()` method, specifically, the code block that returns a `ByteArrayInputStream`. However, it's easy to understand when you know that `getBytes()` provides functionality that's essentially the opposite of what `StringReader` was used for earlier. In other words, while `StringReader` converts native character data to Unicode, `getBytes()` can be used to convert Unicode text into some other format, such as ASCII or ISO-8859-1.

Depending upon the platform and applications you're using, you may find it necessary to include additional `DataFlavor` definitions in `TextSelection` for it to function properly.

Customizing Standard Component Behavior

As mentioned at the beginning of this chapter, drag-and-drop behavior is already built in to the Swing components you'd expect to already have it. For example, you can drag and drop text from and into text components such as `JTextField` and `JTextArea` and likewise files can be dragged from and dropped into `JFileChooser` instances. The reason this support can be built in, though, is because in each case it's intuitively obvious what kind of data can be dropped (e.g., text in the case of a text component), what should happen when that data is dropped (it should be inserted), and how that action affects the component's state (the caret follows the pointer during the drag and the insertion occurs at the caret's location at the time of the drop). In the cases of the `JTable`, `JTree`, and `JList` components, though, it's much less clear how drag and drop—and especially the drop—should behave because those components can support essentially any type of data. In addition, the way that they're used by applications is highly customizable and varies from one application to the next.

As an example of how it's impossible to define one universal set of appropriate drag-and-drop behaviors let's consider the `JList`, which is arguably the simplest of the three component types. A `JList` instance is typically used to represent a read-only list from which zero or more selections can be made. Dragging from such a list seems reasonable, and in fact drag support is already built in, but what about dropping? If drop support is built in, what should be the default behavior as the pointer moves over a list and when the drop occurs? Should the list item under the pointer be selected to indicate that it will be replaced by the drop, or should the space between list items be highlighted to indicate that an insertion will occur upon dropping the source data? As this illustrates, the drag-and-drop behavior that should be provided tends to be very application specific.

Fortunately, the Swing components were designed with this type of customization in mind and by taking advantage of that design you can implement the behavior that's appropriate for your application.

TransferHandler

At the heart of Swing's built-in support for drag-and-drop operations is the `TransferHandler` class that you can use to customize the behavior to meet the needs of your application. `TransferHandler` is defined in the `javax.swing` package and `JComponent` includes the `getTransferHandler()` and `setTransferHandler()` methods that you can use to assign a `TransferHandler` instances to a component, so every Swing component class inherits those methods.

As you'd expect, the Swing components that include predefined drag-and-drop support already have a `TransferHandler` subclass assigned to them upon creation, including the three types that don't automatically provide support for drop operations. You might also expect that to extend the drag-and-drop support for a `JList`, for example, you could simply extend the `JList`-specific implementation of `TransferHandler` and add the appropriate drop support, but unfortunately that's not the case. The `TransferHandler` implementations are defined inside the code associated with a particular look and feel, which is necessary and appropriate because drag-and-drop behavior can vary across look-and-feel implementations. Even if you were willing to tie your customized drag-and-drop behavior to a single specific look and feel, you couldn't do so easily because the TransferHandler subclasses aren't public. In other words, you can't define a CustomListTransferHandler that extends the ListTransferHandler defined by the basic look and feel because that class isn't accessible by your code. Fortunately, defining a custom implementation of TransferHandler isn't difficult and we'll see an example of how it can be done.

Dropping Images on a JTable

To illustrate how to use the TransferHandler class to provide a customized implementation of drop support for a JTable we'll create a simple application that allows files to be dropped on a JTable. For each file that's dropped a row will be appended to the table displaying the location of the file that was dropped and—if the file represents an image format the Java application can process—will also display the dimensions (width and height) of the image the file represents. Figure 10-4 shows an example of how the application's user interface will appear. In this example four files have already been dropped on the table, three of which are image files and one of which is not.

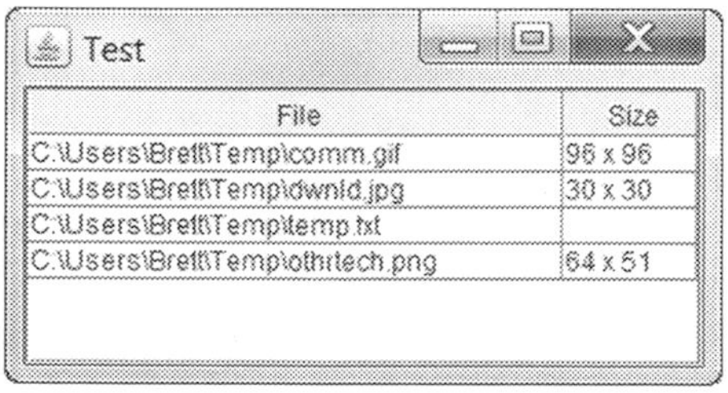

Figure 10-4. *A simple application that allows files to be dropped on a JTable and inserts rows, optionally displaying the dimensions of each image file*

We'll begin by defining a simple Swing application that includes JTable, AbstractTableModel, and DefaultTableCellRenderer subclasses to support the basic user interface as shown in Listing 10-13. It also includes an IconData class that encapsulates a File and, optionally, a Dimension representing the image size if the file does represent an image. Finally, it includes an ImageTableColumn enumeration for encapsulating information about the columns supported by the table.

Listing 10-13. JTable and AbstractTableModel Subclasses That Display File Name and Icon Dimension Columns

```
import java.awt.Component;
import java.awt.Dimension;
import java.io.File;
import java.util.ArrayList;
import java.util.List;

import javax.swing.DropMode;
import javax.swing.ImageIcon;
import javax.swing.JTable;
import javax.swing.ListSelectionModel;
import javax.swing.table.AbstractTableModel;
import javax.swing.table.DefaultTableCellRenderer;
import javax.swing.table.TableColumn;
import javax.swing.table.TableColumnModel;
```

```java
public class ImageTable extends JTable {

  private static final int PREFERRED_WIDTH  = 300;
  private static final int PREFERRED_HEIGHT = 100;

  private static final Dimension PREFERRED_SIZE =
      new Dimension(PREFERRED_WIDTH, PREFERRED_HEIGHT);

  private static final int DIMENSIONS_COLUMN_WIDTH = 60;

  public ImageTable() {
    super(new ImageTableModel());
    initialize();
  }

  private void initialize() {
    setPreferredScrollableViewportSize(PREFERRED_SIZE);
    setDragEnabled(true);
    setDropMode(DropMode.INSERT_ROWS);
    setSelectionMode(ListSelectionModel.SINGLE_SELECTION);
    updateColumnSize();
  }

  private void updateColumnSize() {
    TableColumnModel columns = getColumnModel();
    int dimensionIndex = ImageTableModel.ImageTableColumn.DIMENSIONS.ordinal();
    TableColumn column = columns.getColumn(dimensionIndex);
    column.setMaxWidth(DIMENSIONS_COLUMN_WIDTH);
  }

  @Override
  protected void createDefaultRenderers() {
    super.createDefaultRenderers();
    setDefaultRenderer(Dimension.class, new DimensionRenderer());
  }

  public void addImageIcon(File file, ImageIcon icon) {
    ImageTableModel model = (ImageTableModel)(getModel());
    model.addImageIcon(file, icon);
  }

  static class ImageTableModel extends AbstractTableModel {

    private final List<IconData> iconList = new ArrayList<>();

    public ImageTableModel() {
      super();
    }
```

```java
public void addImageIcon(File file, ImageIcon icon) {
  IconData data = new IconData(file, icon);
  List<IconData> list = getIconList();
  int newRowIndex = list.size();
  list.add(data);
  fireTableRowsInserted(newRowIndex, newRowIndex);
}

@Override
public int getColumnCount() {
  return ImageTableColumn.values().length;
}

@Override
public Class<?> getColumnClass(int columnIndex) {
  ImageTableColumn column = getColumn(columnIndex);
  Class<?> type = column.getColumnClass();
  return type;
}

@Override
public String getColumnName(int columnIndex) {
  ImageTableColumn column = getColumn(columnIndex);
  String name = column.getColumnName();
  return name;
}

@Override
public Object getValueAt(int rowIndex, int columnIndex) {
  Object value;

  IconData data = getIconData(rowIndex);
  ImageTableColumn column = getColumn(columnIndex);
  switch (column) {
    case FILE:
      value = data.getFile();
      break;
    case DIMENSIONS:
      value = data.getIconDimension();
      break;
    default:
      throw new Error("Unsupported column: " + column);
  }

  return value;
}

private ImageTableColumn getColumn(int columnIndex) {
  ImageTableColumn[] columns = ImageTableColumn.values();
  ImageTableColumn column = columns[columnIndex];
  return column;
}
```

```java
  @Override
  public int getRowCount() {
    List<IconData> list = getIconList();
    int count = list.size();
    return count;
  }

  private IconData getIconData(int rowIndex) {
    List<IconData> list = getIconList();
    IconData data = list.get(rowIndex);
    return data;
  }

  private List<IconData> getIconList() {
    return this.iconList;
  }

  enum ImageTableColumn {

    FILE      (File.class      , "File"),
    DIMENSIONS(Dimension.class, "Size"),
    ;

    private final Class<?> columnClass;
    private final String columnName;

    private ImageTableColumn(Class<?> type, String name) {
      this.columnClass = type;
      this.columnName = name;
    }

    public Class<?> getColumnClass() {
      return this.columnClass;
    }

    public String getColumnName() {
      return this.columnName;
    }

  }

  class IconData {

    private final File file;
    private final ImageIcon imageIcon;

    public IconData(File file, ImageIcon icon) {
      super();
      this.file = file;
      this.imageIcon = icon;
    }
```

```java
    public File getFile() {
      return this.file;
    }

    public Dimension getIconDimension() {
      ImageIcon icon = getImageIcon();
      Dimension dimension = (icon != null)
          ? new Dimension(icon.getIconWidth(), icon.getIconHeight()) : null;
      return dimension;
    }

    public ImageIcon getImageIcon() {
      return this.imageIcon;
    }

  }

}

class DimensionRenderer extends DefaultTableCellRenderer {

  public DimensionRenderer() {
    super();
  }

  @Override
  public Component getTableCellRendererComponent(
      JTable table, Object value, boolean isSelected, boolean hasFocus, int row, int column) {
    Object renderValue = value;
    if (renderValue instanceof Dimension) {
      Dimension dimension = (Dimension)renderValue;
      renderValue = dimension.width + " x " + dimension.height;
    }
    Component component = super.getTableCellRendererComponent(
        table, renderValue, isSelected, hasFocus, row, column);
    return component;
  }
}

}
```

Next we'll define a simple subclass of JFrame that creates and displays an instance of the ImageTable class just defined as shown in Listing 10-14.

Listing 10-14. A Simple JFrame Subclass That Creates and Displays an Instance of ImageTable

```java
import java.awt.Container;
import java.awt.GridBagConstraints;
import java.awt.GridBagLayout;

import javax.swing.JFrame;
import javax.swing.JScrollPane;

public class DragTestFrame extends JFrame
{
  private final ImageTable imageTable = new ImageTable();

  public static void main(String[] args) {
    DragTestFrame frame = new DragTestFrame();
    frame.setVisible(true);
  }

  public DragTestFrame() {
    super();
    initialize();
  }

  private void initialize() {
    setTitle("Test");
    buildLayout();
    pack();
    setLocationRelativeTo(null);
    setDefaultCloseOperation(DISPOSE_ON_CLOSE);
  }

  private void buildLayout() {
    GridBagConstraints constraints = new GridBagConstraints();
    Container pane = getContentPane();
    pane.setLayout(new GridBagLayout());
    ImageTable table = getImageTable();
    JScrollPane scrollPane = new JScrollPane(table);
    constraints.weightx = 1;
    constraints.weighty = 1;
    constraints.fill = GridBagConstraints.BOTH;
    pane.add(scrollPane, constraints);
  }

  private ImageTable getImageTable() {
    return this.imageTable;
  }

}
```

Again, this just allows us to display a table but doesn't implement any support for dropping data on the table. To begin implementing drop support let's first define a subclass of TransferHandler called ImageTableTransferHandler as shown in Listing 10-15.

Listing 10-15. Initial Implementation of a `TransferHandler` Subclass That Supports Dropping Images on
ImageTable Instances

```
import javax.swing.TransferHandler;

public class ImageTableTransferHandler extends TransferHandler {

  public ImageTableTransferHandler() {
    super();
  }

}
```

Now that our `TransferHandler` class exists, we can assign an instance of it to each `ImageTable` that's
created by calling the `setTransferHandler()` class mentioned earlier that's defined in the `JComponent` class.
We'll add a new line to the `initialize()` method as shown in Listing 10-16.

Listing 10-16. Creating an Instance of the ImageTableTransferHandler and Using It for Transfers That
Occur for ImageTable Instances

```
private void initialize() {
  setPreferredScrollableViewportSize(PREFERRED_SIZE);
  setDragEnabled(true);
  setDropMode(DropMode.INSERT_ROWS);
  setSelectionMode(ListSelectionModel.SINGLE_SELECTION);
  updateColumnSize();
  setTransferHandler(new ImageTableTransferHandler());
}
```

Our `ImageTableTransferHandler` class is just a shell at this point and doesn't override any of the
behavior it inherits from the `TransferHandler` class, but now we can begin to implement the custom
behavior we want. We'll start by overriding the `canImport()` method to have it display a message whenever
it's called in order to better understand how it's used. Listing 10-17 shows an example of how it might appear.

Listing 10-17. Implementation of the canImport( ) Method That Simply Displays a Message Using Standard
Output

```
@Override
public boolean canImport(TransferHandler.TransferSupport support) {
  System.out.println("Checking to see if we can perform an import...");
  return false;
}
```

The `canImport()` method is called during the drag over the component, which in this case will be an
`ImageTable`, and as its name implies it's responsible for indicating whether the component can "import"
(accept a drop for) the source data. We've currently hard-coded it to always return `false`, so if you run the
application with this implementation and drag files over an `ImageTable` you'll see a no-drop cursor appear.
The more interesting aspect of its behavior, though, is that the message you probably expected to see is never
sent to standard output. The reason for this is that an empty `JTable` like our `ImageTable` class with no rows
by default has a height of 0, so in effect its size is zero and no drag (or drop) ever occurs over it. The content

you see that appears to be part of the table is actually just the table's header (a JTableHeader instance) and the portion below that is occupied by the JScrollPane that contains the table. In other words, the drag never occurs over the table because the table itself isn't visible in the user interface. The easiest solution to this is to use the setFillsViewportHeight() method defined in JTable that—as its name implies—causes the table to fill the viewport in which it's contained even if there aren't enough rows to occupy that space, and we can add this to the initialize() method just as we did the call to assign the custom TransferHandler.

```
setTransferHandler(new ImageTableTransferHandler());
setFillsViewportHeight(true);
```

Now if you rerun the sample application you'll see the message defined earlier being sent to standard output as you drag a file over the ImageTable.

■ **Note**   The canImport() method is overloaded in TransferHandler, and the other implementation accepts a JComponent and an array of DataFlavor instances as arguments. Although that other implementation isn't technically deprecated, you should use the one shown here that takes a single instance of the TransferSupport inner class defined in TransferHandler.

Now that we have a stub implementation of canImport(), what code should really go there? We should check to see if the source of the drag-and-drop operation supports the operation supported by the ImageTable and that the type of data to be dropped is one that's supported. Specifically, we'll support the LINK operation since that's conceptually the most logical one for adding a table entry that is effectively a link to a file, and for the type of data supported we've already determined that files should be dropped. As a result, we can complete the implementation of canImport() as shown in Listing 10-18.

Listing 10-18. Completed Implementation of canImport()

```
@Override
public boolean canImport(TransferHandler.TransferSupport support) {
  boolean importAllowed = isLinkActionSupportedBySource(support)
      && isFileListDataFlavorAvailable(support);
  if (importAllowed) {
    support.setDropAction(LINK);
  }
  return importAllowed;
}

private boolean isLinkActionSupportedBySource(TransferHandler.TransferSupport support) {
  return ((support.getSourceDropActions() & LINK) != 0);
}

private boolean isFileListDataFlavorAvailable(TransferHandler.TransferSupport support) {
  boolean fileListFlavorAvailable = false;
  DataFlavor[] flavors = support.getDataFlavors();
```

```
  for (DataFlavor flavor : flavors) {
    if (DataFlavor.javaFileListFlavor.equals(flavor)) {
      fileListFlavorAvailable = true;
      break;
    }
  }
  return fileListFlavorAvailable;
}
```

With this implemented the pointer correctly changes to indicate that a drop is possible whenever you drag files over the ImageTable, but attempting to perform the drop has no effect on the table's content. To handle the drop action and update the table data we need to also override the importData() method inherited from TransferHandler. That method is called whenever the user indicates that the drop should occur and is used to update the component over which the drop occurs appropriately. In this case the appropriate behavior is for the files dropped to be added to the table and for those files that represent images to have their dimensions shown in the table along with the file. An example of how this can be implemented appears in Listing 10-19. It gets a collection of File instances from the Transferable passed as a parameter, then attempts to create an ImageIcon from each of the files and adds the File and ImageIcon (if one was successfully created) to the table in order to display a new entry.

Listing 10-19. An Implementation of importData()

```
@Override
public boolean importData(JComponent component, Transferable transferable) {
  ImageIcon icon;
  List<File> fileList;

  boolean importOccurred = false;
  ImageTable table = (ImageTable)component;
  if (table != null) {
    fileList = getFileList(transferable);
    for (File file : fileList) {
      icon = createImageIcon(file);
      table.addImageIcon(file, icon);
    }
  }
  return importOccurred;
}


@SuppressWarnings("unchecked")
private List<File> getFileList(Transferable transferable) {
  List<File> fileList;
    try {
    fileList = (List<File>)(transferable.getTransferData(DataFlavor.javaFileListFlavor));
  }
  catch (Exception e) {
    throw new Error("Unable to get transfer data");
  }

  return fileList;
}
```

445

```java
private ImageIcon createImageIcon(File file) {
  ImageIcon icon;

  try {
    URL url = file.toURI().toURL();
    icon = new ImageIcon(url);
    if ((icon.getIconWidth() <= 0) || (icon.getIconHeight() <= 0)) {
      icon = null;
    }
  }
  catch (Exception e) {
    icon = null;
  }

  return icon;
}
```

With these additions made the sample program behaves as expected, allowing you to drop files on the table, at which point it will display the file dropped and, optionally, the size of the icon when appropriate. The complete implementation of ImageTransferHandler appears in Listing 10-20.

Listing 10-20. Complete Implementation of the ImageTransferHandler Class

```java
import java.awt.Component;
import java.awt.datatransfer.DataFlavor;
import java.awt.datatransfer.Transferable;
import java.io.File;
import java.net.URL;
import java.util.List;

import javax.swing.ImageIcon;
import javax.swing.JComponent;
import javax.swing.TransferHandler;

public class ImageTableTransferHandler extends TransferHandler {

  public ImageTableTransferHandler() {
    super();
  }

  @Override
  public boolean canImport(TransferHandler.TransferSupport support) {
    boolean importAllowed = isLinkActionSupportedBySource(support)
        && isFileListDataFlavorAvailable(support);
    if (importAllowed) {
      support.setDropAction(LINK);
    }
    return importAllowed;
  }

  private boolean isLinkActionSupportedBySource(TransferHandler.TransferSupport support) {
    return ((support.getSourceDropActions() & LINK) != 0);
  }
```

```java
private boolean isFileListDataFlavorAvailable(TransferHandler.TransferSupport support) {
  boolean fileListFlavorAvailable = false;
  DataFlavor[] flavors = support.getDataFlavors();
  for (DataFlavor flavor : flavors) {
    if (DataFlavor.javaFileListFlavor.equals(flavor)) {
      fileListFlavorAvailable = true;
      break;
    }
  }
  return fileListFlavorAvailable;
}

@Override
public boolean importData(JComponent component, Transferable transferable) {
  ImageIcon icon;
  List<File> fileList;

  boolean importOccurred = false;
  ImageTable table = (ImageTable)component;
  if (table != null) {
    fileList = getFileList(transferable);
    for (File file : fileList) {
      icon = createImageIcon(file);
      table.addImageIcon(file, icon);
    }
  }
  return importOccurred;
}

@SuppressWarnings("unchecked")
private List<File> getFileList(Transferable transferable) {
  List<File> fileList;

  try {
    fileList = (List<File>)(transferable.getTransferData(DataFlavor.javaFileListFlavor));
  }
  catch (Exception e) {
    throw new Error("Unable to get transfer data");
  }

  return fileList;
}

private ImageIcon createImageIcon(File file) {
  ImageIcon icon;
```

```
  try {
    URL url = file.toURI().toURL();
    icon = new ImageIcon(url);
    if ((icon.getIconWidth() <= 0) || (icon.getIconHeight() <= 0)) {
      icon = null;
    }
  }
  catch (Exception e) {
    icon = null;
  }

  return icon;
  }

}
```

Although we didn't customize the drag behavior for the table, you can do this using the techniques discussed in the previous sections of this chapter in order to fully override the default behavior for a class. Also, although this example focused on JTable behavior, the techniques are essentially identical when implementing drag-and-drop support for JList and JTree instances.

Summary

In this chapter, we covered issues related to Java's drag-and-drop support, including the following:

- The fundamental concepts associated with drag-and-drop operations

- How to add drag support to components so they can be used to initiate drag-and-drop operations

- How to add drop support to components so they can be used to terminate drag-and-drop operations

- Issues related to different types of transfers (e.g., those between Java and native applications, as opposed to a transfer within a single JVM)

- Issues related to the transfer of text data between Java and native applications

- How to implement a custom TransferHandler class in order to customize the drag-and-drop behavior for standard Swing components

CHAPTER 11

■ ■ ■

Printing

Java matured very quickly in most respects after it was first introduced, but for a long time printing was one of Java's weakest points. In fact, Java 1.0 didn't offer any support for printing at all. Java 1.1 included a class called `PrintJob` in the `java.awt` package, but the printing capabilities supported by that class were somewhat crude and unreliable. When Java 1.2 (or "Java 2") was introduced, it included a completely separate mechanism (the *Java 2D printing API*) for printing designed around `PrinterJob` and other classes and interfaces defined in the new `java.awt.print` package. This rendered the `PrintJob`-based printing mechanism (also known as *AWT printing*) largely obsolete, although `PrintJob` has never been deprecated and is still technically a supported class.

Additional changes were made in Java 1.3 when `PrintJob`'s capabilities expanded to allow the setting of job and page attributes using the appropriately named `JobAttributes` and `PageAttributes` classes within the `java.awt` package. With the release of Java 1.3, the printing capabilities were reasonably robust, but some problems still existed in addition to the confusion associated with having two completely separate printing facilities. For one thing, both facilities used an implementation of the `java.awt.Graphics` class for rendering the content to be printed, which meant anything that needed to be printed had to be rendered as a graphical image. In addition, the newer and generally more robust `PrinterJob` facility provided only limited support for setting attributes associated with the job. Finally, neither facility provided a way to programmatically select the target printer.

The biggest change in Java's printing capabilities to date came with the release of Java 1.4, when the Java print service API (application programming interface) was introduced. This third implementation of printing support in Java addressed the limitations that were just described using an implementation of the `PrintService` and `DocPrintJob` interfaces defined in the `javax.print` package. Because this new API represents a superset of the functionality defined by the two older printing facilities, it's the one you should normally use and will be the focus of this chapter.

At a high level, the steps involved in using the Java print service API are straightforward.

1. Locate print services (printers), optionally limiting the list of those returned to the ones that support the capabilities your application needs. Print services are represented as instances of `PrintService` implementations.

2. Create a print job by calling the `createPrintJob()` method defined in the `PrintService` interface. The print job is represented by an instance of `DocPrintJob`.

3. Create an implementation of the `Doc` interface that describes the data you want to print. You also have the option of creating an instance of `PrintRequestAttributeSet` that describes the printing options you want.

4. Initiate printing by calling the `print()` method defined in the `DocPrintJob` interface, specifying the `Doc` you created in the previous step and the `PrintRequestAttributeSet` or a null value.

You'll now examine each of these steps and see how to achieve them.

▨ **Note** Within this chapter I'll use the terms *printer* and *print service* interchangeably because in most cases a print service is nothing more than a representation of a physical printer. The more generic *print service* reflects the fact that the output can theoretically be sent to something other than a printer. For example, a print service might not print the output at all but instead write it to a disk file. In other words, all printers are represented by a print service, but not every print service necessarily corresponds to a physical printer. In practice, though, it's likely you'll almost always send your content to a printer, which is why I'll sometimes use the simpler *printer* term instead of the more technically accurate *print service*.

Locating Print Services

You locate a printer using one of three static methods defined in the PrintServiceLookup class. The simplest of the three methods is lookupDefaultPrintService(), and as its name implies, it returns a reference to the service that represents your default printer.

```
PrintService service = PrintServiceLookup.lookupDefaultPrintService();
```

Although this method is simple and convenient, using it to select which printer to send output to means you're implicitly assuming that the user's default printer will always be able to support the capabilities your application needs in order to be able to print its output correctly. In practice, you'll typically want to select only those printers that are able to handle the type of data you want to print and that support the features your application needs, such as color or two-sided printing. To retrieve the list of all defined printers or to retrieve a list that's limited to printers supporting certain capabilities, you'll want to use one of two other static methods defined in PrintServiceLookup: either lookupPrintServices() or lookupMultiDocPrintServices().

The lookupPrintServices() method accepts two parameters: an instance of DocFlavor and an instance of some implementation of the AttributeSet interface. As you'll see shortly, you can use both of these to limit the list of printers returned by the method, but lookupPrintServices() allows you to specify a null value for either or both of the two parameters. By specifying a null value for both parameters, you're effectively requesting that the method return a PrintService instance for every printer that's available. At this point, you haven't really examined the methods defined in PrintService, but one of them is the getName() method, which returns a String representing the name of the printer. You can display a list of all printers available on your system by compiling and running code like that shown in Listing 11-1.

Listing 11-1. Displaying the Available Print Services

```
PrintService[] services = PrintServiceLookup.lookupPrintServices(null, null);
for (int i = 0; i < services.length; i++) {
    System.out.println(services[i].getName());
}
```

For example, if you have access to printers named Alpha, Beta, and Gamma that are attached to a server named PrintServer, running the previous code produces the following output:

```
\\PrintServer\Alpha
\\PrintServer\Beta
\\PrintServer\Gamma
```

Now let's examine the parameters you can pass to the lookupPrintServices() method and see how they allow you to limit the printers returned to those with only certain capabilities.

DocFlavor

The first parameter you can specify on a call to lookupPrintServices() is an instance of the DocFlavor class, which describes the type of data to be printed and how that data is stored. In most cases, it won't be necessary for you to create a new instance of DocFlavor because Java includes many predefined instances, allowing you to simply pass a reference to one of those instances to lookupPrintServices(). However, let's look at the DocFlavor constructor and methods to understand how an instance is used by a print service.

The two arguments required when creating an instance of DocFlavor are both String instances, with one representing a MIME type and the other being the name of a representation class. As you might expect from the discussion in Chapter 9, the MIME type is used by a DocFlavor to describe the type of data to be printed. For example, if you're printing a GIF file, you'll need to use a DocFlavor that has a MIME type of image/gif. Similarly, you might use a MIME type of text/plain if you're printing text information or text/html for an HTML document.

Representation Class

While the MIME type describes the type of data to be printed, the representation class describes how that data is to be made available to the print service. DocFlavor includes seven static inner classes, with each one corresponding to a representation class and each one corresponding to a different way of encapsulating the data that's to be printed.

Table 11-1 shows the names of the static inner classes defined within DocFlavor and their corresponding representation classes. Note that aside from SERVICE_FORMATTED (which I'll discuss in detail later), each one is described as being associated with either "binary" or "character" data. In reality, the distinction is somewhat artificial because character data is really just a specialized form of binary data, in this case referring to binary data that contains only human-readable characters and perhaps some formatting characters such as tabs, carriage returns, and so on. However, the distinction is important because character-oriented representation classes aren't appropriate for storing the binary data that's to be printed. For example, you wouldn't store a representation of a GIF image in a character array or a String, and you wouldn't make it accessible through a Reader implementation. On the other hand, because "character" data is just a specialized type of binary data, it's entirely appropriate to store text information in a byte array or make it accessible through an InputStream or via a URL.

Table 11-1. DocFlavor's Predefined Representation Classes

Inner Class Name	Representation Class	Data Type
BYTE_ARRAY	[B (byte[])	Binary
CHAR_ARRAY	[C (char[])	Character
INPUT_STREAM	java.io.InputStream	Binary
READER	java.io.Reader	Character
SERVICE_FORMATTED	java.awt.print.Pageable or java.awt.print.Printable	Other
STRING	java.lang.String	Character
URL	java.net.URL	Binary

Each of these static inner classes defined within DocFlavor corresponds to a particular representation class, but remember that I said each DocFlavor instance encapsulates both a representation class and a MIME type that identifies the type of data to be printed. To access an instance of DocFlavor that corresponds to both the representation class and the MIME type of the content you want to print, you'll need to reference an inner class within one of the inner classes listed in Table 11-1. For example, let's suppose you want to print a GIF file that's available on the Web through a URL. In this case, the obvious choice for the representation class is java.net.URL, which is associated with the static class named URL defined within DocFlavor. If you browse the documentation for that inner class, you'll find that it defines a number of static inner classes, each one corresponding to a particular MIME type representing data types commonly supported by printers. Table 11-2 shows the inner classes defined within DocFlavor.URL and their corresponding MIME types.

Table 11-2. *The* DocFlavor.URL *Inner Classes*

Static Inner Class	MIME Type
AUTOSENSE	application/octet-stream
GIF	image/gif
JPEG	image/jpeg
PCL	application/vnd-hp.PCL
PDF	application/pdf
PNG	image/png
POSTSCRIPT	application/postscript
TEXT_HTML_HOST	text/html
TEXT_HTML_US_ASCII	text/html;charset=us-ascii
TEXT_HTML_UTF_16	text/html;charset=utf-16
TEXT_HTML_UTF_16BE	text/html;charset=utf-16be
TEXT_HTML_UTF_16LE	text/html;charset=utf-16le
TEXT_HTML_UTF_8	text/html;charset=utf-8
TEXT_PLAIN_HOST	text/plain
TEXT_PLAIN_US_ASCII	text/plain;charset=us-ascii
TEXT_PLAIN_UTF_16	text/plain;charset=utf-16
TEXT_PLAIN_UTF_16BE	text/plain;charset=utf-16be
TEXT_PLAIN_UTF_16LE	text/plain;charset=utf-16le
TEXT_PLAIN_UTF_8	text/plain;charset=utf-8

Because you'll print a GIF image that's available through a URL, you can access an appropriate DocFlavor instance using the following code:

```
DocFlavor flavor = DocFlavor.URL.GIF;
```

This code creates a reference to the static instance of DocFlavor that has a representation class of java.net.URL and a MIME type of image/gif.

The classes listed in Table 11-2 are defined within the DocFlavor.URL class, but what about the other six inner classes defined within DocFlavor? Again, I'll defer a discussion of SERVICE_FORMATTED until later, but as for the classes associated with binary data types, all three (BYTE_ARRAY, INPUT_STREAM, and URL) include inner classes with the names shown in Table 11-2. So, for example, if you had loaded the GIF data into a byte array, you might instead choose to use code like the following:

```
DocFlavor flavor = DocFlavor.BYTE_ARRAY.GIF;
```

Just as the three DocFlavor inner classes associated with binary data types include their own inner classes, the three associated with character data types include a different set of inner classes, as shown in Table 11-3.

Table 11-3. *CHAR_ARRAY, READER, and STRING*

Static Inner Class	MIME Type
TEXT_HTML	text/html;charset=utf-16
TEXT_PLAIN	text/plain;charset=utf-16

So, for example, if you wanted to print plain-text data that's stored in an instance of String, you could use code like the following:

```
DocFlavor flavor = DocFlavor.STRING.TEXT_PLAIN;
```

Similarly, if the text data represented an HTML document and you wanted to have the data printed as it would appear within a web browser, you could use the following:

```
DocFlavor flavor = DocFlavor.STRING.TEXT_HTML;
```

To summarize, the DocFlavor encapsulates the following two pieces of information:

- Where the data is located/how it's accessed, such as via a URL, a byte array, or a String instance.

- The type of thing the data represents, such as a GIF image, plain text, or an HTML document.

Choosing the Right Printer

Remember that the discussion of DocFlavor began with a desire to make sure the printer you use actually supports the type of data that's to be printed and the delivery mechanism (representation class) you intend to use. This might seem like an unnecessary step, but in reality you may be surprised at which document types a given printer supports. For example, the text-oriented types just described might seem as though they'd be the simplest ones to support, so if your application is printing plain or HTML text, you might be tempted to simply select the first available print service and send the output to that printer. As it turns out, though, many printers don't support the text-based representation classes, and if you attempt to send output to a printer that doesn't support the DocFlavor you select, an exception will be thrown like the following:

```
Exception in thread "main" sun.print.PrintJobFlavorException: invalid flavor
        at sun.print.Win32PrintJob.print(Win32PrintJob.java:290)
        at PrintTest.main(PrintTest.java:11)
```

Now that you've seen how to obtain a reference to a DocFlavor and I've discussed the importance of selecting a printer that supports the selected flavor, I'll show how you can use it to make sure you use a printer that supports the flavor you need. As I discussed earlier, the lookupPrintServices() allows you to specify a DocFlavor as its first argument, and if you specify a non-null value, the method will return only the PrintService instances that correspond to printers that support the specified DocFlavor. For example, the following code will retrieve an array that identifies all printers on your system that can print GIF images that are referenced via a URL:

```
DocFlavor flavor = DocFlavor.URL.GIF;
PrintService[] services  = PrintServiceLookup.lookupPrintServices(flavor, null);
```

Alternatively, if your application has already retrieved a reference to a PrintService and you want to determine whether it supports a particular flavor, you can call the isDocFlavorSupported() method. In the code segment in Listing 11-2, a reference to the default printer is obtained, and an error message will be displayed if it's not able to print a GIF image retrieved via a URL.

Listing 11-2. Checking the Default Printer for GIF Support via URL

```
PrintService service = PrintServiceLookup.lookupDefaultPrintService();
DocFlavor flavor = DocFlavor.URL.GIF;
if (!service.isDocFlavorSupported(flavor)) {
    System.err.println("The printer does not support the appropriate DocFlavor");
}
```

AttributeSet

As you've now seen, a DocFlavor describes the data to be printed and can be used to ensure that a PrintService supports the corresponding type of data. However, your application may also need to select a printer based upon the features that the printer supports. For example, if you're printing a graph that uses different colors to convey information, you might want to see if a given service supports color printing and, if not, either prevent the printer from being used or render a representation of the graph that doesn't rely on colors.

Characteristics such as the ability to print in color, to print on both sides of a page, or to use different orientations (portrait or landscape) are referred to as a printer's *attributes*, and the javax.print.attribute package contains many classes and interfaces you can use to describe those attributes. One of those interfaces is AttributeSet, which was mentioned earlier as the second parameter that can be specified on a call to lookupPrintServices(). As you might expect, an implementation of AttributeSet represents a collection of attributes, and specifying a non-null value on the call to lookupPrintServices() will result in only print services being returned that support those attributes. In other words, if you specify both a DocFlavor and an AttributeSet on a call to lookupPrintServices(), the method will return only those printers that support both the specified flavor and the appropriate attributes.

Attribute

Given that an AttributeSet is a collection of attributes, the obvious question is, how do you go about specifying the attribute values that should make up that collection? The javax.print.attribute package also includes an interface named Attribute, and as you'll see shortly, you create the collection of attributes by adding instances of Attribute to an AttributeSet by calling the add() method. Reviewing the documentation for the Attribute interface reveals that a large number of implementations are defined within the javax.print.attribute.standard package, and it's those classes you'll use. Before you see how that's done, it's helpful to review the other interfaces in the javax.print.attribute package along with their implementations.

Attribute Roles

So far I've described attributes as capabilities of a print service, and while that's largely true, it's really something of an oversimplification, at least in terms of how Java supports attributes. For each different attribute, Java associates it with one or more "role," and the attribute is valid only in the context of the role(s) with which it's assigned. In other words, attributes are used in various places within the Java print service and not every attribute is valid within every context.

To better understand this, consider the OrientationRequested and ColorSupported implementations of Attribute that are defined within the javax.print.attribute.standard package. The OrientationRequested attribute is one you can specify when creating a document to be printed and allows you to specify the orientation (such as portrait or landscape) that should be used when printing the document. In contrast, ColorSupported is an attribute that can be returned when you call the getAttributes() method of the PrintService interface. In other words, OrientationRequested is an attribute you use to pass information to the print service, and ColorSupported is one that the print service uses to provide you with information about the printer's abilities. You can't specify ColorSupported as an attribute when creating a document to be printed because the printer's ability to print in color isn't something your application is able to control.

Interfaces and Implementations

When you first look at the interfaces and classes defined in the javax.print.attribute package, it may appear to present a confusing list of choices when it comes to the interfaces and classes defined there. Aside from the Attribute and AttributeSet interfaces and the HashAttributeSet class that implements AttributeSet, the javax.print.attribute package has four sets of subinterfaces and classes, as shown in Table 11-4 and Figure 11-1.

Table 11-4. *Interfaces and Classes Defined Within the* javax.print.attribute *Package*

Attribute Subinterface	AttributeSet Subinterface	AttributeSet Subclass
DocAttribute	DocAttributeSet	HashDocAttributeSet
PrintJobAttribute	PrintJobAttributeSet	HashPrintJobAttributeSet
PrintRequestAttribute	PrintRequestAttributeSet	HashPrintRequestAttributeSet
PrintServiceAttribute	PrintServiceAttributeSet	HashPrintServiceAttributeSet

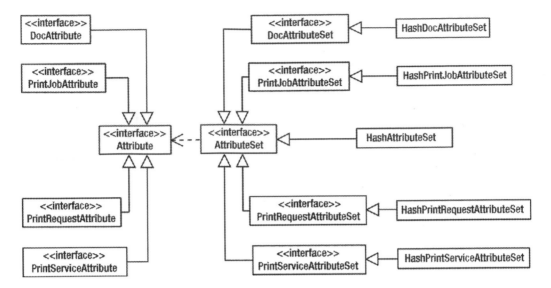

Figure 11-1. *The class hierarchy of a portion of the* `javax.print.attribute` *package*

So, why do you need all these various interfaces and implementations, particularly since the more generalized `Attribute`, `AttributeSet`, and `HashAttributeSet` are provided? The answer is that these specializations are defined to ensure that only the appropriate attributes are used within the role(s) where they're valid. For example, I mentioned that one place where you can use attributes is when creating a document that's to be printed and that some attributes such as `ColorSupported` aren't valid within that context. When creating such a document, you'll use the `DocAttributeSet` interface (or, specifically, its `HashDocAttributeSet` implementation), and the implementation will allow you to add only attributes that implement the `DocAttribute` interface. The four different types of roles are as follows:

- **Doc**: Specified when creating a document that's to be printed to describe how the document should be printed

- **PrintJob**: Attributes returned from the print job to describe the state of the job

- **PrintRequest**: Attributes passed to the print job when a request is made to initiate printing

- **PrintService**: Returned by a `PrintService` to describe the capabilities of the service

To see how this works, let's create an instance of a `DocAttributeSet` and then attempt to set both the `OrientationRequested` and `ColorSupported` attributes for that `AttributeSet`. The `HashDocAttributeSet` defines a no-argument constructor, so you can create an instance easily as follows:

```
DocAttributeSet attrs = new HashDocAttributeSet();
```

Now that you've created the `AttributeSet`, you can call its `add()` method and pass to it instances of `Attribute` implementations. If you examine the documentation for the `OrientationRequested` class, you'll see it includes references to a number of static `OrientationRequest` instances with each one corresponding to a document orientation such as portrait or landscape. To specify the orientation you want, all you need to do is pass a reference to the appropriate static instance to the add() method as follows:

```
DocAttributeSet attrs = new HashDocAttributeSet();
attrs.add(OrientationRequested.PORTRAIT);
```

The ColorSupported class is slightly different but equally simple to use, and it defines two static instances: one that indicates that color printing is supported and another that indicates it's not supported. You can attempt to add a ColorSupported attribute to the DocAttributeSet with code like the following:

```
DocAttributeSet attrs = new HashDocAttributeSet();
attrs.add(OrientationRequested.PORTRAIT);
attrs.add(ColorSupported.SUPPORTED);
```

As mentioned earlier, it's not appropriate to specify whether to support color printing because this isn't something an application is allowed to control. In other words, the ColorSupported attribute isn't valid within the context of a set of document attributes, and as a result, attempting to run the previous code will cause a ClassCastException to be thrown when it attempts to add the ColorSupported attribute.

To understand how this works, remember that each AttributeSet subinterface (in this case, DocAttributeSet) has a corresponding Attribute subinterface (DocAttribute) and an implementation class (HashDocAttributeSet). When an attempt is made to add an attribute, the implementation class tries to cast the Attribute parameter to the corresponding subinterface type, which in turn ensures that only attributes appropriate for that context can be added successfully.

In this case, the add() method of HashDocAttributeSet is first called with an instance of OrientationRequested, and it successfully casts that object to a DocAttribute, because as Figure 11-2 shows, OrientationRequested implements that interface. In contrast, however, passing an instance of ColorSupported fails because ColorSupported doesn't implement DocAttribute.

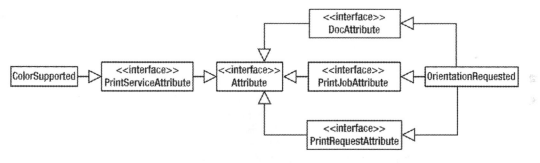

Figure 11-2. *The class hierarchy of a portion of the* `javax.print.attribute` *package*

As this example illustrates, the four different groups of interfaces and classes shown in Table 11-4 ensure that only the appropriate attributes are used within the appropriate context. Notice that a great deal of overlap occurs between roles and the various attributes, so many of the attributes are associated with more than one role. For example, many of the attributes implement both PrintJobAttribute and PrintRequestAttribute because many of the attributes that are maintained and provided to you by a print job correspond to attributes you can specify when you request that printing be initiated. You can, for instance, both specify the job name by adding it to a PrintRequestAttributeSet and retrieve the name of the job during printing by retrieving it from a PrintJobAttributeSet. As a result, the JobName attribute class implements both PrintRequestAttribute and PrintJobAttribute.

AttributeSet and HashAttributeSet

You've now seen why the four groups of subclasses exist, but what about the base AttributeSet interface and the HashAttributeSet superclass? AttributeSet/HashAttributeSet is used in situations where you can't assume that only attributes associated with a single role will need to be stored in a collection. Remember that earlier in the chapter I mentioned that the lookupPrintServices() method allows you to specify an AttributeSet parameter that will limit which print services are returned. On the surface it might appear that it would be better to require that an instance of PrintServiceAttributeSet be specified, but many of the attributes you might want to use don't implement PrintServiceAttribute.

Let's assume you want the lookupPrintServices() method to retrieve only services that support both color printing and landscape printing. Those attributes correspond to the ColorSupported and OrientationRequested attributes, respectively, but notice that those two attribute classes don't share a common role: ColorSupported is a PrintServiceAttribute, and OrientationRequested is associated with all three of the other roles (Doc, PrintRequest, and PrintJob), as shown in Figure 11-2. What this means is that there's no single role-specific AttributeSet interface/class that can contain both a ColorSupported attribute and a Sides attribute.

The way to create an AttributeSet that contains both an OrientationRequested and a ColorSupported instance is to simply use an instance of the generic HashAttributeSet. Unlike its subclasses, it doesn't limit you to adding attributes associated with a particular role, so you can successfully execute the following code:

```
AttributeSet attrs = new HashAttributeSet();
attrs.add(ColorSupported.SUPPORTED);
attrs.add(OrientationRequested.LANDSCAPE);
PrintService[] services = PrintServiceLookup.lookupPrintServices(null, attrs);
```

Printer Selection via User Interface

Up to this point, I've assumed that the printer to be used would be selected programmatically by the application. In practice, however, it's more common to simply display a dialog and allow the user to select which printer to use when printing the output. Fortunately, Java makes it easy to do just that by using the static printDialog() method in the ServiceUI class defined within the javax.print package.

Aside from the location of the dialog to be displayed, the only parameter values that must be specified on the call to printDialog() are the following:

- An array of PrintService instances from which the user can choose.

- The default PrintService.

- An instance of PrintRequestAttributeSet. This is used to populate the dialog that's displayed, and it returns any changes that were made by the user before the dialog was dismissed.

To illustrate how this works, you can use the following simple code segment to display a print dialog:

```
PrintService[] services = PrintServiceLookup.lookupPrintServices(null, null);
PrintService svc = PrintServiceLookup.lookupDefaultPrintService();
PrintRequestAttributeSet attrs = new HashPrintRequestAttributeSet();
PrintService selection = ServiceUI.printDialog(
        null, 100, 100, services, svc, null, attrs);
```

When run, the code produces a dialog like the one shown in Figure 11-3.

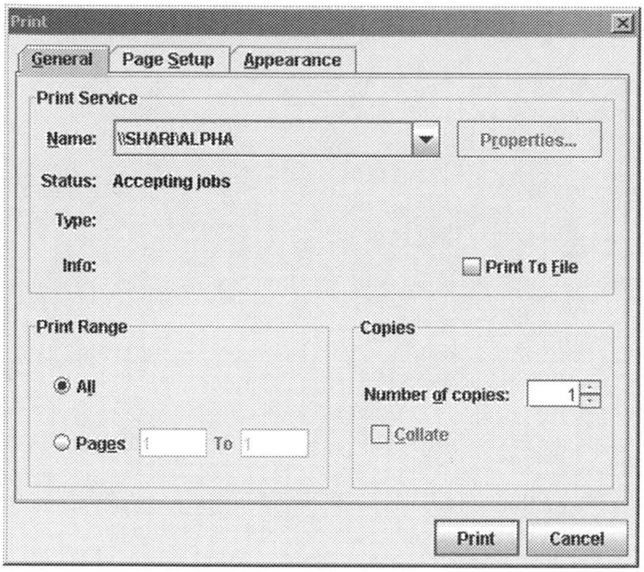

Figure 11-3. *The printer dialog*

As this code illustrates, the value returned from the `printDialog()` method is an instance of `PrintService` that identifies which printer the user selected or null if the user canceled the printer dialog. In addition, the `PrintRequestAttributeSet` is updated to reflect any changes made by the user through the dialog, such as the number of copies to be printed.

By using the `printDialog()` method, you can allow the user to select which printer his or her output will be sent to, providing the kind of functionality that users have come to expect from professional applications.

Creating a Print Job

This is the simplest step involved in printing, because once you've obtained a reference to a `PrintService`, all you need to do is call its `createPrintJob()` method as follows:

```
PrintService service;
.
.
.
DocPrintJob job = service.createPrintJob();
```

As indicated in the code, the value returned from `createPrintJob()` is an instance of `DocPrintJob`, an object that allows you to control and monitor the status of the printing operation. To initiate printing, you'll call the `DocPrintJob` object's `print()` method, but before you do so you'll need to define the document to be printed and optionally a `PrintRequestAttributeSet`. You've already seen how to construct and populate an `AttributeSet`, so I won't review that step; instead, you'll see how you go about defining the document to be printed.

Defining the Document to Print

The next step in printing is to define the document that's to be printed, which is done by creating an instance of an implementation of the Doc interface defined in the javax.print package. Each instance of Doc has two mandatory attributes and an optional one.

- An Object that represents the data to be printed

- An instance of DocFlavor that describes the type of data to print

- An optional DocAttributeSet containing attributes to use when printing the document

Reviewing the documentation for the Doc interface reveals that the javax.print package includes an implementation of the interface named SimpleDoc, which has a constructor that takes three arguments that match the three attributes described previously. To see how to construct an instance of SimpleDoc, let's assume you want to print two copies of a GIF image that's stored at http://upload.wikimedia.org/wikipedia/en/e/eb/Apress-logo.png.

All that's needed to construct a SimpleDoc instance that describes the document to be printed is to create a URL (uniform resource locator) that points to the image, obtain a reference to the appropriate DocFlavor, and pass those two objects to the SimpleDoc constructor as follows:

```
URL url = new URL(
    "http://upload.wikimedia.org/wikipedia/en/e/eb/Apress-logo.png");
DocFlavor flavor = DocFlavor.URL.GIF;
SimpleDoc doc = new SimpleDoc(url, flavor, null);
```

Initiating Printing

The final step involved in printing is to call the DocPrintJob's print() method, passing it the Doc object that describes the data to be printed and optionally an instance of PrintRequestAttributeSet. For the sake of simplicity, I'll assume the default printer supports the flavor and attributes you need, in which case you could use the code shown in Listing 11-3 to print two copies of the GIF file referenced in the previous example.

Listing 11-3. Printing Two Copies of an Image File

```
PrintService service = PrintServiceLookup.lookupDefaultPrintService();
DocPrintJob job = service.createPrintJob();
URL url = new URL(
    " http://upload.wikimedia.org/wikipedia/en/e/eb/Apress-logo.png");
DocFlavor flavor = DocFlavor.URL.GIF;
Doc doc = new SimpleDoc(url, flavor, null);
PrintRequestAttributeSet attrs = new HashPrintRequestAttributeSet();
attrs.add(new Copies(2));
job.print(doc, attrs);
```

Note that in some cases printing is performed asynchronously, in which case the call to print() may return before printing has actually completed. If your application needs to know the status of the print job, you should use a PrintJobListener to monitor its status, as described next.

Monitoring and Controlling a Print Job

To monitor the status of a print job, you can create an implementation of PrintJobListener and register it as a listener by calling the addPrintJobListener() method defined within DocPrintJob. PrintJobListener is defined within the javax.print.event package, and it defines a number of methods that are called to indicate various changes related to the state of the print job, such as when data transfer completes and when the job has failed or requires attention. Although their names are largely self-explanatory, the methods defined within PrintJobListener are listed in Table 11-5 along with a description of when each one is called.

Table 11-5. *Methods Defined Within the* PrintJobListener *Interface*

Method	Description
printDataTransferCompleted()	Data has been successfully transmitted from the client to the print service.
printJobCanceled()	The print job was canceled.
printJobCompleted()	The job has completed.
printJobFailed()	The print job has failed and must be resubmitted for the document to be printed successfully.
printJobNoMoreEvents()	No more calls to any of the methods in this interface will be called for this print job.
printJobRequiresAttention()	An error has occurred that may be recoverable, such as the printer running out of paper.

If you're interested only in a subset of these methods, you may find it convenient to use the PrintJobAdapter implementation class that provides "stub" implementations for each of the methods listed in Table 11-5. In other words, it defines methods that don't do anything when those methods are called, and by overriding only the method(s) that are of interest to your application, you can quickly and easily define your own PrintJobListener implementation as shown in Listing 11-4.

Listing 11-4. Using a PrintJobListener Implementation

```
PrintService service = PrintServiceLookup.lookupDefaultPrintService();
DocPrintJob job = service.createPrintJob();
job.addPrintJobListener(new PrintJobAdapter() {
    public void printDataTransferCompleted(PrintJobEvent event) {
        System.out.println("Data transfer is complete");
    }
    public void printJobNoMoreEvents(PrintJobEvent event) {
        System.out.println("No more events will be received");
    }
});
```

Monitoring Attribute Changes

Aside from monitoring the status of the print job itself, it's also sometimes helpful to monitor changes to the attributes that may change during printing. For example, let's suppose your application is printing a multipage document, and it wants to provide the user with some kind of indication of which page is currently being printed. You can accomplish this by registering a PrintJobAttributeListener with the DocPrintJob and optionally by specifying which attributes are of interest to your application.

The process of registering a PrintJobAttributeListener is similar to the approach you just saw for registering a PrintJobListener and is done using the addPrintJobAttributeListener() method defined in DocPrintJob. One important difference, however, is that addPrintJobAttributeListener() accepts not only a PrintJobAttributeListener but also an optional instance of PrintJobAttributeSet that can be used to specify which attributes are of interest to the listener. By registering an attribute listener, you're indicating you want the listener to be notified of changes to the attributes associated with the print job. If you specify a null value for the PrintJobAttributeSet parameter, the listener will be notified of all attribute changes. However, if you specify a non-null value, the listener will be notified only of attributes that are included in the PrintJobAttributeSet you specify.

To see an example of this, let's create and use an instance of PrintJobAttributeListener to monitor which page is currently being printed. The first step is to create the implementation, which can be done as shown in Listing 11-5. Notice that PrintJobAttributeListener defines only a single attributeUpdate() method that must be implemented.

Listing 11-5. Retrieving and Displaying an Attribute Value

```
PrintJobAttributeListener listener = new PrintJobAttributeListener() {
    public void attributeUpdate(PrintJobAttributeEvent event) {
        PrintJobAttributeSet attrSet = event.getAttributes();
        Attribute attr = attrSet.get(JobMediaSheetsCompleted.class);
        if (attr != null) {
            JobMediaSheetsCompleted sheets = (JobMediaSheetsCompleted)attr;
            System.out.println("Finished printing page " + sheets.getValue());
        }
    }
};
```

Within the attributeUpdate() method, you first retrieve the PrintJobAttributeSet that encapsulates the attribute(s) being reported as having changed. Once that's done, you can attempt to retrieve from the set the specific attribute you're interested in, and if it's found within the set, you cast it to the appropriate class and display a message indicating which page has finished printing.

Once the PrintJobAttributeListener implementation has been created, you can easily register it as a listener using code like that in the following bold line:

```
PrintService service = PrintServiceLookup.lookupDefaultPrintService();
DocPrintJob job = service.createPrintJob();
job.addPrintJobAttributeListener(listener, null);
```

In this case, you specified a null value for the second parameter, which will result in the attributeUpdate() method being called when the value of any attribute changes. Alternatively, you could construct an instance of PrintJobAttributeSet, populate it with the specific type of attribute you want to monitor, and specify that set when adding the listener, as follows:

```
PrintJobAttributeSet attrs = new HashPrintJobAttributeSet();
attrs.add(new JobMediaSheetsCompleted(0));
PrintService service = PrintServiceLookup.lookupDefaultPrintService();
DocPrintJob job = service.createPrintJob();
job.addPrintJobAttributeListener(listener, attrs);
```

With this modification, the `attributeUpdate()` method will be called only when or if the `JobMediaSheetsCompleted` attribute changes for the print job.

When using attribute listeners, it's important to remember that not all attributes will be supported by all print services. If the print service you're using doesn't support the `JobMediaSheetsCompleted` attribute, then the code you've just created won't do anything because that attribute will never be updated.

Canceling a Print Job

You've now seen how to initiate and monitor the status of a print job, but what if the user wants to cancel the job before it has completed? Well, it's important to mention that like many of the other capabilities I've discussed, the ability to cancel a print job will vary from one print service to the next, so you shouldn't assume a print job can be canceled. However, the Java print service API includes an interface called `CancelablePrintJob` that extends `DocPrintJob`, and if the print job that's created by the print service implements `CancelablePrintJob`, you can call its `cancel()` method to cancel the job. Following is an example of how to accomplish this:

```
if (job instanceof CancelablePrintJob) {
    CancelablePrintJob cancelable = (CancelablePrintJob)job;
    cancelable.cancel();
}
```

Introducing Service-Formatted Printing

All the printing you've been doing so far is referred to by the Java print service API as *client formatted*, but earlier in the chapter I mentioned an alternative approach called *service formatted*. Since your application code represents the "client," you might expect service-formatted printing to be easier because the name implies that the print service will do more of the (formatting) work. In reality, though, using service-formatted printing means your code has more control over formatting, and in this case more control means additional complexity.

So, what exactly is service-formatted printing? It's really just a way of integrating the Java print service API we've been using with the older Java 2D printing API that was first introduced in Java 1.3. Java's 2D printing works by passing an instance of `Graphics` to your application when a page is to be printed and allowing your application to draw the output that should appear on the printed page.

A `Graphics` object is a representation of a hardware device onto which graphics can be drawn, such as a monitor or printer, and it includes methods such as `drawImage()`, `drawLine()`, and `drawRect()` that allow you to draw images, lines, and rectangles, respectively, on the corresponding device. `Graphics` instances are most commonly used to have components draw themselves onto a computer monitor, but in this case the `Graphics` object represents a printer, and the same logic that's used to draw a component onto a screen can be used to print that component. In other words, your application can use the Java 2D printing API to have AWT and Swing components draw (or *render*) themselves onto a printed page using the same logic they normally use to draw themselves within a window displayed on your monitor. This is particularly useful for creating What-You-See-Is-What-You-Get (WYSIWYG) printouts, but it can also be helpful when creating more customized output.

To use service-formatted printing, you'll need to choose from one of the three variations that are supported: `PAGEABLE`, `PRINTABLE`, or `RENDERABLE_IMAGE`. The first two are based upon the `Pageable` and `Printable` interfaces defined within the `java.print` package, and the third is related to the `RenderableImage` class defined within the `java.awt.image.renderable` package. To understand how these are used, let's begin by looking at some of the concepts related to how 2D printing works.

Java's 2D printing API supports a resolution of 72 dots per inch (DPI), which means each pixel you draw onto a Graphics object will occupy 1/72nd of an inch (approximately 0.3528 millimeters) on the printed page. That unit of measure (in other words, 1/72nd of an inch) is called a *point* and is used by the 2D printing facility to represent locations and size values. So, for example, a sheet of letter-sized (8.5 inches wide and 11 inches long) paper is 612 (8.5 * 72 = 612) points wide and 792 (11 * 72 = 792) points long. Based on this information, it might seem that you could produce printed output up to 612 points wide and 792 points long on letter-sized paper. However, most printers are physically capable of printing only onto a subset (although normally a very large one) of the total area available on the paper or other media used in printing. That subset is represented as a rectangular area known as the *printable area*, and as you'll see later, it's particularly important to keep this in mind when using service-formatted printing. The portions of a page that are unusable (which I'll call the *hardware margins*) vary from one model of printer to the next, but the shaded area in Figure 11-4 provides an example of the area that may be unavailable. The darker color represents the hardware margins, the lighter color represents user-specified margin settings, and the white rectangle in the center represents the area available for printing.

▓ **Note** Although I refer in this chapter to printing on "paper" and Java even defines a class by that name, the generic term *media* is really more appropriate because many printers support printing to things other than paper (e.g., transparencies).

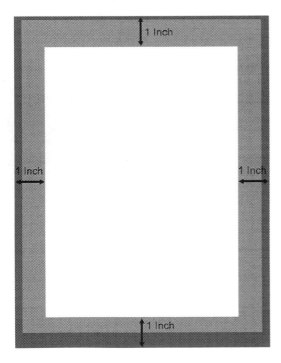

Figure 11-4. Hardware margins, user-specified margins, and the printable area

Hardware margins aren't normally a serious limitation because most applications use margin sizes that are greater than those imposed upon them by the hardware. For example, you might want to have 1-inch margins on each side of a printed text document to improve readability, so Figure 11-4 shows the approximate area of a letter-sized page that's available with margins of that size. The area inside the margins available for printing is known as the *imageable area*, and you'll need to take the size and position of that area into consideration during printing.

Support Classes

To understand how to use the 2D printing API, it's helpful to review the classes that support it. Specifically, you'll examine the Paper, PageFormat, and Book classes and the Printable and Pageable interfaces. Table 11-6 describes these classes and interfaces.

Table 11-6. *Some Interfaces and Classes Defined in the Java 2D Printing API*

Name	Type	Description
Paper	Class	Describes the physical characteristics of a given type of paper
PageFormat	Class	Describes the size and orientation of a page that's to be printed
Printable	Interface	Represents a single printable page
Pageable	Interface	Represents a collection of printable pages
Book	Class	A convenient implementation of the Pageable interface

Figure 11-5 illustrates the relationship between the Java 2D printing API support classes.

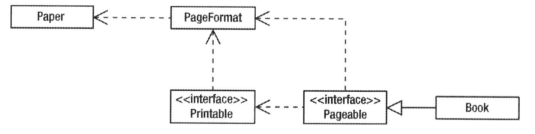

Figure 11-5. *The relationship between the Java 2D printing API support classes*

Paper

The java.awt.print.Paper class encapsulates two pieces of information: the physical size of the paper you're printing on and the size and position of the imageable area. Paper includes a single no-argument constructor that initializes its properties to correspond to U.S. letter-sized paper with 1-inch margins on each side (top, left, bottom, and right) of the page.

It's actually somewhat misleading to suggest that instances of Paper maintain margin information because in reality they don't, at least not explicitly. However, margin sizes can be derived using the paper size and imageable area information. For example, if the imageable area is located 144 points from the left edge of the paper, the paper effectively has a 2-inch (144 / 72 = 2) left margin. The right margin can be similarly calculated by subtracting the width of the imageable area and the width of the left margin from the total width of the paper.

For the most part, the methods defined in Paper are simple accessor and mutator methods that allow you to reference the encapsulated information.

getWidth(), getHeight(), setSize()

These methods allow you to modify and query the physical dimensions of the paper. Those values are maintained as double primitives that identify the paper size in points. For example, since Paper's values default to those of a letter-sized piece of paper, the initial width value of a Paper instance is 612 (8.5 * 72 = 612), and the initial height is 792 (11 * 72 = 792).

setImageableArea(), getImageableX(), getImageableY(), getImageableWidth(), getImageableHeight()

These methods allow you to modify and query the size and location of the imageable area. The setImageableArea() method requires four double parameter values: X position, Y position, width, and height of the paper's imageable area. For example, to set the imageable area for a letter-sized piece of paper that should have 1-inch left and right margins and 1.5-inch top and bottom margins, you could use the code that appears in Listing 11-6.

Listing 11-6. Calculating and Specifying the Values for 1-Inch Margins

```
double paperWidth = 8.5 * 72;
double paperHeight = 11 * 72;
double xMargin = 1.0 * 72;
double yMargin = 1.5 * 72;
double areaWidth = paperWidth - (xMargin * 2);
double areaHeight = paperHeight - (yMargin * 2);
Paper p = new Paper();
p.setImageableArea(xMargin, yMargin, areaWidth, areaHeight);
```

Note that these are point values, so the margin sizes must be converted from inches to points before calling setImageableArea().

clone()

Paper implements the Cloneable interface and overrides the clone() method inherited from java.lang. Object. This allows you to easily create copies of a Paper object.

Using Paper with Alternative Paper Sizes

As you saw previously, it's easy to set the imageable area size for an instance of Paper. Similarly, you'll sometimes want to adjust the paper size and margins to correspond to some type of paper other than U.S. letter size. For example, you could use the code shown in Listing 11-7 to create an instance of Paper that will be used to print to A4-sized pages (210 millimeters wide and 297 millimeters long) with 25-millimeter margins around each edge.

Listing 11-7. Calculating Margins for a Less Common Size of Paper

```
Paper paperA4 = new Paper();
double inchesPerMillimeter = 0.0394;
double widthInInches = inchesPerMillimeter * 210;
double heightInInches = inchesPerMillimeter * 297;
double marginSizeInInches = inchesPerMillimeter * 25;
double widthInPoints = widthInInches * 72;
double heightInPoints = heightInInches * 72;
double marginSizeInPoints = marginSizeInInches * 72;
double availableWidth = widthInPoints - (marginSizeInPoints * 2);
double availableHeight = heightInPoints - (marginSizeInPoints * 2);
paperA4.setImageableArea(marginSizeInPoints, marginSizeInPoints,
          availableWidth, availableHeight);
```

PageFormat

While Paper describes the physical attributes of the paper used in printing, the PageFormat class describes the logical characteristics of one or more printed pages. Depending upon the orientation (portrait or landscape) used when printing, the physical attribute values may be identical to the logical attributes.

An instance of PageFormat is passed to the print() method when it's called so the Printable implementation can determine the size and location of the imageable area on the page and confine its rendering to that region accordingly.

setOrientation(), getOrientation()

These methods allow you to modify and query the orientation value for the page(s) printed using this PageFormat object. The orientation is maintained as an int value that corresponds to one of the following constants defined in PageFormat: PORTRAIT, LANDSCAPE, or REVERSE_LANDSCAPE.

getPaper(), setPaper()

PageFormat maintains a reference to a Paper object, and these methods allow you to obtain a copy of that object and to replace it. The default Paper object corresponds to U.S. letter-sized paper with 1-inch margins on each side.

It's important to understand that getPaper() returns a copy of the PageFormat's Paper object instead of a reference to the original.

Therefore, if you want to modify the paper's size or imageable area values, you must call getPaper(), modify the object returned, and then call setPaper() to update the PageFormat's reference. The following is an example of this:

```
PageFormat pf = new PageFormat();
Paper p = pf.getPaper();
p.setImageableArea(0, 0, p.getWidth(), p.getHeight());
pf.setPaper(p);
```

getMatrix()

This method returns a matrix that can rotate an image appropriately so its orientation is correct when it's printed. However, such rotations are performed automatically and transparently based on the orientation value you select, so you won't normally use this method directly.

getWidth(), getHeight()

These methods return the logical size of the paper, as opposed to the physical size returned by the methods of the same name in Paper. The physical size identifies the actual size of the paper and always produces the same value for a certain type of paper (e.g., U.S. letter size). On the other hand, the logical size represents the paper size that's adjusted based on the selected orientation. If you use portrait orientation, the logical width and height are the same as the physical width and height. However, if you select landscape orientation, you've effectively rotated the paper, although in reality the data itself is logically rotated before it's printed. When either LANDSCAPE or REVERSE_LANDSCAPE is specified for the orientation value, the paper's logical width equals its physical height, and its logical height equals its physical width.

getImageableX(), getImageableY(), getImageableWidth(), getImageableHeight()

In much the same way that getWidth() and getHeight() translate the physical paper size into a logical size, these methods convert Paper's imageable area values based on the selected orientation.

clone()

This method is overridden from the Object implementation to allow you to easily create copies of a PageFormat instance.

Printable

Printable defines a single print() method that's called when a page should be rendered and is passed a reference to a Graphics object that represents the page being rendered. If you're already familiar with Graphics, it's probably because an instance is passed to the print() method of AWT and Swing components when they're displayed as part of a user interface. As you may suspect, because components are already able to render themselves onto a Graphics object, it's easy to print them; you'll see how to do so later in the chapter.

print()

This method is called one or more times during printing so the Printable implementation can render a page of output. Three parameter values are passed to print() that allow it perform the rendering appropriately.

- A Graphics object representing the page being rendered.

- A PageFormat object that describes the logical characteristics of the paper onto which printing will occur.

- An integer value that identifies the page to render. This is necessary because a single Printable instance may be responsible for printing multiple pages.

Some printer jobs produce output that's easy to render, and other times jobs may be complex and involve a large number of rendering operations. For the more complicated printer jobs, it may not be practical to determine in advance how many pages will be printed. For that reason, print() is required to return a value that indicates whether it was able to render the requested page. The value should correspond to one of two constants defined in Printable: PAGE_EXISTS if the page was successfully rendered or NO_SUCH_PAGE if the Printable couldn't render the requested page. When you identify a Printable implementation to PrinterJob and initiate printing, the print() method is called repeatedly until it returns a value of NO_SUCH_PAGE. Therefore, you'd typically include logic similar to that in Listing 11-8 in your print() method to cause the print job to end after printing a single page.

Listing 11-8. Terminating a Print Job Using NO_SUCH_PAGE

```
public int print(Graphics g, PageFormat pageFormat, int pageNumber) {
  if (pageNumber == 0) {
    // Rendering logic would normally go here
    return Printable.PAGE_EXISTS;
  }
  else {
    return Printable.NO_SUCH_PAGE;
  }
}
```

In effect, your print() method is responsible for identifying the printing equivalent of an "end-of-file" condition, and until it does so, PrinterJob will continue to print pages rendered by your Printable.

■ **Note** The page number passed to print() is zero-indexed, meaning that a value of 0 represents the first page, 1 represents the second page, and so on.

Sample Printing Application

It's now possible to create a simple printing application using the classes described previously. The application shown in Listing 11-9 requires the user to specify the name of an image (e.g., a GIF or JPEG) file as the first command-line parameter, and the constructor uses that file to create an instance of java.awt.Image. Although this example illustrates only how to print an image, it's just as easy to print Swing components.

Listing 11-9. Simple Printing Application

```java
import java.awt.*;
import java.awt.print.*;
import javax.print.*;
import javax.print.attribute.*;
import javax.print.attribute.standard.*;
import javax.swing.ImageIcon;

public class ImagePrint {

  protected ImageIcon printImage;

  public static void main(String[] args) throws Exception {
    ImagePrint ip = new ImagePrint(args[0]);
    ip.performPrint();
    System.exit(0);
  }

  public ImagePrint(String fileName) {
    printImage = new javax.swing.ImageIcon(fileName);
  }

  private void performPrint() throws Exception {
    // Remaining code goes here ...
  }

}
```

To print the loaded image, you must define an implementation of `Printable` that will print the image. In this case, an inner class provides the `Printable` implementation shown in Listing 11-10; the `print()` method is implemented as outlined a moment ago and simply uses the `Graphics` class's `drawImage()` method to print the image specified on the command line.

Listing 11-10. Drawing an Image on a Page Using a `Graphics` Object

```java
class MyPrintable implements Printable {

  public int print(Graphics g, PageFormat pf, int pageIndex) {
    if (pageIndex == 0) {
      g.drawImage(printImage.getImage(), 0, 0, null);
      return Printable.PAGE_EXISTS;
    }
    return Printable.NO_SUCH_PAGE;
  }

}
```

Finally, you can obtain a reference to the default print service, create a `DocPrintJob`, and use it to initiate printing as implemented in Listing 11-11.

Listing 11-11. Creating and using a DocPrintJob

```
public void performPrint() throws Exception {
    PrintService service = PrintServiceLookup.lookupDefaultPrintService();
    DocPrintJob job = service.createPrintJob();
    DocFlavor flavor = DocFlavor.SERVICE_FORMATTED.PRINTABLE;
    SimpleDoc doc = new SimpleDoc(new MyPrintable(), flavor, null);
    job.print(doc, null);
}
```

If you compile and execute this application, you may be somewhat surprised by the results. Instead of the image being printed inside the imageable area, it's aligned at the upper-left corner of the page, and a section is missing from both the top and left sides of the image (see Figure 11-6). This occurs because the Graphics object passed to print() is "clipped" to prevent you from drawing outside the imageable area even though the origin (coordinates 0, 0) of the Graphics object corresponds to the upper-left edge of the paper.

Figure 11-6. *By default the drawing is done relative to the upper-left corner of the paper even if a portion of the image falls outside the imageable area*

You can partially solve this issue by reducing the margins and therefore increasing the imageable area, but that doesn't eliminate the problem because the portion of the image outside the hardware margins would still be clipped. A better solution to this problem is to change the coordinates specified on the call to drawImage(). However, an even better solution is to adjust the Graphics object's origin so it corresponds to the corner of the imageable area, instead of the corner of the page. You can do this using translate() as shown in Listing 11-12,

471

which causes all subsequent drawing operations to be offset by the specified number of pixels. Conceptually, you may find it easier to think of translate() as moving the rendered output down and/or to the right when positive translation values are specified or moving up and to the left for negative values.

Listing 11-12. Displaying the Available Print Services

```
public int print(Graphics g, PageFormat pf, int pageIndex) {
   g.translate((int)(pf.getImageableX()),
       (int)(pf.getImageableY()));
   if (pageIndex == 0) {
    g.drawImage(printImage.getImage(), 0, 0, null);
      return Printable.PAGE_EXISTS;
   }
   return Printable.NO_SUCH_PAGE;
}
```

If you make this modification and execute the ImagePrint application, the upper-left portion of the image will be aligned with the upper-left corner of the imageable area, preventing it from being clipped on the top or left sides (see Figure 11-7).

Figure 11-7. By using the translate() method, you can perform your drawing as if the upper-left corner of the imageable area corresponds to the coordinates 0, 0

Scaling

Up to this point, I haven't made any assumptions about the Graphics object passed to the print() method, but in fact it will always be an instance of Graphics2D, which means it supports the capabilities defined within that class associated with the Java 2D API for graphics and imaging. To take advantage of the Graphics2D methods, simply cast the Graphics object as follows:

```
public int print(Graphics g, PageFormat pf, int page) {
    Graphics2D g2d = (Graphics2D)g;
```

■ **Note**   Part of the reason the Java 2D printing API is useful is because you have almost complete control over how the printed output appears. However, another reason that it's worthwhile is because it allows you to use the powerful Java 2D API for graphics and imaging.

One of the capabilities provided by Graphics2D is the ability to perform scaling, which changes the size of the output you render. For example, suppose you modify the scale factor so it renders your output at half its normal size. In that case, an image that's 100 pixels wide and 50 pixels in height will be only 50 pixels wide and 25 in height when rendered and printed. In other words, scaling allows you to shrink or enlarge your output, and you can use this technique to ensure that your data will fit on a printed page.

When you set a scale factor for a Graphics2D object, you normally should use the same value for both the width and the height. This causes your output to have the same proportions it'd have if it hadn't been scaled, while using two different scale values will distort your output. For example, if you're rendering a square but you use one value to scale the width and a different value to scale the height, the shape will be rendered as a rectangle instead of a square.

You'll typically select a scale factor by calculating the value that can be used to make the output as large as possible while still fitting within a single page, and the calculations for doing so are simple. For example, let's suppose you want to print an image that doesn't fit onto a single page like the one shown in Figure 11-8.

To print the entire image on a single page, you could make the changes shown in Listing 11-13 to ImagePrint to ensure that the image being printed fits exactly within the imageable area.

Listing 11-13. Scaling an Image to Fill the Entire Page

```
public int print(Graphics g, PageFormat pf, int pageIndex) {
    Graphics2D g2d = (Graphics2D)g;
    g.translate((int)(pf.getImageableX()),
        (int)(pf.getImageableY()));
    if (pageIndex == 0) {
        double pageWidth = pf.getImageableWidth();
        double pageHeight = pf.getImageableHeight();
        double imageWidth = printImage.getIconWidth();
        double imageHeight = printImage.getIconHeight();
        // Find out what scale factor should be applied
        // to make the image's width small enough to
        // fit on the page
        double scaleX = pageWidth / imageWidth;
        // Now do the same for the height
        double scaleY = pageHeight / imageHeight;
        // Pick the smaller of the two values so that
```

```
    // the image is as large as possible while
    // not exceeding either the page's width or
    // its height
    double scaleFactor = Math.min(scaleX, scaleY);
    // Now set the scale factor
    g2d.scale(scaleFactor, scaleFactor);
    g.drawImage(printImage.getImage(), 0, 0, null);
    return Printable.PAGE_EXISTS;
  }
  return Printable.NO_SUCH_PAGE;
}
```

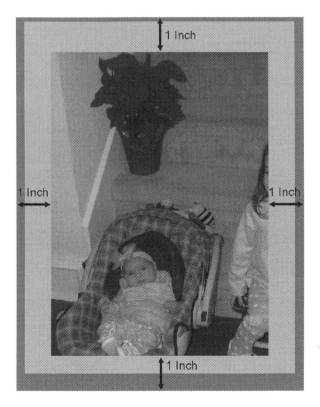

Figure 11-8. *The image is too large to be printed on a single page, so the right and bottom portions of it are clipped outside the imageable area*

With this change made, the image is scaled so it fits exactly within the imageable area, as shown in Figure 11-9. A complete discussion of the Java 2D graphics and imaging API is beyond the scope of this chapter, but by using it along with the Java 2D printing API, you can create professionally formatted output.

Figure 11-9. *Scaling lets you take advantage of the imageable area without having a portion of your output clipped*

Other Support Classes

Although Printable is perhaps the most important interface for you to be familiar with, you may also find it helpful to familiarize yourself with the Pageable interface and the Book implementation of that interface, so I'll close this chapter by briefly reviewing them.

Pageable

In the section "Introducing Service-Formatted Printing," I mentioned that service-formatted printing supports an interface called Pageable, and that interface is useful when your application needs to print multiple pages, particularly when those pages have different formatting needs. The Pageable interface defines a set of methods that can be used to create a collection of Printable/PageFormat pairs, with each pair corresponding to a printed page.

getPrintable()

Given a page number, this method returns the Printable implementation responsible for rendering the page.

getPageFormat()

Given a page number, this method returns the PageFormat that describes the logical characteristics of the page.

getNumberOfPages()

This method should return an int value that identifies the number of pages encapsulated by this Pageable object. Sometimes, however, it may not be possible to provide the page count before the printing occurs. In that case, you should return the UNKNOWN_NUMBER_OF_PAGES constant defined in Pageable.

Book

Book is an implementation of the Pageable interface and defines methods that allow you to add pairs of Printable/PageFormat objects to the collection. In addition to the three methods defined in the Pageable interface, Book implements the methods described next.

append()

This overloaded method has two implementations, although both of them require a Printable parameter and a PageFormat parameter. One implementation assumes that the Printable/PageFormat pair will be used to print a single page, and the other implementation allows you to specify the number of pages that the pair should render. For example, if you've already initialized a number of Printable and PageFormat objects, you could use code similar to that in Listing 11-14 to encapsulate those objects in an instance of Book.

Listing 11-14. Appending Pages to a Book Instance

```
Printable myPrintable1, myPrintable2, myPrintable3;
PageFormat myFormat1, myFormat2, myFormat3;
// ...
Book myBook = new Book();
myBook.append(myPrintable1, myFormat1);
myBook.append(myPrintable2, myFormat2, 5);
myBook.append(myPrintable3, myFormat3);
```

This code segment creates a Book that can print seven pages. The first page will be rendered by myPrintable1, the next five rendered by myPrintable2, and the last page by myPrintable3. When a particular page is to be rendered, the print() method of the associated Printable object is called and is passed a reference to the PageFormat object that was added to the book along with the Printable.

setPage()

While append() adds a Printable/PageFormat pair to the end of the Book's list, this method stores a pair at a specific page location. For example,

```
Book myBook = new Book();
MyBook.append(myPrintable1, myFormat1, 5);
MyBook.setPage(2, myPrintable2, myFormat2);
```

This code segment initializes a Book that can print five pages, with myPrintable1 and myFormat1 used for pages 1, 2, 4, and 5 and myPrintable2 and myFormat2 used for page 3. As is the case with the print() method, the page index values specified on setPage() calls are zero-indexed, meaning that the first page corresponds to a value of 0, so the parameter 2 in the previous arguments to setPage() refers to the third page.

RenderableImage

As its name implies, the RenderableImage interface defined in the java.awt.image.renderable package represents an image that can have operations such as rotation or cropping applied to it in a resolution-independent manner. If your application works with an instance of RenderableImage, you can specify an instance of this class as the object to be printed, as shown in Listing 11-15.

Listing 11-15. Using a RenderableImage Implementation

```
RenderableImage image;
.
.
.
PrintService service = PrintServiceLookup.lookupDefaultPrintService();
DocPrintJob job = service.createPrintJob();
DocFlavor flavor = DocFlavor.SERVICE_FORMATTED.RENDERABLE_IMAGE;
SimpleDoc doc = new SimpleDoc(image, flavor, null);
job.print(doc, null);
```

Summary

In this chapter, I covered the following:

- A brief history of Java's printing capabilities

- How to find print services

- How to limit which services are returned by specifying document flavors and attributes

- How to initiate client-formatted printing

- How to create and control a print job

- How to monitor a print job

- How to use service-formatted printing

- The basics of the Java 2D printing API

CHAPTER 12

■ ■ ■

Introducing JDBC

When your application creates or uses large amounts of data, it's usually necessary for that information to be stored in a database. Although there has been significant growth in the use of NoSQL databases in recent years, the most widely used type of database is still a relational database, and some examples of relational database products are Oracle, DB2, Sybase, MySQL, and Microsoft SQL Server. A relational database product is sometimes referred to as a *relational database management system* (RDBMS, or simply DBMS), while a *database* usually refers to a collection of data managed by a DBMS.

Java's support for relational databases is provided through the Java Database Connectivity (JDBC) API (application programming interface) that's largely contained in the java.sql package and consists of some interfaces and a handful of simple classes. Just as Java programs are intended to work on many different platforms, JDBC is designed to allow your application to communicate with many different database systems.

Using JDBC is simple, and you need to take only a few steps to add database functionality to your application. The steps involved are as follows:

1. Select/obtain a JDBC driver and add the driver code to your CLASSPATH just as you would any other third-party library.

2. Obtain a database connection using DriverManager or a DataSource and a URL that's appropriate for the driver you're using.

3. Create a Statement or an instance of one of its subinterfaces (in other words, PreparedStatement or CallableStatement), and use it to execute SQL commands.

For example, the code shown in Listing 12-1 uses a JDBC driver to connect to an Oracle database, performs a query, and sends the data returned by that query to standard output.

Listing 12-1. JDBC Example

```
String userid = "bspell";
String password = "brett";
// Get a connection
Connection conn = DriverManager.getConnection("jdbc:oracle:thin:@oraserver:1521:projava ",
  userid, password);
// Create a statement for executing SQL
Statement stmt = conn.createStatement();
// Execute a query / SELECT statement
ResultSet resultSet = stmt.executeQuery("SELECT * FROM TEST_TABLE");
ResultSetMetaData rsmd = resultSet.getMetaData();
// Find out how many columns were returned by the query
int count = rsmd.getColumnCount();
```

```
// Loop until all rows have been processed
while (resultSet.next()) {
  // Loop until all columns in current row have been processed
  for (int i = 1; i <= count; i++) {
    // Print out the current value
    System.out.print(resultSet.getObject(i));
    // Put a comma between each value
    if (i < count) {
      System.out.println(",");
    }
  }
  // Start the next row's values on a new line
  System.out.println("");
}
// Close the database objects
resultSet.close();
stmt.close();
conn.close();
```

In this chapter, you'll examine each of the following topics related to using JDBC:

- Selecting and obtaining driver types

- Obtaining a connection to a database

- Executing SQL statements and stored procedures

- Understanding data types defined in JDBC and how they relate to "native" types

- Managing transactions

- Implementing database connection pooling

- Processing errors and warnings generated by JDBC functions

- Debugging guidelines for database applications

SQL Standards and JDBC Versions

Providing a single interface to many DBMS products is difficult because each product supports a unique collection of features and data types. For example, while SQL Server supports a Boolean data type, Oracle doesn't; however, you can simulate Boolean data using numeric fields. Even when two DBMS products provide the same functionality, the way you use that functionality on one DBMS can be very different from the way it's used on the other. Fortunately, JDBC provides a layer of abstraction between your application and the specific details of how to perform a particular task.

Variation between DBMS products has been limited somewhat by organizations that have established standards for Structured Query Language (SQL). The most widely adopted and well-known standard is the SQL2 standard (also known as SQL92), although a more recent standard called SQL3 has emerged. SQL3 is partly an attempt to address what's perceived as a serious limitation of SQL2: its lack of support for object-oriented concepts. When SQL2 was designed, object-oriented programming wasn't yet widely adopted, and the result is that SQL as defined by SQL2 is poorly suited to object persistence. In fact, an entire category of products has emerged to address this problem using technology called *object-relational mapping*; you'll examine that topic in more detail in the next chapter.

The JDBC 1.*x* API specification defined functionality based on the SQL2/SQL92 standard, and support for that specification was included in the Java 1.1 core classes and defined within the java.sql package. When the JDBC 2.0 specification was released, it included some functionality that was expected to be used primarily on application servers and that wasn't originally intended to be included in the Standard Edition of Java. As a result, the JDBC 2.*x* functionality included changes to the "core" java.sql package and also defined a new javax.sql "standard extension" package that contained classes related to the newly defined server functionality. Eventually, however, the javax.sql package became part of the Java Standard Edition, so you'll now find both java.sql and javax.sql if you examine the documentation for that edition.

As you read this chapter, an important point to be aware of is that the features available to your application will depend upon which implementation of JDBC you're using. For example, if you're using an implementation of the JDBC 3.0 API, you won't be able to use features that were added in the 4.0 specification. For that reason, it's obviously desirable to pick an implementation of the latest specification, but that's not always possible depending upon which database you're using. When writing your application, you should ensure you use only those JDBC features that will be available to you, and the way to determine this is to find out which JDBC driver (explained next) you'll be using and consult its documentation to learn which API specification it supports.

JDBC Drivers

The most important part of the java.sql package is its collection of interfaces, because they define how your application interacts with a relational database. One of those interfaces is Driver, and it includes a method that's used to obtain database connections, so in a sense Driver is the starting point for an application's use of JDBC. In reality, you'll rarely, if ever, use Driver directly, but instead you'll rely on other classes and interfaces that provide an additional layer of abstraction around the creation of a database connection. Even so, the phrase *JDBC driver* is used to refer to a library of classes that includes a Driver implementation and the other classes—usually a large number of them—that provide support for JDBC operations to one or more types of DBMS. A JDBC driver is usually packaged as a ZIP or JAR file, and you can obtain drivers from a variety of sources.

Most DBMS vendors supply at least one driver for use with their own database, usually at no cost. However, third parties also sell drivers, and those often provide better performance and/or reliability than the database vendor implementations. Note that it's not necessary for a driver to support all features defined in the JDBC specification for the driver to be considered JDBC-compliant, although most drivers do support most features. If there's a specific feature your application needs, you should test the driver in advance before choosing it or contact the vendor that supplies the driver before purchasing it to ensure that it supports the desired functionality.

Like any other third-party library, a JDBC driver that you obtain for use within your application must be added to your CLASSPATH when the application is executed. For example, if you've downloaded a driver that's packaged as a ZIP file called ojdbc7.jar stored in the C:/brett/temp directory, you could use the following statement to execute an application called MyDatabaseApp and include the driver in your CLASSPATH:

```
java -classpath=C:/brett/temp/ojdbc7.jar MyDatabaseApp
```

Driver Types

JDBC drivers are divided into four categories, or *types*, based on how they connect to the database. Each category has unique advantages and disadvantages, and it's common for driver vendors to provide more than one type of JDBC driver for a database. For example, Oracle provides both a type-2 and a type-4 driver for its namesake DBMS.

Type 1: Connection Through an ODBC Data Source

Microsoft's Open Database Connectivity (ODBC) is conceptually similar to JDBC and is widely used to provide relational database connectivity. In fact, ODBC is provided with the Windows operating system, and you can define an ODBC data source through the Data Sources dialog box, as shown in Figure 12-1.

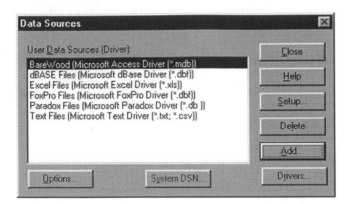

Figure 12-1. *Windows allows you to list the ODBC data sources defined on your system*

A *data source* is simply a way of associating a name with a particular database, and when creating a new data source, you must select the ODBC driver used to access the database, as shown in Figure 12-2.

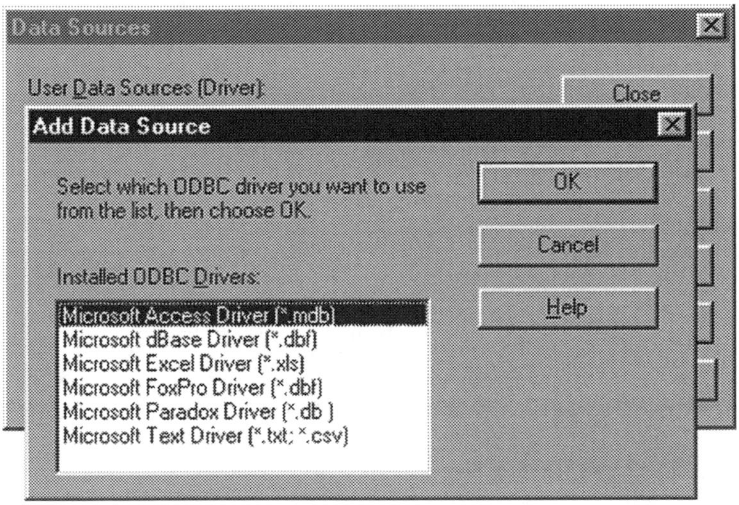

Figure 12-2. *To define a new data source, you must first select the type to create*

The first type of JDBC driver we'll look at, called a *type-1 driver*, provides JDBC access to a database by connecting to it through an ODBC data source instead of by connecting directly to the database. To create a connection using a type-1 driver you specify the name of a data source and the driver will connect to the data source you specified. Subsequent JDBC operations are then performed by calling the equivalent function in the ODBC driver and converting the results returned from those functions into their Java equivalents.

For many years the Java core classes include a type-1 driver commonly referred to as the *JDBC-ODBC bridge driver*. Although the driver wasn't very robust in terms of features it was useful for performing simple tests and for developing small applications. It was particularly useful in the early days of Java when few JDBC drivers (but many ODBC drivers) were available, because it allowed Java applications to connect to any database for which an ODBC driver was present. Now, though, there are probably even more JDBC drivers than ODBC drivers to choose from, and presumably as a result of its greatly reduced usefulness, Oracle removed the bridge driver from Java effective in Java 8.

In practice, type-1 drivers were never considered an ideal solution for database connectivity and the bridge driver had long been described as a "transitional" technology. Besides the obvious disadvantage of needing two different database drivers (one JDBC and one ODBC) to be present, this design is inherently slower than one that communicates directly with a database and is largely a Windows-centric solution because ODBC is primarily focused on providing database access to Windows applications.

Type 2: Connection Through Native Client Networking Code

Most DBMS products provide a client interface that allows you to interact with the database server. For example, Oracle provides the SQL*Plus application that allows you to connect to a database, issue SQL statements, and view the results of those statements (the rows returned from a query). However, before you can use SQL*Plus, you must install Oracle's networking software that allows a client to communicate with the database server.

A type-2 JDBC driver includes both Java and native code, and it communicates with the client-side network software of a particular DBMS. It provides better performance than a type-1 driver does, but it can make distributing your application more difficult since you must ensure that each client has the networking software installed.

Type 3: Connection Through Middleware

This type of driver is written entirely in Java, and it sends database requests to a server component. Those requests are transmitted using a protocol that's not specific to any database, and the server component is responsible for converting it into the appropriate format before forwarding the request to a particular DBMS.

A type-3 driver has the disadvantage of requiring a server-side component, but it does allow you to change the DBMS being used on the server without affecting your client code.

Type 4: Direct Connection to DBMS

A type-4 driver is written entirely in Java, and it communicates directly with a DBMS server using the appropriate protocol for that type of server. For example, in the case of Oracle's type-4 driver, a socket connection is opened between the JDBC application and the database server.

This type of driver is easy to use because the only component needed is the driver itself, which can easily be packaged with a Java application. No other client- or server-side software is required, which simplifies distributing your application.

Table 12-1 summarizes the advantages and disadvantages of the various driver types.

Table 12-1. *Advantages and Disadvantages of Each Driver Type*

Driver Type	Advantages	Disadvantages
1	Allows Java program code to use any database that provides an ODBC driver	Performance may not be as good as a driver of a different type.
2	Performance is generally very good	Uses native code and is therefore platform-dependent.
3	Platform-independent	Requires both a client and a corresponding server implementation.
4	Platform-independent	Performance may not be as good as a driver of a different type.

Obtaining a Database Connection

As mentioned earlier, you can use an implementation of the Driver interface to obtain a database connection, although you shouldn't call the methods in that class directly. Instead, you should request a connection from the DriverManager singleton through its static getConnection() methods.

When you call getConnection(), DriverManager passes the parameter values specified to each registered driver until it finds one that's able to establish a connection using those values. Since the inclusion of JDBC 4.0 in Java 6 all JDBC drivers on the class path have been loaded automatically, although in earlier versions of Java it was necessary to explicitly instantiate the Driver implementation class, which in turn would cause it to register itself with the DriverManager class. For example, in an earlier version of Java you would need to include a line like the following:

```
new oracle.jdbc.driver.OracleDriver();
```

or as follows:

```
Class.forName("oracle.jdbc.driver.OracleDriver");
```

Alternatively, you could have drivers loaded automatically by setting the value of the jdbc.drivers system property when starting a Java Virtual Machine (JVM). The jdbc.drivers property specified the names of the Driver classes to be loaded and was set using the –D option available on most JVM implementations. The following command executes the main() method of the Java class named Test after loading an Oracle driver. Multiple drivers could be specified by separating the fully qualified Driver class names (the package and class names) with the colon (:) character:

```
java –Djdbc.drivers=oracle.jdbc.driver.OracleDriver Test
```

JDBC URL Formats

At a minimum, you must specify a JDBC URL when calling getConnection(), although a user ID and password are usually also needed. The URL identifies the specific database you want to connect to, while the user ID and password provide the authentication information that the database may require before a connection can be created.

The JDBC URL isn't a traditional URL that can be represented by an instance of java.net.URL but is a String value that identifies a particular JDBC driver and database. The general format of a JDBC URL is jdbc:<subprotocol>:<subname>, where the values of <subprotocol> and <subname> vary based on the database you want to connect to and the driver being used. One of the simplest examples of a URL format is that of the previously mentioned bridge driver, where the subprotocol would simply be "odbc" and the subname would be the name of the ODBC data source. For example, to connect to an ODBC data source named projava, you would specify the URL as jdbc:odbc:projava. In practice, JDBC URLs are usually slightly more complex than that. For example, Oracle's type-4 (or *thin-client* as Oracle refers to it) driver requires you to create a <subname> that includes three items:

- The host name of the machine that the DBMS server is running on

- The port number that it uses to listen for incoming connections

- The name of the database to which you want to connect

To use Oracle's thin-client driver to connect to the database projava maintained on a server named oraserve that uses port 1521, you'd specify the following URL:

```
jdbc:oracle:thin:@oraserver:1521:projava
```

Keep in mind that the URL isn't just vendor-specific but driver-specific. For example, besides the thin-client driver mentioned, Oracle also offers a type-2 (or OCI), and to connect to the same database with that driver, you'd instead use the following URL:

```
jdbc:oracle:oci8:@projava
```

Since the format of the URL is driver-specific, you should review the documentation associated with the driver you're using to determine the correct format of a URL.

Connection

A database connection is represented in JDBC by an instance of the Connection class, and as you might expect, an instance of that class is returned by DriverManager's getConnection() methods. The following code illustrates how to obtain a database connection:

```
String url = "jdbc:oracle:thin:@oraserver:1521:projava";
Connection connect = DriverManager.getConnection(url, "bspell", "brett");
```

Obtaining Connections from a DataSource (2.*x* Optional Package)

The technique just described for obtaining a database connection is easy to use, but it does have one drawback. Since you must load a driver and construct a driver- and database-specific URL, this approach causes your application to be tightly coupled to a specific driver and database. Although there are ways to address those weaknesses, no standard solution was defined until JDBC 2.*x*, when the DataSource interface was introduced as part of the optional package.

A DataSource is simply a class that provides a layer of abstraction between your application and the information needed to connect to a database. That information may include the "identity" of the Driver class, the information needed to construct a valid URL, and a user ID and password. Like DriverManager, DataSource provides getConnection() methods that can be used to obtain database connections.

DataSource implementations are widely used by application servers to provide the ability to connect to a database through a combination of JDBC and the Java Naming and Directory Interface (JNDI). JNDI is an API that defines methods used to associate names with resources and provide access to those resources through a *directory*. In this case, the resource would be a DataSource that's able to obtain a connection to a particular database; the following is an example of how JNDI and the DataSource might be used:

```
Context ctx = new InitialContext();
DataSource source = (DataSource)(ctx.lookup("jdbc/projava"));
Connection connect = source.getConnection();
```

With this approach, your application code is coupled only to the name assigned to the database (projava) instead of to a particular driver and URL. In fact, this technique allows both the driver and the information used to connect to the database to be modified without requiring any changes to your source code. So, for example, if you've deployed a web application to an application server and that application uses a database connection, you can change the connection information if necessary without making any changes to the web application code.

DatabaseMetaData

The DatabaseMetaData interface defines a large number of methods that allow you to identify the capabilities of the DBMS and the JDBC driver, as well as allowing you to obtain a description of the contents of the database. For example, you can retrieve the list of schemas defined in the database, the tables within each schema, the columns within each table, and the characteristics of those columns, such as their size and data types. In addition, you can use DatabaseMetaData to identify primary and foreign keys, indices, and many other items.

In general, the methods in DatabaseMetaData fall into one of two categories: those for describing features and functionality and those that describe the contents of the database.

The methods that describe database features and functionality typically return a boolean, an int, or a String; some examples include the following:

- supportsOuterJoins() returns a boolean that indicates whether the database supports outer joins.

- getMaxConnections() returns an int that identifies the maximum number of simultaneous connections that can be open to the database.

- getDatabaseProductName() returns the name of the DBMS product.

In contrast, the methods that describe the contents of the database do so by returning an implementation of ResultSet, an interface described later in the chapter that's normally used in JDBC to represent the results of a query. Examples of this category of method include getSchemas(), which returns a list of schemas defined in the database, and getTables(), which as its name implies returns a list of the tables defined.

Once you've successfully connected to the database, it's possible to obtain a reference to an instance of DatabaseMetaData using code similar to the following:

```
Connection connect = DriverManager.getConnection(url, "bspell", "brett");
DatabaseMetaData metaData = connect.getMetaData();
```

As Figure 12-3 shows, the DatabaseBrowser application in Listing 12-2 allows you to browse the tables in a database, and you accomplish this by using DatabaseMetaData to dynamically identify the accessible tables.

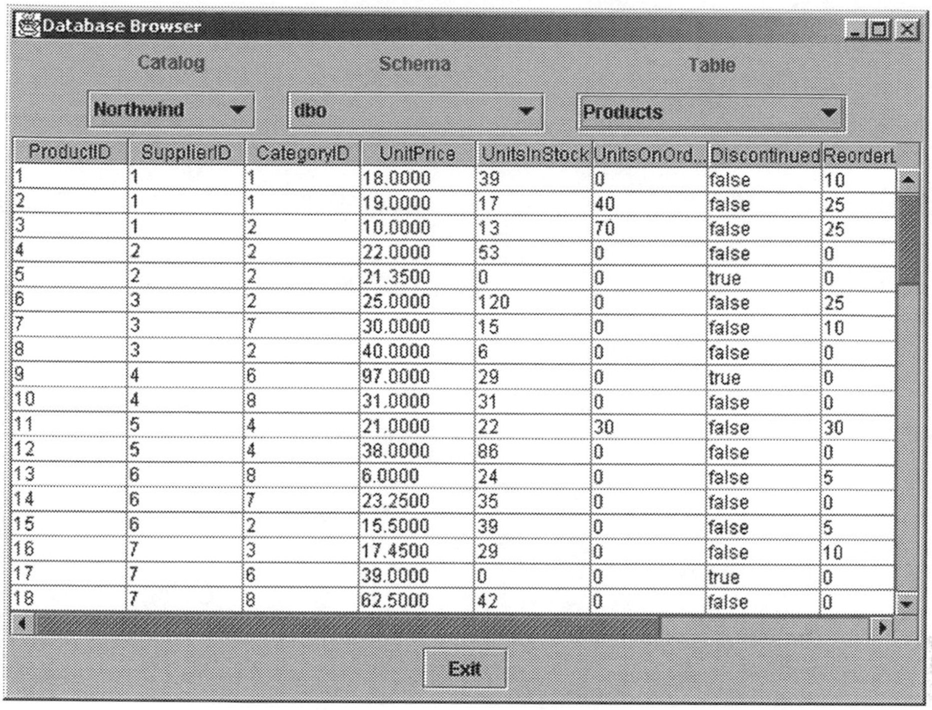

ProductID	SupplierID	CategoryID	UnitPrice	UnitsInStock	UnitsOnOrd...	Discontinued	ReorderL
1	1	1	18.0000	39	0	false	10
2	1	1	19.0000	17	40	false	25
3	1	2	10.0000	13	70	false	25
4	2	2	22.0000	53	0	false	0
5	2	2	21.3500	0	0	true	0
6	3	2	25.0000	120	0	false	25
7	3	7	30.0000	15	0	false	10
8	3	2	40.0000	6	0	false	0
9	4	6	97.0000	29	0	true	0
10	4	8	31.0000	31	0	false	0
11	5	4	21.0000	22	30	false	30
12	5	4	38.0000	86	0	false	0
13	6	8	6.0000	24	0	false	5
14	6	7	23.2500	35	0	false	0
15	6	2	15.5000	39	0	false	5
16	7	3	17.4500	29	0	false	10
17	7	6	39.0000	0	0	true	0
18	7	8	62.5000	42	0	false	0

Figure 12-3. *The `DatabaseBrowser` application allows you to browse the information in a database*

Listing 12-2. `DatabaseBrowser` Application

```
import java.awt.*;
import java.awt.event.*;
import java.sql.*;
import java.util.ArrayList;
import java.util.List;
import javax.swing.*;
import javax.swing.table.*;

public class DatabaseBrowser extends JFrame {

  private Connection connection;
  private JComboBox catalogBox;
  private JComboBox schemaBox;
  private JComboBox tableBox;
  private JTable table;

  public static void main(String[] args) throws Exception {
    DatabaseBrowser browser = new DatabaseBrowser();
  }
```

```
public DatabaseBrowser() throws Exception {
  super("Database Browser");
  ConnectionDialog dialog = new ConnectionDialog(this);
  connection = dialog.getConnection();
  buildFrameLayout();
  setSize(600, 450);
  setVisible(true);
}

private void buildFrameLayout() {
  Container pane = getContentPane();
  pane.add(getSelectionPanel(), BorderLayout.NORTH);
  table = new JTable();
  table.setAutoResizeMode(JTable.AUTO_RESIZE_OFF);
  refreshTable();
  pane.add(new JScrollPane(table), BorderLayout.CENTER);
  pane.add(getFrameButtonPanel(), BorderLayout.SOUTH);
}

private JPanel getSelectionPanel() {
  JLabel label;
  JPanel panel = new JPanel();
  panel.setLayout(new GridBagLayout());
  GridBagConstraints constraints = new GridBagConstraints();
  constraints.gridy = 0;
  constraints.insets = new Insets(5, 10, 5, 10);
  label = new JLabel("Catalog", JLabel.RIGHT);
  panel.add(label, constraints);
  label = new JLabel("Schema", JLabel.RIGHT);
  panel.add(label, constraints);
  label = new JLabel("Table", JLabel.RIGHT);
  panel.add(label, constraints);

  constraints.gridy = 1;
  catalogBox = new JComboBox();
  populateCatalogBox();
  panel.add(catalogBox, constraints);
  schemaBox = new JComboBox();
  populateSchemaBox();
  panel.add(schemaBox, constraints);
  tableBox = new JComboBox();
  populateTableBox();
  panel.add(tableBox, constraints);

  catalogBox.addItemListener(new ItemListener() {
    public void itemStateChanged(ItemEvent event) {
      String newCatalog = (String)(
          catalogBox.getSelectedItem());
      try {
        connection.setCatalog(newCatalog);
      } catch (Exception e) {};
```

```
      populateSchemaBox();
      populateTableBox();
      refreshTable();
    }
  });

  schemaBox.addItemListener(new ItemListener() {
    public void itemStateChanged(ItemEvent event) {
      populateTableBox();
      refreshTable();
    }
  });

  tableBox.addItemListener(new ItemListener() {
    public void itemStateChanged(ItemEvent event) {
      refreshTable();
    }
  });
  return panel;
}

private void populateCatalogBox() {
  try {
    DatabaseMetaData metaData = connection.getMetaData();
    ResultSet resultSet = metaData.getCatalogs();
    List values = new ArrayList();
    while (resultSet.next()) {
      values.add (resultSet.getString(1));
    }
    resultSet.close();
    catalogBox.setModel(new DefaultComboBoxModel(values.toArray()));
    catalogBox.sctSelectedItem(connection.getCatalog());
    catalogBox.setEnabled(values.size() > 0);
  } catch (Exception e) {
    catalogBox.setEnabled(false);
  }
}

private void populateSchemaBox() {
  try {
    DatabaseMetaData metaData = connection.getMetaData();
    ResultSet resultSet = metaData.getSchemas();
    List values = new ArrayList();
    while (resultSet.next()) {
      values.add (resultSet.getString(1));
    }
    resultSet.close();
    schemaBox.setModel(new DefaultComboBoxModel(values.toArray()));
    schemaBox.setEnabled(values.size() > 0);
  } catch (Exception e) {
    schemaBox.setEnabled(false);
  }
}
```

```java
private void populateTableBox() {
  try {
    String[] types = {"TABLE"};
    String catalog = connection.getCatalog();
    String schema = (String)(schemaBox.getSelectedItem());
    DatabaseMetaData metaData = connection.getMetaData();
    ResultSet resultSet = metaData.getTables(catalog, schema, null,
        types);
    List values = new ArrayList();
    while (resultSet.next()) {
      values.add(resultSet.getString(3));
    }
    resultSet.close();
    tableBox.setModel(new DefaultComboBoxModel(values.toArray()));
    tableBox.setEnabled(values.size() > 0);
  } catch (Exception e) {
    tableBox.setEnabled(false);
  }
}

private JPanel getFrameButtonPanel() {
  JPanel panel = new JPanel();
  JButton button = new JButton("Exit");
  button.addActionListener(new ActionListener() {
    public void actionPerformed(ActionEvent event) {
      System.exit(0);
    }
  });
  panel.add(button);
  return panel;
}

private void refreshTable() {
  String catalog = (catalogBox.isEnabled() ?
      catalogBox.getSelectedItem().toString() :
      null);
  String schema = (schemaBox.isEnabled() ?
      schemaBox.getSelectedItem().toString() :
      null);
  String tableName = (String)tableBox.getSelectedItem();
  if (tableName == null) {
    table.setModel(new DefaultTableModel());
    return;
  }
  String selectTable = (schema == null ? "" : schema + ".") +
      tableName;
  if (selectTable.indexOf(' ') > 0) {
    selectTable = "\"" + selectTable + "\"";
  }
```

```
    try {
      Statement stmt = connection.createStatement();
      ResultSet resultSet = stmt.executeQuery("SELECT * FROM " +
          selectTable);
      table.setModel(new ResultSetTableModel(resultSet));
    } catch (Exception e) {};
}

class ConnectionDialog extends JDialog {

private JTextField useridField;
private JTextField passwordField;
private JTextField urlField;

private boolean canceled;
private Connection connect;

public ConnectionDialog(JFrame f) {
  super(f, "Connect To Database", true);
  buildDialogLayout();
  setSize(300, 200);
}

public Connection getConnection() {
  setVisible(true);
  return connect;
}

private void buildDialogLayout() {
  JLabel label;

  Container pane = getContentPane();
  pane.setLayout(new GridBagLayout());
  GridBagConstraints constraints = new GridBagConstraints();
  constraints.anchor = GridBagConstraints.WEST;
  constraints.insets = new Insets(5, 10, 5, 10);

  constraints.gridx = 0;
  constraints.gridy = 0;
  label = new JLabel("Userid:", JLabel.LEFT);
  pane.add(label, constraints);

  constraints.gridy++;
  label = new JLabel("Password:", JLabel.LEFT);
  pane.add(label, constraints);

  constraints.gridy++;
  label = new JLabel("URL:", JLabel.LEFT);
  pane.add(label, constraints);
```

```
      constraints.gridx = 1;
      constraints.gridy = 0;

      useridField = new JTextField(10);
      pane.add(useridField, constraints);

      constraints.gridy++;
      passwordField = new JTextField(10);
      pane.add(passwordField, constraints);

      constraints.gridy++;
      urlField = new JTextField(15);
      pane.add(urlField, constraints);

      constraints.gridx = 0;
      constraints.gridy = 3;
      constraints.gridwidth = GridBagConstraints.REMAINDER;
      constraints.anchor = GridBagConstraints.CENTER;
      pane.add(getButtonPanel(), constraints);
    }

    private JPanel getButtonPanel() {
      JPanel panel = new JPanel();
      JButton btn = new JButton("Ok");
      btn.addActionListener(new ActionListener() {
        public void actionPerformed(ActionEvent event) {
          onDialogOk();
        }
      });
      panel.add(btn);
      btn = new JButton("Cancel");
      btn.addActionListener(new ActionListener() {
        public void actionPerformed(ActionEvent event) {
          onDialogCancel();
        }
      });
      panel.add(btn);
      return panel;
    }

    private void onDialogOk() {
      if (attemptConnection()) {
        setVisible(false);
      }
    }

    private void onDialogCancel() {
      System.exit(0);
    }
```

```java
  private boolean attemptConnection() {
    try {
      connect = DriverManager.getConnection(
          urlField.getText(),
          useridField.getText(),
          passwordField.getText());
      return true;
    } catch (Exception e) {
      JOptionPane.showMessageDialog(this,
          "Error connecting to " +
          "database: " + e.getMessage());
    }
    return false;
  }

}

class ResultSetTableModel extends AbstractTableModel {

  private List columnHeaders;
  private List tableData;

  public ResultSetTableModel(ResultSet resultSet)
      throws SQLException {
    List rowData;
    ResultSetMetaData rsmd = resultSet.getMetaData();
    int count = rsmd.getColumnCount();
    columnHeaders = new ArrayList(count);
    tableData = new ArrayList();
    for (int i = 1; i <= count; i++) {
      columnHeaders.add(rsmd.getColumnName(i));
    }
    while (resultSet.next()) {
      rowData = new ArrayList(count);
      for (int i = 1; i <= count; i++) {
        rowData.add(resultSet.getObject(i));
      }
      tableData.add(rowData);
    }
  }

  public int getColumnCount() {
    return columnHeaders.size();
  }

  public int getRowCount() {
    return tableData.size();
  }
```

```
    public Object getValueAt(int row, int column) {
      List rowData = (List)(tableData.get(row));
      return rowData.get(column);
    }

    public boolean isCellEditable(int row, int column) {
      return false;
    }

    public String getColumnName(int column) {
      return (String)(columnHeaders.get(column));
    }

  }

}
```

Statement

Once you've obtained a database connection through DriverManager or through a DataSource, you can create a Statement object. A Statement allows you to execute SQL commands, and you can create an instance of Statement by calling Connection's createStatement() method:

```
Connection connect = DriverManager.getConnection("jdbc:odbc:projava");
Statement stmt = connect.createStatement();
```

The Statement interface defines four methods for executing SQL commands, and the specific methods used will depend upon the type of statements you're executing and the type of results returned by those statements.

You can reuse a single instance of Statement repeatedly to execute SQL statements, and simple applications usually need to create only one Statement. However, each instance allows only a single SQL command to be active at any given time, so you may sometimes need to create multiple Statement objects. For example, if your application needs to perform a query while the results of a previous query are still being processed, the two queries must be issued from different Statement instances.

executeUpdate()

This method allows you to execute most Data Manipulation Language (DML) statements (INSERT, UPDATE, and DELETE) and Data Definition Language (DDL) statements (CREATE TABLE, CREATE VIEW, etc.). It accepts a single String parameter that represents the SQL statement to be executed and returns an integer value identifying the number of rows that were modified by the statement. The following are examples of how to use executeUpdate():

```
Statement stmt = connect.createStatement();
int rowsChanged = stmt.executeUpdate(
        "UPDATE MYTABLE SET ACCTSTATUS = 0 WHERE CUSTID = 123");
rowsChanged = stmt.executeUpdate(
        "UPDATE HERTABLE SET ACCTBAL = 0 WHERE CUSTID = 123");
```

For DDL commands, a value of zero is always returned by executeUpdate().

executeQuery()

When you want to perform a query (issue a SELECT statement), you can do so using the executeQuery() method. This method requires a String parameter representing the statement to be executed, and it returns a ResultSet that can be used to process the results of the query.

```
ResultSet resultSet = stmt.executeQuery("SELECT * FROM MYTABLE");
```

I'll provide a detailed description of how to use ResultSet later in this chapter.

execute()

In some unusual cases, a single SQL statement can return multiple update counts or ResultSet instances, and you should use this method when you expect that to be the case. Like executeUpdate() and executeQuery(), this method is passed a String parameter representing the statement to be executed, but execute() returns a Boolean value instead of an int or a ResultSet. That value identifies the data type of the first return value and will be true if the first value is a ResultSet or false if it's an integer.

You can iterate through the return values by calling getMoreResults(), which returns a Boolean value with the same meaning as the value returned by execute(). ResultSet instances and integer update counts can be retrieved from the queue using getResultSet() and getUpdateCount(), respectively, but when getUpdateCount() returns a value of -1, the end of the result queue has been reached.

addBatch(), executeBatch()

The executeUpdate() method described previously is simple and easy to use but has one disadvantage: each SQL statement executed is immediately sent to the database. While that isn't a problem as long as a small number of updates are being executed, it can result in poor performance when making many changes to a database. The DBMS server and the client application typically reside on different machines, which means that each invocation of executeUpdate() will incur the overhead associated with a network call. That overhead is usually substantial, and it's much more efficient to transfer a large amount of data in a single network call than it is to transfer smaller amounts of data using many calls.

The addBatch() method can be called multiple times for a Statement and allows you to create a group (or *batch*) of update (INSERT, UPDATE, DELETE) statements. Once you've added the statements you want to include in the batch, executeBatch() will send those statements to the DBMS using a single network call, and the results are returned as an array of int values. Since batch updates greatly reduce network overhead, they can significantly improve an application's performance. Following is a simple example of how to use batch updates:

```
Statement stmt = connect.createStatement();
stmt.addBatch("UPDATE MYTABLE SET STATUS = 5 WHERE CUSTID = 123");
stmt.addBatch("UPDATE HISTABLE SET FIRSTNAME = 'John' WHERE CUSTID = 456");
int[] results = stmt.executeBatch();
```

When all the updates in a batch complete normally, executeBatch() returns an array of integer values, and there will be an array element for each update statement. Like the integer value returned by executeUpdate(), each integer identifies the number of rows the statement changed or will be -2 if that number couldn't be determined.

A JDBC driver may or may not continue executing batch update statements after one of them fails. When an error does occur, a BatchUpdateException is thrown that can be used to retrieve the integer values for the statements that were executed. If the driver continued to execute updates after a failure, the BatchUpdateException's getUpdateCounts() method will return an array of integers for every statement in the batch, including a count value of -3 as the array element for a statement that wasn't executed successfully. If the driver stopped executing statements once a failure occurred, the integer array will contain only count values for the statements prior to the one that failed. Regardless of the outcome, the list of SQL commands in the Statement's batch is cleared once executeBatch() completes. You can also clear the list of statements without executing them by calling the clearBatch() method.

PreparedStatement

When you call one of Statement's execute() methods, the SQL statement specified is "compiled" by the JDBC driver before being sent to the DBMS. In many cases, you'll want to execute multiple statements that are similar and may differ only by a single parameter value. For example, you might execute SQL statements like the following:

```
Statement stmt = connect.createStatement();
stmt.executeUpdate(
    "UPDATE MYTABLE SET FNAME = 'Jacob' WHERE CUSTID = 123");
stmt.executeUpdate(
    "UPDATE MYTABLE SET FNAME = 'Jordan' WHERE CUSTID = 456");
stmt.executeUpdate(
    "UPDATE MYTABLE SET FNAME = 'Jeffery' WHERE CUSTID = 789");
```

Compiling each SQL statement can result in poor performance if a large number of statements are executed. However, this example illustrates the usefulness of PreparedStatement, which is a subclass of Statement. PreparedStatement allows you to compile a statement one time and use substitution parameters to modify the final SQL statement that's executed. In this case, for example, you might create a PreparedStatement using code like the following:

```
PreparedStatement pstmt = connect.prepareStatement(
    "UPDATE MYTABLE SET FNAME = ? WHERE CUSTID = ?");
```

The two question marks (?) in the statement represent substitution parameters, and you can use the setXXX() methods defined in PreparedStatement to specify values for those fields. For example, the code in Listing 12-3 is functionally equivalent to the group of statements used earlier.

Listing 12-3. Using a PreparedStatement

```
PreparedStatement pstmt = connect.prepareStatement(
    "UPDATE MYTABLE SET FNAME = ? WHERE CUSTID = ?");

pstmt.setString(1, "Jacob");
pstmt.setInt(2, 123);
pstmt.executeUpdate();

pstmt.setString(1, "Jordan");
pstmt.setInt(2, 456);
pstmt.executeUpdate();

pstmt.setString(1, "Jeffery");
pstmt.setInt(2, 789);
pstmt.executeUpdate();
```

This approach is much more efficient because the statement is compiled only once, but it's executed several times.

Note that the substitution field index values are one-based instead of zero-based, meaning that the first question mark corresponds to field 1, the second to field 2, and so on.

Another advantage of using a `PreparedStatement` instead of a `Statement` is that it partially insulates your application from the details of creating a valid SQL statement. For example, suppose you attempt to execute the following code:

```
Statement stmt = connect.createStatement();
String insertText = "This won't work";
String sqlText = "UPDATE MYTABLE SET FNAME = '" + insertText + "' " +
                "WHERE CUSTID = 123");
stmt.executeUpdate(sqlText);
```

The SQL statement that's constructed in the code segment listed previously will fail because of the embedded single quote/apostrophe character in the word *won't*. In other words, the SQL statement will contain the following text:

```
UPDATE MYTABLE SET FNAME = 'This won't work' WHERE CUSTID = 123
```

It's possible to solve this problem (and use a `Statement`) by changing each embedded apostrophe into a pair of apostrophes. However, that approach is moderately complex and requires you to perform a conversion on any string that may have embedded apostrophes before using the string in a SQL statement.

A related problem occurs when embedding date values in a SQL statement, since each DBMS can define its own date format. For example, the following statement may be valid for one DBMS but not another:

```
UPDATE ACCTINFO SET DATEOFSALE = '09-FEB-2001' WHERE ACCTNUM = 456
```

A third problem occurs when you want to store binary data in a database. SQL supports text, numeric, and date information but doesn't define a way for you to embed a series of byte values in a SQL statement.

Fortunately, `PreparedStatement` provides an easy solution for all three of these problems. Instead of embedding the data value directly inside the SQL statement, you can simply define a substitution parameter and use a `setXXX()` method to store the appropriate value. When you do so, the JDBC driver assumes responsibility for creating a valid SQL statement, which insulates your application from the details of embedding a particular type of data. For example, you can store a `String` value (with or without embedded quotation marks) in a `PreparedStatement` using code like the following:

```
String insertText = "This won't work";
PreparedStatement pstmt = connect.prepareStatement(
    "UPDATE MYTABLE SET FNAME = ? " +
    "WHERE CUSTID = 123");
pstmt.setString(1, insertText);
pstmt.executeUpdate();
```

You can specify a Date value the same way, as illustrated next. Note, however, that an instance of java.util.Date must first be converted into an instance of java.sql.Date.

```
java.util.Date dateValue = new java.util.Date();
java.sql.Date sqlDate = new java.sql.Date(dateValue.getTime());
PreparedStatement pstmt = connect.prepareStatement(
    "UPDATE ACCTINFO SET DATEOFSALE = ? " +
    "WHERE ACCTNUM = 456");
pstmt.setDate(1, sqlDate);
pstmt.executeUpdate();
```

Finally, an array of byte values can be stored by encapsulating them in a ByteArrayInputStream and storing a reference to that stream using setBinaryStream().

```
byte[] pixelValues;
// ...
PreparedStatement pstmt = connect.prepareStatement(
    "UPDATE APPIMAGES SET IMAGEDATA = ? " +
    "WHERE IMAGEID = 789");
ByteArrayInputStream bais = new ByteArrayInputStream(pixelValues);
pstmt.setBinaryStream(1, bais, pixelValues.length);
```

CallableStatement

CallableStatement is a subclass of PreparedStatement, and this class allows you to execute stored procedures, or programs stored inside a database. Stored procedures are usually written in a proprietary language such as Oracle's PL/SQL, and they typically contain a combination of SQL statements and structured programming instructions. The following is the simplest version of a stored procedure call, where myProcedure is a stored procedure that performs a query:

```
String procedureCall = "{call myProcedure}";
CallableStatement cstmt = connect.prepareCall(procedureCall);
ResultSet resultSet = cstmt.executeQuery();
```

Note that the string used to call the stored procedure is enclosed in braces. This is done because the syntax for calling stored procedures isn't a standard part of SQL, so JDBC supports these calls through its escape syntax. The escape syntax is used for nonstandard SQL extensions that are supported by JDBC, and it indicates to the driver that the escape text must be converted into a form that's appropriate for the DBMS.

Like Java methods, stored procedures may allow you to pass parameter values (in stored procedure terminology, an IN parameter) and may provide a return value (or result parameter). Unlike Java methods, however, stored procedures can return multiple values through OUT parameters, and a parameter can be an IN parameter, an OUT parameter, or both (INOUT). Parameters are identified by question marks in CallableStatement commands the same way that substitution fields are identified for PreparedStatement commands. For example, to call myProcedure and indicate that it returns a result parameter, you could execute the following:

```
String procedureCall = "{?= call myProcedure}";
```

You can specify IN and OUT parameters inside parentheses as illustrated in the following example, where three parameters are specified for myProcedure:

```
String procedureCall = "{?= call myProcedure(?, ?, ?)}";
```

Before calling a stored procedure, you must provide a value for each IN parameter and identify the type of data that will be returned by each OUT parameter. You provide a value for an IN parameter in the same way as you set values for PreparedStatement instances—using the setXXX()methods.

```
String procedureCall = "{?= call myProcedure(?, ?, ?)}";
CallableStatement cstmt = connect.prepareCall(procedureCall);
cstmt.setString(2, "Hello");
cstmt.setInt(3, 123);
cstmt.setBoolean(4, true);
```

Identifying the type of data returned by each OUT parameter is equally simple; you do so using CallableStatement's registerOutParameter() method. When calling that method, you must specify the index of the parameter and an integer value that corresponds to one of the data types defined in java.sql. Types, which is described next. In Listing 12-4, the result parameter is expected to return a numeric value, and the second of the three IN parameters is also declared as an OUT (or more accurately, as an INOUT) parameter that returns character data.

Listing 12-4. Registering Output Parameters

```
Connection connect = null;
String procedureCall = "{?= call myProcedure(?, ?, ?)}";
CallableStatement cstmt = connect.prepareCall(procedureCall);
cstmt.setString(2, "Hello");
cstmt.setInt(3, 123);
cstmt.setBoolean(4, true);
cstmt.registerOutParameter(1, Types.NUMERIC);
cstmt.registerOutParameter(3, Types.VARCHAR);
```

Once the stored procedure has been executed, you can retrieve values from the result, OUT, and INOUT parameters using the getXXX() methods defined in CallableStatement (see Listing 12-5).

Listing 12-5. Retrieving Values Returned by a Stored Procedure

```
String procedureCall = "{?= call myProcedure(?, ?, ?)}";
CallableStatement cstmt = connect.prepareCall(procedureCall);
cstmt.setString(2, "Hello");
cstmt.setInt(3, 123);
cstmt.setBoolean(4, true);
cstmt.registerOutParameter(1, Types.NUMERIC);
cstmt.registerOutParameter(3, Types.VARCHAR);
cstmt.execute();
java.math.BigDecimal bd = cstmt.getBigDecimal(1);
String str = cstmt.getString(3);
```

Named Parameters

In all the code examples you've seen so far, a position index identified which parameter to set or retrieve. However, JDBC supports the ability to reference parameters by name, allowing you to create code that's more readable, as follows:

```
cstmt.setString("Greeting", "Hello");
cstmt.setInt("CustNumber", 123);
cstmt.setBoolean("Registered", true);
```

Keep in mind that, like many JDBC features, support for named parameters isn't universal across JDBC drivers. If you plan to use them you should first consult the documentation for the driver you intend to use to verify that it does include support for named parameters.

ParameterMetaData

Just as the DatabaseMetaData provides metadata about the database, an instance of ParameterMetaData describes the parameters associated with a PreparedStatement. You can use this information to dynamically obtain information about the types of data associated with the parameters in a PreparedStatement, and Listing 12-6 illustrates an example of how you can use it to display the data type name associated with the underlying database column.

Listing 12-6. Displaying a Database Column's Data Type Name

```
PreparedStatement pstmt;
// ...
ParameterMetaData pmd = pstmt.getParameterMetaData();
int count = pmd.getParameterCount();
for (int i = 1; i <= count; i++) {
    System.out.println("Parameter " + i +
            " is associated with a column of type " + pmd.getColumnTypeName(i));
}
```

Note that ParameterMetaData is also available for implementations of CallableStatement, which is a subinterface of PreparedStatement, and ParameterMetaData also allows you to determine the mode (IN, OUT, or INOUT) of each parameter.

JDBC Data Types

SQL defines a number of standard data types, and those types are represented in Java by integer constants defined in the java.sql.Types class. As indicated in Table 12-2, JDBC defines a mapping between each SQL data type and a Java class that's able to encapsulate values of that type. The table lists each SQL type/Types constant, its associated Java class, and an indication of the release in which the type was introduced.

Table 12-2. *SQL Type/Types Constant*

SQL Type/Types Constant	Associated Java Type	JDBC Version
ARRAY	java.sql.Array	2.x
BIGINT	long	1.x
BINARY	byte[]	1.x
BIT	boolean	1.x
BLOB	java.sql.Blob	2.x
BOOLEAN	boolean	3.x
CHAR	String	1.x
CLOB	java.sql.Clob	2.x
DATALINK	java.net.URL	3.x
DATE	java.sql.Date	1.x
DECIMAL	java.math.BigDecimal	1.x
DISTINCT	(See the section "DISTINCT.")	2.x
DOUBLE	double	1.x
FLOAT	double	1.x
INTEGER	int	1.x
JAVA_OBJECT	(See the section "JAVA_OBJECT.")	2.x
LONGVARBINARY	byte[]	1.x
LONGVARCHAR	String	1.x
NCLOB	java.sql.NClob	4.x
NULL	null	1.x
NUMERIC	java.math.BigDecimal	1.x
OTHER	(See the section "OTHER.")	1.x
REAL	float	1.x
REF	java.sql.Ref	2.x
ROWID	java.sql.RowId	4.x
SMALLINT	short	1.x
SQLXML	java.sql.SQLXML	4.x
STRUCT	java.sql.Struct	2.x
TIME	java.sql.Time	1.x
TIMESTAMP	java.sql.Timestamp	1.x
TINYINT	byte	1.x
VARBINARY	byte[]	1.x
VARCHAR	String	1.x

Most of these types should be self-explanatory, but some that may not be are described next.

ARRAY

Most database columns can contain only a single value of a simple data type in each row. However, the SQL3 standard provides support for an ARRAY type that allows you to define columns that contain an array of values in each row.

To store an array in a database column, you can use code like the following:

```
String[] names = {"Jacob", "Jordan", "Jeffery"};
PreparedStatement ps = connect.prepareStatement(
    "UPDATE NAMETABLE SET NAMECOL = ? WHERE EMPLOYEE = 123");
ps.setObject(1, names);
ps.executeUpdate();
```

To read an array of values from a database row, you can use the getArray() method in ResultSet (see Listing 12-7).

Listing 12-7. Retrieving an Array of Values from a ResultSet

```
String[] names;
Statement stmt = connect.createStatement();
ResultSet resultSet = stmt.executeQuery(
    "SELECT * FROM NAMETABLE WHERE EMPLOYEE = 123");
if (resultSet.next()) {
  Array sqlArray = resultSet.getArray("NAMECOL");
  names = (String[])(sqlArray.getArray());
  for (int i = 0; i < names.length; i++) {
    System.out.println(names[i]);
  }
}
```

Alternatively, you can use the getResultSet() method defined in Array instead of getArray(). The following code segment will produce the same output as the one shown previously, but it retrieves the values through a ResultSet instead of an array of String instances:

Listing 12-8. Retrieving an Array via the getResultSet() Method in Array

```
Statement stmt = connect.createStatement();
ResultSet resultSet = stmt.executeQuery(
    "SELECT * FROM NAMETABLE WHERE EMPLOYEE = 123");
if (resultSet.next()) {
   Array sqlArray = resultSet.getArray("NAMECOL");
   ResultSet arraySet = sqlArray.getResultSet();
   while (arraySet.next()) {
     System.out.println(arraySet.getObject(2));
   }
}
```

BLOB, CLOB

When you perform a query and access a value stored in a table row, you normally must retrieve the entire value. For example, if you perform a query that returns table rows containing character data, the full-text value is returned when you call getString() or getObject(). That behavior is acceptable in most cases, but it can be a problem when reading data from columns that contain extremely large values. For example, if a column contains binary data that represents a large audio or video "clip," it may be undesirable or even impossible to read the entire clip into memory at one time because of its size.

SQL3 defines the Binary Large Object (BLOB) and Character Large Object (CLOB) types that are represented by the Blob and Clob interfaces in java.sql. These new types allow you to retrieve and update specific portions of a database column's value instead of requiring that the entire value be read into memory. In addition, the Blob and Clob interfaces define methods that allow you to search for a particular sequence of byte values (for BLOBs) or characters (for CLOBs) without first retrieving the data you're searching against from the database. For example, the following code performs a query, obtains a Clob from the ResultSet, and searches for *Pro Java Programming* in the text stored in the database. If that string is found, up to 100 characters are read from the database starting at the position where the search text was located.

```
ResultSet resultSet = stmt.executeQuery(
    "SELECT * FROM MYBOOK WHERE TEXTID = 123");
Clob myClob = resultSet.getClob("CHAPTERTEXT");
long index = myClob.position("Pro Java Programming", 0);
if (index != -1) {
  String theText = myClob.getSubString(index, 100);
}
```

DATALINK

The JDBC 3.0 specification introduced this data type, and it's used to represent a URL. A URL can be stored as a parameter in a PreparedStatement using the setURL() method and can be retrieved from a query using the getURL() methods defined within ResultSet, as follows:

```
Connection conn;
URL url;
// . . .
PreparedStatement pstmt = conn.prepareStatement(
        "DELETE FROM FAVORITE WHERE BROWSER_HISTORY = ?");
pstmt.setURL(1, url);
```

DATE, TIME, TIMESTAMP

The DATE type defined by SQL represents a date (day, month, and year) value only, TIME represents a time (hours, minutes, and seconds) only, and TIMESTAMP is a combination of a date and a time. Each of these is represented by a java.util.Date subclass defined in java.sql such as the java.sql.Timestamp class.

The java.util.Date class couldn't be used directly to represent a TIMESTAMP because SQL's definition of that type requires that it support nanosecond values, while java.util.Date supports nothing smaller than milliseconds.

DISTINCT

SQL3 supports user-defined types (UDTs) that allow users to define new data types based on existing types. A distinct data type is a UDT that's based on a single existing SQL data type. For example, you might want to create a new type to represent the two-character language codes used by Java's Locale object, which can be accomplished with the following SQL command:

```
CREATE TYPE LANGUAGECODE AS CHAR(2);
```

Once a distinct type has been created, it can be used when defining the columns that make up tables within the database. You can retrieve the value of a distinct data type from a ResultSet by using the getXXX() method that's appropriate for the underlying type. In this case, for example, you'd use getString() to retrieve the value stored in a LANGUAGECODE column.

STRUCT

Structured types are similar to distinct types, but structured types allow you to create more complex data types. Although conceptually similar to classes, a SQL structured type contains only data, while classes typically contain both data and logic. For example, suppose you have a Java class like the following:

```
public class Student {

    public String name;
    public int studentID;
    public java.util.Date dateOfBirth;
    public float testScore;

}
```

In practice, this class would normally contain accessor and mutator methods for its properties, although those are omitted here for the sake of simplicity. In any case, given this Student class, an equivalent structured type could be created using a SQL command similar to the following:

```
CREATE TYPE STUDENT {
    STUDENTNAME VARCHAR(20),
    STUDENTID   NUMERIC(10),
    DATEOFBIRTH DATE,
    TESTSCORE   NUMERIC(5, 2)
}
```

Once a structured type has been created, it can be used when defining the columns that make up database tables.

Since they're conceptually similar to classes, structured types can be useful for providing object persistence.

REF

Just as SQL3's structured types are similar to classes, its new REF type provides functionality similar to that of an object reference, and a SQL3-compliant DBMS will allow you to create columns containing references to structured type instances. For example, if you define the STUDENT structured type described previously, you can define table columns that contain references to instances of STUDENT.

Although conceptually similar to one another, an instance of SQL's REF type doesn't map directly to a Java object reference. You can't, for example, create an instance of the Student class and store a reference to that object in a database. It's possible to obtain access to a REF using the ResultSet's getRef() method that returns an instance of java.sql.Ref. However, Ref doesn't currently provide any useful functionality. Intuitively, you might expect a Ref to allow you to access the values stored in the structured type/object instance, but that isn't the case. To access those values, you must perform a query/SELECT and specify the Ref value in a WHERE clause just as you would a traditional primary key.

JAVA_OBJECT

A DBMS may provide direct support for storing Java objects in the database, and this type identifies columns that contain some type of Java object.

OTHER

This value represents columns that have a type that the JDBC driver was unable to map to a known SQL type.

ResultSet

An instance of ResultSet is returned from executeQuery(), and one or more instances may be returned from execute(). A ResultSet is a representation of the data returned by your query, and it allows you to process the results one row at a time. Before you can process a row, you must move the ResultSet's cursor (pointer) to that row, and the row that's pointed to by the cursor is called the current row. When a ResultSet is created, the cursor is initially positioned before the first row.

You should be aware that the data returned by your query isn't usually stored in the ResultSet object. In most cases, the data remains on the database server and only when the cursor moves to a particular row is that row read from the server and cached by the ResultSet. This allows you to perform queries that return a much larger volume of data than can be cached in your machine's memory.

Instances of ResultSet are sometimes returned by methods in java.sql when no query has been issued explicitly. For example, some of the methods defined in DatabaseMetaData return data in the form of a ResultSet, as previously illustrated in the DatabaseBrowser application in Listing 12-2.

It's helpful to review some ResultSet properties before describing the methods defined in that interface, because its properties determine which of a ResultSet's methods you're able to use for a particular instance and how they function.

Forward-Only vs. Scrollable (Scrollability Type)

Scrollability describes the type of cursor movement that's allowed, and a forward-only ResultSet allows the cursor to be moved forward only one row at a time using the next() method. However, with a scrollable ResultSet, you can use a variety of methods to position the cursor. It can be moved forward or backward, and it can be moved in those directions by any number of rows. In addition, it's possible to move the cursor to a specific row (in other words, to use absolute instead of relative positioning), including the first and last rows in the ResultSet.

Early versions of JDBC only supported the next() method, with the other cursor positioning methods added to ResultSet as part of the JDBC 2.x enhancements. However, even if a JDBC driver is compliant with the 2.x specification, it may not allow you to create a scrollable ResultSet.

You can determine which ResultSet types are supported by calling the supports ResultSetType() method in DatabaseMetaData.

Read-Only vs. Updatable (Concurrency Mode)

ResultSet defines a large number of getXXX() methods that allow you to read column values from the current row (getString(), getFloat(), etc.), and it includes a corresponding updateXXX() method for each getXXX(). While it's always possible to call the read/get methods, a ResultSet's concurrency mode determines whether you can use the write/update methods. As its name implies, a read-only ResultSet allows you only to read the data, while an updatable ResultSet allows you both to read the data and to modify it through the ResultSet.

The updateXXX() methods were added to ResultSet as part of the enhanced functionality of JDBC 2.x, but even some JDBC 2.x–compliant drivers may not support updatable result sets.

However, your application can determine which concurrency modes are supported by calling the supportsResultSetConcurrency() method in DatabaseMetaData.

Update Sensitivity

While you're using a ResultSet to process the results of a query, it's usually possible for other users/applications to modify the rows in the database that were returned by your query. Update sensitivity indicates whether the ResultSet will reflect changes that are made to the underlying data after the ResultSet is created. Those updates are known as "changes by others" to distinguish them from changes made to the data using an updatable ResultSet's updateXXX() methods. If you call a getXXX() method to read data from the current row, a sensitive ResultSet will return the data stored in the underlying database even if the data was changed by another user after the ResultSet was created. However, an insensitive ResultSet doesn't detect such changes and may return outdated information.

Update sensitivity doesn't imply that a ResultSet is sensitive to all types of changes. For example, a ResultSet might be sensitive to row deletions but not to row updates or insertions. In addition, a ResultSet's sensitivity to "changes by others" can be different from its sensitivity to its own changes (modifications to the data made through the updateXXX() methods). However, DatabaseMetaData provides methods that allow you to determine which types of changes are visible for a given ResultSet type.

Holdability

In some cases, you'll use a particular database connection to make changes to data while referencing the data in a ResultSet that was created using that same connection, but this may not always be possible. That's because some implementations will automatically close any open ResultSet instances when the commit() method is called for the Connection used to create those ResultSets. However, you may be able to control this behavior by specifying the cursor *holdability* you need when creating a Statement (or one of its subinterfaces) implementation. In other words, holdability describes the ability of a ResultSet to remain open even when changes are committed for the underlying Connection.

Selecting ResultSet Properties

To set the scrollability, concurrency, and sensitivity properties, you must specify the appropriate values when creating a Statement. The code segments shown earlier used the createStatement() method that doesn't accept any parameter values, but another version of createStatement() allows you to specify two integer values representing ResultSet properties.

```
int resultSetType, resultSetConcurrency;
// ...
Statement stmt = connect.createStatement(resultSetType,
        resultSetConcurrency);
```

The resultSetType parameter represents a combination of the scrollability and sensitivity properties, and it should be assigned one of the following constants defined in ResultSet: TYPE_FORWARD_ONLY, TYPE_SCROLL_INSENSITIVE, or TYPE_SCROLL_SENSITIVE.

The resultSetConcurrency value represents the concurrency mode for ResultSet instances created by this statement and should be assigned the value of either CONCUR_READ_ONLY or CONCUR_UPDATABLE.

You can use these constants and the createStatement() method shown previously to create a Statement that will produce ResultSet instances with the desired properties. For example, you can use code similar to the following to create a Statement and request that the ResultSet instances it creates be scrollable, sensitive to others' changes, and updatable.

```
Statement stmt = connect.createStatement(ResultSet.TYPE_SCROLL_SENSITIVE,
                            ResultSet.CONCUR_UPDATABLE);
```

Note that if you specify a type of ResultSet that's not supported by the driver, it won't generate an error when createStatement() is called.

Instead, the Statement will produce ResultSet instances that match the type you requested as closely as possible. In this case, for example, if the driver supports updatable ResultSet instances but not scrolling, it will create forward-only instances that are updatable.

You may also be able to denote the desired holdability by specifying a third parameter as in the following example and specifying either the HOLD_CURSORS_OVER_COMMIT or the CLOSE_CURSORS_AT_COMMIT constant defined in ResultSet:

```
Statement stmt = connect.createStatement(ResultSet.TYPE_SCROLL_SENSITIVE,
                        ResultSet.CONCUR_UPDATABLE),
                        ResultSet.HOLD_CURSORS_OVER_COMMIT
```

Performance Hints

For drivers that support it, you can provide information that may improve the performance of a ResultSet. As mentioned earlier, a row is normally retrieved from the database only after it becomes the ResultSet's current row, but JDBC allows buffering or *prefetching* of rows by a ResultSet.

The fetch size specifies the number of rows that the ResultSet should retrieve from the database each time it needs to read new rows, and that value is set using the setFetchSize() method. In other words, when the driver is capable of buffering database records, this value identifies the maximum number of records that should be buffered. For example, suppose you execute the following code:

```
ResultSet resultSet = stmt.executeQuery("SELECT * FROM MYTABLE");
resultSet.setFetchSize(10);
```

If you execute the ResultSet's next() method, it should retrieve ten records from the database and store them in a buffer. As your application executes the next() method again to process more records, the ResultSet won't request more data from the database until all ten of the original records have been processed. Once that occurs, the ResultSet will retrieve up to ten more records, and the process will be repeated. Just as performing updates in a batch improved performance by reducing network calls, this type of record buffering can improve performance for the same reason.

You can also suggest a fetch direction to the driver, and doing so may improve its performance by identifying the direction in which you plan to process the records in a ResultSet. You specify the fetch direction using the setFetchDirection() method, and that method requires an integer parameter value that should be equal to FETCH_FORWARD or to FETCH_REVERSE, both of which are constants defined in ResultSet.

Note that the fetch size and fetch direction settings are described as *hints* because the driver may choose to ignore one or both of those values. In fact, a driver may not even support prefetching/buffering of rows at all.

Using ResultSet

Almost all the methods defined in ResultSet fall into one of three categories: cursor positioning, data retrieval, and data modification.

Cursor Positioning

The positioning methods allow you to change the position of the cursor so you can select which row to process. As mentioned earlier, JDBC originally only supported the next() method, which moves the cursor forward one row, and even some newer drivers may not support scrollable ResultSet instances.

The next() method doesn't accept any parameter values and returns a Boolean value that indicates whether another row was found. In other words, the value returned from next() is the ResultSet equivalent of an end-of-file indicator. If it returns true, the cursor points to a valid row that can be processed, but if it returns false, the cursor has moved beyond the last row in the ResultSet.

The following code segment shows how to iterate through the rows in a ResultSet using next():

```
ResultSet resultSet = stmt.executeQuery("SELECT * FROM MYTABLE");
while (resultSet.next()) {
  // Process the current row here
}
```

The other positioning methods mentioned earlier aren't described in detail here, but they're equally simple to use and allow you to move the cursor to any row in the ResultSet. You can use relative positioning to move the cursor forward or back a specified number of rows, or you can use absolute positioning to move the cursor to a specific row. For example, to move the cursor back five rows from its current position, you could execute the following code:

```
ResultSet resultSet;
// ...
resultSet.relative(-5);
```

In addition, positioning methods are provided that move the cursor to (or before) the first row in the ResultSet and to (or after) the last row.

Data Retrieval

The getXXX() methods defined in ResultSet allow you to retrieve data from the current row, and the specific method used determines the type of value returned. For example, getBytes() returns an array of bytes, getString() returns a String instance, getInt() an int value, and so on. In most cases you'll know in advance which data type is stored in a particular column, but if you don't know, you may want to use the getObject() method. When getObject() is called, it returns an Object that's appropriate for the type of data stored in the column, such as a String for character data, a byte array for raw binary data, an appropriate wrapper object for primitive types (e.g., a BigDecimal for numeric data), and so on.

Two implementations are provided for each data retrieval getXXX() method defined in ResultSet: one that accepts an integer parameter and another that requires a String. The integer value represents the position within the ResultSet of the column from which the data should be retrieved and is one-based. For example, to retrieve a String value from the second column, you could use code similar to the following:

```
ResultSet resultSet;
// ...
String columnValue = resultSet.getString(2);
```

The getXXX() methods that accept a String parameter require that the String be equal to the name of one of the columns in the ResultSet.

```
ResultSet resultSet;
// ...
String columnValue = resultSet.getString("FIRSTNAME");
```

Note that some drivers may not allow you to retrieve a column's value more than once and/or require that you must access the columns in left-to-right order. If your application's design makes it necessary to access the data repeatedly, you may need to read the data from the ResultSet and cache it in memory to allow your code to function properly.

Data Modification

When a ResultSet is updatable, you can use its updateXXX() methods to modify the data in the current row, while insertRow() and deleteRow() insert a new row and delete the current row, respectively.

The updateXXX() methods are similar to the getXXX() in that you can specify either a column's name or its index in the ResultSet. For example, to update the third column with a float value, you could execute code like the following:

```
ResultSet resultSet;
// ...
resultSet.updateFloat(3, 123.45f);
```

Modifications you make to the ResultSet's data aren't immediately propagated to the underlying database.

Calling updateRow() causes any changes made to the current row to be saved, while cancelRowUpdates() causes your changes to be discarded.

The refreshRow() method also causes any updates to be discarded, but there's an important difference between it and cancelRowUpdates(). While cancelRowUpdates() causes the row's original values to be restored, refreshRow() actually rereads the row from the database. This can be useful if the information may have changed in a way that can affect the behavior of your application.

Determining the Number of Rows Returned

You'll often want to determine the number of rows returned by a query before processing the `ResultSet` data, and since version 2.*x* JDBC has provided an easy way to determine the number of rows encapsulated by a `ResultSet` but only when the `ResultSet` is scrollable. Specifically, you can use the `last()` method defined in JDBC 2.*x* to move the cursor to the last row in the `ResultSet` and then call `getRow()` to retrieve the index of the current row (see Listing 12-9 for an example).

Listing 12-9. Determining the Number of Records Returned by a Query

```
int recordCount;
Statement stmt = connect.createStatement();
// Get the data
ResultSet resultSet = stmt.executeQuery(
    "SELECT COUNT(*) FROM EMPLOYEE WHERE SALARY < 50000");
// Move the cursor to the last row
resultSet.last();
// Get the current row's index (i.e., the number of rows in the ResultSet)
recordCount = resultSet.getRow();
// Restore the cursor to its previous position
resultSet.beforeFirst();
```

Retrieving Automatically Generated Keys

In many cases, the data you want to store doesn't inherently include a value that can be used as the primary key in a database table. For example, let's suppose you're creating an application that will store information about the customers of a business and you need some sort of unique identifier for each customer. You could require that each customer provide an existing unique identifier such as a Social Security number or a driver's license number, but you have no guarantee that each customer will have either one or will know it and be willing to provide it. As a result, it's often better to use an identifier that's meaningful only within your database and that's unique within that context; for this reason, most database systems support the concept of an autogenerated key. In most cases, this is simply a number (usually an integer) that's automatically incremented each time a new record is added to the table, and you can allow this number to be automatically created and used as the record's primary key.

The only problem with autogenerated keys is that because they're not assigned by your application, there's no way for your code to know in advance what key has been assigned to a given record. For example, let's suppose you create a class like the one in Listing 12-10 that describes a `Customer` as having a unique identifier and a name.

Listing 12-10. A Sample Customer Class That Encapsulates a Name and Identifier

```
public class Customer {

    private int customerID;
    private String name;

    public int getCustomerID() {
    }

    public void setCustomerID(int id) {
        customerID = id;
    }
```

```
    public String getName() {
        return name;
    }

    public void setName(String nm) {
        name = nm;
    }

}
```

Now let's also assume you've created a database table that includes an autogenerated key for the customer identifier and that you've created a method that can add a newly created Customer.

```
public void addNew(Customer customer, Connection conn) throws SQLException {
    PreparedStatement pstmt = conn.prepareStatement(
            "INSERT INTO CUSTOMER (NAME) VALUES (?)");
    pstmt.setString(1, customer.getName());
    pstmt.executeUpdate();
    pstmt.close();
}
```

The problem is that after executing this code you now have an instance of Customer in memory that doesn't contain the unique identifier that was created when the record was added to the database. Fortunately, JDBC 3.0 defines a way to retrieve autogenerated keys like the customer identifier, which is done by calling the getGeneratedKeys() method defined in the Statement interface. That method returns a ResultSet that contains a row for each autogenerated key and can be used to update the Customer object:

```
pstmt.executeUpdate();
ResultSet resultSet = pstmt.getGeneratedKeys();
if (resultSet.next()) {
    int customerID = resultSet.getInt(1);
    customer.setCustomerID(customerID);
}
```

ResultSetMetaData

As described earlier, DatabaseMetaData can determine the capabilities of the DBMS and the JDBC driver, as well as examine the contents of the database. Similarly, ResultSetMetaData can obtain information that describes the columns returned by a query, such as each column's name and the type of data it contains. ResultSetMetaData can also determine the number of columns returned by a query, so you could use a code segment like the one in Listing 12-11 to display the column names and values returned by a query.

Listing 12-11. Accessing the Meta Data of a ResultSet

```
public void printResultSet(ResultSet resultSet) throws SQLException {
  ResultSetMetaData rsmd = resultSet.getMetaData();
  int count = rsmd.getColumnCount();
  for (int i = 0; i < count; i++) {
    System.out.print((i == 0 ? "" : "\t") +
    rsmd.getColumnName(i + 1));
  }
```

```
  System.out.println();
  while (resultSet.next()) {
    for (int i = 0; i < count; i++) {
    System.out.print((i == 0 ? "" : "\t") +
    resultSet.getObject(i + 1));
  }
  System.out.println();
 }
}
```

RowSet

ResultSet instances are by nature somewhat limited in terms of how they can be used, but the RowSet interface that extends ResultSet adds an additional layer of flexibility to ResultSet instances and their supported behavior. For example, a RowSet can provide scrollability and updatability behavior even if you're using a JDBC driver that doesn't support these features, and RowSet implementations also provide a JavaBeans-style notification mechanism that allows the registration of listeners that will be notified of changes to the associated ResultSet/RowSet, such as cursor movement and changes to the underlying data.

There are two varieties of RowSet implementation: connected and disconnected. As the names imply, a connected RowSet is one that uses a database connection to dynamically provide access to the underlying data, while a disconnected RowSet does not use a database connection but instead maintains the data in memory.

There are five different interfaces that directly or indirectly extend RowSet, with each interface providing different functionality.

JdbcRowSet

This is an implementation of connected RowSet—in fact, the only interface representing a connected implementation—that provides the basic RowSet functionality described earlier, specifically, JavaBeans-style event notifications and a scrollable and updatable representation of the underlying ResultSet data.

The concrete implementation of this interface is the JdbcRowSetImpl class, which you can initialize in one of two ways:

- By passing an already-created ResultSet instance to the JdbcRowSetImpl construct that accepts a single ResultSet parameter.

- By providing a Connection or the information needed to create one (URL, user name, and password) along with a SQL query that the JdbcRowSetImpl will use to create a ResultSet.

An example of this second approach is shown in the code that follows, where a Connection instance is passed to the constructor and a query is specified by calling the setCommand() method defined in RowSet:

```
Connection connection;
// . . .
JdbcRowSet rowSet = new JdbcRowSetImpl(connection);
rowSet.setCommand("SELECT * FROM TEST_SCORE");
```

It's also possible to assign parameter values as you would with a PreparedStatement, so you could limit the results of the query with code like that shown next.

```
JdbcRowSet rowSet = new JdbcRowSetImpl(connection);
rowSet.setCommand("SELECT * FROM TEST_SCORE WHERE STUDENT_ID = ?");
rowSet.setInt(1, 12345);  // Return only the record(s) where the student ID is 12345
```

Once you've initialized the JdbcRowSet, you must call the execute() method to indicate that it should perform the assigned query as shown next.

```
JdbcRowSet rowSet = new JdbcRowSetImpl(connection);
rowSet.setCommand("SELECT * FROM TEST_SCORE WHERE STUDENT_ID = ?");
rowSet.setInt(1, 12345);  // Return only the record(s) where the student ID is 12345
rowSet.execute();
```

At this point you can use the RowSet just as you would a ResultSet, but with the additional functionality provided by the RowSet interface.

CachedRowSet

In contrast to JdbcRowSet which represents a connected RowSet, the CachedRowSet interface represents an implementation of a disconnected RowSet. As with JdbcRowSet for which there's a JdbcRowSetImpl class, the CachedRowSet has a corresponding CachedRowSetImpl class, though unlike JdbcRowSetImpl there is no CachedRowSetImpl constructor that accepts an existing ResultSet. Instead, you must provide a Connection or the information needed to create a connection to the JdbcRowSetImpl object and then call its execute() method, at which point it will connect to the database, execute a query, and load all of the data into memory.

In addition to the base CachedRowSet interface, JDBC also includes three interfaces that directly or indirectly extend CachedRowSet: WebRowSet, FilteredRowSet, and JoinRowSet, and Table 12-3 identifies and describes these interfaces.

Table 12-3. *RowSet Interfaces That Extend CachedRowSet*

Name	Extends	Functionality Provided
WebRowSet	CachedRowSet	Ability to serialize and de-serialize the ResultSet data as an XML document.
FilteredRowSet	WebRowSet	Filter the records in the ResultSet based on a Predicate implementation.
JoinRowSet	WebRowSet	Combine two or more RowSet instances as if a join query had been performed.

In summary, RowSet implementations allow you to do things that you wouldn't ordinarily be able to do with the results of a database query, and they can be very useful when your application needs the additional functionality defined by one of these interfaces.

Transactions

Applications often need to make related changes to more than one database table, and it's usually important that either all of the changes succeed or none of them do. The classic example of this is an application that transfers money from one bank account to another, perhaps from a savings account to a checking account, or vice versa (see Listing 12-12). If the two account balances are stored in separate tables, it's necessary to issue two UPDATE statements: one that subtracts the appropriate amount from the first table and another that adds the appropriate amount to the second table.

Listing 12-12. Banking Application

```java
import java.sql.*;

public class TransTest {

  private String url = "jdbc:odbc:banktest";
  private String userid = "bspell";
  private String password = "brett";

  public void transferFunds(float transferAmount, int accountNumber,
      String fromTable, String toTable) throws SQLException,
      InvalidTransferException {
    Statement stmt = null;
    ResultSet resultSet = null;
    Connection conn = DriverManager.getConnection(url, userid,
        password);
    try {
      stmt = conn.createStatement();
      resultSet = stmt.executeQuery("SELECT BALANCE FROM " + fromTable +
          " WHERE ACCOUNTID = " + accountNumber);
      resultSet.next();
      float fromBalance = resultSet.getFloat(1);
      if (fromBalance < transferAmount) {
        throw new InvalidTransferException("Insufficient funds available");
      }
      resultSet.close();
      resultSet = stmt.executeQuery("SELECT BALANCE FROM " + toTable +
          " WHERE ACCOUNTID = " + accountNumber);
      resultSet.next();
      float toBalance = resultSet.getFloat(1);
      fromBalance -= transferAmount;
      toBalance += transferAmount;
      stmt.executeUpdate("UPDATE " + fromTable + " SET BALANCE = " +
          fromBalance + " WHERE ACCOUNTID = " + accountNumber);
      stmt.executeUpdate("UPDATE " + toTable + " SET BALANCE = " +
          toBalance + " WHERE ACCOUNTID = " + accountNumber);
    } finally {
      if (resultSet != null) resultSet.close();
      if (stmt != null) stmt.close();
      conn.close();
    }
  }
}
```

```
class InvalidTransferException extends Exception {

  public InvalidTransferException(String message) {
    super(message);
  }

}

}
```

Unfortunately, this code has a potential problem. It's possible for the application to be interrupted after it has deducted the transfer amount from the checking account but before that amount is added to the savings account balance. If such an interruption does occur, the customer will lose money, which isn't desirable for the customer. Similarly, if the order of the updates is reversed and an interruption occurs, the customer's accounts will collectively contain more money than they did before the transfer was initiated, and that outcome is even less desirable for the bank.

A *transaction* is a collection of related updates that should either fail or succeed as a group. Updates that are part of a transaction are issued in the same way that nontransactional updates are issued, and there's no batch-like facility in JDBC for defining the updates in a transaction. However, methods are available that allow you to define the beginning and end of a transaction, and you must use those methods to make updates part of a transaction.

At any point during a transaction, you can end the transaction and discard (or roll back) the changes that have occurred, which you'll frequently do if one of the updates generates an error. However, if the updates all complete successfully, you'll normally end the transaction and save (or commit) the changes that were made.

When using JDBC, it's not necessary to explicitly identify the start of a transaction because all updates are considered part of a transaction. However, a commit operation is performed by default after each update, which effectively disables transaction processing since a transaction is useful only when it includes multiple updates. You can disable the default behavior (and enable transactions) by passing a value of false to the setAutoCommit() method in Connection.

Connection also defines commit() and rollback() methods that end the current transaction and save or discard the changes that were part of the transaction. Note that only a single transaction can be active for a Connection at any given time, so if your application needs to have multiple transactions active simultaneously, you must obtain a connection for each transaction.

You can easily update the class shown in Listing 12-13 to use transactions to ensure that either both balances are updated or neither one is changed.

Listing 12-13. The Modified Banking Application

```
import java.sql.*;

public class TransTest {

  private String url = "jdbc:odbc:banktest";
  private String userid = "bspell";
  private String password = "brett";

  public void transferFunds(float transferAmount, int accountNumber,
      String fromTable, String toTable) throws SQLException,
      InvalidTransferException {
    Statement stmt = null;
    ResultSet resultSet = null;
```

515

```
Connection conn = DriverManager.getConnection(url, userid,
    password);
conn.setAutoCommit(false);
try {
  stmt = conn.createStatement();
  resultSet = stmt.executeQuery("SELECT BALANCE FROM " + fromTable +
      " WHERE ACCOUNTID = " + accountNumber);
  resultSet.next();
  float fromBalance = resultSet.getFloat(1);
  if (fromBalance < transferAmount) {
    throw new InvalidTransferException("Insufficient funds available");
  }
  resultSet.close();
  resultSet = stmt.executeQuery("SELECT BALANCE FROM " + toTable +
      " WHERE ACCOUNTID = " + accountNumber);
  resultSet.next();
  float toBalance = resultSet.getFloat(1);
  fromBalance -= transferAmount;
  toBalance += transferAmount;
  stmt.executeUpdate("UPDATE " + fromTable + " SET BALANCE = " +
      fromBalance + " WHERE ACCOUNTID = " + accountNumber);
  stmt.executeUpdate("UPDATE " + toTable + " SET BALANCE = " +
      toBalance + " WHERE ACCOUNTID = " + accountNumber);
  conn.commit();
} catch (SQLException sqle) {
  conn.rollback();
  throw sqle;
} finally {
  if (resultSet != null) resultSet.close();
  if (stmt != null) stmt.close();
  conn.close();
}
}

    class InvalidTransferException extends Exception {

      public InvalidTransferException(String message) {
        super(message);
      }
    }
}
```

Note that this code differs from the original implementation in two ways. First, it disables the autocommit feature so that the first account update won't be permanently saved until/unless commit() is called explicitly. Second, it intercepts any SQLException before it's returned to the caller and performs a rollback() on the connection, which will ensure that the data in the database is restored to its original condition when an error occurs. This is important to do because the second update might fail even though the first one had succeeded.

Savepoints

When discussing the rollback() method and its effect on a transaction, I've so far assumed that calling the method will cause all changes to be canceled for the transaction, and in the examples you've seen that's indeed what happens. However, JDBC 3.0 added support for a new concept called *savepoints* that allows you to designate a particular transaction state to which you can roll back without canceling all changes made since the beginning of the transaction.

To understand how this can be useful and see how it's done, let's assume you're saving two sets of changes to a database within a single transaction:

```
Connection conn;
// ...
performFirstUpdate(conn);
performSecondUpdate(conn);
conn.commit();
```

Assuming that an error occurs during the second set of updates, your options are to either commit all the work that has been done or roll back all the work. However, let's suppose in certain circumstances you want to roll back only the changes made in the second set of updates when an error occurs while they're being processed. If you're using a JDBC driver that supports savepoints, you can create a savepoint before starting the second set of updates and roll back only the changes made in that set if an error occurs. An example of this appears in Listing 12-14.

Listing 12-14. An Example of How a Savepoint Can Be Used in a JDBC Application

```
Connection conn;
Savepoint savepoint = null;
// ...
try {
    performFirstUpdate(conn);
    savepoint = conn.setSavepoint();
    performSecondUpdate(conn);
    conn.commit();
}
catch (SQLException sqle) {
    if (savepoint != null) {
        conn.rollback(savepoint);
    }
    else {
        conn.rollback();
    }
}
```

Note that you can have more than one savepoint per transaction, and you can associate a name with each one, allowing you to roll back by specifying that name instead of by providing a reference to the specific Savepoint:

```
Savepoint sp1 = conn.setSavepoint("first");
// ...
Savepoint sp2 = conn.setSavepoint("second");
// ...
conn.rollback("first");
```

Read-Only Transactions

Up to this point, I've discussed transactions only in the context of update operations. While they're often most useful when performing updates, transactions can be used with query operations as well. For example, issuing a SELECT statement twice within the same transaction should result in the query returning the same results the second time as it did originally, even if the underlying data is modified between the two queries. In other words, transactions can be used with query operations to ensure that they return consistent results.

It's important to realize that regardless of the type of SQL statements used, transaction support is provided by the DBMS and not by the JDBC driver. In addition, depending upon how the DBMS implements transaction support, a number of problems can occur when multiple transactions access the same data; the following sections describe those problems. Later, I'll show how you can avoid these scenarios, or at least select which ones your application will allow to occur.

Dirty Reads

A *dirty read* occurs when a table row is modified as part of one transaction and a second transaction performs a query that returns the modified row despite that the modification hasn't been committed. This behavior is inappropriate since the first transaction may choose to roll back the update, in which case the second transaction has effectively read invalid (or "dirty") data.

Nonrepeatable Reads

As mentioned, performing the same query multiple times in a single transaction should produce the same results each time. In some cases, however, the updates or deletions made by one transaction can affect the query results of another transaction. For example, suppose that transaction A performs a query that returns ten rows, after which transaction B deletes one of those rows from the database. If transaction A then executes the same query and only nine rows are returned, a *nonrepeatable read* has occurred.

Phantom Reads

This type of problem is similar to the nonrepeatable read but is related to rows that are inserted. For example, suppose that transaction A performs a query that returns five rows, after which transaction B inserts a new row that meets the criteria specified by transaction A. If A then reissues the query and sees the newly inserted row, a *phantom read* has occurred.

Transaction Isolation Levels

Many applications don't support multiple transactions and won't experience the problems just described. However, for some database-intensive applications where the integrity of the data is important, it's necessary to eliminate these problems or at least control which ones can occur. Most DBMS products provide some degree of control over these problems, and they usually do so through *data locking*. Locking is a technique that makes some or all of the data in a table unavailable while it's being read or updated by a transaction. If other transactions attempt to access locked data, their requests will fail, or more frequently, they will be made to wait until the transaction that caused the lock to occur has ended.

In the simplest case, an entire table can be locked as long as its data is referenced by an active transaction, which will prevent any of the three problems just described from occurring. However, that approach has the disadvantage of making the table's data unavailable to other applications for what could be a large amount of time, and that behavior may be unacceptable. In other words, you should avoid dirty reads, nonrepeatable reads, and phantom reads but only by sacrificing accessibility to the data to some extent.

In practice, the ideal balance between data integrity and data accessibility varies from one application to another. Some applications are more concerned with accessibility to the data, others are primarily concerned with data integrity, and still others may seek a "middle ground" between the two extremes. Since application needs vary, transaction isolation levels are provided to allow an application to select an appropriate balance between accessibility and transaction integrity.

Four transaction isolation levels exist, and each one is represented in JDBC by a constant defined in `Connection`. A given DBMS product may not support all four levels, but you can determine which ones are supported using the `supportsTransactionIsolationLevel()` method defined in `DatabaseMetaData`.

Table 12-4 describes the four isolation levels, with the first one representing maximum accessibility and minimum data integrity and the last one representing the opposite extreme.

Table 12-4. *Four Transaction Isolation Levels*

Isolation Level	Description
Read Uncommitted	This transaction isolation level is represented by the `TRANSACTION_READ_UNCOMMITTED` constant, and it allows dirty, nonrepeatable, and phantom reads to occur.
Read Committed	This level is represented by `TRANSACTION_READ_COMMITTED`, and it allows only nonrepeatable and phantom reads to occur; dirty reads are prevented.
Repeatable Read	This level is represented by `TRANSACTION_REPEATABLE_READ` and allows only phantom reads to occur while preventing dirty and nonrepeatable reads.
Serializable	Dirty, nonrepeatable, and phantom reads are all prevented from occurring when this level is used, which is represented by the `TRANSACTION_SERIALIZABLE` constant.

The default isolation level that's in effect will vary from one DBMS product to the next, although you can determine which one is active for a given `Connection` by calling its `getTransactionIsolationLevel()` method. That method returns an integer value equal to one of the four constants that represent the different isolation levels.

Setting a Connection's Transaction Isolation Level

Once you've selected an appropriate isolation level and ensured that it's available with the DBMS your application uses, you can easily specify the desired level by calling the `setTransactionIsolation()` method in `Connection`.

```
connect.setTransactionIsolation(Connection.TRANSACTION_REPEATABLE_READ);
```

Table 12-5 lists the isolation levels and identifies which types of problems can occur with each one.

Table 12-5. *Potential Problems Associated with Each Isolation Level*

Isolation Level	Dirty	Nonrepeatable	Phantom
Read Uncommitted	Allowed	Allowed	Allowed
Read Committed	Prevented	Allowed	Allowed
Repeatable Read	Prevented	Prevented	Allowed
Serializable	Prevented	Prevented	Prevented

Distributed Transactions

The transaction capabilities discussed up to this point are applicable to changes made to tables in a single database. In some cases, however, you may want to make related changes to tables stored in databases residing on different machines, perhaps involving two completely different DBMS products. For example, you might want to make an update to an Oracle database on one server and a Sybase database on a different machine and need those updates to be made as a single unit. That type of operation is known as a *distributed transaction* and is supported in Java through the Java Transaction API (JTA) and Java Transaction Service (JTS). However, a detailed discussion of distributed transactions is beyond the scope of this book.

Connection Pooling

Creating a database connection is a relatively slow process, and if an application repeatedly opens and closes many connections, it may have a serious negative impact on the speed of the application and thus on its value. However, you can improve performance by using *connection pooling*, a technique that allows existing connections to be reused.

A connection pool manager can be implemented as part of a JDBC driver or as a separate component if the driver doesn't support pooling. The JDBC 2.*x* optional package includes interfaces used to perform connection pooling and partially describes how a connection pool manager should be implemented. If the driver you're using supports JDBC 2.*x*-style connection pooling, you can get an instance of a PooledConnection from a DataSource by calling the getPooledConnection() method. Once you've done so, you can obtain a database connection by calling the PooledConnection object's getConnection() method as shown in Listing 12-15.

Listing 12-15. Using a Pooled Connection Data Source

```
String url = "jdbc:oracle:thin:@myserver:1521:mydata";
String userid = "bspell";
String password = "brett";
OracleConnectionPoolDataSource ocpds = new OracleConnectionPoolDataSource();
ocpds.setURL(url);
ocpds.setUser(userid);
ocpds.setPassword(password);
PooledConnection pool = ocpds.getPooledConnection();
// . . .
Connection conn = pool.getConnection();
```

When a database connection is requested from a pool manager, the manager attempts to provide one from its pool of existing connections, but if that pool is empty, a new connection is created and returned instead. Once an application has finished using a connection, the connection is returned to the pool manager instead of being closed, which allows the manager to avoid the overhead of creating a new connection the next time one is needed.

This description is somewhat misleading because it implies that a true database connection is returned by the pool manager and that the application using the connection is aware of and cooperates with the pool manager by "giving back" connections. In reality, the manager returns a proxy object that maintains a reference to a real database connection created by a JDBC driver. Most of the proxy's methods simply delegate their functionality to the real connection, but the proxy's close() method returns the real database connection to the pool manager instead of closing the connection. Listing 12-16 illustrates how such a proxy might be implemented.

Listing 12-16. Implementing a Proxy

```java
import java.sql.*;

public class ProxyConnection implements Connection {

  private Connection realConnection;

  public ProxyConnection(Connection connect) {
    realConnection = connect;
  }

  public void clearWarnings() throws SQLException {
    realConnection.clearWarnings();
  }

  public void close() throws SQLException {
    // Don't close the real connection. Return it to the pool
    // manager instead. This example assumes the existence of
    // a class named PoolManager that's responsible for connection
    // pool management.
    PoolManager.connectionClosed(realConnection);
  }

  public void commit() throws SQLException {
    realConnection.commit();
  }

  public Statement createStatement() throws SQLException {
    return realConnection.createStatement();
  }

  // etc.
```

In other words, the proxy object maintains a reference to a "real" Connection and intercepts the calls that are made. This design makes connection pooling transparent to your application, because a pooled connection behaves the same way that a nonpooled connection does.

Pooling Properties

Just as you saw earlier that JDBC defines some standard property names that are commonly used across DataSource implementations, the JDBC 3.0 specification includes definitions of properties that are commonly used in connection pooling (see Table 12-6). In most cases, these properties should be set only through a configuration file, but the definition of these standard names makes it more likely that you can (if necessary) replace one JDBC driver with another without having to change your configuration options.

Table 12-6. *Pooling Properties*

Property	Description
initialPoolSize	Number of database connections that should be created when a connection pool is created.
minPoolSize	Minimum number of database connections that the pool should contain. If 0, connections will only be created when they are requested.
maxPoolSize	Maximum number of database connections that the pool should contain. A value of 0 means that there isn't a maximum number that can be available in the pool.
maxIdleTime	Number of seconds that a connection can remain unused in the pool before it's closed. A value of 0 means that unused connections should never be closed.
maxStatements	Maximum number of statements that the pool should be allowed to cache.
propertyCycle	Number of seconds that should elapse between attempts to enforce the behavior associated with other properties.

Errors and Warnings

Errors can occur for many reasons when performing database operations, and most of the methods defined in the java.sql package can throw SQLException, which is described next.

SQLException

Like other Exception subclasses, SQLException includes a message that describes the nature of the error, and it can be retrieved by calling getMessage(). However, SQLException also provides other properties you may find helpful, and the methods used to access them are described next.

getNextException(), setNextException()

These methods allow you to modify or retrieve the reference to the next instance of SQLException in a chain of exceptions. Multiple errors can occur during a single operation in some cases, and this chaining technique allows an instance of SQLException to be created for each error.

getErrorCode()

This method returns an integer value that describes the error, although the meaning of that value is driver-specific. To interpret the meaning of this value, you should consult the documentation associated with the driver and/or the DBMS.

getSQLState()

The SQLState value is a five-character String that identifies the nature of the error that occurred. This value is defined by the X/OPEN SQL standard and is common to all DBMS implementations that have adopted the standard. Since the SQLState provides a specific indication of the type of problem that occurred, your application may be able to use it to recover from an error or otherwise handle (or ignore) it appropriately.

The SQLState consists of two parts: the first two characters, which are unfortunately called the *class*, and the last three characters, known as the *subclass*. A class effectively identifies a high-level type of error, while a subclass identifies a more specific error. Classes and subclasses can be either standard (defined as part of the X/OPEN specification) or implementation-defined (specific to a particular DBMS product). Standard classes and subclasses begin with one of the characters 0–4 or A–H. Subsequent characters and the first character of an implementation-defined class or subclass can be any letter or digit (0–9, A–Z).

Table 12-7 lists some standard classes and subclasses, along with the associated condition (description of the class) or subcondition (description of the subclass). Note that some classes don't have subclasses because the class itself is sufficient to describe in detail the type of problem that occurred.

Table 12-7. *SQL State Values*

Class	Condition	Subclass	Subcondition
00	Successful	000	
01	Warning	000	
		001	Cursor operation conflict
		002	Disconnect error
		003	Null value eliminated in set function
		004	String data right truncation
		005	Insufficient itemdescriptor areas
		006	Privilege not revoked
		007	Privilege not granted
		008	Implicit zero-bit padding
		009	Search condition too long for schema
		00A	Query expression too long for schema
02	No data	000	
07	Dynamic SQL error	000	
		001	using clause doesn't match parameters
		002	using clause doesn't match target
		003	Cursor specification cannot be executed
		004	using clause required for parameters
		005	Prepared statement, not a cursor spec
		006	Restricted data type attribute violation
		007	using clause required for result fields
		008	Invalid descriptor count
		009	Invalid descriptor index

(continued)

Table 12-7. (*continued*)

Class	Condition	Subclass	Subcondition
08	Connection cxception	000	
		001	Client unable to establish connection
		002	Connection name already in use
		003	Connection doesn't exist
		004	Server rejected connection request
		006	Connection failure
		007	Transaction resolution unknown
0A	Feature not supported	000	
		001	Multiple server transactions
21	Cardinality violation	000	
22	Data exception	000	
		001	String data right truncation
		002	Null value without indicator
		003	Numeric value out of range
		005	Assignment error
		007	Invalid DATETIME format
		008	DATETIME field overflow
		009	Invalid time zone displacement value
		011	Substring error
		012	Division by zero
		015	Interval field overflow
		018	Invalid character value for cast
		019	Invalid escape character
		021	Character not supported
		022	Indicator overflow
		023	Invalid parameter value
		024	Unterminated C string
		025	Invalid escape sequence
		026	String data length mismatch
		027	Trim error
23	Integrity constraint violation	000	
24	Invalid cursor state	000	

(*continued*)

Table 12-7. (*continued*)

Class	Condition	Subclass	Subcondition
25	Invalid transaction state	000	
26	Invalid SQL statement name	000	
27	Triggered data change Violation	000	
28	Invalid authorization specification	000	
2A	Syntax error or access rule violation in SQL statement	000	
2B	Dependent privilege descriptors still exist	000	
2C	Invalid character set name	000	
2D	Invalid transaction termination	000	
2E	Invalid connection name	000	
33	Invalid SQL descriptor name	000	
34	Invalid cursor name	000	
35	Invalid condition number	000	
37	Syntax error or access rule violation in dynamic SQL statement	000	
3C	Ambiguous cursor name	000	
3D	Invalid catalog name	000	
3F	Invalid schema name	000	
40	Transaction rollback	000	
42	Syntax error or access rule violation	000	
44	Check option violation	000	
HZ	Remote database access	000	

SQLWarning

SQLException is somewhat unusual in that it's used by JDBC in two different ways. First, as previously noted, it can be thrown by many of the java.sql methods, and in that way it's similar to other exception classes. However, many types of errors can occur that aren't critical and that won't cause your application's execution to be interrupted. For example, if you read a floating-point value into an integer field using the ResultSet's getInt() method, you may lose a portion of the original value. That type of problem may be of interest to your application but in many cases should be ignored, so it doesn't result in an exception being thrown. Instead, an instance of SQLWarning (a subclass of SQLException) is created and appended to a list maintained by the object that generated the warning, which in this example would be a ResultSet. Connection, Statement, and ResultSet can all generate warnings, and each of those classes provides a getWarnings() method accordingly. That method returns the first SQLWarning instance in the object's list, and the list effectively serves as an error log. In other words, when any event generates a warning, an instance of SQLWarning is quietly (without being thrown or otherwise interrupting your application) added to the list of warnings maintained for the object that generated it. In addition to the getWarnings() methods, Connection, Statement, and ResultSet each provide a clearWarnings() method that can be used to remove all warnings currently chained.

Debugging

JDBC provides a logging facility that driver classes can use to display diagnostic information. For example, the driver may generate a message each time one of its classes' methods is called, and/or it may display the SQL statements that are actually sent to the DBMS. Those statements are sometimes different from the ones your code specifies, because the driver often modifies statements before forwarding them to the database, such as when it fills in the parameter values specified for a PreparedStatement. In addition, the message log may contain SQL statements that were issued by the driver itself that don't correspond to any statements explicitly executed by your application.

This logging facility first appeared in JDBC 1.x and can be used by passing a reference to a PrintStream to the static setLogStream() method in DriverManager. For example, you might execute the following code to have the messages sent to standard output:

```
DriverManager.setLogStream(System.out);
```

In JDBC 2.x, the setLogStream() method was deprecated and replaced by setLogWriter(), which is passed an instance of PrintWriter. The following code creates an instance of PrintWriter using System.out and calls setLogWriter() to direct messages to standard output:

```
OutputStreamWriter osw = new OutputStreamWriter(System.out);
PrintWriter pw = new PrintWriter(osw);
DriverManager.setLogWriter(pw);
```

Following is an example of the output that may be produced by this code:

```
Fetching (SQLFetch), hStmt=5312212
End of result set (SQL_NO_DATA)
Free statement (SQLFreeStmt), hStmt=5312212, fOption=1
*Connection.createStatement
Allocating Statement Handle (SQLAllocStmt), hDbc=5311148
hStmt=5312212
Registering Statement sun.jdbc.odbc.JdbcOdbcStatement@63cb330d
*Statement.executeQuery (SELECT * FROM Attribute)
*Statement.execute (SELECT * FROM Attribute)
Free statement (SQLFreeStmt), hStmt=5312212, fOption=0
Executing (SQLExecDirect), hStmt=5312212, szSqlStr=SELECT * FROM Attribute
Number of result columns (SQLNumResultCols), hStmt=5312212
value=8
Number of result columns (SQLNumResultCols), hStmt=5312212
value=8
*ResultSet.getMetaData
*ResultSetMetaData.getColumnName (1)
Column attributes (SQLColAttributes), hStmt=5312212, icol=1, type=1
value (String)=AttributeKey
```

Releasing Resources

One of the characteristics of Java that makes it easy to use is its automatic garbage collection. In most cases, it's acceptable to release a resource simply by eliminating references to the object that represents it, and the same is true to some degree of database resources (for instance, instances of Connection, Statement, and ResultSet). For example, if you create a connection to a database, you can release it by simply dereferencing it as follows:

```
String url = "jdbc:oracle:thin:@oraserver:1521:projava";
Connection connect = DriverManager.getConnection(url, "bspell", "brett");
// ...
connect = null;
```

Although this approach should eventually result in the connection being closed, that won't occur until the garbage collector reclaims the Connection object. However, the garbage collector may never run, and even if it does, this code could result in the connection remaining open (but unused) for a long time. To avoid this problem, you should always explicitly release database resources by calling the close() method that's defined in Connection, Statement, and ResultSet:

```
String url = "jdbc:oracle:thin:@oraserver:1521:projava";
Connection connect = DriverManager.getConnection(url, "bspell", "brett");
// ...
connect.close();
connect = null;
```

Not only will failure to explicitly release resources prevent other applications from using those resources, but it may also degrade the performance of your application if a large number of connections are created. It's particularly important to close connections when connection pooling is in use, since a failure to do so will usually prevent the Connection from being returned to the pool manager until the garbage collector runs.

With this in mind, it's often worthwhile to take advantage of the try-with-resources feature that was introduced in Java 7, which can help ensure that JDBC artifacts like Connection, Statement, and ResultSet instances are closed appropriately even if an exception occurs during processing. Listing 12-17 shows an example of how this can be done.

Listing 12-17. Using Try-with-Resources to Ensure That JDBC Artifacts Are Closed When No Longer Used

```
try
(
  Connection conn = DriverManager.getConnection(
      "jdbc:oracle:thin:@oraserver:1521:projava ", userid, password);
  Statement stmt = conn.createStatement();
  ResultSet resultSet = stmt.executeQuery("SELECT * FROM TEST_TABLE");
)
{
  while (resultSet.next()) {
    // Process ResultSet data here
  }
}
```

The `Connection`, `Statement`, and `ResultSet` interfaces all extend `AutoCloseable`, which is the interface that identifies resources that will be closed automatically when used in a try-with-resources block like the one in Listing 12-17 and using this approach allows you to avoid using multiple nested `try`/`finally` blocks to ensure that the database resources your application creates are closed appropriately.

Summary

In this chapter, you looked at each of the following topics:

- Selecting and obtaining a driver
- Obtaining a connection to a database
- Executing SQL statements and stored procedures
- Understanding the data types defined in JDBC and how they relate to "native" types
- Managing transactions
- Implementing database connection pooling
- Processing errors and warnings generated by JDBC functions
- Debugging guidelines for database applications

CHAPTER 13

■ ■ ■

Internationalizing Your Applications

Occasionally software applications are used by only a small number of people within a limited geographic area, but it has become increasingly common for an application to be used by many people in different parts of the world. In some cases, it's possible to require all your application's users to understand a single language and use the same symbols and formatting for items such as dates, times, and numeric values. However, most users prefer to work with the language and formatting conventions they're most comfortable with, and by taking that into consideration when designing your application, you can accommodate their wishes.

Modifying or designing an application so it supports more than one language and set of formatting conventions is known as *internationalization* (or *i18n*, because 18 characters appear between the *i* and the *n*). As evidenced by its use of Unicode, Java was designed with internationalization in mind, and it provides a number of classes that make it easy to internationalize your applications.

Closely related to internationalization is *localization*, which is the process of ensuring that an application will function appropriately when used in a particular region of the world. The most obvious step you must take to localize an application is to ensure that it displays text in the user's native language. This requires you to provide a translation for each text item that can be written or displayed by the application, and Java doesn't provide any facilities for automatically translating messages. However, it does provide an easy way for you to define collections of text messages, with each collection representing a particular language, and Java makes it easy for your application to select the appropriate translation of a text item. Where internationalization aims to create applications that can support more than one language, localization provides the extra language support for internationalized applications.

In addition to providing a translation for each message, an internationalized application should also display information using the appropriate symbols and conventions when formatting information such as dates, times, and numeric values. For example, the mm/dd/yy (two-digit month, day, and year) format for dates is appropriate for most users in the United States but isn't commonly used in other countries. Similarly, numeric values are represented in different ways in different parts of the world, especially currency values.

Just as an internationalized application must customize the output it produces, it must also handle user input appropriately. If a user is allowed to enter text that represents a number, the application must be able to parse the text and convert it into a numeric type (say, a double or long value). In addition, a date that was entered by the user will typically need to be converted into an instance of a class such as `java.util.Date` before it can be used or stored by the application. It's also sometimes necessary to parse text and isolate individual sentences, lines, words, or characters in the text, which is a complex task to perform for some languages.

In some cases, a user's language can be implicitly identified based on the user's location. For example, a user in the United States or United Kingdom can reasonably be expected to prefer English messages. In other cases, two or more languages may be commonly used in the same country, such as in Canada where both English and French are widely spoken. However, even if two different users share the same language, you can't assume they also share the same formatting conventions for dates, times, and numeric values.

To be able to internationalize your applications, you'll need to know about the following topics:

- Locales

- Resource bundles

- Formatting and parsing

Locales

As just mentioned, a user's country can't always be used to select the language that an application should use, and a language isn't sufficient to determine the formatting conventions for dates, times, and numeric values. However, it's usually true that a region can be defined that has one dominant language and set of formatting conventions, and that region can be defined by geographic, political, or simply cultural boundaries. Java's Locale class identifies such a region, and each instance of Locale contains property values that include the following:

- A language code represented by a String value that corresponds to one of the codes defined by the ISO-639 standard. You can find various information—including a list of language codes—on the Library of Congress web site at www.loc.gov/standards/iso639-2/.

- Similarly, the country code is a String that's assigned the value of an ISO-3166 country identifier, a list of which is available at www.chemie.fu-berlin.de/diverse/doc/ISO_3166.html.

- The variant value is optional and can be omitted, but it may be useful in some cases.

As shown in Table 13-1, the ISO-639 standard defines both two- and three-character language codes. The two-character code is the older representation but the three-character codes are available for a larger number of languages.

Table 13-1. *Sample List of ISO-639 Language Codes, Including One for Which There Is No Two-Character Code*

Language	ISO-639-1	ISO-639-2
English	en	eng
French	fr	fra
German	de	deu
Spanish	es	spa
Coptic		cop

Similarly, ISO-3166 offers more than one way of representing a country. Specifically, there are both two- and three-character alpha representations, along with a three-digit numeric code for each country as shown in Table 13-2. Notice that the language codes are represented using lower case while the country codes are uppercase.

Table 13-2. *Sample List of ISO-3166 Country Codes*

Country	Alpha-2	Alpha-3	Numeric-3
United States	US	USA	840
Canada	CA	CAN	124
United Kingdom	GB	GBR	826
France	FR	FRA	250
Germany	DE	DEU	276

The `Locale` class requires you to use the two-character language code where one is defined or, if none is defined, the three-character code, and for the country code you should use the two-character code. `Locale` does technically support an alternative representation for a region, specifically, the UN M.49 standard, but that is a newer standard and is less often used than the ISO-3166 codes.

The `java.util.Locale` class itself doesn't provide much functionality that's useful for internationalization, but an instance of `Locale` can be passed to some methods defined in Java's core classes, and those methods will produce the results appropriate for that `Locale`. For example, `java.text.NumberFormat` provides a `getNumberInstance()` factory method that creates an object that can be used to format numeric values. If you pass an instance of `Locale` to the factory method, it will return an object that formats numeric values in a manner that's appropriate for the `Locale` you specified. Most of those methods that accept a `Locale` parameter have a counterpart that doesn't accept such a parameter, and those that don't use the default `Locale`. The default `Locale` is simply a static instance of `Locale` that's selected for you based on your operating system settings, and you can query and modify the default through the static `getDefault()` and `setDefault()` methods in the `Locale` class.

Although you can create an instance of `Locale`, some instances are provided for you as predefined constants in the `Locale` class. Some of those constants represent a `Locale` with only a language specified (for example, `Locale.ENGLISH`, `Locale.FRENCH`, and `Locale.GERMAN`), while others represent both a language and a country (for example, `Locale.US`, `Locale.FRANCE`, and `Locale.GERMANY`). In addition to those constants, Java includes the information needed to support a large number of locales; you can obtain an array of those supported by calling the `getAvailableLocales()` method. For each `Locale` identified by that method, Java provides the ability to display dates, times, and numeric values using the conventions appropriate for that `Locale`. In addition, Java provides the ability to parse and compare `String` instances that consist of characters used in the `Locale`.

To create a `Locale`, you must use either the constructor that accepts country and language codes or the constructor that accepts those values in addition to a variant. For example, to create a `Locale` for Spanish used in the United States, you could use the following:

```
Locale cajunFrenchLocale = new Locale("es", "US");
```

In addition to allowing you to access its country, language, and variant values, each `Locale` provides a `getDisplayName()` method that returns the name of the locale. By default, the method returns a name in the language appropriate for the user's default locale. As with many other methods, though, `getDisplayName()`

allows you to explicitly specify a Locale. If you do so, the name returned will be a string that's appropriate for display in the Locale specified. For example, suppose your default locale is set to Locale.US and you execute the following line of code:

```
System.out.println(Locale.US.getDisplayName());
```

When you do so, the output will appear as follows:

```
English (United States)
```

However, you could instead choose to display the Locale's name in a form that's appropriate for a user in France using code like the following:

```
System.out.println(Locale.US.getDisplayName(Locale.FRANCE));
```

Executing this code will produce the following output:

```
anglais (États-Unis)
```

Many times, you'll want to display a representation of a Locale using the language that's associated with that instance, which you can do with code similar to this:

```
Locale someLocale;
// Assign a reference to an instance of Locale to the variable just defined
// . . .
System.out.println(someLocale.getDisplayName(someLocale));
```

Resource Bundles

Perhaps the most obvious step you must take to internationalize an application is to store the text it displays in an external location. For example, suppose you have the following trivial application:

```
public class Hardcoded {
  public static void main(String[] args) {
    System.out.println("The number of arguments entered is " +
                         args.length);
  }
}
```

This small program can't be made to support more than one language or locale without modifying the source code, because the message text is embedded (or *hard-coded*) within the source. However, Java's resource bundles allow you to store strings, image files, or any other type of resource in files outside your application's source code.

Specifically, the java.util.ResourceBundle class allows you to create a separate resource bundle for each Locale you want to support in your code and have the appropriate bundle selected dynamically at runtime.

A ResourceBundle is a class that encapsulates a set of resources, each of which is associated with a unique key value that's an instance of java.lang.String. To access a particular resource, you simply obtain a reference to the ResourceBundle and call its getObject() method, passing a reference to the String that identifies the resource to which you want to obtain a reference. Resources will often be text information that has been localized but can be any object that's needed to internationalize your application. Since instances of String are the most common type of data stored in and retrieved from instances of ResourceBundle, a getString() method is provided in addition to getObject(). The getString() method simply casts the resource you retrieve to a String object.

Note that the resource keys are case-sensitive, so when calling getObject() or getString(), you must ensure the String you specify is capitalized appropriately. If you specify a key that isn't an exact match for a resource defined in the ResourceBundle, a MissingResourceException is thrown.

Once an appropriate ResourceBundle has been created, which you'll see how to do shortly, the Hardcoded application shown previously could be easily modified to remove the embedded message text as follows:

```
import java.util.*;

public class Hardcoded {

  public static void main(String[] args) {
    ResourceBundle myBundle = ResourceBundle.getBundle(
        "MyResources");
//      System.out.println("The number of arguments entered is " +
//                          args.length);
    String msg = myBundle.getString("MsgText");
    System.out.println(msg + args.length);
  }
}
```

In this case, a resource bundle named MyResources was created that contains a resource with a key of MsgText. This modified application loads the resource bundle, obtains a reference to the MsgText resource, casts it to a String, and uses that text to produce its output. With this modified design, you can make the Hardcoded application support more than one Locale, and it will display the message text in the appropriate language for each one.

In the previous example, no Locale was specified on the call to getBundle(), but a different implementation of that method allows you to do so. For example, if you wanted to load the ResourceBundle containing Canadian French messages, you could use code like the following:

```
ResourceBundle myBundle = ResourceBundle.getBundle(
        "MyResources", Locale.CANADA_FRENCH);
```

When you call its getBundle() method, ResourceBundle attempts to load each class file with a variation of the name that was specified. It first looks for classes with the explicitly specified Locale values (in other words, language, country, and variant codes) appended to the name and then to classes with the default Locale's values. For example, if the default Locale is Locale.US in this case, getBundle() will load each of the following files if they exist:

```
MyResources_fr_CA.class
MyResources_fr.class
MyResources_en_US.class
MyResources_en.class
MyResources.class
```

Note that getBundle() also attempts to use the variant name if one is specified, but in this case, both the default (Locale.US) and the explicitly specified instance (Locale.CANADA_FRENCH) have a variant that's set to the empty string (""). In other words, the search order used when loading a ResourceBundle file can be summarized by the following list. In this list, (1) represents the explicitly specified Locale, (2) represents the default locale, and basename represents the String argument passed to getBundle().

```
basename_language(1)_country(1)_variant(1).class
basename_language(1)_country(1).class
basename_language(1).class
basename_language(2)_country(2)_variant(2).class
basename_language(2)_country(2).class
basename_language(2).class
basename.class
```

As you'll see shortly, there's an important reason why calling getBundle() loads each of these classes if they exist instead of simply loading the first one that's found.

Creating a ResourceBundle

ResourceBundle is an abstract class, and although you can create your own direct subclass, you don't need to normally do so. Instead, you'll create a subclass of either ListResourceBundle or PropertyResourceBundle, which are convenience classes provided with Java that make it easier for you to create a ResourceBundle. If you're going to be using images or other objects in your ResourceBundle, then a ListResourceBundle is the one to use, while the PropertyResourceBundle is a better choice for use with text.

ListResourceBundle

Creating a subclass of ListResourceBundle is simple; you need to implement only a single getContents() method that returns a two-dimensional array of key/resource pairs.

To learn how to create a ListResourceBundle subclass, suppose you want to internationalize the application shown in Listing 13-1 that displays a dialog and requests the user to click the button corresponding to the correct answer. Figure 13-1 shows the application in action.

Listing 13-1. JavaQuestion Application

```java
import java.util.*;
import javax.swing.*;

public class JavaQuestion {

  public static void main(String[] args) {
    ImageIcon flagIcon = new ImageIcon("flags/unitedstates.gif");
    String[] options = {"Yes", "No"};
    JOptionPane pane = new JOptionPane(
```

```
        "Is Java an object-oriented programming language?",
        JOptionPane.QUESTION_MESSAGE, 0, flagIcon, options);
    JDialog dlg = pane.createDialog(null, "Java Question");
    dlg.setModal(true);
    dlg.setVisible(true);
    String selection = (String)(pane.getValue());
    boolean selectedYes = (selection == options[0]);
  }
}
```

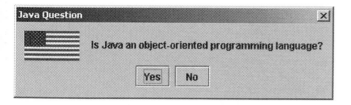

Figure 13-1. *The* JavaQuestion *application displays an icon and prompts the user to answer a question*

As shown in Listing 13-1, this code uses four text resources and an ImageIcon that should be localized based on the default Locale, and a ResourceBundle named MyResources can easily be created like the one in Listing 13-2. As you can see, this class simply defines each resource and maps it to a String key, while the getContents() method returns a reference to the array containing the key/value pairs.

Listing 13-2. Returning the Contents of a ListResourceBundle

```
import java.util.*;
import javax.swing.*;

public class MyResources extends ListResourceBundle {

  private static Object[][] resources = {
      {"WhatIsJava", "What is Java?"},
      {"JavaIsLang", "Is Java an object-oriented " +
          "programming language"},
      {"LabelYes", "Yes"},
      {"LabelNo", "No"},
      {"FlagIcon", new ImageIcon("flags/unitedstates.gif")}
  };

  public Object[][] getContents() {
    return resources;
  }

}
```

If the application that uses these resources is intended to also be used by German-speaking people, you could create an equivalent ResourceBundle called MyResources_de as shown in Listing 13-3.

Listing 13-3. A ListResourceBundle Containing Resources for the German Language

```
import java.util.*;
import javax.swing.*;

public class MyResources_de extends ListResourceBundle {

  private static Object[][] resources = {
      {"WhatIsJava", "Was ist Java?"},
      {"JavaIsLang", "Ist Java eine objektorientierte " +
          "Programmiersprache?"},
      {"LabelYes", "Ja"},
      {"LabelNo", "Nein"},
      {"FlagIcon", new ImageIcon("flags/germany.gif")}
  };

  public Object[][] getContents() {
    return resources;
  }
}
```

This definition of a German-language ResourceBundle illustrates an important point. Although it may be possible for all German-speaking users to share the text in this bundle, it's not appropriate for them to share the same flag icon, since the German language is spoken in more than one country. It wouldn't be correct, for example, to display Germany's flag for a user in Switzerland, although it might be appropriate to use the same text resources for both. Fortunately, Java's internationalization capabilities were designed to easily address this problem.

As mentioned earlier, getBundle() creates a ResourceBundle for each of the variations it finds for the specified bundle name. In this case, both MyResources_de.class and MyResources.class will be loaded if a German Locale (for example, Locale.GERMAN or Locale.GERMANY) is the default or is specified explicitly when getBundle() is called. In addition, the bundles are arranged in a logical hierarchy, and if you request a resource that isn't found in the "lowest" bundle, the hierarchy will be searched until a bundle is found that does contain the resource. In this case, for example, if you request a resource that isn't defined in MyResources_de.class but is defined in MyResources.class, the value from MyResources will be returned.

You can take advantage of this behavior by defining only the resources in a "lower" bundle that should be different from those in a "higher" bundle. For example, to address the issue described earlier of the German flag being returned for Swiss users, it's possible to simply define a new German Swiss (MyResources_de_CH) bundle, like the one in Listing 13-4.

Listing 13-4. *An Additional Resource Bundle Specifically Targeted at German as Spoken in Switzerland*

```java
import java.util.*;
import javax.swing.*;

public class MyResources_de_CH extends ListResourceBundle {

  private static Object[][] resources = {
    {"FlagIcon", new ImageIcon("flags/switzerland.gif")}
  };

  public Object[][] getContents() {
    return resources;
  }
}
```

When a Swiss German bundle is used, the FlagIcon resource will be retrieved from that bundle. Other resources, such as the message text items, will effectively be "inherited" from the MyResources_de bundle because they aren't defined in MyResources_de_CH (see Figure 13-2).

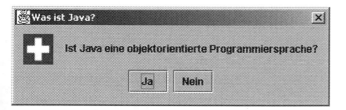

Figure 13-2. *Modifying the application to produce different results depending upon which bundle's resources are used*

With the base (MyResources), German (MyResources_de), and Swiss German (MyResources_de_CH) bundle classes created, you can modify the JavaQuestion application to retrieve its resources from a ResourceBundle (see Listing 13-5 for an example of how this can be accomplished).

Listing 13-5. *Using the Resource Bundles with the Sample Application*

```java
import java.util.*;
import javax.swing.*;

public class JavaQuestion {

  private static ResourceBundle resources =
      ResourceBundle.getBundle("MyResources");

  public static void main(String[] args) {
    ImageIcon flagIcon = (ImageIcon)(resources.getObject(
        "FlagIcon"));
    String[] options =
      {resources.getString("LabelYes"), resources.getString("LabelNo")};
    JOptionPane pane = new JOptionPane(
```

```
            resources.getString("JavaIsLang"),
            JOptionPane.QUESTION_MESSAGE,
            0, flagIcon, options);
        JDialog dlg = pane.createDialog(null,
            resources.getString("WhatIsJava"));
        dlg.setModal(true);
        dlg.setVisible(true);
        String selection = (String)(pane.getValue());
        boolean selectedYes = (selection == options[0]);
    }
}
```

PropertyResourceBundle

The ListResourceBundle in the previous example included an ImageIcon, but in practice, your bundles will often contain only text data. In addition, it's somewhat inconvenient to recompile a ListResourceBundle class each time a new resource is added, updated, or deleted. However, in addition to the ListResourceBundle, Java also includes the PropertyResourceBundle, and it provides a more convenient way to package text resources.

Specifically, you can create a properties file, which is a flat file containing key/value pairs, with a pair on each line and the key and value separated by an equal (=) sign. For example, you could create a properties file containing the previously defined German messages.

```
WhatIsJava=Was ist Java?
JavaIsLang=Java ist eine objektorientierte Programmiersprache
LabelYes=Ja
LabelNo=Nein
```

Unlike ListResourceBundle, you don't need to define a new Java class to use a PropertyResourceBundle. Instead, you create a file with a .properties extension and add property information to it like that shown previously. When you call getBundle(), it will search for properties files in addition to ResourceBundle subclasses, and getBundle() will automatically create a PropertyResourceBundle when it finds a .properties file. If it doesn't find a match after searching, it will go to the base filename if available. For example, with these messages stored in a file named ResourceTest_de.properties, you could access them using the following code:

```
ResourceBundle bundle = ResourceBundle.getBundle(
    "ResourceTest", Locale.GERMAN);
```

Locale-Sensitive Formatting and Parsing

Creating localized messages is only one of the tasks you must perform to internationalize your applications. You must also ensure that dates, times, and numeric values are formatted appropriately for the Locale when displayed, and your applications must be able to parse these data types correctly when they're entered by a user. For example, if you provide a text field that allows a user to enter a date value, you'll typically want to convert the text entered in that field into an instance of a class used to represent a date, such as java.util.Date or one of the classes that are part of the new Date and Time API (application programming interface).

The Date and Time API introduced in Java 8 is the preferred mechanism for representing and manipulating date and time values and we already saw in Chapter 3 how to perform those operations. However, if you're using an earlier version of Java or you need to maintain code based on one of those versions it can be helpful to be familiar with how to perform date processing using the older classes, and this section provides that information.

Java provides the ability to format and parse date, time, and numeric values by creating instances of java.text.NumberFormat (for numeric values) and java.text.DateFormat (for dates and times). Both of those classes provide factory methods that allow you to obtain a formatter for a specified Locale or for the default Locale. For example, the following five lines of code obtain formatters that use the default Locale's date, time, numeric, currency, and percent conventions, respectively:

```
DateFormat dateFormatter = DateFormat.getDateInstance();
DateFormat timeFormatter = DateFormat.getTimeInstance();
NumberFormat numberFormatter = NumberFormat.getNumberInstance();
NumberFormat currencyFormatter = NumberFormat.getCurrencyInstance();
NumberFormat percentFormatter = NumberFormat.getPercentInstance();
```

These Format objects actually provide two types of functionality. First, they allow you to convert the value of a Java object or primitive (for example, an instance of Date or a long value) into a text string that's formatted according to the conventions of the appropriate Locale. Second, they allow you to perform the opposite type of conversion, where a string (perhaps one entered by your application's user) can be converted into an appropriate object or primitive type. For example, DateFormat converts java.util.Date instances into text and can convert a text representation of a date into an instance of Date.

Formatting and Parsing Dates

Date values are represented differently in various locales, even in those that use the same language. As noted earlier, the mm/dd/yy format is the most commonly used format in the United States, but much of the rest of the world (including other English-speaking regions) uses dd/mm/yy instead.

Even within a single Locale, different date formats are often used. For example, each of the following represents a format in which a date might be displayed in the United States:

```
03/19/00
March 19, 2000
Sunday, March 19, 2000
```

To obtain a reference to a DateFormat object that can be used to format and parse dates, you can call the static getDateInstance() method in the DateFormat class. When calling getDateInstance(), you can specify a Locale, and if you don't do so, a DateFormat object is returned that will format dates based on the conventions of your default Locale. In addition, getDateInstance() allows you to specify a style, which is an integer value that's equal to one of four constants defined in DateFormat: SHORT, MEDIUM, LONG, or FULL. The style value indicates how detailed a description of the date will be produced by the DateFormat instance. For example, SHORT generates brief strings (for example, "03/19/00"), while MEDIUM, LONG, and FULL each provide increasingly more detailed date representations (for example, FULL generates "Sunday, March 19, 2000"). In the following sections, you'll get to see by example what effect each of these constants has on the output.

Formatting Dates

Once you've created an instance of DateFormat, you can use it to convert the value of a java.util.Date instance into a text string by calling the DateFormat's format() method. The following code segment creates a LONG-style DateFormat that will use the conventions that are appropriate for the predefined FRANCE Locale and uses the Dateformat object to display the current date:

```
DateFormat formatter = DateFormat.getDateInstance(DateFormat.LONG,
    Locale.FRANCE);
System.out.println(formatter.format(new java.util.Date()));
```

Running this code segment will produce the following output line:

```
19 mars 2000
```

If you'd like to see the various formats that are included for the version of Java you're using, you could write an application that uses the static getAvailableLocales() method defined in Locale to display the various formats for a given date using each Locale (see Figure 13-3).

Date Viewer

English (United States)

Selected date: Tuesday, November 14, 2000   **Refresh**

○ Short ○ Medium ○ Long ● Full

Locale	Short	Medium	Long	Full
Byelorussian (Belarus)	14.11.00	14.11.2000	аўторак, 14, лістапа...	аўторак, 14, лістапа...
Bulgarian	00-11-14	2000-11-14	Вторник, 2000, Ноем...	Вторник, 2000, Ноем...
Bulgarian (Bulgaria)	00-11-14	2000-11-14	Вторник, 2000, Ноем...	Вторник, 2000, Ноем...
Catalan	14/11/00	14/11/2000	14 / novembre / 2000	dimarts, 14 / novembr...
Catalan (Spain)	14/11/00	14/11/2000	14 / novembre / 2000	dimarts, 14 / novembr...
Catalan (Spain,Euro)	14/11/00	14/11/2000	14 / novembre / 2000	dimarts, 14 / novembr...
Czech	14.11.00	14.11.2000	14. listopad 2000	Úterý, 14. listopad 2000
Czech (Czech Republi...	14.11.00	14.11.2000	14. listopad 2000	Úterý, 14. listopad 2000
Danish	14-11-00	14-11-2000	14. november 2000	14. november 2000
Danish (Denmark)	14-11-00	14-11-2000	14. november 2000	14. november 2000
German	14.11.00	14.11.2000	14. November 2000	Dienstag, 14. Novem...
German (Austria)	14.11.00	14.11.2000	14. November 2000	Dienstag, 14. Novem...
German (Austria,Euro)	14.11.00	14.11.2000	14. November 2000	Dienstag, 14. Novem...
German (Switzerland)	14.11.00	14.11.2000	14. November 2000	Dienstag, 14. Novem...
German (Germany)	14.11.00	14.11.2000	14. November 2000	Dienstag, 14. Novem...
German (Germany,Eu...	14.11.00	14.11.2000	14. November 2000	Dienstag, 14. Novem...
German (Luxembourg)	14.11.00	14.11.2000	14. November 2000	Dienstag, 14. Novem...
German (Luxembour...	14.11.00	14.11.2000	14. November 2000	Dienstag, 14. Novem...
Greek	14/11/2000	14 Νοε 2000	14 Νοέμβριος 2000	Τρίτη, 14 Νοέμβριος 2...
Greek (Greece)	14/11/2000	14 Νοε 2000	14 Νοέμβριος 2000	Τρίτη, 14 Νοέμβριος 2...
English (Australia)	14/11/00	14/11/2000	14 November 2000	Tuesday, 14 Novemb...
English (Canada)	14/11/00	14-Nov-00	November 14, 2000	Tuesday, November 1...
English (United Kingd...	14/11/00	14-Nov-00	14 November 2000	14 November 2000
English (Ireland)	14/11/00	14-Nov-00	14 November 2000	14 November 2000

Figure 13-3. *Some of the many different date formats associated with various locales*

Parsing Dates

Just as you'll want your application to display dates according to the local conventions, you'll also want it to be able to convert a date string entered by a user into an instance of java.util.Date. To convert a string representation of a date into an instance of Date, simply create an instance of DateFormat and use its parse() method as follows:

```
public static void main(String[] args) throws ParseException {
  DateFormat formatter = DateFormat.getDateInstance(DateFormat.SHORT);
  java.util.Date dateValue = formatter.parse(args[0]);
}
```

Note that a ParseException is thrown if the date string passed to the parse() method doesn't represent a valid date as defined by the appropriate Locale's formatting conventions. There will also potentially be an ArrayIndexOutOfBoundsException thrown if no argument is provided.

Parsing and DateFormat's Leniency Mode

As mentioned earlier, you can use instances of DateFormat to convert String representations of date and time values into instances of Date. For example, the application in Listing 13-6 converts the first command-line parameter into a Date value using the SHORT form of the default Locale's date-formatting conventions:

Listing 13-6. A Simple Application That Uses a DateFormat for Parsing Date Text

```
import java.text.*;
import java.util.Date;

public class DateTest {

  public static void main(String[] args) throws ParseException {
    DateFormat formatter = DateFormat.getDateInstance(DateFormat.SHORT);
    Date theDate = formatter.parse(args[0]);
    System.out.println(theDate);
  }
}
```

In most cases, entering an invalid date string will result in the parse() method throwing a ParseException. However, in some versions of Java, you can enter text that doesn't represent a valid date without an exception being thrown. For example, you might execute the following application while using the Java 1.1 core classes:

```
java DateTest 02/09/hello
```

Depending upon the version of Java you're using, the invalid date ("02/09/hello") may incorrectly produce the following results:

```
Mon Feb 09 00:00:00 CST 0001
```

In this case, the invalid year ("hello") was converted to a value of 0001. This occurs because the DateFormat's leniency mode is enabled, which causes it to attempt to "guess" what date the String was intended to represent.

In most cases, you'll want DateFormat's parse() method to both convert and validate the date that was entered. In other words, the main purpose of parse() is to convert a String into a Date, but it's also responsible for ensuring that the text it converts represents a valid date. However, the previous code segment may fail to correctly notify your application (by throwing a ParseException) that the date was invalid. To ensure it does so, you can call the setLenient() method as in Listing 13-7, specifying that lenient parsing of dates should be disabled.

Listing 13-7. Enabling Lenient Parsing in the Sample Application

```
import java.text.*;
import java.util.Date;

public class DateTest {

  public static void main(String[] args) throws ParseException {
    DateFormat formatter = DateFormat.getDateInstance(DateFormat.SHORT);
    formatter.setLenient(false);
    Date theDate = formatter.parse(args[0]);
    System.out.println(theDate);
  }
}
```

Formatting and Parsing Times

If you want to format and/or parse time values instead of dates, you can use the getTimeInstance() factory method defined in DateFormat as in the following code segment:

```
DateFormat formatter = DateFormat.getTimeInstance();
```

Like getDateInstance(), the getTimeInstance() method allows you to specify a style (and optionally a Locale); Figure 13-4 shows some of the combinations.

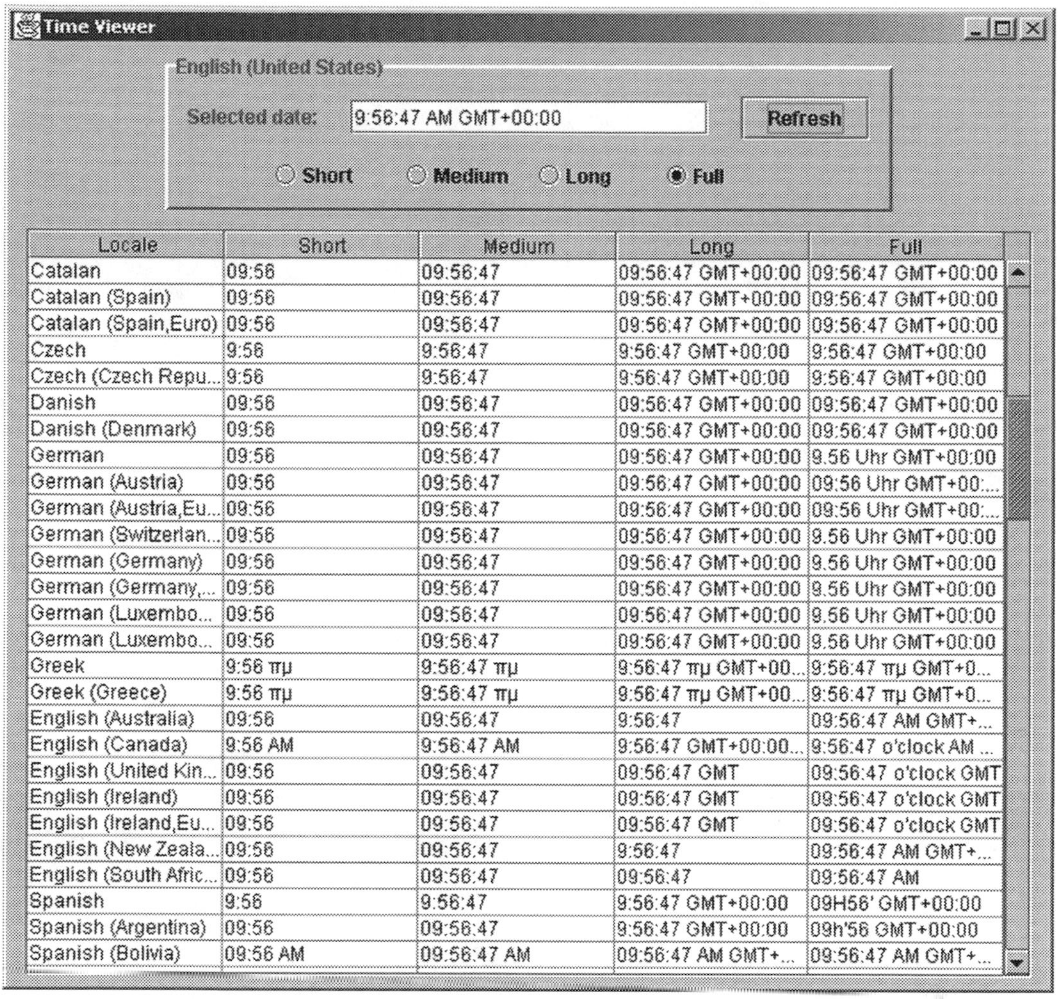

Figure 13-4. *Previewing how the current time is displayed using various combinations of format and locale*

Formatting and Parsing Numeric Values

While DateFormat allows you to format and parse date and time values, NumberFormat allows you to format and parse numeric values. In this context, *numeric values* refers collectively to plain numeric values as well as currency and percentage values, although a different factory method is provided for each of the three types. To obtain a reference to a formatter/parser for plain numeric data, use the getNumberInstance() method in NumberFormat. As with DateFormat, you can specify a Locale, but NumberFormat doesn't support different styles.

NumberFormat provides format() methods that can be passed either a long value or a double value, so you can pass any numeric primitive type to those methods for formatting. For example, given the following code segment:

```
NumberFormat formatter = NumberFormat.getNumberInstance(Locale.US);
System.out.println(formatter.format(123456.78));
```

543

executing the code will produce the following output:

```
123,456.78
```

There isn't as much variation in the way that numbers are formatted around the world as there is variation in how dates and times are displayed, but there are some differences. For example, the United States and many other countries use the period (.) to represent the decimal point and commas (,) or a space to separate every three characters to the left of the decimal. However, other countries (for example, Germany) reverse the meaning of these two characters, using the comma to represent the decimal point and the period as the digit separator. For example, suppose you modify the previous code segment as follows:

```
NumberFormat formatter = NumberFormat.getNumberInstance(Locale.GERMANY);
System.out.println(formatter.format(123456.78));
```

Executing this code will produce the following output:

```
123.456,78
```

Like DateFormat instances, NumberFormat objects can be used for both formatting and parsing, and while DateFormat's parse() method returns an instance of java.util.Date, NumberFormat's parse() returns an instance of java.lang.Number. However, Number provides convenience methods that allow you to retrieve the encapsulated value as any primitive type, so it's easy to convert a numeric String into a given type. For example, you could use the following code segment to convert the first command-line parameter into an int value:

```
public static void main(String[] args) throws ParseException {
  NumberFormat formatter = NumberFormat.getNumberInstance();
  int value = formatter.parse(args[0]).intValue();
}
```

With Locale set to GERMANY, this code will take the figure "123,45" and return "123" as a result. As with DateFormat, NumberFormat's parse() method will throw a ParseException if the string that's parsed doesn't represent a valid number.

NumberFormat Example

Although the conventions used for percentage and plain numeric values don't vary much from one Locale to the next, the conventions used for currency values vary widely (see Figure 13-5).

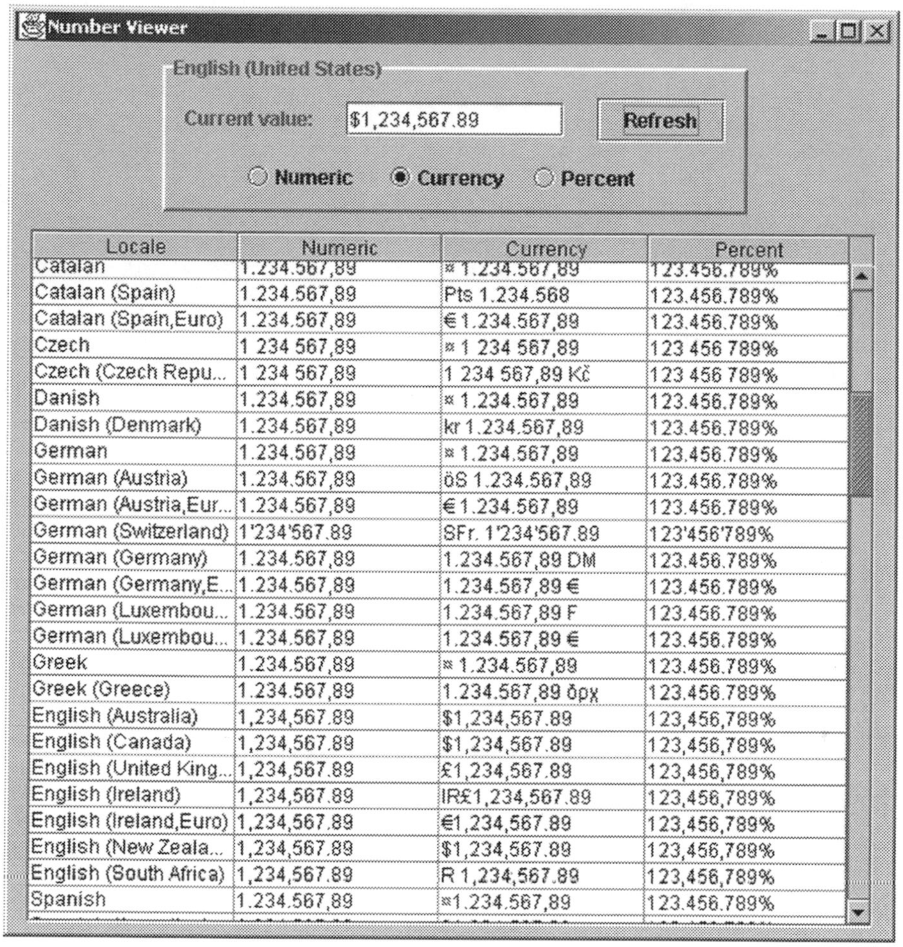

Locale	Numeric	Currency	Percent
Catalan	1.234.567,89	¤ 1.234.567,89	123.456.789%
Catalan (Spain)	1.234.567,89	Pts 1.234.568	123.456.789%
Catalan (Spain,Euro)	1.234.567,89	€ 1.234.567,89	123.456.789%
Czech	1 234 567,89	¤ 1 234 567,89	123 456 789%
Czech (Czech Repu...	1 234 567,89	1 234 567,89 Kč	123 456 789%
Danish	1.234.567,89	¤ 1.234.567,89	123.456.789%
Danish (Denmark)	1.234.567,89	kr 1.234.567,89	123.456.789%
German	1.234.567,89	¤ 1.234.567,89	123.456.789%
German (Austria)	1.234.567,89	öS 1.234.567,89	123.456.789%
German (Austria,Eur...	1.234.567,89	€ 1.234.567,89	123.456.789%
German (Switzerland)	1'234'567.89	SFr. 1'234'567.89	123'456'789%
German (Germany)	1.234.567,89	1.234.567,89 DM	123.456.789%
German (Germany,E...	1.234.567,89	1.234.567,89 €	123.456.789%
German (Luxembou...	1.234.567,89	1.234.567,89 F	123.456.789%
German (Luxembou...	1.234.567,89	1.234.567,89 €	123.456.789%
Greek	1.234.567,89	¤ 1.234.567,89	123.456.789%
Greek (Greece)	1.234.567,89	1.234.567,89 δρχ	123.456.789%
English (Australia)	1,234,567.89	$1,234,567.89	123,456,789%
English (Canada)	1,234,567.89	$1,234,567.89	123,456,789%
English (United King...	1,234,567.89	£1,234,567.89	123,456,789%
English (Ireland)	1,234,567.89	IR£1,234,567.89	123,456,789%
English (Ireland,Euro)	1,234,567.89	€1,234,567.89	123,456,789%
English (New Zeala...	1,234,567.89	$1,234,567.89	123,456,789%
English (South Africa)	1,234,567.89	R 1,234,567.89	123,456,789%
Spanish	1.234.567,89	¤1.234.567,89	123.456.789%

Figure 13-5. *Previewing how a currency value is displayed using various combinations of format and locale*

MessageFormat

The ResourceBundle class provides a convenient way to encapsulate messages, but it's often necessary to insert strings inside those messages before displaying them. For example, suppose you want to display a message describing the number of users who are logged into an application. You might display a message like the following one, changing the integer at the beginning of the message to display the appropriate numeric value:

```
10 users are currently logged on.
```

On the surface, it may seem you can simply define the non-numeric portion of the text in a message and append it to the number of users. For example:

```
ResourceBundle bundle;
int userCount;
// ...
// The ResourceBundle includes a CurrentUsers key that's associated with
// the message shown below:
//
// users are currently logged on.
//
String msgText = (String)(bundle.getObject("CurrentUsers"));
System.out.println(userCount + msgText);
```

The problem with this approach is that when the "users are currently logged on," text is translated to another language; thus it may not be grammatically correct to simply append the message text to the numeric value. For example, the equivalent message in Spanish is as follows:

```
Entran a 10 utilizadores actualmente.
```

One way of addressing this is to break the message into two segments: one that represents the text that should precede the numeric value and the other containing the text that follows it. In the English ResourceBundle, the text that precedes the value would be empty, while the Spanish version would be assigned an "Entran a" value. However, that approach would require you to define multiple resources for each message that contains substitution parameters (for example, the numeric value). Splitting a single message into multiple resources would make your code more confusing and make the ResourceBundle file maintenance (in other words, updating and deleting messages) more tedious and error-prone. Fortunately, Java provides the java.text.MessageFormat class that allows you to format messages with substitution parameters. It does this by allowing you to format strings into pattern strings at the places you specify in your code.

To use MessageFormat, simply create an instance using the constructor that accepts a single String parameter. That String should represent message text with substitution parameters identified by numeric values in braces, as follows:

```
{0} users are currently logged on.
```

To format this message properly, you must construct an array of objects and pass that array to the format() method of the MessageFormat you created. When you do so, the substitution parameter values embedded in the message text will be replaced by a String representation of the corresponding object in the array. In this case, only a single substitution parameter has a value of 0, so you can construct an array that contains a single object representing the number of users logged on.

```
Object[] values = {new Integer(userCount)};
```

The 0 value in the message identifies the index of the array element that should be placed in the substitution field, which in this case is an Integer representing the user count.

You can pass the array of values to the format() method, and it will produce a String representing the message text with the substitution parameter values embedded within it. For example, suppose you've defined a properties file like the following one that's suitable for use by a PropertyResourceBundle:

```
CurrentUsers={0} users are currently logged on.
```

To format this text with the substitution parameter, simply create an instance of MessageFormat and call its format() method, passing an array of objects that should be used for the substitution parameters. In this case, a single parameter is specified, so the array needs to contain only a single Object, and any additional instances are ignored.

```
ResourceBundle bundle = ResourceBundle.getBundle("FormatMessages");
int userCount;
// ...
// The ResourceBundle includes a CurrentUsers key that's associated with
// the message shown below:
//
//    users are currently logged on.
//
String msgText = (String)(bundle.getObject("CurrentUsers"));
MessageFormat msgFormat = new MessageFormat(msgText);
Object[] values = {new Integer(userCount)};
System.out.println(msgFormat.format(values));
```

If the value of userCount is 15, the previous code segment will produce the following output:

```
15 users are currently logged on.
```

Since it allows you to dynamically construct messages based on their substitution parameters, MessageFormat allows you to avoid creating code that's specific to a Locale. For example, when a Spanish equivalent of the ResourceBundle is created, the substitution parameter can simply be moved to the appropriate location within the message.

```
Entran a {0} utilizadores actualmente.
```

In effect, MessageFormat shifts the responsibility for creating grammatically correct output from the Java programmer to the person who provides message translation.

I used a single substitution parameter in this example, but it's equally simple to specify multiple parameters when using MessageFormat. For example, you might want to create a message with the following text:

```
$123.40 was deposited at 10:49 AM on March 21, 2000.
```

In this case, a currency value, date, and time are included in the message output, and the date and time should be derived from a single instance of java.util.Date. To accomplish this, you might initially create a message like the following:

```
Deposit={0} was deposited at {1} on {1}.
```

Note that the second object in the array is referenced twice in this message, and in fact, MessageFormat allows you to use an object as many times as you want. In addition, it has no requirement that you must use each object in the array within the message, so it's valid for the array to contain extraneous objects. In this example, there's no reason to add elements to the array that aren't used in the message, but in practice, you may want to format() an array that's used for other purposes within your application.

Given the message defined previously, you could create code like that in Listing 13-8 to display the message.

Listing 13-8. An Example of Using MessageFormat

```
ResourceBundle bundle = ResourceBundle.getBundle("FormatMessages");
float depositAmount = 123.4f;
// ...
String msgText = (String)(bundle.getObject("Deposit"));
MessageFormat msgFormat = new MessageFormat(msgText);
Object[] values = {new Float(depositAmount), new java.util.Date()};
System.out.println(msgFormat.format(values));
```

However, executing this code doesn't produce the desired results but instead produces output similar to the following:

```
123.4 was deposited at 3/21/00 10:49 AM on 3/21/00 10:49 AM.
```

This occurs because the message text defined earlier doesn't contain any information that specifies how the data should be formatted. When you don't do so, the default Locale's formatting styles for numbers and date/time values are used. However, MessageFormat allows you to provide information within the message text that describes how the values should be formatted. For example, you could make the following changes to display the first parameter as a currency value, the second parameter as a SHORT-style time, and the third as a LONG-style date:

```
Deposit={0,number,currency} was deposited at {1,time,short} on {1,date,long}.
```

Making this modification to the message text results in the output being correctly formatted.

```
$123.40 was deposited at 10:49 AM on March 21, 2000.
```

The second item you can specify in the substitution field is referred to as the *element format* and must be one of the following: time, date, number, or choice. The third item is the *element style* and must be short, medium, long, or full for date/time values or currency, percent, or integer for numeric values. The choice element format is useful when the message text that should be displayed is dependent upon the value of the substitution parameter; I'll describe how to use choice later in this chapter.

Specifying a Locale

When you create an instance of MessageFormat, it uses the default Locale to format the substitution values using instances of DateFormat, NumberFormat, and ChoiceFormat. For example, if the default Locale is equal to Locale.US, date and time values are formatted using US formatting conventions, but you can change the Locale used by a MessageFormat instance by calling its setLocale() method. However, once you've modified the Locale, you must reapply the message pattern, using applyPattern() as in Listing 13-9.

Listing 13-9. Using a Locale with MessageFormat

```
ResourceBundle bundle = ResourceBundle.getBundle("FormatMessages");
float depositAmount = 123.4f;
// ...
String msgText = (String)(bundle.getObject("Deposit"));
MessageFormat msgFormat = new MessageFormat(msgText);
msgFormat.setLocale(Locale.FRANCE);
msgFormat.applyPattern(msgFormat.toPattern());
Object[] values = {new Float(depositAmount), new java.util.Date()};
System.out.println(msgFormat.format(values));
```

This code displays the same message shown earlier, but it uses French currency and date/time formatting conventions as follows:

```
F123,40 was deposited at 10:49 AM on mars 21, 2000.
```

Specifying a Format Object

When you specify a Date object as a parameter, MessageFormat creates an instance of DateFormat that it uses to convert the Date's value to a String. Similarly, numeric values are formatted using instances of NumberFormat that are constructed automatically.

In most cases, it's appropriate to allow MessageFormat to construct DateFormat, NumberFormat, and ChoiceFormat objects for you. However, you'll sometimes want to construct one explicitly and have it used by MessageFormat. For example, you might want to change the previous code so it displays dates using Italian formatting standards while still allowing other fields to be formatted using the default Locale. To accomplish this, you could use the setFormat() method as in Listing 13-10.

Listing 13-10. Calling the setFormat() Method for a MessageFormat

```
ResourceBundle bundle = ResourceBundle.getBundle("FormatMessages");
float depositAmount = 123.4f;
// ...
String msgText = (String)(bundle.getObject("Deposit"));
MessageFormat msgFormat = new MessageFormat(msgText);
DateFormat timeFormat = DateFormat.getTimeInstance(
    DateFormat.LONG, Locale.ITALY);
msgFormat.setFormat(1, timeFormat);
DateFormat dateFormat = DateFormat.getDateInstance(
    DateFormat.LONG, Locale.ITALY);
msgFormat.setFormat(2, dateFormat);
Object[] values = {new Float(depositAmount), new java.util.Date()};
System.out.println(msgFormat.format(values));
```

If your default Locale is equal to Locale.US, the output from this code segment will appear as follows:

```
$123.40 was deposited at 9.46.22 CST on 22 marzo 2000.
```

Note that the index value specified on setFormat() corresponds to the index of a substitution field, not a substitution value. In other words, that index identifies the zero-based location of the substitution field within the message, where the first field corresponds to a value of 0, the second to a value of 1, and so on. Don't confuse this with the values within the substitution fields themselves (for example, {0}, {1}, and so on), which represent indices into the array of parameter values.

In addition to the setFormat() method, MessageFormat also provides setFormats(), which allows you to specify an array of Format objects (for example, instances of NumberFormat or DateFormat). For example, the code segment in Listing 13-11 shows the same output as the previous one, but it uses a slightly different approach. It retrieves the array of Format objects built by the MessageFormat instance and overrides the second and third substitution formats with instances that use the Locale for Italy.

Listing 13-11. Using the setFormats() Method to Set Multiple Formats in One Invocation

```
ResourceBundle bundle = ResourceBundle.getBundle("FormatMessages");
float depositAmount = 123.4f;
// ...
String msgText = (String)(bundle.getObject("Deposit"));
MessageFormat msgFormat = new MessageFormat(msgText);
Format[] formats = msgFormat.getFormats();
formats[1] = DateFormat.getTimeInstance(
    DateFormat.LONG, Locale.ITALY);
formats[2] = DateFormat.getDateInstance(
    DateFormat.LONG, Locale.ITALY);
msgFormat.setFormats(formats);
Object[] values = {new Float(depositAmount), new java.util.Date()};
System.out.println(msgFormat.format(values));
```

ChoiceFormat

When creating a message that contains a numeric value, it's often not sufficient to simply insert the number into the message, because the text may be grammatically incorrect for some values. For example, the message described earlier that identifies the number of logged-on users can display each of the following:

```
0 users are currently logged on.
1 users are currently logged on.
2 users are currently logged on.
```

Notice that the message produced when a single user is logged on ("1 users are currently logged on.") is grammatically incorrect. In addition, a better message when there are zero users would be "No users are currently logged on." Attempting to produce these results by modifying the Java source code would result in the same type of Locale-specific coding that appeared earlier, but the ChoiceFormat class provides a solution to this problem.

To create an instance of ChoiceFormat, you can use the constructor that accepts two parameters: an array of double values in ascending order and an array of String instances. When you call ChoiceFormat's format() method and pass it an instance of a numeric wrapper class (for example, Integer, Float, Byte, and so on), it returns one of the String values from the array based on the value of that numeric object. For example, suppose you create a ChoiceFormat using the following code:

```
double[] limits = {0d, 1d, 2d};
String[] values = {"x < 1", "1 <= x < 2", "x >= 2"};
ChoiceFormat cf = new ChoiceFormat(limits, values);
```

This ChoiceFormat defines three ranges of numbers: less than one, between one and two, and greater than or equal to two. Note that the first value in the list (in this case, zero) is effectively ignored with respect to defining ranges, but you must include it and ensure that it's less than the second value. Given this ChoiceFormat, you can call its format() method and pass it instances of a Number subclass such as Integer. Passing a value that's less than one will cause the first String to be printed, while a value greater than or equal to one but less than two causes the second value to be printed. Finally, values greater than or equal to two cause the third message to be printed. For example, you might execute code like the following:

```
System.out.println(cf.format(new Integer(0)));
System.out.println(cf.format(new Integer(1)));
System.out.println(cf.format(new Integer(2)));
```

Compiling and executing this output will produce the following results:

```
x < 1
1 <= x < 2
x >= 2
```

As you may suspect, you can use ChoiceFormat to resolve the problem with the value of a substitution parameter affecting the appropriate grammar in a message. For example, you could write the code in Listing 13-12 to generate the appropriate output based on the number of users who are logged on.

Listing 13-12. Using a ChoiceFormat to Handle Variations Based on a Numeric Value

```
ResourceBundle bundle = ResourceBundle.getBundle("FormatMessages");
int userCount;
// ...
//   The ResourceBundle includes a CurrentUsers key that's associated with
//   the message shown below:
//
//       {0} currently logged on.
//
Integer countValue = new Integer(userCount);
String msgText = (String)(bundle.getObject("CurrentUsers"));
double[] borderValues = {0d, 1d, 2d};
String[] descriptions = {"No users are", "One user is", "{0} users are"};
ChoiceFormat choice = new ChoiceFormat(borderValues, descriptions);
Object[] values = {choice.format(countValue)};
MessageFormat msgFormat = new MessageFormat(msgText);
msgFormat.applyPattern(msgFormat.format(values));
values[0] = countValue;
System.out.println(msgFormat.format(values));
```

This code segment first creates a ChoiceFormat that contains the String that's appropriate for the number of logged-on users. It then uses MessageFormat to add that String to the message stored in the ResourceBundle and finally uses MessageFormat again to insert the number of users (when that number is greater than 1).

Besides being somewhat confusing, this code has another serious drawback: portions of the message text are embedded within it. This is a problem that ResourceBundle and MessageFormat are intended to eliminate. Fortunately, MessageFormat provides a way to use ChoiceFormat objects without creating them directly as was done here. Just as it's possible to specify an element format for date, time, and numeric values (in other words, DateFormat and NumberFormat instances), it's also possible to specify one for ChoiceFormat values. To do so, you simply specify choice for the element format and create an element style that represents the limit values and the String that corresponds to each one as follows:

```
CurrentUsers=
  {0,choice,0#No users are|1#One user is|2#{0} users are} currently logged on.
```

Notice that a substitution parameter with an index of zero appears in two places in this message. It's used first at the beginning of the message, where it identifies the choice value, and again within the third and final message that can be produced by the choice. In each case, that parameter represents the number of users who are logged on, and it's first used by the choice to select which of its three text strings should be used. For example, if there are ten users logged on, MessageFormat uses the choice to create the following intermediate message:

```
{0} users are currently logged on.
```

Once the choice has been processed, MessageFormat will perform its normal processing that causes the number of users to be inserted into the message to produce the following correct output:

```
10 users are currently logged on.
```

To use this new message, you can simplify the previous code segment as shown in Listing 13-13.

Listing 13-13. Using ChoiceFormat Implicitly by Embedding It Within the Message Pattern

```
ResourceBundle bundle = ResourceBundle.getBundle("FormatMessages");
int userCount;
// ...
String myText = (String)(bundle.getObject("CurrentUsers"));
MessageFormat mf = new MessageFormat(myText);
Object[] vals = {new Integer(userCount)};
System.out.println(mf.format(vals));
```

By implicitly using ChoiceFormat this way, you can ensure your messages are grammatically correct while still maintaining the separation of message text from application code.

Using Formatter and String's format() Method

An alternative to using MessageFormat is to use the static format() method defined in the String class, which provides functionality that's similar to what MessageFormat offers. In reality, String.format() is just a convenience method that uses the Formatter class defined in the java.util package. Although the functionality is similar to that of MessageFormat, the Formatter approach is based on conventions long used in the C programming language's printf() function.

The MessageFormat and Formatter classes use very different notation but provide very similar functionality, although Formatter is slightly more flexible and arguably easier to use. For example, if you want to format text with a single String substitution parameter value you can use code like the following:

```
String pattern = "My name is %s";
System.out.println(String.format(pattern, "John"));
```

Executing this produces the following output:

```
My name is John
```

Similar to the how the MessageFormat.format() method is used, the static String.format() method accepts a pattern and zero or more argument values which—again like with MessageFormat—are specified as varargs. The most obvious difference is how the substitution field is specified, specifically in this case with "%s". The percent (%) sign identifies a substitution field, while the "s" indicates how the value should be formatted and is referred to as the "conversion" value. One important difference between this approach and that of MessageFormat is that MessageFormat requires you to specify the position of the argument that should be used to fill in the substitution parameter. With Formatter you can omit the position value, which will cause it to use the argument that corresponds to position of the substitution field. In other words, the first argument will be displayed in the first substitution field, the second argument in the second field, etc. To better illustrate this let's assume that you want to display both a first and last name, in which case you can use code like the following:

```
String pattern = "Hello there %s %s";
System.out.println(String.format(pattern, "John", "Smith"));
```

Executing this code will produce the following output:

```
My name is John Smith
```

Note that the percent sign and the conversion value are the only two parts of a specifier that are required. As we'll see, other values can be included to provide additional customization with respect to how the formatting is done, but the first character in a substitution field must begin with the percent sign and end with a conversion character.

As mentioned earlier, Formatter does allow you to specify the index of the argument that should be used to fill in a substitution field just as is required when using MessageFormat, though so far we've omitted the index values. To specify which argument should be used just embed an integer value immediately after the percent sign and follow it with a dollar sign ($), and the corresponding argument will be used instead of the one that corresponds to the placement of the field. For example, we can use the following code to display the last name and then the first name even though they appear in the opposite order in the argument list:

```
String pattern = "Hello there %2$s, %1$s";
System.out.println(String.format(pattern, "John", "Smith"));
```

Executing this code produces the following output:

```
Hello there Smith, John
```

As this example implies, the "s" conversion generates a String representation of the value by calling the toString() method of the argument specified. In the previous examples both the arguments were already String instances and calling toString() for a String object results in that object simply returning a result to itself. To illustrate this point you can create and run the following code, which creates a Date object and then sends two identical lines to standard output—one the result of calling the Date object's toString() method directly and another by calling String.format() with the Date passed as an argument and the "s" conversion specified:

```
Date date = new Date(0l);
System.out.println(date);
System.out.println(String.format("%s", date));
```

The following is the output generated by running this code on a system configured for use in the United States:

Wed Dec 31 18:00:00 CST 1969

Wed Dec 31 18:00:00 CST 1969

As you'd expect, there's a conversion type specifically for date/time values, specifically, the "t" conversion, and it can be combined with additional characters referred to as "suffix characters" to output only a specific component of a date such as the date's hours, minutes, seconds, day of the week, and so on. For example, to send the current day of the week to standard output you could use code like the following which uses the "a" suffix character to display the abbreviated name ("Sun," "Mon," "Tue," etc.) of the specified Date's day of the week:

```
Date date = new Date(0l);
System.out.println(String.format("%ta", date));
```

Running this code sends "Wed" to standard output. Alternatively, you can display the full name of the day of the week by using the "A" suffix character instead, and the following code displays "Wednesday" instead of "Wed":

```
Date date = new Date(0l);
System.out.println(String.format("%tA", date));
```

This lowercase/uppercase variation is also supported for display abbreviated (two-digit) or full (four-digit) year values using the "y" and "Y" suffix characters, respectively, as well as the abbreviated or full month name through "b" and "B." In other cases, however, there's no relationship between the lower- and uppercase versions of a suffix character. For example, "M" represents the minutes within the hour (00-59) while "m" represents the month formatted as a two-digit value.

On the other hand, the majority of the conversion characters do support the use of an uppercase equivalent and this does have a consistent meaning: use of an uppercase character indicates that the generated text should be converted to uppercase. So, for example, running the following code will generate "WEDNESDAY" instead of "Wednesday" because the uppercase "T" indicates that the generated text is to be in all caps:

```
Date date = new Date(0l);
System.out.println(String.format("%TA", date));
```

An uppercase variant of the conversion character is supported for all conversion types that potentially generate alphabetic characters, so, for example, instead of the "s" conversion character we used earlier you could specify "S" to indicate that the alpha characters generated should all be uppercase.

In general, the conversion types are categorized by the type of argument object supported. For example, the "d," "o," and "x" conversion types support "integral" (Byte, Short, Integer, Long, and BigInteger) arguments and format them as decimal, octal, or hexadecimal values, respectively. Similarly, the "e," "f," "g," and "a" conversion types accept floating point (Float, Double, and BigDecimal) argument types and format them in various different ways.

Two unique conversion types worth mentioning are the "%" and "n" values. The "%" conversion type essentially represents an "escape" usage of the percent sign (%). In other words, if you need to embed that symbol in your output you can easily do so by embedding two sequential occurrences of the character as follows:

```
System.out.println(String.format("I support you %d%%!", 100));
```

Running this code produces the following output:

```
I support you 100%!
```

The "n" conversion type is a convenient way of embedding in the output the line separator character or sequence of characters used by the platform on which the code is running. For example, Windows uses a carriage return + linefeed combination to represent a line separator, while most other systems use the linefeed by itself to indicate a line break.

One place where using "%n" can be helpful is in the case of another convenience method that uses Formatter, specifically the printf() methods added to the PrintStream class. An instance of PrintStream is used to represent standard output and standard error, so the you can abbreviate statements like the ones used earlier by calling printf() instead of println().

```
System.out.printf("I support you %d%%!", 100);
```

Note, however, that printf() is more like the print() method—and unlike println()—in that it doesn't append line separator text to the output. What this means is that if you want your output to appear on a line by itself you'll typically need to explicitly insert a line separator, and this is where the "n" conversion comes in handy. To have System.out.printf() behave more like System.out.println(), just include "%n" at the end of the formatter pattern as follows:

```
System.out.printf("I support you %d%%!%n", 100);
```

Like MessageFormat, Formatter also provides the ability to create custom formats for substitution parameter values. For example, when using a floating point value as an argument you might want to specify the exact number of digits that should be displayed to the right of the decimal point. This value is referred to as the "precision" and can be accomplished by using code like the following:

```
Float value = 123.456F;
System.out.printf("%.2f%n", value);
```

Running this code will produce the following output:

```
123.45
```

You can also specify a value that indicates exactly how wide the formatted value should be, and this value is referred to as the width. As you might expect, the width is specified before the period (.) character in contrast to the precision that we just specified after it. For example, to produce a string that's exactly eight characters long you could use the following:

```
Float value = 123.456F;
System.out.printf("%8.2f%n", value);
```

Running this code produces the following, with two blank spaces preceding the numeric text:

```
123.45
```

For additional custom you can take advantage of Formatter's flags, which largely are used to support further customization of numeric output. For example, if you want the padding on the left to be done using zeroes instead of spaces you could use the "0" flag that indicates this as shown here.

```
System.out.printf("%8.2f%n", value);
```

Running this now generates output similar to that in the previous example, but with a pair of leading zeroes instead of spaces.

```
00123.45
```

Other flags indicate that negative numbers should be enclosed in parentheses, whether a sign (+/-) should be displayed, and so on.

Now that we've discussed different ways of formatting data that's to be displayed for the user, it's helpful to consider how internationalization can be supported by doing essentially the opposite: processing data that has been entered by a user or some external system.

Parsing Text Data

You'll often find it necessary to parse text information that has been entered by a user. For example, you may need to split text across multiple lines if it's displayed in a component that's too narrow to display the string on a single line. In other cases, you may want to identify each word or sentence that was entered or simply process each character. These are all relatively easy operations to perform in English, but some other languages have complex rules that govern what's considered a sentence or a word. Even identifying a single character can be complex, particularly in some Asian languages, because a single logical character in one of those languages can be represented by a sequence of multiple Unicode characters. Fortunately, Java provides the BreakIterator class that can be used to parse text using the rules for a given Locale.

BreakIterator

To use a BreakIterator, you must obtain an instance of the appropriate type from one of the factory methods that are defined; those methods are getCharacterInstance(), getWordInstance(), getLineInstance(), and getSentenceInstance(). Two implementations of each of those methods are provided: one that accepts a Locale parameter and another that uses the default Locale.

Once you've obtained a BreakIterator, you must identify the String that's to be parsed by calling the setText() method. The BreakIterator works by maintaining an index value in the text, and when you call a method to locate the next break position, that index is adjusted appropriately. The next() method moves the index to the next boundary in the text field and returns the position of that boundary or a value of BreakIterator.DONE when no more boundaries can be found. For example, the code segment in Listing 13-14 shows how you can identify sentence boundaries using a BreakIterator.

Listing 13-14. An Example of How to Use BreakIterator

```
BreakIterator bi = BreakIterator.getSentenceInstance();
String sent = "This is a sentence! Is this a sentence too? " +
    "This is the last sentence.";
bi.setText(sent);
int lastIndex = bi.first();
int currentIndex = bi.next();
while (currentIndex != BreakIterator.DONE) {
  System.out.println(sent.substring(lastIndex, currentIndex));
  lastIndex = currentIndex;
  currentIndex = bi.next();
}
```

If you compile and execute this code, it will produce the following output:

```
This is a sentence!
Is this a sentence too?
This is the last sentence.
```

Note that BreakIterator provides methods for moving both forward and backward through a string to identify its boundaries, although you'll typically process them in a forward direction as was done here. You should also be aware that the whitespace characters (spaces in this example) are grouped with the sentence they follow. For example, the first two sentences shown previously will each include a trailing space, since a space is included in the sample text between each of the three sentences.

Character Iteration

As mentioned earlier, identifying each character in a String is trivial in some languages but not in others. For example, characters with accents such as the *ä* and *ë* characters that represent one logical character can be represented by two "physical" characters: the base character (for example, *a* or *e*) followed by a diacritical mark (¨). By using BreakIterator, you can identify each individual logical character within a String, regardless of how it's stored.

Word Iteration

Although relatively simple for English text, identifying word boundaries can be complex in some languages, but BreakIterator allows you to do so easily. When using a word iterator, boundaries are identified on each side of punctuation characters as well as around the words themselves. For example, the following sentence will be broken into eight separate pieces:

```
This is a test.
```

The eight pieces that a word iterator will identify are the four words within the sentence, the three whitespace regions (in other words, the space characters) between those words, and the period at the end of the sentence.

Line Iteration

Line iteration is useful when you need to find an appropriate location within a String where the text can be split across lines. For example, you might do so if implementing word wrap behavior like that found in JTextArea, where a single word isn't allowed to span multiple lines. In the case of English text, line boundaries occur at spaces and at hyphens, since it's considered acceptable to split a hyphenated word across two lines.

Sentence Iteration

As illustrated earlier, this type of BreakIterator allows you to identify the beginning and end of sentences.

BreakIterator Example

Listing 13-15 provides an application that allows you to test the behavior of the various types of BreakIterator. It produces a user interface like the one shown in Figure 13-6, which allows you to select a Locale and a BreakIterator type (character, word, line, or sentence), enter some text, and have the text parsed by a BreakIterator.

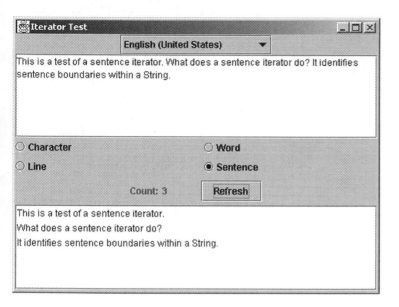

Figure 13-6. *BreakIterator contains sophisticated logic for identifying sentence breaks*

When the text is parsed by pressing the Refresh button, the boundaries identified by the BreakIterator are used to add the separate pieces of text to a JList, allowing you to scroll to view all of the parsed items. Listing 13-15 provides the full text of this code.

Listing 13-15. Testing BreakIterator

```
import java.awt.*;
import java.awt.event.*;
import java.text.*;
import java.util.*;
import javax.swing.*;

public class IteratorTest extends JPanel {

  private JComboBox localeButton;

  private JTextArea textArea;

  private JRadioButton charButton;
  private JRadioButton wordButton;
  private JRadioButton lineButton;
  private JRadioButton sentButton;

  private JLabel countLabel;
  private JButton refreshButton;
```

```java
private JList itemList;
// Create a window for the Iterator test
// and make sure that later components will fit
public static void main(String[] args) {
  JFrame f = new JFrame("Iterator Test");
  f.setDefaultCloseOperation(JFrame.EXIT_ON_CLOSE);
  f.setContentPane(new IteratorTest());
  f.pack();
  f.setVisible(true);
}

public IteratorTest() {
  buildLayout();
  refreshDisplay();
}

private void buildLayout() {
  setLayout(new GridBagLayout());
  GridBagConstraints gbc = new GridBagConstraints();

  // Set up the contents of the Locale combo box
  gbc.gridx = 0;
  gbc.gridy = 0;
  localeButton = new JComboBox(Locale.getAvailableLocales());
  localeButton.setRenderer(new LocaleListCellRenderer());
  localeButton.setSelectedItem(Locale.getDefault());
  add(localeButton, gbc);

  gbc.gridwidth = GridBagConstraints.REMAINDER;
  gbc.fill = GridBagConstraints.BOTH;
  gbc.weightx = 1;

  // Set up the input area panel
  gbc.gridy++;
  gbc.weighty = 1;
  textArea = new JTextArea(5, 20);
  textArea.setLineWrap(true);
  textArea.setWrapStyleWord(true);
  JScrollPane jsp = new JScrollPane(textArea,
      JScrollPane.VERTICAL_SCROLLBAR_AS_NEEDED,
      JScrollPane.HORIZONTAL_SCROLLBAR_NEVER);
  add(jsp, gbc);

  // Add a panel for the choice buttons
  gbc.gridy++;
  gbc.weighty = 0;
  add(getTypePanel(), gbc);
```

```
    // Add a panel for the refresh button and the count label
    gbc.gridy++;
    add(getCountPanel(), gbc);

    // Add a panel for the parsed output
    gbc.gridy++;
    gbc.weighty = 1;
    itemList = new JList();
    add(new JScrollPane(itemList), gbc);
  }

  // Create the panel for the choice buttons
  private JPanel getTypePanel() {
    JPanel panel = new JPanel();
    panel.setLayout(new GridLayout(2, 2, 20, 0));
    charButton = new JRadioButton("Character", true);
    panel.add(charButton);
    wordButton = new JRadioButton("Word");
    panel.add(wordButton);
    lineButton = new JRadioButton("Line");
    panel.add(lineButton);
    sentButton = new JRadioButton("Sentence");
    panel.add(sentButton);

    // Add the buttons to a group
    ButtonGroup group = new ButtonGroup();
    group.add(charButton);
    group.add(wordButton);
    group.add(lineButton);
    group.add(sentButton);
    return panel;
  }

  // Create a panel for the refresh button and the count label
  private JPanel getCountPanel() {
    JPanel panel = new JPanel();
    JLabel label = new JLabel("Count:", JLabel.RIGHT);
    panel.add(label);
    countLabel = new JLabel("", JLabel.LEFT);
    Dimension size = panel.getPreferredSize();
    size.width = Math.min(size.width, 100);
    countLabel.setPreferredSize(size);
    panel.add(countLabel);
```

```java
    // Add the refresh button
    refreshButton = new JButton("Refresh");
    refreshButton.addActionListener(new ActionListener() {
      public void actionPerformed(ActionEvent event) {
        refreshDisplay();
      }
    });
    panel.add(refreshButton);
    return panel;
  }

  private void refreshDisplay() {
    int startIndex, nextIndex;
    Vector items = new Vector();
    // Get the input text
    String msgText = textArea.getText();
    // Set the locale and prepare the iterator
    Locale locale = (Locale)(localeButton.getSelectedItem());
    BreakIterator iterator = null;
    // Work out which button is selected and set the iterator
    if (charButton.isSelected()) {
      iterator = BreakIterator.getCharacterInstance(locale);
    }
    else if (wordButton.isSelected()) {
      iterator = BreakIterator.getWordInstance(locale);
    }
    else if (lineButton.isSelected()) {
      iterator = BreakIterator.getLineInstance(locale);
    }
    else if (sentButton.isSelected()) {
      iterator = BreakIterator.getSentenceInstance(locale);
    }
    iterator.setText(msgText);
    startIndex = iterator.first();
    nextIndex = iterator.next();

    // Find the breaks in the input text
    // and add the substrings for output
    while (nextIndex != BreakIterator.DONE) {
      items.addElement(msgText.substring(startIndex, nextIndex));
      startIndex = nextIndex;
      nextIndex = iterator.next();
    }
    countLabel.setText(Integer.toString(items.size()));
    itemList.setListData(items);              // Output the parsed input
  }

  // Combo box to select the available locales
  class LocaleListCellRenderer extends DefaultListCellRenderer {
    public Component getListCellRendererComponent(
        JList list, Object value, int index,
```

```
        boolean isSelected, boolean hasFocus) {
      Locale locale = (Locale)(value);
      return super.getListCellRendererComponent(
          list, locale.getDisplayName(),
          index, isSelected, hasFocus);
    }
  }
}
```

Text Comparisons and Sorting

It's sometimes necessary for your application to compare instances of String to one another, such as when the text items in a collection are being sorted. For example, you might want to sort a list of names alphabetically, which you'd accomplish by comparing the names to one another.

Although Java's String class provides compareTo() and compareToIgnoreCase() methods, those methods may not return the correct results when comparing non-ASCII characters. As with parsing, the rules that govern String comparisons are simple in some cases but not in others. Fortunately, the java.text package includes the Collator class that can be used to perform Locale-specific comparisons of strings, and you can obtain an instance of Collator by calling the getInstance() method. Like many of the other methods related to internationalization, two implementations of getInstance() are available: one that accepts a Locale argument and another that doesn't. The no-argument version returns a Collator that's appropriate for the default Locale, while the implementation that accepts a Locale parameter returns a Collator that sorts based on the conventions of the specified Locale.

Once you've obtained a reference to a Collator object for the appropriate Locale, you can call the compare() method that accepts two String parameters and returns an int value. The return value indicates the relative value of the first string to the second, as shown in Table 13-3.

Table 13-3. *Values Returned by the* compare() *Method Defined in* Collator

Relative Values of the String Parameters	Value Returned by **compare()**
First string less than the second string	Less than zero
First string equal to the second string	Zero
First string greater than the second string	Greater than zero

The following code segments illustrate how to perform a comparison that will work correctly regardless of the user's Locale:

```
String first, second;
// ...
Collator coll = Collator.getInstance();
int result = coll.compare(first, second);
if (result < 0) {
  System.out.println("First String is less than second");
}
else if (result == 0) {
  System.out.println("First String is equal to the second");
}
else if (result > 0) {
  System.out.println("First String is greater than the second");
}
```

Sorting the objects in a java.util.List implementation is even easier, since the Collections class in java.util provides a static sort() method you can use. For example, if you create a Vector containing String values and you want to sort those values, you can pass that Vector as a parameter to the sort() method in Collections. The only requirements for using sort() are that each object in the List must implement the java.lang.Comparable interface (which is true of most wrapper classes) and that a comparison between any two of the elements is meaningful. In general, for a comparison to be meaningful, the two elements must be instances of the same type of object.

By default, the sort() method in Collections sorts using the rules for the default Locale. However, you can create a Collator instance and pass that to the sort() method along with the List implementation to have the items in the list sorted according to the Locale associated with your Collator object. For example, if your default Locale isn't equal to Locale.JAPAN but the text to be sorted was entered by a Japanese user, you could use code such as the following to ensure that the sorting is performed correctly:

```
// This Vector will contain the items to be sorted
Vector textItems;
// ...
Collator coll = Collator.getInstance(Locale.JAPAN);
Collections.sort(textItems, coll);
```

Collator Strength

Sorting is sometimes not as simple as it may appear, even when sorting English text that contains only simple Latin characters. For example, depending upon the circumstances, it may or may not be the case that "hello" should be considered equal to "Hello"; in addition, for languages where characters can be used with or without an accent (for example, "pêche" vs. "péché"), it may or may not be desirable to consider the presence or absence of accents when comparing String values. Fortunately, the Collator class allows you to select a strength value that determines which type of differences between characters (if any) will be ignored.

The four strength values supported by Collator are represented by constants defined in that class: PRIMARY, SECONDARY, TERTIARY, and IDENTICAL. These constants define how closely two characters must match one another for them to be considered equal. Although the specific rules for making that determination are Locale-specific, some generalizations can be made. For example, it's commonly the case that a primary difference means that two characters represent different letters of the alphabet, and the difference between *A* and *B* is primary, but the difference between *A* and *a* isn't. A secondary difference between two characters indicates that their accents are different or that one has an accent while the other doesn't. For instance, the difference between *é* and *ê* is considered a secondary difference. Finally, a tertiary difference in this case refers to the case of the letter, such as when comparing *e* to *E*. As described in Table 13-4, the four constants defined in `Collator` allow you to specify how closely two characters must match one another for them to be considered equal.

Table 13-4. *Collator Strengths and Types of Differences*

Collator Constant	Type of Differences Considered Significant
PRIMARY	Primary
SECONDARY	Primary and secondary
TERTIARY	Primary, secondary, and tertiary
IDENTICAL	All

`IDENTICAL` differs from `TERTIARY` in that it differentiates between precomposed characters with accents and combined characters with accents. By setting the strength of a `Collator`, you can control how items are sorted; the following is an example of how to set the strength:

```
Collator coll = Collator.getInstance();
coll.setStrength(Collator.PRIMARY);
```

Decomposition Mode

The `Collator` class also supports a decomposition mode that determines how composed characters are handled by the `Collator` instance. Examples of composed characters are those that contain accents, which are usually broken down (or *decomposed*) for comparison operations. For example, the *é* character in "péché" would be decomposed into two characters: the base letter (lowercase *e*) followed by the acute character (´). In other words, when it's decomposed, "péché" is seven characters long instead of five, and the purpose of this decomposition is to ensure that the result of a comparison is correct.

Depending upon the language being used, it may or may not be necessary for `Collator` to perform decomposition. For example, decomposition isn't necessary at all when comparing only English text. Since decomposition causes comparison operations to run more slowly, you may choose to disable decomposition entirely if you're certain your application will only ever compare `String` values that don't require it.

If your application can be used with languages that require some level of decomposition, you must choose between *canonical decomposition* (the default value for instances of `Collator`) and *full decomposition*. Canonical decomposition is appropriate for most languages and will provide correct comparisons for all canonical variants defined in the Unicode 2.0 standard. However, if your application supports Katakana characters, for example, you may find it necessary to use full decomposition despite its relatively slow performance. For information on which character sets require full decomposition, you should visit the Unicode home page at `www.unicode.org/`. (Katakana characters are traditional Japanese handwriting.)

Each of the composition modes is represented by a constant defined in Collator, and you can modify and query a Collator's mode using the setDecomposition() and getDecomposition() methods. The three constants representing composition modes are NO_DECOMPOSITION, CANONICAL_DECOMPOSITION, and FULL_ DECOMPOSITION; the following is an example of how to use them:

```
Collator coll;
String first, second;
// ...
// We may be comparing Katakana characters
coll.setDecomposition(Collator.FULL_DECOMPOSITION);
int result = coll.compare(first, second);
```

Internationalizing an Application

You'll now briefly examine the steps you must take to internationalize an existing application. In this case, the application is a simple program that allows the user to maintain a collection of instances of the Person class shown in Listing 13-16.

Listing 13-16. Person Class

```java
import java.util.Date;

public class Person implements java.io.Serializable {

  private String firstName;
  private String lastName;
  private String address;
  private Date dateOfBirth;

  public Person(String fn, String ln, String addr, Date dob) {
    super();
    setFirstName(fn);
    setLastName(ln);
    setAddress(addr);
    setDateOfBirth(dob);
  }

  public Person() {
    this(null, null, null, null);
  }

  public void setFirstName(String fn) {
    firstName = fn;
  }

  public String getFirstName() {
    return firstName;
  }
```

```java
public void setLastName(String ln) {
    lastName = ln;
}

public String getLastName() {
    return lastName;
}

public void setAddress(String addr) {
    address = addr;
}

public String getAddress() {
    return address;
}

public void setDateOfBirth(Date dob) {
    dateOfBirth = dob;
}

public Date getDateOfBirth() {
    return dateOfBirth;
}
}
```

As shown in Figure 13-7, the EditPersonList application allows entries to be added, updated, and deleted, and it stores those entries in a disk file named people.ser. Listing 13-17 shows the code for the EditPersonList application.

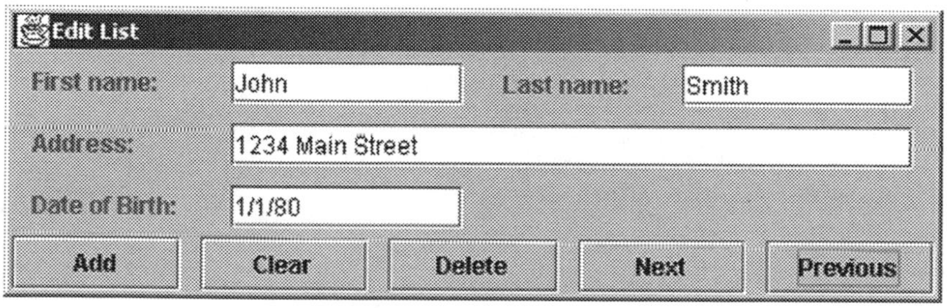

Figure 13-7. *A simple application that allows data to be edited and stored*

Listing 13-17. EditPersonList Application

```java
import java.awt.*;
import java.awt.event.*;
import java.io.*;
import java.text.*;
import java.util.*;
import javax.swing.*;

public class EditPersonList extends JFrame {

    private Vector personList;
    private int currentIndex;

    private JButton addButton;
    private JButton deleteButton;
    private JButton clearButton;

    private JButton nextButton;
    private JButton previousButton;

    private PersonPanel personPanel;

    public static void main(String[] args) throws Exception {
        EditPersonList epl = new EditPersonList("Edit List");
        epl.setDefaultCloseOperation(JFrame.EXIT_ON_CLOSE);
        epl.setVisible(true);
    }

    public EditPersonList(String title) throws Exception {
        super(title);
        buildLayout();
        File f = new File("people.ser");
        if (f.exists()) {
            FileInputStream fis = new FileInputStream(f);
            ObjectInputStream ois = new ObjectInputStream(fis);
            personList = (Vector)(ois.readObject());
        }
        else {
            personList = new Vector();
        }
        currentIndex = 0;
        displayCurrentPerson();
        pack();
    }

    private void buildLayout() {
        Container pane = getContentPane();
        personPanel = new PersonPanel();
        pane.add(personPanel, BorderLayout.CENTER);
        pane.add(getButtonPanel(), BorderLayout.SOUTH);
    }
```

```java
private JPanel getButtonPanel() {
  JPanel panel = new JPanel();
  panel.setLayout(new GridLayout(1, 5, 10, 0));
  addButton = new JButton("Add");
  panel.add(addButton);
  clearButton = new JButton("Clear");
  panel.add(clearButton);
  deleteButton = new JButton("Delete");
  panel.add(deleteButton);

  nextButton = new JButton("Next");
  panel.add(nextButton);
  previousButton = new JButton("Previous");
  panel.add(previousButton);

  addButton.addActionListener(new ActionListener() {
    public void actionPerformed(ActionEvent event) {
      Person p = new Person();
      if (personPanel.updatePerson(p)) {
        personList.addElement(p);
        currentIndex = personList.size() - 1;
        displayCurrentPerson();
      }
      savePersonList();
    }
  });

  clearButton.addActionListener(new ActionListener() {
    public void actionPerformed(ActionEvent event) {
      personPanel.clear();
    }
  });

  deleteButton.addActionListener(new ActionListener() {
    public void actionPerformed(ActionEvent event) {
      personList.removeElementAt(currentIndex);
      if (currentIndex >= personList.size()) {
        currentIndex = personList.size() - 1;
      }
      savePersonList();
      displayCurrentPerson();
    }
  });

  nextButton.addActionListener(new ActionListener() {
    public void actionPerformed(ActionEvent event) {
      currentIndex++;
      displayCurrentPerson();
    }
  });
```

```java
    previousButton.addActionListener(new ActionListener() {
      public void actionPerformed(ActionEvent event) {
        currentIndex--;
        displayCurrentPerson();
      }
    });

    return panel;
  }

  private void displayCurrentPerson() {
    if ((currentIndex >= 0) && (currentIndex < personList.size())) {
      personPanel.displayPerson((Person)
                 (personList.elementAt(currentIndex)));
    }
    else {
      personPanel.clear();
    }
    previousButton.setEnabled(currentIndex > 0);
    nextButton.setEnabled(currentIndex < personList.size() - 1);
  }

  private void savePersonList() {
    File f = new File("people.ser");
    try {
      FileOutputStream fos = new FileOutputStream(f);
      ObjectOutputStream oos = new ObjectOutputStream(fos);
      oos.writeObject(personList);
      oos.close();
    } catch (IOException ioe) {};
  }

  class PersonPanel extends JPanel {
    private JTextField firstNameField;
    private JTextField lastNameField;
    private JTextField addressField;
    private JTextField dobField;

    public PersonPanel() {
      buildLayout();
    }

  private void buildLayout() {
    JLabel label;
    setLayout(new GridBagLayout());
    GridBagConstraints gbc = new GridBagConstraints();
    gbc.weightx = 1;
    gbc.fill = GridBagConstraints.HORIZONTAL;
    gbc.insets = new Insets(5, 10, 5, 10);
```

```
  gbc.gridy = 0;
  label = new JLabel("First name:", JLabel.LEFT);
  add(label, gbc);

  firstNameField = new JTextField(10);
  add(firstNameField, gbc);

  label = new JLabel("Last name:", JLabel.LEFT);
  add(label, gbc);

  lastNameField = new JTextField(10);
  add(lastNameField, gbc);

  gbc.gridy++;
  label = new JLabel("Address:", JLabel.LEFT);
  add(label, gbc);

  gbc.gridwidth = GridBagConstraints.REMAINDER;
  addressField = new JTextField(10);
  add(addressField, gbc);

  gbc.gridwidth = 1;
  gbc.gridy++;
  label = new JLabel("Date of Birth:", JLabel.LEFT);
  add(label, gbc);

  dobField = new JTextField(10);
  add(dobField, gbc);
}

public void clear() {
  firstNameField.setText("");
  lastNameField.setText("");
  addressField.setText("");
  dobField.setText("");
}

public void displayPerson(Person p) {
  firstNameField.setText(p.getFirstName());
  lastNameField.setText(p.getLastName());
  addressField.setText(p.getAddress());
  DateFormat formatter = DateFormat.getDateInstance(DateFormat.SHORT);
  dobField.setText(formatter.format(p.getDateOfBirth()));
}
```

```
    public boolean updatePerson(Person p) {
      String firstName = firstNameField.getText();
      String lastName = lastNameField.getText();
      String address = addressField.getText();
      Date dateOfBirth = null;
      DateFormat parser = DateFormat.getDateInstance(DateFormat.SHORT);
      try {
        dateOfBirth = parser.parse(dobField.getText());
      }
      catch (ParseException pe) {
        JOptionPane.showMessageDialog(this, pe.getMessage(),
            "Invalid Date",
            JOptionPane.ERROR_MESSAGE);
        return false;
      }
      p.setFirstName(firstName);
      p.setLastName(lastName);
      p.setAddress(address);
      p.setDateOfBirth(dateOfBirth);
      return true;
    }
  }
}
```

No String comparisons are performed in this class, and the only parsing operation occurs when a String entered by the user is converted into a Date instance. Therefore, you can internationalize this class simply by removing the Locale-specific text that's embedded within it. Specifically, those strings are the JFrame's title, the JOptionPane's title, the JButton labels, and the text displayed within the user interface panel (PersonPanel).

Although a String is specified for the name of the file that's used to store the People instances, that name isn't visible to users of the application and doesn't need to be stored in the ResourceBundle.

Since all the resources that must be isolated from the source code are text strings, you can create a PropertyResourceBundle like the following one named PeopleResources.properties:

```
FrameTitle=Edit List
Button_Label_Add=Add
Button_Label_Clear=Clear
Button_Label_Delete=Delete
Button_Label_Next=Next
Button_Label_Previous=Previous
Label_Text_FirstName=First name:
Label_Text_LastName=Last name:
Label_Text_Address=Address:
Label_Text_DOB=Date of Birth:
Dialog_Title_Invalid_Date=Invalid Date
Menu_Locale=Locale
```

Although you can use any identifiers/keys you find appropriate, it's usually helpful to use names that describe how the resource is used (for example, Button_XXX for button labels, Label_XXX for JLabel text, and so on). This can provide an intuitive clue that helps you to determine how and/or where a particular resource is used within your application.

With a file defined that contains the resources, it's easy to modify the EditPersonList class so that it uses the external resources instead of embedding the messages (see Listing 13-18).

Listing 13-18. EditPersonList Class

```java
import java.awt.*;
import java.awt.event.*;
import java.io.*;
import java.text.*;
import java.util.*;
import javax.swing.*;

public class EditPersonList extends JFrame {

  private Vector personList;
  private int currentIndex;

  private JButton addButton;
  private JButton deleteButton;
  private JButton clearButton;

  private JButton nextButton;
  private JButton previousButton;

  private PersonPanel personPanel;

  private static ResourceBundle resources =
      ResourceBundle.getBundle("PeopleResources");

  public static void main(String[] args) throws Exception {
    EditPersonList epl = new EditPersonList(resources.getString("FrameTitle"));
    epl.setDefaultCloseOperation(JFrame.EXIT_ON_CLOSE);
    epl.setVisible(true);
  }

  public EditPersonList(String title) throws Exception {
    super(title);
    buildLayout();
    File f = new File("people.ser");
    if (f.exists()) {
      FileInputStream fis = new FileInputStream(f);
      ObjectInputStream ois = new ObjectInputStream(fis);
      personList = (Vector)(ois.readObject());
    }
```

```
  else {
    personList = new Vector();
  }
  currentIndex = 0;
  displayCurrentPerson();
  pack();
}

private void buildLayout() {
  Container pane = getContentPane();
  personPanel = new PersonPanel();
  pane.add(personPanel, BorderLayout.CENTER);
  pane.add(getButtonPanel(), BorderLayout.SOUTH);
}

private JPanel getButtonPanel() {
  JPanel panel = new JPanel();
  panel.setLayout(new GridLayout(1, 5, 10, 0));

  addButton = new JButton(resources.getString("Button_Label_Add"));
  panel.add(addButton);
  clearButton = new JButton(resources.getString("Button_Label_Clear"));
  panel.add(clearButton);
  deleteButton = new JButton(resources.getString("Button_Label_Delete"));
  panel.add(deleteButton);

  nextButton = new JButton(resources.getString("Button_Label_Next"));
  panel.add(nextButton);
  previousButton = new JButton(resources.getString("Button_Label_Previous"));
  panel.add(previousButton);

  addButton.addActionListener(new ActionListener() {
    public void actionPerformed(ActionEvent event) {
      Person p = new Person();
      if (personPanel.updatePerson(p)) {
        personList.addElement(p);
        currentIndex = personList.size() - 1;
        displayCurrentPerson();
      }
      savePersonList();
    }
  });

  clearButton.addActionListener(new ActionListener() {
    public void actionPerformed(ActionEvent event) {
      personPanel.clear();
    }
  });
```

```java
    deleteButton.addActionListener(new ActionListener() {
      public void actionPerformed(ActionEvent event) {
        personList.removeElementAt(currentIndex);
        if (currentIndex >= personList.size()) {
          currentIndex = personList.size() - 1;
        }
        savePersonList();
      displayCurrentPerson();
      }
    });

    nextButton.addActionListener(new ActionListener() {
      public void actionPerformed(ActionEvent event) {
        currentIndex++;
        displayCurrentPerson();
      }
    });

    previousButton.addActionListener(new ActionListener() {
      public void actionPerformed(ActionEvent event) {
        currentIndex--;
        displayCurrentPerson();
      }
    });

    return panel;
}

private void displayCurrentPerson() {
  if ((currentIndex >= 0) && (currentIndex < personList.size())) {
    personPanel.displayPerson((Person)
              (personList.elementAt(currentIndex)));
  }
  else {
    personPanel.clear();
  }
  previousButton.setEnabled(currentIndex > 0);
  nextButton.setEnabled(currentIndex < personList.size() - 1);
}

private void savePersonList() {
  File f = new File("people.ser");
  try {
    FileOutputStream fos = new FileOutputStream(f);
    ObjectOutputStream oos = new ObjectOutputStream(fos);
    oos.writeObject(personList);
    oos.close();
  } catch (IOException ioe) {};
}
```

```java
class PersonPanel extends JPanel {
  private JTextField firstNameField;
  private JTextField lastNameField;
  private JTextField addressField;
  private JTextField dobField;

  public PersonPanel() {
    buildLayout();
  }

  private void buildLayout() {
    JLabel label;
    setLayout(new GridBagLayout());
    GridBagConstraints gbc = new GridBagConstraints();
    gbc.weightx = 1;
    gbc.fill = GridBagConstraints.HORIZONTAL;
    gbc.insets = new Insets(5, 10, 5, 10);

    gbc.gridy = 0;
    label = new JLabel(resources.getString(
        "Label_Text_FirstName"), JLabel.LEFT);
    add(label, gbc);

    firstNameField = new JTextField(10);
    add(firstNameField, gbc);

    label = new JLabel(resources.getString(
        "Label_Text_LastName"), JLabel.LEFT);
    add(label, gbc);

    lastNameField = new JTextField(10);
    add(lastNameField, gbc);

    gbc.gridy++;
    label = new JLabel(resources.getString(
        "Label_Text_Address"), JLabel.LEFT);
    add(label, gbc);

    gbc.gridwidth = GridBagConstraints.REMAINDER;
    addressField = new JTextField(10);
    add(addressField, gbc);
    gbc.gridwidth = 1;
    gbc.gridy++;
    label = new JLabel(resources.getString(
        "Label_Text_DOB"), JLabel.LEFT);
    add(label, gbc);

    dobField = new JTextField(10);
    add(dobField, gbc);
  }
```

```
  public void clear() {
    firstNameField.setText("");
    lastNameField.setText("");
    addressField.setText("");
    dobField.setText("");
  }

  public void displayPerson(Person p) {
    firstNameField.setText(p.getFirstName());
    lastNameField.setText(p.getLastName());
    addressField.setText(p.getAddress());
    DateFormat formatter = DateFormat.getDateInstance(DateFormat.SHORT);
    dobField.setText(formatter.format(p.getDateOfBirth()));
  }

  public boolean updatePerson(Person p) {
    String firstName = firstNameField.getText();
    String lastName = lastNameField.getText();
    String address = addressField.getText();
    Date dateOfBirth = null;
    DateFormat parser = DateFormat.getDateInstance(DateFormat.SHORT);
    try {
      dateOfBirth = parser.parse(dobField.getText());
    }
    catch (ParseException pe) {
      JOptionPane.showMessageDialog(this, pe.getMessage(),
          resources.getString("Dialog_Title_Invalid_Date"),
          JOptionPane.ERROR_MESSAGE);
      return false;
    }
    p.setFirstName(firstName);
    p.sctLastName(lastName);
    p.setAddress(address);
    p.setDateOfBirth(dateOfBirth);
    return true;
  }
 }
}
```

Changing the Locale at Runtime

In many cases, it's acceptable to always use the default Locale or to require the user to select a Locale when logging on and use that Locale for the duration of the user's session. However, you'll sometimes want to allow users to change their Locale preference while the application is running. Although providing this capability requires more work, it's usually not technically difficult to do so. Normally all that's necessary is to provide methods that will update the user interface components when the Locale selection changes. For example, you can change the EditPersonList application as shown in Listing 13-19 to provide a menu with one JRadioButtonMenuItem for English and another for German. When you click one of those buttons, the ResourceBundle is reloaded based on the selection and the messages are updated as shown in Figure 13-8.

Listing 13-19. Modified `EditPersonList` Application

```java
import java.awt.*;
import java.awt.event.*;
import java.io.*;
import java.text.*;
import java.util.*;
import javax.swing.*;

public class EditPersonList extends JFrame {

  private Vector personList;
  private int currentIndex;

  private JButton addButton;
  private JButton deleteButton;
  private JButton clearButton;

  private JButton nextButton;
  private JButton previousButton;

  private PersonPanel personPanel;

  private JMenu localeMenu;

  private static ResourceBundle resources =
      ResourceBundle.getBundle("PeopleResources");

  public static void main(String[] args) throws Exception {
    EditPersonList epl = new EditPersonList(resources.getString("FrameTitle"));
    epl.setDefaultCloseOperation(JFrame.EXIT_ON_CLOSE);
    epl.setVisible(true);
  }

  public EditPersonList(String title) throws Exception {
    super(title);
    buildLayout();
    File f = new File("people.ser");
    if (f.exists()) {
      FileInputStream fis = new FileInputStream(f);
      ObjectInputStream ois = new ObjectInputStream(fis);
      personList = (Vector)(ois.readObject());
    }
    else {
      personList = new Vector();
    }
    currentIndex = 0;
    displayCurrentPerson();
    pack();
  }
```

```
private void buildLayout() {
  JMenuItem menuItem;

  Container pane = getContentPane();
  personPanel = new PersonPanel();
  pane.add(personPanel, BorderLayout.CENTER);
  pane.add(getButtonPanel(), BorderLayout.SOUTH);

  JMenuBar jmb = new JMenuBar();
  localeMenu = new JMenu(resources.getString("Menu_Locale"));
  jmb.add(localeMenu);

  ButtonGroup group = new ButtonGroup();

  menuItem = new JRadioButtonMenuItem(
      Locale.ENGLISH.getDisplayName(Locale.ENGLISH), true);
  localeMenu.add(menuItem);
  menuItem.addActionListener(new ActionListener() {
    public void actionPerformed(ActionEvent event) {
      resources = ResourceBundle.getBundle(
          "PeopleResources", Locale.ENGLISH);
      updateLabels();
      pack();
    }
  });
  group.add(menuItem);

  menuItem = new JRadioButtonMenuItem(
      Locale.GERMAN.getDisplayName(Locale.GERMAN));
  localeMenu.add(menuItem);

  menuItem.addActionListener(new ActionListener() {
    public void actionPerformed(ActionEvent event) {
      resources = ResourceBundle.getBundle(
          "PeopleResources", Locale.GERMAN);
      updateLabels();
      pack();
    }
  });
  group.add(menuItem);

  setJMenuBar(jmb);
}

private JPanel getButtonPanel() {
  JPanel panel = new JPanel();
  panel.setLayout(new GridLayout(1, 5, 10, 0));
```

```java
addButton = new JButton(resources.getString("Button_Label_Add"));
panel.add(addButton);
clearButton = new JButton(resources.getString("Button_Label_Clear"));
panel.add(clearButton);
deleteButton = new JButton(resources.getString("Button_Label_Delete"));
panel.add(deleteButton);

nextButton = new JButton(resources.getString("Button_Label_Next"));
panel.add(nextButton);
previousButton = new JButton(resources.getString("Button_Label_Previous"));
panel.add(previousButton);

addButton.addActionListener(new ActionListener() {
  public void actionPerformed(ActionEvent event) {
    Person p = new Person();
    if (personPanel.updatePerson(p)) {
      personList.addElement(p);
      currentIndex = personList.size() - 1;
      displayCurrentPerson();
    }
    savePersonList();
  }
});

clearButton.addActionListener(new ActionListener() {
  public void actionPerformed(ActionEvent event) {
    personPanel.clear();
  }
});

deleteButton.addActionListener(new ActionListener() {
  public void actionPerformed(ActionEvent event) {
    personList.removeElementAt(currentIndex);
    if (currentIndex >= personList.size()) {
      currentIndex = personList.size() - 1;
    }
    savePersonList();
  displayCurrentPerson();
  }
});

nextButton.addActionListener(new ActionListener() {
  public void actionPerformed(ActionEvent event) {
    currentIndex++;
    displayCurrentPerson();
  }
});
```

```java
    previousButton.addActionListener(new ActionListener() {
      public void actionPerformed(ActionEvent event) {
        currentIndex--;
        displayCurrentPerson();
      }
    });

    return panel;
  }

  private void displayCurrentPerson() {
    if ((currentIndex >= 0) && (currentIndex < personList.size())) {
      personPanel.displayPerson((Person)
                (personList.elementAt(currentIndex)));
    }
    else {
      personPanel.clear();
    }
    previousButton.setEnabled(currentIndex > 0);
    nextButton.setEnabled(currentIndex < personList.size() - 1);
  }

  private void savePersonList() {
    File f = new File("people.ser");
    try {
      FileOutputStream fos = new FileOutputStream(f);
      ObjectOutputStream oos = new ObjectOutputStream(fos);
      oos.writeObject(personList);
      oos.close();
    } catch (IOException ioe) {};
  }

  private void updateLabels() {
    setTitle(resources.getString("FrameTitle"));
    personPanel.updateLabelText();
    localeMenu.setText(resources.getString("Menu_Locale"));
    addButton.setText(resources.getString("Button_Label_Add"));
    clearButton.setText(resources.getString("Button_Label_Clear"));
    deleteButton.setText(resources.getString("Button_Label_Delete"));
    nextButton.setText(resources.getString("Button_Label_Next"));
    previousButton.setText(resources.getString(
        "Button_Label_Previous"));
  }

  class PersonPanel extends JPanel {
    private JTextField firstNameField;
    private JTextField lastNameField;
    private JTextField addressField;
    private JTextField dobField;
```

```java
    private JLabel firstNameLabel;
    private JLabel lastNameLabel;
    private JLabel addressLabel;
    private JLabel dateOfBirthLabel;

    public PersonPanel() {
      buildLayout();
    }

      private void buildLayout() {
//       JLabel label;
        setLayout(new GridBagLayout());
        GridBagConstraints gbc = new GridBagConstraints();
        gbc.weightx = 1;
        gbc.fill = GridBagConstraints.HORIZONTAL;
        gbc.insets = new Insets(5, 10, 5, 10);

        gbc.gridy = 0;
        firstNameLabel = new JLabel(resources.getString(
            "Label_Text_FirstName"), JLabel.LEFT);
        add(firstNameLabel, gbc);

        firstNameField = new JTextField(10);
        add(firstNameField, gbc);
        lastNameLabel = new JLabel(resources.getString(
            "Label_Text_LastName"), JLabel.LEFT);
        add(lastNameLabel, gbc);

        lastNameField = new JTextField(10);
        add(lastNameField, gbc);

        gbc.gridy++;
        addressLabel = new JLabel(resources.getString(
            "Label_Text_Address"), JLabel.LEFT);
        add(addressLabel, gbc);

        gbc.gridwidth = GridBagConstraints.REMAINDER;
        addressField = new JTextField(10);
        add(addressField, gbc);

        gbc.gridwidth = 1;
        gbc.gridy++;
        dateOfBirthLabel = new JLabel(resources.getString(
            "Label_Text_DOB"), JLabel.LEFT);
        add(dateOfBirthLabel, gbc);

        dobField = new JTextField(10);
        add(dobField, gbc);
      }
```

```java
    public void clear() {
      firstNameField.setText("");
      lastNameField.setText("");
      addressField.setText("");
      dobField.setText("");
    }

    public void displayPerson(Person p) {
      firstNameField.setText(p.getFirstName());
      lastNameField.setText(p.getLastName());
      addressField.setText(p.getAddress());
      DateFormat formatter = DateFormat.getDateInstance(DateFormat.SHORT);
      dobField.setText(formatter.format(p.getDateOfBirth()));
    }

    public boolean updatePerson(Person p) {
      String firstName = firstNameField.getText();
      String lastName = lastNameField.getText();
      String address = addressField.getText();
      Date dateOfBirth = null;
      DateFormat parser = DateFormat.getDateInstance(DateFormat.SHORT);
      try {
        dateOfBirth = parser.parse(dobField.getText());
      }
      catch (ParseException pe) {
        JOptionPane.showMessageDialog(this, pe.getMessage(),
            resources.getString("Dialog_Title_Invalid_Date"),
            JOptionPane.ERROR_MESSAGE);
        return false;
      }
      p.setFirstName(firstName);
      p.setLastName(lastName);
      p.setAddress(address);
      p.setDateOfBirth(dateOfBirth);
      return true;
    }

    public void updateLabelText() {
      firstNameLabel.setText(resources.getString("Label_Text_FirstName"));
      lastNameLabel.setText(resources.getString("Label_Text_LastName"));
      addressLabel.setText(resources.getString("Label_Text_Address"));
      dateOfBirthLabel.setText(resources.getString("Label_Text_DOB"));
    }

  }
}
```

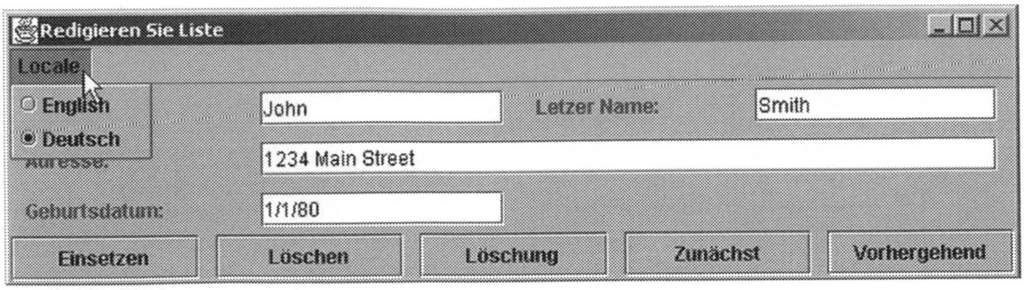

Figure 13-8. *Dynamically changing the* Locale *that's used*

Notice that the main difference between this modified version of EditPersonList and the previous implementation is the presence of methods that update the displayed text. In addition, JLabel instances that were defined locally within a method are assigned to class-level instance variables so that the labels can be modified when the Locale changes.

For this modified EditPersonList class to work, you should also define a file that contains the German language equivalent of the English text defined earlier. The following is an example of this, which could be stored in a file called PeopleResources_de.properties:

```
FrameTitle=Redigieren Sie Liste
Button_Label_Add=Einsetzen
Button_Label_Clear=L\u00F6schen
Button_Label_Delete=L\u00F6schung
Button_Label_Next=Zun\u00E4chst
Button_Label_Previous=Vorhergehend
Label_Text_FirstName=Vorname:
Label_Text_LastName=Letzer Name:
Label_Text_Address=Adresse:
Label_Text_DOB=Geburtsdatum:
Dialog_Title_Invalid_Date=Unzul\u00E4ssiges Datum
Menu_Locale=Locale
```

native2ascii

As the previous example illustrates, you can embed characters with a PropertyResourceBundle file just as with a Java source code file: using \unnnn, where *nnnn* is the hexadecimal value of the Unicode character you want to define. In fact, this may be the only way you can enter characters that aren't included in the character set supported by your keyboard. The problem with this approach is that it's not convenient if a user whose keyboard supports the characters is editing the file. For example, a German user editing the PeopleResources_de.properties file defined previously would probably prefer to enter the accented character directly instead of entering each character's Unicode value.

As you can see, it's sometimes desirable to represent characters with their Unicode value but not always. Fortunately, Java provides the native2ascii utility that allows you to convert files between these two formats. In addition, you should use only ASCII characters when creating class names.

By default, native2ascii converts a file that contains "native" (in other words, non-Latin 1) characters into a format that contains the Unicode representation of those characters, but it also allows you to perform the reverse operation. For example, to convert the \unnnn characters in the PeopleResources_de.properties file shown previously into their native equivalents, you could enter the following:

```
native2ascii -reverse PeopleResources_de.properties PeopleResources_de.native
```

The -reverse option indicates that native2ascii should convert Unicode (for example, \unnnn) characters into their native equivalents, and the converted output will be stored in a file named PeopleResources_de.native. That file will contain the converted contents of the original PeopleResources_de.properties file.

```
FrameTitle=Redigieren Sie Liste
Button_Label_Add=Einsetzen
Button_Label_Clear=Löschen
Button_Label_Delete=Löschung
Button_Label_Next=Zunächst
Button_Label_Previous=Vorhergehend
Label_Text_FirstName=Vorname:
Label_Text_LastName=Letzer Name:
Label_Text_Address=Adresse:
Label_Text_DOB=Geburtsdatum:
Dialog_Title_Invalid_Date=Unzulässiges Datum
Menu_Locale=Locale
```

Similarly, you can reconvert this file with native characters using the following command that produces output identical to that found in the original PeopleResources_de.properties file:

```
native2ascii PeopleResources_de.native PeopleResources_de.unicode
```

You can also use the -encoding option with native2ascii, which will cause it to use the character encoding that you specify when performing conversions between native and Unicode values. If you do so, you must specify the canonical name of an encoding that's supported by Java's InputStreamReader and OutputStreamWriter classes.

Summary

In this chapter you looked briefly at locales and resource bundles. You learned how the formatting for dates and currency varies with locale and how you need to keep this in mind when producing applications for an international market.

To make your applications internationalized and localized, you used MessageFormat and ChoiceFormat in conjunction with resource bundles. This has enabled the appropriate information to be displayed for the locale in which the application is run.

Because characters can vary from language to language, you've had to learn a little about parsing characters. BreakIterator is there to help you with this.

CHAPTER 14

■ ■ ■

Using XML

Although the two aren't inherently tied together, the eXtensible Markup Language (XML) and Java are often discussed in the same context. This chapter explains why that's the case and provides an overview of XML, along with a description of some of the tools available and when and how to use them. You'll look at the following:

- What XML is and how to create an XML document

- Parsing and validating XML documents using the Document Object Model (DOM)

- Using XML namespaces to eliminate ambiguities where a document uses multiple Document Type Definitions (DTDs)

- Transforming XML documents with eXtensible Stylesheet Language Transformations (XSLT)

Like the HyperText Markup Language (HTML), XML is an implementation of the Standard Generalized Markup Language (SGML). Although SGML is extremely flexible and powerful, it's also complex and difficult to use, and XML is an attempt to provide most of SGML's functionality without its complexity. The *extensible* part of XML means that, unlike HTML, you're free to define your own tags, which as you'll see is a very useful feature.

The following listing provides a simple example of an XML document; one of the first things you may notice is how much it resembles HTML:

```
<?xml version="1.0" ?>

<book>
  <title>Pro Java Programming</title>
  272103_1_EnBrett Spell</author>
  <publisher>Apress</publisher>

  <tableOfContents showPageNumbers="Yes">
    <tocEntry>Printing</tocEntry>
    <tocEntry>Cut And Paste</tocEntry>
    <tocEntry>Drag And Drop</tocEntry>
  </tableOfContents>
</book>
```

Some differences between XML and HTML aren't obvious from this example. For one, blank lines and indentation (the whitespace) in an HTML document are largely ignored, but as you'll see in detail later, that's not the case with XML. Another difference is that XML is case-sensitive, while HTML normally isn't.

XML vs. HTML

XML is much more than just an improved version of HTML, and it's helpful, when trying to understand how and why XML is useful, to compare it to HTML and to review some of HTML's weaknesses. For example, suppose you construct the following HTML document that's similar to the previous XML document:

```
<html>
<center><h1>Pro Java Programming</h1></center>
<h4>Brett Spell</h4>
<b>
<h3>Table Of Contents</H3>
<ul>
  <li>Printing</li>
  <li>Cut and Paste</li>
  <li>Drag and Drop</li>
</ul>
</b>
<h4>Apress</h4>
<img src="http://www.apress.com/ApressCorporate/supplement/1/421/bcm.gif"
     alt="Cover Image" />
</html>
```

When viewed in a web browser, this document produces a display like the one shown in Figure 14-1.

Figure 14-1. *The HTML document describes the information to be displayed and also how that information should be formatted*

588

Although similar from a purely conceptual standpoint, an important difference emerges when you compare the HTML document with its XML equivalent. The HTML version is a combination of data (a book's name, author, and publisher) and instructions called *tags* (<center>, <h1>, and <h4>) that describe the relationships between the data items and how they should be displayed. In some cases, such as <li>, the tag both describes the structure of the data and implicitly describes how it should be displayed. In other words, the data in an HTML document is tightly coupled to the tags used to control how the data is displayed; as in the case of object-oriented design, tight coupling is undesirable because it limits reusability.

For example, suppose you want to print the information contained in the previous HTML document instead of displaying it in a web browser. One option is to produce printed output that's similar (or identical) to the output produced by displaying the document in a browser. However, you might instead want to create printed documentation that has a different format from the browser display. Printed output obviously has different characteristics from a browser display, and it may be inappropriate or impossible to use the same characteristics in both cases. For one thing, it's common to use a black-and-white laser printer, while browsers normally assume they're used with a color monitor. Therefore, using different colors to highlight some portion of a document may be appropriate for a browser but inappropriate for printed output. Similarly, while hyperlinks are commonly embedded in HTML documents, they're not helpful when viewing printed output. In the following example, the HTML document contains a reference to another chapter that can be accessed by clicking the hyperlink text:

```
The DataFlavor class is covered more thoroughly in the chapter on
<a href="http://www.apress.com/projava/cutpaste.html">cut and paste</a>.
```

When printing this information, it might be more appropriate to refer to a page number or perhaps to include endnotes that describe the URLs referenced within the document (see Figure 14-2).

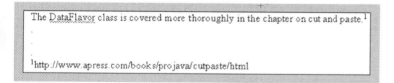

Figure 14-2. *When printing, it's often helpful to format data differently from the way it was displayed*

In addition to printing, many different media can be used for representing data besides a web browser. You might prefer to display the data on a device with a less powerful user interface such as that provided by a cell phone. Alternatively, you may want to display the data using an interface that's more flexible than the one offered by a browser, such as a Swing-based "thick-client" application interface.

The important thing to realize is that you'll sometimes need to be able to present more than one view of your data, but HTML makes this difficult at best. On the surface, it may seem that the data within an HTML document could be displayed in other forms by parsing the document and converting its contents. Unfortunately, it often isn't practical for at least two reasons.

- Because an HTML document doesn't contain information that describes its data

- Because HTML documents aren't required to be well-formed documents

In the next sections, you'll first examine the significance of having information that describes the data (sometimes referred to as *metadata*) and then you'll see what *well-formed* means and why it's important.

Describing the Data

Let's assume you attempt to create code that parses the HTML document defined earlier. To display the data in some arbitrary format, the parsing code must be able to identify specific portions of the data within the document such as the author, publisher, and so on. Unfortunately, this is difficult to do reliably because no information in the document indicates that a particular piece of data represents some specific type of information. Although a human reader might easily guess that *Apress* refers to the publisher, it's not feasible to expect a software application to make the same deduction. You could "hard-code" an application so that it assumes that the second <h4> tag in a document identifies the book publisher, but that approach is inflexible and unreliable. If the order of the tags changes, or if an additional <h4> tag is inserted prior to the existing ones, the technique would no longer work correctly. In other words, scanning for <h4> tags is inappropriate because that tag doesn't describe the type of data that follows it; it simply describes how the data is to be displayed.

In contrast, XML describes only the data and doesn't include tags that explicitly describe how the data is displayed. For example, the <publisher> tag defined in the earlier sample XML document indicates what type of data follows it without specifying how that information should appear. By building an application that "understands" the significance of a <publisher> tag, you can create code that reliably interprets the contents of XML documents, even if their contents change.

Well-Formed Documents

Although the HTML document defined earlier qualifies as a well-formed document, it's not necessary that this be true for HTML to be considered valid, at least not by most browsers. However, well-formed documents are much easier to parse correctly and are easier for applications to represent internally. The following list summarizes the characteristics of a *well-formed* document:

- The document must contain an end tag for each start tag, except for empty elements (described in a moment).

- Attribute values must be enclosed in quotes, either double or single quotes.

- Special characters used to define tags, called *markup-start characters*, must be represented by their equivalent escape sequences (described later).

- The document can't contain any overlapping tags (the most recently opened tag must be the first to be closed).

Unlike HTML, XML documents must always be well-formed. This means they're easy to parse and easy to represent in memory using collections of objects. Before learning how you can do this, however, it's important to understand each of the four characteristics of a well-formed document so you'll know how to create a valid XML document.

Matching Start and End Tags

In most cases, each start tag (for example, <html>, <center>, <h1>, and so on) in the HTML document has a corresponding end tag (</html>, </center>, and </h1>) that identifies the tag's effective range. Each pair of start and end tags is collectively referred to as an *element*, an important term I'll use frequently through this chapter. However, browsers generally don't require you to specify end tags in HTML documents; you could omit most of the tags in the sample document without affecting how the document is displayed. This lenient approach doesn't have any significant advantage, however; in fact, it has the disadvantage of making HTML documents more difficult to parse reliably. Since ease of parsing is important for its intended purpose, XML requires that each start tag have an end tag, with the exception of empty elements.

While it may appear that the `<img>` tag in the HTML document violates this rule and therefore prevents the document from being well-formed, that isn't the case. This is an example of an *empty element*, or an element for which it isn't necessary or meaningful to put information between the start and end tags. Since the attributes (`src` and alt) within the `<img>` tag contain all the information needed by the element, you don't need to provide a corresponding `</img>` tag. Instead, in XML the start tag is identified as defining an empty element by ending it with a combination of the forward slash and a greater-than character, as shown in the following tag. In contrast, other tags are terminated with the greater-than character only.

```
<img src="http://www.apress.com/ApressCorporate/supplement/1/421/bcm.gif"
     alt="Cover Image" />
```

Attribute Values and Quotation Marks

Some HTML tags allow you to specify attributes, where an attribute/value pair consists of an attribute name and a value that's assigned to the attribute, with the two separated by an equal (=) sign. For example, the following `<img>` element contains two attributes named src and alt:

```
<img src="http://www.apress.com/ApressCorporate/supplement/1/421/bcm.gif"
     alt="Cover Image" />
```

As this example illustrates, you can enclose attribute values within quotation marks, and you must do so for each attribute value that contains embedded spaces (as in the case of the previous alt attribute). In contrast, when the value doesn't contain spaces, it's not only possible to omit the quotation marks, but excluding them is common practice. For example, the following variation of the `<img>` tag (in which the quotation marks around the src attribute's value have been removed) is considered valid HTML:

```
<img src=http://www.apress.com/ApressCorporate/supplement/1/421/bcm.gif
     alt="Cover Image" />
```

Unfortunately, this causes those documents to be more difficult to parse, since it complicates the task of identifying the end of an attribute value. XML documents also allow you to specify attributes, but to ensure that the elements and their attributes can be parsed easily you must place quotation marks around each attribute value. Therefore, while the previous `<img>` tag may be valid as part of an HTML document, it isn't acceptable in XML.

Representing Markup-Start Characters

Some characters such as the less-than (<) sign, greater-than (>) sign, and ampersand (&) have special meanings in the context of an XML document and can't be used directly in the document. For example, if you modified the *Cut and Paste* and *Drag and Drop* text from the earlier sample HTML document to read *Cut & Paste* and *Drag & Drop* as shown in the following code, a parser will fail to process the document correctly:

```
<ul>
  <li>Printing</li>
  <li>Cut & Paste</li>
  <li>Drag & Drop</li>
</ul>
```

In fact, one of the things the ampersand is used for is to allow you to embed these special characters into documents indirectly by providing an abbreviated name for each one that can be used in place of the character. To use the abbreviated name, place an ampersand before the name and a semicolon after it, and each sequence will be replaced with the character that it represents when the document is loaded. Table 14-1 lists some of the characters for which abbreviated names have been defined and the sequences you should use to represent those characters in XML documents.

Table 14-1. *Special Characters in XML*

Name	Character	Equivalent Sequence
Less-than sign	<	<
Greater-than sign	>	>
Apostrophe	'	'
Quotation mark	"	"
Ampersand	&	&

For example, if you want to embed a less-than sign in a document, you can use the < string instead of the less-than (<) sign itself. Similarly, to embed ampersands into a document, you code & instead, as shown in the following code:

```
<ul>
  <li>Printing</li>
  <li>Cut &amp; Paste</li>
  <li>Drag &amp; Drop</li>
</ul>
```

When a document containing the previous sequences loads, each occurrence of & will be replaced with & during the processing of the document. As you'll see, these sequences are examples of entity references, and I'll describe them in more detail later in this chapter.

Overlapping Elements

Two elements overlap when one element "contains" a start tag but doesn't contain the associated end tag. For example:

```
<ul>
  <li>Printing</li>
  <li>Cut and Paste</li>
  <b>
  <li>Drag and Drop</li>
</ul>
</b>
```

Instead of the unordered list (<ul>) element being contained entirely within the bold (<b>) element, the two now overlap, and the bold property applies only to some of the items in the unordered list instead of to all of them. Although overlapping tags are often created accidentally and are confusing at best, they're tolerated by most browsers. Unfortunately, they not only make parsing an HTML document more difficult but also greatly increase the complexity involved in creating a representation of such a document.

To better understand this point, suppose you've created a set of classes used to represent the structure of an HTML document you're parsing. For example, you might create a class called UnorderedList that contains a collection of ListItem objects, and those objects might be maintained in a Vector or Hashtable. As long as there are no overlapping tags, creating such a representation of the document's contents and characteristics is reasonably simple; you can do so by creating an object hierarchy, as shown in Figure 14-3.

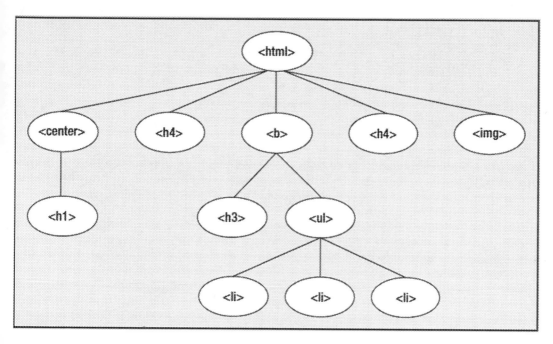

Figure 14-3. *If a document is well-formed, the relationship between the elements is a hierarchical one, with each descendent contained between its parent's start and end tags*

However, when the document is modified as shown previously to contain overlapping nodes, it's not possible to use a hierarchical tree structure to represent its contents.

When and Why to Use XML

Now that you understand some of the deficiencies associated with HTML, you may still be wondering when and why you'd use XML. It's obviously easier to parse and to represent internally than HTML, but when is it useful to take advantage of those characteristics? One use for XML that I've already mentioned is for providing multiple views of data. In effect, the XML document defines the data model, and you can create more than one view of that model based upon the needs of your application. You'll examine this capability in more depth later in the chapter when I discuss the eXtensible Stylesheet Language (XSL), which allows you to transform an XML document's content into some other form such as HTML.

Another significant application of XML is for representing data that's to be transferred between different applications. Since XML describes data and is easy to parse but isn't tied to a particular programming language, it allows you to transfer information between applications easily, even if those applications reside on different operating systems or are written in different programming languages. In fact, it's often said that just as Java provides interoperability across platforms for executable code, XML provides the same type of interoperability for data.

An important variation of this is when businesses use XML to submit various types of electronic documents to other businesses, including purchase orders, invoices, and so on. In the past, the preferred technology for doing this was Electronic Document Interchange (EDI) and the X12 standards. X12 defines a number of electronic documents and a specific format for each one, and many organizations use it. However, those documents are somewhat inflexible and complex, and EDI hasn't been as widely adopted as many had predicted. In contrast, XML allows companies to easily create their own formats for electronic documents that can be changed without requiring the company's business partners (or a standards organization) to first update their application code.

One other use of XML that's worth mentioning is for creating configuration files. In the early days of Windows, it was common for applications to create and use their own initialization (`.ini`) file that contained configuration information. Although simple to implement and easy to edit, those files are somewhat restrictive and have been largely abandoned by Windows applications in favor of the Windows registry, which contains a hierarchical collection of configuration information, allowing each application to reference values stored in its "branch" of the registry tree, as shown in Figure 14-4.

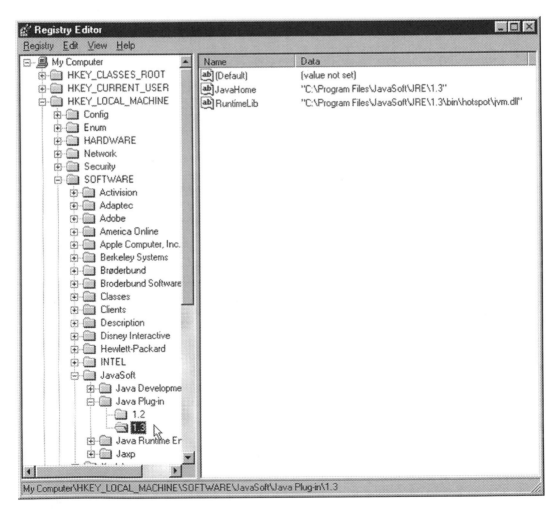

Figure 14-4. *One of XML's strengths is its ability to allow you to provide configuration parameters like those found in the Windows registry*

Since an XML document represents a collection of hierarchical data, it's a good candidate for the type of configuration information that's stored in the Windows registry. In fact, version 1.1 of the Enterprise JavaBeans specification requires deployment descriptors to be written in XML instead of the serialized object representation required by the 1.0 specification. A deployment descriptor is essentially a configuration file that describes how an Enterprise JavaBean is to be used, such as which users are allowed to access the bean. While the serialized object approach was convenient for the Enterprise JavaBeans server, it complicates how users can edit the deployment descriptor. The advantage of using XML is that it's both human-readable and can be parsed easily, which means it represents a format that's convenient for both humans and software.

Creating an XML Document

Because creating and editing XML documents can take place with simple text editor/word processor applications, it's easy to create a new document. Aside from the requirement that it be well-formed, there are almost no restrictions on what an XML document must contain. However, let's review the document that was defined at the beginning of this chapter; it illustrates some important points.

```
<?xml version="1.0" ?>

<book>
   <title>Pro Java Programming</title>
   272103_1_EnBrett Spell</author>
   <publisher>Apress</publisher>

   <tableOfContents showPageNumbers="Yes">
     <tocEntry>Printing</tocEntry>
     <tocEntry>Cut and Paste</tocEntry>
     <tocEntry>Drag and Drop</tocEntry>
   </tableOfContents>

</book>
```

Unlike the rest of the file, the first line doesn't describe the data in the document. Instead, it's a processing instruction, sometimes simply referred to as a PI; you can use processing instructions to provide special information to applications that may process the document's contents in some way. In this case, the instruction identifies the file as an XML document and specifies which version of XML was used to create the document. Although only the version attribute was specified here, the instruction actually supports two other attributes: encoding and standalone. As its name implies, encoding indicates which character set was used to construct the document, while standalone (which must be assigned a value of yes or no) indicates whether the document contains references to other files. For example, a file that doesn't contain external references and that was created using the UTF-8 character set might contain the following instruction:

```
<?xml version="1.0" encoding="UTF-8" standalone="yes" ?>
```

You'll often see the encoding attribute used at the beginning of an XML document, but standalone is rarely specified.

Root Elements

One other point to make concerning the structure of an XML document is that it must have only one element at the outermost level, and that element is known as the root element. In the previous document, the <book> element contains all the other data elements, and only the <?xml> processing instruction lies outside that element, so <book> is the root element. Since there may be only one root element, it's not valid, for example, to include another element at the same level in the document, as in the following listing:

```
<book>
  <title>Pro Java Programming</title>
...
</book>

<tableOfContents>
...
</tableOfContents>
```

In general, the *prolog* (the part of an XML document before the root element's start tag) consists of an optional <?xml> declaration, zero or more comments, processing instructions, and whitespace characters, followed by an optional DTD. A DTD describes the structure to which the data should conform and is used by validating parsers to ensure that a document is correct, but the details of defining a DTD aren't included in this chapter.

Components of an XML Document

Like HTML, XML allows you to use elements (with or without attributes) within the root element, and those elements can contain text or other elements. For example, the following <tableOfContents> element contains a showPageNumber attribute with a value of "Yes", together with three other elements, each of which contains text data:

```
<tableOfContents showPageNumbers="Yes">
  <tocEntry>Printing</tocEntry>
  <tocEntry>Cut and Paste</tocEntry>
  <tocEntry>Drag and Drop</tocEntry>
</tableOfContents>
```

Empty tags are valid in XML, so both of the following elements are acceptable:

```
<exampleElement></exampleElement>
<exampleElement/>
```

XML also allows you to specify comments within your documents in the same way you do within HTML.

```
<!-- This is a comment -->
<title>Pro Java Programming</title>
272103_1_EnBrett Spell</author>
<publisher>Apress</publisher>
```

A similar but more powerful feature of XML is its support for CDATA (character data) sections, which are portions of the document that are never parsed. The beginning of such a section is identified by <![CDATA[and terminated with]]>, and everything between those character sequences is ignored by an XML parser. For example,

```
<title>Pro Java Programming</title>
<![CDATA[
The <title> element identifies the title of this book. I can put open tags
without close tags (or vice versa) here because this entire block will be
ignored by XML parsers.
]]>
272103_1_EnBrett Spell</author>
<publisher>Apress</publisher>
```

On the surface, it may appear that a CDATA section is functionally identical to a comment, but an important difference exists. Some parsers may examine the text in a comment block, and although the text is generally ignored, using reserved characters (for example, <, >, and &) in a comment may cause the parser to fail. However, the information in a CDATA block is always ignored by a parser, so you can include any information between the <![CDATA[and]]> delimiters without affecting the parsing of the document. In fact, you can even include text that would normally be interpreted as XML tags without being concerned about the parser attempting to parse and validate the information.

Parsing and Validation

I've mentioned that one of XML's most important features is its ability to be parsed and validated easily, and as you might expect, Java's core libraries include classes that allow you to perform those operations. The classes are part of the Java API for XML Processing (JAXP) and are contained within the javax.xml package and its subpackages, along with org.w3c.dom and org.xml.sax and their subpackages. The latter two packages contain the specific implementations that correspond to the primary standards that have emerged for parsing XML: DOM and the Simple API for XML (SAX). Although DOM and SAX both represent techniques for parsing, they represent two very different approaches to doing so, and they both have their own strengths and weaknesses.

DOM was defined by the World Wide Web Consortium (W3C) and is the more powerful of the two technologies, allowing you to parse, validate, and update an XML document. This is usually done by reading the entire document into memory, where it's maintained as a hierarchical collection of objects. By modifying that collection of objects, you can change the structure and content of the document in memory, after which you can save the updated document again to some external location. In addition, DOM allows you to create an entirely new document, which as you'll see later is a very useful feature.

In contrast, SAX was created as a result of a mailing list discussion and provides sequential, read-only access to the document's contents. In other words, SAX doesn't provide any facility for creating or modifying a document, and it doesn't allow you to examine an arbitrary portion of the document. (It doesn't provide "random access" to the document's contents.) Instead, it allows you to register various types of listeners with a parser, and the parser will notify the appropriate listener for each portion of the document it processes. This approach is sometimes referred to as *event-based* because it treats each portion of the document as an event for which it sends a notification. Although some programmers may not find this approach intuitive, SAX is simple to use and has the advantage of not requiring that the entire document be loaded into memory at once. While that may not be a significant advantage for smaller documents, it can be an important factor when processing extremely large XML files.

Note that in this chapter, DOM refers to W3C's DOM Level 2 recommendation, where a recommendation is simply a completed standard. As of this writing, JAXP supports DOM Level 2, although it's likely at some point in the future to support the newer Level 3 specification. For the full details of DOM, see `www.w3.org/DOM/`.

Similarly, SAX refers to version 2.0 of the SAX standard, which is the version used by JAXP's current SAX parser implementation, although the SAX 2.0 specification is now available at `www.saxproject.org/`.

Parsing with the DOM Implementation in JAXP

As described earlier, DOM is more powerful than SAX in some ways and can be more intuitive, especially if you're already familiar with hierarchical tree structures such as those used by Swing's `JTree` component. In fact, although no direct relationship exists between `JTree` and DOM, you may find it helpful to review Chapter 7, which covers `JTree`, because much of the terminology defined there relating to tree structures applies to DOM as well.

As mentioned earlier, a SAX parser scans an XML document sequentially and reports the contents of the document through events. In contrast, a DOM parser creates a collection of objects in memory that represents the document's contents, and those objects are implementations of the interfaces defined in the `org.w3c.dom` package (see Figure 14-5).

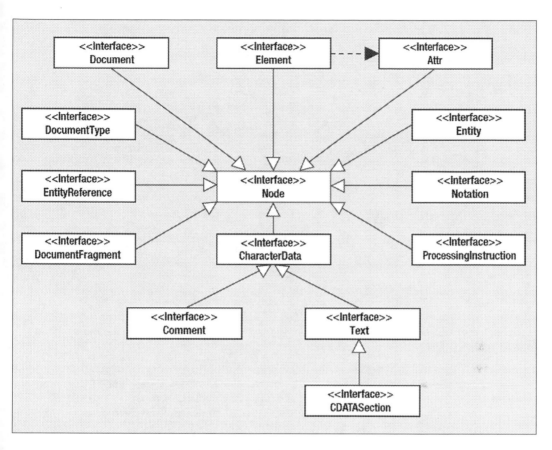

Figure 14-5. *A class diagram that illustrates the relationships between the classes and interfaces used by the DOM parser in JAXP*

With a few exceptions, each interface represents some particular type of information found in an XML document, and using a hierarchical collection of these objects, DOM is able to create a structure that mimics the document's contents. For example, suppose you process the following XML data with a DOM parser:

```
<tableOfContents showPageNumbers="Yes">
  <tocEntry>Printing</tocEntry>
  <tocEntry>Cut and Paste</tocEntry>
  <tocEntry>Drag and Drop</tocEntry>
</tableOfContents>
```

DOM will represent the `<tableOfContents>` element with an object that implements the `Element` interface, and that object will contain a reference to a single `Attr` representing the `showPageNumbers` attribute. In addition, the `Element` object will contain a child node for each of the `<tocEntry>` items, and they in turn will each contain a single `Text` node representing the text between the start and end tags of each element. Figure 14-6 illustrates this, but it omits what can be an important detail—that nodes are also created for whitespace such as carriage returns, linefeeds, tabs, and spaces. It's possible in many cases to ignore the nodes that represent whitespace, although, as you'll see later in the chapter, it's important at other times to realize that they may be present.

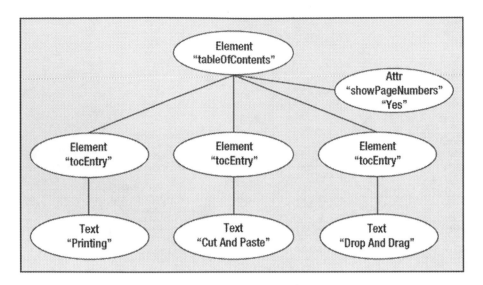

Figure 14-6. *An example of the heirachical nature of the elements with a DOM tree*

Creating a representation of the document in this manner causes a DOM parser to use more memory resources than a SAX parser uses, but DOM's approach offers two advantages.

- While SAX allows you to examine the document's contents in a sequential manner only (from beginning to end), the DOM interfaces include methods that allow you to navigate through the tree's nodes in any direction. That's possible because the nodes are stored in memory and maintain references to one another, and you can move from parent to child (and vice versa) and from one sibling to another.

- Since the collection of objects effectively represents a copy of the parsed document, it allows you to make changes to the document's contents and structure programmatically. Once you've made changes or created a new document, you can save them by converting the object structure back into an XML document.

Parsing an existing document using the JAXP implementation of DOM is extremely easy to do; you can do this by obtaining an instance of DocumentBuilder using the following code:

```
DocumentBuilderFactory factory = DocumentBuilderFactory.newInstance();
DocumentBuilder builder = factory.newDocumentBuilder();
```

Once you've gotten a reference to a DocumentBuilder, you can parse an existing document or create a new one easily. The DocumentBuilder class includes a number of parse() methods that accept various types of input (a String, a File, or an InputStream) representing an XML document. As the name and return type imply, parse() parses the document, creates a representation of it in memory, and returns a reference to that representation to the caller in the form of a Document object. You'll examine the Document interface in more detail shortly, but for now it's sufficient to recognize that it's a representation of an XML document that's stored in memory. In the meantime, the following is an example of how to use parse():

```
DocumentBuilderFactory factory = DocumentBuilderFactory.newInstance();
DocumentBuilder builder = factory.newDocumentBuilder();
java.io.File xmlFile = new java.io.File("C:/brett/temp/mytest.xml");
Document doc = builder.parse(xmlFile);
```

600

Creating a new (empty) document in memory is equally simple; you do this by calling the
newDocument() method instead of parse().

```
DocumentBuilderFactory factory = DocumentBuilderFactory.newInstance();
DocumentBuilder builder = factory.newDocumentBuilder();
Document doc = builder.newDocument();
```

As mentioned earlier, it's sometimes necessary or desirable to validate a document while it's being
parsed. Whether or not you plan to perform validation, you should keep in mind that the DocumentBuilder
can throw an exception when the parse() method is called and design your code accordingly.

You'll now examine the various interfaces used to support the JAXP implementation of DOM, because
it's necessary to have some familiarity with these interfaces before you can use DOM effectively.

Node

This interface is the superinterface of many of the other DOM interfaces that include the Document interface
mentioned earlier, and as you'd expect, Node defines methods that are shared by many of the different types
of objects that represent portions of an XML document.

getNodeType( )

This method allows you to easily determine which type of XML document item is represented by this node.
It returns a short value corresponding to one of the constants defined in Node, which are listed in Table 14-2.

Table 14-2. *Node Type Constants*

Node Constant	Associated Interface Name
ATTRIBUTE_NODE	Attr
CDATA_SECTION_NODE	CDATASection
COMMENT_NODE	Comment
DOCUMENT_FRAGMENT_NODE	DocumentFragment
DOCUMENT_NODE	Document
DOCUMENT_TYPE_NODE	DocumentType
ELEMENT_NODE	Element
ENTITY_NODE	Entity
ENTITY_REFERENCE_NODE	EntityReference
NOTATION_NODE	Notation
PROCESSING_INSTRUCTION_NODE	ProcessingInstruction
TEXT_NODE	Text

The code segment in Listing 14-1 illustrates how you can use this method to determine the type of
document item a given Node represents.

Listing 14-1. Using getNodeType( ) to Provide Different Types of Processing per Node

```
protected void displayTree(Node node) {
  short nodeType = node.getNodeType();
  switch (nodeType) {
    case Node.DOCUMENT_NODE:
      printDocument((Document)node);
      break;
    case Node.ELEMENT_NODE:
      printElement((Element)node);
      break;
    case Node.TEXT_NODE:
      printText((Text)node);
      break;
    default:
  }
}
```

getNodeName( )

This accessor method allows the caller to retrieve a reference to the node's name property, although the usage of that property varies from one Node subclass to another. For example, an Element node uses the name property to contain the element or "tag" name (for example, *book* for a <book> element), while an Attr node uses the name property to store the name of the attribute. Table 14-3 summarizes the values of this property.

Table 14-3. getNodeName( ) Properties

Node Subinterface	Value/Usage of nodeName Property
Document	#document
Element	Element/tag name
Attr	Attribute name
Text	#text
Comment	#comment
CDATASection	#cdata-section
ProcessingInstruction	Instruction target
EntityReference	Name of entity referenced
DocumentFragment	#document-fragment
DocumentType	Name of DTD as defined in <!DOCTYPE>
Entity	Entity name
Notation	Notation name

Note that there's no corresponding setNodeName( ) method defined in Node, which is because the node's name is normally specified when the Node object is created and is immutable.

Some of the Node subinterfaces listed in Table 14-3 define an additional accessor method that returns the same value as getNodeName(), which provides a more intuitive way to access the value. For example, you can call getTarget() to retrieve the instruction target of a ProcessingInstruction object instead of calling the more generic and less intuitive getNodeName(). Table 14-4 lists these interfaces, along with the method that returns the value stored in the node name property in each case.

Table 14-4. *Node subinterfaces with convenience methods for retrieving values*

Node Subinterface	Convenience Method
Element	getTagName()
Attr	getName()
ProcessingInstruction	getTarget()
DocumentType	getName()

getNodeValue( ), setNodeValue( )

Like the nodeName property, nodeValue's usage varies from one node type to the next, and in many cases the getNodeValue() method returns null. Table 14-5 summarizes the use of this property.

Table 14-5. *Node Value Usage*

Node Subinterface	Value/Usage of nodeValue Property
Document	Null
Element	Null
Attr	Attribute value
Text	Text encapsulated by the node
Comment	Comment text
CDATASection	Text data stored in section
ProcessingInstruction	Instruction data (all text after the target)
EntityReference	Null
DocumentFragment	Null
DocumentType	Null
Entity	Null
Notation	Null

Just as some of the interfaces define more intuitively named methods that allow you to access the node name property, two of them also provide accessor/mutator pairs for the node value property. For example, you can call setData() to update the data portion of a Processing➡ Instruction instead of calling setNodeValue(). Table 14-6 lists the interfaces that provide this convenience and includes the names of the relevant methods.

Table 14-6. *Attribute and Processing Instruction Convenience Methods*

Node Subinterface	Accessor Method	Mutator Method
Attr	getValue()	setValue()
ProcessingInstruction	getData()	setData()

getAttributes( )

Although the majority of the methods defined in the Node interface are used by most or all of its subclasses, this one is meaningful only for objects used to represent elements in an XML document (an Element). Since that's the case, I'll provide a detailed discussion of getAttributes in the overview of the Element interface and its methods instead of here. It returns null for other types of Node.

appendChild( ), insertBefore( ), removeChild( ), replaceChild( )

As their names imply, these methods add, replace, and remove child nodes from the node for which the method is called. While appendChild() simply adds a new node to the end of the list of children, insertBefore() allows you to insert a node into a specific location within the list. You'll use these methods when you want to modify the structure of a document that was loaded by a DOM parser.

getChildNodes( ), getFirstChild( ), getLastChild( )

You can use these methods to obtain either a complete list of the node's children (getChildNodes()) or a reference to the first or last entry in the node's list of children (getFirstChild() and getLastChild(), respectively). The getChildNodes() method returns an object that implements the NodeList interface; this object is similar to Java's Vector class but is much less sophisticated. In fact, NodeList defines just two methods: getLength(), which indicates how many objects are in the collection, and item(), which returns a reference to one of the Node items based on an index value. For example, Listing 14-2 shows how to obtain a list of children from a Node, uses the NodeList object to retrieve a reference to each one, and prints its String representation.

Listing 14-2. *Obtaining and Using a List of Child Nodes*

```
org.w3c.dom.Node parentNode;
org.w3c.dom.NodeList nodeList;
// ...
nodeList = parentNode.getChildNodes();
int count = nodeList.getLength();
for (int i = 0; i < count; i++) {
  node = nodeList.item(i);
  System.out.println(node.toString());
}
```

getNextSibling( ), getPreviousSibling( )

It's sometimes useful to be able to access the siblings of a given node, and these methods allow you to do just that. When you call getNextSibling() for a node, the method returns a reference to the sibling of the node that appears next in their parent's list of children, while getPreviousSibling() returns a reference to the previous sibling. A null value is returned by getNextSibling() if this node is the last one in the parent's list of children or if getPreviousSibling() is called for the first child node in a list.

hasChildNodes( )

If the node for which this method is called has any children, hasChildNodes() returns true; false indicates it doesn't currently have any children.

getOwnerDocument( )

Each Node object is associated with a particular Document, and this method returns a reference to that Document instance unless this Node is itself a Document, in which case it returns null.

cloneNode( )

A copy of this node is returned by cloneNode(), and that copy will either be a deep copy or a shallow copy depending upon the value of the Boolean parameter that's passed. If you specify a value of true, a deep copy is returned, which means that the entire subtree defined by this node is also copied and returned, while false indicates that only this node should be copied. In other words, a *shallow copy* is a copy of this node only, and a *deep copy* is a copy of this node and all of its descendents.

Document

As mentioned earlier, the Document interface is implemented by an object that represents an entire XML document, and a Document is returned by the DOM parser's parse() method. In other words, the object returned by parse() is the starting point from which you can begin to examine (or update) the document.

getDocumentElement( )

A Document object maintains a reference to the Node that represents the XML document's root element, and you can use this method to obtain access to that node. In fact, the first thing you'll do after calling a DocumentBuilder's parse() method often will be to invoke this method on the Document object returned so you can begin to process the elements representing the document's content as illustrated in Listing 14-3.

Listing 14-3. Obtaining a Reference to the Root Element

```
DocumentBuilderFactory factory = DocumentBuilderFactory.newInstance();
factory.setValidating(true);
DocumentBuilder builder = factory.newDocumentBuilder();
Document doc = builder.parse(uri);
Element rootElement = (doc.getDocumentElement());
```

If you executed this code using the XML document defined at the beginning of this chapter, for example, the getDocumentElement() method will return a reference to the object representing the <book> element.

getDocType( )

Just as a Document represents an XML document, a DocumentType represents a DTD. Each Document can maintain a reference to a DocumentType object, and this method allows you to access that object. If there's no DTD associated with the object, getDocType() returns a null value. Note that although the Level 1 DOM specification allows you to retrieve some of a document's DTD information, it doesn't allow you to modify that data or create a new DTD.

createAttribute( ), createCDATASection( ), createComment( ), createDocumentFraction( ), createElement( ), createEntityReference( ), createProcessingInstruction( ), createTextNode( )

These all represent factory methods that allow you to create instances of the various types of nodes without coupling your code to the JAXP-specific classes used to represent those types. In other words, by using only interfaces and factory methods, you can create application code that's not coupled to any particular DOM implementation.

getElementsByTagName( )

You can use this method to obtain a NodeList that encapsulates all Element nodes in the document with a particular name or a list of all Element nodes in the document regardless of their names. To obtain a list of all elements, pass a String value of * to getElementsByTagName( ); specifying any other value causes it to return only the elements that have a name equal to the specified string. The code in Listing 14-4 shows how you can use this method.

Listing 14-4. Retrieving Elements with a Specific Tag Name

```
Document document;
NodeList list1, list2;
// ...
// Obtain a list of elements representing all of the elements in the
// document.
list1 = document.getElementsByTagName("*");
// Obtain a list of all elements with a tag/node name of "tocEntry".
list2 = document.getElementsByTagName("tocEntry");
```

getImplementation( )

An object that implements the DOMImplementation interface is returned by getImplementation( ), and that interface defines a single hasFeature( ) method. That method accepts two String parameter values: the name of a feature and a version number, and it returns true if the DOM parser that created the Document supports the specified feature. This is intended to allow applications to query a parser's capabilities in an implementation-independent manner, but version 1.0.1 of the JAXP DOM parser reports that it supports only version "1.0" of the "XML" feature.

Element

As already mentioned, this interface is used by objects that represent elements within the XML document. As you might expect, most of the methods defined in Element provide functionality that allows you to create, update, remove, and retrieve attribute values.

setAttribute( ), setAttributeNode( )

These methods allow you to add an attribute value to the element or to replace the value associated with an existing attribute.

The setAttribute( ) method requires two String parameters, the first of which represents the attribute's name and the second of which represents its value. If an attribute with the specified name already exists, its value is updated, but if it doesn't already exist, a new Attr object is created and added to this element's list of attributes.

The setAttributeNode() method works the same way, but instead of passing two String values, you must pass it a reference to an object that implements the Attr interface. As described in a moment, that interface is used by objects that encapsulate the name and value associated with element attributes.

getAttribute( ), getAttributeNode( )

Both of these methods are passed a String parameter that represents the name of an attribute, and both of them return the value associated with the specified attribute. However, while getAttribute() returns only a String representing the attribute's value, getAttributeNode() returns the entire Attr object. getAttributeNode() returns a null value if no attribute with the specified name exists, while getAttribute() returns an empty string if the attribute can't be found.

removeAttribute( ), removeAttributeNode( )

As their names imply, these methods allow you to remove an attribute from the element, and they differ only in how they require you to identify the attribute to be removed. To use removeAttribute(), you must pass a String representing the attribute's name, while removeAttributeNode() requires you to specify the Attr node object to be removed.

getTagName( )

This method is provided as a convenience and is functionally identical to the getNodeName() method inherited from the Node interface. In other words, both getTagName() and getNodeName() return a String representing the name of the element.

normalize( )

This method causes the parser to combine adjacent Text nodes that are descendents of this element, which can make processing simpler and more efficient. In addition, some operations may be sensitive to changes in the tree's structure, and such changes can occur if a document is stored and reloaded without first being normalized. For example, suppose you create two new Text nodes and add them to an element as shown in Listing 14-5.

Listing 14-5. Creating and Appending a Pair of Text Nodes

```
Document document;
Text text1, text2;
Element element;
// ...
text1 = document.createTextNode("Matrix ");
text2 = document.createTextNode("Resources");
element.appendChild(text1);
element.appendChild(text2);
```

If you save and reload this document, it's likely that the text that was stored in the two separate (but adjacent) nodes just created will be stored in a single node that contains a value of Matrix Resources; however, you can force the nodes to be merged immediately by calling the normalize() method:

```
element.appendChild(text1);
element.appendChild(text2);
element.normalize();
```

getElementsByTagName( )

This method performs the same task as the method of the same name in the Document interface, but the difference is that only elements that are descendents of this one are included in the search. In other words, instead of returning a list of all elements in the document with a particular name (or all elements in the document when * is specified), this method returns only matching elements that are descendents of this node.

Attr

Objects that are used to represent an attribute should implement this interface, which defines methods for accessing and modifying the attribute's value and for retrieving its name. Note that Attr objects aren't child nodes of the element they describe.

getName( )

Like getTagName( ), this method is provided as a convenience and is functionally equivalent to getNodeName( ). In other words, the implementations of getName( ) and getNodeName( ) in Attr both return a reference to a String representing the attribute's name.

getValue( ), setValue( )

This pair of accessor and mutator methods allows you to retrieve and update the value associated with an attribute.

getSpecified( )

This method returns a Boolean value that allows you to distinguish between attribute values that were actually specified in the XML document and those that are default values specified in the document's DTD. A value of true is returned if the value was specified in the XML document or if the value has been set/modified by a call to the Attr object's setValue( ) method. However, if the attribute's value was derived from its definition in a DTD and its setValue( ) hasn't been called, getSpecified( ) returns false. Note that if setValue( ) is called, this method will return true even if the value passed to the setValue( ) method is the same value that was already assigned to the attribute.

CharacterData

CharacterData is a subclass of Node, and like Node, CharacterData defines methods that are shared by other interfaces used to represent portions of an XML document. Specifically, CharacterData is the superclass of the Text, Comment, and CDATASection interfaces that are described in a moment. Each CharacterData subclass encapsulates text ("character data") information, and this interface defines methods for setting, retrieving, and modifying that text. In fact, many of the methods described next are similar to methods defined in Java's StringBuffer class.

getLength( )

This method returns an integer value that represents the number of characters in the text string associated with this node.

setData( )

You can use this method to set the text value associated with this node by passing a reference to a `String` object representing the new value.

getData( ), substringData( )

These methods return all (in the case of `getData()`) or part (`substringData()`) of the text associated with this node. Both return a `String` value, and `substringData()` requires two integer parameters: one specifying the starting index of the portion of the text to return and another representing the number of characters to be retrieved.

appendData( )

You must pass a `String` parameter to this method, and the characters in that `String` are appended to the text data maintained by this node.

replaceData( )

You can use this method in place of `setData()` when you want to replace only a portion of the character data encapsulated by the node. To do so, you must pass the following parameter values:

- An integer representing an index into the existing text value
- An integer representing the number of characters to be replaced
- A `String` representing the data that's to replace the specified portion of the target

For example, the code segment in Listing 14-6 illustrates how to replace the word *is* with *was* in an object that implements `CharacterData`.

Listing 14-6. Replacing Data in a Text Node Using `replaceData()`

```
CharacterData charData;
// ...
charData.setData("This is a test");
// The word "is" has an index of 5 (it's the sixth character in the string)
int start = 5;
// The word "is" has a length of 2 (it's two characters long)
int length = 2;
charData.replaceData(start, length, "was");
// The following line prints "This was a test");
System.out.println(charData.getData());
```

609

insertData( )

The appendData( ) method allows you to append characters onto the end of the existing value, but you'll often need to insert characters at some arbitrary location other than the end. When that's the case, you can use this method, which requires you to pass an index value that describes where the text should be added and a String representing the text to be inserted. For example, the following code illustrates how to add text to the beginning of the existing value instead of at the end:

```
CharacterData charData;
// ...
charData.insertData(0, "This text is being inserted at the beginning");
```

deleteData( )

When you need to delete characters from the existing node value, you can call deleteData( ) to do so. You must pass two integer values to this method: one representing the position of the first character to delete and another representing the number of characters to be deleted.

Text

This interface is one of the subinterfaces of CharacterData and is used to represent text within an XML document. Objects that implement this interface can be added as children to an Element node to describe the data between the element's start and end tags. For example, suppose you create an XML document that contains the following elements:

```
<outer>Java and <keyword>XML</keyword> are good</outer>
```

When a DOM parser processes this portion of the document, the <outer> element will contain three child nodes in the following order:

- An instance of Text containing the first portion of the text (*Java and*).

- An Element representing <keyword> that in turn contains one child—a Text object with a value of XML.

- Another Text object containing the remainder of the text (*are good.*).

Figure 14-7 illustrates these nodes.

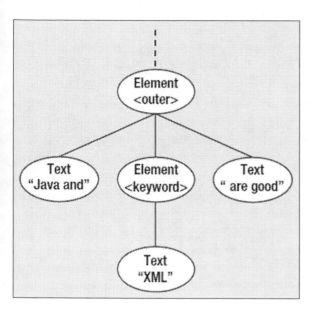

Figure 14-7. A representation of how the XML data is stored internally after it's parsed

It's important to realize that from a DOM parser's perspective, there's no difference between text that represents meaningful information (for example, *Java and*) and text that represents whitespace (linefeed and character return characters, tabs, and spaces). If you were to create an <example> element such as the following one, it too would have three child nodes. The second child would represent the empty <myInner> element, while the first and third children would represent the whitespace that precedes and follows that element in the document text, respectively.

```
<example>
  <myInner/>
</example>
```

splitText( )

This is the only method defined in the Text interface and is essentially the opposite of the "normalization" operation described previously that's available through the Element interface. In other words, while Element's normalize() method combines adjacent Text entries into a single entry, this method causes the Text object to be split into two separate (but adjacent) instances of Text.

The only parameter passed to this method is an integer that indicates the position at which the Text object's character data should be split. The characters up to and including the character at the position you specify will remain in the existing node, and any characters after that will be added to a new Text node. That new node will then be inserted into the parent node's list of children so it immediately follows the original Text node, as shown in Figure 14-8.

611

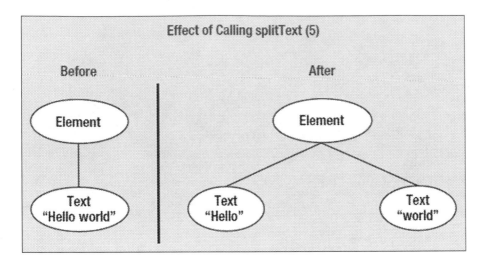

Figure 14-8. *As its name implies,* splitText() *splits a text element into two elements*

You'll use this method when you want to insert new elements or other data between two portions of text in an XML document. Once you've called splitText(), you can insert child nodes between the original Text node and its newly created sibling.

Comment

No methods are defined in this interface, so an implementing class includes only those that are inherited from CharacterData. As you might expect, an instance of Comment encapsulates the text specified in a comment in an XML document. For example, the following entry results in the creation of an object that implements Comment and that has a data value of *This is a comment*:

```
<!-- This is a comment -->
```

CDATASection

Just as the Comment interface encapsulates the text stored in an XML document's comment, this interface (which is a subclass of Text) contains the text stored in a CDATA section. If the following entry were part of an XML document, it'd result in the creation of a CDATASection with a value of *This is some text data*:

```
<![CDATA[This is some text data]]>
```

ProcessingInstruction

The intuitively named ProcessingInstruction interface is implemented by objects that represent processing instructions found in XML documents, and this interface defines the following three methods.

getTarget( )

As you may recall from the discussion of processing instructions and the SAX parser, the instruction target is the text that immediately follows the first question mark (?) and precedes the whitespace or the end of the instruction. For example, the target in the following example is myTarget:

```
<?myTarget doSomething moreInfo?>
```

getData( ), setData( )

The *instruction data* is any text information inside a processing instruction that follows the target value, and these methods allow you to retrieve and set the instruction data associated with this node. In the processing instruction shown previously, the instruction data is doSomething moreInfo.

EntityReference

This represents an entity reference that's embedded within an XML document. This may be an entity that you've defined inside a DTD or one of the predefined entities described earlier that are used to represent special characters such as the less-than (<) sign, greater-than (>) sign, ampersand (&), and so on. For example, the following code contains a sequence (&) that represents such a reference, and that sequence will be converted into an EntityReference object when processed by a DOM parser:

```
<someText>I can't embed the ampersand character (&amp;) directly</someText>
```

getNodeName( )

This is the only method that allows you to retrieve the name of the referenced entity. For example, the previous entry in an XML file results in the creation of an EntityReference object with a node name of amp, so calling getNodeName( ) returns that String value.

DocumentFragment

No methods are defined in this interface, which doesn't correspond to a specific portion of an XML document, but DocumentFragment has a property that can be useful. Like all Node subclasses, it can contain child nodes, and it can be added as a child to other nodes. However, when a DocumentFragment is added as a child of some other node, the DocumentFragment's children, rather than the DocumentFragment itself, will be added. Therefore, DocumentFragment provides a convenient container object for a collection of nodes that you want to make children of some other node (for example, when rearranging a document or implementing cut-and-paste functionality). Using DocumentFragment avoids the overhead of using a Document to hold the nodes.

DocumentType

This interface provides a partial representation of the DTD associated with an XML document and allows you to access (but not update) some of the information in the DTD.

getName()

Use this method to return the DTD's name, which is the first value that appears after the DOCTYPE keyword. For example, the name of the DTD referenced in the following code is book:

```
<?xml version="1.0" ?>
<!DOCTYPE book SYSTEM "./bookgram.dtd">
```

getEntities()

This method returns a collection of Entity objects encapsulated within a NamedNodeMap collection object; I'll describe the Entity interface in a moment.

You should recall the earlier discussion of the NodeList interface that's used by classes that provide a simplistic Vector-like functionality, which allows you to access a node based on its position within the collection/list. NamedNodeMap provides that same functionality, but it also allows you to assign each entry in the collection a name or "key" value that can be used to access the entry. In this case, the NamedNodeMap represents a collection of Entity objects, and the name/key value for each one is its name. For example, the following <!ENTITY> definition results in an Entity entry in the NamedNodeMap with a name/key of currentYear:

```
<!ENTITY currentYear "2000">
```

getNotations()

Just as the previous getEntities() method returns a NamedNodeMap that's a collection of Entity objects, this one returns a NamedNodeMap representing a collection of Notation instances. Like with Entity, I'll describe the Notation interface in a moment.

Entity

A DOM parser uses an implementation of this interface to represent entities that are defined in a DTD. For the three methods described next, assume that the following NOTATION and ENTITY definitions exist in the DTD:

```
<!NOTATION symbols "-//W3C//ENTITIES Symbols for XHTML//EN  ">
<!ENTITY HTMLsymbols SYSTEM "xhtml-symbol.ent" NDATA symbols>
```

getPublicId()

This method returns the public identifier of the entity, which in this case is -//W3C//ENTITIES Symbols for XHTML//EN; a null value indicates that no public identifier was specified for the entity.

getSystemId()

This method returns the system identifier of the entity, which in this case is xhtml-symbol.ent; a null value indicates that no system identifier is specified for the entity.

getNotationName()

When called for an unparsed entity, this method returns the name of the notation associated with the entity, which in this case is symbols. A value of null is returned by this method when called for a parsed entity.

getNodeName()

This method isn't defined in the Entity interface but is inherited from Node and returns the name of the entity (for example, HTMLSymbols).

Notation

This class represents a notation that's defined in a DTD, and a collection of Notation instances can be retrieved by calling the getNotations() method for a DocumentType object.

getPublicId()

As its name suggests, this method returns a String representing the notation's public identifier.

getSystemId()

As its name suggests, this method returns a String representing the notation's system identifier.

Traversing a Document with DOM

Now that you've examined the DOM interfaces, you'll see how to use them to examine an XML document and create a hierarchical collection of objects in memory. Each Element node can contain its own child nodes that can be other Element nodes, and those children may have their own child nodes, and so on, for a theoretically infinite number of levels, as shown in Figure 14-9.

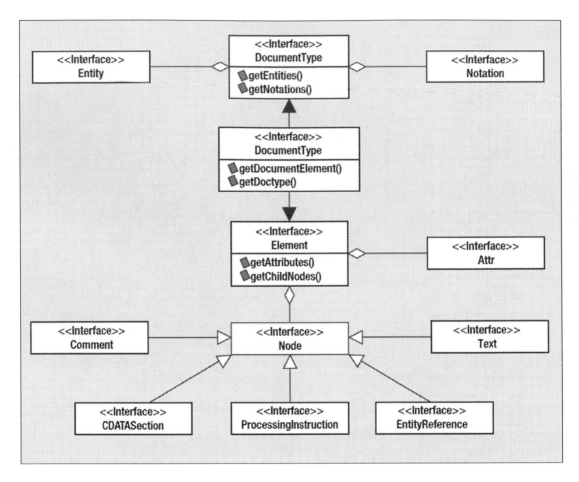

Figure 14-9. *The relationships that exist for the various interfaces used to represent a document maintained internally by a DOM parser*

As mentioned earlier, the DocumentBuilder class includes a parse() method that returns a Document object representing an XML document that's stored in memory. Once you have access to the Document object, you can call getDocumentElement() to obtain a reference to the XML document's root element or getDocumentType() if you intend to examine the document's DTD. The following code segment illustrates how you can use the JAXP classes to create a DOM parser, load and parse a document, and obtain access to its root element:

```
String uri;
// ...
DocumentBuilderFactory factory = DocumentBuilderFactory.newInstance();
factory.setValidating(true);
DocumentBuilder builder = factory.newDocumentBuilder();
Document doc = builder.parse(uri);
Element rootElement = doc.getDocumentElement();
```

As you've seen, the Node interface includes methods that allow you to access a node's parent, children, or siblings, and it's easy to use them to navigate through a document structure.

For example, suppose you're given an Element node and you want to display the subtree that it represents as it appeared in the original XML document. In other words, you not only want to examine the object structure but also want to actually reverse the parsing process and convert the objects back into an XML document. You can do this quite easily by creating code that traverses the tree, identifies which type of item each Node represents, and processes the node accordingly. Listing 14-7 shows an outline of such an application.

Listing 14-7. Initial DOMTest Implementation

```java
import javax.xml.parsers.*;
import org.w3c.dom.*;

public class DOMTest {

  public static void main(String[] args) throws Exception {
    DOMTest dt = new DOMTest(args[0]);
  }
}

public DOMTest(String uri) throws Exception {
  DocumentBuilderFactory factory =
      DocumentBuilderFactory.newInstance();
  factory.setValidating(true);
  DocumentBuilder builder = factory.newDocumentBuilder();
  Document doc = builder.parse(uri);
  displayTree(doc.getDocumentElement());
}

protected void displayTree(Node node) {
  short nodeType = node.getNodeType();
  switch (nodeType) {
    case Node.ELEMENT_NODE:
      printElement((Element)node);
      break;
    case Node.TEXT_NODE:
      printText((Text)node);
      break;
    case Node.COMMENT NODE:
      printComment((Comment)node);
      break;
    case Node.CDATA_SECTION_NODE:
      printCDATA((CDATASection)node);
     break;
    case Node.ENTITY_REFERENCE_NODE:
      printEntityReference((EntityReference)node);
     break;
    case Node.PROCESSING_INSTRUCTION_NODE:
      printProcessingInstruction(
          (ProcessingInstruction)node);
      break;
    default:
  }
}
```

```
protected void printElement(Element node) {
  // ...
}

protected void printText(CharacterData node) {
  // ...
}

protected void printComment(Comment node) {
  // ...
}

protected void printCDATA(CDATASection node) {
  // ...
}

protected void printEntityReference(EntityReference node) {
  // ...
}

protected void printProcessingInstruction(ProcessingInstruction node) {
  // ...
}
}
```

Except for Element instances, each type of Node subclass object can be converted into an appropriate text representation easily. In fact, all the previous printXXX() methods except printElement() can be completed with a single statement that wraps the node data in an appropriate character string as shown in Listing 14-8.

Listing 14-8. Generating Text Representations of Various Node Types

```
protected void printText(CharacterData node) {
  System.out.print(node.getData());
}

protected void printComment(Comment node) {
  System.out.print("<!--" + node.getData() + "-->");
}

protected void printCDATA(CDATASection node) {
  System.out.print("<![CDATA[" + node.getData() + "]]>");
}

protected void printEntityReference(EntityReference node) {
  System.out.print("&" + node.getNodeName() + ";");
}

protected void printProcessingInstruction(ProcessingInstruction node) {
  System.out.print("<?" + node.getTarget() + " " + node.getData() + "?>");
}
```

Processing Element nodes is slightly more complex because they can have attributes and child nodes that must be included in the output, but the start and end tags can easily be generated.

```
protected void printElement(Element node) {
  // ...
  System.out.print("<" + node.getNodeName());
  // ...
  System.out.print(">");
  // ...
  System.out.print("</" + node.getNodeName() + ">");
}
```

To include an element's attribute values inside its start tag, you must retrieve a reference to its attribute list by calling the getAttributes() method. After that, iterate through the list and generate output for each one, placing quotes around its value. Listing 14-9 shows an example of how this can be done.

Listing 14-9. Embedding Elements in a Node's Start Tag

```
protected void printElement(Element node) {
  Attr attr;
  System.out.print("<" + node.getNodeName());
  NamedNodeMap attrs = node.getAttributes();
  int count = attrs.getLength();
  for (int i = 0; i < count; i++) {
      attr = (Attr)(attrs.item(i));
      System.out.print(" " + attr.getName() + "=\"" + attr.getValue() +
                        "\"");
  }
  System.out.print(">");
  // ...
  System.out.print("</" + node.getNodeName() + ">");
}
```

You must also ensure that all of an element's child nodes are included in the generated output, but this is even easier to accomplish. Simply obtain a reference to the list of children by calling getChildNodes() and then call the displayTree() method for each one. This causes the entire tree structure to be processed using *preorder traversal*, a term that's described in Chapter 7, discussing JTree. Stated simply, however, it means that a node is processed/displayed before its children instead of afterward and an example of how this can be implemented appears in Listing 14-10.

Listing 14-10. Preorder Traversal Implementation in the printElement() Method

```
protected void printElement(Element node) {
  Node child;
  Attr attr;
  System.out.print("<" + node.getNodeName());
  NamedNodeMap attrs = node.getAttributes();
  int count = attrs.getLength();
  for (int i = 0; i < count; i++) {
      attr = (Attr)(attrs.item(i));
      System.out.print(" " + attr.getName() + "=\"" + attr.getValue() +
                        "\"");
  }
```

619

```
    System.out.print(">");
    NodeList children = node.getChildNodes();
    count = children.getLength();
    for (int i = 0; i < count; i++) {
        child = children.item(i);
        displayTree(child);
    }
    System.out.print("</" + node.getNodeName() + ">");
}
```

With the `printElement()` method in place, you can now use the `DOMTest` application to print the contents of an XML document's root element. To do this, simply compile the code and execute it, passing a string that represents a URI (uniform resource identifier) to the `main()` method as shown in the following code:

```
C:\brett\temp>java DOMTest file:/c:/brett/temp/booktest.xml
<book><title>Pro Java Programming</title>272103_1_EnBrett Spell</autho r><publisher>
Apress</publisher><tableOfContents showPageNumbers="Yes">
<t ocEntry>Printing</tocEntry><tocEntry>Cut and Paste</tocEntry><tocEntry>
Drag and Drop</tocEntry></tableOfContents></book>
```

Although this application provided a reason for you to see how to traverse a DOM tree, it really wasn't necessary to implement this functionality at all. That's because the DOM implementation supplied with the JAXP download contains `toString()` methods that do essentially the same thing as the `printXXX()` methods. In fact, the simplified version of `DOMTest` in Listing 14-11 will produce the same output as the code just created.

Listing 14-11. Displaying the Text Representation of a Document

```java
import javax.xml.parsers.*;
import org.w3c.dom.*;

public class DOMTest2 {

  public static void main(String[] args) throws Exception {
    DOMTest2 dt = new DOMTest2s(args[0]);
  }

  public DOMTest2(String uri) throws Exception {
    DocumentBuilderFactory factory =
        DocumentBuilderFactory.newInstance();
    factory.setValidating(true);
    DocumentBuilder builder = factory.newDocumentBuilder();
    Document doc = builder.parse(uri);
    System.out.println(doc.getDocumentElement());
  }

}
```

It may be tempting to take advantage of this functionality if you're using the JAXP parser, but you should keep in mind that this behavior isn't part of the DOM standard.

Editing Documents with DOM

You can use DOM to edit a document in essentially the same way you use it to scan the document. In addition to the methods that allow you to access node values and navigate through an object structure, DOM also provides methods that allow you to add, modify, and delete nodes from the tree. For example, given the XML document shown in Listing 14-12, suppose you want to assign a value of no to the showPageNumbers attribute value in the <tableOfContents> element.

Listing 14-12. An XML Document to Be Edited

```
<?xml version="1.0" ?>

<book>
  <title>Pro Java Programming</title>
  272103_1_EnBrett Spell</author>
  <publisher>Apress</publisher>

  <tableOfContents showPageNumbers="yes">
    <tocEntry>Printing</tocEntry>
    <tocEntry>Cut &amp; Paste</tocEntry>
    <tocEntry>Drag &amp; Drop</tocEntry>
  </tableOfContents>
</book>
```

Once the document has been loaded into memory, the root element can be accessed and its children searched until the <tableOfContents> element is located. After that's done, you can use a call to setAttribute() to set the showPageNumbers value to no, as shown in Listing 14-13.

Listing 14-13. Locating a Node and Modifying Its Value

```
import javax.xml.parsers.*;
import org.w3c.dom.*;

public class DOMTest3 {
  public static void main(String[] args) throws Exception {
    DOMTest3 dt = new DOMTest3(args[0]);
  }

  public DOMTest3(String uri) throws Exception {
    DocumentBuilderFactory factory =
        DocumentBuilderFactory.newInstance();
    factory.setValidating(true);
    DocumentBuilder builder = factory.newDocumentBuilder();

    Document doc = builder.parse(uri);
    Element rootElement = doc.getDocumentElement();
    NodeList children = rootElement.getChildNodes();
    Node current = null;
    int count = children.getLength();
```

```
    for (int i = 0; i < count; i++) {
      current = children.item(i);
      if (current.getNodeType() == Node.ELEMENT_NODE) {
        Element element = (Element)current;
        if (element.getTagName().equalsIgnoreCase("tableOfContents")) {
          element.setAttribute("showPageNumbers", "no");
        }
      }
    }
    System.out.println(doc.getDocumentElement());
  }
}
```

If, on the other hand, you want to delete the <tableOfContents> tag completely instead of modifying its attribute, you can use the removeChild() method, as shown in Listing 14-14.

Listing 14-14. Removing a Node

```
import javax.xml.parsers.*;
import org.w3c.dom.*;

public class DOMTest4 {

  public static void main(String[] args) throws Exception {
    DOMTest4 dt = new DOMTest4(args[0]);
  }

  public DOMTest4(String uri) throws Exception {
    DocumentBuilderFactory factory =
    DocumentBuilderFactory.newInstance();
    factory.setValidating(true);
    DocumentBuilder builder = factory.newDocumentBuilder();

    Document doc = builder.parse(uri);
    Element rootElement = doc.getDocumentElement();
    NodeList children = rootElement.getChildNodes();
    Node current = null;
    for (int i = 0; i < children.getLength(); i++) {
        current = children.item(i);
        if (current.getNodeType() == Node.ELEMENT_NODE) {
          Element element = (Element)current;
          if (element.getTagName().equalsIgnoreCase("tableOfContents")) {
            rootElement.removeChild(element);
          }
        }
      }
    System.out.println(doc.getDocumentElement());
  }
}
```

When removing nodes like this, keep in mind that you're removing not only the node you specify on the call to removeChild() but all of its descendents as well. In this case, for example, removing the <tableOfContents> element results in the removal of the three <tocEntry> elements that are its children, those three nodes' children, and so on.

In other words, removeChild() effectively eliminates the entire subtree defined by the node that you pass as a parameter value.

Creating and Adding New Nodes

Creating and adding new nodes are equally simple, since the Node interface includes methods such as appendChild(), insertBefore(), and replaceChild(). Creating a new node is something you haven't done before, although you may remember that the Document interface includes factory methods that return instances of the different types of Node objects. In most cases, these methods require a single parameter that represents the name of the node to be created, and the following is an example of how you might create a new Element node:

```
Document doc = builder.parse(uri);
// ...
Element myNewElement = doc.createElement("tocEntry");
```

Once the new element is created, you can call its mutator methods to modify its state, and once it's properly initialized, you can add it to the object structure. The following code creates a new Element representing a <tocEntry>, creates a new Text node containing Help, makes the Text node a child of the new Element, and inserts that element before the second child of the <tableOfContents> node, as shown in Listing 14-15.

Listing 14-15. Adding a Node to the Tree

```
import javax.xml.parsers.*;
import org.w3c.dom.*;

public class DOMTest5 {

  public static void main(String[] args) throws Exception {
    DOMTest5 dt = new DOMTest5(args[0]);
  }

  public DOMTest5(String uri) throws Exception {
    DocumentBuilderFactory factory =
        DocumentBuilderFactory.newInstance();
    factory.setValidating(true);
    DocumentBuilder builder = factory.newDocumentBuilder();

    Document doc = builder.parse(uri);
    Element rootElement = doc.getDocumentElement();
    NodeList children = rootElement.getChildNodes();
    Node current = null;
    int count = children.getLength();
```

```
    for (int i = 0; i < count; i++) {
      current = children.item(i);
      if (current.getNodeType() == Node.ELEMENT_NODE) {
        Element element = (Element)current;
        if (element.getTagNamc().equalsIgnoreCase("tableOfContents")) {
          // Get the list of <tocEntry> items
          NodeList tocitems = element.getElementsByTagName("tocEntry");
          // Obtain a reference to the second one
          Node secondChild = tocitems.item(1);
          // Create a new <tocEntry> element
          Element newTOCItem = doc.createElement("tocEntry");
          // Create a new "Help" text node
          Text newText = doc.createTextNode("Help");
          // Make it a child of the new <tocEntry> element
          // <tocEntry>Help</tocEntry>
          newTOCItem.appendChild(newText);
          // Add the new <tocEntry> element to <tableOfContents>
          element.insertBefore(newTOCItem, secondChild);
        }
      }
    }

    System.out.println(doc.getDocumentElement());
  }
}
```

In effect, this is equivalent to making the following addition to the original XML document:

```
<tableOfContents showPageNumbers="Yes">
  <tocEntry>Printing</tocEntry>
  <tocEntry>Help</tocEntry><tocEntry>Cut &amp; Paste</tocEntry>
  <tocEntry>Drag &amp; Drop</tocEntry>
</tableOfContents>
```

This illustrates an important point that may not be obvious. Although it may appear that the original <tableOfContents> node had only three children, it has at least seven: four Text nodes representing whitespace in addition to the three <tocEntry> Element nodes. If the tree has been normalized (which it typically will be after it's first constructed), there will be exactly seven child nodes. However, it's possible that one "section" of whitespace consists of up to two sequential Text nodes (for example, a linefeed followed by a tab). In any case, when adding data nodes to a tree as in this example, you may also want to add a Text node representing whitespace as well. Although whitespace has no impact upon a parser's ability to process the document or upon the logical organization of the document, you want to add it for the sake of readability. In this case, you can add whitespace easily by inserting the bold code in Listing 14-16.

Listing 14-16. Adding a Whitespace Node

```
// ...
for (int i = 0; i < count; i++) {
  current = children.item(i);
  if (current.getNodeType() == Node.ELEMENT_NODE) {
    Element element = (Element)current;
    if (element.getTagName().equalsIgnoreCase("tableOfContents")) {
      // Get the list of <tocEntry> items
      NodeList tocitems = element.getElementsByTagName("tocEntry");
      // Obtain a reference to the second one
      Node secondChild = tocitems.item(1);
      // Create a new <tocEntry> element
      Element newTOCItem = doc.createElement("tocEntry");
      // Create a new "Help" text node
      Text newText = doc.createTextNode("Help");
      // Make it a child of the new <tocEntry> element
      // <tocEntry>Help</tocEntry>
      newTOCItem.appendChild(newText);
      // Add the new <tocEntry> element to <tableOfContents>
      element.insertBefore(newTOCItem, secondChild);
      // Create another text node containing a linefeed and
      // two tabs to use for whitespace
      newText = doc.createTextNode("\n\t\t");
      // Insert it before the new <tocEntry> we added
      element.insertBefore(newText, secondChild);
    }
  }
}
// ...
```

This inserts a linefeed and two tab characters after the newly inserted `<tocEntry>` element (before the element that follows it) so that when converted into XML, the document's contents will appear as shown in the following code:

```
<tableOfContents showPageNumbers="Yes">
  <tocEntry>Printing</tocEntry>
  <tocEntry>Help</tocEntry>
  <tocEntry>Cut &amp; Paste</tocEntry>
  <tocEntry>Drag &amp; Drop</tocEntry>
</tableOfContents>
```

Creating a New Document

All of the Document instances you've used so far were created when the parse() method read and processed an existing document, but you'll sometimes want to create a new object collection that's not associated with an existing XML document. As you saw earlier, JAXP's DocumentBuilder class contains a newDocument() method that you can use to obtain a new (and empty) Document object and an example of its use appears in Listing 14-17.

Listing 14-17. Initial DOMTest Implementation

```
import javax.xml.parsers.*;
import org.w3c.dom.*;

public class DOMTest6 {

  public static void main(String[] args) throws Exception {
    DOMTest6 dt = new DOMTest6();
  }

  public DOMTest6() throws Exception {
   DocumentBuilderFactory factory =
       DocumentBuilderFactory.newInstance();
   factory.setValidating(true);
   DocumentBuilder builder = factory.newDocumentBuilder();
   Document document = builder.newDocument();

   // ...
 }

}
```

Once you've created a new Document object, the first Element child you add to it will become the document's root element, and you can add other nodes as described previously and as done in Listing 14-18.

Listing 14-18. Creating and Appending a Child Element to a New Document

```
import javax.xml.parsers.*;
import org.w3c.dom.*;

public class DOMTest6 {

public static void main(String[] args) throws Exception {
  DOMTest6 dt = new DOMTest6();
}

public DOMTest6() throws Exception {
  DocumentBuilderFactory factory =
      DocumentBuilderFactory.newInstance();
  factory.setValidating(true);
  DocumentBuilder builder = factory.newDocumentBuilder();

  Document document = builder.newDocument();
  // Create a new Element object
  Element rootElement = document.createElement("book");
  // Make it the root element of this new document
  document.appendChild(rootElement);

  System.out.println(document.getDocumentElement());
 }
}
```

Transforming XML Documents

I've already pointed out that using XML allows you to separate your data from instructions that describe how the data is displayed. However, I haven't mentioned how to convert an XML document into some format that's appropriate for display, such as an HTML document. For example, you should recall that an HTML document and a similar XML document were defined at the beginning of this chapter. Since the HTML version contains information that describes how to format the data, it's possible to view that document in a browser and have it display the data appropriately. In contrast, the XML document doesn't contain any such display guidelines.

One option for converting an XML document into some other format is to use DOM to examine the document's contents and write an appropriate representation, but this can be a complex and difficult task depending upon the size and complexity of the document. In addition, writing Java code to perform the formatting means you must change that code when you want to change the structure of the output. Fortunately, an alternative approach exists that makes it reasonably simple to define a set of rules that describes how an XML document should be transformed. That alternative is XSL. XSL is a standard created by the World Wide Web Consortium, and its purpose is to allow you to create stylesheets for XML documents, where a *stylesheet* is simply a file that describes how information should be transformed.

XSL allows you to do two things that are (technically, at least) distinct from one another: rearrange the structure of your document's nodes and describe what output should be generated for each node. In other words, you can convert a document from one XML grammar to another or even from one XML format to some non-XML format such as HTML, RTF, PDF, and so on.

You'll now see how to create an XSLT file that will transform the XML document at the beginning of this chapter into the equivalent HTML document. First, you should create a file called booktran.xsl that contains the following three lines. The first line is the XML declaration you've already seen, and the next line is the stylesheet declaration, which identifies the namespace that will be used to refer to XSLT instructions:

```
<?xml version="1.0"?>
<xsl:stylesheet xmlns:xsl="http://www.w3.org/1999/XSL/Transform" version="1.0">
</xsl:stylesheet>
```

To specify how XML data is formatted, you must create templates, which are elements containing transformation instructions and data. In this case, for example, when a <book> element is encountered, you want an HTML document to be generated that contains the same data found in <book> but with HTML tags that describe how to format the data. Therefore, you can create a template like the following one that will generate the <html> and </html> tags when <book> is encountered:

```
<?xml version="1.0"?>
<xsl:stylesheet xmlns:xsl="http://www.w3.org/1999/XSL/Transform" version="1.0">

<xsl:template match="book">
<html>
</html>
</xsl:template>

</xsl:stylesheet>
```

To embed information from one of the elements, you can use the value-of instruction as shown in the following code. This instruction generates output from the text found between the start and end tags of the specified element. In this case, it's used to extract the book's title, author, and publisher from the XML document.

```
<?xml version="1.0"?>

<xsl:stylesheet xmlns:xsl="http://www.w3.org/1999/XSL/Transform" version="1.0">

<xsl:template match="book">
<html>
<center><h1><xsl:value-of select="title"/></h1></center>
<h4><xsl:value-of select="author"/></h4>
<h4><xsl:value-of select="publisher"/></h4>
</html>
</xsl:template>

</xsl:stylesheet>
```

For example, given the XML document at the beginning of this chapter, the previous XSLT document will extract the contents of the <title>, 272103_1_En, and <publisher> elements, enclosing the title within an <h1> tag and the author and publisher within <h4> tags. To actually perform this transformation, however, you need an XSL processor.

Performing an XSL Transformation

Like SAX and DOM, you must obtain an XSLT processor before you can use the technology, but again, Java includes an implementation for your use. The first step in doing so is to obtain an instance of the TransformerFactory class defined within the javax.xml.transform package.

```
TransformerFactory factory = TransformerFactory.newInstance();
```

As you might expect, a TransformerFactory returns instances of Transformer, and those instances can be used to transform XML documents based on the instructions in a stylesheet. However, since the Transformer relies upon the stylesheet to perform the transformation, you're required to identify the source of the stylesheet data when you create the Transformer. You can do this using an implementation of the Source interface defined in javax.xml.transform; fortunately, Java provides convenient implementations of that interface. One implementation is StreamSource, which represents a data source as a stream that corresponds to a File, a Reader, or an InputStream. Let's suppose the stylesheet defined previously is stored in C:\brett\temp\styletest.xsl and you want to create a Transformer that uses it to process an XML document. In that scenario, you could use code like that shown in the following:

```
File file = new File("C:/brett/temp/styletest.xsl");
Source source = new StreamSource(file);
```

Now that you've seen how to define a Source, you can easily create a Transformer using the following code:

```
TransformerFactory factory = TransformerFactory.newInstance();
File file = new File("C:/brett/temp/styletest.xsl");
Source source = new StreamSource(file);
Transformer transformer = factory.newTransformer(source);
```

628

Finally, to perform the transformation, you need to create another Source implementation that identifies the XML document to be transformed along with a Result implementation that identifies where to send the transformed output. As was the case with Source, JAXP provides convenient implementations of the Result interface, including the StreamResult class that allows output to be sent to a File, an OutputStream, or a Writer. For example, to create a Result implementation that will send the transformed data to standard output, you could use code like the following:

```
Result result = new StreamResult(System.out);
```

Now that you've seen how to create Source and Result implementations, you can easily transform an XML document stored in C:\brett\temp\mytest.xml using a stylesheet stored in C:\brett\temp\styletest.xsl and send it to standard output using the code in Listing 14-19.

Listing 14-19. Transforming an XML Document and Displaying It in Standard Output

```
TransformerFactory factory = TransformerFactory.newInstance();
File file = new File("C:/brett/temp/styletest.xsl");
Source source = new StreamSource(file);

Transformer transformer = factory.newTransformer(source);
file = new File("C:/brett/temp/mytest.xml");
source = new StreamSource(file);
Result result = new StreamResult(System.out);
transformer.transform(source, result);
```

Running this code with the stylesheet defined earlier and the XML document listed at the beginning of this chapter produces the following output:

```
<html>
<center>
<h1>Pro Java Programming</h1>
</center>
<h4>Brett Spell</h4>
<h4>Apress</h4>
</html>
```

Although this example is a trivial one, XSLT provides a robust facility for performing translations. A complete discussion of its capabilities is beyond the scope of this chapter, but you can find more information at www.w3.org/TR/xslt/ or refer to *XSLT 2.0 Programmer's Reference* by Michael Kay (Wrox Press, 2004).

Introducing XPath

Before continuing, it's helpful to closely examine the values of the select attributes associated with the value-of instructions you created. Although it may not be apparent, these are examples of XPath (XML Path Language) values. XPath is an expression language used to select nodes in an XML document tree, specify conditions for different ways of processing a node, and generate text from the tree. Here it simply provides a way to refer to specific nodes in the XML document. XPath is a separate standard from XSL/XSLT, but as this example illustrates, it's used to identify document nodes referenced during transformations. Fortunately, XPath is somewhat intuitive, since the notation used is similar to what you're probably already accustomed to using when referring to directories in a file system.

For example, suppose you issue the command dir . in a DOS/Windows environment. The single period character (.) represents the current directory, so this command will list all the files in the current directory and all its subdirectories. For example, if your current directory is C:\brett\temp, the previous command will list all files and subdirectories contained by that directory. Similarly, issuing the command dir xslt from that same directory will list the contents of the xslt subdirectory (C:\brett\temp\xslt).

Given these examples, you may already realize how this relates to XPath. In the template that's defined to handle <book> elements, the "current node" is the <book> element being processed, and a path such as author or publisher refers to the element directly below the current one. In other words, the value-of instruction simply includes the text found between the start and end tags of the node identified by the XPath value. In this case, that means the <title>, 272103_1_En, and <publisher> values.

At this point, you need to add two things: the table of contents information and the publisher's logo image. You can easily reproduce the table of contents header using the techniques already described and shown in Listing 14-20.

Listing 14-20. Including an Element for the Table of Contents Header

```
<?xml version="1.0"?>

<xsl:stylesheet xmlns:xsl="http://www.w3.org/1999/XSL/Transform" version="1.0">

<xsl:template match="book">
<html>
<center><h1><xsl:value-of select="title"/></h1></center>
<h4><xsl:value-of select="author"/></h4>
<b>
<h3>Table Of Contents</h3>
</b>
<h4><xsl:value-of select="publisher"/></h4>
</html>
</xsl:template>
```

On the other hand, including the <tocItem> entries in the output is slightly more complex because there are several such entries and because they aren't directly below the <book> element being processed. That isn't really a difficult problem to solve because XPath allows you to refer to the <tocItem> entries from the <book> template. However, since you have multiple such entries, you must use the for-each instruction to define a loop that will process each one of them and an example of how this can be done appears in Listing 14-21.

Listing 14-21. Including a Loop That Will Generate an Element for Each Entry

```
<?xml version="1.0"?>

<xsl:stylesheet xmlns:xsl="http://www.w3.org/1999/XSL/Transform" version="1.0">

<xsl:template match="book">
<html>
<center><h1><xsl:value-of select="title"/></h1></center>
<h4><xsl:value-of select="author"/></h4>
<b>
<h3>Table Of Contents</H3>
```

```
<ul>
<xsl:for-each select="tableOfContents/tocEntry">
</xsl:for-each>
</ul>
</b>
<h4><xsl:value-of select="publisher"/></h4>
</html>
</xsl:template>

</xsl:stylesheet>
```

With this loop in place, you can easily generate output for each <tocEntry> element. Note the use of the single period (.) for the select value, which in the context of the loop refers to the value between the start and end tags of the <tocEntry> element. An implementation of this is found in Listing 14-22.

Listing 14-22. Including a List Item for Each `tocEntry` Element

```
<?xml version="1.0"?>

<xsl:stylesheet xmlns:xsl="http://www.w3.org/1999/XSL/Transform" version="1.0">

<xsl:template match="book">
<html>
<center><h1><xsl:value-of select="title"/></h1></center>
<h4><xsl:value-of select="author"/></h4>
<b>
<h3>Table Of Contents</H3>
<ul>
<xsl:for-each select="tableOfContents/tocEntry">
<li><xsl:value-of select="."/></li>
</xsl:for-each>
</ul>
</b>
<h4><xsl:value-of select="publisher"/></h4>
</html>
</xsl:template>

</xsl:stylesheet>
```

Finally, you can add the <img> tag that will display the cover image, although you have at least two ways to accomplish this. One approach is to explicitly embed the information in the document, as shown in Listing 14-23.

Listing 14-23. Embedding an IMG element in the Document

```
<?xml version="1.0"?>

<xsl:stylesheet xmlns:xsl="http://www.w3.org/1999/XSL/Transform" version="1.0">

<xsl:template match="book">
<html>
<center><h1><xsl:value-of select="title"/></h1></center>
```

631

```
<h4><xsl:value-of select="author"/></h4>
<b>
<h3>Table Of Contents</H3>
<xsl:for-each select="tableOfContents/tocEntry">
<li><xsl:value-of select="."/></li>
</xsl:for-each>
</b>
<h4><xsl:value-of select="publisher"/></h4>
<img src="http://www.apress.com/ApressCorporate/supplement/1/421/bcm.gif" alt="Cover Image" />
</html>
</xsl:template>

</xsl:stylesheet>
```

However, if you prefer to avoid explicitly identifying the file in your XSL document, you can use entity references instead as in Listing 14-24.

Listing 14-24. Using an Entity Reference to Refer to an Image File

```
<?xml version="1.0"?>
<!DOCTYPE xsl:stylesheet SYSTEM "pubinfo.dtd">

<xsl:stylesheet xmlns:xsl="http://www.w3.org/1999/XSL/Transform" version="1.0">

<xsl:template match="book">
<html>
<center><h1><xsl:value-of select="title"/></h1></center>
<h4><xsl:value-of select="author"/></h4>
<b>
<h3>Table Of Contents</H3>
<xsl:for-each select="tableOfContents/tocEntry">
<li><xsl:value-of select="."/></li>
</xsl:for-each>
</b>
<h4><xsl:value-of select="publisher"/></h4>
<img src="&logoFile;" alt="&logoText;"  />
</html>
</xsl:template>

</xsl:stylesheet>
```

This latter approach also requires that a `pubinfo.dtd` file be created with the following contents:

```
<!-- pubinfo.dtd -->
<!ENTITY logoFile "http://www.apress.com/ApressCorporate/supplement/1/421/bcm.gif">
<!ENTITY logoText "Coverage Image">
```

The output produced by this stylesheet is shown in Listing 14-25.

Listing 14-25. The HTML Output Generated by XSL

```
<html>
<center>
<h1>Pro Java Programming</h1>
</center>
<h4>Brett Spell</h4>
<b>
<h3>Table Of Contents</H3>
<li>Printing</li>
<li>Cut and Paste</li>
<li>Drag and Drop</li>
</b>
<h4>Apress</h4>
<img alt="Cover Image"
     src="http://www.apress.com/ApressCorporate/supplement/1/421/bcm.gif "></html>
```

Creating and Using Additional Templates

Although the previous approach is acceptable for a relatively simple XML document, it has one design flaw that can be significant. Specifically, all processing takes place inside a single template, and if your document's structure is complex, you'll be forced to put a large amount of code inside that template. This is roughly equivalent to creating a large, "monolithic" method in Java or some other programming language, where that method performs many different steps in a complex algorithm. Such a method becomes difficult to understand and maintain, so it's usually desirable to separate the functions by placing them in different methods (or templates in this case). A good candidate for such a change is the code that handles the <tableOfContents> elements and its <tocItem> subelements, since that code accounts for roughly half of the logic inside the existing template.

You can easily create a new template that handles only <tableOfContents> elements, as shown in the following code; it contains essentially the same instructions that were present in <book>. The only exception is that the <tocEntry> items are referenced from a location relative to the <tableOfContents> entry instead of the <book> element. Therefore, you must change the path used in the for-each instruction to reference each <tocEntry> from tableOfContents/tocEntry to tocEntry. An example of how this might be done appears in Listing 14-26.

Listing 14-26. Using a More Granular Approach to Templates

```
<?xml version="1.0"?>
<!DOCTYPE xsl:stylesheet SYSTEM "pubinfo.dtd">

<xsl:stylesheet xmlns:xsl="http://www.w3.org/1999/XSL/Transform" version="1.0">

<xsl:template match="book">
<html>
<center><h1><xsl:value-of select="title"/></h1></center>
<h4><xsl:value-of select="author"/></h4>
<h4><xsl:value-of select="publisher"/></h4>
<img src="&logoFile;" alt="&logoText;"/>
</html>
</xsl:template>
```

```
<xsl:template match="tableOfContents">
<b>
<h3>Table Of Contents</H3>
<xsl:for-each select="tocEntry">
<li><xsl:value-of select="."/></li>
</xsl:for-each>
</b>
</xsl:template>

</xsl:stylesheet>
```

Although you might expect the template associated with the `<tableOfContents>` element to be called automatically, that's not the case. Only the template that handles the root element will be called automatically, and to use any other templates, you must explicitly "call" them using the `apply-templates` instruction. This instruction causes the XSLT processor to handle the specified child element(s) of the current element and embed the results in the output being created. For example, to include the `<tableOfContents>` element output between the text created for the `272103_1_En` and `<publisher>` elements, you need to make the modification shown in Listing 14-27.

Listing 14-27. Applying Another Template to Generate Content

```
<!-- ... -->

<xsl:template match="book">
<html>
<center><h1><xsl:value-of select="title"/></h1></center>
<h4><xsl:value-of select="author"/></h4>
<xsl:apply-templates select="tableOfContents"/>
<h4><xsl:value-of select="publisher"/></h4>
<img src="&logoFile;" alt="&logoText;"/>
</html>
</xsl:template>

<!-- ... -->
```

This command will again generate a file `booktest.html` containing the content shown in Listing 14-28.

Listing 14-28. Final HTML Output Generated by the Modified XSL

```
<html>
<center>
<h1>Pro Java Programming</h1>
</center>
<h4>Brett Spell</h4>
<b>
<h3>Table Of Contents</H3>
<li>Printing</li>
<li>Cut and Paste</li>
<li>Drag and Drop</li>
</b>
<h4>Apress</h4>
<img alt="Cover Image"
     src="http://www.apress.com/ApressCorporate/supplement/1/421/bcm.gif "></html>
```

Although the whitespace isn't quite the same as that of the HTML document defined earlier in the chapter, the two documents are functionally identical from a browser's perspective.

Summary

In this chapter, you looked at the following:

- What XML is and how it differs from HTML
- How an XML document is formed
- How to parse XML documents using the DOM API
- How to transform XML documents using XSLT
- The role of XPath in transformations

CHAPTER 15

■ ■ ■

Adding Annotations

A very useful part of Java is its support for annotations, which are used to define what is sometimes referred to as *metadata*. To understand what benefits this feature provides, it's helpful to first realize that the definition of metadata is "data about data." In other words, metadata is information that describes other data. An example of where metadata has long been used in Java is the java.sql package that contains DatabaseMetaData, ResultSetMetaData, and the relatively new ParameterMetaData interfaces. As implied by the definition just mentioned and by their names, these classes encapsulate data that describes a database, a ResultSet, and parameter information, respectively. For example, ResultSetMetaData allows you to find out how many columns are represented within a ResultSet, the data types associated with those columns, and so on.

In contrast to the classes defined in java.sql, Java's support for annotations allows you to include in your source files information that describes the elements of your code such as classes, methods, and parameters. To understand how this is useful, we'll briefly examine another way that earlier releases of Java supported metadata, specifically, through the @deprecated tag used by the javadoc tool. The @deprecated tag identifies a method that programmers are discouraged from using, typically because a preferred alternative exists that should be used instead. To illustrate how this works, let's assume you've created and compiled a class like the one in Listing 15-1. Notice that a javadoc-style comment block has been defined for the getText() method.

Listing 15-1. A Simple Class for Retrieving Text

```java
public class Server {

    /**
     * @deprecated Use the getText() method in the NewAndImprovedServer class
     * instead.
     */
    public String getText() {
        return "Hello world!";
    }

    public String getMoreText() {
        return "Hello galaxy!";
    }

}
```

As mentioned, the presence of the @deprecated tag means that programmers are discouraged from using this method, and as this example illustrates, the tag also should contain text that tells what should be used in place of this deprecated method. Now let's further assume you create and compile a class like one in Listing 15-2 that attempts to use the deprecated method.

Listing 15-2. Compiling a Class That References Another Type with a Deprecated Method

```java
public class Client {

    public static void main(String[] args) {
        Server server = new Server();
        System.out.println(server.getText());
    }
}
```

Compiling this class without specifying any options will result in a warning being generated like the following:

```
Note: Client.java uses or overrides a deprecated API.

Note: Recompile with -deprecation for details
```

Recompiling with the -deprecation option as instructed generates output like the following:

```
Client.java:5: warning: getText() in Server has been deprecated
        System.out.println(server.getText());
```

An important point to realize is that you'll receive these deprecation warnings even if the source file isn't present. That's possible because the Java compiler actually includes in the Server.class file a flag that indicates the getText() method has been deprecated. Later, when the compiler attempts to compile Client.java, it scans the Server.class file, notes that the method is deprecated, and generates a warning. It's worth pointing out that @deprecated is unique in this sense; most javadoc tags are intended to be used only when the javadoc tool parses source code and no remnant of any other tag is included in a class file generated by a Java compiler.

Just as it's a good example of how metadata is useful, the @deprecated tag is also an example of why Java needed a better way of allowing programmers to include metadata in their source files. After all, the javadoc tags are embedded within comment blocks that could otherwise be ignored by Java compilers, and since other tags are ignored, @deprecated amounts to a nonstandard (or at least unusual) way of using a javadoc tag. In addition, even in the case of @deprecated where a flag is stored in the compiled class file, there's no trivial way for an application to determine which tags were specified. Fortunately, the annotation facility provides an improved way of specifying metadata and for processing that data programmatically.

Using Annotations

As you'll see later, the annotation facility in Java allows you to define custom annotations, but Java also includes some predefined annotations that are useful. For example, one of the predefined annotations is a replacement for the @deprecated tag, and the replacement is named (intuitively enough) Deprecated. To use an annotation, simply specify it before the element you want to apply it to by putting an at (@) sign followed by the name of the annotation. For example, to replace the @deprecated javadoc tag with the Deprecated annotation, make the changes shown in bold in Listing 15-3 to the Server class. Note that putting the annotation(s) on a separate line isn't required; it's customarily done this way to improve the readability of the code.

Listing 15-3. Adding a @deprecated Annotation to a Method

```
public class Server {

    @Deprecated
    public String getText() {
        return "Hello world!";
    }

    public String getMoreText() {
        return "Hello galaxy!";
    }

}
```

In addition to providing a simpler and "cleaner" way of marking a deprecated method, annotations provide several advantages, one of which is that you can apply them to a wider range of program elements. For example, you can apply javadoc only at a package, class, or method level, but you can apply annotations to any of the following:

- **Annotations**: An annotation can itself have annotations.

- **Constructors and methods**: This is perhaps the most common usage.

- **Fields**: You can apply annotations to static or instance variables defined within a class.

- **Local variables**: You can apply annotations to variables defined and used inside methods.

- **Package**: You can associate annotations with an entire package.

- **Parameter**: You can assign annotations to individual method parameters.

- **Type**: A class, interface, or enum definition can have annotations.

Each of the foregoing represents some kind of declaration, and prior to Java 8 declarations were the only place where you could define annotations. As of Java 8, however, annotations can be assigned any time a type is referenced, such as in conjunction with generics. For example, you can now define a statement like the one following:

```
List<@NonNull String> names = new ArrayList<>();
```

The value of this may not be immediately obvious, especially given that none of Java's predefined annotations is valid when used this way. However, the real power of annotations lies in the fact that not only can you define your own custom annotations but you can then write code that uses those annotations to perform useful functions. In fact, the @NonNull annotation shown in this example is an actual custom annotation defined and used by the FindBugs source code analysis tool to detect potential errors that Java's predefined annotations can't identify.

Another advantage of annotations over javadoc comments is that it's easy to determine programmatically which annotations are present for a given element. Before you see how to do this, though, you should review the API (application programming interface) documentation for the java.lang package, specifically, the section "Annotation Types Summary." Annotations are defined in a way that's very much like creating a class or an interface, and they're included in the API documentation along with other components.

Now that you know that annotation definitions resemble those of classes and interfaces, writing code that refers to an annotation becomes somewhat more intuitive. For example, let's suppose you want to write a code segment that examines the methods defined in the Server class and displays the names of those that are deprecated. You can write most of that code using the reflection capabilities that have long been a part of Java, as shown in Listing 15-4.

Listing 15-4. Retrieve and Loop Through an Array That Represents the Methods in a Class

```
Class myClass = Server.class;
java.lang.reflect.Method[] methods = myClass.getMethods();
for (int i = 0; i < methods.length; i++) {
    // Check for annotations here
}
```

To see if a given annotation is present, you can use the isAnnotationPresent() method and simply refer to the annotation using its Class object as shown in Listing 15-5.

Listing 15-5. Checking a Method for the Presence of the @deprecated Annotation

```
Class myClass = Server.class;
java.lang.reflect.Method[] methods = myClass.getMethods();
for (int i = 0; i < methods.length; i++) {
    if (methods[i].isAnnotationPresent(Deprecated.class)) {
        System.err.println("Method '" + methods[i].getName() + "' is deprecated");
    }
}
```

As this simple example illustrates, applications can easily access annotation information without having to scan a source file or a class file. Thus the implication is that it's easy for development tools and user applications to take advantage of annotations in any way that's helpful. As a Java programmer you'll typically include annotations in your applications but won't need to process them yourself, so it's sufficient to realize that annotations provide a flexible mechanism for defining metadata that's easy to use. In fact, annotations are heavily used by some of the most popular frameworks associated with Java applications such as Spring, Hibernate, and many others. Again, this usage of annotations by powerful and popular frameworks illustrates that most of the value provided by annotations isn't in the ones predefined by Java (though those are useful) but lies in the ability to define and process custom annotation types.

As you may have noticed when reviewing the API documentation, Deprecated isn't the only annotation defined in the java.lang package but is accompanied by the intuitively named Override and SuppressWarnings annotation types, along with the SafeVarargs and FunctionalInterface. As its name implies, Override allows you to mark a method that's intended to override a superclass method, while SuppressWarnings lets you indicate to a Java compiler that it shouldn't generate warnings for specific elements.

Override

For an example of how to use `Override`, let's assume you create a subclass of `Server` called `AdvancedServer` and you override the `getMoreText()` method as in Listing 15-6.

Listing 15-6. A Subclass of the Server Class

```
public class AdvancedServer extends Server {

    public String getMoreText() {
        return "Hello universe!";
    }

}
```

If you're wondering why it's useful to mark a method as overriding a superclass method, consider what would happen if you do one or more of the following:

- Forget to include `extends  Server` in the class definition

- Specify an "incorrect" method name such as `getAdditionalText()` or later change the superclass method name without also changing the overriding subclass method

- Change the superclass method signature by adding an argument without an equivalent change in the subclass

For example, let's suppose you make a change to the `getMoreText()` method defined in `Server` but you forget to also modify the `AdvancedServer` subclass as mentioned.

```
public String getMoreText(String name) {
        return "Hello " + name;
}
```

It's still possible to compile `AdvancedServer` successfully, but the `getMoreText()` method no longer overrides the superclass implementation. Instead, two methods with that name can be called: one (defined in `AdvancedServer`) that accepts no arguments and another (defined in `Server`) that accepts a single `String` parameter. Assuming that this is the result of an oversight on the part of the programmer, using an instance of `AdvancedServer` can produce unexpected results.

Fortunately, the `Override` annotation allows you to mark methods that are intended to override a superclass implementation; you specify it on the `getMoreText()` method as is done in Listing 15-7.

Listing 15-7. Using the @Override Annotation

```
public class AdvancedServer extends Server {

    @Override
    public String getMoreText() {
        return "Hello universe!";
    }

}
```

Once you make this modification, attempting to compile `AdvancedServer` will result in an error being generated because the `getMoreText()` method no longer overrides the `Server` implementation.

```
AdvancedServer.java:3 getMoreText(java.lang.String) in AdvancedServer cannot

override getMoreText(java.lang.String) in Server; overridden method is final
```

In other words, the `Override` annotation ensures that a subclass can and does override a superclass method. Note that using this annotation won't have any effect on the error message you receive if you try to compile code that overrides a `final` method. That's because doing so is already invalid since by definition a `final` method is one that can't be overridden.

Although you're not required to use this annotation, doing so can reduce the number of programming errors that go undetected at compile time by identifying methods that you expect override other methods. Without this type of error checking, your application might wind up with code that incorrectly calls the older superclass implementation of a method when you expect it to execute what you thought was an overriding implementation in the subclass. This type of mistake can be difficult and time-consuming to find when testing and debugging your code, which is why `Override`'s ability to bring these mistakes to your attention at compile time is so helpful.

FunctionalInterface

As described in Chapter 3, Java 8 introduced support for functional programming through the use of Lambda expressions and a functional interface is one that has only a single unimplemented method. You can enforce this convention at compile time by using the `@FunctionalInterface` annotation to indicate that a given interface is intended to be a functional interface. If a type annotated with this value is found not to qualify as a functional interface the compiler will issue an error message.

SuppressWarnings

As you might expect, the purpose of this annotation is to allow you to indicate that warnings should be suppressed that would otherwise occur. For example, let's suppose you want to be able to compile the `Client` class without receiving a warning related to its use of the deprecated `getText()` method in `Server` and without suppressing any other deprecation warnings. In that case, you could use the `SuppressWarnings` annotation as in Listing 15-8.

Listing 15-8. An Example of the `@SuppressWarnings` Annotation's Use

```java
public class Client {

@SuppressWarnings(value="deprecation")
public static void main(String[] args) {
    Server server = new Server();
    System.out.println(server.getText());
}

}
```

Elements

Notice that SuppressWarnings is very different from the previous two we looked at in that it includes what appears to be a property assignment within a pair of parentheses. In fact, it's a property assignment, although in the context of annotations the properties are referred to as *elements*. If you review the API documentation for SuppressWarnings, you'll see it does indeed contain an element called value that represents a String array; an array is used because it's possible to specify more than one type of warning you want to suppress. If you do want to specify multiply warning types, you should put a list of strings within braces ({}) and separate them with commas, just as you'd do when defining a String array.

```
@SuppressWarnings(value={"deprecation", "fallthrough"})
```

However, because it's so common for annotations to use a single element named value, a simpler syntax is supported; the following shows an example of how you can use it:

```
@SuppressWarnings("deprecation")
```

In the case where an annotation supports multiple elements, you can specify a value for each one by separating them with commas. For example, if you want to use an annotation named Author that had firstName and lastName elements, you can specify something like the following:

```
@Author(firstName="Brett", lastName="Spell")
```

Given that annotations support elements, it's easy to guess that the element defined in SuppressWarnings specifies which type(s) of warning should be suppressed, and in this case you want to suppress deprecation warnings. However, it's probably less clear how you could have known what to specify for the element in this case. After all, the API documentation for SuppressWarnings doesn't mention deprecation or any other value that you can or should assign to the element; it simply indicates that SuppressWarnings includes an element named value that represents a String array.

You'll see what meaningful values you can specify for SuppressWarnings, but before I explain this, it's worthwhile to make an important point related to annotations. Specifically, you should realize that the tool that will use the annotation is responsible for dictating which values are valid for the annotation's elements. For example, the tool that will use SuppressWarnings is your Java source code compiler, so it's that compiler that will dictate which element values are useful. To get a list of the nonstandard options supported by your compiler you can issue the following command:

```
javac -X
```

If you're using the reference implementation of Java one of the options displayed will be the lint option. That option is essentially the compiler-level version of SuppressWarnings, and the option values displayed correspond to the values you can specify for the annotation's element. As a result, one of the lines of output generated when you issue the previous command will look like the following code. Specifying an option with a minus (-) sign in front of it means that the corresponding type of warning should be disabled (turned off), while specifying the version without the minus sign means that the warning type should be enabled.

```
-Xlint:{all, cast, deprecation, divzero, empty, unchecked, fallthrough, path, serial,
finally, overrides, -cast, -deprecation, -divzero, -empty, -unchecked, -fallthrough,
-path, -serial, -finally, -overrides, none} Enable or disable specific warnings
```

Note that in the case of the lint option, you can enable or disable warnings, but in the case of SuppressWarnings, you can only disable (*suppress*) them. As a result, the valid choices for the annotation are as follows:

- cast
- deprecation
- divzero
- empty
- unchecked
- fallthrough
- path
- serial
- finally
- overrides

You've already seen that deprecation refers to deprecation warnings and we'll now briefly examine the other values listed.

cast

Disables warnings related to cast operations, such as redundant casts as in the following example:

```
List<String> testList = new ArrayList<>();
// ...
String value = (String)(testList.get(0));
```

In this case the explicit cast operation isn't needed because the List can only contain String values and the get() call will automatically cast the returned value to a String.

deprecation

Disables the warnings that indicate the presence of a reference to a deprecated class, method, or field. The following example uses the deprecated setHours() method defined in the java.util.Date class and will generate a warning unless that type of warning is disabled:

```
Date date = new Date();
date.setHours(1);
```

divzero

This option corresponds to the warning generated when the compiler detects an attempt to divide by zero, as in the following fragment:

```
int value = 123 / 0;
```

empty

The empty option controls whether the compiler warns you about an empty if block as in the following example:

```
int age;
// . . .
if (age < 18);
```

On the other hand, it won't warn you of empty else statements like the following:

```
if (age < 100) {
    System.out.println("The person is less than 100 years old");
}
else;
```

unchecked

To understand what causes an unchecked warning, let's consider the code in Listing 15-9 that creates and uses a collection without specifying the type of objects stored in the collection.

Listing 15-9. Creating and Using a Collection Without Specifying a Generic Type

```
import java.util.*;

public class NewTest {

    public static void main(String[] args) throws Exception {
        List list = new ArrayList();
        list.add("Hello");
    }

}
```

If you attempt to compile the code, you'll see a message like the following:

```
Note: NewTest.java uses unchecked or unsafe operations.

Note: Recompile with -Xlint:unchecked for details
```

Recompiling as instructed with the –Xlint:unchecked option provides somewhat more information. In particular, note the unchecked text that appears within the brackets ([]) in the warning message.

```
NewTest.java:7: warning: [unchecked] unchecked call to add(E)

as a member of the raw type java.util.List
        list.add("Hello");
```

This more detailed explanation at least makes it clear that the compiler failure happens because you attempted to add a String to a List for which no type was specified. In other words, the call to add() is "unchecked" because the compiler doesn't know what type of object you intended to store in the List and therefore can't verify that adding a String is appropriate. At this point, you have several options, one of which is to specify a type.

```
List<String> list = new ArrayList<String>();
list.add("Hello");
```

Alternatively, you could simply add a SuppressWarnings annotation to the method (or the class), specifying unchecked for the element value.

```
@SuppressWarnings("unchecked")
public static void main(String[] args) throws Exception {
```

In many cases, however, your best option is to simply suppress the warnings at the compiler level, which allows you to maintain your code in a state that allows it to be successfully processed by compilers that support both Java 5 and earlier releases.

```
javac -Xlint:-unchecked NewTest.java
```

fallthrough

A *fallthrough* refers to a switch statement that contains a case for which no break or other statement prevents execution from *falling through* to the following case, as illustrated in Listing 15-10:

Listing 15-10. An Example of "Falling Through" a Case by Omitting a Break or Other Control Flow Instruction

```
switch (myValue) {
    case 1:
        doWork(); // This is a fallthrough
    case -1:
        doMoreWork();
        break;
    default:
        isZero = true;
        break;
}
```

Although it's sometimes useful to deliberately code a switch statement this way, fallthroughs can also be the result of accidentally omitting a break statement, and the SuppressWarnings annotation allows you to control whether a fallthrough results in a warning being generated.

path

Specifying an incorrect path location when compiling or executing programs is a common source of problems. For example, let's say you intend to compile a class; you want to include in the classpath a JAR file stored in the D:\java\jars directory, and you think the name of the file is dbcp.jar. In that case, you might execute a command like the following:

```
javac -classpath D:\java\jars\dbcp.jar NewTest.java
```

Now let's assume either that the JAR file isn't really located in the D:\java\jars directory or that you mistype the name on the command line. In most cases you'll receive a compiler error if your code references a class that's found in the JAR file, but depending upon various factors related to your code and your environment, it's possible you might not receive an error. In addition, even if you do receive an error stating that a class couldn't be found, you might not know that the missing class was supposed to be in the dbcp.jar file. Ideally, the compiler should tell you when you've specified a path entry (classpath or sourcepath) that it can't find, and this option is intended to allow you to control whether it does so. If your classpath or source path includes a file or directory that doesn't exist but you want to avoid having a warning generated, you can use the -Xlint:-path option to prevent a warning from being issued.

serial

When you create a class that's serializable, it's often desirable to define a serialVersionUID for the class to ensure appropriate compatibility across different versions of that class. The specifics of how to do this and when it's appropriate are outside the scope of this chapter, but you should simply understand that this value allows you to suppress warnings related to a missing serialVersionUID.

finally

Warnings of this type indicate that a finally block exists that can't complete normally, as in the following code (see Listing 15-11):

Listing 15-11. A try/catch/finally Block That Can Never Return the Values from the try or catch Block

```
try {
    doWork();
    return 123;
}
catch (Exception e) {
    // Handle exception here
    return 456;
}
finally {
    // The following return will not be executed
    return 789;
}
```

The values specified in the try and catch blocks will never be returned because the code inside the finally block will always be executed after them, with the result that the value returned by this code will always be 789. If you want to suppress warnings related to this situation, you can specify a SuppressWarnings annotation with finally, or you can specify the appropriate option during compilation.

overrides

This determines whether the compiler will generate warnings related to certain conditions affecting method overriding. For example, suppose that you have one method with an array parameter.

```
public void doStuff(Integer[] numbers)
```

And then you create a subclass that has a similar (but not quite identical) method signature that uses varargs.

```
public void doStuff(Integer... numbers)
```

In practice a vararg is treated as an array, but these two method signatures are slightly different, and when enabled the overrides option will cause this condition to generate a warning.

Creating Custom Annotations

Java includes some useful predefined annotations, but what makes annotations potentially even more powerful is that you can easily define your own. For example, let's suppose you're creating server objects for use with Java's Remote Method Invocation (RMI) and you want to define an annotation that would allow you to mark a class as representing a remote object. Before you see how easy it is to do this, define a simple remote interface like the one in Listing 15-12 for use with a server object.

Listing 15-12. A Remote Interface Definition

```
import java.rmi.*;

public interface Test extends Remote {

    public String getText() throws RemoteException;

}
```

Next, you can create a simplistic implementation of the remote interface like the one in Listing 15-13.

Listing 15-13. A Simple Remote Interface Implementation

```
import java.rmi.*;
import java.rmi.server.UnicastRemoteObject;

public class SimpleTest extends UnicastRemoteObject implements Test {

    public SimpleTest() throws RemoteException {
    }

    public String getText() {
        return "Hello world!";
    }

}
```

CHAPTER 15 ░ ADDING ANNOTATIONS

Now you can begin to create the annotation. Assuming you don't need to specify any properties/elements for the annotation, you can easily create one as shown next. Note that except for the inclusion of an at (@) sign, the code is identical to the code you'd use to define an interface.

```
public @interface RemoteObject {
}
```

Once you've created and compiled this annotation definition, you can add the appropriate annotation to the SimpleTest class.

```
@RemoteObject
public class SimpleTest extends UnicastRemoteObject implements Test {
```

Until now, you've marked only individual methods with annotations, but as this example illustrates, the use of annotations isn't limited to methods.

To continue with the example, let's suppose you want to allow the programmer to specify the name of the remote interface to use with the implementation class. You can easily accomplish this by adding a String element to the RemoteObject annotation.

```
public @interface RemoteObject {

    public String value();
}
```

Once again, the most notable characteristic of the Annotation definition is how closely it resembles an interface definition. An important difference, though, is that as mentioned earlier, it's possible to specify a default value for the elements. In this case, for example, you could define a default value of RemoteInterface by making the following change to the code:

```
public @interface RemoteObject {

    public String value() default "RemoteInterface";

}
```

At this point you've successfully defined a new Annotation type, but it's worthwhile to consider refining the type further. For example, you've defined this annotation for the purpose of identifying classes that represent remote objects, but what would prevent you from annotating (for example) a method or even a parameter with this new type? In fact, with the current definition of RemoteObject, it's entirely possible to assign this annotation to any program construct (package, class, method, parameter, and so on) that supports annotation, and if you modify the SimpleTest class as is done in Listing 15-14, it will compile successfully.

Listing 15-14. Adding the Custom Annotation to a Method

```
import java.rmi.*;
import java.rmi.server.UnicastRemoteObject;

public class SimpleTest extends UnicastRemoteObject implements Test {

    public SimpleTest() throws RemoteException {
    }
```

```
@RemoteObject
public String getText() {
    return "Hello world!";
}

}
```

This obviously isn't what you wanted for the new annotation type, because it's only meaningful to say that a particular object is a "remote object," so ideally it shouldn't be possible to specify the annotation type for a single method. Fortunately, the annotation facility allows you to control which program elements an annotation type can be successfully applied to, which is done by annotating the annotation. To see how this is done, you should examine the API documentation for the java.lang.annotation package, which contains (among other things) an annotation type called Target. As the documentation indicates, Target specifies the "kinds of program element to which an annotation type is applicable." In other words, if you want your custom annotation to be used only at a class level, you can use Target to enforce that behavior.

Target

Examining the documentation for Target reveals that its single element is an array of ElementType instances, where ElementType is a type-safe enumeration that defines enumeration constants for the supported program elements mentioned earlier that are supported by annotations. Specifically, the supported types are those listed in Table 15-1.

Table 15-1. *Enumeration Constants Defined Within* ElementType

Type	Description
ANNOTATION_TYPE	Used to annotate other annotations (as with Target).
CONSTRUCTOR	Can be used to annotate constructors.
FIELD	Annotates fields (static or instance variables) within a class.
LOCAL_VARIABLE	Annotation can be used with variables defined and used within methods.
METHOD	Allows the annotation to be used with methods.
PACKAGE	The annotation can be associated with a package.
PARAMETER	Indicates that the annotation can be used with method parameters.
TYPE	Can be used to annotate a class, interface, enumeration, or annotation.
TYPE_PARAMETER	Supports the use of the annotation with a generic type, such as in List<@NonNull String>.
TYPE_USE	Allows the annotation to be used with any type, such as in a cast.

So how exactly do you annotate the annotation type (RemoteObject) to ensure it can't be used with methods or other inappropriate types? You can simply add the code highlighted in Listing 15-15 to the annotation. Note that it's necessary to import ElementType and Target for the file to compile successfully, just as it would be if you were referencing them in a class or (nonannotation) interface.

Listing 15-15. Using Java's Predefined @Target Annotation to Annotate the Custom Annotation Type

```
import java.lang.annotation.ElementType;
import java.lang.annotation.Target;

@Target(ElementType.TYPE)
public @interface RemoteObject {

    public String value() default "RemoteInterface";
}
```

After you've made this change and recompiled the RemoteObject annotation type, attempting to compile the SimpleTest class with the annotated method shown earlier will generate a compiler error like the following:

```
SimpleTest.java:9: annotation type not applicable to this kind of declaration
    @RemoteObject public String getText() {
```

One final point is worth making: since Target defines an array of ElementType values, it's possible for you to specify more than one type when using the Target annotation. For example, if you want to allow the RemoteObject annotation to be used at both a class and a package level, you can change the definition to include both types.

```
@Target({ElementType.TYPE, ElementType.PACKAGE})
public @interface RemoteObject {
```

Retention

At this point, let's suppose you've created and compiled the implementation of the SimpleTest class shown in Listing 15-16.

Listing 15-16. Another Class That Uses the @RemoteObject Annotation

```
import java.rmi.*;
import java.rmi.server.UnicastRemoteObject;

@RemoteObject
public class SimpleTest extends UnicastRemoteObject implements Test {

    public SimpleTest() throws RemoteException {
    }

    public String getText() {
        return "Hello world!";
    }

}
```

Now let's assume you create code that attempts to examine the class in order to see what annotations are associated with it. You did this earlier in the chapter when you wrote a code segment to examine the Server class in order to see if it was tagged with the Deprecation annotation, so you can use similar code to accomplish essentially the same thing here. An example of how this might appear is found in Listing 15-17.

Listing 15-17. Checking for the Presence of the RemoteObject Annotation

```
public class ScanTest {

    public static void main(String[] args) throws Exception {
        Class<SimpleTest> myClass = SimpleTest.class;
        if (myClass.isAnnotationPresent(RemoteObject.class)) {
            System.out.println("It is a RemoteObject");
        }
        else {
            System.out.println("It doesn't appear to be a RemoteObject!");
        }
    }

}
```

Surprisingly enough, running the code results in a message being displayed that indicates that SimpleTest isn't annotated with the RemoteObject type, even though you've clearly defined it as such. To understand this, let's go back to the earlier discussion of the javadoc tags and how @deprecated is unique in that it's the one tag for which information is stored in the class file as part of compilation. The other tags are ignored by the Java compiler because it simply doesn't care about them; only the javadoc tool performs any processing on the other tags, and it uses the Java source code (.java) file as input, not the class files created by the Java compiler. In other words, the @deprecated tag represents information that needs to be included in the compiled class file, while all other javadoc tags represent information that's useful only within the source code.

This difference between the context in which the tags are needed is a common theme, which is why another feature of Java's annotation facility is that it allows you to define a retention policy for annotations. Like Target, the Retention annotation is used to annotate other annotations, and it's defined within the java.lang.annotation package. It allows you to specify one of three retention policies, each of which corresponds to an instance of the RetentionPolicy enumeration type. The three retention policies are as follows:

- SOURCE: The annotation information is stored only within the source file, and no remnant of it should be stored in a class file generated from that source file.

- CLASS: The annotation information is stored within the class file when the source code is compiled, but the information isn't loaded into memory as part of the class definition. This is the default if you create a custom annotation but don't specify a retention policy.

- RUNTIME: The annotation data is stored within the class file and loaded into memory when the class definition is loaded.

At this point it should be apparent why the ScanTest class was unable to detect the SimpleTest annotation in the previous code example. Because you didn't specify a retention policy for the RemoteObject annotation, it defaulted to the CLASS policy, which means the annotation information wasn't included in the class information when the class definition was loaded into memory. In other words, you can detect an annotation programmatically at runtime only if the annotation has a retention policy of RUNTIME. Otherwise, the information will be omitted at the point when the source is compiled (with a policy of SOURCE) or when the class is loaded (with a policy of CLASS).

Now that you know how annotation information is maintained, you can update the RemoteObject definition as shown in Listing 15-18 if you want to allow the information to be included in the class and runtime definition.

Listing 15-18. Defining an Annotation So That It's Present at Runtime

```
import java.lang.annotation.ElementType;
import java.lang.annotation.Retention;
import java.lang.annotation.RetentionPolicy;
import java.lang.annotation.Target;

@Target(ElementType.TYPE)
@Retention(RetentionPolicy.RUNTIME)
public @interface RemoteObject {

    public String value() default "RemoteInterface";
}
```

Once you've made this change, you should recompile the RemoteObject annotation and the SimpleTest class. Once you've done so, you can rerun the ScanTest application, and it will now correctly indicate that SimpleTest is annotated as a RemoteObject.

Documented

After making all of the changes described so far to the SimpleTest and related types, you'll now see what happens if you run the javadoc utility to generate documentation for SimpleTest. Viewing the generated API documentation for SimpleTest doesn't provide any indication that SimpleTest is annotated as a RemoteObject even though you know it has been marked as such and that information is available in all circumstances (in the source, in the class, and at runtime), as shown in Figure 15-1.

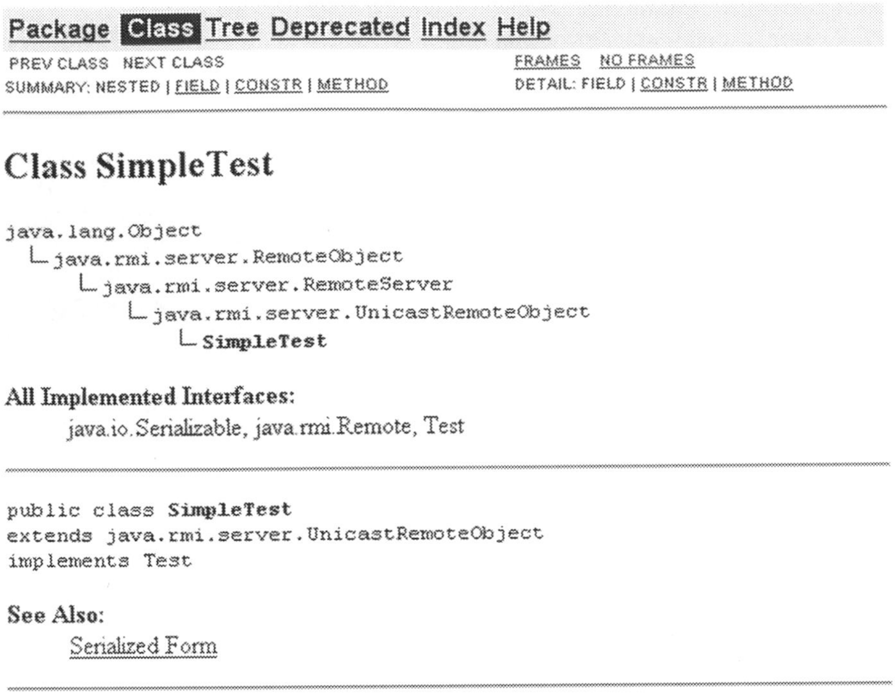

Package **Class** Tree Deprecated Index Help

PREV CLASS NEXT CLASS
SUMMARY: NESTED | FIELD | CONSTR | METHOD

FRAMES   NO FRAMES
DETAIL: FIELD | CONSTR | METHOD

Class SimpleTest

```
java.lang.Object
  └ java.rmi.server.RemoteObject
     └ java.rmi.server.RemoteServer
        └ java.rmi.server.UnicastRemoteObject
           └ SimpleTest
```

All Implemented Interfaces:
> java.io.Serializable, java.rmi.Remote, Test

```
public class SimpleTest
extends java.rmi.server.UnicastRemoteObject
implements Test
```

See Also:
> Serialized Form

Figure 15-1. *With the current implementation of* RemoteObject, *no indication of its use is provided in the API documentation created by* javadoc

This is because annotations are by default not identified in the documentation generated by javadoc, but you can change this behavior by using the Documented annotation defined in the java.lang.annotation package. Like Target and Retention, Documented annotates other annotation types, and you can add it to the list of annotations specified for the RemoteObject annotation type as shown in Listing 15-19.

Listing 15-19. Adding the @Documented Annotation

```java
import java.lang.annotation.Documented;
import java.lang.annotation.ElementType;
import java.lang.annotation.Retention;
import java.lang.annotation.RetentionPolicy;
import java.lang.annotation.Target;

@Documented
@Target(ElementType.TYPE)
@Retention(RetentionPolicy.RUNTIME)
public @interface RemoteObject {

    public String value() default "RemoteInterface";

}
```

Once you've made this change and recompiled RemoteObject, rerunning the javadoc utility for the SimpleTest class causes the API documentation to include an indication that SimpleTest is annotated as a RemoteObject, as shown in Figure 15-2.

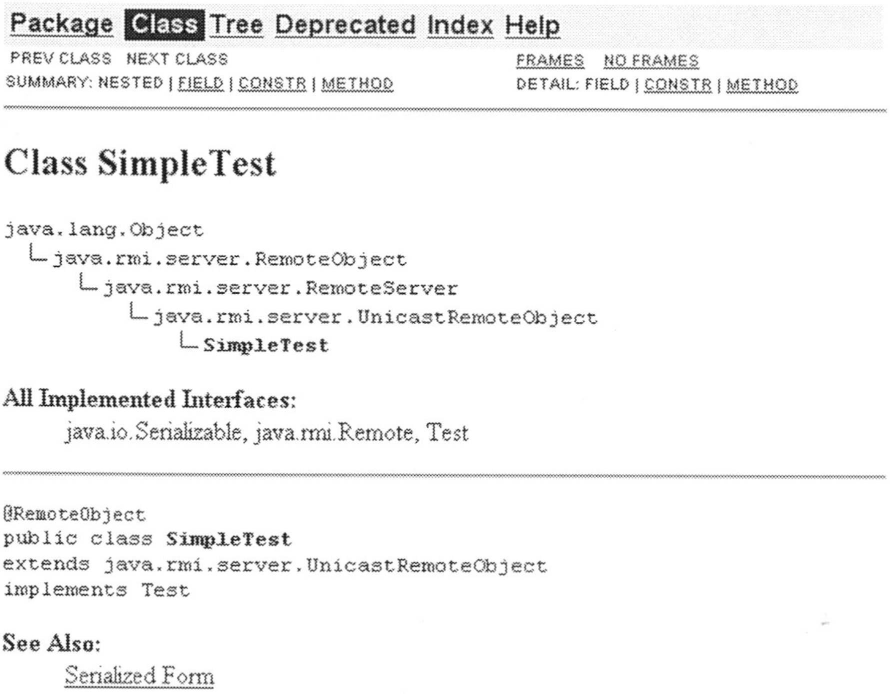

Package **Class** Tree Deprecated Index Help

PREV CLASS   NEXT CLASS   FRAMES   NO FRAMES
SUMMARY: NESTED | FIELD | CONSTR | METHOD   DETAIL: FIELD | CONSTR | METHOD

Class SimpleTest

```
java.lang.Object
  └ java.rmi.server.RemoteObject
      └ java.rmi.server.RemoteServer
          └ java.rmi.server.UnicastRemoteObject
              └ SimpleTest
```

All Implemented Interfaces:

      java.io.Serializable, java.rmi.Remote, Test

```
@RemoteObject
public class SimpleTest
extends java.rmi.server.UnicastRemoteObject
implements Test
```

See Also:

      Serialized Form

Figure 15-2. *Specifying the Documented annotation causes the javadoc tool to include in its output an indication that the annotation was used*

Inherited

You've now seen how to define and apply a RemoteObject annotation to a class, but you might be wondering what happens when you create a subclass of that class. In other words, does annotating a given class mean that its subclasses are associated with the same annotation? To find out, let's suppose you create a ComplexTest class that extends the SimpleTest class created earlier.

```
public class ComplexTest extends SimpleTest {

    public ComplexTest() throws java.rmi.RemoteException {};

}
```

Now let's assume you modify the ScanTest class defined earlier so that it examines the ComplexTest class (instead of SimpleTest) for the presence of the RemoteObject annotation. An implementation of this is provided in Listing 15-20.

Listing 15-20. Defining a Reference to the ComplexTest Type

```java
public class ScanTest {

    public static void main(String[] args) throws Exception {
        Class<ComplexTest> myClass = ComplexTest.class;
        if (myClass.isAnnotationPresent(RemoteObject.class)) {
            System.out.println("It is a RemoteObject");
        }
        else {
            System.out.println("It doesn't appear to be a RemoteObject!");
        }
    }

}
```

If you recompile and execute this code, it will indicate that ComplexTest isn't annotated as a RemoteObject. As this example illustrates, an annotation by default will not be "inherited" by the subclasses of an annotated class. In this case and many others, however, it's entirely appropriate for subclasses to inherit annotations, and fortunately the java.lang.annotation package contains an annotation that can be used to address this. Specifically, the Inherited annotation can indicate that an annotation should be inherited; the code highlighted in Listing 15-21 shows an example of how you can use it.

Listing 15-21. Defining Annotation Inheritance

```java
import java.lang.annotation.Documented;
import java.lang.annotation.ElementType;
import java.lang.annotation.Inherited;
import java.lang.annotation.Retention;
import java.lang.annotation.RetentionPolicy;
import java.lang.annotation.Target;

@Documented
@Inherited
@Target(ElementType.TYPE)
@Retention(RetentionPolicy.RUNTIME)
public @interface RemoteObject {

    public String value() default "remoteName";

}
```

If you make this change and recompile the code, the ScanTest application will indicate that ComplexTest is indeed a remote object.

Repeatable

Although it's typically only useful to specify an annotation once, there may be times when you want to use an annotation multiple times in the same location, and as of Java 8 this can be allowed for a custom annotation by specifying the Repeatable annotation when defining your custom type. Repeatable takes a single parameter that identifies the type to be repeated, as in Listing 15-22.

Listing 15-22. Defining a Repeatable Annotation

```
import java.lang.annotation.ElementType;
import java.lang.annotation.Repeatable;
import java.lang.annotation.Target;

@Repeatable(CodeModification.class)
@Target({ElementType.METHOD, ElementType.TYPE})
public @interface CodeModification {
    public String programmerName();
    public String explanation();
}
```

Once defined, the annotation can be used repeatedly on a single element of an appropriate type, so in this case the CodeModification annotation could be assigned to a class or method more than once.

```
@CodeModification(programmerName="John Smith" explanation="Updates for Java 8")
@CodeModification(programmerName="Jane Doe" exaplanation="Bug fix")
public class DemoTest {
```

Replacing External Metadata

In the discussions up to this point I've focused on using annotations to replace metadata that's internal to Java source code files, such as the @deprecated tag used by javadoc. In reality, however, there are even more cases where metadata is stored outside the source code, and those uses provide an even better opportunity for using metadata. In fact, you've already seen an example of this type of "external" metadata in the case of the SimpleTest remote object and its remote interface defined in Test. In that case you have an interface (Test) that effectively represents metadata because its sole purpose is to identify which methods within the implementation class can be called remotely. It'd be convenient to simply have the Java compiler create the remote interface dynamically upon compilation by assuming that each public method within the implementation class can be called. As long as the user is required to explicitly define and maintain the remote interface, that file largely represents a nuisance because it requires the programmer to do extra work initially. In addition, because its method signatures must match those of the implementation class for it to work correctly, any changes to the implementation will need to be reflected in the remote interface. In other words, when a programmer goes to add, change, or remove a remote method, the change must be made in two places: the implementation class and the remote interface.

Another example that's closely related and that illustrates work that's even more tedious is that of an Enterprise JavaBean (EJB). Prior to the EJB 3.0 specification creating even a simple EJB required you to define at least four separate files, with three of these largely or entirely made up of what amounts to metadata.

- The implementation class itself

- A remote interface similar to one you'd create for an RMI server object

- A home interface that defines constructors you can use to create or retrieve an EJB instance

- An XML-based deployment descriptor that identifies the other three classes and that describes how the EJB will be used

To illustrate this point, let's create a simple EJB that does nothing but return a *Hello world* string. Begin by defining the remote interface that appears in Listing 15-23.

Listing 15-23. A Simple Enterprise JavaBeans (EJB) Interface

```
import java.rmi.RemoteException;
import javax.ejb.EJBObject;

public interface MessageGenerator extends EJBObject {

    public String getMessage() throws RemoteException;

}
```

Assuming that you want to provide only a single no-argument constructor/lookup method, the home interface is also reasonably simple to create. However, like the remote interface, it essentially represents an unnecessarily tedious way of specifying metadata and an example of this appears in Listing 15-24.

Listing 15-24. Defining a Home Interface

```
import java.rmi.RemoteException;
import javax.ejb.CreateException;
import javax.ejb.EJBHome;

public interface GeneratorHome extends EJBHome {
    public MessageGenerator create() throws RemoteException, CreateException;
}
```

Next you can create the implementation itself as is done in Listing 15-25.

Listing 15-25. An EJB Implementation Class

```
import javax.ejb.*;

public class SimpleMessageGenerator implements SessionBean {

    private SessionContext context;

    public SimpleMessageGenerator() {
    }
```

```
    public void ejbCreate() throws CreateException {
    }

    public void setSessionContext(SessionContext theContext) {
        context = theContext;
    }

    public void ejbActivate() {
    }

    public void ejbPassivate() {
    }

    public void ejbRemove() {
    }

    public String getMessage() {
        return "Hello world!";
    }

}
```

Finally, you must create the deployment descriptor as in Listing 15-26.

Listing 15-26. A Deployment Descriptor XML Document

```
<?xml version="1.0" encoding="UTF-8"?>

<!DOCTYPE ejb-jar PUBLIC
'-//Sun Microsystems, Inc.//DTD Enterprise JavaBeans 1.1//EN'
'http://java.sun.com/j2ee/dtds/ejb-jar_1_1.dtd'>

<ejb-jar>
  <display-name>testejb</display-name>
  <enterprise-beans>
    <session>
      <description>Message generator bean</description>
      <display-name>Generator</display-name>
      <ejb-name>Generator</ejb-name>
      <home>GeneratorHome</home>
      <remote>MessageGenerator</remote>
      <ejb-class>SimpleMessageGenerator</ejb-class>
      <session-type>Stateless</session-type>
      <transaction-type>Container</transaction-type>
    </session>
  </enterprise-beans>
  <assembly-descriptor>
    <container-transaction>
      <method>
        <ejb-name>Generator</ejb-name>
        <method-intf>Remote</method-intf>
```

```
        <method-name>*</method-name>
      </method>
      <trans-attribute>NotSupported</trans-attribute>
    </container-transaction>
  </assembly-descriptor>
</ejb-jar>
```

This example is obviously a contrived one since you're not likely to create an EJB just to return a message, but it does reveal a weakness related to the creation of EJBs. Specifically, there's a significant amount of repetitive, tedious work involved in implementing even a simple bean. Some of that tedium is related to the implementation class, but a significant portion of it is because several external files (the home and remote interfaces and the deployment descriptor) are little more than external metadata files, sometimes called *side files*.

Fortunately, since the introduction of annotations, changes to the Enterprise Edition of Java have been made that eliminate much of the tedious work associated within defining an EJB. In fact, with EJB 3.0 or later, you can replace the previous four files with a simplified version of the implementation class that uses annotations as is done in Listing 15-27.

Listing 15-27. An EJB 3.0-Compliant EJB That Uses Annotations to Simplify the Definition

```java
import javax.ejb.*;

@Remote @Stateless
public class SimpleMessageGenerator {

public SimpleMessageGenerator() {

public String getMessage() {
        return "Hello world!";
    }

}
```

As you can see, aside from the Remote and Stateless annotations, this file is virtually identical to a so-called plain old Java object (POJO) and lacks the complexity of the EJB implementation class and support files you created earlier. Not all of the simplification is because of metadata, however; other changes were made to the EJB specification that facilitated this simplified implementation.

As previously mentioned, it isn't just the creation of EJB specification that has benefited from the introduction of annotations. Widely used frameworks like Spring, Hibernate, and many others have been able to significantly reduce the time and complexity needed for their use by offering the option of adding metadata directly to the related files as was done here instead of requiring the tedious construction of a separate XML file.

Summary

You've now seen how to use annotations in Java applications and how they can be detected and processed. You typically won't need to write code to do such processing yourself but will simply take advantage of behavior that's implemented by a vendor that provides you with development tools. However, as this example illustrates, significant potential exists for simplifying and otherwise streamlining the development process by automating the creation and synchronization of source implementations and their related and dependent side files.

In this chapter, you examined the following topics:

- What metadata is and examples of how it has long been used within Java

- How to define metadata using both predefined and custom annotations

- How to locate metadata using Java's reflection capabilities

- How annotations have greatly simplified the development of Enterprise JavaBeans

Index

▧ H

▧ I

▧ J, K